C0-AUL-867

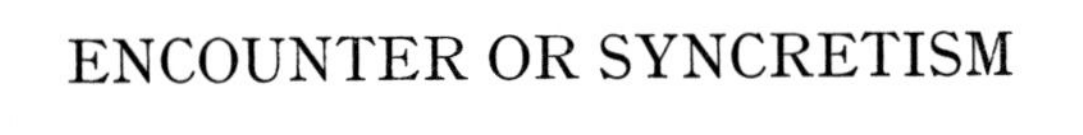

ENCOUNTER OR SYNCRETISM

The Tenjukoku-*mandara*

CORRIGENDA

p. XII, line 7: 494: 495.

p. 4, line 1: *Kakure-Kirishitan*: Kakure-Kirishitan.

p. 11, line 24: Boutelier: Bouteiller.

line 25: He: She.

p. 46, line 25: head, 神, *kami*,: head, kami.

p. 51, ft. nt. 1: Sycześniak: Szcześniak.

p. 52, line 10: *Takama*: Takama.

p. 56, line 9: ō-omi: *ō-omi*.

p. 66, line 16: intirely: entirely.

p. 67, line 27: kamu: Kamu.

p. 77, ft. nt. 1, read: Such as Nakamura Kichiji for instance.

p. 83, line 13: mots: most.

p. 85, last line: footnote 4: footnote 3.

p. 94, line 10: disguished: disguised.

line 11: is as far: in as far.

p. 112, line 33: *tenson* tribe: *Tenson* tribe.

p. 115, line 18: ō-omi: *ō-omi*.

p. 119, line 2: *Takama*: Takama.

p. 124, line 11: to the Yamato: to the Yamato plain.

p. 142, line 3: chapter: chapters.

p. 150, line 10: reverent: reverend.

p. 160, last line: in a bundle of: in a bundle.

p. 162, line 17: *Mahāparanibbana-suttam*: *Mahāparinibbana-suttam*

p. 189, line 6: tribul: tribal.

line 26: Ik: Iki.

p. 192, ft. nt. 4: line 5: t'ien: *t'ien*.

line 12: *Santalaceae, Santalum album*: Santalaceae, Santalum album.

line 16: *euonymus*: euonymus.

line 19: *Betula Schmidtii*: Betula Schmidtii.

p. 217: line 8: e The Korean Immigrants: e Korean Immigrants.

p. 243, ft. nt. 3, line 2: districts: provinces.

p. 266, ft. nt. 1: 625: 645 (twice).

p. 267, line 17: *iro*: *hiro*.

p. 299, ft. nt. 2, line 4: officesof: offices of.

p. 310, ft. nt. 4, line 4 up: Shitenn-ji: Shitennōji.
p. 324, line 24: Nahiwa: Naniwa.
p. 329, line 24 and 27: Sshime: Ishime.
p. 330, line 15: districts: provinces.
p. 349, ft. nt. 3: Bhaiṣajyaguru Vaidūrya: Bhaiṣajyaguru-vaidūrya
p. 382, last line: Kakushi: Yakushi.
p. 393, line 12: referredto: referred to.
p. 403, line 2 up: Jūkyū: Jūkyō.
p. 409, line 10 up: sourcers: sources.
p. 430, line 17: *tenjukoku*: *Tenjukoku*
p. 453, line 1: *Takama no hara*: Takama *no hara*
p. 467, line 12 up: fulfil: fulfill.

ENCOUNTER OR SYNCRETISM

THE INITIAL GROWTH OF JAPANESE BUDDHISM

BY

J. H. KAMSTRA

LEIDEN
E.J. BRILL
1967

This book was printed with financial support of the Netherlands Organization for the Advancement of Pure Research (Z.W.O.)

PRINTED IN THE NETHERLANDS

TABLE OF CONTENTS

INTRODUCTION

Such words as 'dialogue', 'encounter' and 'discussion' belong to the terms in current use in discussions or writings concerning the mutual relationships of religions, which have become well-worn jargon. Here it is frequently noticeable, that at each 'encounter' or 'dialogue' many who utilize these words do not appear to progress much further than a monologue, during which the partner is permitted to listen calmly to how 'openmindedly' he is being considered.

The same can often be said of discussions concerning non-western religions. Here dialogues are often entered into with religions which may be totally non-existent, except perhaps in the thoughts of the 'encounterers'. They repeatedly attempt to conceive of other religions as analogous to their own. As Christianity is unimaginable without its own scripture and a continually recurrent reconsideration of it, as well as being inconceivable without a systematology developed by dogmatists and exegetes, these authors feel that non-western religions can also only exist by the grace of their individual scripture and systematology. Such religions as result from these two (conceptions) are then discussed. We do not wish to deny the value of these dialogues here, as amongst those other religions many may be found in which scripture and a certain doctrinal train of thought certainly do play an important role. However, in this manner one can scarcely achieve realistic discussion with the actual practitioner of these religions. One is readily inclined to label the religion of the man in the street as being impure, syncretic and 'heretical', from the standpoint of scripture or some systematology or other. In this one is doing an injustice to the practice of these religions themselves. It will always remain impossible to realize an encounter with them as long as authentic value is not attributed to the actual practice; as long as the religion as incarnated in its participants is not also chosen as starting point of that 'discussion'. One will then come to the realization that various forms borrowed from other religions have, in their actual practice, not merely remained foreign components but have achieved a totally new interpretation. That in itself alone justifies the authenticity which the actual experience by the members of these religions deserves.

All of this is equally valid with regard to Japanese Buddhism. This, too, in its own character is not to be understood from the standpoint of certain Hīnayāna- and Mahāyāna schools. Here also it is indefensible to deduce an entire system,[1] without further evidence, from a certain religious phenomenon, whether this be an image or a Sūtra. In examining its true nature, actual and practical experience of the various sections of Japanese society will also have to be taken into account. In this research we have made what is, in as far as we know, an initial (and therefore, in many respects, incomplete) attempt to gauge the separate character of the most ancient Japanese Buddhism in its relationship with the Japanese national character.

Various considerations have brought me to this research into the initial phase of Japanese Buddhism. Along with many other colleagues, I have personally experienced over a period of years in Japan the problem of the laborious acceptance of Christianity. This problem was accentuated by the fact that at the same time many new, post-war, religions of local origin gained enthusiastic approval in the eyes of more than one-third of the Japanese population.[2] Naturally, in this situation, comparison of Christianity to these religions comes into being. The none too flattering fact to Christianity emerges logically, that here a religion which is Western, un-Japanese, not adapted to the local situation, far too highly based on speculation and relying too much on large and expensive institutions, really contrasts sharply with a group of indigenous religions which have built themselves entirely on the Japanese national outlook and on the major national post-war problems. Only these latter succeeded in combining the Western mental attitudes useful to Japan with its own ancient religious popular tradition. That combination is, in almost all of these religions, the result of extreme elasticity, receptivity and a highly delicately balanced perception. Regardless of what a new development may

[1] Cf. August Karl Reischauer, for example, in *Studies in Japanese Buddhism,* New York 1917. He considers that the image which King Sŏng of Paekche in Korea sent to the Japanese emperor Kimmei was one of Amitābha. Cf. p. 80. Also, the system of Amidism was immediately linked with this image. Cf. op. cit., p. 105.

[2] Cf. the most important works on this: Werner Kohler, *Die Lotus Lehre,* Zürich 1962; H. van Straelen and C. B. Offner, *Modern Japanese Religions,* Tōkyō 1963; A. Bairy, *Japans neue Religionen in der Nachkriegszeit,* Bonn 1959.

be, it is accurately noted, and, if useful, absorbed into these religions.

Here I have repeatedly asked myself whether this was also the case in past ages in genuine Japanese religions; in other words, whether we are dealing with a Japanese national characteristic. This would then consist of an almost unfettered receptivity of all that is new. In order to solve the above problem, I next asked myself: Did Buddhism in Japan's antiquity on its arrival, just as Christianity today, superimpose itself as a closed system on the structure of Japanese society? Or did it permeate from the bottom upwards? How did it grow to a national religion and a genuine popular movement? This research is an attempt to find an answer to all of these questions.

We have made this initial period of Japanese Buddhism the subject of our study not because we desire, as a kind of antiquary, to disassociate ourselves from the problems of modern Japan, but because the answer to these problems concerning such important questions as syncretism and adaptation has its roots in antiquity. This study of the manner in which the Japanese in antiquity encountered and accepted Buddhism is therefore, in my firm opinion, capable of throwing some light on forces which, naturally combined with many other and more modern elements, are active even to day. However much a nation may evolve in the course of centuries, certain facets will always characterize it. Dutch straightforwardness and (often impertinent and tactless) honesty have also not just come to light in our press during the last decade. On the basis of this type of characteristic, which repeatedly recurs in history, one encounters something one could call the 'eternal Dutchman'. This is valid in no lesser degree for the Japanese.

His desire for what we call syncretism has always characterized every religious revival in his history. The teachings of the *honji-suijaku*, 本地垂迹, and of *ryōbu-shintō*, 両部神道,[1] in which Shintō deities became the avatāras of Buddha and vice versa all Buddhas came under the protective guardianship of Shintō deities, is nearly as old as Japanese Buddhism itself. The failure of Christianity in Japan can be ascribed to the fact that it does not wish to harmonize with these syncretistic tendencies. Nevertheless, even Christianity has not remained free from this. Amongst the many disuniate

[1] Cf. this work, p. 468 ff.

Nagasaki Christians, the so-called *Kakure-Kirishitan*, 隱切支丹, many images of Christ and Mary have also become Shintō deities and bodhisattvas. Therefore it is also highly important to present-day Japanese religious problems to follow the process of Japanese syncretism from scratch. For the sake of this research we must point out two considerations at this stage which lend it its own special distinction. The first concerns Japanese antiquity, the second Japan's oldest mentality.

As far as antiquity is concerned, recent studies have brought to light that it had totally different aspects to those attributed or willfully ascribed to it.[1] As a result of this, Japan's most ancient, venerable and frequently deified emperors have become semblances as well as constructions which, for the benefit of a calendar system which was introduced later, had to fill up more than a thousand years. In proportion to the deeper antiquity to which the chronicles of Japan's oldest sources referred, they became increasingly unmasked as inventions which actually were to prove the historical situation of the eighth century. In the light of these facts, can one still accept facts which those chronicles recount with regard to Buddhism for example, knowing that these also probably served to 'historify' and legitimize the situation of the eighth century?

In connection with these queries concerning Japanese antiquity,

---

[1] Of these studies we mention: 1) The work by Kadowaki Teiji, *Jimmu Tennō*, Tōkyō 1957. This is a critical study of the historical material concerning Japan's 'first' emperor, Jimmu.

2) The collective work *Tennō no Rekishi* (History of the emperors), in which the most important historical problems surrounding the imperial house in particular are set out. It was achieved with extensive editing. Matsukawa Jirō has taken the lion's share in this. It was published in Tōkyō in 1959.

3) References for all this research and the material required are provided by the six-part work *Daigaku Nihon-shi* (Japanese history for university education), which was also brought about by the united efforts of a team of specialists as: Abe Makoto, Imai Rintarō, Inoue Kaoru. It was published in Tōkyō in 1958.

4) These problems are also touched upon in both works by Tsuda Sōkichi: *Nihon Jōdaishi no Kenkyū* (Study of Japan's primeval history) and *Nihon Koten no Kenkyū* (Study of the Japanese classics). They were published by the same publisher as the previous work, in 1963. We also refer the reader to many articles, quoted by us, in Japanese periodicals such as: *Shūkyō Kōron, Shigaku Zasshi, Chōsen Gakuhō, Minzoku-gaku Kenkyū, Kokugakuin Zasshi*, etc.

we have dedicated a separate chapter to Japan's actual origin and to the special structure of its most ancient sources.

Concerning Japan's oldest religious mentality, examination of Japan's oldest sources will lead us to entirely different conclusions than those recently deduced from these. It is clear from the above that, in order to comprehend this, we must not start from one or other Buddhistic system, but from the phenomenon of Japanese religiosity itself, as indicated by the sources as based on their various re-interpretations. By means of a critical approach to those sources I have attempted to penetrate to forms of religiosity for which there is probably no place in any single system, as they move between the systems and are accounted syncretism because of this. These forms constituted to those who believed in them a creed of authenticity equal to that which the systems themselves offered. Should the systems themselves in this study receive less attention, there will be other elements which must be taken into closer account. Some of them occur in all religions, others remain limited to the Asiatic continent. What elements are these? We believe that especially syncretism, Shamanism, Buddhistic forms such as Maitreyanism and Amidism, Shintō forms and the social structure of Japan have dictated Japan's religious mentality of the first century of the existence of Japanese Buddhism. We will conclude this introduction with a few remarks about demythologisation and Japanese names.

1. Syncretism

The first element, syncretism, has also been given a place in the title of this work: Encounter or Syncretism. In so doing we have sought after a formulation of the tensions in the oldest Japanese Buddhism. One might be able to formulate these even differently in the following question: In the confrontation between Japan's national religions and the most ancient Buddhism, was the main concern an encounter or an amalgamation, which we label syncretism?

The term encounter has gained a very peculiar sense especially in modern anthropology. An encounter only occurs between two persons, between an 'I' and a 'You'. It is made up of a conscious and voluntary positioning of my entire personality confronting someone else's. This definition of position results in a conscious acceptance or rejection of the other. In this not only are his personal characteristics concerned, but also his entire personality. His acceptance or rejection also includes this fact of his being different from myself. Such an acceptance can also take place in the emotional sphere, without its becoming conscious. It is, however, clear that one can only accept or reject the other when one knows him completely, otherwise only a fiction concerns both and not himself; in this case the personal core is not penetrated. In the latter case the image of the other merely becomes one charged with the observer's personal emotion and petrified fiction. Then it can readily diverge from the reality of the other. Here one has only experienced the other as an extension of oneself, not yet as the other himself. One can scarcely call this a genuine encounter.

A real existential encounter can only take place if the 'I' and the 'You' are experienced as the true I and You, without any projections. By the latter we mean a disproportionate enlargement, originating in various subjective motives, and a distortion of the original reality. The acceptance or rejection of the other in the latter sense not only encompasses some warped fiction of mine about him, but the actual existing reality of himself. It means my enriching myself with something which actually exists outside myself. This can only be thanks to the real encounter which precedes this.

This real, existential encounter is, however, not easily brought about. Processes must be activated in both 'encounterers' which will eventually lead to mutual contact. Therefore each encounter is preceded by the desire for, and an inclination towards, this encounter. It grows from a discontent with always being shut up within oneself, the fear of becoming too rigid and choking in one's own structure and a surfeit of this. All of this calls into being a desire to enrich oneself with the unknown, the new and the fascinating, which lives in the other. The position which one takes up with regard to one's own structure (often tied to tradition) and the ascendancy and charm of that which is new in the other, will both determine either the internal change or the inflexible opposition which result from the initial encounter with the other.

This anthropology of encounter is equally valid in the field of comparative religion. Here too one meets with a real and an unreal 'encounter', which, in their turn, are at two levels: a personal and an impersonal, abstract level.

At the personal level it is the encounter with the religion of another person in which his religion is experienced as exactly belonging to that person, as something which additionally defines his being different from me. The acceptance of this religion (= conversion) will render me very dependent on him, as this religion belongs very personally to him. In this one will often only be able to recognize the systematology of one or other religion with difficulty. However, there is also an imaginable acceptance of a religion which does not come to life in another person, but which exists as an abstract structure and system. Here, however, one will have to ask oneself whether, on the plane of such inter-personal relationships (where religion also takes a place) such an 'abstract' acceptance is possible at all; in other words, whether the acceptance or rejection of a religion is, ultimately, something which is canalized, especially in a society such as that of Japan, by human relationships and encounters. Especially among such practically minded East Asiatics as the Japanese, such abstract acceptance is likely to occur infrequently. Conversions amongst them will therefore usually be achieved as a result of previous human encounters.

One might go even further and consider this encounter as entirely separate from any individual, as if two different religions themselves were concerned in this. It is unnecessary to comment that the latter is only an abstraction as every encounter between religions mutually can initially only be brought about by and in human individual or community relationships. There can only be question of this abstract encounter between religions mutually after it has been phenomenologically established how these religions, seen as mental outlooks of individual persons, have "appreciated" each other in the encounter of these persons. That might take place in two ways. The 'foreign element' of the new religion may either be entirely discovered even before it has been accepted or rejected, or one may become stuck fast somewhere along the road to that discovery. In the latter case little more would be left of the new religion than a caricature, of which one does not know what really corresponds with the new religion.

These two possibilities also play a part in this work. In the encounter between Buddhism and Japanese popular religion both were realized. Therefore one must ask a double question with regard to sixth-century Japanese Buddhism: did the first Japanese who discovered Buddhism in a foreigner, recognize this as Buddhism also? In that case there was not only a personal encounter, but also a real encounter with Buddhism itself. Then he could accept it without confusing it with his own religion. Had he not indeed admitted its being different? This conscious knowledge would be conducive to assimilation rather than to syncretism.[1]

The second question is: did this Japanese meet this Buddhist foreigner without this also being an encounter with his Buddhism itself? In that case he did not see much more in Buddhism than a religious phenomenon, which, if necessary, he could invest with categories from his own religious mental world. His acceptance of the religious world of the other here contains the genesis of entirely new and original data. This resulted partly from discontent with his own religious thinking, as it limped along behind the changes of his time, partly from the results of the encounter. As a result of this an entirely new syncretic religion came into being, which henceforth began to move between Buddhism and his own old religion. The unity and organism of this were established by the 'believer' himself, in whom the new data continued to contrast with the old contents of belief, until they had achieved a new organic unity and harmony.

We do not wish to call this course of events outright syncretism. One should not only consider this concept as an alternative to the true encounter, as if there, where there was no encounter, only syncretism would remain. Because there also where a truly existential encounter has taken place, there was room for syncretism, if one is to interpret this as a mutual appropriation of each others beliefs. Others, however, are likely to prefer to see assimilation in this.[2] This latter encounter can only be ascribed to the fact that one does not desire to shut oneself off from the other in the loneliness of the personal 'I'. Especially with the Japanese this grew into syncretism in a higher degree than with us, as in his country there has not been so much conscious clarification of metaphysical conceptions, owing to the fact that metaphysical interests and thought

[1] There are not many known publications concerning syncretism. Concerning the concept syncretism cf. É. Cornelis, *Valeurs chretiennes des Religions non chrétiennes*, Paris 1965, pp. 75-99. With regard to popular belief and syncretism, M. de Jong in "Mysterieuze machten in het volksgeloof" (Mysterious powers in popular belief), *Streven*, 1960, no. XIII, part II, pp. 126 ff. considers syncretism to be a cross between an historical layer in popular belief and a natural layer. Here he gives some startling examples of Christian syncretism.

[2] Cf. É. Cornelis, op. cit., p. 76.

are unavoidably lacking in most East Asiatics with their strong attachment to concrete reality.

Between these two forms of encounter, real and unreal, and those of syncretism, conscious and unconscious, Japanese Buddhism of the sixth century is suspended. In the last three chapters of this work especially we hope to show that at that time there was merely an encounter, which became stuck fast along the road. It led to syncretism, which was the fruit of an only partial existential encounter. Buddhism had not, as yet, been accepted as the 'other'.

2. Shamanism

Modern students of comparative religion do not agree on the exact meaning and extent of this concept. It is therefore difficult to define this term so that all discrepancies concerning it can be ironed out. This is, also, not the intention of this work. Nevertheless we shall attempt to give a description which is, in our opinion, justifiable, so that the reader comprehends what we mean when we use the word shaman further on in this work. This description of the term does not necessarily indicate that we heedlessly agree with all the opinions of the various authors on this subject. We shall attempt to arrive at our own description of Shamanism by the use of the opinions of these authors.

The word shaman is derived from the Tungusian word *samâr*. However, it appears to originate from India and is related to the Sanskrit word *śramana*, which means priest. [1] One can not, however, deduce from this etymology that it might also owe its origin in Northern Asia to Buddhism. In Japan, for instance, Shamanism had existed for years before Buddhism travelled to this country. Here there is a strong similitude between the Japanese word *kami*, the leaders in Japan's pre-Buddhist society, and the Turco-Tartar name for shaman: *qam*. Shamanism was indeed stronger in Japan before the advent of Buddhism than afterwards. Therefore one can scarcely agree with Eliade in stating that it was especially instigated by Buddhism.[2]

Now what is Shamanism? In Shamanism we encounter an age-old Siberian and Northern Asiatic phenomenon, in which the lead is played by a male or female charismatic person, who ascends either to heaven or to a higher power in a trance. This phenomenon we

[1] Cf. M. Eliade, *Le Chamanisme*, Paris 1951, pp. 430 ff.

[2] Op. cit., p. 433.

describe as Shamanism. It is not permissable simply to describe this, in accordance with Findeisen,[1] as religion. Findeisen's description of Shamanism is narrowly connected with his outlook on religion. We find it hard to agree with his opinion that religion is only constituted by feeling and emotion or traces of a cult [2]) of a higher power. One will certainly have to allow room in the definition of religion [3]) for that higher power as a *terminus ad quem*. Now in Shamanism "das Heilige" as a *terminus ad quem* may vary in each case. It varies from the soul of a defunct person to the Supreme Being itself. Therefore we cannot call it a religion, but a religious phenomenon which is traceable throughout all religions: it is "eine Institution innerhalb einer anderen Religion".[4]

---

[1] Hans Findeisen, *Schamanentum*, Stuttgart 1957, p. 14.

[2] Findeisen, loc. cit., p. 14, by appealing to Nathan Söderblom, attempts to give substance to his premise that religion does not depend on imagery, but on the *feeling* (sensitivity) and the *affect* of primitive man towards a higher power, or on the words and gestures as expressions of the respect for this power. Can this be maintained? If the *terminus ad quem* is kept outside the definition of religion, then religion becomes merely a humanism. When making such a definition, one cannot exclusively argue from one or other *a priori*, as here the noetic plane is equally concerned. Therefore, in defining the specific nature of religion, one must start from existing religions, those of highly developed cultures as much as those of primitive peoples. Now these religions are not only defined and classified by the human relations to a higher being, but also by the individual nature of this higher being itself. It is arguable as to which of these two elements are primary for the definition of religion. It cannot, however, be said that they are not both necessary constituents for it.

[3] If, with G. Mensching, *Die Religion*, Berlin 1959, p. 18, one defines religion as: "erlebnishafte Begegnung mit dem Heiligen und antwortendes Handeln des vom Heiligen bestimmten Menschen", one is deficient in the definition of the being of religion, if '*Das Heilige*' is not itself concerned. Otherwise a totally different classification is arrived at, which wholly ignores the historically developed religions. Thus Christianity as a religion is not only distinguished from Islam by a principally differently experienced form of its relationship to both god and man, but also by the *terminus ad quem*, the actual nature of the Higher Being itself. The Trinity, eternally fruitful in love, and the lonely Allah both equally define the difference between the religions. The concept utilised by Mensching of '*Lebensmitte*' as "Besonderheit sowohl der Begegnung mit dem Heiligen als auch der Antwort auf sie", however adequate a generalisation for all religions it may be, does not suffice to differentiate them from each other. Here '*Das Heilige*' also plays a part.

[4] Cf. the discussion in Band IX of the "Ursprung der Gottesidee" by Annemarie von Gabain, in *Anthr.*, vol. 51, 1950, p. 1072.

If Shamanism is not identical with religion, but belongs amongst the phenomena common to all religions, such as mysticism, spiritualism, Yoga, etc., one may ask oneself what place it takes among these. The answer to this question is very narrowly connected with the inquiry into the real nature of Shamanism. Of what does this consist?

Eliade [1] sees the "phénomène originaire" in Shamanistic ecstatic experience, the primeval phenomenon, which takes shape in various ways according to the historical and religious situation. He finds this specifically expressed in the "ascension" of the shaman.[2] Findeisen finds the spiritualistic element especially noteworthy in this ecstatic experience.[3] We believe, however, that he exaggerates this particularly from personal experience.

Dom. Schröder [4] also sees moreover the internal change of being in the ecstatic experience itself, which the shaman wishes to establish in his trance. He contends that the latter is the essential characteristic of Shamanism. But even this does not adequately distinguish Shamanism from mysticism and Yoga, which also do attempt similar inward changes of being. Therefore, Schröder contends, this trance only becomes a totally Shamanistic trance owing to the fact that it is at the service of the entire community, i.e., he continues by describing Shamanism as "eine institutionelle und formgebundene Verbindung des Menschen mit dem Jenseits im *Dienste der Gemeinschaft*".[5] M. Boutelier also points out this social aspect. He opines that the shaman can not execute his office without general recognition and an official social consecration.[6]

---

[1] M. Eliade, *Le Chamanisme*, p. 436.

[2] Ibid. Cf. also the abbreviated summary of his opinion in a more recent article: M. Eliade, "Recent Works on Shamanism", in *H.o.R.*, vol. 1, 1961, p. 154: "As an experience, ecstasy is a non-historical phenomenon; it is a primordial phenomenon in the sense that it is co-extensive with human nature. Only the religious *interpretation* given to ecstasy and the techniques designed to prepare or facilitate it are historical data. That is to say, they are dependent on various cultural contexts, and they change in the course of history."

[3] Findeisen, op. cit., p. 15, describes Shamanism as "Eine alte spiritistische Religion, die in Nordasien alle anderen religiösen Bereiche, Anschauungen und Sitten weitgehend durchsetzt und sich angeglichen hat."

[4] In "Zur Struktur des Schamanismus", *Anthr.*, vol. 50, 1955, pp. 848 ff.

[5] Loc. cit., p. 879.

[6] Marcelle Bouteiller, *Chamanisme et Guérison magique*, Paris 1950, p. 269. We believe that the social characteristic, together with many others,

Without this social characteristic it is difficult to distinguish Shamanism from mysticism or spiritualism. Considering this social position of the shaman it is clear, that he might also play an important political part. This is indeed not only the case in some Siberian areas, or in pre-Buddhist Tibetan Shamanism, but also in pre-Buddhist Japan.[1] Besides these two, there were also other characteristics.

Goldammer [2] points out in particular the irrational element in Shamanism, which also establishes its charismatic character. The latter distinguishes the shaman from the priest, who is bound by established laws. Several of these characteristics may be recognized in A. Waley's [3] analysis of nine primeval Chinese shaman songs. Here one finds the shamans riding to meet the spirits in carriages drawn by mythical creatures, which are strongly reminiscent of the fiery chariot of the Old Testament shaman, Elijah.

In the light of the above we believe that the phenomenon of Shamanism is so complex that one can scarcely reduce it to one characteristic feature. Rather do we see the sum of all these phenomena in Shamanism. Wherever one is lacking, it becomes dubious whether we are still dealing with Shamanism.

These phenomena are:

1. The ecstatic element, which is made up of an inward change in the shaman.
2. The social element: the shaman always has his own position in society, which is often the part of leader.
3. The irrational and extrovert element which distinguishes him from the mystic and the yogi.
4. The charismatic element which places him opposite the 'legal' priest.

---

gives Eliade's ecstasy, described above, its religious interpretation of Shamanistic ecstasy.

[1] Cf. Findeisen, op. cit., p. 15: "Sie stellen nicht selten die politischen Führer ihrer Sippenbände." We have described the political leaders in Japanese Shamanism in Chapter II, pp. 83 ff.; the political, or state Shamanism of Tibet is described by R. de Nebesky-Wojkowitz, *Oracles and Demons of Tibet*, The Hague 1956, pp. 428 ff.

[2] Cf. Kurt Goldammer, *Die Formenwelt des Religiösen*, Stuttgart 1960, p. 364.

[3] Arthur Waley, *The Nine Songs, A Study of Shamanism in Ancient China*, London 1956, p. 14.

5. The different Weltanschauung, by which Shamanism becomes a Eurasian phenomenon.
6. The spirits and the deities who equally define his being, and who distinguish between one shaman and another.

Japanese Shamanism is very strongly determined by dependence on the spirits of ancestors. This ancestor Shamanism did not, as Eliade believes, develop from Buddhism but from far older influences. Thus the presence of ancestor worship—whether or not in connection with Shamanism—can readily be explained by the racial relationship of the Japanese people to the Chinese.[1] As far as the latter is concerned, we must point out that it is very difficult to decide which elements of this ancestor worship are of Japanese and which of Chinese origin, in other words, which have been present amongst the Japanese people from the start and which later became incorporated from China into the existing Japanese. Shamanism could have come into being there under Ainu or other Northern Asiatic influences.

Although less sharply distinguished, all of these elements may be found in the phenomenological description by Goldammer in his work *Formenwelt des Religiösen.*[2] He lays fairly strong emphasis on faith healers. However, one should not consider the working sphere of the shamans as being only in this field. They could be equally as important to national politics as in healing disease.

From the above closer definition of Shamanism, the degree of relationship to other religious phenomena such as asceticism, mysticism, yoga and primitive Buddhism also follows. They all

---

[1] As far as that ethnological relationship is concerned, cf. Egon Freiherr von Eickstadt, "Rassentypen und Typendynamik von Asien", in *Historia Mundi*, Munich 1952, I. Band, pp. 150-151: 3) "Die Drei Siniden Stufen". Neither here, nor on the map on p. 149, are Chinese elements in Japan mentioned. They were, however, as present in Japan as in Korea. The antiquity of Shamanism in Japan over and above that of Buddhism has been established, as it was met with just as much amongst Japan's oldest inhabitants: the Ainu. Cf. Werner Kohler, *Die Lotus-Lehre*, p. 270: "Das Schamanentum ist bei ihnen (Ainu) nachgewiesen und mit dem hocharktischen Schamanentum in Zusammenhang gebracht worden." The establishment of this fact renders unnecessary the consideration of the theses by Ohlmark and Eliade on the southern or northern expansions of Shamanism.

[2] Cf. p. 158.

pursue more individual purposes. Just as in spiritualism, the social character only comes in the second place. Of Yoga in particular it must be stated especially that it can not be divorced from the Indian mentality, just as little as Buddhism or Hinduism. Eliade says of this:[1]

"Le Yoga constitue une dimension spécifique de l'esprit indien, à tel point que partout où ont pénétré la religion et la culture indiennes on rencontre également une forme plus ou moins pure du Yoga. Dans l'Inde, le Yoga a été intégré et valorisé par tous les mouvements religieux hindouistes aussi bien qu' „hérétiques". It is unavoidably a technique which is equally defined by its object. This can only be realized within the confines of the Indian Weltanschauung. Therefore it is extremely doubtful whether one can separate this from this mental approach, so that one could, even in Europe, speak of a Christian Yoga.[2]

Primitive Buddhism too might be accounted amongst these phenomena, that is to say, Buddhism in its "original" concept, which, by means of the *anatta* teaching, consciously disassociated itself from the existence or non-existence of the *terminus ad quem*, but nevertheless remained a specifically Indian technique owing to its bonds with the Indian cyclical view of the world. If we are to separate this from this view of the world only a general human phenomenon remains. Of this we can say with Conze: [3] "The essence of this philosophy of life has been explained with great force and clarity by Thomas à Kempis, in his *Imitation of Christ*."

Western counterparts of the detailed way which is called Buddhism can therefore be seen in such works as *Ascent of Mount Carmel* by Johannes à Cruce and in various passages of the *Exercitia spiritualia* by Ignatius de Loyola.

This basic Buddhistic pattern of the "Four Noble Truths" and the "Eightfold Way" was only later linked with various forms of "Das Heilige". Owing to this, Hīna-, Mahā-, Tantra-, and Vajrayānistic religions came into being. The name Buddhism changed

---

[1] Cf. M. Eliade, *Le Yoga*, Paris 1960, p. 355.

[2] Cf. M. Eliade, op. cit., pp. 411-412. These pages give the detailed literature concerning this. Amongst modern publications, J. M. Déchanet's work deserves mentioning, which is: *La Voix du Silence*, Paris 1961, as an attempt to construct Christian Yoga.

[3] Edward Conze, *Buddhism*, London 1952, p. 11.

from a phenomenon current in many religions to a collective name of religions which vary from monism to mono-theism and polytheism.[1] This has left a wide field for Shamanism as well.

The fact that Shamanism, as we described it above, is also practised by women does not change its nature, as it is practised by men and women in equal degree.[2] Japanese Shamanism especially was almost exclusively practised by women. This is only owing to the fact that the important positions in pre-imperial Japan were practically only held by women. There are even symptoms which indicate that there must have been a matriarchy at that time. Eder [3] says of the present-day forms of Shamanism in Japan:

"Dafür, dass der Schamanismus fast nur von Frauen betrieben wird, dürfen wir nicht einfach bloss zu psychologischen Gründen, wie etwa grössere Empfänglichkeit der Frauenseele zum Glauben an übernatürliche Vorgänge, greifen, sondern die Tatsache des Mutterrechtes in Alt-Japan muss ebenfalls in Rechnung gestellt werden." These female shamans have exercised great influence on the very oldest Buddhism in Japan. This is shown by the historical figure of Empress Suiko, to which we shall return in chapter six.

3. Maitreyanism and Amidism

In Japanese Buddhism these two groups especially have played an enormous rôle. Owing to a particularly Western predominant preference for what we called above "original" Buddhism—because this corresponded most fully to the oldest texts—these two have been greatly forced into the background. As a result of this, the opinion is very generally widespread in the West, that Japan's Buddhism is really little more than Zen Buddhism. Actually the above-mentioned categories have defined the entire history of Japan's religious life and have contributed to the foundation of new categories and sects which have the greatest recruiting force amongst the Japanese people. In the Middle Ages in Japan these were Shin-*shū*, Jōdo-*shū* and especially Nichiren-*shū*. The new, post-war Japanese religions with the greatest and most explosive

[1] Cf. Christmas Humphrey, in: *Buddhism*, London 1954, p. 12: "Buddhism is in fact a family of religions."

[2] Cf. B. A. G. Vroklage, *De Godsdienst der Primitieven*, Roermond 1949, p. 371.

[3] Cf. Mathias Eder, "Schamanismus in Japan", *Paid.*, Heft VI, Mai 1958, p. 379.

growth, such as the Sōka-gakkai and the Risshō-kōsei-kai, which wish to bring about nothing less than a modern revival of the religion of Nichiren, have proved that even today Japanese popular religion is not of a very different nature than in the sixth or seventh century. We believe that just because of this these two groups can enable us to understand the true Japanese popular mentality. We shall return at some length to the true nature of these two categories in the third chapter.

4. Shintō and Ujigami Beliefs

There is mention in various places in this work of Shintō or *ujigami* belief. It is not permissible to see synonyms in these two terms. Here we encounter a starting point and an end point of a development which has needed many centuries. *Ujigami* belief, that is to say the religious convictions which were connected with Japan's oldest social structure, stood, together with other forms which were more or less disconnected, at the beginning of a centuries-long development. Shintō formed a later, streamlined and systematised termination of this.

There was first mention of true Shintō [1]) in the year 647, when Emperor Kōtoku, 孝德 (645-654) decreed: [2] "In accordance with the will (or the nature) of the gods,[3] my children must rule." According to Kōno Shōzō [4] the word in the Japanese text was used

[1] Cf. Shimonaka Yasaburō, *Shintō Daijiten*, Tōkyō 1940, part 2, p. 282, cols. II, III; W. Gundert, *Japanische Religionsgeschichte*, Stuttgart 1935, p. 32.

[2] Cf. *Nihonshoki*, 25th. *maki*, Kōtoku, Taika 3rd. year, 4th. month; Kuroita Katsumi, Maruyama Jirō, *Kokushitaikei Nihonshoki*, part 1, Tōkyō 1963, p. 239; Karl Florenz, *Die Historischen Quellen der Shinto-Religion*, Göttingen 1919, p. 350. Cf. W. G. Aston, *Nihongi*, vol. II, *T.P.A.S.*, 1896, Supp. I, p. 226.

[3] The Japanese text gives: 惟神, *kannagara*. The following notation has been added in the text: "*Kannagara* is also called: according to the way of the gods or the nature of the gods". In this the emphasis falls more on the accordance with the gods than on the gods themselves. This 惟神 is also read as *yuishin*, *kore kami* or *tada kami*. *Kannagara*—incorrectly limited by some to Amaterasu—shows similarity to *yawaragi*, prized especially by Shōtoku Taishi in 'his' constitution of twelve articles, as Japan's national virtue. (Cf. p. 389): the harmonious agreement to the will of the gods. Cf. Kōno Shōzō, "Kannagara no michi", *M.N.*, vol. III, July 1940, no. 2, pp. 9-31, especially pp. 11-23. See also the notes by D.C. Holtom concerning the word *kannagara* in the same article, pp. 27-28.

[4] Op. cit., p. 23.

for: in agreement with the will of the gods, *kannagara*, 唯神, in order to differentiate between the Japanese indigenous religions and the other foreign ones. This was also expressed in the opinion of a chronicler of Emperor Yōmei (586-588): [1] "The emperor has accepted Buddha's teaching and has, moreover, respect for the *paths of the gods.*" In the first text *kannagara*, in an additional remark, is clarified by *shin-dō*, 神道, the path of the gods. In the second text there is mention, without further ado, of *shin-dō* = Shintō.[2] Thus Shintō was projected from the very beginning as a local religion in contrast to *butsudō*: The way of Buddha, or Buddhism. Thus it became a concept which, in the course of time, absorbed all kinds of forms of religiosity which lay outside Buddhism. Gradually Confucian, Taoist and even elements affiliated to Buddhism began to belong to this, in as far as they received a position in the world picture of the gods (the *kami*). That this was a true *world* picture follows from the fact that especially in later Shintō there was no longer room for a heaven and a hereafter.[3] It was—and still is—a real religion, because it strove after a harmonious agreement with the will of the gods. In this pantheon were included not only the sun goddess Amaterasu, as was emphatically contended in times of too extreme nationalism, but also the ancestors of famous Japanese families and sometimes even living emperors themselves.[4]

Now in this centuries-long process of development of the fairly liberal and therefore nebulous Shintō, which primarily modelled itself on the systematism of Buddhism, the *ujigami* belief belonged to the initial phase. By this last observation we do not want to deny that besides the religion of Japan's oldest *uji*-society—which we call *ujigami* belief here—there were also religious cults such as ancestor worship and nature worship, which belonged just as much to the initial phase of Japanese Shintō.[5] The same processes therefore, in which *ujigami* belief was concerned, obtained equally in these other cults. We have treated of these only en passant in this

---

[1] Cf. p. 366.

[2] Ibid.

[3] Cf. Gamo Toshimasa, "Holtom no bankin no shintōron" (The recent Shintō discussions by Holtom), *K.G.Z.*, vol. 54, no. 2, June 1953, p. 53.

[4] Gamo Toshimasa, op. cit., p. 52.

[5] Concerning this see further: Shimonaka Yasaburō, op. cit., part 2, p. 282 (column I) to p. 284 (column II).

work, because their growth processes are harder to follow step by step. Generally they ran parallel to those of *ujigami* belief.

5. Social Structure

The last of the elements which has defined Japan's religious mentality in a very special manner has been its *pre*-Buddhist social structure. To a very great extent this made possible, and influenced, the advent of Buddhism. It formed the framework in which the encounter between Buddhism and the Japanese took place. This Buddhism then can only be comprehended within this framework. In as far as this is concerned, it is not very different from Western Christianity, which also owes its character largely to our western society. Therefore we have dedicated the second chapter of this work to this social structure of Japan.

6. Demythologisation

In various places in this work demythologisation is mentioned, but here it has not the existentialist meaning attributed to it by Bultmann and others in their interpretations of Holy Scripture. Here it is intended to give an historical and comparative X-ray of Japan's most ancient sources, so that out of, and from behind these Japanese myths and chronicles the intentions and characteristics of the authors and editors of these texts may come to light. In this way it is not only possible to encounter all sorts of anachronisms but it is also possible to uncover an historical development quite different to that which is actually suggested in these texts. The meaning of a personal and existential engagement must therefore not be looked for here.

In the light of a deeper insight into Japanese antiquity and the religious mentality which is implanted in its social structure, sketched in the first three chapters, we can experience the adventure of Japan's encounter with Buddhism in the last three chapters. From this encounter Japan's own folk mentality will unveil itself especially in the fifth and sixth chapters.

At the end of this introduction we must add one comment concerning the repeatedly recurrent Japanese names in this work.

In various places in this work personal names—frequently the length of an entire line—occur. In these not only the given name and family name of the persons concerned are incorporated, but also often titles, ranks, geographical and other descriptions of the person. In order to assist the reader somewhat on his way, we shall analyse some of these often recurring personal names. On this basis it will not be difficult to both understand and analyse other names. One of the most recurrent names is: *Soga no Umako no sukune no ō-omi*. Here Soga is the clan name; *no* means: of. Umako is the given name. *Sukune* is a kind of noble and untranslateable title.[1] Ō-*omi* indicates the great *omi*. An *omi* was the leader of a clan related to the emperor. As there were many dozens of these clans, there were also many dozens of *omi*. The leader of all these *omi* was called the great *omi*: *ō-omi*. Therefore one might translate this long name as follows: Umako, the *sukune* and leader of the *omi* of the Soga clan. In the same way one can translate the name of the antagonist of this Umako: *Mononobe no Yuke no Moriya no ōmuraji* by Moriya of Yuke of the clan Mononobe, leader of the *muraji* (the *muraji* were the antagonists of the *omi*).

There were also geographical personal names. One of them is: *Katsuraki no omi, Onara,* that is to say Onara (given name), the *omi* of Katsuraki (one of the districts of the Yamato area in Central Japan). *Ki no Omaro no sukune* is translateable by Omaro (given name), the *sukune* (title) of Ki (a territory lying on the bay of Ōsaka). Other names again were personal descriptions. One of the best known was *Umayado,* door of the horsestable, or: *Toyoto mimi no mikoto*: the imperial prince (= *mikoto* [2]) of the purple ears. These were two names for Shōtoku Taishi, Father of his Country, which indicate his birth place or his particular bodily features. Other names will be explained where they occur.

In the long names, descriptions such as *no* = of, and titles such as: *atae, sukune, ō-omi, ōmuraji, mikoto, hime* etc. are italicised so that the actual names stand out better. For the transcription of the

[1] This word—originally an official title in China—was especially used in the *Kojiki,* probably Japan's oldest manuscript, as an honorific for the *omi* group (cf. p. 123). Moreover, in the *Nihonshoki* it was also associated with the ancestors of various *omi*. For instance, one of them was the Soga patriarch Takeuchi *no sukune no mikoto* (cf. p. 64). This *sukune,* 宿禰, was supposed to stem from *sō* (祖), patriarch, and *na* (名), name. Particularly in the southwest corner of Yamato this became the title of the large clans or *shizoku*. Cf. Watanabe Naohiko, "Sukune no shiteki igi" (The historical meaning of sukune), *K.G.Z.*, vol. 63, nos. 10, 11, Oct., pp. 15-23; especially pp. 22-23.

[2] This word was reserved for emperors and imperial princes. Cf. Watanabe Naohiko, op. cit., p. 23; for derivation of this word see p. 83, footnote 3.

Japanese names and words Katsumata Senkichiro's: *Kenkyusha's New Japanese-English Dictionary* (Tōkyō 1954) has been followed and for the Chinese: R. H. Mathews' *Chinese-English Dictionary* (Cambridge, Mass., 1963). For the Korean words and names I took the advice of the Korean expert of the Leiden' University Prof. Dr. F. Vos. It goes without saying that the variant spellings in quotations remain untouched. For all the Japanese names and almost all the Chinese and Korean names we give also the Chinese transcription. This transcription is omitted only in case of a few Korean and Chinese names without any importance for our text and which only occur once.

CHAPTER ONE

THE GENESIS OF PRE-BUDDHIST JAPAN

The supposed origin of the Japanese empire has, for a long time, been something with which no one in Japan could, or might, meddle. According to Japan's oldest sources, the foundation of this country as a nation was dated as being in the year 660 B.C. This was supposedly done by Jimmu, 神武, the son of the gods, and first emperor. Thus it was attempted to establish the Japanese imperial house as the oldest still governing institution and dynasty in the world. This data has already been doubted openly in the West for a long time. In Japan everyone had to accept this up to 1945 as being well-established, as it all had a place in the dogmas which were supposed to maintain the Japanese war machine. Since then this has become more and more widely unacceptable in Japan as well. Nowadays there is general agreement that Japan began to exist as a nation not long before the fifth century A.D. This date is not far removed from that at which Buddhism came to the country. Therefore much research concerning Japan's origins also serves in placing the very earliest beginnings of Buddhism in a totally different framework than was the case hitherto.

A phenomenological inquiry into the beginnings of this Buddhism therefore demands that the results of all investigations into the beginning of the Japanese nation should be equally taken into account. This motivates the first two chapters in the lay-out of this work. Both are especially concerned with the origin of pre-Buddhist Japan. Moreover, emphasis is specifically laid on this origin itself in the first chapter. The unique nature of the Japanese people and the initial growth of their society form the theme of the second chapter. The wholly individual influence which has resulted from these on the origin and initial development of Japanese Buddhism induced us to treat of these two aspects in a separate second chapter.

From what we have briefly indicated above, it will be clear that much research into Japan's antiquity is still only in its elementary stages. Therefore it is not surprising that there are still many dubious points attached to it. Various reasons can be given for this.

One of the most important is probably that the pre-war Japanese government for a long time made it impossible for its own historians to study Japan's antiquity calmly and honestly. The government also established an educational system which was based on the supposition of the divine origin of the emperor. All of this has left traces in the generation alive today. For these who now wish to interpret the old sources differently from pre-1945 and want to 'de-mythologise' them, are still considered pioneers. Many post-war scientists can only hesitantly overcome the above-mentioned well-established assumptions. Amongst the few who [in imitation of previous Japanese thinkers such as Kamo Mabuchi (1697-1769) and Motoori Norinaga (1730-1801)] dared to doubt some nationalistic dogmas before 1945, and dared to pursue their own historical research, Tsuda Sōkichi was one of the greatest. He was sent to jail for some time for his publication *Shindaishi no Kenkyū* (trans.: Study of the history of the era of the gods). His free and brave vision was, however, honoured by various prizes in Japan after the war. Therefore the younger generations consider him a high and unassailable authority. By himself he already counts as a symbol for the fact that Japan's historical sciences have now taken an entirely individual and far from dull road. From this one can readily explain the great uncertainty of many modern Japanese historians with regard to antiquity. This chapter will therefore have to start with a brief glance at that road.

a. The history of Japanese historical science

Though Japanese historical science has taken a very individual road, it was only after the war that it became possible to study all of the questions surrounding the origin of the Japanese state freely and without hindrance. Up to 1945 Japanese historians lacked the freedom and the right to do this. Excessive nationalism formed an obstacle for a long time to these studies. Therefore the tale of Japanese history has, from the first, been a tale of official opposition and resistance.

Although historical studies had been dabbled in from the eighth century onwards, nevertheless there was no historical science, in the full sense of the word, worth mentioning till the beginning of the Meiji period (1868), when the school of von Ranke especially, with its critical use of all historical data, gained much support from

Japanese historians.[1] Earlier there had already been various doubts amongst such scholars as Ban Nobutomo (1773-1846) and Aoyama Emi (1776-1843) concerning the chronology of Japan's mythical origin and that origin itself. From then on these doubts became noticeably strengthened by intense study with stronger arguments.[2] This was provided by such scholars as Naka Michiyo (†1908), Kume Kunitake (1839-1931), Kida Teikichi (1871-1939), not to mention Tsuda Sōkichi (1873-1961). As most doubts were centered around the historicity of Japan's oldest writings, the *Kojiki* and the *Nihonshoki*, they were accompanied by a critical consideration and de-mythologising of these sources themselves.

However progressive the government might be in those days, it nevertheless took good care that not too much publicity was given to this research. Thus there was no question that the results of this research should reach the school books. Scientific publications containing discoveries about Japan's antiquity which were unwelcome to the government were suppressed without more ado. Thus Dr. Kume Kunitake [3] who, in a publication, connected Shintō with the Chinese cult of Heaven was so violently attacked by many Shintoists who called themselves 'folklorists', that he had to resign his professorship at the Imperial university of Tōkyō. Kida Teikichi was also dismissed from the same university in 1911 when he treated of Japan's historical northern and southern dynasties with the same considerations in a textbook intended for teachers. Tsuda Sōkichi was imprisoned in 1940 when he published a critical study of antiquity on the occasion of the 2600th anniversary of the empire. Chicanery of this nature destroyed any desire for honest historical research up till 1945.[4]

The ferocity with which historians of those days were opposed becomes comprehensible from the fact that the government of those days propagated mainly that which these historians most doubted. The best example of this is the institution of the celebration of the founding of the empire, the so-called '*kigensetsu*', (feast of *kigen*), 紀元節.[5] This was supposed to add colour to the

[1] Cf. John Young, *The Location of Yamatai*, Baltimore 1957, p. 174.

[2] For this and other data see, i.a., Kadowaki Teiji, *Jimmu Tennō*, Tōkyō 1957, p. 45 ff.

[3] See Kadowaki Teiji, loc. cit.

[4] Ibid. See also John Young, op. cit. p. 92.

[5] See Kadowaki Teiji, op. cit. pp. 17-35. Suzuki Shūchū points out, that

officially disseminated opinion that Japan was of divine origin, for had it not been founded in 660 B.C. by Jimmu, descendant of the sun goddess Amaterasu 天照? This mythical tale of Japan's foundation can be found in that country's oldest sources. Especially from 1872 on, the government gave these opinions its full support. On November 23 of that same year the *kigensetsu* was promulgated. On January 23, 1873 the date of this feast was also definitely established, after more than eight decrees had been published within a fairly short time, each of which stipulated a different date for this feast. At the same time other festivities were removed from the official calendar. These were especially the most ancient feasts, in connection with the harvest and the seasons. They were celebrated on January 7, March 3, May 5, July 7 and September 9. They are also sometimes indicated by the collective name *gosetsukun* 五節句.[1] The celebration of *kigensetsu* was instituted together with two other feasts. Thus the calendar of feasts henceforth contained: February 11, the *kigensetsu*; April 3, feast of the emperor Jimmu and November 3 the *tenchōsetsu*, 天長節. This last had been established by Emperor Kōnin (770-781 A.D.). After being unobserved for more than a thousand years it was again unearthed because, as an Imperial celebration, it lent itself extremely well to the new emperor cult.[2] The feast of *kigensetsu* was originally planned only for the court and government officials. The common people considered it to be not much more than a '*wake mo wakaranu hi*', 'a meaningless day'.[3] The government had clearly indicated by its entire legislation concerning this feast, that it itself was uncertain as to when precisely the Japanese empire had been founded. As

---

this question is still alive. However, one is now more inclined to see the origination of the nation embodied in the figure of Shōtoku Taishi, the Buddhist 'champion' and actual Father of the Fatherland at the beginning of the seventh century. Some wish to institute a feast of the foundation of the nation round him, because he was supposed to have been the first designer of a constitution. Today amongst the Japanese also, there are various objections to this. We need only refer to our final chapter for this. See Suzuki Shūchū, "Kenkoku hi no mondai" (Problems surrounding the day of the foundation of the nation), *Shūkyō Kōron*, vol. 28, 1958, no. 2, (Feb.), pp. 26, 27.

[1] See Kadowaki Teiji, op. cit., p. 34.

[2] For further details concerning politics surrounding these feasts, see Kadowaki Teiji, op. cit., pp. 31-34.

[3] See Kadowaki Teiji, op. cit., p. 36.

we shall see, it was impossible that the government should know this.

These, and many other measures were aimed at emphasising the absolutism and specially the divine descent of the emperors. In each decree, however boringly formulated,[1] this intention was brought forward. General conscription and compulsory education for instance, had to be maintained under this banner. Resistance from the local nobility was crushed by an appeal to this. In 1889 the constitution was founded even more on the divinity of the emperors. The first day of January 1900 saw the ceremonies of the celebration of the feast of *kigen*. Despite various incidents and national discontent, the policy of the government remained based on this until the end of the last war. As the propaganda for this increased, healthy and free development of historical science was made commensurately impossible. Many historians landed in jail owing to their opposition to the *kigensetsu*. We have mentioned Tsuda Sōkichi. The founders of the now powerful Sōka-gakkai also belonged amongst these.[2] 1945 brought the first complete freedom to study Japan's origin. Since then these ex-prisoners will, naturally, have been the first to re-write the history books. Just as the national historians many years previously, so the man in the street discovered an entirely different development than that which he had been led to believe in prior to 1945. For him too the Japanese nation no longer began in 660 B.C., but a thousand years later, i.e. shortly before Buddhism crossed to Japan. This gave a powerful jolt to the opinions of many. Kadowaki [3] writes of this:

"It is strange that, on the basis of material of more than a thousand years ago, all the facts surrounding Emperor Jimmu were, without further ado, accepted as truth. This is very strange for a country such as ours, with the smallest number of illiterates in the world. We shall have to examine critically as to who this Emperor Jimmu was, and not just allow ourselves to agree with the opinion of one or other historian."

---

[1] This unvarying formulation was: "The emperor is a son of the Goddess Amaterasu. He possesses genuine divine descent. All countries and peoples exist only for him. He and Amaterasu are the parents of Japan." See Kadowaki Teiji, op. cit., p. 36.

[2] Cf. J. H. Kamstra, "Sōkagakkai, Japans grösste Gefahr", *Z.M.R.* 44, 1960, no. 2 (April), p. 44.

[3] Op. cit., p. 36.

Now that this research has been taken up again after the war, we must not be surprised that numerous questions still remain unanswered concerning Japanese antiquity. The study of this is still in its infancy. Before arriving at definite conclusions the confidence which, owing to more than sixty years of fanatical propaganda, has been lost, will have to be regained. Only then will the results of this study also achieve respect in wider circles.

b. Recent results of source investigation

Despite the somewhat somber utterance of Kadowaki quoted above, various results have already been achieved. These also cast an entirely different light on the growth of Japanese Buddhism. These results are especially due to the study of the oldest sources of and about Japan, archeological finds, and the erstwhile East Asiatic historical constellation. They have all brought to light that Japan's history in the period between 660 B.C. and the fourth century A.D. was nothing more than a projection, which had mainly come into being in the eighth century. As a result of this a totally different image concerning the origin of Japan as a nation has evolved. There is no longer room for a divine figure such as Jimmu, and he is reduced to an absurdity. In this we do not wish to contend that we should also simultaneously deny his oldest sources, namely the *Kojiki* and the *Nihonshoki*, because they inspired this absurdity. A more critical study of these can equally confirm the results of the latest studies and aid in reconstructing the true picture of the Japan of antiquity. Owing to this research the true image is also gradually freed from its growth towards Buddhism. The first indications of this image appear from:

1 *The Chinese sources concerning Japan*

The oldest writings about Japan known to us originate from China. They indicate a very individual cross section of Japan's historical situation in antiquity. These are principally the *Hou Han-shu*, 後漢書, the *Wei chih*, 魏志, and the *Sung-shu*, 宋書.

The collection, which, although compiled fairly late (in 445 A.D. by Fan Ye (398-445 A.D.)) nevertheless contains the oldest data on Japan, is called the *Hou Han-shu*. This treats of the most important events concerning the Chinese later Han dynasty (25-220 A.D.). A special part of this is dedicated to 'The Barbarians of the East' and is therefore called *Tung-i chuan*, 東夷伝, traditions concerning the 'Eastern Barbarians'.[1] This introduced Japan to the Chinese as follows: [2]

"The *Wa* dwell on mountainous islands south-east of Han (Korea) in the middle of the ocean, forming more than one hundred communities. From the time of the overthrow of Chao-hsien (Northern Korea) by Emperor Wu (140-87 B.C.), nearly thirty of these communities have held intercourse with the Han (dynasty) court by envoys or scribes. Each community has its king, whose office is hereditary. The King of Great Wa resides in the country of Yamadai. The commandry of Lo-lang is twelve thousand *li* [3] from that country . . ."

Concerning the government of this region of the *Wa* peoples, the *Hou Han-shu* gives us the following: [4]

"In the second year of the Chien-wu Chung-yüan era (57 A.D.), the Wa country Nu sent an envoy with tribute who called himself *ta-fu*. This country is located in the southern extremity of the Wa country. Kuang-wu bestowed on him a seal.[5]

In the first year of the Yung-ch'u era (107 A.D.), during the reign of An-ti (107-125), the King of Wa presented one hundred sixty slaves, making at the same time a request for an imperial audience. During the reigns of Huan-ti (147-168) and Ling-ti (168-189), the country of Wa was in a state of great confusion, war and conflict raging on all sides. For a number of years, there was no ruler. Then a woman called Pimiko appeared. Remaining unmarried, she occupied herself with magic and sorcery and bewitched the populace. Thereupon they placed her on the throne. She kept one thousand female attendants, but few people saw her. There

---

[1] See Ryūsaku Tsunoda, *Japan in the Chinese Dynastic Histories*, South Pasadena 1951, p. 3, footn. 1.

[2] Ryūsaku Tsunoda, op. cit., p. 1. These texts may also be found in abbreviated form in Ryūsaku Tsunoda, Wm. Theodore de Bary, Donald Keene, *Sources of Japanese Tradition*, New York 1964, vol. I., p. 7 ff.

[3] A *li* is, in this case, slightly more than an English mile; cf. Ryūsaku Tsunoda, *Japan in the Chinese Dynastic Histories*, p. 4, ft. nt. 5.

[4] Ryūsaku Tsunoda, op. cit., pp. 2, 3.

[5] This seal was found in the Edo period (1600-1868) in the area of Hakata, not far from the present-day town Fukuoka. It is now generally accepted that this find is a forgery of a later date. See Okabe Nagaaki, "Kigensetsu no mondai" (Problems surrounding Empire Day), *Shūkyō Kōron*, vol. 27, 1957, no. 3, (March), p. 5; J. Edward Kidder, *Japan before Buddhism*, London 1959, p. 92; Ryūsaku Tsunoda, op. cit., p. 5, ft. nt. 12.

was only one man who was in charge of her wardrobe and meals and acted as the medium of communication. She resided in a palace surrounded by towers and stockade, with the protection of armed guards. The laws and customs were strict and stern.

Leaving the queen's land and crossing the sea to the east, after a voyage of one thousand *li*, the country of Kunu is reached, the people of which are of the same race as that of the Wa. They are not the queen's subjects, however."

These more or less similar data can also be found in the *Wei chih*, the collection of chronicles which were compiled circa 297 A.D. —150 years earlier than the *Hou Han-shu*—by Ch'ên Shou (233-297 A.D.). It treats of the most important events in the state of Wei, one of the three realms into which China disintegrated in the period of 220-268 A.D. The Wa peoples also appear here in a part dedicated to the Eastern Barbarians: the *Tung-i chuan*. As the compiled text of the *Wei chih* is older than that of the *Hou Han-shu*, it is not impossible that the compiler of the *Hou Han-shu* has delved into the *Wei chih* for various parts of his *Tung-i chuan*. In any case the agreement between the material of both texts is striking.[1] In our second chapter [2] we shall return to various details of this *Wei chih*.[3] In this text also there is mention of the people of Wa,[4] who dwelt in the Japanese islets fanning out through thirty minor states and maintained friendly relations with the Wei dynasty. The *Wei chih* has the most to relate about the federation of thirty minor states. Of these some are easily identified even today, such as the islands Tsushima and Iki, the natural bridge between South Korea and West Japan. The situation of others can no longer be established. Therefore there has been considerable discussion over the last hundred years, about the geographical situation and the extent of this federation. Together with the Horyūji question (in which it is debatable as to whether or not

---

[1] This was also the case for the texts concerning the Puyŏ in both works. Ikeuchi Hiroshi considers, as far as this is concerned, that the *Tung-i chuan* of the *Hou Han-shu* is a copy of that of the *Wei chih*. Ikeuchi Hiroshi, "A Study on the Fuyü", *T.B.*, no. VI, 1932, p. 27.

[2] P. 81 ff.

[3] See for the translated English text: Ryūsaku Tsunoda, op. cit., pp. 8-16.

[4] This term was written 倭. Until some time in the T'ang period, the Chinese used this to indicate the Japanese. See further Ryūsaku Tsunoda, op. cit., p. 4, ft. nt. 2. John Young gives a summary concerning the use of this word in the Chinese chronicles, op. cit., p. 28.

this famous temple burnt down in the seventh century) this, for a long time, formed the only problem of antiquity which was of interest.[1] Two groups of opinions grew from the discussions about this, which even today still have fervent proponents, namely the Kyūshū- and the Yamato groups.[2] The first group situates all the minor states of the Wei chronicle without more ado in Kyūshū, the second spreads them out up to the region of Yamato, the surroundings of the present-day towns of Nara and Ōsaka. The first group sees no more than large villages in all of these little states, which all together could therefore never have extended to the Yamato area. The Yamato group, however, was more inclined to transpose the point of gravity of this federation to Yamato, as this has always been its only center of gravity politically and culturally in Japanese traditions. It need not be stressed that the pre-war Japanese nationalism also played a part, as Yamato was very closely connected with the imperial traditions. The Kyūshū opinion, the junior of the two, finds more supporters amongst historians who do not wish to be connected with nationalism. However, they too are not blind to the major role which the Yamato plain has played in Japan's history.

Which of these two is right? The answer to this question is very important to those who wish to form any idea of the origin of the Japanese empire and the role which Yamato played in this. According to the oldest sources, the emperors resided right from the beginning in the plain of Yamato. According to the defenders of the Yamato opinion, that was certainly the case in the second century A.D. Thus a continuity must have existed between the federation of the *Wei chih* and the emperors of Yamato before them. To support this idea they ascribed to the empire of that period a region stretching from the island of Tsushima to the plain of Yamato. Many of them at the same time identified the female leader of the federation, Himiko, with the most prominent empress of the *Kojiki*: Empress

---

[1] Cf. Okabe Nagaaki in: "Nichi-shi-kō to shijō no Taishi" [(Shōtoku) Taishi and the historical relations between China and Japan], *Shūkyō-Kōron*, vol. 25, 1955, no. 4, p. 65: "The most important study after the Meiji period (that is to say, after 1912) was made up of the Hōryūji and the Himiko dispute."

[2] Matsukawa Jirō, "Tennōshijō no bōten" (Unclear points in the history of the Emperors), *Tennō no Rekishi*, pp. 20-122, has expatiated on the problems of the Yamato and Kyūshū groups. Especially on pp. 39, ff. See John Young, op. cit., for the entire historical development of this matter.

Jingū, 神功. However, not all supporters of the Yamato group agree with this latter identification, as Jingū—according to the traditional chronology of the *Nihonshoki*—was supposed to have lived more than a hundred years after Himiko. For the supporters of the Kyūshū opinion, however, there could not possibly be question of such a continuity as it is precisely the existence and the authority of the emperorship at that time which they query.[1] Both groups' arguments more or less by-pass each other. The Yamato group attempts to twist the Wei chronicles on the basis of the emperorship. The Kyūshū group starts more or less with the Wei texts and allows the existence or non-existence of the emperorship—at least in Kyūshū—to depend on them.

We attribute the most value to the arguments of this latter group. A federation, which certainly encompassed the islands of Tsushima and Iki, had apparently developed itself from Korea. These islands served as a bridge to Japan. Therefore it is more likely to have had its focal point in Kyūshū. Yamato, situated more than thirteen hundred kilometers from Tsushima and inaccessible at that time owing to bad communications, could scarcely satisfy the demands made on the government centre of such a federation. In saying this we do not wish to deny that Yamato itself could have been a centre of political power at this time. We do not know. It is, however, too far-fetched, to distort and interpret the relatively small distances which are mentioned in the Wei chronicles, to such a degree that Yamato becomes accessible. If one is to accept that the imperial family resided in Yamato even at that time, one will have to accept a second centre of power in Kyūshū also.

Another interesting particular which these chronicles offer, is the fact that the entire federation of states was ruled by a woman. Namely, there was the head of the central Wa state: Pei-mi-hu, 卑弥呼, or Pimiko, Sino-Japanese Himiko, also occasionally read as Himeko (= princess).[2] The Chinese chroniclers called her a witch and a develish teacher, who misled the population. In the second chapter we hope to show [3] that she was, in fact, a governor and a priestess. She succeeded to a male ruler, under whom the federation

---

[1] Tsuda Sōkichi, *Nihon Koten no Kenkyū*, part 1, p. 570: "No continuity existed between Himiko and an empress of Yamato: the land of Yamadai (name of the federation) was therefore not identical to Yamato."

[2] For both these versions, see Ryūsaku Tsunoda, op. cit., p. 5, ft. nt. 15.

[3] P. 87, ff.

had fallen into decay. Her rise to power meant a re-awakening for the country and the government. Towards the end of the second century she had succeeded in projecting herself as a symbol of federal unity. In particular the continuous threat from the geographical indefinable country of Kunu had led to this.[1]

We indicated above, that some of the supporters of the Yamato group intended to emphasise that this Himiko was none other than the Empress Jingū, the mother of Emperor Ōjin, 応神.[2] According to the official dates of the *Nihonshoki*, she ruled from 201-269 A.D., that is, about a hundred years after Himiko. It is hard to prove, from the scant details of the *Wei chih*, whether they were identical. The principle argument against it still remains the impossibility that Yamato [3] could have been the centre of the federation. In addition to this, there is also the refusal of some of the supporters of the Yamato group to investigate critically whether the second century emperorship existed. We hope to point out also, that it has now been established that the data which the *Kojiki* and the *Nihonshoki* give us concerning this, are highly dubious, as the material for these old manuscripts was not assembled until a few centuries later. Naturally this research forces us to ask ourselves whether emperors were general in Japan at that time. In how far this question becomes justified by discoveries at a later date, we shall refer to later.

Other Chinese sources have also given us information concerning

---

[1] According to supporters of the Kyūshū opinion, this must have made up approximately the southern half of Kyūshū. Some protagonists of the Yamato opinion prefer to assume that this area was in the northern areas of Honshū.

[2] According to the traditional count she reigned between 201 and 269 A.D. The compilers of the *Nihonshoki* were the first to allow her to co-exist with Himiko, by inserting the notes of the *Wei chih* in the Jingū chronicles. This occurred in her 39th, 40th and 43rd year. See Kuroita Katsumi, Maruyama Jirō, *Kokushitaikei Nihonshoki*, Tōkyō 1962, part 1, p. 257. Nevertheless, Himiko certainly lived earlier. Her government concurred with the reign of Emperor Ling, 靈, of the late Han dynasty, i.e. between 180 and 190 A.D. Cf. Matsukawa Jirō, op. cit., p. 28 and p. 70.

[3] An important argument was, in this, the similarity of the name Yamato (大和) to Yamadai (邪馬台), the name of the federation. The supporters of the Kyūshū opinion however, also had their own pendants for this Yamadai, such as: Yamato *no* kōri (Higo, Kyūshū) or the Kumaso area of south Kyūshū, Ryūsaku Tsunoda, op. cit., p. 4, ft. nt. 4. For further literature concerning this, see Bruno Lewin, *Aya und Hata*, Wiesbaden 1962, p. 4, ft. nt. 9.

some of the Japanese emperors. For instance, we know that between the years 413 A.D. and 502 A.D. there was certainly contact between Japan and the Chinese southern dynasties. These were in particular the Sung, 宋, (420-479 A.D.) and the Ch'i, 齊, (479-502 A.D.) dynasties. These relations are shown in the collections of chronicles of that period, the *Sung-shu* and the *Sui-shu*,[1] 隋書. The *Sung-shu*, compiled by Shên Yuëh (441-513 A.D.) was particularly important, as in this the names of the Japanese emperors of that period are mentioned. These are: [2] 讃, Ts'an (Sino-Jap.: San), 珍, Chên (Sino-Jap.: Chin), 済, Ch'i (Sino-Jap.: Sai), 興, Hsing (Sino-Jap.: Kō), and finally, 武, Wu (Sino-Jap.: Bu). It is difficult to correlate all these figures with various Japanese emperors of the *Kojiki* and the *Nihonshoki*. This explains the vast disagreement which exists regarding this point. There is general agreement to the extent that they are considered successors of Ōjin, who is considered by many to be the actual founder of the Japanese realm. That might then have been: Nintoku, 仁徳, in whom many see only an invented simulacrum,[3] then Hanzei 反正, Inkyō, 允恭, Ankō, 安康, and Yūryaku, 雄略.[4] The reason that these figures are mentioned may be ascribed to the fact that they all ruled during the fifth century in Japan. But it remains difficult to date them more closely.

In a letter which, according to the same *Sung-shu*, King Wu sent to the Chinese court in 478 A.D., the following can be read: [5]

"Our land is remote and distant; its domains lie far out in the ocean. From time of old forebears have clad themselves in armour and helmet and gone across the hills and waters, sparing no time for rest. In the east they conquered fifty-five countries of hairy men; and in the west, they brought to their knees sixty-six countries of various barbarians. Crossing the sea to the north, they subjugated ninety-five countries. The way of government is to keep harmony and peace; thus order is established in the land . . ."

---

[1] See Ryūsaku Tsunoda, op. cit., pp. 22, 24 for the *Sung-shu* mentioned and quoted here.

[2] For the actual Chinese text, see: *Daigaku Nihon-shi*, pp. 40, 41; Ryūsaku Tsunoda, op. cit., pp. 22, 23.

[3] As a projection from a later period, which served to embody the Confucian virtue of 仁, *jên*, Sino-Jap.: *jin*, magnanimity, in Ōjin's time. Cf. Tsuda Sōkichi, *Nihon Koten no Kenkyū*, part 2, p. 39 ff.

[4] See note 4 on page 33.

[5] The Chinese text may be found, i.a., in *Daigaku Nihon-shi*, part 1, pp. 40, 41. See Ryūsaku Tsunoda, op. cit., p. 23 for the English text.

This text proves that in 478 A.D. the unity of the Japanese state was a fact owing to the influence of more powerful figures than Himiko. Here one can ask oneself whether the federation of states, of which there is mention in the Wei chronicles, did not initially begin to become a part of the empire situated at Yamato at this time. This confederation of states would then have been of the same limited size as that of the respectively 55, 66 and 95 small states, of which there is mention in this text. The vast number of these small states causes one to suspect that they were not much more

---

[4] How far opinions differed concerning this, may be seen from the following table:

Data	*Nihon-shoki* a)	*Sung-shu*	Ts'i chronicle	Hara b)	Hashi-moto c)	Matsu-moto d)	Naoki e)
310	Ōjin						
399	Nintoku				Ōjin	Ōjin	Ōjin
405	Richū						
410	Hanzei						
415		Ts'an (Ōjin or Nintoku)		Nintoku (= Ts'an)			
420							
425					Nintoku		Nintoku
430		Chên (Hanzei)					
435	Inkyō				Richū		
440				Richū	Hanzei		
445		Ch'i (Inkyō ?)				Nintoku	Hanzei
450				Hanzei	Inkyō		
455	Ankō	Hsing (Ankō ?)				Inkyō	Inkyō
460					Ankō		
465	Yūryaku	Wu (Yūryaku)		Inkyō		Ankō	
470					Yūryaku		Ankō
475				Ankō			
480						Yūryaku	
485	Seinei	478 (letter from Wu)	479 (Anto Becomes C.-in-C. (of Army))	Yūryaku			
490	Kenzō						Yūryaku
502	Ninken						

Notes: a) Until 1945 the dates of the *Nihonshoki* were the officially adopted ones. The *Kojiki* has no dates, but merely indicates the ages of the emperors.
b) and c) are based on Kadowaki's survey, op. cit., p. 209.
d) For this opinion, see Matsukawa Jirō, op. cit., pp. 93 ff.
e) Article by Naoki Kojirō in *Daigaku Nihon-shi*, part 1, pp. 25 ff.

For the identification of these Chinese emperors with the Japanese, see A. Wedemeyer, *Japanische Frühgeschichte*, Tōkyō 1930, pp. 98-107.

than large agricultural communities. In any case, this *Sung-shu* confirms—in contrast to the *Wei chih*—that Japan was ruled by powerful rulers in the fifth century, who are comparable to some of the imperial figures found in its own sources. What, however, happened before that period in the imperial house, we can only learn from Japanese archeology.

2 *Japanese archeology*

The existence and achievements of the five rulers mentioned in the *Sung-shu*, are particularly confirmed by burial mounds. These huge funerary monuments often built up in the shape of a keyhole, can be found without much difficulty all over central Japan. Kidder [1] in particular has described them. Those who wish to investigate their position with regard to earlier periods of Japanese archeology, need only be referred to his book.[2] These burial mounds form the proof of the origin of an entirely new culture and funeral customs, which remain inexplicable from Japan's archeological past. The start of these burial mounds can be dated at the end of the third, early fourth century. Prior to that time the dead were not buried in such tumuli, not even dead rulers. The most extensive graves date from the fifth century, the period of the abovementioned five emperors. One of the largest of these burial mounds is now generally ascribed to Emperor Nintoku. This Nintoku grave, situated on the eastern edge of the town of Sakai near Ōsaka, belongs to the largest grave monuments in the world. It is more than 108 feet high, nearly 2695 feet long and is surrounded by a large moat.[3] The erection of this mound was an exertion which, without exaggeration, may be compared to the laborious building of the Egyptian pyramids. Besides the objects which were normally buried with the dead in earlier periods and cultures, artefacts were found here which indicate a greater dependence on the horse than previously. Moreover, these graves specifically show many points in common with those of North Korea and the North Asian continent. In so far they bear witness to an unheard of break with

---

[1] J. E. Kidder, *Japan before Buddhism*, London 1959.

[2] J. E. Kidder, op. cit., pp. 145 ff.

[3] J. E. Kidder, op. cit., pp. 146, and 150, 151. An even larger grave was the one which originated in the seventh century, known as Ishibutai and belonging to Soga no Umako, situated near Shimanoshō. See J. E. Kidder, op. cit., p. 159.

Japan's previously existing cultural pattern. This is inexplicable from the customs of the previously existing fishing and farming population. It may be dated at the end of the third century. This break did not originate in South Korea or Kyūshū, as the oldest burial mounds and also the largest concentration of them may be found in the Yamato district. The interest in the horse—often religious—which is shown by various remains in these graves, probably indicates a Northern Asiatic nomad tribe. This tribe might have entered from the North of Korea into Japan and come to a standstill in the plain of Yamato. There it began to intermingle with the existing population, of which in future it made up the top stratum. This is the only explanation for the sudden upsurge of the burial mound culture with relation to earlier cultures. From Japan's archeological situation alone it remains incomprehensible.

As the imperial house was so narrowly connected with this funerary cult, we cannot avoid accepting that this must have entered Japan only in the third or fourth century, though the road it followed is unclear. It is obvious that at that time there was, as yet, no imperial house in the strict sense of the word. Here we still have only to do with a nomadic tribal chieftain. This leadership was hereditary, just as that of other North Asiatic and Tungusian tribes. The successors of these tribal chieftains could grow into powerful rulers and immediate predecessors of the imperial house, by extending their territory and influence.

It follows from the late arrival of this so-called 'imperial race' to Japan, that it was not yet there at the time of Himiko. The Japan of the emperors began shortly before the first burial mounds came into existence. Thus this opinion makes an end of the so-called 'divine descent' of the emperors. The pioneers of this theory are especially Kida Teikichi,[1] Oka Masao,[2] Egami Namio,[3] and Kado-

[1] See F. Vos' inaugural speech: *Volken van één stam* ? (Peoples of one tribe ?) for a clear exposition of the opinion of Kida about the *Tenson-minzoku*, the Celestial Grandson peoples. The Hague 1959, pp. 6 ff.

[2] Oka Masao, in his 'Culture complex' hypothesis, explains the origin of the Japanese people as coming from five population groups, which merged and united with each other. These groups were: an ethnical group of Melanesian origin; an Austro-Asiatic group; a north-eastern Asiatic Tungusian group; a south-eastern Asiatic group of Austronian origin and finally an altaic group, which first conquered all the tribes of Manchuria and Korea at about the beginning of our era. In the fourth century it crossed to Japan. This group, in contradistinction to the first two, was patriarchal. They

waki Teiji.[1] As their hypotheses partly take place in pre-history, it is difficult to verify them entirely. However, the reverse is equally true.

It is self-evident that the above reconstruction of the origin of the Japanese emperorship can find no justification in the eyes of many. It is, inevitably, difficult to free oneself emotionally from the old myth of the emperors, which formed an important part of the entire school curriculum up till 1945. Liberation from such convictions, impressed from childhood, necessarily demands a free and independent train of thought. Even for those who managed to achieve this, a calm and objective opinion on these questions remains difficult. Against this background we can understand the criticism which Matsukawa Jirō aims at Egami Namio, one of the supporters of the above-mentioned opinion:[2] "Egami airs only illusions which spring from his prolific fantasy in his new theory." Matsukawa himself, on the contrary, is of the opinion, that the imperial lineage could not possibly have come from Korea into

---

recognised Amaterasu or Takamimusubi as deities. This opinion of Oka Masao was tested in 1948 on those of Egami Namio, Yawata Ichirō, et al., in a discussion concerning the origin of the Japanese people. This discussion was published in *Minzoku-gaku Kenkyū*, vol. 13, no. 3 (1948), under the titel "Nihon-minzoku-bunka no Genryū to Nihonkokka no Keisei (Origin of the Culture of the Japanese people and the Forming of the Japanese State)", on pp. 207-277. Matsukawa Jirō based his article "Tennōshijō no bōten" on this discussion. See *Tennō no Rekishi*, pp. 107, ff. for the opinion mentioned above. See also Joseph M. Kitagawa, "Prehistoric Background of Japanese Religion, *H.o.R.*, vol. II, 1963, no. 2, pp. 308, 309.

[3] Egami Namio has further based his hypothesis on the abovementioned opinion of Oka Masao. He believes that the last group, according to him, the horse riding tribe (*kiba-zoku*), crossed from the southern tip of Korea to Kyūshū and travelled on from there to Yamato. There, in the fifth century, it became the founder of the Japanese nation. Cf. "Nihon-minzoku-bunka no Genryū . . .", p. 241 ff.; J. M. Kitagawa, op. cit., pp. 310 ff.; Matsukawa Jirō, op. cit., p. 114.

[1] Cf. Kadowaki Teiji, op. cit., pp. 105, 106. He deduces a political development into larger states from the growth in circumference and height of the burial mounds. The struggle of the prehistorical and mythical Jimmu might have taken place in this period, that is to say, the third and fourth centuries. Those in opposition to Jimmu in this struggle, were the members of the original population. This opinion, according to Kadowaki, reached publication for the first time in the *Yamato Times*, in an article by Ikeda Gendai: "Atarashii Yamato no Rekishi (the new history of Yamato)".

[2] Op. cit., pp. 121, 122.

Japan, as there is only mention in the *Kojiki* and the *Nihonshoki* of raids by the people of Yamato into Korea, and not vice versa. According to him the break in the development of the old cultures was not due to some invasion or other, but to an internal revolution This argument, however, cannot be justified, as in the works aforementioned there is merely mention of strife between the imperial house of Japan, which had already developed, and Korea; not of a conflict which had something to do with the origination of that imperial house itself. Tsuda Sōkichi, as one of the opponents of this invasion theory, also believes that the imperial house was established in the second or third century within Japan itself.[1] According to his views, it acted aggressively only outside and not within Japan. That is specifically shown in the battle against Korea. The same, however, is valid for him as for Matsuwaka, i.e. that he also almost exclusively depends on the *Kojiki* and the *Nihonshoki*. We shall return more closely to these two sources in the following pages. In connection with Tsuda's opinion, we must here point out that in these sources there is also repeated mention of internal enemies such as the *Ebisu* 夷 and the *Tsuchigumo* 土蜘蛛, two frequently recurrent names, which could both be freely translated by 'barbarians'.[2] In all the despatches concerning these opponents, one gets the impression that here one has to do only with Japan's original population.[3] Matsukawa and Tsuda, despite their critical attitude towards the Japanese sources, have followed them too closely, without taking the above-mentioned archeological and other data from the history of the surrounding countries into account.

Other proponents of the revolution theory want to reconstruct a proof from the inscription which was inscribed on a 17 foot commemorative column, which was discovered in 1882 on the site of the old Koguryŏ (= North Korea) capital T'ong'gu (Chinese: T'ung-kou) in Southern Manchuria. On this column the heroic deeds of King Kwanggaet'o (Chinese: Kuang-kai-t'u) 広開土, (391-412 A.D.) of Koguryŏ are exalted. According to the same

[1] In *Nihon Jōdaishi no Kenkyū*, p. 451.

[2] The Ebisu, Tsuchigumo, Kumaso and others counted equally as tribes, which, just as the great opposers of Yamato from Izumo, did not participate in the Japanese nation.

[3] One can find these data in almost every *maki* of the *Kojiki* and *Nihonshoki*, but also in superabundance in the *Fudoki*.

inscription it was erected in 414 A.D. This column is of high historical value especially to Japan and Korea. In addition to the above-mentioned Chinese manuscripts, this is the oldest historical witness concerning the Japanese. It amplifies the Chinese manuscripts. In these latter these relationships and wars with China itself are primarily in the foreground. Military operations and other occurrences in which China did not participate, only received scant attention. On this column, however, various military operations are mentioned which took place outside the Chinese sphere of influence. Thus, i.a., the Puyŏ [1], 夫余, are mentioned here. It is of importance to Japanese history because it records various Japanese invasions, victories and defeats.[2] According to this stone, the *Wa* overthrew the vassals of Koguryŏ in Southern Korea, Paekche and Silla in 391 A.D. In 399 A.D. Koguryŏ marched on Paekche, which had broken its pact with Koguryŏ. In 400 A.D. Koguryŏ came to the aid of Silla under the leadership of King Kwanggaet'o against the *Wa* and in the years 404 A.D. and 407 A.D. Kwanggaet'o succeeded in overwhelmingly defeating the *Wa.* [3] The inhabitants of *Wa*, of whom there is mention on this column are the same *Wa* people of whom there is mention in the Chinese chronicles. The facts which this inscription records, however, cannot be allowed to count as arguments against the invasion theory, as the occurrences recorded there, took place only at the beginning of the fifth century, that is to say, some time after the invasion of the 'imperial race'. The invasion occurred more than a century earlier.

Both supporters and opponents of the invasion theory have, however, left one argument out of consideration. This places not only the development, nature and structure of the new imperial race, but also the growth of Japan's religious mentality, namely Buddhism, in an entirely new light. This argument is to be found in the state of affairs abroad at that time. If, namely, the 'imperial'

---

[1] Cf. Chapter III, p. 198, ft. nt. 4.

[2] Cf. B. Szcześniak, "Japanese-Korean Wars in A.D. 391-407 and their Chronology", *J.R.A.S.*, 1946, parts 1 and 2, pp. 54-66. In this context especially p. 59.

[3] For the literal text of all of these texts, see Sakai Kaizō, "Kōtaiō-himen no chimei ni tsuite (On the local names in the suscription of the Hotĕ-wang monument)", *C.G.*, no. 8, 1955 (Oct.), pp. 51, 52; *Daigaku Nihon-shi*, part 1, p. 40; see furthermore B. Szcześniak, op. cit., pp. 60, 61; Emil Gaspardone, "La Chronologie ancienne du Japon", *J.A.*, tome CCXXX, Avril, Juin, 1938, pp. 235-277, especially pp. 264, 265.

race operated from outside the Japanese island territory, then it is obvious that it began migrating owing to various foreign involvements. It is hard to accept in the first place that population movements which concerned not only Western Europe but also the lands on the periphery of Japan such as Korea and North China, should just have ignored the Japanese islands. The possibility that Japan was influenced by these is also confirmed by the fact that from the end of the fourth century Japan's relationship with the population of these areas increased noticeably.

It is, however, hard to trace which tribes or peoples were concerned in the invasion of Japan. Only those tribes have remained known to us which, in one way or other also played a part in the history of China. This is owing to the fact that this land alone recorded the movements of the tribes in its state chronicles. By the use of these we cannot identify but are able to estimate the tribes which must have invaded Japan.

The people who have most influenced China's history were denigratingly called the Five *Hu*, 胡, that is to say, the Five Barbarians, by the Chinese themselves. They owe this name to the fact that they flooded China in five consecutive waves. The beginning of these invasions in China occurred at the same time as the arrival of the 'imperial tribe' in Japan. These *Hu* were nomadic people, who, relying on their fleet horses,[1] knew how to render the local population serviceable to themselves. They have influenced world history as far as West Europe. The Huns of Attila (434-453 A.D.) and the Mongol tribes of Genghis Khan, which threatened Europe and Japan in the thirteenth century were related to them. This is proved by the names of these five barbarian groups. Those were the Hun tribes such as the Liu and the Kie, Tibetans such as the Fu- and Chang families and especially the Tungusian Hsien-pi, 鮮卑, and T'opa, 拓跋, which respectively founded the powerful Yen-, 燕, and Wei, 魏, realms.[2] Dwelling on the edges of the Chinese empire, they exercised pressure in various directions on it. This often occurred simultaneously, so that they subdivided the large

---

[1] Cf. Wolfram Eberhard, *Lokalkulturen im alten China, T.P.*, suppl. vol. XXXVII, Leiden 1942, pp. 13 ff.

[2] Cf. O. Franke, *Geschichte des chinesischen Reiches*, Berlin 1936, II. Band, p. 63. As far as the Yen realms are concerned, cf. G. Schreiber, "The History of the former Yen Dynasty", *M.S.*, XIV (1949-1955), pp. 374-480; XV (1956), pp. 1-141.

Northern Chinese 'cake' into many small states amongst themselves. The Tibetan tribes operated on the west side of the empire. The Huns often attempted to invade China from the North, but they were overwhelmingly conquered and exterminated in 352 A.D. by the Hsien-pi, so that no trace of them any longer remains. These Hsien-pi and their strongest grouping, the T'opa,[1] who ruled the longest of any, coveted the north-eastern edge of the Chinese empire for themselves. The T'opa ruled there in the Wei kingdoms which began to coexist in 386 A.D. with the Yen kingdoms of the Hsien-pi. Eventually they were to absorb these within their elastic borders. Hence these last two tribal groupings operated in an area which was situated near to Japan and Korea.

Under the influence of all these movements on the northern border of Korea, one of the tribes related to the Five *Hu* migrated and used the Korean peninsula as a bridge to reach Japan. In the third chapter we hope to make clear from Korean mythology, that this tribe must have split off from the Puyŏ nomadic peoples settled at that time in South Manchuria. In particular, the Korean myths show that the ruling houses of almost all the Korean states descended from these Puyŏ.[2] The agreement between Japanese and Korean myths,[3] and also other data (for instance, archeological [4]), render a similar relationship of the Puyŏ to what Kida calls [5] the '*tenson*', 天孫, "Heavenly Grandson" tribe highly probable. This is also the more likely because it has been established that this '*tenson*' tribe had 'passed through' Korea over a long period.

These suspicions, however, cannot be confirmed by genuine historical facts, as these are unavoidably lacking. Chinese data also leave a gap of 170 years [6] between the earliest *Wei chih* data and the oldest of the *Sung-shu*. This gap is between the years 250 A.D. and 421 A.D. The Kwanggaet'o column mentioned above, which

---

[1] The T'opa were not only related to the Hsien-pi on a linguistic basis. Schreiber, op. cit., pp. 388, 389, expressly points out how far the Chinese of their period saw a Hsien-pi state in them. On the basis of this Schreiber refutes the opinion, although the T'opa may have fought against the Hsien-pi; op. cit., p. 405, ft. nt. 105.

[2] Cf. Chapter III, pp. 191 ff.

[3] See p. 44 ff.

[4] See Chapter III, pp. 188 ff.

[5] See p. 35, ft. nt. 1.

[6] Cf. Ryūsaku Tsunoda, op. cit., for the final Japanese date in the *Wei chih*: ± 250, on p. 16; for the earliest date of the *Sung-shu*: 421, on p. 22.

describes the period 391-414 A.D. subtracts another thirty years from this. Therefore this invasion could have taken place after 250 A.D. and before 390 A.D.

Nevertheless, despite this, not all indications of such an invasion are missing. In particular in Japanese mythology, handed down to us by the *Kojiki* and the *Nihonshoki*, various indications can be found which not only have something to do with Korea, but even with the racial territory of the Puyŏ, i.e. Manchuria. Although nothing is known of the Puyŏ language, as the Puyŏ disappeared entirely from history, it may be surmised that it has contributed to the origin of Manchurian. Now particularly in Japan's own religion, Shintō, and its most 'holy' mythology, various indications related to this may be found. It may be said of the religion and especially of the mythology of a nation, that in these its own nature and ideology are most completely expressed. If we now apply this to Japan, then it is of interest that the most important basic principles of Shintō can not only be better understood from the Manchurian, but also bring to light a clear relationship with this language.[1]

One of these basic principles is expressed by the word *musubi*, i.a. written 産霊, or 結び. We shall show more explicitly in the second chapter that this has been one of the central conceptions from which Shintō has evolved.[2] In the *musubi* one must recognize the elemental force which alone could make the deeds of gods and men truly successful. When the mythical divine couple Izanagi, 伊弉諾, and Izanami, 伊弉冊, began creating heaven and earth, they required a great deal of force for originating the land, mountains and rivers. The deification of this force was a *musubi*: Takamimusubi, 高魂命, who effected the work of creation of this couple.[3] The same Takamimusubi always accompanied Amaterasu, under the name of Takagi *no kami*, 高木神, in her most important deeds, such as the creation of the Japanese nation.[4] At the Japanese

[1] For the following data cf. Jean Romieux, "Mythes du Japon ancien vus à la lumière de la linguistigue comparative", *M.S.G.*, VIII 1946, pp. 63-93.

[2] Chapter II pp. 105 ff., ft. nt. 3.

[3] See Sasaya Ryōzō, "Musubi-gami no shinkō (Beliefs regarding the Kami of Musubi)", *K.G.Z.*, vol. 64, 1963, nos. 8, 9, Aug., Sept., p. 84.

[4] Sasaya Ryōzō, op. cit., p. 85. According to the *Kojiki*, Takagi *no kami* was another name for Takamimusubi. Cf. *Kojiki*, 1st *maki*, Ame-waka-hiko; Kuroita Katsumi, Maruyama Jirō, *Kokushitaikei Kojiki*, Tōkyō 1962, p. 37. Sasaya Ryōzō, op. cit., p. 86, therefore calls *musubi* the divine power which remains in the objects, also after the divine touch.

'coronation' feasts, the feast of *niiname*, 新嘗, when the emperor was robed in the imperial garments, he was simultaneously enriched with the partite soul of Amaterasu, who resided in these garments. The robing was a magical endowment with the *musubi*, who made the person thus enrobed one with Amaterasu herself.[1] These two examples suffice to illustrate that this *musubi* belief lies at the root of Japanese Shintō.[2] It is therefore not surprising that this word *musubi* is always taken as a proto-Japanese word. Now this word can also be found in Manchurian and Mongolian.[3] This also proves to be the case with other words.

In various places in this work we shall encounter the word '*Ame*', 天, heaven, (or *Ama* in composite forms). This word also shows a similar relationship. Of the related names of deities we mention especially Ame *no* Uzume *no mikoto*, 天鈿女命.[4] In this name both *Ame*, *Uzume* (goddess of dancing, mimicry)[5] and *mikoto* indicate Manchurian relationship. This goddess of dancing was also a *musubi*. It is known of her that she contrived to lure Amaterasu from her cave with an obscene dance, as a result of which the darkness vanished and the sun began to shine again.[6] This relationship between Japanese and Manchurian is undoubtedly established in the following concepts, which occur in practically every Shintō rite, such as *matsuri*=sacrificial service to the gods; *hara(h)i*= purification; and *imi*=abstention.[7] Also the names of various other

[1] Sasaya Ryōzō, op. cit., p. 91; see also p. 354.

[2] It was older in the Japanese mythology than the Ōminaka-nushi, modelled after the Chinese T'ien-ti. Sasaya Ryōzō, op. cit., p. 83.

[3] Cf. J. Romieux, op. cit., p. 68.

[4] Cf. J. Romieux, op. cit., pp. 87, 88.

[5] Sasaya Ryōzō, op. cit., pp. 87, 88.

[6] This follows from a phonetic comparison as well as a comparison of the meaning of these words as they co-exist in both tongues:

Japanese		*Manchurian*	
Phonetic	*Meaning*	*Phonetic*	*Meaning*
Musubi	Knot, fasten	*Fosomi*	Fasten
Ame	Heaven	*Abka*	Heaven
Udzu	"Fille tourbillonante"	*Ondo*	To pantomime, to practise immoral deeds

Cf. T. Romieux, op. cit., pp. 68, 78, 79, 82.

[7] See J. Romieux, op. cit., pp. 77, 78.

important gods such as Susa *no* O, 素戔嗚, and Ninigi *no mikoto*, 瓊瓊杵命, who constitute the hard core of Japan's myths and remain incomprehensible from the Japanese, first become meaningful from Manchurian.[1]

Thus far we have compared Manchurian with Japanese and have been able to note specifically in the most inherent Japanese concepts a strong Manchurian relationship. The fact that there is, in Manchuria and Korea, a very strong attraction to the South and to Japan, is equally proven by Manchurian, in which both the 'South' and 'forwards' and the 'North' and 'backwards' are identical.[2]

Comparison of Japanese with Korean gives various pointers to the fact that this Manchurian tribe (of the Puyŏ) passed through Korea and crossed from there to Japan. According to the *Kojiki* [3] the descent of the 'Manchurian' grandson of Amaterasu, Ninigi *no mikoto*, took place on the mountain Tsukushi *no* Himuka *no* Takachiho *no* Kushifuru-*take*, 竺紫日向之高千穗之久士布流多氣, literally: The Kushifuru peak of the (mountain) Takachiho of Himuka (Hyūga region) of Tsukushi (= the N.E. of Kyūshū). Of all of the words of this name, only 'Kushifuru' demands clarification, as it has simply been added to the term for mountain peak. The Korean philologist Ch'oe Hyŏnbae (Tschö Hyönbä) supported by Kanazawa, says of this Kushifuru: [4]

---

[1] See J. Romieux, op. cit., pp. 84-87, 89-90.

[2] See Chapter III, p. 187, ft. nt. 1.

[3] *Kojiki*, 1st *maki*, Itsutomo no o; Kuroita Katsumi, Maruyama Jirō, op. cit., p. 44: "They descended on the Tsukushi no Himuka no Takachihō no Kushifuru-take."

[4] Ch'oe Hyŏnbae (Tschö Hyonbä) in "Beziehungen zwischen Korea und Japan in alter Zeit", in *Koreanica, Festschrift Professor Dr. André Eckardt zum 75. Geburtstag*, Baden-Baden 1960, p. 27.

See in particular Kanazawa Shōzaburō, "Chōsen Kenkyū to *Nihonshoki* (A Study of Korea and the *Nihonshoki*)", *C.G.*, no. 1, May 1951, p. 74. In this connection he points out in particular, that in the *Shōjiroku*, a genealogical register from 814, prominent people in Japan were called Soshihori, i.e., people from Silla, loc. cit. He also points out the narrow relationship to the *Kushifuru* of the *Kojiki* and the *Nihonshoki*. Udō Masamoto, says, furthermore, of this *Kushifurū*: "The place of Takachihō was also sometimes named *Kushi(furu)-hi-mine* (槵日峯), the sun peak Kushi(furu), with regard to Korea. From the top of this mountain there was a view over Kyūshū, Shikoku, Chūkoku (central Honshū) and one got the feeling that Korea lay far away to the north-west. This explains the remark of the Tenson (= Ninigi

"Die Ortschaft, in der Ninigi, ein Enkel Isanagi's zum erstenmal in Japan erwähnt wird, heisst Hyūga no takechiho no Kusi-puru take oder Hyūga no takechiho no Sopori take = "Bergspitze". Wie oben untersucht,[1] so entspricht sipuru dem Sopori und Somori und ist nur ein anderer Name für Silla (S.E.-Korea). Ku in Kusipuru ist der Stamm des heute noch gebräuchlichen adjektivischen Verbums k'ŭda "gross sein". Aus dieser Wortähnlichkeit, ja Gleichheit von Kusipuru mit "gross" Sori-(Sora)-pol (Feld, Gemeinde) kann geschlossen werden, dass Ninigi in Japan sein Reich mit dem gleichen Namen wie Silla, also mit Sopori (= Sorapŭl) belehnte."

The importance of this name is shown further by the fact that from this peak, according to the same place in the *Kojiki*, one could see Korea, because it was situated opposite Kara (= South Korea).[2] We do not want to linger over these philological comparisons any longer, because we are convinced, together with J. Romieux, that the close relationship of Japanese with Korean and other altaic languages is: "Un point si bien établi que nous pouvons nous dispenser d'illustrer d'exemples." [3]

Apart from these, there are also other arguments to be found in Japanese sources, which are indicative of Korean influence. They originate from a more recent mythology. We are slightly apprehensive of comparing the tale of the descent of Ninigi *no mikoto*,

---

no mikoto), that this land lay opposite Korea and that the land was shone on by the morning and evening sun." Udō Masamoto in "Kodai-Nihon no Taiyō-shinkō to sono bunji-hyōgen (Worship of the sun in the literature of old Japan)", *K.G.Z.*, vol. 59, nos. 10 and 11, 1958, Oct., Nov., p. 127. It follows from this, that this Kushifuru peak was also a directive towards Korea and sun worship.

[1] Namely, a few lines earlier, he writes: "Wo ist nun das eben genannte Sosimori? Ursprünglich hiess es Sosi-pŏl. Der S- und R-Laut sind verwandte Laute und wechseln häufig. Dem Sosi entspricht das koreanische Sori und Sora. Auch der Wandel von M- und P-Laut kann in beiden Sprachen nachgewiesen werden. Mori ist gleich pŏri und pŏl. Sosimori ist mit sorapŭl gleichbedeutend. So heisst noch heute ein Dorf in Silla. Pŭl, pŏl ist das heutige 'pad' = 'Feld'". This may also be found in Kanazawa Shōzaburō, op. cit., pp. 74, 75 and p. 85.

[2] See Chapter II, p. 116, ft. nt. 3.

[3] J. Romieux, op. cit., p. 64. For further similarities see also Ch'oe Hyŏnbae, op. cit., pp. 24-31, and the article mentioned on p. 43, ft. nt. 4 by Kanazawa Shōzaburō. For a more elaborate exposition of other linguistic similarities, see F. Vos, op. cit., pp. 13-18.

the so-called *Tenson-kōrin*, 天孫降臨, story, with that of the Korean Tan-gun, as it does not appear to be entirely impossible that both tales are modelled on the Chinese.[1] The tale of the Korean Ama *no* Hiboko *no mikoto*, 'Prince Heavenly Spear of the Sun', who crossed from Silla in South Korea to Japan, is, in our opinion, a better example.[2] Therefore this Ama *no* Hiboko deserves our special attention, as he was closely related to the Japanese imperial house. To be exact, he was the progenitor of Empress Jingū, mother of Ōjin, the one whom we shall call Japan's first historic emperor in this chapter. Thus, according to the *Kojiki* and the *Nihonshoki*, Korean blood therefore entered the Japanese imperial race for the first time via Empress Jingū.[3] The name 'Prince Heavenly Spear of the Sun' indicates that Ama no Hiboko also had something to do with sun worship. We shall return to the similarity in this sun worship further in the third chapter.[4]

This figure (shrouded in myths), together with the other data, could be an indication of the fact that the Puyŏ tribe which crossed from Korea to Japan, also dwelt in Korea itself for some time. Perhaps there too, it overlapped the Korean population, before doing the same with regard to Japan's original population. It was certainly not the only tribe to cross into Japan. The stone circles, for instance, which have been found on Hokkaido, indicate an invasion of a Tungusian tribe which must have taken place in the fifth century.[5] The tribe, which later expanded into the imperial

---

[1] It is probably not to be excluded, that a Chinese model has served for both myths, which was specifically used to accentuate the divinity of the imperial house. See Udō Masamoto, op. cit., p. 125.

[2] Cf. *Kojiki*, 2nd *maki*; Kuroita Katsumi, Maruyama Jirō, op. cit. p. 106: "Once there was a son of the king of Silla, called Ame *no* Hiboko, 天之日矛. He crossed the sea."

See also the *Nihonshoki*, 4th *maki*, Suinin third year, 3rd month; Kuroita Katsumi, Maruyama Jirō, *Kokushitaikei Nihonshoki*, part 1, p. 177:

"In the third year, spring, third month, the son of the king of Silla Ama *no* Hiboko came." Cf. W. G. Aston, *Nihongi*, *T.P.J.S.*, 1896, supplement I, vol. I, p. 168.

In the *Fudoki* also a wealth of texts concerning him may be found. Cf. Takeda Iukichi, *Fudoki*, Tōkyō 1938, pp. 202, 209-212, etc. See also A. Wedemeyer, op. cit., pp. 138-146. Bruno Lewin, op. cit., p. 8.

[3] See Ōjin's genealogy in A. Wedemeyer, op. cit., pp. 142, 143.

[4] Cf. Chapter III, p. 208 ff.

[5] Cf. Martin Gusinde and Sano Chiye, "Stone circles in Northern Japan", *Anthr.*, vol. 55 (1960), pp. 441-455.

race, also bore all the characteristics which were specific to such Tungusian tribes. Egami says of this: [1] "In the Yayoi-[2] period and in the burial mound period which followed it, the magically symbolic, popular, S.E. Asian agricultural characteristics decreased strongly. Simultaneously the present-day warlike, N. Asian characteristics, or rather the characteristics of horseriding peoples, became dominant. The aforementioned periods make these actual differences clearly obvious. The stages in this development are abrupt." One can add others to these characteristics. One of them is the nomadic inclination, especially present in the blood of the first emperors, to change residence continuously. This habit continued to exist until the end of the sixth century. Furthermore, they organised the immigration of large numbers of Koreans, who had to pay for their lack of knowledge of agriculture. In this they did not differ from the Hsien-pi and the T'opa,[3] who did the same in China. In addition, a far stronger emphasis than before was laid on patriarchy. All Japanese sources relate with how much severity they fought and eradicated the last remnants of matriarchy in Japan.[4] Genuine patriarchal qualities emerged simultaneously into the foreground. One has only to think of the sun cult and the many phallic fertility rites. The Japanese language also could not disguise the influence of the North Asian tribes. We hope to show later the extent to which the word *uji*, in the sense of clan, has parallels in Tungusian and Korean languages.[5] The Japanese word for deity and clan head, 神, *kami*, occurs in more or less the same sense in *kam* or *qam* [6] in Turkish or Tartar. There, however, it had rather the special sense of shaman, a function which was similar to that of the Japanese clan head, the *uji no kami*. We hope to return to this in the second chapter.

From all of the above it follows, that the great migrations of the third and fourth centuries on the Eurasian continent halted just as little for the Japanese islands as they did in Europe for Scandinavia or England. Just as much as China and Korea, Japan had

---

[1] Kadowaki Teiji, op. cit., p. 111.

[2] For the Yayoi period, cf. J. E. Kidder, op. cit., p. 23.

[3] See p. 39.

[4] Cf. Joseph Schwientek, "Der Synkretismus von Shinto und Buddhismus in Japan", *Anthr.*, vol. 22 (1927), pp. 430-439.

[5] Cf. Chapter II, pp. 74 ff., ft. nt. 1.

[6] Cf. M. Eliade, *Le Chamanisme*, pp. 17, 18 and 430.

encountered all the political and religious trends which set China and Korea in motion from that time. It is therefore obvious, that the emperorship, as a result of this continental stamp, influenced the religious situation in Japan otherwise than has often been thought.

More follows from this. Now that it has been established, on the basis of all of the above, that the Japanese emperorship began only at the end of the third, early fourth century, it is clear, that one may no longer attribute any historical value to all those imperial figures who, according to Japanese sources, supposedly lived before that time. This disposes of fifteen emperors of Japan's impressive imperial list. This equally confirms the fact that Emperor Jimmu, who played such an important part in the divine heritage of the emperors, was *not* the founder of it. Moreover, we hope to show from Japan's own sources, that he was only an invention, which first came into being only in the 7th century A.D., therefore 12 hundred years after his 'reign'. It is now generally agreed, that Ōjin should be given the first place on the imperial list. In the old list he occurs in the sixteenth place. This follows from the fact that, according to the official calculation, he is supposed to have reigned between 270 and 310 A.D.,[1] the period in which the invasion of the imperial race took place. As, however, this calculation also is unsettled in relation to this period, it is uncertain whether he actually ruled at such an early date. Therefore various questions still remain with regard to the true first emperor. We believe that there are adequate indications in the Japanese sources that Ōjin was the first emperor.

3 *The Japanese sources*

However definitely these determinations may result from the Chinese sources mentioned above, from Japanese archeology and from the state of the Eurasian continent, they can nevertheless also be confirmed from the Japanese sources. Here we are especially concerned with the *Kojiki* and the *Nihonshoki*, re-edited c. 700 A.D. from other material. Despite the fact that until recently this material appeared to suggest the opposite, it can also lead to the same conclusions, if only it be considered critically. Thus it can even be deduced from these sources, that Jimmu as an emperor must have

[1] See Kadowaki Teiji, op. cit., p. 129.

been a fiction of a far later period. They also confirm the dubious historical value of his first fourteen successors. We owe that to the fact that all of these imperial figures were first established in these sources after Buddhism had gained a strong foothold in Japan. In the following table we have collected all these imperial figures according to their Chinese short names. After these names we have cited the periods of reign ascribed to them prior to 1945.[1]

No.	Name	Reign
1.	Jimmu	660-585 B.C.
2.	Suizei 綏靖	581-549 B.C.
3.	Annei 安寧	548-511 B.C.
4.	Itoku 懿徳	510-477 B.C.
5.	Kōshō 孝昭	475-393 B.C.
6.	Kōan 孝安	392-291 B.C.
7.	Kōrei 孝霊	290-215 B.C.
8.	Kōgen 孝元	214-158 B.C.
9.	Kaika 開化	157-98 B.C.
10.	Sujin 崇神	97-30 B.C.
11.	Suinin 垂仁	28 B.C.-70 A.D.
12.	Keikō 景行	71-130 A.D.
13.	Seimu 成務	131-190 A.D.
14.	Chūai 仲哀	192-200 A.D.
15.	Jingū	201-269 A.D.
16.	Ōjin	270-310 A.D.

As far as Jimmu is concerned, one can determine, by the use of Japan's own sources, the period and conditions in which his mythical stature must have been established. Namely, that was after the sixth century, when many emperors established their residence in Iware.[2] If one connects this place name Iware, 磐余, with that of the region of Yamato, in which it was situated, the actual Japanese name of Jimmu: Yamato-Iware-*hiko* [3] results. The additional word *hiko* conveys the sense of prince. Hence his Japanese name is not much more than a geographical indication. The word Iware plays a very important part in the history of the emperors of antiquity. The Japanese sources mention that Jimmu touched land not far from the presentday Ōsaka on his campaign from Kyūshū to Yamato. Just in this area there is a village which bears one of the names of Emperor Ōjin, namely Ōmuta or Honda, 譽田. His mother, Empress Jingū, had named Ōjin Ōmuta-bekkō in the third year of her reign. The meaning of this name is: The Special Prince Ōmuta. He lived with her in her Waka-sakura, 稚櫻, palace, the Palace of the 'Fresh' Cherries. This latter was located in the village of Iware. Emperor Richū, 履中, (400-405 A.D.) too is

[1] See also footnote 4 on p. 33.

[2] Situated in the neighborhood of the present-day town Sakurai in the Nara prefecture.

[3] For this word there were three methods of writing: 神日本磐余彦, 神倭伊汲礼昆古 or 大和國磐余彦.

supposed to have resided in this palace. Emperor Seinei, 清寧, (480-484 A.D.) lived in the Mikakuri, 甕栗, palace, also situated in Iware. In the sixth century the emperors Keitai (507-531 A.D.), Senka (536-540 A.D.) and Yōmei (586-588 A.D.) lived there. These Iware residences of the emperors of the fifth and sixth centuries formed the basis on which, at that time, the Japanese realm was built. This place name Iware must therefore have been idealized into a specific person, Jimmu, who grew into a myth as founder of this realm. We shall see later on how he received the Chinese name Jimmu under Chinese influence. In the fifth chapter we hope to show how this Iware particularly was ideally situated as an imperial residence, as it lay in the centre of the habitation areas of the fiercely warring clans.[1] The history of Jimmu, or Iware-*hiko*, originated from this period and served these clans as a kind of peg to which they could hang their own relationship to the imperial house. According to Kadowaki [2] this was already an accomplished fact in the chronicles of 620 A.D. Furthermore, there is also his grave, which can prove that he was only a fictitious emperor, or merely a local village headman. For a long time this was held to be Japan's oldest grave monument. In the event, however, it appears that throughout the centuries there has been so much meddling with it, that the latest date can no longer be ascertained. The oldest fragments of this grave which still exist, date only from the fifth and sixth centuries A.D. Therefore the Jimmu of the *Kojiki* and the *Nihonshoki* probably never existed, except perhaps as a local and insignificant village headman.

All of this does not mean to say that we should ignore, along with Jimmu himself, all of the tales about him. One of the dissectors of these tales, Kadowaki [3] does not allow that they originated before the third or fourth century A.D. Probably they belonged to the history of Ōjin. In that case, Jimmu has been divided into two, in order to gratify another clan. Thus Jimmu could have originated as a replica of Ōjin. We can support this point of view with other arguments as well from the same sources. Thus it is indeed significant, that here we can discover a very strong similarity between the two figures of Ōjin and Jimmu. It was related of both that they gained their victories after they had consulted an oracle. Both were

[1] See map on p. 470.
[2] Op. cit., p. 105.
[3] Loc. cit.

great conquerors: Jimmu mythically, Ōjin historically as well. Additionally, the Japanese sources intentionally devote plenty of room in the chronicles to both. The Chinese names also, which were ascribed to them far later, indicate this parallelism. Together with yet another imperial figure, Sujin, who was supposed to have lived in the period between Jimmu and Ōjin, they were the only ones who possessed a Chinese name which was made up of the word *jin*, Chinese: *shên*, 神, Japanese : *kami*.[1] The Japanese names of these emperors also show this parallelism. Both Sujin and Ōjin are called by their Japanese names: Hatsu-kuni-shirasu-*sumera-mikoto*, a long word, which is indicative of: the emperor, the first ruler of the nation.[2] Later this parallel will also be shown with regard to religion. We therefore believe that Jimmu, Sujin and Ōjin were nothing other than three different projections of the actual founder of the Japanese empire. These were circulated by the clans of the fifth and sixth centuries, who wished to outdo each other. These projections were connected to each other by the editors of the abovementioned sources, because they could very well serve to bridge the period which was supposed to start in the year 660 B.C. We have already pointed out that the Chinese sources already mentioned here, together with the Japanese burial mounds, brought to light, that this founder lived at the time which officially coincided with that of Emperor Ōjin. This does not, however, mean to say that Emperor Ōjin was this founder in the way in which he is described in the Japanese sources. One should, for instance, consider the fact that his mother was pregnant 13 months with him.[3] He too is a projection. Nevertheless, he answers to historical reality more than Jimmu and Sujin, especially when he has something to do with the feats of arms of which there is mention on the

[1] This character 神 only occurs in the names of 神武 Jimmu, 崇神 Sujin, and 応神 Ōjin. Also in that of 神功, Jingū. Many do not accept her sovereignty.

[2] That Jimmu was a mythologisation of Ōjin, is interconnected with this name. See the article concerning this by Takasaki Masahide, "Kojiki-denshōron (Commentary on the *Kojiki* tradition)", *K.G.Z.*, vol. 63, 1962, no. 9, Sept., p. 13. Furthermore, on the basis of a critical comparison of the first emperors, he says that "we see in Jimmu and his successors the same (persons) as in Ōjin and the six who succeeded him." Op. cit., p. 19. See also Kadowaki Teiji, op. cit., p. 199.

[3] Matsukawa Jirō, op. cit., p. 80, attempts to prove by the use of statistics of German medical doctors, that such a pregnancy was impossible.

Kwanggaet'o memorial stone already mentioned.[1] A penetrating examination of the imperial names of his predecessors renders their existence improbable.[2]

After this brief sketch of Japan's modern outlook on the origin of its imperial house it will surprise no one, that at the present stage of preliminary investigation, undertaken hesitantly by only a few, there still remain many doubts and unproven suppositions. Amongst all of this, however, it has been irrefutably established that the Japanese Empire came into being only at the end of the fourth century, in a manner which is, even in rough outline, still not entirely clear to us. From what we now know of the imperial race, it is certainly clearly evident that the Japanese people, just as every other race in the world, is a mixed race. The original purpose of the *kigensetsu*, which aimed at proving precisely the opposite, is also entirely and scientifically cancelled by this. This is no news to Western Japanologists, as they have never regarded the Japanese as a pure race. For many Japanese, however, it meant a severe shock. Kadowaki writes of this:[3]

"That we, as Japanese, are of a mixed breed, need not shame us. One should not consider a pure race to be something good, if only because such a race does not exist anywhere on earth. We must once and for all accept scientific facts as truth. In as far as that is concerned, we must liberate ourselves from our ancestry."

This passage does prove how difficult it still is, even for the Japanese alive today, to reconcile themselves to this idea which is so self-evident to us. Therefore we must not be surprised that the racial problem which is bound up with the imperial descent has been the cause of the picture of the origin of Japanese Buddhism being, historically, totally mutilated. Shōtoku Taishi, Father of the Fatherland, was so particularly strongly idealized because he had to disguise an all too great dependence on foreign countries. The main reason for this may be found in Japan's oldest sources, which

[1] Sycześniak, op. cit., p. 59, especially attempts to prove this. This is, however, unprovable, as the dates of the *Nihonshoki* concerning this period of reign give absolutely no support.

[2] See Kadowaki Teiji, op. cit., p. 135: "In the *Nihonshoki* and the *Kojiki* many emperors are mentioned prior to Ōjin, but we cannot accept these as historical realities. We must view the period before Ōjin as the time in which our country achieved its political unity. The chronicles before Ōjin are highly mythical; those after him recount historical facts."

[3] Op. cit., p. 54.

have fostered the imperial deification the most. Therefore one must admire the audacity with which, in post-war Japan, not only have the mythical origins of the Japanese empire been unravelled, but also particularly the study of the origin and demythologising of the oldest sources has been taken in hand. It is owing to this that the origin of Japanese Buddhism also has come to appear in a totally different light.

c. The evidence of Japanese sources

Although we have excluded the mythical origin of the Japanese empire as historical data in the preceeding pages, nevertheless this does not give us the right to ignore these myths and the sources which describe them without further ado. These myths were not counterfeits but mistaken historical reconstructions of primeval happenings, which, in the thoughts of the people of the seventh century, comprised the foundation of the Japanese state. As such they form a very valuable testimony to the beliefs of those days.

Despite all the historical inexactitudes, the Japanese sources remain Japan's oldest documents. Without them we know nothing more of Japan's antiquity than that which we can conclude from archeological finds of that period. Many chronicles in these sources may also possess historical value if only we sift them critically and classify them. We have already indicated the tragedy of the fact that various Japanese historians cannot progress so far.

It is understandable that it was a tour de force to voice any criticism of the sources in opposition to their opinions. Nevertheless there were various people who dared to do this, and sometimes risked severe punishment in so doing. One of these pioneers was, for example, Arai Hakuseki (1656-1725), who dared to locate the old Japanese heaven *Takama no hara*, 高天原, in Ise. He was overshadowed by the great champion of the original "Japanese" ideals, free from foreign intervention: Motoori Norinaga (1730-1801). Hirata Atsutane (1776-1843), less of a scientist but active propagator of the same ideals, followed in Motoori's footsteps. Ban Nobutomo (1775-1848) investigated the chronology of the sources less tendentiously than Motoori and Hirata, sincerely and calmly, in a penetrating manner. We have already indicated at the beginning of this chapter such textual critics as Kume Kunitake and Tsuda Sōkichi. The latter has become just as much a pioneer for many of the younger generation.[1] Just as the "Formgeschichtliche Schule" in the West resolved Holy Scripture, thus he analysed the Japanese sources. In this way he attempted to penetrate to historical facts which had remained hidden until now. With this study society of the sixth century was unveiled as well as the way in which Buddhism had gained a position in it.

1 *Genesis of Japan's Oldest Sources*

Thus far there has been repeated mention of Japan's oldest sources. Nevertheless, we shall have to consider the individual nature, genesis and content of them more closely, as they are our chief source of information concerning antiquity and Buddhism. The sources are—we have already indicated them where necessary—especially the *Kojiki* and the *Nihonshoki*. The collection of topologies, usually called *Fudoki* (= topology), originates from a far later period in its final recension, just as does the *Shoku-Nihongi*, 続日本紀, the collection which links up with the *Nihonshoki*, i.e.: the *Fudoki* originated between 713 and 733 A.D., the *Shoku-Nihongi* initially in 797 A.D. [2] The controversies concerning Japanese antiquity rest entirely on facts related by the *Kojiki* and the *Nihonshoki*. Therefore our attention is especially drawn to these two works. The individual nature of these two sources can be deduced from their names. The word *Kojiki* [3] 古事記, means: The chronicles of old occurrences. *Nihonshoki*, 日本書紀, may be translated by: The chronicles of Japan's manuscripts. If we compare these names with each other, then the *Nihonshoki*, in contrast to the *Kojiki*, appears to be supported by various written sources. Namely, in the *Nihonshoki* other sources are also repeatedly quoted. Such references are usually introduced by the words: "*issho iwaku*", 一書日, that is to say: 'One or other manuscript makes mention' . . . etc.

The contents of both works concern the primeval period of Japan's history. The *Kojiki* relates that from 660 B.C. up to and including the death of Empress Suiko (628 A.D.). The *Nihonshoki* encompasses

[1] Especially in his *Nihon Koten no Kenkyū* and his *Nihon Jōdaishi no Kenkyū*.

[2] For the *Fudoki* see Chapter II, pp. 96 ff.

[3] This was translated by Florenz as: "Geschichte der Begebenheiten im Altertum." Cf. Karl Florenz, *Die historischen Quellen der Shinto Religion*, Göttingen 1919, p. 3.

the same period but continues until the year 696 A.D. The *Kojiki* follows no single calendar. Therefore the facts mentioned there are hard to date, in contrast to the *Nihonshoki*, which does date them. The greater part of both sources is written in a fairly businesslike, chronicle style. However, running through these businesslike and often sober chronicles, there are page-long stories, which, in their verbosity break entirely with the businesslike chronicle tone. Such passages can best be encountered in the descriptions of the myths of Japan's origin. Here and there they are richly embroidered with long songs and verbose expositions about various heroic deeds of the gods. The 'younger' parts, which concern the periods after 500, provide more officially neutral chronicles than the older ones. It can be deduced from this, that these works were not only written by businesslike officials, but also by other people, such as monks for example.

The *Kojiki* is divided into three scrolls. Such a scroll is called a *maki*. The first part treats of the mythology of the gods, the second and third of the conquests of Jimmu and Japan's further history up to and including Suiko. That same construction may be met with in the *Nihonshoki*. This latter work, however, is divided into thirty *maki* 巻, or scrolls. The *Kojiki* has a less official character than the *Nihonshoki*, which was supposed to pass as the state chronicles. We shall meet with both types of chronicle writing in the following chapters.

As far as the history of the genesis of these sources is concerned, we must not be satisfied with accepting the dry decrees about it in the *Nihonshoki* and the *Shoku-Nihongi*. They too have originated from certain ambitions and various philosophies. These have influenced the specific nature and the truth content of them to an important degree.

The origin of these works was also, to a great extent, connected with the script itself. Was it not essential that, before one could start on state chronicles, there should be a script. Initially no script was known. It was borrowed from China. We do not know when this happened. The very oldest text is to be found on a commemorative stone in the prefecture of Kumamoto on Kyūshū.[1] This dates from the fifth or from the beginning of the sixth century. The use of script is shown nowhere in the superabundance of finds of

---

[1] Cf. *Daigaku Nihon-shi*, part 1, p. 41, for the literal text.

earlier times. Therefore it is difficult to decide whether the script was there before the fifth century. It is not very probable.

From this it follows that Japan's oldest tales were probably handed down only verbally. We know with certainty that the possibility of recording them in writing existed only from the fifth century on. Whether this possibility was realized immediately, is not, as yet, too obvious. Certainly the Japanese were initially at a loss as to what to do with the copious Chinese character script. That is proved by the fact that, at first, it was used almost exclusively by Korean immigrants, usually of Chinese origin. As Japan's first chroniclers, they stood apart from the rest of the Japanese population, which had only a low level of development.

Therefore, in order to be written, Japan's traditions had virtually to be translated into Chinese first. That is actually what happened. The *Kojiki*, *Nihonshoki* and *Shoku-Nihongi* and the *Fudoki* for instance are therefore collections of Chinese texts translated from Japanese, rather than completely Japanese manuscripts.

This translation was unavoidable as polysyllabic Japanese does not have too much in common with monosyllabic Chinese. In addition, both differ noticeably from each other in grammar. Therefore we need not be surprised that nowhere in the lines of the *Kojiki*—except for the introduction to it—is there mention of a command to write state chronicles. Japanese was, at that time, simply not ripe for this. This only occurred after two types of Japanese script, parallel to each other, had been developed from the Chinese; i.e. the *hiragana*, 平仮名, and the *katakana*, 片仮名. The Chinese texts of the *Kojiki* and the *Nihonshoki* were later rendered readable to the Japanese by adding the Japanese reading of the text to the Chinese characters in small *hira*- or usually in *katakana* (which later received the special name of *furigana*, 振り仮名, litt. 'added writing'). However, the history of chronicle-writing did not wait until the *furigana* was devised.

The *Nihonshoki* records several chronicles which allow the origin of Japan's oldest sources to be surmised. The first may be found under the 28th year of the reign of Empress Suiko, 推古, which corresponds to the date 620 A.D. There it is written: [1]

"That year the *kōtaishi*, 皇太子, entered into discussion with the

---

[1] *Nihonshoki*, 22nd *maki*, Suiko 28th year, Kuroita Katsumi, Maruyama Jirō, *Kokushitaikei Nihonshoki*, part 2, p. 159. Cf. W. G. Aston, op. cit., vol. II, p. 148.

ō-omi Shima, 嶋, with a view to writing the chronicles of the emperors, of the lands (provinces), of those of the *omi, muraji, tomo no miyatsuko, kuni no miyatsuko,* of the hundred and eighty *be* (guilds) of the ordinary people."

The *kōtaishi,* the imperial prince, who is mentioned in this text, is no less than Shōtoku Taishi. Many now see in him the real founder of the Japanese nation. How far this is justifiable we hope to determine in our last chapter. He was to die a year after this decree. The name ō-omi Shima stands for Soga Umako, 蘇我馬子. Sometimes he is also referred to by his given name alone: Umako. He was the most important representative and imperial councillor of the Soga clan.[1] In the following chapters we shall return to this figure more closely. Furthermore, various titles of notables, such as *omi, muraji,* etc.[2] are mentioned in this text. These titles were conferred only on the leaders of the various clans which were then known to Japan. They really did exist around the year 620 A.D. That is also shown by other texts of that period. We therefore believe that here we are dealing with an authentic text. The fact that this decree was made just in the reign of Empress Suiko (593-628) was not accidental, but entirely a result of the constellation of that age. In this period the Soga clan had succeeded in gaining its strong grip on the imperial house, after the murder of Emperor Sushun (587-592), 崇峻, in 592, instigated by the same Soga Umako, and the defeat of the other clan Mononobe, 物部, Soga's opponents, in 587. Also as a result of this, Umako contrived to have Buddhism recognised as the state religion and to reach the summit of his power. It is obvious that these chronicles too had to serve in some way or other to glorify him and his clan. We do not know precisely what these chronicles looked like, because on June 12, 645, his son Emishi, who had meanwhile succeeded him as head of the clan, was so hemmed in by his enemies that he could only find a way out by death. Before he laid hands on himself, he first attempted to burn these chronicles. On that occasion the imperial chronicles were destroyed by fire, those of the provinces, however, were rescued by a certain Fumano-*fuhito* Esaka, 般史惠尺.[3] There-

---

[1] He is to play an important part especially in Japan's primeval Buddhism. Cf. Chapter V for this.

[2] *Omi, muraji, tomo no miyatsuko* and *kuni no miyatsuko* were titles of nobility of that period. Cf. Chapter II, p. 125 and ff. for this.

[3] Cf. *Nihonshoki,* 24th *maki,* Kōgyoku 4th year, 6th month; Kuroita

fore in the remaining part something of the relations between the clans must have been preserved. It is, however, difficult to point out those passages in the *Kojiki* and the *Nihonshoki* which go back to these salvaged collections.

After this, there was to be no mention of chronicles in the *Nihonshoki* until the date of 681.[1] In that year Emperor Temmu, 天武, (673-686) gave Prince Kawashima, 川嶋, and others the order to set down 'the imperial chronicles and all occurrences of antiquity.' As a result of the great interest taken in literature at that time, they even received remuneration under his reign. Most people are of the opinion, that this was the first large collection of material, from which the *Nihonshoki* originated. Others, such as Hayashiya and Iwahashi prefer to see in this the material for the *Kojiki*.[2]

The last *Nihonshoki* text concerning the origin of the chronicles is to be found in 691. In the fifth year of the reign of Empress Jitō, 持統, (690-697) eighteen clans received, according to an imperial command, the privilege of also compiling their chronicles.[3] Kadowaki's conclusion is: [4] 'It is not difficult for us to imagine here that these ancestral chronicles formed the material for the *Nihonshoki*.' The last recension of the *Nihonshoki* was put in hand, according to Kadowaki et al. in 714,[5] on the 10th of the 2nd month,

Katsumi, Maruyama Jirō, op. cit., part 2, p. 210: "12th day, when Soga *no omi* Emishi, 蘇我臣蝦夷, and his people were on the point of being put to death, they burnt all the imperial chronicles, national chronicles, and rare treasures.

Fune *no fumubito* Esaka, 船史惠尺, was able quickly to snatch the burning chronicles of the *kuni* (provinces). He gave them to Naka *no* Ōe." Cf. W. G. Aston, op. cit., vol. II, p. 193.

[1] Cf. Kadowaki Teiji, op. cit., p. 72. *Nihonshoki*, 29th *maki;* Kuroita Katsumi, Maruyama Jirō, op. cit., part 2, p. 357; Cf. W. G. Aston, op. cit., vol. II, p. 350.

[2] We are much inclined to this latter opinion as even the name of the *Kojiki* as *collection of ancient tales* can be found back in this decree. Namely, it speaks of the most ancient tales: 上古諸事. According to its contents also, the *Kojiki* offers older tales than the *Nihonshoki*.

[3] Cf. *Nihonshoki*, 30th *maki*, Jitō 15th year; Kuroita Katsumi, Maruyama Jirō, op. cit., part 2, p. 411:

"Orders were given to the eighteen clans to offer the chronicles of the ancestral graves (to the empress)."

The names of these clans or *uji* are given here. Cf. W. G. Aston, op. cit., vol. II, p. 403.

[4] Kadowaki Teiji, op. cit., p. 190.

[5] *Shoku-Nihongi*, 6th *maki*, Gemmei, Wadō 7th year; Kuroita Katsumi,

when Empress Gemmei, 元明, (707-715) gave Fujimaro, 藤麻呂, and others the command to compose 'the history of the nation'. Hayashiya [1] believes that the *Kojiki* originated as a result of the abovementioned recensions of 620 and 681, while the *Nihonshoki* supposedly originated in those of 691 and 714. He believes that he can elucidate the discrepancies between the two works from these recensions which were independent of each other. If Hayashiya's supposition is correct, then the *Nihonshoki* should be more dependable than the *Kojiki*, as it came into being in a far more peaceful and settled era. That is confirmed by the fact that the *Nihonshoki* offers a far greater diversity of opinions and occurrences. This historical reliability is progressively reduced, however, the further we remove from the year 700, and penetrate antiquity. It would be going too far if we were to engross ourselves in the question as to which of the two was edited first. Of far greater importance is the question as to what happened to the material of these sources, before both achieved their final edition. Naoki Kojirō writes of this in the *Daigaku Nihon-shi*: [2]

"In the period which preceeded the Nara period, when the emperorship achieved its heights in such figures as Temmu and Jitō, the editing of the old chronicles was accomplished. The *Kojiki* was compiled by Yasumaro, 大安万呂, at the behest of Emperor Temmu in 714, from material which Hida-Are 稗田阿礼 had collected. The responsibility (for the definite form of the *Kojiki*) lay with Toneri Shino, 舎人親王, (676-735) (= Hida-Are).[3] This was

---

Maruyama Jirō, *Kokushitaikei Shoku-Nihongi*, Tōkyō 1963, part 1, p. 55. In the text itself there is mention of 撰 = chosing. Therefore there must have been material available. Perhaps this was the result of the collection of the chronicles of the 18 clans. Cfr. J. B. Snellen, "Shoku-Nihongi, Chronicles of Japan, continued from 697-791", *T.A.S.J.*, Sec. Ser., XIV 1937, p. 263. Snellen's translation here is entirely different. His translation of the *Shoku-Nihongi* runs only up to the 7th *maki*, Reiki 1st year. For *Shoku-Nihongi* quotations of a later date than the 1st year of Reiki therefore is in this work no reference made to J. B. Snellen.

[1] Cf. Kadowaki Teiji, op. cit., p. 190.

[2] Part 1, p. 70.

[3] These persons are mentioned in the introduction to the *Kojiki*. It must not be entirely believed that the *Kojiki* text was by Emperor Temmu. Namely, Empress Gemmei had given Yasumaro the order to sort all the material. Hida-Are had an extremely good memory and had to memorise these sorted texts as a kind of archive, and then later *read* them to Emperor Temmu. Temmu ascribed the *Kojiki* to his own name in the prologue, for

important material for the history of the Yamato court. There is still much discussion as to the historical reliability of this. In particular, the material antedating the sixth century is highly problematical. Although one can uncover the imperial and national chronicles of those periods, the material has, however, been twisted and deformed in later ages for several reasons. There is most question of such 'ornamentations' in the *Nihonshoki*, but in the *Kojiki* also such passages are to be found. These falsifications kept step with the revolutions which took place during those two hundred years of forgery. Therefore much may be found there which is of no value whatever."

From this conclusion of *Daigaku Nihon-shi* it is obvious that we cannot unreservedly accept the text as it reached its final edition. The text itself also will have to be critically examined. Though the final edition of the *Kojiki* and the *Nihonshoki* lay in the first decade of the eighth century, it is obvious, that the material from which these works originated was much older. How old can usually only be initially decided after a detailed analysis of the individual texts. By the use of a few general facts which occur everywhere throughout this material, it is possible to establish something more definite concerning this antiquity. We shall show this in particular by use of the chronology of the sources and the problems surrounding the names of emperors.

2 *The chronology of Japan's oldest sources*

Only the *Nihonshoki* mentions a chronology of Japan's oldest sources. The *Kojiki* merely reports the ages of the emperors.[1] Nevertheless, there was a certain chronology, which was important to both works. This, moreover, not only served as a means for giving dates, but also as a frame for the construction of both works. It was connected with the so-called *kanshi* (干支) system.

The calendars which the *Nihonshoki* used for its dating were

political considerations, not because he had participated so greatly in its composition. Consult Iwahashi Koyata, "Temmu tennō to *Kojiki* (Emperor Temmu and the *Kojiki*)", *K.G.Z.*, vol. 63, 1962, no. 9, Sept., pp. 50, 51 on this. Therefore Yasumaro simply wrote down what Hida-Are dictated to him. Iwahashi Koyata, op. cit., pp. 52, 53. There are opinions, founded on the basis of the special title *tone*(*-ri*), that Hida-Are was a woman. This problem is however, hard to decide.

[1] Cf. A. Wedemeyer, op. cit., p. 4. He has collected all these calculations of the *Kojiki* together here.

based on this system which was imported from China. The oldest inscription which testifies to the existence of such a calendar in Japan, dates from the year 503 A.D. It is to be found in a painting of the temple of Sumida, 隅田, in the prefecture of Wakayama. The year *mizunoto-hitsuji* is mentioned here, one of the years of this *kanshi* system. This would have been equivalent to 503 A.D. It is, however, accepted, that this inscription came into being only far later, as at that time Japan scarcely maintained any relations with China and Korea. Such an involved system as this must therefore have reached Japan at its earliest at the beginning of the seventh century. The oldest *Nihonshoki* report of a calendar is certainly of a far later date. It says [1] of Emperor Kimmei, whom we shall meet again in connection with the introduction of Buddhism to Japan, that in 553 he sent ambassadors to the South Korean state Paekche. These returned later with 'doctors, soothsayers and calendar scholars.' Some fifty years later, in 602 A.D., the famous Korean monk and scholar Kanroku, 觀勒, [2] came to Japan, with manuscripts of calendrics, astrology and geography. From that time on there was adequate opportunity for chronologers, and other interested people, to qualify themselves in the science of calendars. We can therefore safely assume, that at the end of the sixth, early seventh century, the Chinese *kanshi* system was adapted to apply to Japanese relationships and chronicles. It is therefore pointless to establish the antiquity of the entire series of emperors, with Wedemeyer, by use of this system, which was so belatedly imported.[3]

In what did this *kanshi* system consist? Its nature can be discovered in the word *kanshi* itself. *Kan*, 干, is an indication of the Five Elements, after these had been divided by *yin* and *yang* into two groups of five, the older named *e* and the younger 'brother' named *to*. Thus there were in total ten '*kan*', or rather, five pairs of older and younger brothers. *Shi*, 支, has two meanings, namely 'nucleus' and

---

[1] See Chapter V, p. 292, ft. nt. 1.

[2] *Nihonshoki*, 22nd. *maki*; Kuroita Katsumi, Maruyama Jirō, *Kokushi-taikei Nihonshoki*, part 2, p. 140:

"10th year (602), 10th month. The monk of Paekche, Kanroku (W. G. Aston, op. cit., vol. II, p. 126: Kwal-leuk) came. He offered books on calendrics, astrology and geography, together with literature about *donko*, 遁甲 (that is to say, the art of prognosticating the future from the behaviour of the human eye), and all kinds of arts." Cf. W. G. Aston, loc. cit.

[3] Cf. A. Wedemeyer, op. cit., pp. 3-24.

'something which is divided within itself'. This original meaning was later extended to that of the two verbs for division and addition. Therefore *shi* is a means by which the above-mentioned ten *kan* may be subdivided further. Of these *shi* there were twelve altogether: the twelve signs of the zodiac. In the following table we have arranged the ten *kan* and the twelve *shi* according to the *kanshi* system.

KAN	*Character*	*Sense*	*SHI*	*Character*	*Meaning*
1) *kino-e*	甲	wood	1) *ne*	子	rat
2) *kino-to*	乙		2) *ushi*	丑	ox
3) *hino-e*	丙	fire	3) *tora*	寅	tiger
4) *hino-to*	丁		4) *u*	卯	hare
			5) *tatsu*	辰	dragon
5) *tsuchino-e*	戊	earth	6) *mi*	巳	snake
6) *tsuchino-to*	己		7) *uma*	午	horse
7) *kano-e*	庚	metal	8) *hitsuji*	未	sheep
8) *kano-to*	辛		9) *saru*	申	monkey
			10) *tori*	酉	bird
9) *mizuno-e*	壬	water	11) *inu*	戌	dog
10) *mizuno-to*	癸		12) *i*	亥	swine

In this system the years are indicated by combining one of the ten *kan* with one of the twelve *shi*. Thus 120 combinations can be brought about. They are not all used, as in the *kanshi* system only the odd numbers of both series are allowed to combine with the even numbers of both. The odd numbers of the one series, however, are not allowed to coincide with the even numbers of the other. Thus only sixty combinations are possible. These sixty combinations provide a sequence of sixty years. Each series starts with the year *kinoe-ne* and ends with *mizunoto-i*. This series therefore begins and ends as follows:

1. *kinoe-ne*
2. *kinoto-ushi*
3. *hinoe-tora*
4. *hinoto-u*
5. *tsuchinoe-tatsu*
6. *tsuchinoto-mi*
7. *kanoe-uma*
8. *kanoto-hitsuji*

9. *mizunoe-saru*
10. *mizunoto-tori*
11. *kinoe-inu*
12. *kinoto-i*
13. *hinoe-ne*
14. *hinoto-ushi*

etcetera

57. *kanoe-saru*
58. *kanoto-tori*
59. *mizunoe-inu*
60. *mizunoto-i*

This sixty-year sequence[1] has not been arbitrarily fitted into the Japanese chronicles. More principles were called in to establish it. These can be found formulated in the scarcely translateable text of the Calendar Book: *P'iao-yüan* 表元 (Sino-Jap.: *Hyō-gen*).[2] According to this work an unknown revolution must have taken place at the time of the earth's creation. As a result of a constellation in which the numbers three and five recurred repeatedly, this had no catastrophic results. In order to avoid major disasters in the future also, these numbers had to determine the sequence of years according to the *kanshi* system. The system of the sixty-year

[1] The use of it may be read from the following table:

DATES			KAN	SHI
531	591	1911	*kanoto-*	*i*
532	592	1912	*mizunoe-*	*ne*
533	593	1913	*mizunoto-*	*ushi*
534	594	1914	*kinoe-*	*tora*
535	595	1915	*kinoto-*	*u*
536	596	1916	*hinoe-*	*tatsu*
537	597	1917	*hinoto-*	*mi*
538	598	1918	*tsuchinoe-*	*uma*
539	599	1919	*tsuchinoto-*	*hitsuji*
540	600	1920	*kanoe-*	*saru*
541	601	1921	*kanoto-*	*tori*
542	602	1922	*mizunoe-*	*inu*
543	603	1923	*mizunoto-*	*i*
544	604	1924	*kinoe-*	*ne*
545	605	1925	*kinoto-*	*ushi*
546	606	1926	*hinoe-*	*tora*
547	607	1927	*hinoto-*	*u*
548	608	1928	*tsuchinoe-*	*tatsu*
549	609	1929	*tsuchinoto-*	*mi*

[2] This passage is quoted by Emil Gaspardone, op. cit., pp. 240, 241: "La voix du ciel ne s'éloigne pas grandement, elle revient après trois ou cinq."

cycle was founded on this, also sometimes called *gan*, 元. The sequences of this *gan* also were made up according to these, and other sacred numbers. Twenty-one of these *gan* together formed a *bo*, 部. This latter therefore covered a period of 1260 years.[1] On the basis of these and other principles, various applications of the *kanshi* system or calendars came into being. These calendars were given a somewhat mystical meaning, as they had to prevent all manner of disaster. The fundamental sacred numbers had to guarantee good luck and prosperity.

On the basis of various calendars with separate calculations and applications, the *kanshi* system has been inserted into the history of Japan. These calendars have 'fabricated' a large part of Japan's oldest history. This is shown by the way in which these calendars were inserted into Japan's history. As the calendars were founded on revolutions in primeval times, so in the insertion of them into Japan's chronicles, important revolutions in the history of that time were pre-supposed. These had always to coincide, in the calendar, with a revolutionary year. Kadowaki [2] calls 601 A.D. one such a revolutionary year, as Shōtoku Taishi published the 'Seventeen Article Constitution' at that time. If one now calculates backwards, using one *bo* = 1260 years, then one again arrives at such a revolutionary year, i.e. 659 B.C., the year of Jimmu's ascension to the throne. In the first year of Emperor Temmu also, 681 A.D., various changes took place. If one now calculates according to another application of the *Kanshi* system, i.e. the *Gihō* 儀鳳 calendar,[3] the entire sequence of 1341 years of this calendar beginning at 681 and working back, then one arrives at the same date of Jimmu's

[1] Cf. Gaspardone, op. cit., p. 241, note 1. No explanation is given for the fact as to why 21 times 60 = 1360 and not 1260. This is not Gaspardone's mistake, but lies in the Chinese text quoted by him. Kadowaki only mentions 1 *bo* equalling 1260 years. Op. cit., p. 206.

[2] Cf. Kadowaki Teiji, op. cit., pp. 200 ff.

[3] The calendars used in the *Nihonshoki* were the Gihō- and the Genka-calendar. The Gihō (儀鳳) calendar was achieved in China in the T'ang period (618-907), under the first name of Lin-tê calendar. It was given the name of Gihō calendar in Silla (Korea). From there it arrived in Japan. The dates of the period up to Empress Jitō (687-697) were sustained from the year 604 according to this calendar, just as the long period from Emperor Jimmu until Emperor Ankō. The remainder of the *Nihonshoki* was dated by the Genka (元嘉) calendar, which originated in China in the Sung period (420-477) and reached Japan via Paekche. See Kadowaki Teiji, op. cit., pp. 207 ff.

reign. Thus the calendar might have been established either under or after Shōtoku Taishi, or under or after Temmu. We shall see in the fifth chapter that the 'Seventeen Article Constitution' was ascribed to Shōtoku Taishi only owing to piety, as it was probably never published. Thus the year 601 lapses. It is therefore obvious, that 681 was chosen as the starting point of the calendar for the chronicles. This would thus only have been established after that date. If one accepts, along with Motoori Norinaga et al., that the final edition of the *Kojiki* was already arrived at in 681, it becomes clear why no *kanshi* system may be discovered in the *Kojiki*. It was not yet in existence. It was only introduced before the *Nihonshoki* reached its final recension, that is to say before 691, or 714.

From this calendar history it appears that only those facts can be dated with certainty which took place after the year 681 A.D. Giving a date for facts before that date grows commensurately more difficult according to their increasing distance from 681. It is nearly impossible, on the basis of these calendars, accurately to date occurrences of a century earlier to the day and month, unless one can justify it from other sources.

The institution of these calendars, however, also had other consequences. These were especially related to the Japanese emperorship. On the basis of recent discoveries concerning Japan's antiquity, we have seen that the material which comes under consideration at the beginning of the seventh century for the *Kojiki* and the *Nihonshoki* could, at the most, only be some three hundred years old at the time of the final recension of both sources. Nevertheless this had to be spread out over a period of 1260 years or even more. How was it possible to compose a list of emperors which would account for all those years? One possibility lay in extending especially the lives of the oldest and least known emperors as far as possible. This did indeed take place. This may be seen from the fact that only the lives of the first emperors reached almost Old Testament proportions in both the *Kojiki* and the *Nihonshoki* In the *Kojiki* Jimmu reached the age of 137, in the *Nihonshoki* 127. This difference in ages in both sources could be proof of this state of affairs. Of the first fifteen emperors, twelve died at an age of over 100. The patriarch of the Soga clan, councillor to Emperor Ōjin, Takeuchi, grew (as a result of the longevity of the emperors under whom he served) to be several hundred years old. As a result of this extension, there were naturally not enough chronicles. Thus it can be explained that the chronicles about Jingū in the *Nihon-shoki*, could suddenly jump from the thirteenth year to the thirty-ninth year of her reign.

There was another possibility in so far as new emperors were contrived by, for instance, turning local rulers into emperors, or permitting one and the same emperor to re-occur in the chronicles under various names and in different periods. That the latter also took place, can be proved by comparison of their Chinese and Japanese names.

3 *The names of the emperors*

Until now, we have repeatedly indicated the leaders of the Japanese nation by the word 'emperor'. With this we do not want to suggest that Japan's very oldest royal leaders had the power and the territory which, according to our conceptions, belong to an emperor. This title arises rather from the impossibility of reproducing the entire nature of these rulers in an adequate title. As we shall see in the following chapter, their power was, initially, extremely limited. They only became 'emperor' in the full sense of the word in 645, when their function and name was copied from that of the Chinese emperors. This entirely individual character of Japan's oldest sovereigns must always be born in mind when using the word 'emperor'; the word gained a different interpretation in each period. This development can, i.a., be read into the names of the emperors.

The emperors of Japan's antiquity had two kinds of names. In order to ascertain this, one has only to glance at the *Kojiki* and the *Nihonshoki*. Though the emperor had 'from the first' his own Japanese name, later another, Chinese one was added. This Chinese name was usually not a translation of his original Japanese name, but rather a definite characterisation of his personality. Parallel to this were his two titles of address, which are also used in the oldest sources. The Japanese title was *sumera no mikoto* or *ō-kimi*, the Chinese *tennō*. We are accustomed to assume as much as emperor in these untranslateable titles, although they have a totally different emotional value and background. When the emperors were given their Japanese titles, we do not know. The Chinese title, *tennō*, 天皇, that is to say 'Heavenly Ruler' only arose under Empress Suiko. This is proved by three inscriptions, which date respectively from 596, 607 and 608. Before this word came into fashion, the word *ō-kimi* was much used. This contains the meaning of great ruler. The word *tennō* was considered to be the Japanese pendant of the Chinese *T'ien-ti*, 天帝, 'Heavenly Emperor'.[1] This title visualized the earthly opponent of the Pole star [2] which, in China, was considered to be the central point where the celestial quarters met.

It is held by some that at the time of Empress Suiko this concept began to be applied to the imperial leader of the bureaucratic form of government, who therefore began to be called *tennō*. As, however, at that time there was, as yet, no mention of governmental officialdom, we share Tsuda's opinion, that this ideology was only added in 645, after the Taika-reformation.[3] Therefore we can hardly agree with Kadowaki in believing that Shōtoku Taishi created this role of spiritual and temporal supreme head of bureaucracy.[4] Therefore the word *tennō* could only be naturalized after 645. This also shows in the fact that especially the Confucian protagonists of the emperor idea only intirely gained power after 645, with the Confucian clan of the Nakatomi, 中臣. Although this new function was only established halfway through the seventh century, all preceding *ō-kimi* were mentioned from this date on in the chronicles, for instance, not by their Japanese titles usual until then but by the Chinese *tennō*. This, however, was not enough. Soon the individual emperors as well, even those who had been long dead, began to be given Chinese personal names.

It is not known who the namegiver was. It is, however, agreed that the emperors before Ōjin received their Chinese names only in the eighth century. According to some [5] the Chinese poet Omi *no* Mifune, 淡海三船, supplied all the emperors from Jimmu until Jitō with such names. That must have been towards the end of the eighth century. From Emperor Mommu, 文武, (697-707) on, the emperors themselves began to use these names, although they also

---

[1] For this emperor theory, see J. J. M. de Groot, *Universismus*, Berlin 1918, pp. 80 ff.; M. Granet, *Danses et Légendes de la Chine Ancienne*, tome II, Paris 1959, p. 616. The opinion given here is held by Tsuda Sōkichi, *Nihon Jōdaishi no Kenkyū*, pp. 464, 465.

[2] Cf. Kiyohara Sadao, *Shintōshi*, Tōkyō 1939, p. 114. In China the Pole star was accounted the principle star as it is the link of the heavenly quarters. In Japan this Pole star belief became common property certainly from the beginning of the ninth century on.

[3] Tsuda Sōkichi, op. cit., pp. 476, 477.

[4] Kadowaki Teiji, op. cit., p. 175.

[5] As Kadowaki Teiji on p. 211.

retained their Japanese names. The Chinese nomenclature was not highly original. Many names, for instance, display a striking similarity to those of the small South Korean state Silla. There too one might encounter such names as Mommu, Kōshō, Shōtoku, and even Jimmu.[1] Tsuda,[2] however, believes that Chinese sources suggested these names. Therefore Korean and Japanese rulers' names probably go back to a Chinese original, as the writers, also in both areas, were at least of Chinese descent, if not Chinese.

If we continue comparing the Chinese names of the first fifteen Japanese emperors to each other, then the first, tenth and fifteenth, namely those of Jimmu, 神武, Sujin, 崇神, and Ōjin, 応神, appear to be composed of the Chinese character *shên*, 神, Sino-Jap.: *jin*. We have already remarked on this. This character is also used in the sense of the Japanese word *kami*. Both the Chinese *shên* and the Japanese *kami* can mean superman or deity, with all the gradations which lie between those two concepts. We agree with Kadowaki [3] that this did not just happen by chance. These three figures have been used in order to bridge various periods. Thus Sujin stood on the threshold between the eras of the celestial gods and the heroes. The last hero of this latter period would, in his turn, have been Ōjin. He formed the beginning of the history of ordinary mortals. Thus the figures of Jimmu, Sujin and Ōjin served to project Japanese history backwards in various stages up to the year 660 B.C.

The same is suggested by the Japanese imperial names. These were used in front of the Chinese imperial names. They were impractical in daily use. Thus Jimmu was called: *Kamu-Yamato-Iware-hiko*, and his successor Suizei: *kamu-nuna-kawa-mimi*. If one looks at the 'construction' of these names, then they appear to fall into five groups. In the table given below Kadowaki [4] has attempted to coordinate these groups:

1. Kamu group

   (2 names) i.e.: Kamu-*yamato-iware-hiko* (Jimmu) and Kamu-*nuna-kawa-mimi* (Suizei).

---

[1] This happened because the same characters were being used: 文武, Mommu; 孝昭, Kōshō; 聖徳, Shōtoku and even 神武, Jimmu.

[2] Op. cit., pp. 474 ff.

[3] Op. cit., p. 199.

[4] Op. cit., p. 201.

2. Yamato-neko-hiko group

   (4 names) i.e.: Ō-yamato-neko-hiko-*suki-tomo* (Itoku).

   The following emperors belonged to this group: Itoku, Kōrei, Kōgen and Kaika.

3. Tarashihiko group

   (4 names) i.e.: *Waka*-tarashihiko (Seimu).

   Kōan, Keikō, Seimu and Chūai belonged to this group.

4. Iri-hiko-iso group

   (2 names) i.e.: *Mimaki*-iri-hiko-iso-*nie* (Sujin)

   Sujin and Suinin belonged to this group.

5. A group of imperial names which cannot be ascribed to any of the above 4 categories. These are Annei, Kōshō and Ōjin.

The four centres to which, according to this table, the Japanese names of the first fifteen emperors are pegged, probably go back to various sources. According to Kadowaki [1] that must have been seven or nine. This can very easily be brought into connection with the imperial decree of 691 A.D. to compile the chronicles of eighteen different clans. In the light of this decree it does not seem improbable, that these groups of emperors resulted from clan traditions. Figures who, in this tradition, merely functioned as local chieftains and not as rulers of the entire empire, could be absorbed into the *Nihonshoki* which was to be newly compiled in 714 and into the *Kojiki* of 681, as those who had to bridge the period between 660 B.C. and 300 A.D. Thus the chronology became the framework on which all these local traditions were threaded together and on which they were exhibited. The fact that the clan traditions especially have contributed to a considerable extent to this, may be seen from an analysis of the contents of the sources themselves.

4 *The Japanese sources as clan history*

Comparison of the contents of these sources shows that, despite much editing, traces of the original clan traditions could not be eradicated. In the second chapter we shall, by use of these comparisons, attempt to define the emperor's living image as known among the major clans.[2] Thus one can still trace which clan traditions were

[1] Op. cit., pp. 202, 203.

[2] P. 128, and ff.

used in the composition of the *Kojiki* and the *Nihonshoki*. An example of these may be found in Kadowaki,[1] who deduced it from 'an eastern tale of conquest' concerning Emperor Jimmu.[2] This is recorded both by the *Kojiki* and the *Nihonshoki*. Nevertheless there is some difference in each. The version in the *Nihonshoki* is more detailed than that in the *Kojiki*. The major differences between both versions of this conquest only really come to light in the invasion of the Yamato plain by Jimmu. According to the *Kojiki* there was scarcely any battle in Yamato-Kashihara, 橿原, while on the contrary, the *Nihonshoki* allows a severe struggle to take place there. This was the strife against the *kuni-tsu-gami*, 国ツ神, that is to say, the land gods, actually little more than local and inimical heroes.[3] In this account especially the *Nihonshoki* devotes liberal space to the members of the Ōtomo, 大伴, clan. This is shown, amongst other things, by the battle hymn, which Jimmu's army broke into in its battle against the revolutionary Naga-sune-*hiko*, 長髄彦. In this hymn the destruction of the enemies was sung and ridiculed.[4] It terminates in inexplicable exclamations, which apparently had to be roared forth by all the clan members immediately prior to the struggle. Now this was the clan song of the Ōtomo. This is proved by the fact that it is called the Kume, 久米, song in the *Nihonshoki*.[5] According to Kadowaki this song belonged to the sept of the *Kume-be*, 久米部, which belonged to the Ōtomo clan.[6] The song itself is supposed to stem from the end of the fifth century, as in it there is mention of the struggle against the *ebisu* (barbarians), who were destroyed at that time by, i.a., Ōtomo *no* Takehi *no muraji*, 大伴武日連. Thus the Jimmu story had something to do with the ancestral tales of the Ōtomo clan, of which Ōtomo *no* Takehi *no muraji* was the leader. This clan needed the Jimmu creation for the benefit of its relations with the imperial house,

[1] Op. cit., pp. 88 ff.

[2] The *Tōseiden*, 東征伝, in this campaign by Emperor Jimmu from East Kyūshū to the plain of Yamato is related. For the description of this, see Karl Florenz, op. cit., pp. 222-240; J. M. Martin, *Le Shintoïsme*, tome 1, Hongkong 1924, pp. 80-82.

[3] Cf. Kadowaki Teiji, op. cit., p. 90.

[4] See K. Florenz, op. cit., p. 236 for this hymn.

[5] *Nihonshoki*, 3d *maki*, Jimmu, *tsuchinoe-uma*, 12th month, 4th day, Kuroita Katsumi, Maruyama Jirō, op. cit., part 1, p. 127; K. Florenz, loc. cit.; W. G. Aston, op. cit., vol. I, p. 127.

[6] Op. cit., p. 90.

and therefore bound traditions of its own past to him. This must have happened at the time when this clan reached its supremacy.[1] This occurred before the ascendency of the Mononobe clan at the beginning of the sixth century. By using data known to us from the *Nihonshoki* and the *Kojiki* concerning other clans like that of the Mononobe, it is not difficult to detach entire portions of the *Nihonshoki* as being traditions, which originally belonged to these clans. Therefore this example of the Ōtomo is only one of many. It suffices to illustrate the origin of the oldest Japanese sources. It follows from the above that the chronicles of the *Nihonshoki* and the *Kojiki* should be dated according to the age of the various clans.

The very 'oldest' chronicles of Jimmu were closely connected with the traditions of the Ōtomo clan, and thus those of Sujin linked up with the Mononobe, and the Ōjin chronicles were interwoven with the Soga clan.[2] We shall return to this later.[3] It follows from this peculiar composition of the Japanese sources that they do not straightforwardly give sober and businesslike reports of Japan's oldest political facts, but are rather registers of all the mutual ambitions and rivalries of the clans. If one does not take the specific nature of these sources into account, and follows the text of the *Kojiki* and the *Nihonshoki* slavishly, without discounting their entirely individual origin, one could easily caricature the real image of Japan's genesis. This is equally valid for other data from these sources, such as those concerning Buddhism. In the light of these clan rivalries, and later and further on also of anti-Korean sentiments and embarrassment about national primitiveness, they were used not only to describe the actual historical course of events, but also to camouflage and blur it.

Chinese sources, Japanese archeology and the international political constellation all show that, despite all pre-war fanatical belief in the divinity of the emperors, Japan's genesis came at the same time as the migrations in the West. The growth and development of the Japanese state ran almost parallel to that of many

---

[1] The hey-day of the Ōtomo is dated according to the age of the burial mounds in their area: these date from the time of Keitai (507-531).

[2] Cf. Kadowaki Teiji, op. cit., p. 95: "A reconstruction is also possible with regard to the Mononobe chronicles, just as much as with regard to the Ōtomo ones."

[3] Cf. Chapter II, pp. 128 ff.

western Germanic states. The Japanese sources confirm that this was a growth process in which local and clan interests played an important part. Furthermore, it follows, that just as Christianity was implanted during the growth process of the western states, Buddhism had its place in Japan in one of the first phases of the nation's development. Though, however, there are very many sources which teach us how Christianity has grown into all the western Germanic states, in Japan we have only the *Nihonshoki* at our disposal, by use of which we can follow the origin of Japanese Buddhism. When we use these manuscripts, we shall always have to bear in mind Emperor Temmu's words to his editors in the prologue to the *Kojiki* text: [1]

"We have heard that the imperial annals and old traditions which are in the possession of various families, are contradictory to truth and even contain lies. If one does not correct these aberrations now, then the purpose of these writings will be worthless."

This exhortation of Temmu's will indubitably have led to a great deal of truth remaining in the *Kojiki* and the *Nihonshoki*. Meanwhile, however, many inaccuracies had already crept in, which the editors could no longer brand as such, besides other veiled truths which were equally unrecognizable as they were acceptable to the mentality of that period. Even at the time of Emperor Temmu, a not entirely disguised revulsion against many foreign and non-Japanese importations already belonged to this outlook.

Standing at a reasonable distance from all this, it is easier for us, in many regards, to catch both kinds of mistakes by use of the information discussed in this chapter, however much that same distance may increase many of these attempts at investigation. Though I may exhibit few certainties as a result of this study, it is nevertheless worthwhile now to continue research into the encounter of Japan with Buddhism.

---

[1] See *Kojiki*, 1st *maki*; Kuroita Katsumi, Maruyama Jirō, *Kokushi-taikei Kojiki*, p. 3.

CHAPTER TWO

ORIGIN OF PRE-BUDDHIST SOCIETY

It is clear that Japan's 'new genesis' throws an entirely different light on the social structure into which Buddhism was implanted. The traditional image of this, encountered, i.a., in the older Japanese and Western authors, is thus broken down and rendered obsolete in many respects. The phenomenon of Shamanism especially, and the regressive matriarchy which accompanied it, and, no less, the late origination of the emperorship, make us suspect an entirely different growth of Japan's society than had been known hitherto. As a result, Shintō and Buddhism also underwent a different development. This is due to Japan's religious mentality—as everywhere else—being shaped to a great extent by the specific nature of its society.

This is particularly plain from the fact that the role of the emperors in Japanese history did not begin until far later than had always been presupposed. From this it is clear that the introduction or refusal of Buddhism did not concern only the emperors, but was equally important to the powerful clans surrounding them. The previous chapter showed that these clans also provided the material for the records of the imperial history. It is obvious that they did not contribute less to that history than the emperors themselves. The vast power and independence which they maintained, created the possibility that, according to the membership of one or other clan, the attitude towards religion also varied. Therefore, just as did the imperial house, these clans too moulded Shintō and Buddhism. It was owing to the protection of one of those clans that Buddhism could prosper on Japanese soil.

Besides this specifically Japanese situation, it is generally true of religion, that it is always tied to a certain society and becomes defined by it. We need only consider the history of the Roman Catholic Church in The Netherlands. In the course of centuries it began to differentiate sharply from that of, for instance, Italy and Spain, owing to the gradual integration of even the Calvinist inclined elements of Dutch society. As a result of that, it is not imaginary that there could be Italians who would see Protestantism in Dutch Roman Catholicism rather than their own belief. Therefore an outsider will always have to remain aware of these characteristics when studying this Roman Catholicism. This is no less valid for Japan's religious outlook, and especially for its Buddhism, which one must not just measure against the Indian pattern, and then brand as unorthodox because it has managed to develop differently. A Dutchman also will not tolerate that his Roman Catholic experience should be called unorthodox by an Italian or a Spaniard, just because it does not agree with certain forms in Italy or Spain. Japanese Buddhism has become something specific to Japan's society. Therefore its growth is unthinkable without implicating the entirely specific development and nature of this society.

Now how did this society, which Buddhism was to encounter in the sixth century, grow? On the basis of new developments I believe that I must accept that it was accomplished in two different phases.

The first stage encompasses the growth of the population which inhabited Japan already, before the advent of the imperial race. The structure of this population may be found in the previously mentioned *Wei chih*. Here and there it also comes to light in Japan's oldest sources as a terminal phenomenon.

In the second stage the imperial race coalesces with it. As a result of this a more complicated society was to originate. In the lowest strata the old structure continued to exist, however, its superstructure was to change entirely. This was to be decided by the emperor and the clans, which, together with him, were to rule the old society. This double development of Japanese society was accompanied by a religious growth. Thus, on the one side, groups came into existence which were noted for a very severely shuttered and conservative mentality, as they refused all outside influence. On the other side there were to be other groups who went so far in their progressiveness that they even fused their religious ideas. The exponents of this latter group were especially the emperors. This was due to the fact that gradually they began to count as the supporters of all opinions alive in the various sections of the population. Therefore we shall be able to follow particularly in these emperors the development of Japan's oldest religious forms.

First Phase: Pre-Imperial Society

It is not too easy to sketch the growth process of Japanese society in its initial period, as we do not know too much about it. We only know the structure of society in Japan's seventh and eighth century. In addition we have a few details from the *Wei chih* (and the *Hou Han-shu*) as well as a few sporadic texts from the *Kojiki, Nihonshoki* and the *Fudoki*. In the previous chapter we saw that these three latter manuscripts certainly do not belong to the period before the origin of the imperial house, and that they only give a picture of Japan's fourth and fifth century which was projected backwards from the seventh and eighth century. In as far as the Japanese sources are concerned, we shall have to be satisfied with this picture, as it is from this alone that we can obtain any insight into Japan's pre-imperial society. A Japanese work such as the *Shoku-Nihongi* for instance, gives us no information whatever concerning this initial period. Furthermore, the *Wei chih* and the *Hou Han-shu,* which was inspired by it, give little grip on this period. Here we move in an area of hypotheses, about which the historians can give us little certainty. By using extreme hypotheses, we want to attempt to reconstruct this pre-imperial society.

The projection of the Japanese sources is of great importance to this reconstruction. It was this in particular, which shows us the primeval peculiarities of Japanese society, which also existed when Japan first encountered Buddhism. Namely, when this began here in the sixth century, there was scarcely mention of a central government. This was owing to the lack of the requisite system of officials. This was only achieved under the Taika reformation of 645 which, moreover, tumbled the entire design of the Japanese state and society. This took place for the benefit of a bureaucracy orientated more towards China. It was only this reformation which gave the emperor his powerful central position. The chronicles of the Japanese sources had, however, already ascribed it to him in earlier periods.

1 *The Uji*, 氏.[1]

Despite all the uncertainties concerning Japan's oldest period, the historians and archeologists are nevertheless in agreement that

[1] This word *uji* forms the most important concept in Japan's oldest society. Words such as *uji no kami, ujibito* and *ujigami* illustrate this. Therefore we ought here to investigate more closely the etymological background of this word. *Uji* was written 氏 in Chinese characters, Chin.: shih. Later in Sino-Japanese it was also pronounced *shi*. Nevertheless, the old Japanese

in pre-imperial Japan all power resided with the leaders of the villages and centres of communal interest, into which the old Japan was subdivided. These leaders were called *uji no kami*. One can translate this term by 'governors of the *uji*'. *Uji* is the name for such a small independent community. Those who stood under the direct authority of the *uji no kami* were named, i.a., *ujibito*, that is to say '*uji* people'. Each *uji* stood, in some manner, under the protection of its private deity, the *ujigami*, which is not to be confused with the leader of the *uji*, the *uji no kami*.

The word *uji* does not stem from the Chinese. It is of Japanese origin. One can find many pendants for it in the Korean, Mongolian and Tungusian languages, which are pronounced more or less in the same way. They all carry the sense of family, posterity or enclave. According to its verbal meaning, *uji* is therefore a demarcated family community. Excavations in the Kinki, 近畿, area, that is to say, the area round Ōsaka and Kyōto, have confirmed the existence of such closed dwelling communities. The most important data concerning these is given by the above mentioned *Wei chih*. The reference in this to the more than thirty small states in Kyūshū can only have indicated such *uji*. Now what is such an *uji*? Most opinions think it to be an autonomous dwelling community. The federal bond, in which they co-existed, did not limit its independence severely. The *Wei chih* explains this to us. This federation served rather to be able to withstand the inimical Kuna state, than to coalesce these tiny part states into a larger unit. Only it appears that the religious influence of a figure such as Himiko reached

word *udi*, from which *uji* developed, had little phonetically to do with this Chinese *shi*. It was closely connected to the Korean *ul*, as the Japanese *d* is similar to the Korean ㄹ = *r* or *l*. This Korean *ul* has the meaning of family or enclosure, within which the family dwelt. A pendant to this may yet be found in the Mongolian *uru-q* (the *q* is supposed to be a later addition), which has the meaning of 'related to the mother's side'. *Use* in Manchurian and Mongolian conveys the meaning of seed. This word can also be found, somewhat changed, in Tungusian: *usa*, son. In one of the Ryūkyū languages a similar word occurs, namely: *utuza*, member of the family. In an old Japanese dialect *ushira* means house or entry. In the language of the Ainu *utari* means: member of the same family. By use of these parallels, the concept *uji* can be rounded off to family community. For these data see Ōno Susumu, *Nihongo no Rekishi* (History of the Japanese Language), Tōkyō 1959, pp. 38-52. For similar word tracing see Oka Masaō, "Nihonminzoku-bunka no Genryū . . .", *Minzoku-gaku Kenkyū*, vol. 13, no. 3 (1948), pp. 222, 223.

farther than her own small area. Federal unity is even supported to a large extent by her function of priestess. We shall return to this more closely in our discussion of the function of the *uji no kami*. Most Japanese authors, amongst them Fukuō, Nakamura and Tsuda,[1] consider the *uji* as being fairly evolutionary. They are therefore easily inclined to see a cross section of the later *uji* society in the situation depicted by the *Wei chih*. Originally—according to them—this development must have started from independent *uji* living beside each other. Most *uji* were not much larger than a village at that initial point. Therefore, according to their theory, such *uji* formed the earliest and very oldest cell structure of Japanese society.

Until now, we have only described these *uji* roughly, without closely tracing their specific nature. In what did this consist? Should one consider the *uji* as a large family which was held together by a communal patriarch? Or was it far rather a working community, made up of various families not related to each other, who did not recognize a communal patriarch, but only their leader or one or other deity as a symbol of unity? The question here is therefore whether this principle of the unity of the *uji* was formed by the special tasks of the *uji*, or by its ancestry. The implications of these hypotheses are already apparent for the religious development of Japanese society, which approximately started with these *uji*. Because it is clear, that its specific nature will again be reflected in the choice of the protective deities of the *uji*. Were these ancestral deities, or were they more concerned with the various tasks of the *uji*? This is of importance because these deities in their turn, absorbed into a larger Shintō connotation in later Japan, continued to play their part. Now just on this question of the specific nature of the *uji*, opinions differ extremely. Fukuō [2] sees a family community of *uji no kami* and *ujibito* in the *uji*. According to him the functions of each community were defined by the degree of relationship to the *uji no kami*. In accordance with the expanding interests of these family communities, non-relatives also were to begin

---

[1] Fukuō Takeichirō, *Nihon Kazoku Seidoshi* (History of the Japanese Family System), Tōkyō 1956; Nakamura Kichiji, *Nihon Shakaishi*, Tōkyō 1956; we have already pointed Tsuda Sōkichi out. For the historical location and later development of this society, see: Friedrich Tappe, *Soziologie der Japanischen Familie*, Münster 1955, pp. 11-20.

[2] Fukuō Takeichirō, op. cit., p. 10.

belonging to this *uji*. They were absorbed into this *uji* bond, not as free *ujibito*, but as servants and slaves. In the same sense the *ujigami* is supposed to be a deified ancestor of the *uji no kami*. Therefore he was only accessible to the other family members and not to those who did not belong to the family. Therefore he had no meaning to the other servants and slaves.

We share the opinion of Tsuda and many others [1] that the *uji* should rather be seen as a corporation and a group with common interests than as a family community. Tsuda founds his opinion on an analysis of the word '*ie*' [2] or '*he*', which means house. According to him, this word has something to do with '*hettsui*', the hearth, which was the most important place in the house, because the oven god lived there. This deity was separate from every family connection. He was equally respected by the members of the family of—and by outsiders to—the *uji no kami* alike, as spy and telltale of all the good and evil of the community.[3] Another opinion points out that the Korean word '*he*', which is closely related to the Japanese, has the impartial meaning of 'entrance'.[4] This stood open not only to family members but also to non-family members. These two opinions are, however, not adequately decisive for the corporation theory. More is achieved, if one argues from the angle of all *ujigami* still known to us. These are, admittedly, often depicted in the *Kojiki* and the *Nihonshoki* as being the ancestors of one or other *uji*. We believe, however, that this only occurred later. The trend of the tribal patriarchy of the *ujigami* dates from the time when the most prominent *uji* wanted to suggest their relationship to the imperial house for political benefit. Furthermore, Confucian influences have (also, however, at a far later date) contributed to it. Moreover, if one also considers the names of these so-called 'tribal deities', then it appears that none of them bear the name of the *uji* to which they belonged. Shibata indicates that these names point to a totally different relation of the *ujigami* to the *uji*. This in connection with the fact that they can be reduced either to a *musubi* or to a deity of fire or light. The oldest of these

---

[1] Such as Fukuō Takeichirō and Nakamura Kichiji for instance.

[2] See Tsuda Sōkichi, *Jōdai Nihon no Shakai oyobi Shisō* (Japan's Society and ideology in antiquity), Tōkyō, p. 380.

[3] For this oven and fire god see Kiyohara Sadaō, *Shintōshi*, pp. 167 ff.

[4] Cf. Nakamura Kichiji, op. cit., pp. 63-64.

two types of *ujigami* are, according to him, the *musubi*.[1] As we have seen in the first chapter,[2] they were little other than an impersonal growth force, which produced the rice and other fruits of the field, and also humans. Everything which had the slightest connection with fertility led back to them. Therefore these impersonal deities were predominantly related to the activities of the *uji*, who mostly concerned themselves only with agriculture. The *musubi* did not belong to one or other group of members of a family. They were the protective deities of everything and everyone who belonged to a certain *uji*. From the standpoint of this train of thought, the specific nature of the *uji* must rather have existed in a work community than in a family community.

Therefore an *uji* was originally nothing other than an agricultural community, the members of which farmed communally. Their numbers were decided by the extent of the territory. They were bound to each other by the land. This land was communally rather than privately owned. This may be deduced from the system of land division[3] instituted afterwards in 645 A.D., which was specifically intended as a measure which would terminate this collective land owning. Nevertheless this collectively owned land had transferred amongst the most powerful *uji* to the hands of the *uji no kami*, who gradually came to consider it as his private property. The fact of the originally collectively owned property is still apparent in the Shintō ritual for the *tsumi*, 罪, the sins. In that there is mention of the so-called *shikimaki-tsumi*,[4] which consisted of the taking into private possession of a piece of land owned by an entire community. This appropriation was considered as an infraction of the rights of the entire group, in which no individual property was countenanced. The individuality of the sepa-

---

[1] Cf. Shibata Minoru, "Sōsen sūhai no genryū (Origin of ancestor worship)", in: *N.S.K.*, part III, pp. 26-32. See further Chapter II, p. 105 ff., ft. nt. 3.

[2] p. 41 ff.

[3] Sino-Jap.: *handensei*, 班田制, Cf. Nakamura Kichiji, op. cit., p. 68.

[4] There were three kinds of infringement: *shikimaki*, *kushizashi*, and *asenawa*. *Shikimaki*, literally 'frequent sowing' consisted in the repeated sowing of seed on a piece of land where this had already been done. The last person to sow had the right to the harvest. This shows the joint ownership of the land. *Kushizashi* consisted of the appropriation of a public piece of land, by staking it off with stakes. *Asenawa* was doing this with ropes and cords. Cf. Nakamura Kichiji, loc. cit.

rate members was important in as far as they contributed to the entire *uji*. The soil was tended by the whole group. The separate tasks such as making pottery, sowing and harvesting of certain crops, were only planned in as far as they concerned the whole community. One cannot heedlessly compare these *uji* to the Russian kolkhos. They were different; the mutual differences between their members were not only defined by the tasks which they carried out as part of the *uji*. There was also a strong class distinction. This is shown by the particularized composition of the *uji*, which we will explain in the following paragraph.

2 *The Ujibito and Other Members of the Uji*

In the *uji*, the *ujibito* 氏人, which literally means '*uji* people', were those who stood immediately under the *uji no kami*. Originally they were supposed to have been little other than a few families living together, who wished to provide their livelihood communally. For the benefit of the organisation they had a leader in the *uji no kami*. However much most Japanese authors may be led by evolutionary theories in depicting the origin of these *uji*, one will nevertheless have to be very careful in portraying this state of affairs, as it is equally possible that the *uji* have grown from a decadent, but somewhat more complicated society. In any case, we know nothing about that origin. Therefore it is also difficult to say whether the most 'primitive' *uji* consisted only of *ujibito* and an *uji no kami*. We can, however, say that, as the *uji* and the various necessities of life in it expanded, other kinds of people also began to participate in that *uji*. Therefore many people were incorporated in that *uji*, who were in no way related to the 'original' families. As land and soil communities the *uji* permitted similar infiltrations of freemen and slaves.[1] The freemen would gradually belong to the *ujibito*, the slaves would be subdivided amongst the *uji* and classed according to their degree of serviceability. They were not part of the property of the *ujibito*, but of the *uji*; together with the cattle and the land they formed part of the stock of the community. Thus the *ujibito* grew to be the immediate managers and, moreover, seconds-in-command under the absolute rule of the *uji no kami* of the total property of the *uji*. Amongst the other members of

---

[1] Cf. Takatori Masaō, "Kodai minshū no shūkyō (The religion of mankind in antiquity)", *N.S.K.*, part 2, Tōkyō 1959, p. 35.

the *uji* there was no abrupt change between freemen and slaves. There were many gradations. The number of these 'additional' members varied according to the size of the *uji*. The largest group by far which followed that of the *ujibito* was encompassed by the *be*, 部, or *tomo*, 伴. The guilds of the potters, saddlers, carpenters, etc. belonged to this, but also all of those who were in one way or another useful to the *uji*. These were not only prisoners or slaves, but also entire *uji* which had been subjugated, who, together with their original property began to belong to the conquering *uji* and even bore the name of their conquerors in the future. These *be*-groups too had their own leaders, the *tomo no miyatsuko*, 伴造, literally 'the builders of the *tomo*'. They, or their forefathers, had also been *uji no kami*, when their own *uji* was still independent. This second group also, just as much as the *uji* itself, was not made up of an anonymous mass. It also knew its own classes in accordance with the gradations which existed between freemen and slaves. The *tomo no miyatsuko* had preserved their own responsibility and authority in this, although they were dependent upon another *uji*, along with the whole group. Many centuries later the immigrants from Korea were to belong to this *be*-group. They were often to receive their own appointed villages and settlements, in which they had relative independence and where they could lead their own, Korean way of life. It is partly due to this that Buddhism could gain a secure foothold in Japan. We shall return to this group at the end of the third chapter.[1]

The various layers indicated here in the *be*-group were only classified by their own titles after the Taika reformation. Thus the structure in this *be*-group was even more strongly demarcated.

As a consequence of conquests and the like, the slaves, who were called *yakko*, 奴,[2] were also to be added to this *be*-group. They belonged to the soil, and were re-sold along with the soil to others. Of these slaves, some could maintain an existence befitting a human being; they could marry and dwell in their own cottages. Others, however, were not much more than cattle and were treated as such. The picture of Japanese society at its first stage, as depicted

---

[1] P. 217 ff.

[2] Nakamura Kichiji, op. cit. pp. 78 ff.

above, is particularly supported by data from the *Kojiki* and the *Nihonshoki*.[1]

In the *Wei chih* an almost similar structure may be found, although it has not been indicated by the same nomenclature. Thus one can see in the small states mentioned in this manuscript further developments of the *uji*, which were federally administered by Himiko. We refer to the Tsunoda translation [2] for the full text of this. We will only quote a few passages here, which also illustrate the aspects of *uji* society treated above. Concerning the relationship of the *ujibito* to the lower classes, here one can read the following: [3]

"Ordinarily, men of importance have four or five wives; the lesser ones, two or three. Women are not loose in morals or jealous."

This text shows that here we are dealing with various classes, in which the standard of prosperity is defined more or less by the number of women. We read of the relations between these classes: [4] "There are class distinctions among the people, and some men are vassals of others."

That class distinction is also apparent in the modes of address: [5] "When the lowly meet men of importance on the road, they stop and withdraw to the roadside. In conveying messages to them or addressing them, they either squat or kneel, with both hands on the ground. This is the way they show respect. When responding, they say 'ah', which corresponds to the affirmative 'yes'."

From all this one may deduce that there must have been a deep gulf between superiors and inferiors, which permitted little possibility of contact between these two groups. Possibly this limitation of the classes provided the possibility for Buddhism to reach Japan without being noticed initially.

The *Wei chih* shows as well that there were also slaves outside these two classes. Amongst the gifts which Himiko and her successor Iyo, 壱与, sent to China there were often slaves. Of Himiko the *Wei chih* says concerning this: [6]

"In answer to the Queen of Wa (Himiko), an edict of the Emperor,

---

[1] It is impossible to refer to all these data here. However, we shall refer to some occasionally.

[2] Ryūsaku Tsunoda, *Japan in the Chinese Dynastic Histories*, pp. 8-16.

[3] Ryūsaku Tsunoda, op. cit., p. 12.

[4] Ibid.

[5] Ryūsaku Tsunoda, op. cit., p. 13.

[6] Ryūsaku Tsunoda, op. cit., p. 14.

issued in the twelfth month of the same year (238), said as follows: 'Herein we address Pimiko, Queen of Wa, whom we now officially call a friend of Wei. The Governor of Tai-fang, Liu Hsia, has sent a messenger to accompany your vassal, Nashonmi, and his lieutenant, Tsushi Gori. They have arrived here with your tribute, consisting of four male slaves and six female slaves, together with two pieces of cloth with designs, each twenty feet in length.' "

It says of Iyo that her delegation "visited the Court and presented thirty male and female slaves." [1]

In the same text there is a passage which is moreover the oldest information concerning Japanese criminal law, which explains where those slaves came from: [2]

"There is no theft, and litigation is infrequent. In cases of violation of law, the light offender loses his wife and children by confiscation; as for the grave offender, the members of his household and also his kinsmen are exterminated."

We must accept that the confiscated women,[3] children and kinsmen were all transferred as slaves to the property of the injured party. In this, this criminal code confirms that the *uji* was a community of interests, in which only the rights of that community stood in the foreground. Those of the individual were so repressed that even personal crimes were recouped from the entire community. This is explained by the fact that the entire community was responsible for the offences of each member belonging to it.

This attitude was maintained until the seventh century. Therefore we shall have to take it into account even in our appreciation of the process of conversion to Buddhism. Here too the interests of the community prevailed so strongly over those of the individual that there was no room left for an individual conversion for instance. Therefore, if there is some mention in the Japanese sources concerning a conversion to Buddhism, one will have to realize that this conversion did not remain limited to one person. It was rather the conversion of an entire society which surrounded that person. This can be ascertained from the first Japanese conversions to Buddhism.

For the same reason one will have to see entire groups in various places in the chronicles where there is mention of one single person. Bruno Lewin has pointed this out with regard to the non-Japanese

---

[1] Ryūsaku Tsunoda, op. cit., p. 16.

[2] Ryūsaku Tsunoda, op. cit., p. 12.

[3] In the Chinese text there is mention of: 沒, confiscate.

immigrants.[1] Names such as Achi and Wani belonged to leaders of an entire group, which had immigrated in its entirety to Japan with them at its head. Nevertheless, despite the depreciation of that individuality, there was only one person in each *uji* who was, to a high degree, the only person capable of influencing the whole *uji* philosophically as well. That person was the

3 *Uji no Kami,* 氏の上

The tasks of the various members of the *uji* were not laid down by the *ujibito* or the *be* on a democratic basis, but lay with the *uji no kami,* literally 'the head of the *uji*'. Who was this *uji no kami*? In him one must see the spiritual and political leader of the entire *uji,* who decided its weal and woe. He had not always been this. Originally he was indeed no more than its mots important leader. With the growth of his power he was gradually to expand into the real large property owner and absolute ruler of the *uji.* With this, the whole property holding of the *uji,* with people and land, turned into his private property. Thus, in his *uji,* he grew from primus inter pares to an absolute spiritual and temporal leader who, in accordance with his name, towered over his *uji.*[2] His name, written 上, has something to do with the word written 神 for *kami* [3] which means

[1] Cf. Bruno Lewin, op. cit., p. 20.

[2] 氏 in the word 氏の上, *uji no kami*; *kami* has the meaning of lord and of above, ascend.

[3] For ages there have been different opinions about the word *kami.* The actual origin of it is likely to remain obscure. *Kami* is a word with very many meanings. The real root of it appears to be somewhere near which has the meaning of something *raised,* something *situated high.* Everything which is litterally or figuratively high, may be called *kami*: 上. Thus, in antiquity, the leader of the priests was called *kami* (伯), as was the head of police (尹). *Kami* also indicated: higher official (頭); politician (正); soldier (督); and the protector of a certain area (守). Areas in the neighbourhood of the capital were called *kami* (上一). Upstream is still called *kawakami* (川上). The highest physical member of man, his hair on his head, is called *kami* (髪). Furthermore, all superhuman agencies were called *kami* (神). These *kami* may be encountered in the *Kojiki* for instance, everywhere. Here not only the gods of heaven and earth, or the souls of the humans worshipped in temples as gods are mentioned, but also all hidden forces of nature which are concealed in plants, animals, mountains and rivers. It is understandable, that Japan is called the country of the 8.000.000 gods or *kami.* See Kiyohara Sadaō, *Shintōshi,* p. 8. We must, however, point out at the same time, that in antiquity the deity was not only indicated by *kami.* Originally other words were also used which indicate supreme power or divinity. Until the Nara

divinity. Only in the seventh century did they begin writing both with separate characters. A *kami* was someone who, in one way or

---

period (710-793) these were, for instance, *tama*, *mono*, *chi*, *hi* or *mikoto*. For the use of these words see Anzu Sunahiko, "Kami to Mikoto", *K.G.Z.*, vol. 59, 1958, no. 10, 11, Oct., Nov., pp. 8-18, especially p. 8.

It is difficult to decide whether the concept of divinity, 神, *kami*, is derived from 上, exalted, or vice versa. Here one cannot argue from the various meanings which may be ascribed to the syllables *ka* and *mi* by use of the Chinese characters. Because these characters were imported into Japan only after the word *kami* had already been given both meanings. For these arguments see Tsuda Noritake, *Shintō Kigenron*, Tōkyō 1920, pp. 45-47. (Hence *kami* was supposed, i.a., to derive from *kakureta* (隠) *mi* (身), concealed body; or *kakuri* (隠) *mi* (身) hidden spirit.) See also Kiyohara Sadaō, op. cit., pp. 7-9. (Hence *kami* was supposed to derive, i.a., from *Arakajimi* (明神), god of clarity; thus *kami* would be an abbreviation of *kajimi*.)

Others derive this word from *arakami* (明見), clearly visible, or from 牙 = *kabi*. In this latter derivation *ka* would have the meaning of vague, difficult to perceive and misty, *bi* indicated spiritual. For all of these solutions see also D. C. Holtom, "The Meaning of Kami", *M.N.*, vol. III, 1940, Jan., no. 1, pp. 5-17. However, all these solutions are retrospective reconstruction and therefore too synthetic. More realistic are the arguments based on the difference in accentuation between: 上, *kami*, and: 神, *kami*, although Kamo Mabuchi (1679-1769) announced: "*Kami* (= 神) may be read as *kami* (= 上). This *kami* also sounds like *kami* or *kamu*." Nevertheless Yamamoto has proved from the use of words in the old sources that there was a definite difference. See D.C. Holtom, op. cit., p. 23. This difference is apparent furthermore from the phonology of *kami* in these two senses. Cf. D. C. Holtom, op. cit., p. 24.

Moreover, we are much inclined towards the explanation encountered in Tanaka Yoshito, *Shintō-gairon*, Tōkyō 1942, pp. 36, 37: "According to the *Nihonshoki*, the word *kanki* (干岐) supposedly occurred in the original chronicles of Kaya (Mimana). According to the *Nihonshoki-tsūyaku*, both kings and their families were indicated by that name in those areas.

In Korea and Mongolia the word *kanki* and especially, the word *kan* were used from antiquity to indicate both king and deity. Thus the word *kami* was used by all Eastern peoples. Its own locality of derivation is, however, hard to ascertain." Concerning this word *kanki* see also Suematsu Yasukazu, *Mimana Kōbōshi* (History of the rise and fall of Mimana), Tōkyō 1949, p. 28. Therefore this word may very easily have been an extension of the Turco-Tartar *qam* or *kam*. Cf. M. Eliade, *Le Chamanisme*, p. 430. There *qam* had the meaning of Shaman. We shall later point out that Shamans in Japan also were so much identified with the deity that they themselves became that deity. We mentioned above the word *mikoto* as one of the indications for the concept deity. *Mi* (= honorific)-*koto* (Jap. ritual instrument, often used by Shamans during their trances, cf. this chapter, p. 90.) was, however, also highly involved in Shamanism. Cf. Jean Romieux,

another, excelled the ordinary person. This word is extremely elastic as it embraces all the meanings which lie between one in a superior position and a deity itself. Therefore the word *uji no kami* offered the possibility of seeing in him a kind of personification of the godhead, or, in any case, someone who stood in a very close relationship to the gods. We believe that even his entire authority rested on that relationship, and that his day-to-day and temporal government was a result of that divine tie. In the community which he ruled, he had absolute authority. This can mainly be explained by the fact that he was supposed to be the concrete actualization of the will of the gods. Therefore he was principally a priestly figure. With regard to the very oldest *uji no kami*, it is furthermore remarkable, that many of them in antiquity were women. Their influence was so extensive and particular that one involuntarily recalls that of the Shamans in present-day Siberian tribes. We shall therefore have to investigate these particular spiritual properties of the *uji no kami* more closely in the following pages.

One may find these depicted in many of the old tales of the

"Mythes du Japon Ancien vus à la lumière de la Linguistique comparative", *M.S.G.*, vol. VIII, 1946, pp. 79-82. Seen in the light of the characters mentioned above, the Shaman changed from 上 to 神. Nevertheless, we still agree with many Western and Japanese authors that, despite the close connection between both characters, it still remains difficult to decide which of the two was actually primary. We must also point out that, in our translation of the Japanese word *kami* by deity, we must bear in mind that here we are not dealing with a transcendential god, but with a concept which (in contrast to our Western concept of divinity) allows for "8.000.000" various meanings. Therefore we agree with Grousset, who writes: "Notre mot 'dieu' est d'ailleurs impropre pour rendre l'idée japonaise du 'kami'. Ce mot signifie simplement 'haut', 'supérieur', 'transcendant'. Est 'kami' tout ce qui, dans la nature, est doué de pouvoirs spéciaux (bons ou mauvais). Amaterasu-o-mikami (grande-honorable kami) l'est tout autant qu'un brin d'herbe ou un grain du sable. Les forces vives de la nature n'ont pas besoin d'être personnifiées par des nymphes ou des esprits, elles sont "esprits", elles sont "kami par elles mêmes." Cf. René Grousset, *La Face de l'Asie*, Paris 1955, p. 323. Holtom's conclusion from Japanese opinions concerning this word also implies this. He describes *kami*: "Saturated with the atmosphere of the Divine, the Sacred and the Holy." D. C. Holtom, "The meaning of Kami, Chapter II, Interpretation by Japanese Writers", *M.N.*, vol. III, no. 2, July 1940, p. 53. We would prefer to explain this Japanese concept of deity in the sense of the antique *musubi*: The primeval power which creates and effects all things, with which all things are charged. See our exposition concerning this on pp. 105 ff. ft. nt. 4.

Kojiki, Nihonshoki and *Fudoki*. These descriptions, however, run entirely parallel to those of the *Wei chih*. We shall have to look at the texts concerning this 'Shamanism', and also what we might call (with some reservations) matriarchy, in greater detail, as many characteristics of it, as suggested in these texts, have also played a part in the later emperorship of the sixth and seventh century, which was so great that we must render the entire origin of Buddhism dependent on this.

a. The Wei chih.

In our first chapter, namely in the argument concerning the origin of the Japanese imperial lineage, we pointed out various passages from the *Wei chih* with references to a kind of female Shamans. The most elaborate passage is as follows: [1]

"The country formerly had a man as a ruler. For some seventy or eighty years after that there were disturbances and warfare. Thereupon the people agreed upon a woman for their ruler. Her name was Pimiko (= Himiko). She occupied herself with magic and sorcery, bewitching the people. Though mature in age, she remained unmarried. She had a younger brother who assisted her in ruling the country. After she became the ruler, there were few who saw her. She had one thousand women as attendants, but only one man. He served her food and drink and acted as a medium of communication. She resided in a palace surrounded by towers and stockades, with armed guards in a state of constant vigilance."

According to this translation, she 'occupied herself with magic and sorcery'. The Chinese text states that she practiced 鬼道, *kuei-tao*.[2] The meaning of this word is 'the path of souls (of the dead)'. This word conveyed rather the meaning of fiendish practices to the Chinese chroniclers. That is also obvious from their addition 'she bewitched the people'. Matsukawa Jirō [3] ascribes this attitude to the fact that these authors did not recognize the phenomenon of Shamanism. It was, however, known at that time in China. We shall see in the third chapter that Chinese Shamanism, also sometimes called 'Wu-ism', might already be found in China before the

[1] Ryūsaku Tsunoda, op. cit., p. 13. The actual Chinese text may be found in *Daigaku Nihon-shi*, part 1, pp. 39, 40.

[2] 鬼道 *kuei-tao*, the path of the spirits of earth. See Chapter III, p. 149, footnote 5.

[3] Cf. Matsukawa Jirō, *Tennō no Rekishi*, p. 29.

beginning of our era.[1] It is additionally of interest to note that this Chinese Wu-ism was also mainly practised by women. It was, however, at times highly respected in China and sometimes violently attacked. The emissaries who, in Japan, encountered a phenomenon similar to their own Wu-ism, only show their dislike in their tales, but not that here they were meeting something entirely new. One can also come across that same dislike in Chinese texts concerning Wu-ism. Arthur Waley points out that this contempt expanded in China particularly after state Confucianism became the state religion there.[2]

The fact that the estimation of the Wa peoples for Himiko was something quite different to that held by the Chinese writers of the *Wei chih* is shown by the description of the great respect which Himiko enjoyed. This respect was based rather on the fact that she was more of a spiritual than a temporal leader of the federation. How else can one explain that she left her governmental tasks to a man. One can read of this respect in the description of her funeral: [3]

"When Pimiko (= Himiko) passed away, a great mound was raised, more than a hundred paces [4] in diameter. Over a hundred male and female attendants followed her to the grave."

From this too may be seen that she enjoyed special respect amongst the population because of her spiritual leadership. Nevertheless, I do not believe that we have a right to call her a Shaman solely on the basis of these texts. She undoubtedly had some properties which might mark her as a Shaman. One cannot expect of such an old political chronicle as this, that in it all the elements which define Shamanism could be assembled without more ado. The Chinese chronicler only intended giving a national chronicle, not a theological treatise concerning Shamanism. Though these elements are not assembled here, this does not mean to say that Himiko was not a Shaman also.

The report cited above contains indications that she maintained relations (not further described) with the hereafter. These were also in some way connected with the soothsaying and clairvoyance

---

[1] See Chapter III, pp. 149 ff.

[2] Arthur Waley, *The Nine Songs*, London 1955, pp. 11, 12.

[3] Ryūsaku Tsunoda, op. cit., p. 16.

[4] A *ho* (歩) is six *shaku* (尺) and 4 *sun* (寸), approximately 1.92 metres.

mentioned in this text.[1] Consequently it may be seen that she did not maintain these relations from personal motives only, but in order to 'bewitch the people'. If one separates this sketch from the emotionality of the Chinese chroniclers, then it can best be seen as: she was a mediator with the gods for the people. In this function she felt herself closer to the gods than to her own people; this may be seen from her seclusion described in this text. Contact with the people, necessary for several practical measures and orders, was maintained by one man only. Therefore her spiritual function was primary. It was to this that she owed her task as temporal governor. The success of her rule depended on the fact that she practised 'the path of souls'. This description too might be valid as an amateurish and incomplete definition of her Shamanism. This can be met with again in her successor Iyo, who, just as she, achieved the same office after a man had failed in governing.[2]

"Then a king was placed on the throne, but the people would not obey him. Assassination and murder followed; more than one thousand were thus slain. A relative of Pimiko named Iyo, a girl of thirteen, was made queen and order was restored."

This translation does not express the sense of the Chinese text correctly. Namely, here there was no mention of 'a relative of Himiko', but 'Himiko returned'.[3] Therefore this text is not only important because it states that Iyo was a priestess, but also that Himiko returned in order to entrust the monarchy to her. This is slightly surprising, as in the previous pericope of the *Wei chih*, her funeral had just been described. Here her return can only have occurred in a Shamanistic trance, during which Iyo united herself with Himiko's soul, through which she too gained the capacity of freeing the country from all disturbances. Himiko's return remains inexplicable in any other context than this ecstasy, seen as a Shamanistic trance.

Despite the aversion to this among the chroniclers, sufficient

---

[1] Ryūsaku Tsunoda, op. cit., p. 12: "Whenever they undertake an enterprise and discussion arises, they bake bones and divine in order to tell whether fortune will be good or bad. First they announce the object of divination, using the same manner of speech as in tortoise shell divination; then they examine the cracks made by the fire and tell what is to come to pass."

[2] Ryūsaku Tsunoda, op. cit., p. 16; *Daigaku Nihon-shi*, loc. cit.

[3] In the text it is said of Himiko: 復立. This can only be translated as: Himiko returned.

material has nevertheless been assembled in their accounts concerning Himiko and Iyo which would indicate Shamanism. Only these female Shaman figures appear capable of restoring the country to law and order, although the entire society of that period did appear to be predominantly patriarchal according to the *Wei chih.* This appears from the extremely lowly position of women at that time. Therefore Himiko was not made eminent as ruler and leader of the federation by the matriarchy of that era, but by her Shamanism. This was very easily possible, as this either stood or fell by its recognition or repudiation by the entire society. That it was practised by women is perhaps an indication of the fact that it was an archaic survival from a time when it partly determined another —mainly matriarchal—society.

In this Shamanism the way also lay open to the deification of Himiko. Namely, according to the above-mentioned text, she lived in great seclusion. That withdrawn life made her, in the eyes of her subjects, someone who lived very close to the gods and kept herself distant from everyday affairs. It can be imagined that thus she was gradually identified with those gods. Many of the heroes of the *Kojiki* and the *Nihonshoki* who were placed in the various divine heavens as gods, prove that this actually happened repeatedly. We can therefore imagine that a figure such as Amaterasu was also originally a Shaman like Himiko, who, according to Eder [1] was sublimated and mythologised into a deity.

b The Japanese sources

Will the Japanese sources confirm the picture given above from the *Wei chih*? I believe that these sources offer an abundance of material which points in the same direction concerning the Japanese *uji no kami* of the first phase.

In the *Wei chih* a concrete summary of the deities to whom Himiko stood in relation is lacking. Also the actual nature of those 'fiendish practices' is not clearly described. A far more accurate picture of this may be found in the *Nihonshoki*. The best typification of the spiritual function of the *uji no kami* is to be found in Emperor Ōjin's mother, Jingū. We noted in the first chapter [2] that she was often identified with Himiko, so that Matsuwaka [3] for instance,

[1] M. Eder, "Schamanismus in Japan", *Paid.*, 6. Heft, Mai 1958, p. 375.

[2] Cf. p. 31.

[3] Matsukawa Jirō, op. cit., p. 29, uses the Jingū material to illustrate the

sees only one and the same person in both. Though this latter is scarcely tenable, both figures nevertheless form the best illustration of the spiritual function which the *uji no kami* held in his or her *uji*. This is shown by the following *Nihonshoki* text concerning the Shamanism of Jingū.

After an introduction concerning her personalia, her chronicles begin as follows: [1]

"The Empress chose a propitious day. On it she entered the great hall of worship. She herself undertook the function of *kannushi*, 神主.[2] She let Takeuchi *no sukune*, 武内宿禰 [3] strum on the *koto* 琴.[4] She gave the task of *saniwa(bi)to*, 審神者,[5] to Nakatomi *no* Ikatsu, 中臣烏賊津. Numerous and extensive ribbons had been affixed to both extremities of the *koto*. Loudly and pleadingly she called upon the deity: 'Who is the god who last imposed his will on the Emperor, now deceased? I would like to know his name.' Only after seven nights and seven days did she receive an answer: 'The name of the god who lives in the palace of the Fifty Small Shattered Bells, situated in the district of Momotsu-tawarai, 百傳度逢, in the land of the Kami-kaze, 神風, (the god of the wind) Ise, 伊勢,[6] is: The spirit of the *tsuki-sakaki*, 橦賢木,[7] The Princess of Mukatsu, 向津 (litt.: from the other side of the sea = Korea), which is situated far from the heavens.' Again she asked: 'Are there other gods as well as these?' This question was answered by: 'I am the one who appeared from the ears of the ribbon reed (Eularia japonica). I live in the district of Ota *no* Ata-kushi (or -fushi) *no* Awa, 尾田吾田節之淡.' Again she asked: 'Are there any others?' To this the reply came: 'Yes, the god Tama-kushike-iri *hiko*, 玉籤入彦, the ruler

Himiko figure. However, this opinion is untenable, as has been explained in Chapter I.

[1] Cf. *Nihonshoki*, 9th *maki;* Kuroita Katsumi, Maruyama Jirō, *Kokushi-taikei Nihonshoki*, part 1, pp. 241, 242.

[2] *Kannushi* was the actual leader of divine worship. This is the present-day name for Shintō priest.

[3] See p. 124 for Takeuchi.

[4] For the meaning of this stringed instrument, see ft. nt. 1 on p. 84.

[5] That is to say, the liturgical conductor of the *koto* music. This function occurred only in such oracles as these. Karl Florenz, op. cit., p. 277, ft. nt. 6 calls him: "Der welcher die Göttersprüche deutet."

[6] Situated in the south-eastern corner of Yamato.

[7] *Matsurigoto* in the sense of government was written 政治; in the sense of religion it was written 祭礼. See Matsukawa Jirō on this, op. cit., p. 29.

(litt.: the representative) of all that moves in the heavens and in space, the terrifying Kotoshiro-nushi, 事代主.' Then she asked whether there were any others. She received the answer: 'Whether there are any more or not, we do not know.' To this the *saniwabito* said: 'No answer is forthcoming, however, he will speak again later.' Then yet another answer came: 'In Tachibana, 橘, of the land Hyūga, 日向, at the bottom of a small narrows of the sea, there there are gods, who live there and come into being as fresh (verdant) water plants. They are named the gods of the man of the Uppermost (Visible), of the Middlemost, and of the Deep Hollow.' Again it was asked whether there were more gods. To this the response came: 'Whether there be more or not, we do not know.' It was not further revealed whether there were more. Only after this did she receive the words (revelations) of the gods. In observation of this, they were worshipped. After this Kamo *no* Wake, 鴨別, the ancestor of Kibi *no* omi, 吉備臣, was sent out on her orders to attack the province of the Kumaso, 熊襲."

The text from the *Nihonshoki* cited above belongs as such in the second phase of this chapter. Was there not already mention of an emperor and other figures such as Takeuchi and Nakatomi, who were too closely connected to the imperial House. In this, however, we must also take the new conclusions of the first chapter into account. Now the second phase first began with the imperial house. As we have seen, this only reached Japan with Ōjin. Jingū is depicted in the sources as his mythical mother. As such she has something to do with the second phase. As governor, however, she belongs equally to the first and to the second phase. There are, however, also other reasons why I prefer to give her a place in the first phase. Because the female ruler described here and the entire oracle in which she takes the main part as *kannushi*, belongs rather in the first than in the second phase. The function which is practised by Jingū here is entirely of one piece with Himiko's spiritual leadership. Just as Himiko, her practical political and governmental rule resulted from her position as a priestess. Her trance included both the sacrificial service to the gods and her practical governmental policy. In the *Kojiki* and the *Nihonshoki* this was indicated by the general word *matsurigoto*. This is used both in the sense of national management and of divine worship. This word permits of suspecting how closely the unity of the state and religion was personified at that time by the figure of the *uji no kami*. For the

Japanese of antiquity that unity was not laid down constitutionally, but brought about and experienced in a concrete person: the *uji no kami*. He only decided in what proportion those two stood to each other. This was the case not only in the *uji no kami* of the first, but also of the second phase. Indeed, the emperors had access to the same unlimited power, by which they could activate the entire spiritual, military and religious potential of the nation for whatever ends. This remained the case until the year 645.

The prestige and the charismatism of the personality of the *uji no kami* played an important part in everything. All the more so, because it was not limited by constitutional bonds.

In the text cited above, a kind of oracle is depicted which opens the struggle with Japan's previous inhabitants, here called *Kumaso*. This oracle involuntarily reminds one of that of Delphi, which so often made history in Greece. Could one not also call the Pythia of Delphi a Shaman, as she was an interpretess of the gods to the people and led a secluded life comparable to that of Himiko? This question could be an attempt to find the link between the Japanese and the Greek religious mentality. The difference between Pythia and Jingū is not entirely owing to the fact that here we are dealing with two different cultures. The Pythia was more of a neutral figure, which stood between various nations. She was therefore accessible to friend and foe. She had only to gather the will of the divinity and pass it on. However, her function was not, as was the case with Himiko and Jingū, entrusted to her by a certain community. Therefore she stood outside society to a greater extent.

This was all completely different in the case of Jingū and Himiko. Their contact with the gods was also *matsurigoto*. They were engaged in the community which they themselves led. Owing to this social aspect, the *matsurigoto* belonging to both of them was rather Shamanism than a function of the Pythia.

The trance which co-defines the concept 'Shamanism' is not mentioned in both the texts quoted above. This does not, however, mean to say that it was lacking. The return of Himiko in order to appoint Iyo, and the discussion of Jingū with the gods could not just take place without this tranee, which united them both with the gods invoked. We therefore believe that both these texts indicate true Shamanism owing to the social and extatic elements.

As far as Jingū is concerned, there are more texts in the *Nihon-shoki* which bear witness to her Shamanism. The Japanese sources

—also the *Nihonshoki*—do indeed intend to register the destruction of these female *uji no kami* of the first phase by the emperors and heroes of the second phase. Therefore one can without difficulty recognize the victory of the patriarchy over the matriarchy, despite the fact that there was but little left of it according to the *Wei chih*. Nevertheless, it was not entirely exterminated. A few remnants of it even created the possibility for Buddhism to penetrate to imperial circles also, so that it could be brought out from here as a state religion.

There are also other reasons for investigating these texts more closely. Firstly, they show how these Shamans were regarded in later ages. In addition, the local sketches of the *Fudoki* offer the possibility of more closely localizing their working area among the Japanese islands. As reports of destruction concerning the *uji no kami* of the first phase, they form the proof that there actually was a first phase.

In reading all of these texts we must also realize that though they may have originated at an early date, they were subjected to the censorship of the final recension at the beginning of the eighth century which was strongly bound to the imperial house and patriarchal Chinese influences. One of the intentions of this final recension was to depict the dominion of the imperial house as an age-old historical reality. Therefore it is not surprising that all the important figures (as well as those not connected with the imperial house) of Japanese antiquity were made subject to this purpose. Due to this alone they owed their place in these sources. That Jingū is an exception to this is due to the fact that she was rendered as Ōjin's mother. The Jingū text has therefore been left as it was. Some tales were even added to it, in which she was also implicated in the struggle against the *uji no kami* of the first phase. This makes the Jingū chronicle all the more interesting in comparison to other texts from the *Nihonshoki* and the *Fudoki*. Namely, if this text has slid through the meshes of the final recension of the eighth century, then which edition is it the result of? In the text itself there is mention of Takeuchi, the patriarchal ancestor of the Soga. It does not appear very acceptable that in 681, at a time of extreme anti-Soga feeling, he should have been added to this text. We have seen, moreover,[1] that various authors opine that this recension resulted in

[1] See Chapter I, p. 57 ff.

the *Kojiki*. Therefore I believe that this text is a rescued remainder of the edition which was begun in 620 under the reign of Empress Suiko. Under her the Soga group reached the apex of its power. The figure of Takeuchi fits into that. At this point the matriarchal figure of Empress Jingū became a valuable symbol for the Empress Suiko, living at that time. If this assumption is correct, then this text proves that such figures remained in high esteem well into the period of Empress Suiko's reign. Hence this respect was probably far greater than would superficially appear from the Japanese sources. Its final recension has indeed disguished all matriarchal trends as well as those indicative of Shamanism is as far as possible.

I therefore believe that the fundamental note in other texts of the *Nihonshoki* in the description of similar Himiko figures differs all the more, as all of these have been more thoroughly cleansed of the influences mentioned above. This is also valid for the *Fudoki* texts. This is why Shamanism is no longer here linked to the imperial house. On the contrary, there is a strong inclination to depict female Shamans as enemies of the imperial house. This is probably due to the late institution of the imperial house as much as to the repeated revisions of the *Nihonshoki* data. In the *Nihonshoki* the struggle against such female rulers is especially related under the reigns of the 'emperors' Jimmu, Keikō, Chūai and Jingū, hence under a regime of which we have seen in the first chapter that it never existed. In this there is mention in one place only of figures who also had any religious meaning. This may be found in the chronicles of Emperor Jimmu, under the year *tsuchinoto-hitsuji*, the second month, 20th day:[1]

"In the second month, 20th day, the Emperor ordered his army leaders to bring the army into readiness. Now at that time, on the Hata, 波哆, cape (cape, Jap. *okasaki* 丘岬) of the Sofu, 層富, district[2] dwelt someone named Niiki *tobe*, 新城戶畔; below the Wani, 和珥, slope Kose *hafuri*, 居勢祝, lived, and at the Hosomi *no* Nagara, 臍見長柄, cape someone who was called I-*hafuri*, 猪祝. Relying on their power, these three Tsuchigomo (land spiders) refused to go to the court. The Emperor sent a division of his troops and destroyed them all."

---

[1] Cf. *Nihonshoki*, 3rd *maki*, Jimmu Tennō, year *tsuchinoto-hitsuji;* Kuroita Katsumi, Maruyama Jirō, op. cit., part 1, pp. 128-129; Cf. W. G. Aston, op. cit., vol. I, pp. 129, 130.

[2] District, Jap.: *kowari*, 郡; several *kowari* together formed a *kuni*, 國, which may henceforward be translated by province.

In this text three women are mentioned. The term 'land spider' which is often used in the *Nihonshoki* and the *Fudoki* to indicate these female rulers, is usually applicable to both male and female. However, in these works it usually concerns women. This may be seen from the above-mentioned text. The word *tobe*, 戸畔, which is attached here to the word Niiki, means *hime*, 姫, princess. *Hafuri*, 祝, attached in this case to, respectively, Kose and Ki, has a more religious meaning as seer or priestess. Kadowaki [1] sees in a *hafuri* a woman with a very close connection to a certain deity, for instance, the clan god of the Mononobe, Ōmiwa *no* kami, 大三輪神. On the basis of the meaning of these two words, it becomes dubious whether Niiki *tobe* was a kind of Shaman. The other two figures, however, Kose *hafuri* and I-*hafuri* must certainly have been *uji no kami* of the dimensions of Himiko. Each report concerning the destruction of these land spiders is worded in the same way in the *Nihonshoki* and the *Fudoki*. This standard formulation does not bear much witness to the originality of that report. Therefore the historical core of all these tales of land spiders is probably only established by the fact of the land spiders themselves.

If one is to believe the *Nihonshoki*, Emperor Keikō contributed most to their destruction. From his case it is more clear than in Jimmu's case, that here we are dealing with women. However, in two places in the description of his campaign to Kyūshū, against various lawless robbers, his degree of respect towards some of these female rulers becomes apparent. Both texts may be found in the account of the twelfth year of his reign.[2] The first is as follows:

"Ninth month, fifth day. There was a princess who was called Kamunashi *hime*, 神夏磯媛. She had very many followers and was *hitoko no kami*, 魁帥 (= *uji no kami*) throughout the entire country."

A few lines farther on there is mention that the emperor came into contact with another *hitoko no kami*, Hayatsu *hime*, 速津媛. These two princesses provided him with all kinds of useful information concerning the struggle against the four and five dangerous land spiders, who dwelt not far from both their districts. The text says of this that "they were strong and disposed over many dependents."

---

[1] Cf. Kadowaki Teiji, op. cit., pp. 106, 107. Also see Chapter IV, p. 273, ft. nt. 7 for the meaning of *hafuri*.

[2] Cf. *Nihonshoki* 7th *maki*, Keikō, 12th year, 9th month, 5th day; Kuroita Katsumi, Maruyama Jirō, op. cit., part 1, p. 202; Cf. W. G. Aston, op. cit., pp. 192, 193.

Owing to their advice, the emperor succeeded in overthrowing them all.[1] The dwelling place of the two princesses mentioned here was in the north eastern region of Kyūshū.

It is also told of Empress Jingū that she went to Kyūshū to conquer 'land spiders'.[2] Shortly after the oracle text quoted previously, the *Nihonshoki* says of her:

"Twenty-fifth day. She went to the Yamato, 山門, area (not to be confused with that of Nara and Kyōto; this lay in N. Kyūshū) and there killed the land spider Taburatsu *hime*, 田油津媛."

The above-mentioned texts are only a few excerpts from the many tales of land spiders which may be found in the *Nihonshoki*. However, by far the most stem from the *Fudoki*. Before investigating these texts further, we shall first discuss what this *Fudoki* actually means.

The name *Fudoki*, 風土記, itself can give an answer. This word has the same meaning as the Japanese *chishi*, 地誌, which means topography. The *Fudoki* is a collection of topographical data, mainly from the eighth century, concerning Japanese districts and villages. Descriptions of popular customs, sagas, etymological expositions concerning geographical names and changes of names have also been included in it.

Its composition was started in 713, when Empress Gemmei ordained[3] that "the names of the Kinki (= Yamato) area and all the provinces of the Seven Highways (that is to say, the whole of Japan) be written down; to this also belonged the products of the individual districts, such as silver, copper, all kinds of crops and trees, animals, fish, insects, etc.; furthermore the size of the areas, the origin of the names and the names themselves of mountains, rivers and plains. Also the various tales which were handed down by the elders, should be inscribed in historical registers." As the *Fudoki* is not expressly mentioned in this decree, it is generally accepted that mainly the *Shoku-Nihongi* owes its existence to it.

---

[1] Cf. *Nihonshoki*, 7th *maki*, Keikō, 12th year, 10th month; Kuroita Katsumi, Maruyama Jirō, op. cit., part 1, p. 203, Cf. W. G. Aston, op. cit., p. 194.

[2] *Nihonshoki*, 9th *maki*, Jingū, Chronicles from before her accession to the throne, 3rd month; Kuroita Katsumi, Maruyama Jirō, part 1, p. 243; Cf. W. G. Aston, op. cit., pp. 226, 227.

[3] Cf. *Shoku-Nihongi*, 6th *maki*, Gemmei, Wadō, 6th year, 5th month, 2nd day; Kuroita Katsumi, Maruyama Jirō, *Kokushitaikei Shoku-Nihongi*, part 1 (no. 1), p. 52. Cf. J. B. Snellen, "Shoku-Nihongi", *T.A.S.J.*, Sec. Ser. XIV, 1937, p. 257.

Nevertheless, there are many who are of the opinion that this was also the initial incentive towards the origin of Japan's oldest geography.

The *Fudoki* is compiled, according to its list of contents, from six collections, which originated in various parts of Japan. Therefore these have come into being during various periods. They were the *Fudoki* of: Hitachi (now the prefecture of Ibaragi, after 715); Izumo (the eastern part of the present-day Hiroshima prefecture, after 733); Harima (nowadays the Hyōgo prefecture, ± 715); Bungo (now the prefecture of Oita, 713); Hizen (nowadays the Nagasaki and Saga prefectures, which also came into being after 715); and the last collection, called *Itsubun*, 逸文. This *Itsubun* was made up of various data which had been encountered in the literature of the ninth and tenth century concerning Japan's topology.[1] Of all these collections, only the *Fudoki* of Izumo is complete.

The tales concerning land spiders may be found in all of the collections of the *Fudoki*. Most of them originate from the *Hizen-fudoki*, that is to say, from the area of the present-day prefectures of Saga and Nagasaki. It is interesting to note here that this area, under the name Matsuro, 末盧, formed one of the small states of Himiko's federation.[2] It may be seen from the following pericope that according to the *Fudoki* also, figures dwelt here who were equivalent to Himiko.[3]

"Here previously *tsuchigumo* (land spiders) lived, namely the women Ō-yamada, 大山田, and Sa-yamada, 狭山田. They appropriated the land of the village Shimoda, 下田. If one offered them divine respect in their forms of human or horse, they certainly answered all prayers. When this occurred, it was said of them: 'These are wise women'. Therefore the entire region was called after these wise women (= Sakashime 賢女), the district Sakashime."

In the same *Hizen-fudoki* the mystical ascendancy of women over men in the Matsu-ura, 松浦, district is mentioned:[4]

"In the fourth month of spring the women of that region went out fishing. Then they caught trout. The men, however, did not succeed in catching these."

---

[1] See the introduction by Takeda Iukichi, *Fudoki*, Tōkyō 1938, pp. 3-8.

[2] Namely, Matsuro, 末盧, is the same as the present-day Matsu-ura(gun), 松浦(郡), the northern part of the prefecture of Nagasaki.

[3] Cf. Takeda Iukichi, op. cit., p. 250.

[4] Cf. Takeda Iukichi, op. cit., p. 251-252.

Various of these rulers reigned from mountain tops. Thus the Ōtome-yama, 孃子山, is mentioned in the same *Fudoki*: [1]

"When the same emperor (= Keikō) was travelling round here, there was a land spider here Yasome, 八十女 (meaning: 80 women). She lived on the top of a mountain and came into opposition to the emperor's orders. He then sent soldiers against her and destroyed her. This mountain was named after her Ōtome-yama, that is to say, Girls Mountain."

In the *Bungo-fudoki* there is only one mention of land spiders as opposed to more than nine land spider passages in the *Hizen-fudoki*. Here the imperial patriarch Ninigi *no mikoto* is connected with the land spiders: [2]

"According to the *Fudoki* of the village Chiho, 知鋪, which is situated in the Usuki, 臼杵, district of the Hyūga region (the present-day prefecture Miyasaki), Amatsu Hikobiko-ho *no* Ninigi *no mikoto* 天津彦々火瓊々杵尊, climbed the twin peak of the mountain Takachiho, after he had left his heavenly rock seat and had escaped the eight-fold cloud. At that time it was very dark everywhere, and day could not be distinguished from night. Therefore it was difficult for the people to recognize roads and distinguish colours. This was owing to the presence of land spiders. They were called: Ō-tsuwa, 大鉗 (large pillory) and O-tsuwa, 小鉗 (small pillory). Both did nothing else than tearing up rice plants. If they had been left to their own devices, it would never have become light again. Ō-tsuwa, however, left; therefore the sun and moon began to shine again."

Outside Kyūshū there are also two other regions where, according to the *Fudoki*, land spiders supposedly dwelt. The first lay in the extreme northeast corner of the island Honshū, in the region of Mutsu, 陸奥, which encompasses the present-day prefectures of Fukushima, Miyagi, Iwate and Aomori. In this same area Shamanism may be encountered even today. From the various forms it is apparent that this descends from the period before Buddhism.[3] According to the *Fudoki* we are here dealing with eight powerful

---

[1] Cf. Takeda Iukichi, op. cit., p. 257.

[2] Cf. Takeda Iukichi, op. cit., pp. 352-353.

[3] Cf. M. Eder, op. cit., pp. 376-381. Here, i.a., he points out expressions such as *Kamitsuke*, in which pre-Buddhistic Shamanism may still be recognized. Op. cit., p. 373.

land spiders of the Barbarians (Jap.: *ebisu*) [1] who were rendered harmless during the reign of Emperor Keikō by the mythical hero and conqueror Yamato-takeru *no mikoto*, 日本武尊. The *Fudoki* text is more or less similar to the texts already quoted. This also applies to the land spider of which there is only brief mention in the *Hitachi-fudoki*, and to that of Harima of which there is only a single mention.[2]

All of these texts from the *Fudoki* are too limited in their descriptions to draw any conclusions from them with regard to Shamanism of antiquity. If necessary, one can assemble from them all the elements which together define Shamanism. In the light of the *Wei chih* and the above quoted Jingū text they do, however, all together, form a strong indication of original Shamanism. Here indeed persons are concerned, however summary and superficial their description, who, by their spiritual and ruling activities do not differ greatly from Himiko and Jingū. They are all on the same plane. This becomes especially apparent when comparing the Chinese sources which were mentioned in the previous chapter to the Japanese data which are cited here. Namely, in the *Sung-shu* it was Emperor Wu who assimilated innumerable small states in Japan and Korea. Those must have been small states which the *Wei chih* described some time earlier, and of which only the two female rulers Himiko and Iyo are known to us. The small states which the emperors of the Japanese sources fought about were ruled by figures similar to Himiko. Chinese and Japanese texts confirm one another as well as the existence of Shamanism which was tied to these female *uji no kami* of the first phase.

Furthermore, if one very carefully marks all of the *Fudoki* texts mentioned above according to their origin on the map of Japan, then it appears that the phenomenon of 'land spiders' (or Shamanism), as seen from Yamato, belonged to Japan's outlying regions. The largest concentration of this occurred in the extreme west of Japan at the greatest possible distance from Yamato. The map shows that the tribes which had established the emperorship since the fourth century in Yamato were also those who forced back this old matriarchal Shaman culture as far as possible to the outermost northern and southern borders. It points out that Shamanism was

---

[1] Cf. Takeda Iukichi, op. cit., pp. 292-293.
[2] Ibid.

most strongly represented in those tribes which were not a part of the people to whom the imperial tribe belonged. That is why the 'land spiders' of Mutsu are expressly called barbarians (= *ebisu*).

Although this Shamanism of the first phase was driven back to the far corners of the realm, it was not entirely and wholly repressed.[1] Much of that which was common to these regressive matriarchal tribes was readily accepted by the new tribes of Yamato. Shamanism, practised by women, equally began to define their lives. One cannot deny this, as otherwise it cannot be imagined how the descendants of these tribes could accept a purely Shamanistic figure at the time of Empress Suiko, and later such as Jingū. Then it is equally incomprehensible that the ancestral goddess Amaterasu, a result of Shamanism, could become the leader among Japan's national gods. This was also illustrated by the trout-catching women of the *Hizen-fudoki*. Even according to a more recent manuscript such as the *Manyōshū*, 萬葉集, it was the mother in the home who carried out the worship of the gods.[2] That this Shamanism (mainly linked to women) was still alive at the end of the sixth century, may be seen from the entire figure of Empress Suiko (593-628). At the end of the sixth century she was brought forward as an empress by Soga Umako because she, just as Himiko, was a priestess.[3] This is shown by her own, Japanese, name which was Toyomike Kashikiya *hime*, 豐御食炊屋姫. This long term may be translated as 'princess who prepares the sacrifices to the gods'. This original name moreover expresses her specific function in the society of that period. In the first place she was very closely linked to the worship of the gods. Therefore her *matsurigoto* must have lain, in the first place, in the field of religion for her as an empress.

With these remarks concerning the Shamanism of antiquity it is not contended that every empress of the past must therefore have been a Shaman. Empress Kōgyoku, 皇極 (642-645), for instance, only owed her empress-ship to the politics of her son, Naka *no* Ō-e, 中大兄. The latter could achieve more for the nation as prince regent than as an emperor. Another empress of that period, Genshō,

---

[1] Cf. Joseph Schwientek, "Der Synkretismus von Shinto und Buddhismus in Japan", *Anthr.* 22 (1927), pp. 430-439.

[2] Higo Kazuo, "Jōteiki (Chronicles of Empresses)", *Tennō no Rekishi*, p. 231.

[3] Higo Kazuo, op. cit., p. 232.

元正 (715-724), attempted to dabble in emancipation of women from 715, at the Japanese court. She did not do this because she was a Shaman, but because her Chinese contemporary, Empress (Tsê-t'ien) Wu (684-705), 武, after whom even her period of reign was called (as T'ien pao, Heavenly Empress), inspired her to do this. Thus it can be explained that in her reign, owing to her exertions, as many famous poetesses as poets might be found in Japan. Nevertheless, some of the old influences must have intermingled here. This can be seen from the sequel to the *Nihonshoki*, the *Shoku-Nihongi*. This says of her: [1]

"The *Tennō* had an extremely deep knowledge of the gods."

Thus the *Wei chih* and the Japanese sources have proved that the *uji no kami* of the first phase were often women and Shamans. Furthermore, they lived in great seclusion, left the government to others and considered their spiritual functions as their true task, from which all of their other duties naturally flowed.[2] Their withdrawnness resulted in their own subjects, starting with the lower orders, enlarging upon their spiritual authority. For the subjects they became incarnations of the protective deity of the *uji*. Not infrequently they were even identified with this deity.

4 *The Ujigami*, 氏神

In each *uji*, the *ujigami* stood even above the *uji no kami*. He was considered as being the deity of the *uji*, from whom the *uji no kami* ultimately received all his authority and influence. Little is known about the origin and nature of this. The general indication *ujigami* came into being only in the eighth century. This is shown by three texts of that time.[3] Until then this word did not exist.

---

[1] Cf. *Shoku-Nihongi*, 7th *maki*, Genshō, Reiki 1st year; Kuroita Katsumi, Maruyama Jirō, op. cit., p. 63.

[2] Fukuō Takeichirō, op. cit., p. 10, says of this: "They absorbed the spirits of the *ujigami* and reproduced them within themselves. All orders, governmental and others, were issued as revelations of the *ujigami*."

[3] These three texts are:

1) *Manyōshū* no. 380 is as follows: "In the fifth year of Tempyō, 天平, (733), winter, eleventh month, when the sacrificial service of the *ujigami* of the Ōtomo was celebrated."
Cf. Sasaki Nobutsuna, *Manyōshū*, Tōkyō 1958, pp. 109 and 135.

2) *Shoku-Nihongi*, 34th *maki*, Kōnin, 8th year (777), 7th month, 16th day; Kuroita Katsumi, Maruyama Jirō, op. cit., part 2 (no. 4), p. 435: "The *naidaijin*, 内大臣, who was *hiroki*, 従 (title), of the second

This may be explained by the fact that until then the Japanese were simply not ready for classification and regularization of the various *ujigami*. This was only achieved with the construction of the Japanese State itself. The regularization of the state and the new political ranks also evoked the necessity of regulating the world of the gods. The new order was not established by use of military force, but especially as a result of the institution of a strictly organised bureaucracy. The late use of a conception of names such as *ujigami* can also be explained by the fact that the Japanese of that period was too literally-minded to speak of his gods in general terms. In addition, the *uji* themselves had been too independent as religious units to feel a need for deities which bridged several *uji*. Hence this word probably reached Japan under Chinese influence.

The oldest texts also do not give us too much concerning the specific nature of these *ujigami*. There is no mention of them in the *Wei chih* at all. The *Kojiki* and the *Nihonshoki* do repeatedly mention such deities, but it remains difficult, however, to recognise the *ujigami* of the first phase here. They are represented in these sources as if they had stood under the supremacy of the imperial gods from time immemorial. One need only read the tale concerning the descent of the gods from heaven, the *Tenson-kōrin*, to realize this.[1] One can conclude that here, for the most part, gods are concerned who belong in the second phase.

At the time when the *uji* were still independent, that is to say, prior to Emperor Ōjin, the *ujigami* were merely village gods, who, in protecting the harvest protected the *uji* also. This is proved by the names they were given. In connection with female Shamanism, many of them were probably imagined as goddesses. One need only recall Amaterasu and her pendant in Ise, the Rice Goddess 豐宇気毘賣 Toyo-uke *no hime*.[2] The sphere of influence of these

---

degree, namely Fujihara *no asomi* Rōtsugi, 藤原朝臣良繼, was ill. His *ujigami* Kashima *no sha*, 鹿嶋社, received the distinction of *masa*, 正 (title), third degree . . .".

3) *Shōsōinbunsho*: "Chūhōki, 中宝亀, third year (772), tenth month, 28th day," mentions: "The feast of my *ujigami*".

See further: Shibata Minoru, "Sōsen sūhai no genryū", *N.S.K.*, part 3, Tōkyō 1959, p. 34.

[1] For instance, in Karl Florenz, op. cit., pp. 69 ff.

[2] Toyo-uke *no hime* was probably the original goddess of the Yamato

deities was no larger than the *uji* itself. Only within the *uji* were they its spiritual and lasting symbol. Therefore only the members of each *uji* celebrated their feasts. These had no meaning whatsoever for outsiders.

When the *uji* was later assembled in a more federal union, and various conglomerations of *uji* came into being, the power and the influence of the *ujigami* grew in accordance with that of the *uji* and they began to enjoy recognition in wider circles. When large and powerful *uji* subjected lesser *uji*, the *ujigami* of these lesser *uji* shared their fate. Thus a divine hierarchy came into being. We can imagine how this divine hierarchy was introduced into various myths. In these myths the *ujigami* of the conquerors formed the upper layer. Thus one and the same *ujigami* could, at one stroke, become the most supreme after a conquest by his *uji*, even over and above the *ujigami* of the conquered *uji*. The developments of the second phase confirm this course of events. For instance, it was owing to this that more than 104 *uji* resorted to the *ujigami* Nigihayahi *no mikoto*, 饒速日命, of the *uji* of the Mononobe.[1] As such an *uji* grew to national significance, its *ujigami* could expand commensurately to a national deity. However, this could not take place without the spiritual power which had previously been held by the *uji no kami* of the conquered *uji* being also concentrated in the hands of the most powerful *uji*.

As far as the nature of these *ujigami* is concerned, it has been established that they were certainly not ancestral gods. In this we do not wish to deny the fact of ancestral gods in Japan. The *Kojiki*, *Nihonshoki* and other Japanese sources are full of it. However, this ancestor worship only reached Japan fairly late. Tsuda,[2] amongst others, has proved this. He has analysed various ancestral figures of the most important *uji* and has convincingly shown that though they were sometimes seen as deities, they were not considered *ujigami*. Later it has, however, been attempted to render them as *ujigami* in retrospect. In order to allow them a share of the homage which in reality was due to the *ujigami*, they had to be

---

area. Later she was supplanted from her initial position by the 'imperial' goddess Amaterasu. Her temple in Ise, erected in the same grandiose style as that of Amaterasu, still points to this. See J. M. Martin, *Le Shintoïsme*, part II, Hongkong 1924, p. 228.

[1] Cf. Shibata Minoru, op. cit., p. 26.

[2] *Nihon Jōdaishi no Kenkyū*, pp. 117 ff.

cunningly sneaked into the temple of the existing *ujigami*. Tsuda says of this: "Figures, which had been established as ancestors, had to be connected in one way or other to the deities already extant in popular beliefs in order that they might receive their own divine worship. This clearly shows that *ujigami* were originally not ancestral deities." [1]

Therefore the specific nature of the *ujigami* must not be sought after particularly in tribal relations, but in the fact that they protected the fairly heterogeneous *uji*. A few lines further, Tsuda says of this: [2] "*Ujigami* were deities in whom the entire *uji* believed because they protected it. Ancestral gods, tied only to a certain person or family, could not possibly be described so generally. Moreover, in the *Kojiki*, such ancestral gods always had, after their own names, the additional, special, title *soshin*, 祖神, which means ancestral deity, and not the title of *ujigami*. That too is proof of the fact that the *ujigami* were not ancestral gods. Therefore the *ujigami*, according to their nature, were deities with an individual religious cult. That is very logical, because they were inevitably the object of popular belief."

We not only know that the *ujigami* were not ancestral deities, but that there are also sufficient positive indications known about them, which reveal something of their true nature to us. We have already noted [3] that many consider them to be the original and impersonal roots of the *uji*. Many Japanese are inclined to agree with Spencer in placing magic at the beginning of Japan's religious development. In this they are supported by the theory of the impersonal *ujigami*. Nevertheless, this latter need not be an a priori, Spencerian argument, as, moreover, an entirely different concept of community lodges behind this. It has already been proved by the criminal code described in the *Wei chih* and mentioned previously, that a community which thinks less individually is more readily inclined to ascribe purely personal achievements to the community. If one also bears in mind that a community owes its unity to the land and the soil, one can imagine that it is unlikely that it will interpret its *ujigami* personally. As far as that is concerned, it differs entirely from a community where the personality and the individuality of each separate member prevails. The fact

---

[1] Op. cit., p. 119.

[2] Tsuda Sōkichi, op. cit., p. 121.

[3] See this chapter, p. 77 ff.

that, initially, absolutely no divine images were known is a supplementary confirmation that Japan did indeed think less individually. Real images only arrived with Buddhism. After that it was still to take more than two centuries before a national Japanese deity was represented as a human. This was the god Tado, 多度.[1] Until that time, *ujigami* were only seen impersonally and not in human proportions. This does not mean to say that the Japanese knew no images whatsoever before the advent of Buddhism. In the moats of the large burial mounds thousands of human images, baked of clay, called *haniwa*, 埴輪, have been found to prove this. Therefore the lack of divine images should not be ascribed to the fact that the technical skill was deficient, but rather that a deity was considered as being something other than a kind of 'Superman'. Furthermore, there are also the names of the *ujigami* which underline this impersonal character.

One of those who have examined these names is Shibata Minoru.[2] He has examined those of the *ujigami* of the most important *uji* in order to ascertain more of their specific nature. In this he particularly compared the *uji* which, in the ninth century provided the most important support to the imperial house. In this research he came across two groups in particular: that of the so-called *musubi*, and that of the fire or light gods. This subdivision is indeed valid for the *uji* of the second phase, but it can also, nevertheless, serve as an illustration for those of the first phase, all the more so because several of them continued to exist in the second phase. Of these two kinds of *ujigami*, the oldest were the *musubi*, derived mainly from agriculture.[3] According to various indications, these were not

---

[1] Cf. Takatori Masaō, op. cit., p. 58.

[2] Shibata Minoru, op. cit., pp. 26 ff.

[3] Although we cannot accurately tie down the use of this concept *musubi* to either the first or second phase, nevertheless, we shall have to investigate this important concept more closely here.

We shall attempt to approach this concept by use of the etymology of *musubi*, as well as by use of Japanese mythology and a few Shintō rites.

1) ETYMOLOGICAL APPROACH

The word *musubi* is written in two ways. We shall take this double spelling as starting point for an etymological approach to this word. Originally it was written: 產霊. This can best be translated by 'spiritual power'. Shibata Minoru, loc. cit., very specifically here thinks of a neutral force. Besides these Chinese characters, there was also a close connection to *umu* in the term *mu*(*subi*), 'to be borne', and *umasu*, 'bring into the world'. From here

only older, but also actually different from the fire or light (sun) gods.

---

musubi gains the sense of force which goes out from its enclosure. This meaning of birth still remains in such words as *musuko* (son), *musume* (daughter), *mushi* (insect). Therefore in this *musu* lies something of the spirit inherent to the matter, which forces it towards the outside world. Cf. Tanaka Jigohei, *Amaterasu Ōmikami*, Tōkyō 1959, p. 59. The *hi* or *bi* suffixed to this *musu* is a directive to the spiritual character of this spirit. See also Sasaya Ryōzō, "Musubi-gami no shinkō", *K.G.Z.*, vol. LXIV, 1963, nos. 8, 9; Aug., Sept., pp. 83-111, especially p. 84. According to Sasaya Ryōzō, loc. cit., the more magical *yufu*, 結, which means: the tying of the spirit to matter, was put after this word *musu*. In Chapter I, pp. 41 ff. we pointed out that *musubi* in this more mystic sense of tying was closely related to the Manchurian *fosomi*. This concept is also linked to *iwau*, (derived from *yufu*, *yuwau*), which is usually translated by: the celebration of a religious feast. In reality and origin this *iwau*, however, means: avoidance of the escape of the *musubi* from the material; the enclosure, coagulation of spirits in a certain (mago-religious) object. Thus *iwau* was also a magical technical term, which was used in a primeval force chained to matter and closely linked to it.

A second spelling was: 魂. This actually means *tama*, soul. In connection with the foregoing, one might call this: the deepest basis of reproduction. On the human plane this was especially: *Mioya no mitama*, 祖霊 = soul of the ancestors, and, for rice: *Uka no mitama*, 穀霊 = soul of the rice. M. Eder translates this by: "Erlauchter Geist der Nährung". Cf. Mathias Eder, "Die 'Reisseele' in Japan und Korea", *Folk. St.*, vol. XIV (1955), p. 242. Eating rice was therefore a union of these two souls, often considered as a kind of coitus. This coitus reunited these two souls which had been separated from each other by a dramatic murder in antiquity. At some of the harvest festivals in the country this was plastically enacted. Cf. Shibata Minoru, op. cit., p. 32. Thus every meal and harvest became a typically Japanese "dramatische Darstellung des Urzeitsgeschehens". (Cf. Ad. E. Jensen, *Mythos und Kult bei Naturvölkern*, Wiesbaden 1960, p. 260). This murder can still be seen illustrated in that of Ōgetsuhime, J. M. Martin, op. cit., p. 229.

2) In Japanese MYTHOLOGY the *musubi* was ascribed a highly important role. When the divine parents, the heavenly Izanagi and the earthly Izanami, with their mutual love (Jap.: *majiwari*) began to bring forth the entire world and all that was in it, they could not realize this by themselves. Yet another, specific force was requisite for the origination of land, rivers and mountains. This personified force in their creative work was Takamimusubi. Only this could make fully effective the energy of the two deities. It was also capable of implementing the descent to earth of Ninigi *no mikoto*. At this time it bore the name of Takagi *no mikoto*, 高木命 (or *kami*). Under this name it was always closely connected with Amaterasu, whom it always had to accompany closely as her active power. Amaterasu was also assigned the aid of other *musubi* for the execution of her task. Thus the *musubi* Uzume

The close link of the *musubi* to agriculture can be seen from the fact that in them the growing force in plants, animals and people

---

no mikoto lured Amaterasu from her cave by dancing, and by so doing brought back the daylight. Cf. K. Florenz, op. cit., pp. 39, 40.

Such *musubi* were also closely connected to the origination of the imperial court. The influence of the *musubi* was gradually forgotten when, during the Heian period, attention was almost exclusively given during court ceremonial to the imperial tribal deities, and not to the *musubi* which had brought about the actual links with those tribal deities. Cf. Sasaya Ryōzō, op. cit., p. 89.

The earthly counterpart of the two divine *musubi* Takami and Uzume was the god Sarume, 猿女. Sarume actually conveys the same meaning as Sachime, lady Fortune. When Amaterasu lost her soul, she became powerless. She had to call in the aid of this Sarume to regain her powers. Dying (= *shinu*) and expiring (= *shinaburu*) in Japanese are almost similar. In archaic Japanese *shinau* means expiring, losing one's soul. On the other hand the cause of health was the Sachi: this returned one's powers. Cf. Sasaya Ryōzō, op. cit., p. 88. In this context Sarume returned Amaterasu's powers to her.

3) The meaning of the *musubi* has also been preserved in some RITES AND CUSTOMS. The best example of this is the feast of *niiname*. This was actually the feast of the imperial taking of office and was similar to the imperial coronation usual in Europe. This feast had a deep religious significance. At the feast of *niiname* the emperor was robed in a very old and ceremonial robe while he himself had to recite the numerals laden with *musubi* power from one to ten. This robe owed its venerability to the fact that it was believed that the partite soul of Amaterasu dwelt in it. Those enrobed in it were brought into contact with 'the holy body', as the divinity itself resided in this robe. This contact with the partite soul of Amaterasu was realized by a *musubi*, namely Uzume *no mikoto*, the same one, who with raised attire, lured Amaterasu from the cave. During this 'robing', Uzume bound the partite soul of Amaterasu to her imperial descendant. This binding of the soul is called, as we noted above, *musubu*. In the ideology of the ancient Japanese, the imperial power and authority was thus effected by the *musubi*. For the feast of *niiname* see further pp. 354 ff. and footnote 2 on p. 354. According to Sasaya Ryōzō, op. cit., p. 92, the five companions of Ninigi *no mikoto* on his descent from heaven must be considered at the same level as this *musubi*. They too were *musubi* who had to care for the growth to maturity of the imperial scion.

This *musubi* belief, later destroyed by court ceremonial, is still alive amongst the population, embodied in figures such as Ebisu, 恵比須, and Daikoku, 大黒, who have the same function towards the people as Sachime or Sarume had towards Amaterasu. The *musubi* were also closely connected with water. This is easily understood as there is an inescapably close connection between the growing force in plants and animals, and water. Therefore drinking of, and washing with, water on entering Japanese Shintō temples does not only symbolize cleansing or aleviating thirst, but also the enrichment of a new *musubi*. The *mizu no ōhimo*, 水大紐 (the water cord), also called

was centered. The germinal force of rice and coitus between men and women owed their strength and success to these *musubi*.[1] Now this close link to agriculture places them in the structure of the first phase of Japan's development, which depended entirely on agriculture. The nomadic tribes of the second phase naturally initially did not require these agricultural deities. Therefore they brought entirely different gods with them: the fire and light gods, who, in the second phase, were to be the *ujigami* of the nobility surrounding the emperor, with, at the apex, the imperial matriarch, the Sun Goddess Amaterasu. With the latter, however, one must bear in mind that she was a typical compromise-deity of the first and second phase: for as a deified Shaman of the first phase she person-

---

mizuhiki, 水引き, is a cord of paper string in use even today, with which presents are tied up attractively. Originally the good *musubi* had to be tied to the gift. The offering of a gift, so inherent to day-to-day Japanese etiquette, is therefore also a religious gesture: the gift of creativity. Far more important than the present itself is the *musubi* dwelling in it. Hence the great care and respect with which, even today, gew-gaws are wrapped. This cannot be explained by the fact that, for a Japanese, the wrapping is of greater importance than the contents, as I, a real Westerner, have sometimes heard it explained, but because first and foremost the wrapping expresses the *musubi* which dwells in the trifles.

Finally, the numerals themselves were originally rather indications of the *musubi* which dwelt in the matter, than indications of the matter itself. Summarizing, we can therefore ascribe to the *musubi* divine primeval powers, which brought matter into movement. Cf. D. C. Holtom, "The Meaning of Kami, Chapter III, Kami considered as Mana", *M.N.* vol. IV. 1941, no. 2 pp. 351-394. Here he attempts to reduce the Japanese concept of divinity to the Mana type; see p. 253. Now in *musubi* we have a specific Japanese word for this, with almost the same meaning, which, moreover, as is shown by its own etymology and place in the Japanese Weltanschauung, is more capable of adequately expressing the Japanese concept of divinity than the concept of Mana utilized by D. C. Holtom. For further data and particulars concerning the *musubi* belief, see the extensive article previously mentioned by Sasaya Ryōzō.

At the end of this exposition one is likely to ask why these *musubi* held such a lowly position in the *Kojiki* and the *Nihonshoki*. We are much inclined towards Sasaya Ryōzō's explanation (op. cit., p. 88)—on the basis of our own determinations concerning these sources in Chapter I—that these chronicles, in the first place, served to produce a genealogy of the emperors. In this the importance of these contact deities disappeared. In this Shintō was mainly based on the *Kojiki* and the *Nihonshoki* and thus was led to underestimate the actual meaning of the *musubi*.

[1] Cf. M. Eder, op. cit., pp. 242-244.

ified a deity of the second phase. In the myths also, it can be seen here and there how the agricultural gods and *musubi* were simply pushed aside by light gods. This can even be found in the history of the famous tribe of the Nakatomi. This *uji* always considered Tsuhaya-*musubi no mikoto*, 津速魂命, as its *ujigami*. He, however, had to give way as soon as the Nakatomi began to practise their priestly officies at the imperial court, as these offices were not intended for this *musubi*, but for the Sun God Hi *no kami*, 日之神.[1]

Not too much is known about the temples and the divine worship of these *musubi*. Whether the *ujigami* possessed their own temples right from the beginning is unknown. We know only of temples which were built for the *ujigami* of the second phase. The oldest of them was certainly not accomplished before the sixth century. This is supposed to have been the Ishigami, 石神, temple of the *uji* of the Mononobe. Up till now the most famous is the Kasuga, 春日, temple of later date, near Nara, where three *ujigami* of the Fujihara, 滕原, tribe are venerated.[2]

As the *uji* was one large community of interests with the *ujigami* as symbol, divine worship was not only confined to the *uji no kami* or other prominent members of the *uji*. It was accessible to everyone who belonged to the *uji*. People from other *uji* were not admitted. They are not likely to have been very interested in venerating and worshipping the *ujigami* as they were only aware of their tie to the *ujigami* of their own *uji*. These ties owed their origin and existence similarly to the soil and the interests of the *uji* itself. Thus there were actually just as many religions as there were independent *uji*. This religious situation was later of immense importance to the spread of Buddhism. Namely, if this Buddhism could once succeed (if necessary, under the aegis of the *uji no kami*) in penetrating an *uji* and ensuring a place beside the *ujigami* with its Buddha images, then it could find acknowledgement from every member of the *uji* without more ado, and not just from one or other exclusive group only. Owing to the fact that the foreign *uji* had nothing to do with the divine worship within the individual *uji*, Buddhism could, in favourable isolation, remain unnoticed by undesirable outsiders. Thus a kind of incubation and process of adaptation became gradually not only more in tune with the mentality of this *uji*, but also,

[1] Shibata Minoru, op. cit., p. 29.

[2] For this see Shimonaka Yasaburō, *Shintō Daijiten*, Tōkyō 1940, part 1, p. 178, column I and II.

via this *uji*, with the mentality of other *uji*. After this period of incubation it would, thus made entirely suitable to Japan's own society, be able to win over the other *uji*.

Now that we have considered so many aspects of the *ujigami* itself in the foregoing lines, we must also investigate their relation to the *uji no kami*. The *uji no kami* had an entirely specific task towards the *uji* and the education of a certain religious mentality in his subjects. The Shamans especially, who lived in solitude and were considered to be close to their *ujigami*, had great authority among the ordinary people with their pronouncements concerning those *ujigami*. This may even have identified them occasionally with the *ujigami* themselves. The *uji no kami* could contribute most to the stature of the *ujigami* as he was their mouthpiece. With this, at least in the primitive *uji* of the first phase, he was the only personality who could manipulate the religious mentality of the entire *uji*. If Buddhism could later succeed in converting such an *uji no kami*, then via him it could become common property of the whole *uji*. However, the condition for this remained that the old interconnection of the *uji*, and also, in a certain sense, its *ujigami* beliefs, were preserved. The more powerful and larger that *uji*, the wider would be the circle within which that acceptance could take place. The danger, however, that might be connected with this was that Buddhism would be viewed as an element which had actually come to belong to that *uji*. Thus it could become a modality of the *ujigami* belief. If that *uji* was so powerful that even the future emperors were educated in it, then such an *uji no kami* could also assure that it became a united State religion. We hope to show that this actually happened. Before this could happen, however, various tribes of the second phase had to be superimposed on the existing structure of the first phase. A society of their own grew from this, in which the structure of the first phase was also integrated.

Second Phase: The Imperial Society

The imperial or *Tenson* tribe superimposed itself on the society previously described, in the third or fourth century. This too had a wholly specific structure. It is self-evident that the social pattern of the conquering peoples was imposed upon the conquered. As, however, in this case it was a minority that was concerned—as we have seen in the first chapter—it was impossible to destroy everything which had existed, and hence something of the old forms continued into the new society which now came into being. Thus, matriarchy was repressed, without its disappearing entirely. Ancient Shamanism also continued. The same must have happened with the religious opinions of the old population. As these were the most resistant, they were not easily eradicated by the *Tenson* clan. As there was no destruction of the old population and its habits, a kind of fusion between both societies must have been arrived at.

This process of fusion was possibly comparable to that which was simultaneously taking place in North China. In this country its course was hard to follow step by step. The reason for this is, inter alia, also the fact that the Chinese saw this fusion differently than we do in the West. A Chinese has worded this as follows: [1] "Für uns Chinesen fliessen der blutmässige, oder wie man auch zu sagen pflegt, der 'völkische' und der kulturelle Einfluss in den einen *Ethnischen* zusammen; während der Westen also die eine Legierung eingehenden Bestandteile bewertet und von ihnen aus das Ergebnis festzulegen versucht, legen wir für *die Bewertung die entstandene Legierung zu Grunde*. Ich will damit sagen, dass für uns bei allen am Konfuzianismus einzumessenden Werten die Rasse und damit auch ihre Einmischungen unbeachtet gelassen werden."

Despite these beautiful sentences, there have still remained in China some vestiges of racial discrimination in all rapid adaptations of foreigners to the Chinese culture. Probably this should be called a shift of accent. Nevertheless it remains a fact that several of the groups of the Five Hu, for instance, disappeared entirely, without their being slaughtered. Just as so many other tribes, they began to be a part of the Chinese people. The Hsien-pi rulers, the so-called Mu-jung, 慕容, are an example of this. Schreiber [2] says of them that immediately they accepted the Chinese influence, they enjoyed not only the respect of the local Chinese notables, but also that of the southern Chinese court.

In Japan also a similar mentality has indubitably played its

---

[1] Lin Tsiu Sen, *China und Japan*, Zürich (no date), part 1, p. 150.

[2] Gerard Schreiber, "The History of the Former Yen-Dynasty", in *M.S.*, vol. XV, fasc. 1, p. 125: "As soon as the Mu-jung became sinicized, they gained the respect of the local high officials and even of the court in the South."

A few lines prior to this quotation, it seems that Schreiber supports the same view as Lin Tsiu Sen: "The resentment of the Chinese against foreigners was not primarily based on racial difference. The non-Chinese peoples surrounding China were regarded as inferior because they did not follow the Chinese codes of etiquette and ethics."

part, all the more so as we all know that the Japanese very easily accepts innovations, not only in the field of economics, but also in philosophy. Therefore it is very difficult to discover the limits in this conglomeration of tribes and races, which divided them or differentiated them from each other. Nevertheless, we shall attempt to recover these limits within the second phase, between which philosophical shifts also took place.

1 *Structure of the imperial or* Tenson *tribe*

The second phase of Japan's development was introduced with the advent of the 'imperial' race. In the previous chapter we saw that this tribe was also called *Tenson* (Divine Grandson) or *kiba*, 騎馬, (Horse-riding) *-zoku*, 族 (*zoku* = tribe). The invasion by this tribe left intact much that had been built up during the first phase. Only a new top was set upon the peoples of the first phase, after the old top had crumbled as a result of the 'land spiders' being destroyed, or having been made serviceable to the 'emperor' and the nobility related to him. Before this conflict between the leaders of the first and second phases was reached, their tribes also had grown towards each other, through conquests and the formation of federations. This took place from two central areas: the imperial tribe spread from the area of Yamato and the (Himiko) tribes of the first phase from Kyūshū. Hence, according to the Japanese sources, the struggle between these two groups was fought mainly in this latter area. That is shown especially by the *Fudoki* texts, quoted above.[1] After this struggle the particular structure of the 'imperial' tribe was imposed upon the remaining population. This specific nature and structure of the *Tenson-zoku* can best be discovered in some of the tales of heroes in the *Kojiki* and the *Nihonshoki*, several of which are connected with the advent of the imperial house in Japan. This is recounted in various versions as a mythical, primeval occurrence. We shall limit ourselves to two of them, which we have chosen because they specifically show the structure of the *tenson* tribe.

The first of these two relates the *Tenson-kōrin*: the descent of the Celestial Grandson from heaven. We shall confine ourselves to a few of the details important to this work from this well-known story, and refer to Florenz [2] for the whole translation of the *Kojiki* text.

[1] Cf. pp. 97, ff. of this chapter

[2] See K. Florenz, op. cit., pp. 69-71.

In this myth the grandson of Amaterasu, Ninigi *no mikoto*, is ordered by her to descend from heaven. His descent, which means the origin of Japan's history, moreover brought with it the origin of the world's oldest dynasty, of which he himself was the patriarch. For the structure of the imperial race, the fact that he (according to the *Kojiki* [1]) was accompanied by a total of five gods is of importance. Just as Ninigi *no mikoto* sired the imperial house,[2] so the five gods who accompanied him were the progenitors of the clans which were closely connected to the emperorship. Hence the imperial ancestor was surrounded by a 'Fünferschaft' of five clans. In the description of the sacrifice also, which Ninigi *no mikoto* offered after his *Tenson-kōrin*, not only the names of the five gods are mentioned, but also those of the clans of which they became patriarchs.[3] The most important of them were: Ame *no* Koyane *no mikoto*, 天兒屋命, and Futotama *no mikoto*, 太玉命, who represented the clans of Nakatomi and the Imibe, 忌部. These clans were to come to the fore in political life after 645 in Japan. Moreover, it was just they who were given the special task of being responsible for the religious ceremonies of the *ujigami*. This happened only after previously important clans such as the Ōtomo, Mononobe and Soga had disappeared from the political stage. This shows that this text was re-edited after 645. Not only the names of these gods or clans were important to the structure of the Japanese imperial house, but also the fact that we are dealing with *five* gods here. The text from the *Tenson-kōrin* specifically states: "He appointed these five as his companions and descended from heaven with them." [4] If we disassociate this text from its mythical garb, then it states: the emperor came, together with five clans, to Japan.

There is yet another text in the *Kojiki*,[5] which confirms a similar five-fold clan structure. Here there is mention of a pact, *ukehi*, 宇気比, between the Storm God Susa *no* O and his sister Amaterasu.

---

[1] *Kojiki*, 1st *maki*; Kuroita Katsumi, Maruyama Jirō, *Kokushitaikei Kojiki*, Tōkyō 1963, p. 43, line 7; K. Florenz, op. cit., p. 69.

[2] This list of imperial ancestors began as follows: Izanagi—Amaterasu—Oshi-ho-mimi *no mikoto*—Ninigi *no mikoto*, etc.

[3] Cf. p. 114.

[4] *Kojiki*, loc. cit.: Awasete itsu tomo no Ō wo sashikuwaete Amorimasashime tameki." Translation: "He appointed these five companions and descended from heaven".

[5] Cf. *Kojiki*, 1st *maki*; Kuroita Katsumi, Maruyama Jirō, op. cit., p. 17 and ff.; cf. K. Florenz, op. cit., p. 31-34.

According to this pact they had both put themselves under an obligation to produce progeny. Accordingly Amaterasu had three daughters. Susa *no* O hung his sister's five strands of pearls on his right and left temples, his hair and his wrists, and thus produced five male gods. They were brought up, however, by Amaterasu. Thus, in these myths, both the matriarch of the Japanese imperial house, Amaterasu, and her grandson Ninigi *no mikoto* are connected with five figures who were, in both cases, the ancestors of clans which felt themselves related to the imperial lineage and which, together with the emperors had taken possession of Japanese territory.

Not everyone agrees with this conclusion. For instance, Tsuda Sōkichi [1] is of the opinion that the numbers five and three were initially smuggled, together with the ancestor cult, into these myths under Chinese influence in the seventh century. According to him, they can throw no light on the specific structure of the *Tenson* tribe in its very first stage. However, we cannot share this opinion as it is opposed by indications amongst tribes in North Korea, to which it was so closely related.

In the previous chapter [2] we pointed out the strong relationship of the Japanese emperorship to Korean tribes. Now at the time of the rise of the *Tenson* tribe, a similar tribal structure could be found in Korea. For instance, in the *Kao-chü-li chuan*, 高句麗伝, of the *Wei chih* and the *Tung-i chuan* of the *Hou Han-shu*, there is mention of the five clans of the Koguryŏ, the present-day North Korea.[3] The *Tung-i chuan* of the *Wei chih* reports of the Fu-yü (or Puyŏ which we encountered in the first chapter) that they also had five clans. The totem names of those clans were at least expressed in the naming of their officials.[4] According to the afore mentioned

[1] See Tsuda Sōkichi's opinions et. al., in the article by Matsukawa Jirō, "Tennōshizoku no Shutsuji (Origin of the Imperial *Shizoku*)", *Tennō no Rekishi*, p. 106, ff. See also the discussion between Oka Masaō, Egami Namiō and Yawata Ichirō concerning this and other questions: "Nihon-minzoku-bunka no genryū to Nihon-kokka no keisei", *Minzoku-gaku Kenkyū*, vol. 13, no. 3, pp. 222,ff. (1948).

[2] Cf. p. 40 ff.

[3] Concerning this see Mishina Shōei, "Kokuryō no Gozoku ni tsuite (On the five clans of Koguryŏ)", *C.G.*, no. 6, 1954, Aug., pp. 13-57. For the Chinese texts, cf. pp. 13, 14.

[4] This is shown by the following text concerning the Fu-yü in the *Wei chih*: "The country is under the rule of a monarch, and all his officials are named

Chinese manuscripts, these peoples were already living in North Korea and on the Manchurian border in the second century A.D. In that same period, not earlier, the imperial tribe must also have passed through the territories of these peoples on its way to Japan. On the basis of all this, it seems obvious that the five-fold clan structure, which we encountered in the above mentioned myths, was certainly present right from the beginning. Hence it was no invention of the seventh or eighth century, nor produced by the Chinese respect for the sacred numeral three or five. Therefore the above mentioned *Kojiki* myths must have been supported by a situation which, de facto, no longer existed in the seventh or eighth century. From the end of the fifth century on the Japanese sources no longer mention five important clans, but merely the appointment of only two important imperial advisers, who came as leaders from the two most strongly opposed clans. As early as the sixth century, these two leaders often had more power than the emperor himself.[1] They are recorded by untranslateable titles such as *ōmuraji*, 大連, or ō-*omi*, 大臣. These titles indicated to their contemporaries that they followed the emperor directly in rank. Therefore if the *Nihonshoki*, in the above mentioned *Tenson-kōrin* account, had not permitted Ninigi *no mikoto* to descend from heaven with five gods but with two only, then that would have mirrored the situation in the sixth century, when the emperor ruled with his *ō-omi* and *ōmuraji*.[2] This number, two, may be ascribed to the imperial dependence upon the two most powerful clans. Moreover, in this *Nihonshoki* text also, the belief in this five-fold clan structure is not disguised. Immediately after the *Nihonshoki* version of this legend, another tradition of it is mentioned. This other version is introduced with the two words *issho iwaku*, an introduction which

---

after domestic animals, as *Ma*(horse)—*chia* (house or family), *Niu*(ox)—*chia*, *Chu*(pig)—*chia*, *Kou*(dog)—*chia*, *Ch'üan* (canine)—*chia*. . ." It is clear that these officials have descended from the clans, after whose totem animals they were named. For this text cf. Ikeuchi Hiroshi, "A Study on the Fu-yü", *T.B.*, 1932, no. 6, p. 36. See further Matsukawa Jirō, op. cit., pp. 108, 109; Wolfram Eberhard, *Kultur und Siedlung der Randvölker Nord Chinas*, pp. 16, 17.

[1] See Chapter IV, p. 239 regarding this matter.

[2] Cf. *Nihonshoki*, 2nd *maki*, *Tensonkōrin*; Kuroita Katsumi, Maruyama Jirō, *Kokushitaikei Nihonshoki*, part 1, pp. 62, 63; cf. W.G. Aston, op. cit., pp. 67, 68.

indicates tales quoted from other sources. In approximately the same number of lines as the actual *Nihonshoki* legend, it is then related of Ninigi *no mikoto* that he descended from heaven with five companions. According to the names mentioned here, his companions were identical with those of the *Kojiki*.[1] With this even the texts of the *Nihonshoki* prove that the imperial tribe had the same clan structure as the Korean and Manchurian peoples of the fourth century and earlier.

Yet another text from the *Kojiki* [2] can confirm that the imperial tribe actually did reach Japan from Korea. When Ninigi *no mikoto*, after his descent, gave the gods Ame *no* Oshihi *no mikoto*, 天忍日命, and Amatsu Kume *no mikoto*, 天津久米命, the order to make the firstborn sacrifice, he said: "This place lies opposite the land of Kala." [3] This term "the land of Kala" —or, Sino-Jap.: Kankoku, 韓国,—is still the indication for South Korea. In the third century this country was divided between three tribal areas, which were all called Kala countries: Ma-han, 馬韓 (Sino-Jap.: Bakan); Pyŏn-han, 弁韓 (Sino-Jap.: Benkan) and Chin-han, 辰韓 (Sino-Jap.: Shinkan). It is not easy to discover a five-fold structure here. Indeed, the imperial tribe shared its quintuplescence rather with the North Korean Koguryŏ and the Puyŏ. This too is an argument in favour of the Puyŏ. In any case, in this text the imperial house, personified by Ninigi *no mikoto*, is brought into context with the Kala country.

The five-fold clan structure is further shown by a closer investigation of the Tungusian word *xala*. Various parallels of this word also exist in other Asiatic languages.[4] Thus, amongst Tungusian tribes such as the Bilal and the Kumal, the word *kala* is used in the sense of family. Amongst all of the Tungusian tribes it conveyed the meaning of exogamous clan. This is also the case in Manchurian. Mongolian and the Tagul dialect know the word *xala* as family, clan. The Old Turkish word *kayas* also had something to do with

---

[1] Op. cit., p. 69, last lines.

[2] Cf. *Kojiki*, 1st *maki*; Kuroita Katsumi, Maruyama Jirō, *Kokushitaikei Kojiki*, p. 44.

[3] K. Florenz, op. cit., p. 72, Anmerkung 8, here translates *Karakuni* by: ". . . .ödes Land," and thus does not apply this word to Korea. This is, however, untenable, as in the *Kojiki* and in the *Nihonshoki* themselves, Korea is consistently called the land of '*Kan*', 韓.

[4] Cf. Ōno Susumu, *Nihongo no Rekishi*, pp. 50 ff. See also Oka Masaō, et. al., op. cit., pp. 222, 223.

this. In Korea *kala* and *kaya* mean exogamous clans. They also have this meaning in the *Wei chih.*[1] According to Oka,[2] the '*han*' in the names of South Korean tribal areas Ma-han, Pyŏn-han and Chin-han originally also had something to do with this. In Japanese there are still some words which are made up with this root *kala.* Those are *ugara, yakara, takara, tomogara* and *kara.* The word (*u*)*kara* has the sense of family, group of members of the family, who certainly are not allowed to intermarry. Words such as *yakara, takara* or *tomogara* indicate rather a corporation of *ugara* or *kara.* These are linked not by family relations but by the land or the soil. Hence it can also be considered as an exogamous *uji.* Though it might be quintuply structured, it nevertheless has much in common with the *uji* of the first phase. This certainly facilitated the amalgamation of both types of *uji.*

This also throws some new light on the *Tenson* tribe. The close relationship to the clans in Korea indicates that the 'imperial' tribe must have been such an exogamous *yakara,* which encompassed several *kala.* Hence it was also exogamous. That is shown by the fact that the emperors took their wives from the 'conquered' population.[3] With these wives a limited matriarchy entered the patriarchal imperial tribe. This consisted of the right, granted to empresses and imperial concubines, to have their own dwelling. There they could educate their children, often future emperors. As a result of this, the *ujigami* beliefs of the conquered population entered the imperial house. Thus the exogamous character of the imperial tribe has contributed a great deal to its amalgamation with the indigenous population. Nevertheless, the emperor could remain lord and master as leader of the most powerful tribe. Hence gradually, from his nearest relatives leaders of other *yakara* grew.

In the foregoing we have attempted to reconstruct the 'pure' image of the imperial tribe, as it entered Japan at the time of its pre-history. The strong relationship which this tribe shared with the North Asiatic peoples allows us to extend these characteristics

---

[1] Cf. Ōno Susumu, op. cit., p. 50.

[2] See note 4 on page 116.

[3] Cf. Kadowaki Teiji, *Jimmu Tennō*, pp. 203-206. This gives a list of all the wives of emperors who lived between Sūjin and Ōjin's periods. Many of them were descended from beyond the Yamato area. According to this survey, the tendency, especially among the later emperors, grew stronger to find wives from areas outside Yamato.

with a few properties which all of these peoples had in common. In this we refer to the reconstruction which Wolfram Eberhard [1] composed as picture of his Tungusian T'opa. He developed this on the basis of data concerning peoples of similar ethnical structure and geographical environment.

According to him the tribe decided the actual 'state'. The leadership of this tribe was inherited and patriarchal. Within this tribe various families lived. However, the family of the supreme leader made up a kind of nobility. As the space within the tents permitted of only a few people, families were compelled to erect new tent communities continually. These, in their turn, became independent. Together these families formed "einen gemeinschaftlich nomadisierenden Verband". Actually, most of the North Asiatic tribes fit into this scheme.

Although we know little of the original Japanese imperial tribe, these characteristics may yet be traced back by use of the Japanese sources. For instance, the entire composition of these manuscripts indicates the hereditary nature of the emperorship, as they actually became degraded to little more than ancestral records. In the wars against Korea—again from these sources—it may be seen that all the families surrounding the emperor belonged together. Because the armies, recruited by the various heads of clans in their own territories, marched under their individual leadership, but nevertheless together, to Kyūshū, and from there to Korea. The patriarchal quality of these tales can be seen, for instance, in the triumphant stories of Ōjin in the strife against the land spiders. Hence the imperial tribe also fitted into Eberhard's scheme, and was equally related to the Korean and North Asiatic tribes at China's borders.

According to Eberhard's scheme, the position of the tribal chieftain was also defined to a great extent by the tribal religion. Now amongst all of the aforementioned tribes Shamanism was very popular, although it cannot be discovered in which forms it was experienced, nor what its relations were to the tribal religion. It is therefore hard to define this more narrowly. Hence it can be explained that Eberhard sees the belief of the T'opa generally in the recognition of "eine Unzahl von Göttern, durch Zauberpraktiken und Schamanismus".[2] In reality this description is just as applicable

[1] Wolfram Eberhard, *Das Toba-Reich Nord Chinas,* Leiden 1949, pp. 277, 278.

[2] Wolfram Eberhard, op. cit., p. 237.

to the population under T'opa rule as to the T'opa themselves. None of this offers much grip on the identity of the *Tenson-zoku*. However, it does not impede a relationship with the Puyŏ, who indeed also had a five-fold clan system.[1] However, little of this relationship can be traced in the *Kojiki* and the *Nihonshoki*. The contribution of this nomadic tribe was apparently so limited that it was entirely overwhelmed by the spiritual climate of the tribes of the first phase.

However little is known about this imperial tribe, it is certain that it steadfastly directed Japan towards the political, spiritual and Shamanistic powers which animated similar tribes in North-East Asia. This considerably facilitated the process of adaptation to Buddhism, which also reached Japan via that North and East Asiatic route. The introduction to that process was made up of the amalgamation of these nomadic tribes with Japan's indigenous population of the first phase.

2 *Amalgamation with Japan's original population*

Now how did this amalgamation set about? We have already pointed out that a Japanese, just as a Chinese, is more inclined to see his people as a closed unit than as an amalgam composed of various components. That, however, does not obviate that even in the Japanese sources the processes which permit one to suspect how that amalgam came about can be traced. Thus the emperors, together with their surrounding clans, began to form the apex of the local population. The myth of this amalgamatory process may be found in the *Kojiki*.[2] It is the tale of the oath taken by Amaterasu and Susa *no* O, daughter and son of the primeval parents Izanagi and Izanami.

This Susa *no* O was such a nuisance to Izanagi that he decided to send him to hell. In order to put off this exile for as long as possible, Susa *no* O invented all kinds of pretexts. Amongst others, he decided to seek for help from his sister Amaterasu, who reigned over *Takama no hara*. When he arrived he found her, to his great surprise, heavily armed. Despite all his declarations concerning his

---

[1] Amongst several, for instance Kida Teikichi, post-war authors especially such as Matsukawa Jirō, op. cit., p. 113, and Egami Namiō, op. cit., *Minzoku-gaku Kenkyū*, vol. 13, no. 3, p. 274, are of the opinion that the tribal race descends from this Fu-yü.

[2] *Kojiki*, 1st *maki*; Kuroita Katsumi, Maruyama Jirō, op. cit., pp. 17 ff.

good intentions, Amaterasu continued to insist on a visible sign of his goodwill. At this Susa *no* O proposed the following: let us produce children by turns.

Amaterasu had first turn. She broke her brother's sword into three pieces which she had first dipped in a well and clamped between her teeth. After this she blew them with her breath as gods before her. Thus three goddesses came into being.

Then Susa *no* O hung the five strings of pearls which belonged to his sister round his right and left temples, hair and both wrists. Imitating Amaterasu he produced five gods. Hereupon he said: Because I have a red heart, I have won with my test. After that he devoted himself to all kinds of excesses. The five gods who had been called into life by Susa *no* O with Amaterasu's pearl necklace were looked on by Amaterasu as her own children. Susa *no* O did similarly with the three goddesses.

In these myths two gods stand opposite each other as exponents of two different peoples: Amaterasu represents Japan's oldest population, and the rough, rebellious Susa *no* O the new nomadic tribe. In antiquity, until 809, it was believed he was a Korean deity. Only then, at the imperial orders of Emperor Kammu, 桓武 (781-805), all manuscripts which suggested a common descent for Japanese and Koreans had to be handed in. The tale shows the collision between these two population groups. Hence this story can be put in the following historical context. Having penetrated Amaterasu's territory, that is, the earlier population's land, the symbolic emperor's figure Susa *no* O encountered so much opposition that an annihilating blow threatened. However, as a result of a mutual pact, they became brother and sister to each other. Instead of fighting, they bore each others' children. Hence matriarchy was preserved in the bringing up of the children. Thus the amalgamation of the population of that era was described mythically.

Thus the *ō-kimi* (the 'emperor'), with his surrounding clans, managed to gain power over the whole country from a political point of view, and to tie it to him. This did not, however, take place without major concessions, by the conquerors also. Because as a result of the specific natures of both amalgamated groups matriarchy nevertheless continued to exist, especially in bringing up children. Owing to this, the conquered tribe could still have some ascendency in the field of religion and culture. This mutual amalgamation was possible only because in the long run both groups contrived to accept each other. This acceptance was not as difficult as in China, where too great cultural differences impeded an assimilation, especially of the Chinese part of the population. Moreover, for the ruling nomads this also meant, for most of them at least, an impossible effort. Inescapably, in China the rule held good: "Nur der Bauer ist höherer Mensch, der Viehzüchter bleibt ein Niederer."[1] On the contrary, in Japan a more harmonious assimilation took place. It eradicated the sharp differences on both sides. For this reason it is so difficult to discover a clearly defined division in the Japanese sources between the influences of the people of both phases.

3 *The relationship between the emperor* (ō-kimi) *and the clans* (shizoku)

In contradistinction to the *Wa* peoples, who are mentioned in the *Wei chih,* the imperial nomad tribe settled in the afore mentioned Yamato area. Since the invasion by this tribe, this formed the actual base from which Japan of the sixth century was built up. It has remained Japan's political and cultural centre of gravity since that time, although it shares this place for the last hundred years with Tōkyō. Here the encounter with Taoism and Confucianism took place. Buddhism too underwent its initial incubation period in specifically this area. The invasion of this area was achieved during the fourth and fifth centuries from the south-west. This is also shown by the situation of the old burial mounds.[2] The entrance to the Yamato plain via the Yamato river was blocked in Ōjin's day by many bogs. That is why there is mention in the tales of Jimmu of this southern way along the bed of the river Ki *no gawa,* 紀川, to reach the Yamato plain. Owing to major exertions under the emperors Ōjin and Nintoku, these morasses were drained at the end of the fourth, early fifth century. With the help of technical experts from Korea, brought to Japan by these emperors, many rice

---

[1] Lin Tsiu Sen, op. cit., 1st part, p. 153.

[2] Hence the grave ascribed to Ōjin lay in the narrows of the Yamato plain; that of his successor, Nintoku, was situated further to the west, east of the present-day town Sakai. Cf. Kadowaki Teiji, op. cit., pp. 129, 137; J. E. Kidder, *Japan before Buddhism,* pp. 145 ff. This may also be deduced from the situation of the imperial palaces. See Higuchi Kiyoyuki, "Jōdai gūshidensetsu-chi no kenkyū (Study of the Geography of the antique remains of palaces according to tradition)", *K.G.Z.,* vol. LXII, 1961, no. 9, Sept., pp. 33-43.

paddies were made. Before this happened, however, the Yamato plain had already been subdivided as the tribal territory of the invading nomad tribe between the various clans which belonged to this tribe. These clans had managed to seize land for themselves, which they managed independently. Others were unwelcome. Thus they established various centres of power in the Yamato area, which were to become involved with each other in serious competition as the imperial influence grew, in order to gain the most influence on the imperial house.

The various clans which surrounded the imperial race were called *shizoku*, 氏族. This word is made up of two concepts: 氏, *shi* = *uji* and 族, *zoku* = *yakara*. It indicates a kind of bridge between the old *uji* and a summit organisation, in which the largest part of the previously existing *uji* took a subordinate place. Hence a *shizoku* commanded an unknown potential. With this they gradually attempted to out-trump each other and the emperors. The relationship between the imperial house and the *shizoku* was therefore of the greatest importance in every political and religious development during the first centuries of the empire.

This becomes apparent as we investigate these *shizoku* further. The most powerful was that of the Mononobe. At the end of the fifth century and during most of the sixth the government of the country lay more or less in their hands. Together with the Nakatomi *shizoku* they have attempted to oppose Buddhism in every way possible. This *shizoku* had been the first to advance through the gateway of invasion into the Yamato plain, and had gone as far as possible. They must therefore have been the oldest *shizoku* in the Yamato plain. This explains why they were pressed against the Kasagi, 笠置, mountain range in the east. The encircling ranges threw them entirely back amongst themselves. Their reticence and conservative ideology, which became apparent in the struggle against Buddhism, can be traced back to this local isolation.[1] In any case, owing to the lack of any through road which might admit some traffic, they could dedicate themselves undisturbedly in their own territory to the devotions of their own *ujigami*, Ōmiwa and Ishigami. Hence this local situation can, by itself alone, explain

---

[1] Nagano Tadashi, "Kōi sōkō monogatari no honjitsu (Actuality of the stories about the Imperial ranks and their mutual relations)", *Tennō no Rekishi*, p. 267.

the fierce conservatism which this *shizoku* displayed in the fifth and sixth centuries.

However, the Mononobe were not the only ones to settle in the Yamato plain. Together with them other *shizoku* which felt themselves related to them entered the Yamato plain. Among these belonged the Nakatomi. Especially after 600, they were, as successors to the Mononobe, the great opponents of the progressive *shizoku* of the Soga. Their dwelling area lay to the south of that of the Mononobe. One of the five companions of Ninigi *no mikoto*, namely Ame *no* Koyane *no mikoto*, was their *ujigami*. In the sixth century they, together with the Mononobe, were to form a front against Buddhism, which other *shizoku* wished to propagate. Later they were to admit to being won over by Buddhism and, especially after 645, they became fiery proponents of it, although by that time they had changed their name to Fujiwara.

Another group which made history at the same time as the Mononobe had chosen its clan area in the plain of Akitsu 秋津. This lay in the south-western corner of the Yamato plain, at the point where the prefectures of Wakayama, Nara and Ōsaka now border on each other. Here specifically there were many large keyhole graves, which date from the fifth century, the same time in which these Ōtomo *shizoku* played a very great part in various wars. For instance, they overcame the older clans of the Katsuraki, 葛木, and Heguri, 平群; their important position at that time is shown by the fact that it was they who provided much of the material for the tale of Jimmu.

Together all these clans, with many more smaller ones, formed one large group. They were led by the first and most powerful *shizoku*. The leaders of these clans were indicated by the untranslateable title of *muraji*, 連. In the year of accession to office the chief *shizoku* was given the title of *ōmuraji*, 大連, by the emperor; that is to say, the 'great *muraji*'. At the time of the rise of Buddhism the Mononobe filled this supreme position.

In opposition to the *muraji* group there was another, the leaders of which also bore a special title, namely *omi*, 臣. They called their leader *ō-omi*, 大臣: the 'great *omi*'. One of the characteristics of this group was that they belonged to the family of the emperor. The most important *shizoku* of this large group was especially the Soga in the sixth century. Its leaders were, at that time, the strongest exponents of Buddhism. It must have been the last tribe to enter the Yamato plain. This can be deduced from the fact that they inhabited the area nearest to the entrance to this plain, namely the south-west corner of Hirano, 平野. Here they dwelt on the slopes of the mountain Katsuraki.

They were pressed up against the slopes by other *shizoku* within the mountain ranges surrounding the Yamato plain. As a result of this, all kinds of rivalries broke loose in the Yamato plain between them and their neighbours, and they were forced to expand. The limits of their territory changed like a piece of elastic, according to what pressure was exercised by, for instance, the Mononobe. As they lived close to the entrance to the Yamato, they were also more susceptible to various external influences. That this was indeed the case is proved by the fact that they lodged the most immigrants from Korea and also the first Buddhists in their own area. This accessibility also had other benefits, because it also provided them with the most modern techniques imported from Korea, such as irrigation systems, spinning, ironwork and, finally, script. This gave them an immeasurable superiority over their opponents, the *muraji* group, whom they were eventually to conquer as the Mononobe. The Soga *shizoku* was not only progressive, they were also young. This can be seen in the part which they played, according to the Japanese sources. Though the Mononobe provided, for instance, most of the Kyūshū legends about Jimmu, and the Ōtomo those about Jimmu's conquest of Yamato,[1] and though the *Fudoki* mentions relations with the Ōtomo, Mononobe and Nakatomi in various places, in these older texts there is no mention of the Soga *shizoku*.[2] The first figure to be mentioned here is the aged chancellor Takeuchi, who served under Empress Jingū (201-269) and also under the Emperors Ōjin (240-310) and Nintoku (313-399). If one is to believe the *Nihonshoki*, he must have held office for more than 150 years. This indicates that the Soga attempted during the Suiko recension to enlarge their image by sneaking this important figure into the chronicles specifically of those emperors who had taken such an important position in Japanese history. At the time of the introduction of Buddhism, as the most powerful *shizoku* they had plenty of opportunity to do this.

Just as the Mononobe did in the east of the Yamato area, so the

[1] Cf. Kadowaki Teiji, op. cit., p. 167.

[2] There are five reports in the *Fudoki* on the Nakatomi, five on the Mononobe, nine on the Ōtomo, none, however, on the Soga.

Soga formed the apex of a large group of *uji* and *shizoku* in the south-west. Amongst these too there were groups who had previously exercised great influence on the imperial house, such as the Katsuraki and the Heguri.[1] In the sixth century these two groups of hundreds of *uji* were inimically opposed to each other.

Between these two groups there were also the 'turncoats', the *uji* who did not know whether they were really *muraji* or *omi*. Usually this led to severe conflicts with both groups. Even at the time of Emperor Inkyō (412-454) the struggle grew so ferocious that he found himself forced to intervene.[2] In order to establish the identity of the group of these hesitants he instituted the 'boiling water test', the so-called *kukatachi*, 盟神探湯. The leaders of the quarrelling factions had to put their hands into a pot of boiling water in order to prove their honesty. In this harsh way the identity of the doubting *uji* was established. According to Nagano Tadashi,[3] this "pre-Confucian and pre-Buddhist usage, which was popular especially in noble circles", was used to examine eighty different *uji*. Thus the *uji* of the Wani, 和珥, which was actually of Korean origin,[4] was changed from *muraji* to *omi*, and the Nakatomi, which was initially *omi*, became *muraji*. Whether this divine justice was applied under the personal supervision of the emperor himself is unknown.[5]

Later this dual system was to be ruptured by the emperors with even more titles and distinctions. This happened especially in the seventh and eighth centuries. These titles were laid down in personal decrees, which can be found in the *Nihonshoki* under the years 603, 663 and 674. In 685 an eightfold system was made, in which all the *uji* were divided into *mahito*, 眞人, *asomi*, 朝臣, *sukune*, 宿禰,

---

[1] Cf. Kadowaki Teiji, op. cit., p. 90: "Though there is proof that the *shizoku* of the Katsuraki and the Heguri are older than those of the Ōtomo and the Mononobe, they nevertheless did not provide any specific ancestral histories, as they had already fallen into decay after the emperors Yūryaku (457-479) or Ninken (488-498)."

[2] Cf. *Nihonshoki*, 13th *maki*, Inkyō 4th year, 9th month, 28th day; Kuroita Katsumi, Maruyama Jirō, *Kokushitaikei Nihonshoki*, part 1, pp. 339, 340; K. Florenz, op. cit., p. 293; W. G. Aston, op. cit., pp. 316, 317.

[3] Cf. Nagano Tadashi, op. cit., p. 265.

[4] According to the *Kojiki*, Wani, just as Achiki, had already come from Korea to Japan under Ōjin.

[5] Cf. Nagano Tadashi, op. cit., p. 265.

imiki, 忌寸, *michinose*, 道師, *omi*, *muraji* and *inaki*, 稲置,[1] mostly untranslateable names which cannot even be transposed into the titles of our Western feudal system such as count, duke or baron, because they had an entirely different background. These titles honoured not so much the *uji*, but rather the *uji no kami* of the *uji*. However, we are not concerned with all these titles in *shizoku* society of the sixth century, excepting the dual system of *omi* and *muraji*. These titles, also called *kabane*, 姓, were all of a later date, however much used in earlier texts of the *Nihonshoki*.

The foregoing has shown that the entire struggle for power between the *shizoku* is strongly tied to the tribal lands of Yamato. This was almost split into two by the conflict. Nevertheless, the greatest *shizoku* also had many possessions outside this tribal land. Various comments from the *Fudoki* prove this. Thus we know of the Ōtomo, Mononobe and Nakatomi that they had vast properties both in north and in south Japan under their private rule, which were sometimes called after them. This shows the far-reaching influence of these *shizoku*.

Amongst all this *shizoku* influence, what became of the position of the actual leader of this *tenson* tribe? If we mark off the areas inhabited by the *omi* and *muraji* in the Yamato tribal lands, finally nothing remains for the emperor's clan. Yamato was entirely divided up between the two competing *shizoku*, as may be seen from our map (see p. 470).

It is known of the emperors that they did possess their own territories. These were indicated by special names such as: *miyake*, *mita*, *hajiro*, and *kojiro*.[2] They could not, however, have been

[1] See for the arrangement of all these degrees and ranks:

for 603: Ch. VI, p. 389, ft. nt. 3.

for 663: *Nihonshoki*, 27th *maki*, Tenchi 3d year, 2nd month; Kuroita Katsumi, Maruyama Jirō, op. cit., part 2, pp. 287, 288; cf. W. G. Aston, op. cit., vol. II, pp. 280-281.

for 685: *Nihonshoki*, 29th *maki*, Temmu 13th year, 10th month; Kuroita Katsumi, Maruyama Jirō, op. cit., part 2, p. 372; cf. W. G. Aston, op. cit., vol. II, p. 364, 365.

[2] *Miyake* (written 屯食 or 屯家) was a term from the era in which taxation did not, as yet, exist. A *miyake* encompassed the following: a *tabe* (田部), a piece of land, was brought under cultivation and its harvest was kept in storage for the emperor: the *miyake*. *Mita* (屯田) was the name of the field in which the imperial rice was cultivated. Furthermore, there were similar areas, such as the *hajiro* (名代) and the *kojiro* (子代). The original area

situated in the actual tribal land of Yamato, but outside it, especially in Kyūshū and North Japan. This creates an entirely specific problem: namely, can it be contended by this that the emperor, just as the other *shizoku*, had a private geographical tribal area, or not? I agree with Kadowaki [1] that "present-day school books mistakenly speak of *miyake*, *mita*, *hajiro* and *kojiro* of the *ō-kimi* as if these decided their own jurisdiction area." On the other hand, nowhere in the *Nihonshoki* can we find confirmation of the opinion of Nagano [2] which states that the *ō-kimi* and their families inhabited their own tribal area, which was wedged between the territories of the *muraji* and the *omi* in Yamato. Thus one can search in vain for texts which indicate territorial conflicts between the imperial house and the other *shizoku*; though there are enough about those amongst the *shizoku* themselves. Moreover, both the *Kojiki* and the *Nihonshoki*, especially in the chronicles concerning the oldest periods, are full of texts from which the residences of the *ō-kimi* may be deduced. We shall encounter this again in the fourth chapter. Those texts show that, according to what political use could be made of the situation, they settled inside the dwelling area of Soga, Mononobe or neutral *shizoku*. For instance, Emperor Kimmei lived closer to the Mononobe; Yōmei and Suiko, however, lived within the tribal territory of the Soga. Hence the emperor was at liberty to settle where he pleased and, especially until the second half of the sixth century, they moved repeatedly. Therefore the emperors were, in contrast to the settled *shizoku*, almost the only ones in the Yamato district who, together with their near relatives, continued the original nomadic existence. Why they did this is unknown. It was probably a kind of conservatism, supported by religious motives. Now they can no longer be traced.

It is interesting that, owing to this form of conservatism, they maintained their mobility among the *shizoku*. It also made them highly receptive to everything going on among the various *shizoku*. Various, and more and more divergent philosophies, which origi-

---

belonging to the emperors was called *mi-agata* (御県). Such areas were spread all over the country from Kyūshū to the plain of Kantō (the Tōkyō plain). In the sixth century the Soga especially were to fight the Mononobe violently for the possession of these territories. The murder of Emperor Sushun at the end of the sixth century had something to do with this.

[1] Kadowaki Teiji, op. cit., p. 124.

[2] Op. cit., p. 267.

nated in the valleys of the Yamato plain amongst them, thus found a sounding-board in the emperor. Syncretically they congregated in him. This made him an incarnation of this many-branched and far-reaching *shizoku* belief. This indubitably gave him an authority beside which the leadership of the various *shizoku* paled.

Owing to this extensive power, it was often he alone who could move the mutually inimical leaders of the *shizoku* towards larger, national interests. Hence the emperor could, in the fourth century also, advance on Korea at the head of an expeditionary force recruited from the *shizoku*, in order to capture many Korean technical experts, in particular those who were necessary to the institution of rice-growing in the Yamato plain and in the neighbouring Kawachi, 河内, plain, and for the requisite irrigation.[1]

It was also owing to this generally acknowledged authority that the emperors could take the initiative in projects which far exceeded the capacity of one single *shizoku* and required a national approach. Such major works were: the draining of swamps, the building of rice lakes in the hills for irrigation of the slopes, the construction of mammoth burial mounds such as those of Ōjin and Nintoku, and the digging of the Naniwa 難波 canal. Against all the interests of the local *uji no kami*, he represented in his person the federal government; in this he was a kind of hereditary American President on a smaller scale.

4 *The* shizoku *view of the emperorship*

This imperial image, raised above the *shizoku*, changes in the *Kojiki* and the *Nihonshoki* with every emperor until 645. These same sources permit us to see this emperorship in yet another way, namely through the eyes of the three most powerful *shizoku* who, especially in the sixth century, defined Japan's political course. This threefold view is not a description of the contemporary emperorship, although it dates entirely from the sixth century.

---

[1] Cf. Kadowaki Teiji, op. cit., p. 132. The success of this war may also be seen from the construction of rice ponds, which are mentioned even under Ōjin. For instance in the *Nihonshoki*, 10th *maki*, Ōjin, 7th year, Kuroita Katsumi, Maruyama Jirō, op. cit., part 1, p. 272: "In September of the seventh year the inhabitants of Koguryŏ, Paekche, Imna and Silla (therefore from all Korean territories) came to Japan. At that time Takeuchi *no sukune* gave all the peoples of Kara (=Korea) the order to build a pond. This pond is called 'Pond of the People of Kara'."

It was far rather a retrospective projection of Japan's very first emperors. Of these there were no historically responsible reproductions. Their views of the emperorship made incarnations of their own *shizoku* mentality of the oldest emperors. Thus Jimmu, Sujin and Ōjin, the three 'divine' emperors, appear as sublimated *uji no kami* of the three most important *shizoku*. This threefold view can still be traced, as the *Kojiki* and the *Nihonshoki* are merely *shizoku* traditions linked to each other.[1] The ruling *shizoku* of the sixth century, i.e. the Ōtomo, Mononobe and Soga have contributed most to this. Therefore their mentality is set out best in them. It could most adequately be incorporated in the old sources by projection as old, no longer extant, figures. The series of fifteen fictitious emperors allowed enough possibilities for this.

The most powerful *shizoku* of the sixth century certainly did this. Here it is of interest that they, for the benefit of their position at court, also chose the most powerful figures of the series of fifteen. Actually, it was the other way round, as the *shizoku* rendered them as the most powerful. Their ascendency can still be seen from their posthumous Chinese names.[2]

Of these three, the 'oldest' emperor was particulalry linked with the Ōtomo traditions. We have already pointed out that the Ōtomo, even above the Mononobe and the Soga, had much influence on Japanese political life until 547. It is therefore obvious, that their traditions must also have been much older than those of the other two *shizoku*. The history of the Ōtomo *shizoku* has not, however, been written at that same time. This was due to script only coming to Japan at the beginning of the sixth century. Hence, as written traditions they originate, at the earliest, from the first half of the sixth century. Therefore they still remain as the oldest core of the *Nihonshoki*. Using the Kume song in the first chapter, we have already pointed out the unmistakeable Ōtomo characteristics in the Jimmu chronicles. Now what does the imperial image look like, that the Ōtomo have projected?

For the Ōtomo the emperor counted as the conqueror; he who set out from Kyūshū to fight the leaders of the local population, who, at the time of the Ōtomo were particularly strong in Kyūshū. These leaders were nevertheless to be deified in their anonymity as

---

[1] Chapter I, pp. 68 ff.
[2] Chapter I, p. 66 ff.

'land-gods', Jap.: 國ッ神, *kuni-tsu-kami*. In the Jimmu tale the new imperial tribe still fought the old, local inhabitants. In the Kume song the main accent was on their destruction. Hence fierce enmity must still have existed between the populations of both phases. Jimmu's strife against the *uji no kami* of the original population illustrates that he had not yet grown into the omnipotent symbol of the combined spiritual power of both conquerors and conquered: the emperorship was not yet a sign of national unity.

This was entirely different in the Sujin chronicles. Sujin was the tenth emperor. Some, amongst whom Matsukawa,[1] opine that he was the original founder of the emperorship. Jimmu, according to his posthumous Chinese name, may have been called the fighting divinity, but Sujin stood for 'he who worships the gods'. This name is not only confirmed by his chronicles. It was also closely connected with the Mononobe who, according to the chronicles, had been particularly charged with the divine worship of the gods. This proves the close link between the Mononobe and Sujin. One can even ask oneself, whether this divine respect given to Sujin is not attributable to the fact that his mother was a Mononobe.[2] She was probably, as were so many princesses at that time, a Shaman or priestess at court. His close connection to the Mononobe is also apparent from other facts. In the eighth month of the seventh year of his reign he specifically charged the ancestor of the Mononobe, Ikashikoo, 伊舌色雄, on the advice of his soothsayers, with the making of a special sacrifice to the gods. In this it is interesting to note that the sacred utensils for the sacrifice had been made by 'eighty hands', that is to say, by very many members of the Mononobe-*shizoku*.[3]

---

[1] op. cit., p. 112.

[2] Cf. *Nihonshoki*, 5th *maki*, Sujin 1st year; Kuroita Katsumi, Maruyama Jirō, op. cit., part 1, p. 157:
"Mimaki-iri-hiko Isonie *sumera-mikoto*, 御間城入彦五十瓊殖天皇 was the second son of Waka Yamato-neko Futohihi *no sumera-mikoto*, 稚日本根子大日日天皇 (= Emperor Kōrei). His mother was called: Ikashikome *no mikoto*, 伊香色謎命, and was the daughter of the patriarch of the Mononobe-*uji* Ō-heso-kino, 大綜麻杵." Cf. W. G. Aston, op. cit., vol. I, p. 150.

[3] Cf. *Nihonshoki*, 5th *maki*, Sujin 7th year, 8th month; Kuroita Katsumi, Maruyama Jirō, op. cit., part 1, p. 161:
"The Emperor spoke: 'Now we shall be prosperous and healthy.' By means of soothsaying he ascertained whether he should appoint the forefather of the Mononobe *no muraji* Ikashikoo as sharer of the sacrifices to the gods.

Approximately one line after this appointment, the *Nihonshoki* typifies Sujin as follows: "*Katate agametamau ama-tsu-kami kuni-tsu-kami*", that is to say: he had a deep respect for the gods of heaven and earth.[1]

If we compare these Sujin chronicles with those of Jimmu, then the progress and difference become clearly apparent. Jimmu believed that he still ought to fight the land-gods. Sujin, however, already respected the deities of the conquered peoples. By so doing he managed to make himself the symbol of the mutual racial amalgamation. As the *uji no kami* of everyone, he had at one stroke become the sounding-board of every *ujigami* without exception. This was, however, far from easy, as there were very many, i.e. 800,000.[2] This is understandable owing to the close ties of the *ujigami* to various districts and population groups. The great respect of one could easily lead to dissension among supporters of other gods. Therefore he had the gods removed from his palace, to separate temples.[3]

This decision was made after he 'had examined the 800,000 gods

---

This was right. Furthermore by means of soothsaying it was inquired if, on this occasion other gods should also be worshipped. This was not right." Cf. W.G. Aston, op. cit., p. 153.

Of these eighty Mononobe-hands (according to Aston, op. cit., p. 154, 'hands of the eighty Mononobe') there is mention in the eleventh month of that same year; Kuroita Katsumi, Maruyama Jirō, loc. cit.; K. Florenz, op. cit., p. 246.

[1] Cf. *Nihonshoki*, 5th *maki*, Sujin 1st year; Kuroita Katsumi, Maruyama Jirō, op. cit., part 1, p. 157.

[2] 800.000 here means very many. Cf. Chapter IV, p. 244, ft. nt. 1. K. Florenz, op. cit., p. 244 (see the following number, for instance) translates incorrectly by 80 myriad.

[3] Cf. *Nihonshoki*, 5th maki, 7th year, 11th month; Kuroita Katsumi, Maruyama Jirō, op. cit., part 1, p. 161:

"After that he discovered, by soothsaying, that it was right to celebrate the feasts of other gods. Thus he came to celebrate the feasts of the 800.000 gods apart. After this he established the temples of the gods of heaven and of earth, the *kamudokoro*, 神地 (litt.: earth of the gods, that is to say the rice fields belonging to the temple grounds), and the *kamube*, 神戸 (litt.: the gods-*be*, those who should cultivate this land). Only after this did an end come to the epidemic. The land too came slowly to rest. The five kinds of grain began to grow again and there came abundance to the people once more". See also K. Florenz, op. cit., pp. 246, 247; W. G. Aston, op. cit., p. 154.

himself'.[1] The Mononobe tale permits this to happen in two ways. One means of examination lay in investigating the cracks and lines which occurred in burning the shell of a tortoise. These lines could deny or confirm a previously posed question. This was a primeval Chinese procedure, and it is mentioned in the Sūjin chronicles of the seventh year.[2]

Another method of questioning lay in the Shamanistic trances of the princesses at the imperial court. It is expressly stated of the Princess Totobi-momoso, 迹迹日百襲, that she was 'overcome' (*kami-kakarite*) by the deity. Her oracle gave occasion for the institution of a separate feast for the divinity who had entranced her.[3] Therefore separate priests were also appointed, amongst whom the Mononobe. Such princesses must be accounted of the first phase and Japan's oldest ethnic group. As a result of their religious activities, they gained access to the court. From the chronicles of Keikō, which are also a Mononobe part of the *Nihonshoki*, we quote the following text from the twelfth year of his reign, concerning a similar female ruler: [4]

[1] See the translation on p. 131, ft. nt. 3.

[2] For this technique see H. G. Creel, *La Naissance de la Chine*, Paris 1937, pp. 178, 179. The following chronicle, to be found in the *Nihonshoki*, 5th *maki*, Sujin 7th year, 2nd month; Kuroita Katsumi, Maruyama Jirō, op. cit., p. 159, proves the existence of this: "Would it not be right to order that by means of divine tortoises the cause of the disasters should be discovered?" Cf. W.G. Aston, op. cit., p. 152. K. Florenz, op. cit., p. 244, Anmerkung 8, believes in the historicity of this text, and therefore considers this tortoise method not improbable. However, this objection is invalid as these texts also are projections from a later date, at which time the Chinese procedure with tortoises was already widely known.

[3] Cf. *Nihonshoki*, 5th *maki*, 7th year, 2nd month; Kuroita Katsumi Maruyama Jirō, op. cit., pp. 159, 160:

"The *Tennō* went to the Kamu-asachi, 神淺茅, -plain (literally the plain of the shallow China grass). Here he collected the 800.000 gods and questioned them by means of soothsayers. These brought the princess Yamato-totobi-momoso, 倭迹迹日百襲, to inspiration (*kami-kakarite*) and answered by her mouth. Why is the *Tennō* distressed by the disorder in this land? If he would worship me properly, it would of a certainty come to peace again. To this the emperor asked: Who is the deity who has thus instructed me? The answer was: I am a god who lives within the limits of the Yamato area and I am called Ōmono-nushi *no kami*, 大物主神. When he had received this divine command, he had the feast of this god celebrated in accordance with the divine instruction." Cf. K. Florenz, op. cit., pp. 244, 245; W.G. Aston, op. cit., pp. 152, 153.

[4] Cf. *Nihonshoki*, 7th *maki*, Keikō 12th year, 9th month, 5th day; Kuroita

"The emperor sent Take-moroki, 武諸木, the ancestor of many *omi*, Unade, 菟名手, the ancestor of the *omi* of Kuni-saki, 國前, and Natsuhana, 夏花, the ancestor of the noblemen of the Mononobe, ahead of him and ordered them to look at the local situation. Now a woman dwelt there called Kamunashi *hime*, 神夏磯媛, who had many supporters. She was the *hitoko no kami*, 魁帥 (= *uji no kami*), of the entire countryside. When she heard that the emissaries of the *tennō* were coming, she tore up a *sakaki* tree, 賢木,[1] from the Shitsu, 磯津, mountain. On the topmost branch of it she hung the Yatsuka, 八握, sword, on the middle branch the Yata, 八咫, mirror, and on the lowest the shimmering pearl of Yasaka. 八尺.[2] She hoisted a white flag on the bows of her ship. Thus she set out to meet them, with the prayer: 'send no soldiers. My people are definitely not in revolt against you.'"

In this *Nihonshoki* text the same three symbols are mentioned which are named in the *Nihonshoki* tale of the descent from heaven, the *Tenson-kōrin*: they were the three signs from heaven which Ninigi *no mikoto* brought to earth on behalf of Amaterasu from heaven. In this tale a female ruler is mentioned who possessed symbols which are preserved in Ise as the three jewels of Shintō. In view of this text, one can ask whether these symbols were inherited by the imperial race from Japan's original population, to which that female ruler belonged. The possibility of this transposition is suggested by this text, as they were not inimical to each other, in contrast to many other 'land spiders'. This is apparent from the advice which she later gives in the struggle against those land spiders. Here the three jewels indicate one of the first phases of the Amaterasu cult. Owing to the exogamous character of the imperial house, this cult could infiltrate via the imperial wives and even spread into becoming the imperial tribe's religion. Simultaneously the female Shamans of the first phase, on whom this religion relied, entered the imperial court. This can explain how they, as princesses at court, maintained close relations with these gods. Did they not descend from these female Shamans? This leads to Sujin's decree, which charged two of them with the divine worship

Katsumi, Maruyama Jirō, op. cit., part 1, p. 202; cf. W. G. Aston, op. cit., pp. 192, 193.

[1] 榊: Cleyera ochracea, the sacred Shintō tree. This is shown by the character which is made up of the radicals: 木, tree and 神, *kami*.

[2] 137) Yatsuka, Yata and Yasaka themselves also have the meaning of, respectively, sword, mirror and pearl.

for the most important gods of that time: Amaterasu and the local deity Yamato *no* Ōkuni-tama, 日本大国魂.[1]

Thus these women and princesses could bring Shamanism of the first phase to the court and introduce the gods with whom they were closely linked. This was all facilitated as something of the old matriarchy still continued to exist at the court of the *ō-kimi*. The imperial consorts did not move in with the emperors, but maintained separate establishments, where the ruler would visit occasionally. It was not difficult for these 'foreign' imperial wives to introduce their *ujigami* amongst the princes and emperors. Had they dwelt at the emperors' court themselves, then they would never have succeeded in contriving, for instance, that Amaterasu was magnified into an imperial divinity. At the Japanese court something similar could take place via these foreign women to that which happened at Solomon's court, who was converted from his original monotheism by his wives.

This makes it clear that Amaterasu, as deified Shaman of the first phase, was more popular amongst the empresses than amongst the emperors.[2] It is, however, unclear, to which gods the sympathy of the emperors was extended. Later, the war god Hachiman became very popular among them.[3] As an oracular divinity he gave just as

---

[1] *Nihonshoki*, 5th *maki*, Sujin 6th year; Kuroita Katsumi, Maruyama Jirō, op. cit., p. 159:

"In the sixth year people began to travel around everywhere. Revolutions also broke out. All this violence was difficult to restrain by wise policy. From dawn to dusk he (= the emperor) was afraid and he therefore prayed the heaven and earth gods for (the punishment of his) guilt. Chiefly he did so to the two gods Amateru ōmikami (= Amaterasu) and Yamato *no* Ōkuni-tama by worshipping them in his palace. As he was really afraid of their power he did not feel happy living together with them (under one roof). Therefore he ordered princess Toyo-suku-iri, 豊金秋人, to worship Amateru ōmikami in the Yamato village Kasanuhi, 笠縫, and set up an *hiorogi*, 神籬, (temple). He commisioned princess Sunaki-iri, 渟名城入, with the divine worship of Yamato *no* Ōkunitama." Cf. K. Florenz, op. cit., pp. 244, 245; W. G. Aston, op. cit., p. 152,153.

[2] Cf. Matsukawa Jirō, op. cit., p. 86: "Prior to Emperor Meiji (1852-1912) there was not one among the many hundred emperors except for Empress Jitō (686-697) who had particularly great respect for the Ise temple. That does give us a somewhat odd feeling."

[3] This is particularly obvious in the chronicles of the sixth and seventh centuries. Therefore Hachiman is certainly younger than Amaterasu. There is mention of him only for the first time in 767, in connection with the appointment of the monk Dōkyō, 道鏡, as chancellor to Empress Shōtoku.

much advice as Amaterasu, but this did not happen before the eighth century.

This shows that, despite the fact that the authority of the old *uji no kami* in future combined in the emperor's person, the practical experience of divine worship and contact with the gods themselves still belonged to the female members of the court or to other Shamans. The male deity Hachiman made no exception to this.[1] Thus Shamanism of the first phase survived all the revolutions and wars, and discovered adequate meeting points in the Shamanism present among the new nomadic tribe of the *ō-kimi* to be able to continue existing. What religion there was at the time of the Mononobe, lay in the hands of these female Shamans and princesses. The above mentioned *Nihonshoki* text indicates that they were descendents of female Shamans and land spiders of the first phase.

The separation of religion and court under Sujin did not bring with it a division between religion and state. Sujin's measures were merely attempts to ensure a greater personal neutrality.[2] By localising the entire divine worship at various points and by delegating it to others, the *ō-kimi* himself could more easily than before continue as the general spiritual head of the nation, without having to be tied down to certain gods. Externally this made it possible for the emperorship to display a certain openness and an accompanying impartiality towards the various trends of the local religions. This could be the reason why it is now so difficult to trace the original *ujigami* of the imperial race. Was this a totem god or Takamimusubi?[3] Was it Amaterasu or Hachiman? This

[1] In the chronicles of Empress Shōtoku for instance, contact with Hachiman was always achieved by a priestess.

[2] Cf. Nakamura Kichiji, *Nihon Shakaishi*, p. 97. Proof of this may be seen in the chronicles of the successor to Sujin, namely Suinin, which recount 99 years of his reign in 18 pages. Twice there is mention here of the fact that he hung his armament in the temples. Cf. *Nihonshoki*, 6th *maki*, Suinin 27th year; Kuroita Katsumi, Maruyama Jirō, op. cit., part 1, p. 186: "He gave orders to the *kamu-tsukasa* (priest-officials) to determine, by soothsaying the weapons for the sacrifices to the gods." Cf. W. G. Aston, op. cit., p. 178. Cf. also Kiyohara Sadaō, *Shintōshi*, p. 193: "In 55 (Suinin 39th year) all temples received a bow and a sword and in 57 1000 swords were hung in the temple of the god Ishigami, 石上. They counted as swords for the gods". Cf. *Nihonshoki*; Kuroita Katsumi, Maruyama Jirō, op. cit., p. 189; W. G. Aston, op. cit., pp. 183, 184.

[3] Matsukawa Jirō, "Tennō-shijō no Bōten", *Tennō no Rekishi*, pp. 114 and 115, opines that Takamimusubi had more to do with the imperial tribe,

problem cannot be solved by the light of the *Kojiki* or the *Nihon-shoki* alone. We believe that the individual nature of the imperial nomadic tribe is indicative of the 'animal' parents of Jimmu as being the very oldest *ujigami* of the imperial tribe. Under the influence of the tribes of the first phase they were first pushed aside by a *musubi*—however Manchurian that name may be—and later by the compromise divinity Amaterasu. We have already indicated in the foregoing that later, under Chinese influence, she was given a mighty opponent in Hachiman.

The vague, undefined attitude of the emperors of the sixth century towards Buddhism also explains this impartiality. With regard to Japanese syncretism it was important. As the mentality of someone who was not bound to a definite form of *ujigami* belief but nevertheless wanted to remain the spiritual head of the nation, it could absorb all kinds of *ujigami* beliefs as a result of its indetermination. In this accessibility of the emperors lay the very first impetus towards syncretism.

Thus, through the Mononobe ideal of Sujin (the *ujigami* emperor par excellence), we can nevertheless estimate the true open nature of the imperial mentality. The nomadic character of the imperial tribe cannot be ignored in this. The different natures and the sensitivity of the *shizoku* forced Sujin to an openness which is not to be found in the older descriptions of Emperor Jimmu. Jimmu, the conqueror, was certainly still far from respecting the gods of those he conquered. Sujin not only respected them but, via the princesses, returned them to their previous sphere of existence. He even built their own temples for them.

The third (and Soga) Emperor Ōjin did not differ too extremely from the foregoing Mononobe creation, Sujin. We have encountered him already in the first chapter. Officially he was Japan's sixteenth emperor. We have, however, already noted that of all sixteen he was the first and only one who really existed. Amongst all his names there was one, his posthumous Chinese name, Ōjin, 応神, which also really typified him. The meaning of this word Ōjin is 'he who answers to the will of the gods'.[1] This special title can scarcely be

---

and Amaterasu was associated more with the people who populated Japan before the *Tenson* tribe. We believe rather more in Takamimusubi being older with regard to Amaterasu on the basis of her task described in footnote on pp. 106, 107.

[1] Cf. Kadowaki Teiji, op. cit., p. 216.

taken as an indication of his government, as is the case with Jimmu and Sujin, because during his reign there is hardly any mention of outstanding religious activity. It has more to do with the fact that he, in accordance with the will of the gods consulted by his mother, came into the world after a pregnancy of thirteen months. Therefore the name Ōjin is very closely connected with the chronicles of his parents, Chūai and Jingū. Now despite the individual Soga character of these chronicles, they nevertheless show great similarity to those of Sujin. Here, even more so than in Sujin's chronicles, it is apparent that the fate of the emperors depended more on one or other Shaman. In these Soga chronicles this was Jingū. She entered into contact with the gods in order to gain directives for the war in Korea. In the *Nihonshoki* the following is recorded about this under the eighth year of her husband, Chūai's reign: [1]

"Ninth month, fifth day. The emperor turned to all his ministers in order to consult with them about an attack on Kumaso.[2] Then *the empress received a revelation from a divinity* which was as follows: 'Why does the emperor worry about the fact that Kumaso does not submit? This is indeed a spineless land. Is it really worth the effort of raising an army and attacking it? There is, however, another land which exceeds it, a land full of richness, similar to the eyes of a beautiful woman. It can be found on the other side of the sea (Jap.: *mukatsu-kuni*, 向津國: Korea) and is blinding to the eyes. Gold may be found there, and silver, and it is rich in colour.[3] This land is called Takufusuma, 栲衾, Silla'." [4]

The emperor would not listen to this divine hint. Therefore he was told by the same god, in the same story: "Thou shalt not conquer this land. The child, of which the empress is pregnant, will gain it." The end foretold here was not long in coming. After recounting his vain strife against the Kumaso, the *Nihonshoki* continues: [5]

"In his ninth year, the fifth day of the second month in the Spring, the emperor became ill and died. He was 52 years old."

---

[1] Cf. *Nihonshoki*, 8th *maki*, Chūai 8th year, 9th month; Kuroita Katsumi, Maruyama Jirō, op. cit. part 1, pp. 236-237.

[2] The eastern half of the island Kyūshū.

[3] K. Florenz, op. cit., p. 276, translates this by 'washed silken materials'

[4] K. Florenz, loc. cit., translates this Takufusuma by "Papiermaulbeerdecken". Cf. W. G. Aston, op. cit., p. 221: 'Silla of the coverlets of Paper Mulberry' (Broussonetia papyrifera).

[5] loc. cit.; Kuroita Katsumi, Maruyama Jirō, op. cit., part 1, p. 237; W.G. Aston, op cit., p. 222.

This entire story served to illustrate that Ōjin, in contrast to Chūai, behaved in accordance with the will of the divinity. Therefore this tale is really an explanation of the name Ōjin, he who accords with the divinity. That divine preference for Ōjin Amaterasu was also vouchsafed by the mouth of his mother Jingū to the Soga patriarch Takeuchi, in the following *Kojiki* account: [1]

" 'I inform you that the ruler of this country is the child which still lies in the womb of your empress (= Jingū).' To this Takeuchi answered: 'Terrifying, great god, what manner of child lies in the womb of the divinity?' (Jingū identified here with the divinity)[2] She said: 'It is a boy' ".

In these texts the Soga showed their attitude to the specific nature of the emperorship by the mouth of their patriarch. Their vision did not differ too extremely from that of the Mononobe. Just as in previous texts, here too even the *matsurigoto* in the sense of national government by prominent Shamans such as Jingū took place. Perhaps this Takeuchi also had something to do with Shamanism, as he interviewed the divinity for the common weal.

Despite this, there were also noticeable differences between this Soga emperor and the Mononobe model Sujin. These were particularly expressed by the fact that his religious mentality did not remain limited to Japan alone. How could this be otherwise, seeing that he descended on his mother's side from the Korean Ama *no* Hiboko? Religious forms which existed at that time in Korea therefore certainly met with his appreciation and interest. How otherwise was the study of the works of Confucius to begin during his reign? He entrusted the education of his son to the Korean Achiki. The immigration of Koreans also, who built many rice paddies, was started during his reign.

In these lines, it is of little importance whether or not the facts mentioned actually took place. In Ōjin we encounter the embodiment of the specific Soga mentality and their imperial ideals, which is of the utmost importance here. The Soga view was an expansion of that of the Mononobe, as even foreign philosophies such as Confucianism could begin to belong to the religious content of this

---

[1] Cf. *Kojiki*, 2nd *maki*; Kuroita Katsumi, Maruyama Jirō, *Kokushitaikei Kojiki*, p. 95.

[2] Here she is called *kami*. However this is not written 上 but 神. Therefore she was considered to be a kind of superhuman being; a shaman or the deity itself. Cf. footnote on p. 84.

emperor's image. Simultaneously, however, they continued to see in their emperor the strong links with Shamans such as Jingū. As far as this is concerned, they did not lag behind the Mononobe with their Sujin. In the eyes of the Mononobe or Soga the emperor was not himself a Shaman, but they were highly dependent on this Shamanism as it had become the integrating component of their *matsurigoto*.

Finally, if we compare these three views, as linked to these emperors, to each other, then we must leave undecided the difficult problem as to whether we are here dealing with a three-fold illumination of one and the same imperial figure, who is supposed to lie in the vast burial mound ascribed to Ōjin. There are many arguments for this. The most important is probably the *shizoku* proofs discussed here. However, absolute certainty will probably never be gained on this, as long as other possibilities are not excluded. It can indeed be equally argued that the three historical centres of these emperors' pictures go back to hero figures within the circle of the individual *shizoku* itself. The only historical datum for this threefold view is the fact that these three imperial figures embodied the imperial image which was alive amongst the most powerful *shizoku* of the sixth century. Therefore it is the illustration of an evolution which took place in the sixth century in the Yamato plain; a shifting of mentality of similar dimensions such as we are experiencing in Japan and Europe today. This threefold illumination also shows something to be seen of the emperors of the sixth century under whom the three *shizoku* reached their political apex. Thus the Ōtomo also typified Emperor Keitai, under whom they served. The Mononobe picture is equally valid for their Emperors Kimmei and Bidatsu and that of the Soga for the Emperors Yōmei and Suiko. We shall return to this in the three last chapters.

We have been able to observe, by use of the above mentioned sources, the mental growth of the emperorship from provincialism to nationalism, and from nationalism to internationalism. In this the emperors themselves were little more than spiritual ideals which were alive in various *shizoku* and which led to various encounters between the *shizoku*. These conflicts were to break out especially amongst the three most powerful *shizoku* of the sixth century. This disunity had various consequences. The Mononobe were brought, by their conservatism, to lower a kind of *ujigami* curtain, behind which they could nurse it. On the other hand, the extensive international accessibility of the Soga brought them so far that they welcomed all immigrants, together with their religious opinions. They did, however, take care that their own *ujigami* beliefs did not founder. Even after accepting Buddhism, they remained faithful to it. The following chapters remove any doubt on that score.

Nevertheless, through the individual colouring given to the imperial image by the various *shizoku,* the awe-inspiring imperial authority continued to exist. Inevitably it personified everything amongst the large and small *shizoku.* Therefore it can certainly not be rated lower than that of its North Asiatic spiritual kindred, such as the great promoter of Maitreyanism, Fu Chien [1] at the end of the fourth century, or the T'opa emperor who was acclaimed as the living Maitreya of his era at a not much later date.[2] Just as these emperors, the *ō-kimi* counted as the incarnation not only of all the gods of the original nomad tribe, but also of the newly conquered tribes of the first phase.

On the other hand, this authority must also be related to the society of that era. At that time there was no bureaucracy, which could immediately execute or implement all the orders of the *ō-kimi.* For this he was always dependent on his *shizoku,* which knew how to exploit this dependence to the full. If the *ō-kimi* could not manoeuvre between the two most powerful *shizoku,* then serious quarrels arose, which were sometimes even decided by his own death. As so little contact between the head of state and the people was possible, owing to the entire lack of a bureaucracy, the influence of the *ō-kimi* reached no further than the most prominent leaders of the *shizoku.* He met them only. The people themselves were, however, ruled by the local *uji no kami,* not by the emperors. The *uji no kami* were absolute lords and masters of the population. Not the distant *ō-kimi* but the small *uji no kami* himself decided in

[1] Cf. E. Zürcher, *The Buddhist Conquest of China,* p. 188

[2] Wolfram Eberhard, *Das Toba-Reich Nord Chinas,* p. 229, contends that this was Emperor T'ai-tsu. E. Zürcher, op.cit., p. 414, note 14, also apparently supports this, although he mentions Fa-kuo (+ 420) instead of Tao-ko as court chaplain to T'ai-tsu. However, one can search in vain among the T'opa emperors for a T'ai-tsu. The name T'ai-tsu occurs in the *Sung-shu* under the second year of Yüan-chia (A.D. 425). Cf. Ryūsaku Tsunoda, *Japan in the Chinese Dynastic Histories,* p. 22. T'ai-tsu wên-ti was the posthumous name under which the third emperor of the Liu Sung dynasty, Liu I-lung (407-453) was canonized. Cf. Ryūsaku Tsunoda, op. cit., p. 25, no. 4.

each *uji* what the religion of the people was to be. This state of affairs continued until the reign of Emperor Meiji in the previous century.[1]

Thus, we believe, Japan had grown towards its encounter with Buddhism at the beginning of the sixth century. Before we go on to explore Japan's acceptance or denial of it, we shall take a closer look at how Buddhism grew towards Japan in China and Korea.

---

[1] Cf. Takeda Shizuko, "Tennōsei to shūkyō (Emperorship and religion)", *Gendai Shūkyō Kōza* (Studies of modern religion), Tōkyō 1956, p. 168:

"The position of the emperors prior to Meiji was radically different to that of emperors hereafter. Just as the Pope of Rome, he was veiled in a mysterious cloud. He had the power to appoint the *shōgun*, who were to exercise the daily government. Thus he could cut short or strengthen their positions at will. There lay the true power of the emperors. In the Tokugawa period he was called 'his imperial majesty'. Nevertheless his influence did not reach the common people. During the Nara and Heian periods, until the Tokugawa era, the *kimi*, that is to say the actual ruler, was, to the population, the person under whose immediate authority they stood."

CHAPTER THREE

ORIGIN OF PRE-JAPANESE BUDDHISM

We have attempted in the two previous chapter to follow Japan's growth towards its encounter with Buddhism. The question which concerns us in this third chapter begins on the other side: we are going to relinquish Japan temporarily and discuss how Buddhism grew towards Japan.

As far as this is concerned, it is an historically established fact that Buddhism reached Japan via China and Korea. The processes which ripened this religion for its encounter with Japan were therefore especially to be found in these areas. Therefore, in this chapter, a closer look will be taken at the Buddhism of these countries, prior to its crossing to Japan. Hence this chapter falls into two parts, the first of which treats of China and the second of Korea.

Part One

A. CHINA AND BUDDHISM

It would be an oversimplification to imagine that the Buddhism which reached Japan was that of Buddha, because this was already changed on its arrival in China at the beginning of our era. Had Śākyamuni been alive then it would have been unrecognisable to him in many aspects as, even in India itself, it had inclined towards many specifically Indian philosophies and religions since his death. Zimmer writes of this: [1]

"The Buddha had begun as a Hindu. Moreover, the Hindu gods had attended him (according to the Buddhist legend) at every stage of his progress. He remained, in other words, within the sphere of India's traditional philosophy, only approaching its classic problem of release (*mokṣa*) from a fresh and revivifying point of view. The range of his interests and effort corresponded precisely to that of the contemporary Brāhmanic thinkers. And so, in due time, the systems came practically together. Sharing ideas, problems and methods, their protagonists argued out the same questions

---

[1] Heinrich Zimmer, *Philosophies of India*, New York 1956, pp. 530, 531.

in the same city and village, parks and courtly gardens, until at last the practical distinctions between their two approaches disappeared."

On its arrival in China Buddhism had already spread itself extensively in many Hīnayāna schools, some of which laid the foundations for Mahāyāna persuasions such as the Mādhyamika and the Vijñānavādin.

Despite those inherent Indian developments, it had not ripened before its encounter with China. That could be ascribed to the fact that its growth took place against the background of Indian schools only, although they were not Buddhist. These schools were all strongly tied to the area of their origin. It therefore appeared to every Chinese as a system which was complete, but also foreign. Therefore, also, little could be found in it concerning the Chinese outlook.

Therefore it is not surprising that this Buddhism, during the first centuries after its arrival in China, can only be typified as translated Buddhism. This is all the more so as, originally, it desired to be nothing other than a replica of its Indian original. This, however, does not mean to say that it did not also gradually search the Chinese mentality for points of contact which would render it acceptable to every Chinese. So nevertheless, a kind of amalgam was achieved between Indian Buddhism and the Chinese popular mentality: between Mahāyāna Buddhism and Taoism mingled with Confucianism [1]; furthermore between Buddhist opinions concerning *nirvāṇa* and the rooted Chinese belief in the beneficence and holiness of a long life prior to death.

Just as Buddhism slowly changed since its origin according to the varying situations it found itself in, it also admitted of growth towards the moment of its encounter with Japan's entirely specific position. In the previous chapters we have seen how only a few *shizoku* at the beginning of the sixth century exposed Japanese society to an encounter with Buddhism. Here, however, one must also ask oneself in how far this Buddhism had already incorporated the entirely specific nature of that society before the encounter.

[1] Cf. Genjun Sasaki, "Hīnayāna-schools in China and Japan", *Pr. du B.*, 1959, pp. 501, 502: "The brilliant outburst of Buddhist literature is due to the assimilation between Taoist and Buddhist philosophies. The tenets of Taoism is the philosophy of non-reality. The Chinese native philosophy of "Voidness" and the Indian Buddhist philosophy of non-reality".

Obviously this is closely connected with the way which it followed up to Japan. Now it is noteworthy that the oldest Japanese Buddhism received its shape in the same areas where the 'imperial tribe' also originated, namely North East Asia. In the following pages we hope to show that Buddhism was here forced from its original by the mentality of the East Asiatic and Tungusian tribes into new adaptations and deviations. Simultaneously this related it to the inherent nature of the 'imperial tribe'.

This result was mainly owing to various Hu rulers in North China. The Hun Liu Yüan, 劉淵, at the end of the third century and the Tibetan Fu Chien,[1] 苻堅, after 376 had especially applied themselves to this end. When the frontiers of their realm of Kansu stretched to the present-day North Korea [2] there was a possibility of two currents flowing in opposite directions, of Shamanism from the north and Buddhism from the south-west. Before these two rulers achieved Buddhism, they made dubious efforts to be more Chinese and Confucian than Buddhist. To this end they wished to appear to their subjects as *T'ien-tzŭ*, 天子, Sons of Heaven. For this they utilised slogans such as: "The ruler who satisfies the people is no stranger to the Chinese. He may rightfully make the position of T'ien-tzŭ, the Son of Heaven, his own." [3] These aspirations of the emperors of the 'Barbarians' were radically punished by the Chinese themselves. Fu Chien had to pay for this in 385 with defeat. Thereafter their successors were more concerned to base their authority on Buddhist ideology. For instance, various T'opa emperors believed that in this they had an adequate counterweight against the Confucian ambitions of the Chinese nobility. Other T'opa rulers, however, such as Hsiao Wên-ti, 孝文帝, (471-499), believed that they still had a chance of being recognised as T'ien-tzŭ by the Chinese. Their attempt, however, met with equally little success. These aspirations of the rulers could not endanger Buddhism. On the contrary, under these foreign rulers it was given a chance to measure up to the mentality of the indigenous population. The only condition for this was relative peace. Owing to the extensiveness of the northern realm this new Buddhist incubation could complete itself over a wide area. This was especially possible because in all

---

[1] A good comparison of these two rulers is to be found in Wolfram Eberhard, *A History of China*, London 1950, pp. 139, 140.

[2] Cf. O. Franke, *Geschichte des Chinesischen Reiches*, part 2, p. 83.

[3] O. Franke, op. cit., p. 149.

of those areas between Turkestan and North Korea, in the plethora of tribes and peoples, religious opinions could be found which were more or less identical. These were particularly characterised by Shamanism, which was present according to all of the essential indications enumerated by us in the introduction.[1] Furthermore, amongst all these peoples the conviction of the existence of the soul after death was alive. It was accepted that these souls dwelt in a place to which the Shaman could occasionally ascend.[2] In this spiritual world, identified by Shamanism, such Buddhist ideas as *nirvāṇa*, transmigration or rebirth, and *anatta*, in the sense of a total extinguishing of the 'I', were hard to accept. This had already become apparent in the South Chinese history of Buddhism, where it had encountered similar difficulties. We shall return to this later.[3] These developments of South Chinese Buddhism were not of immediate importance to Japan's oldest and original Buddhism. Namely, it will appear from this and the following chapters that, in the first place, this Buddhism in Japan was an extension of North Chinese Buddhism.

On its way to Japan, Buddhism had to integrate all of this if it wished to be meaningful not only to monks but also to the North Asian masses. It had to give a compromise solution between these sharply defined extremes. We hope to show in this chapter that this was found in Maitreyanism and Amidism. These two trends in Buddhism succeeded in changing Buddhism from a monkish rule into a national religion. This fact is of particular importance to Japanese Buddhism as even today Amidism is the backbone of the national religion and Buddhism of this country.

This development is particularly indebted, as we shall explain, to Shamanism, which prevailed in China and its outlying territories. Shamanism, the Buddhist answer to it (namely Maitreyanism and Amidism) and both their positions in North Chinese society, all together formed the initial incitements to a growth process from which, in our opinion, Japanese Buddhism of the sixth

[1] This is not surprising as the cradle of all Shamanism lies specifically in these districts. H. Findeisen, *Schamanentum*, p. 15, says of this Shamanism that it "alle anderen religiösen Bereiche, Anschauungen und Sitten weitgehend durchsetzt und sich angeglichen hat".

[2] Compare the general typification of Shamanism of the peoples of that era in: Wolfram Eberhard, *Das Toba-Reich Nord Chinas*, pp. 228, 229.

[3] pp. 152 ff. of this Chapter.

century arose. For this reason we have further defined these three facets in the following pages.

I *Shamanism of the Chinese and the North Chinese frontier peoples*

North Chinese history can superabundantly confirm that there were ideological clashes between the Chinese and their non-Chinese neighbours. Thus the difference in class between the Chinese farmers and the nomadic North Asians was far too great.[1] In addition, the inacceptability of the non-Chinese was laid down in set practical Confucian principles, which established being or not being Chinese.[2] The presence of Shamanism in both did, despite these racial differences among these two population groups, smooth the way for Buddhism which built further on it. Buddhism on the Indian model had no grasp on this. Wolfram Eberhard noted this amongst the Chinese farmers and nobles of the T'opa realm.[3] We shall now look more closely at this Shamanism of both Chinese and non-Chinese.

It has been adequately established of China's oldest religious forms that they were closely linked to Shamanism. Thus one can find many indications of Shamanism in the tales of the oldest legendary emperors. Though classical Chinese chronology wished to place these figures in the third millenium B.C., in reality they were merely projections from the time of the beginning of our era. They were used to give a place in history to the ancestors of the influential noble families of the Han period (208 B.C.-220 A.D.).[4]

---

[1] A good example of this may be found in the T'opa realm, cf. W. Eberhard, op. cit., pp. 276-278.

[2] Thus W. Eberhard, op. cit., p. 236, says of the Chinese in the T'opa realm: "Einmal zeigt die chinesische Gentry ihre Verachtung gegen jeden Nicht-Konfuzianer deutlich (denn ein solcher gehört nicht zur Schicht!); die Regeln des Konfuzianismus aber sind schwer zu lernen. Die Fremden konnten sie in der ersten Zeit beim besten Willen selbst nicht erlernen."

[3] Cf. W. Eberhard, op. cit., p. 237.

[4] Cf. W. Eberhard, "Geschichte Chinas bis zum Ende der Hanzeit", in *Historia Mundi*, Munich 1953, part II, p. 567.

Descriptions of these prehistoric figures can be found in Marcel Granet, *Danses et Légendes de la Chine Ancienne*, Paris 1959, Tome II, p. 278, 280. For their historicity see M. Granet, op. cit., p. 601. The collection in which these legends have been incorporated dates from Szŭ-ma Ch'ien, 司馬遷.

He lived from 145 to 86 B.C. and wrote the collection under the name of *Shih-chi*, 史記. He was an extremely good compiler, and took care that much was preserved for future generations. Nevertheless, many of his tales had

If one agrees with M. Eliade[1] in considering a kind of ascension into heaven as one of the most important characteristics of Shamanism, then prehistoric China knew Shamanism. To this end we shall cite two examples only.

The first concerns the last of China's legendary 'Five Sovereigns': Shun, 舜.[2] He is supposed to have lived from 2255 to 2205 B.C. He was namely the first person who could really fly. We believe that this cannot just be branded as Shamanism, as we consider that a few more factors are requisite to Shamanism than just an ascent into heaven. Therefore that flight of Shun's was probably rather a magic activity. The interesting part of this appears to us to be the matriarchal character, all the more so as this too was closely tied to China's Shamanism. Namely, Shun was supposed to have learnt this magical flight from two women, who were sisters of each other. Only after this event did they both become his wives. This tale illustrates a strong religious ascendancy of the women over the men. Now can one deduce from this, that at the time of the origination of this story, that is to say, around the beginning of our era, Chinese magic, marked down as Shamanism by Eliade, was *entirely* in the hands of women? Such a conclusion goes a little too far as here there is merely question of matriarchal terminal phenomena. The fact that the ordinary boy Shun, by his marriage to these two women, who were moreover daughters of his predecessor Yao, 堯, inherited all Yao's sons, vassals and other possessions does not affect the matter at all.[3]

---

been corrupted by Taoists and Confucians before he compiled them. After his death also they attempted to utilize the material collected by him for their own ends. It appears, however, that he himself had nothing to do with these corruptions. Eugen Feifel, *Geschichte der chinesischen Literatur*, Darmstadt 1959, pp. 145, 146, says of him: "Sein hervorragender wissenschaftlicher Standpunkt, sein klarer, leichtverständlicher Stil verdienen uneingeschränktes Lob". See also M. Granet, op. cit., vol. I, p. 31, who defines his mentality as: "fidéisme rationaliste, qu'on peut appeller esprit critique".

Wolfram Eberhard says of all of these old Chinese legends: "Die heutige Forschung lehnt alle Textangaben über die Zeit der Hsia-Dynastie als unhistorisch ab". Op. cit., pp. 565, 566.

[1] *Le Chamanisme*, p. 437.

[2] The story is to be found in M. Granet, op. cit., tome I, p. 282.

[3]) M. Granet, op. cit., tome II, p. 611. For the matriarchy see M. Eliade, op. cit., p. 394.

W. Eberhard considers this 'matriarchy' to be merely a trick of later nobility in order to prove their descent from the emperors. (op. cit., p. 568).

The second example which Eliade also calls Shamanistic consists of the dance of Shun's successor, the Great Yü, 大禹, (2205-2197 B.C.). According to Granet this dance was so laden magically that after it one could survive even the most extreme trials.[1] Furthermore, it guaranteed power over the gods and ancestors, and thus also over the continued existence of the dynasty. The town in which it took place was made holy by it and became the hub of the world.[2] The manuscript in which this dance is described has not, in contradistinction to other texts of that period, been spoilt by all kinds of interpolations from the Han period.[3] Therefore this dance was probably one of China's oldest magic practices. It was closely connected with the two complementary principles *yin*, 陰, and *yang*, 陽, who regulated everything. Indeed, Emperor Great Yü knew the secret of uniting these two principles with each other, by means of the sacred dance.[4] Though the origin of these principles probably went back to the separation of the sexes as a result of the exogamy,[5] they certainly owed their sacred meaning to the trances, of which Yü's dance was one.

The religious forms which were projected in retrospect in such pre-historic figures as Shun and Great Yü from the Han period to cover a few thousand years probably did exist in reality at that time.[6] It may, however, be doubted whether they existed in the full sense of the word Shamanism.[7] Indubitably, various characteristics mentioned by us in the introduction can be recognised. Thus the ascent into heaven and the dance described above were probably both charismatic. The social aspect could also easily be traced. It

---

1) Marcel Granet, upon whom Eliade, op. cit., p. 394, is inclined to rely, does give an opinion concerning the terrific magical force which was accumulated in the dance but indicates nowhere, not even in his conclusions, that here we are dealing with a Shaman dance. Of this kind of dance he says, in tome II, p. 616: "Une vertue nouvelle s'inaugure par des danses qui servent à expulser un ordre vieilli".

Concerning this dance of the Great Yu, see further M. Granet, op. cit., tome II, pp. 549-579.

2 Op. cit., p. 616.

3 Op. cit., pp. 610, 611. Concerning the interpolations, cf. op. cit. p. 619.

4 Cf. M. Granet, op. cit., p. 496.

5 Cf. M. Granet, op. cit., p. 615. Further see also Arthur Wright, *Buddhism in Chinese History*, Stanford California 1959, p. 12; M. Eliade, *Images et Symboles*, Paris 1952, pp. 166-168.

6 Cf. M. Granet, op. cit., pp. 610, 611.

7 As Eliade contends, cf. *Le Chamanisme*, pp. 394, ff.

can, however, be doubted whether an internal change of being similar to a kind of identification with the godhead took place in these emperors. We believe that this transcendental element is lacking: the activities performed were of great magical import, but not religious. They intended a magic conquest of the world, but not, however, a relation with the deity. For this reason one cannot designate this Shamanistic; at the most it can be seen as magical phenomena related to Shamanism.

For the same reasons also the Chinese emperor himself cannot be called a Shaman, as if the imperial sacrifice to heaven, which was actually established far later, were a stylised and instituted Shamanistic trance, which had compensated the charismatic character of the Shaman by rich ritual.[1] This cannot, however alluring, be proved. With this we do not want to say that ancient China did not recognise any Shamanism at all, but only that the above mentioned phenomena are only indications of Shamanism, but not proof. The fact that there must have been genuine Shamanism at that time can mainly be deduced from the fact that, at a later date, it occurred throughout the whole of China.

Later genuine Shamanism did certainly occur in China because the transcendental element and the internal change of being, which were lacking in the cases mentioned above, were present in it. This was practised both by men and women. Male Shamans were called *hsi*, 覡; female *wu*, 巫.[2] As the number of *wu* [3] far exceeded that of the *hsi*, the word Wu-ism, derived from *wu*, grew to be the Chinese name for Shamanism as used by both Eliade and Waley.[4] Now these *wu* and *hsi* were, from time to time, possessed by the *shên*, 神, that is to say, the souls of the departed dead, or by the *kuei*, 鬼, the devils and demons.[5] Neither de Groot nor Granet definitively call

---

[1] This is implied by J. J. M. de Groot, *The Religious System of China*, Leiden 1910, vol. VI, book II, p. 1205:

"We have now had before us sufficient evidence to perceive, that in the second and first centuries before our era the Wu-ist priesthood actually was the priesthood proper of China, even for the highest man in the world under heaven".

[2] M. Eliade, op. cit., p. 399.

[3] Cf. de Groot, op. cit., p. 1201: "The prevalence of Wu-ism in those four parts of the empire involves the probability that it existed in all its parts".

[4] M. Eliade, op. cit., p. 398; Arthur Waley, *The Nine Songs*, p. 9.

[5] According to de Groot, op. cit., p. 1211, both *shên* and *kuei* in China meant the souls of the dead. In this *kuei* meant rather the soul of the body.

this phenomenon Shamanism.[1] Waley, however, has clearly indicated that these *wu* were indeed true Shamans. He states: "Indeed the functions of Chinese *Wu* were so like those of Siberian and Tunguz Shamans that it is convenient to use Shaman as a translation of *Wu*." [2] He points out that the above mentioned elements were present. In a dialogue, which dates from the fifth century B.C., they are described: [3] "The Shaman . . . is a person upon whom the Bright Spirit has descended, attracted to him, because he is particularly vigorous and lively, staunch in adherence to principles, reverent and just; so wise that in all matters, high and low, he always takes the right side, so saintly (*shêng*) that he spreads around him a radiance that reaches far and wide . . ." In this Wu-ism de Groot sees the actual priesthood of China.[4]

Later Taoists especially have taken on much of this Wu-ism.[5] The social character of it must have lost a great deal of value, however much the other Shamanistic characteristics—according to Eliade, all of the characteristics [6]—remained recognisable. Despite this, this Wu-ism must always have preserved its social nature, however small the group. De Groot writes of this: [7] "The *Wu* have ever remained what they probably were from the night of time: men and women possessed by spirits or gods, and consequently acting as seers and soothsayers, exorcists and physicians, invokers

---

It belonged to the earth and also returned to the earth after death. The *shên*, on the contrary, was the heavenly soul, which was only united with the *kuei* during the life on earth, but returned to heaven after death. These souls were actually aspects of *yin* and *yang*, who were given concrete shape in the human spirit in the union of *shên* and *kuei*. Cf. further Tsuda Sōkichi, *Shina Bukkyō no Kenkyū* (Studies of Chinese Buddhism), Tōkyō 1957, pp. 103 ff. Hence death was something of both heaven and earth. Tsuda S., op. cit., p. 97.

This was also closely connected with the worship of the *shên*, but not of the *kuei*. From later Han onwards, the *shên* was only considered as something present in the *living* body, not as that which remained of man after death; Tsuda S., op. cit., p. 143.

[1] Namely in the works of both authors quoted above, in which there is specific mention of Wu-ism.

[2] A. Waley, op. cit., p. 9.

[3] Ibid.

[4] See p. 149, footnote 1.

[5] Cf. M. Eliade, *Le Chamanisme*, p. 395.

[6] Op. cit., p. 401.

[7] Op. cit., p. 1212.

or conjurors *bringing down gods* or sacrifices, and performing other sacerdotal functions, occasionally indulging also in imprecation, and in sorcery with the help of spirits. This fact is evidenced by Chinese literature of every age . . ." Thus in reality did the most ancient Chinese Shamanism reach us by means of this Wu-ism.

Though the *wu* were important in China itself, Shamanism lay far more deeply anchored in the northern neighbouring tribes. Something is known to us about this from the Chinese chronicles only. Thus we know that the Shamanism of the Huns (Chin.: Hsiung-nu, 匈奴) played an important part in locating and pursuing sorcerers.[1] Later also, after the advent of Buddhism in similar Hsiung-nu dominions, it does not appear to have lost power. Even Buddhist monks became Shamans here; they made flights to heaven and prophesied the future.[2] It is known of the rulers of the various Yen realms of the Hsien-pi that they were buried on mountain tops. There they also sacrificed to the gods. Possibly these scanty indications concerning the beliefs of the Yen realms also contain indications towards Shamanism. We do not know.[3]

The strength of Shamanism among the T'opa is illustrated by the fact that it was legalised by means of Buddhism. The most highly Shamanistic elements were adopted from it.[4] Under the rule of the T'opa emperor Tao Wu-ti, 道武帝 (386-409), it is known that in the year 400 an entire series of sacrificial services was conducted by *wu*.[5] It is known of these same *wu* that they abused the countenance, that they revelled. Thus sexual extravagance among the *wu* and the *hsi* caused the T'opa emperor Hsiao Wên-ti in the year 472 to take measures which limited their activities. Here de Groot comments that this merely revoked their official functions. Their Shamanism might be exercised as before. Thus it can be explained that the emperors, later, once again ordered them to resume their official services, without there being any mention in this command of their

---

[1] Cf. J. J. M. de Groot, op. cit., pp. 830 ff.

[2] Cf. W. Eberhard, *Das Toba-Reich Nord Chinas*, pp. 228, 229.

[3] For Shamanism under Fu Chien see E. Zürcher, *The Buddhist Conquest of China*, p. 146. For that of the Yen realms, see G. Schreiber, in *M.S.*, Vol. XIV, pp. 333, 349, 423 and 450, where, although there is no specific mention of Shamanism, the mountain burials of the Yen rulers are discussed.

[4] W. Eberhard, *History of China*, pp. 154, 155. See also E. Zürcher, op. cit., p. 146.

[5] Cf. J. J. M. de Groot, op. cit., p. 1234.

other Shamanistic practices.[1] Though the decrees of this latter emperor were very negatively formulated, nevertheless they prove irrefutably the high position which these Shamans filled at court.

With the above we have roughly defined Shamanism of the northern edge of China. In the second part of this chapter we shall see that this also influenced the religious life of the Koreans to a great extent. Now we shall see what kind of an answer Buddhism in China found to this.

2 *The Buddhist answer to this Shamanism and the tenets deduced from it*

As Shamanism was and still is incontrovertibly a phenomenon which influenced the entire North Asiatic continent, every religion existing in this continent had to take it into account. Also Buddhism. Therefore it is important to know what kind of an answer Chinese Buddhism gave to it. Before investigating this any further, we must realise that Buddhism went a double way in China. North and South China had both undergone, especially since the invasions of the Five Hu, an entirely specific political development. The South remained free of all 'barbarian' domination, but the North did not. Thus both became isolated from each other. Approximately parallel to this, Buddhism also went an entirely individual and different way in the North and the South. It moved at different levels in both areas. In the South it certainly counted as a foreign religion up to the beginning of the fourth century, which was wholly incapable of exercising any influence on Chinese society. That is apparent, for example, from the fact that it is scarcely mentioned in the *San-kuo chih*, 三國志, the state chronicles of the San-kuo 三國, the 'Three Realms' (220-265), which date from the time when the North and the South formed one and the same country. The oldest Buddhist apologetic literature only came into being in the fourth century.[2] Prior to this time it led a meagre existence and was accounted a religion for foreigners. Therefore in the first few centuries it did not get much further than being a dubious translation, almost illegible to the Chinese, of old *sūtras*.[3]

The situation of this Buddhism is depicted in the following

[1] Cf. J. J. M. de Groot, op. cit., p. 1235.

[2] Cf. E. Zürcher, op. cit., p. 72.

[3] Cf. Genjun Sasaki, op. cit., pp. 500-505, in which he summarizes these translation activities systematically.

description by the hand of the Hun dictator Huan Hsüan, 桓玄 (369-404):[1]

"Formerly, there were among the people of China hardly any Buddhists. The monks were mostly barbarians, and, moreover, the (Chinese) rulers did not have contacts with them. It was only therefore that (the government) could tolerate their local customs, and did not restrain them (in the practice of their creed)." Of greater importance and more general is the letter which the Buddhist Hsi Ts'o-ch'ih (+ ca. 383) wrote in 365 to his teacher Tao-an, 道安:[2] "More than four centuries have passed since the Great Doctrine spread to the East. Although there were sometimes rulers in the border regions or private individuals who became devotees, yet (in general, only) the ancient teachings of China were practised by former generations." There are no reasons to doubt this Buddhist evidence, as it is anything but apologetic and therefore honest and truthful.

The Chinese attitude depicted in the above mentioned texts can also be seen in Taoism, which partially originated from the ancient Shamanism. This considered the highest human ideal to be realised in a long and contented life-time, embodied in the ancient of years who does not die because he is so virtuous.[3] Naturally this was hard to reconcile with Buddhism which was strongly directed towards flight from this world. The Chinese inevitably found it difficult to accept this life as grief, from which he must be liberated. A *nirvāṇa*, which was accounted even as an improvement and reward for this earthly life, was unacceptable to him.

On the contrary, they were inclined to see all of this in reverse. To them, life on earth was primary. Tsuda, de Groot, Zürcher and many others[4] have all pointed out this typical Chinese mentality. Making use especially of Tsuda's definitions,[5] we shall describe this

---

[1] Cf. E. Zürcher, loc. cit.

[2] Ibid.

[3] Cf. Tsuda Sōkichi, op. cit., p. 220.

[4] Cf. Tsuda Sōkichi, op. cit., pp. 92-113; pp. 143-160; pp. 213-242; M. Granet, *La Religion des Chinois*, Paris 1951, pp. 24, 25; O. Franke, op. cit., part II, pp. 203 ff.; E. Zürcher, op. cit., pp. 11 ff.

[5] Tsuda S. has especially developed this problem in the third chapter of his *Shina Bukkyō no Kenkyū*. There, in 180 pages he has depicted the entire growth of this Chinese soul belief, which raised various difficult problems both for the *sūtra* translations and in the disputes concerning the immortality of the soul. Cf. Tsuda Sōkichi, op. cit., pp. 144-159; 160-230.

briefly. In this we shall particularly attempt to indicate the areas of contact, where the Chinese mentality touches on Buddhism. Tsuda specifically tries to approach this mentality from the various magic practices with which the dead were surrounded. These practices were aimed at rendering the dead innocuous to the living. These rites could certainly not make the dead any more contented.[1] Rites for gods and spirits in antiquity served only to make life on earth happier.[2] Hence the Chinese sign, 壽, *shou*, long and contented life, has not been placed for nothing in every Chinese house, even to our own Western Chinese restaurants, on walls, lamps and cutlery. Continued existence of the soul after death was believed in.[3] After some time, however, it was doomed to discontinue existing independently. At most it might continue alive in posterity.[4] This, however, never happened owing to previous services, because these were paid for during this life, or became posterity's debt.[5] This became the basis for the later Confucian view, that no sacrifices were required any longer for anyone who had been dead for more than seven generations.[6] From that moment on, his individuality was almost entirely extinct, and he could no longer be a danger to his descendents. He had reached the point at which he would be absorbed into the impersonal and mass soul of the tribe.[7] This popular belief might also be found in the circles of the intelligentsia, although here it was slightly more rationalized. To them the soul ceased at the same time as the body. Thereafter it was no more than a kind of breath, 氣, *ch'i*, which was absorbed after death by the world soul, the *yü-chou-ch'i*, 宇宙氣.[8] They alone were no longer interested in the services for the dead held by the common people because there was little advantage to be gained by this,[9] although

---

[1] Tsuda Sōkichi, op. cit., p. 237: "The souls of the ancestors were *shên*, 神, and possessed the same powers and functions generally ascribed to these *shên*. They themselves neither gained nor lost anything in the divine worship.

[2] Tsuda Sōkichi, op. cit., p. 236.

[3] Cf. M. Granet, op. cit., pp. 24, 25 for the belief in souls after death.

[4] Ibid.

[5] Cf. Tsuda Sōkichi, op. cit., p. 216.

[6] Cf. Takatori Masao, "Kodai minshū no shūkyō", in *N.H.S.K.*, Tōkyō 1959, part II, pp. 20, 21.

[7] Cf. M. Granet, op. cit., p. 25, who mentions: "incorporation de la masse ancestrale au sol domestique".

[8] Tsuda Sōkichi, op. cit., pp. 222-224.

[9] Tsuda Sōkichi, op. cit., p. 123.

they adhered to it for appearances. Narrowly viewed, Chinese ancestor worship was therefore an abbreviated form of self-interest.

At an even later date this belief in the soul was to be entirely extinguished. During the Wei and Tsin, 晋, dynasties (that is to say, from 220-420) the idea that in death not only the body but also the soul ceased to exist gained more and more ground.[1] During that same period the *shên* had only something to do with the *living* body, no longer anything to do with that which remained after the death of the person.[2]

It need scarcely be mentioned that Buddhism had but few points of contact with the above mentioned Chinese ideology. Buddhism was indeed built up against a background of the diametrically opposed Indian cosmology, which specifically sought after flight from this life, which would guarantee its unrepeatableness. Therefore it was hard to accept the Buddhist theory of *saṁsāra* in China.[3] In this light the adaptation problems become understandable, against which later Amidists also had to fight, and which Zürcher summarises pregnantly as follows: [4]

"The theory which in Indian Buddhism constitutes the very essence of the doctrine by which it is most sharply distinguished from other schools of thought, viz. the doctrine of the non-existence of the permanent ego (*anātmya*) was completely misunderstood by the Chinese, monks and laymen alike, before the fifth century A.D. The Chinese (not unreasonably) were unable to see in the doctrine of rebirth anything else than an affirmation of the survival of the soul' (*shên*, 神) after death (神不滅)."

There are many examples from that very first period which illustrate how various Buddhist concepts were warped according to the mentality depicted above. Thus concepts such as *ātman*, *puruṣa* and *pudgala* in the oldest *sūtra* translations were translated by the Taoist *shên*.[5] Only after the third century was this *shên* to be substituted by 我, *wo*, I, but even this did not solve all of the problems.[6] Obviously other concepts also were given a wholly

---

[1] Tsuda Sōkichi, op. cit., p. 143.

[2] Ibid., further p. 123.

[3] Tsuda Sōkichi, op. cit., p. 123.

[4] Cf. E. Zürcher, op. cit., p. 11; see the same chapter, footnote 58 for the part of the Amidists in this.

[5] See Tsuda Sōkichi, op. cit., pp. 146, 147.

[6] Cf. Tsuda Sōkichi, op. cit., pp. 153-157.

different content. For instance, *saṁsāra* grew to be viewed as rebirth to improve life on earth; if necessary in a different heaven somewhere on earth. The *bodhi* grew to be considered in the perspective of *shêng-t'ien*, 生天. This is a kind of earthly heaven in which the souls of the dead arrived after they had been freed by the *T'ien-jên*, 天人, a kind of angels or men who had finally achieved the Tao, from the torments of the *kuei*, 鬼, the demons or earth spirits. Naturally here there is no mention of a true *bodhi*.[1] The interesting part of this term *shêng-t'ien* is that it was almost exclusively used on epitaphs for the dead, which were inscribed on images of Maitreya.[2] Tsuda [3] sees in this term a twisting of the Buddhist ideology towards the Taoist theory of the holy hermits; those who withdrew to the hills in order to learn the art of growing old there. These developments did not make it hard for Maitreyanism, and later Amidism, to connect their heaven and release doctrines to it. Thus these inaccurate translations formed the initial impulses for later popular Buddhism; all the more so because there were no official institutions in Chinese Buddhism which could undo these deviations by anathemas. Leaving this aside, Buddhism was driven further towards a compromise with popular belief by the Chinese view of the life of the monks.

The life of the monk, who left his parental home, thus withdrawing from the duties of the parental home, was considered at that time by every right-minded Chinese as an offence. This led to fierce disputes against the institution of the *saṅgha* and celibacy. It was considered to be a violation by the individual of rights which, according to the Confucian *pietas filialis*, belonged only to the community.[4]

In the foregoing paragraphs we have illustrated how Chinese popular beliefs actually began to define the path of Chinese Buddhism. This also occurred amongst the Chinese upper classes. We have already drawn attention to this casually. Only, in the circles of the Chinese intelligentsia, other speculations were added. According

---

[1] Cf. Tsuda Sōkichi, op. cit., p. 241; the heaven here mentioned was also supposed to be somewhere on earth. Cf. Tsuda Sōkichi, op. cit., p. 216.

[2] Tsuda Sōkichi, op. cit., p. 242.

[3] Ibid.

[4] For these latter questions concerning monks and their celibacy, see E. Zürcher, op. cit., pp. 254-288.

to Zürcher [1] these speculations centred round two rather existential-seeming complexes. The first of these encompassed the *hsüan-hsüeh*, 玄学, doctrine. This may be translated as 'doctrine of the mysteries'. It involves all kinds of speculations concerning the polarity between two principles which lie at the root of everything in existence. Those principles are *pen-wu*, 本無, and *mo-yu*, 末有. *Pen-wu* is a kind of general description of what one is not naturally. *Mo-yu* is a principle with a certain finality, it indicates that to which one finally inclines. Here we are therefore dealing with two opposite poles, which are very closely connected ontologically and functionally. Together they form the mystery of mysteries. In the power plane between these two principles there is dynamic tension, which supplied material to a superfluity of opinions. It is not hard to realise that these principles also lie entirely in the field of the terrestrial.

The second complex was called *ming-chiao*, 明教, the doctrine of names. This is intended to set out the principles by use of which one can endow someone with functions and titles which agree with his true capacities. According to the *ming-chiao* everyone has his own *fên*, 分. This *fên* may be translated as 'portion of properties'. It is absolute and irrevocable. No one can change anything in his own *fên*. Now this *ming-chiao* is incorporated within the Taoist ideal of *wu-wei*, 無為, which literally means 'doing nothing'. The actual meaning of this latter principle is as follows: one must not oppose one's individual capacity and nature. Based on this thought, Taoism voiced its own theory of the holy man. This is not only someone who is rewarded with the happiness of a long life, but moreover also possesses the gift of acting in accordance with the *fên* of all things. Hence he is universal and all-embracing, and his capacities reach beyond those of ordinary people. This *fên*, or 'allotted portion', is the basis of the class distinction amongst the nobility. This latter is, however, unacceptable to the Buddhist *karma* doctrine and most especially to the Mahāyāna doctrine which denies all differences. Indeed, this '*fên* fatalism' does not admit of an improvement of one's lot, either in a future life or with regard to a previous existence.[2] Moreover, it is limited strictly to *this* life.

[1] E. Zürcher, op. cit., p. 87.

[2] In the Weltanschauung of the Chinese and Japanese Hossō-*shū*, 法相宗, it may yet be found as 'Fremdkörper'. We pointed this out in the manuscript

These speculations among Buddhist monks were gradually to increase. However, this did not assist Buddhism on its way, as all of these principles were too highly directed towards this life to offer Buddhism any hold. The most intellectual circles would not easily become converted to Buddhism by this. Naturally, these principles could not release a popular movement at all. Nevertheless Buddhism was gradually changed by this. That is shown, for instance, by the fact that Buddhist and Taoist monks began to use each others' terminology.[1] By means of sacrifices to Buddha it was even attempt-

---

of our doctoral thesis, *The Hīna- and Mahāyānism of the Japanese Nara-sects*, Nijmegen 1962, pp. 70 and 71: "The Hossō sect genuinely finds itself on the borderline of the large and small vehicle. On the one side it has fully distanced itself from all Hīnayāna doctrines, as a comparison to the doctrine of Sarvāstivādin and Sautrantika fully proves.

As a genuine Vijñānavādin sect, it has attempted to reduce the multiplicity of the phenomena to the unity of the absolute. On the other hand, it did retain elements of Hīnayāna, as it ascribed so much reality to the five sources which constitute four of the five classes, that these could determine the existence and non-deliverance of humanity because they could not be destroyed by the gnosis alone. This runs directly contrary to the basis concept of the Vijñānavādin and of the Mādhyamikas, which actually opened a via media as a possibility for everyone. Its cosmology gives no reason for characterising it as Hīnayāna as this is wholly integrated in its doctrine, and, on the basis of this doctrine, Hīnayāna becomes little more than a cosmology of illusions and not of existing things. What moved Hsüan-tsang, 玄奘, when he devised this sect? Did he consciously incorporate some Hīnayāna elements in a Mahāyāna doctrine, because he considered them an actual addition to his system? This may have been the case as regards the cosmology, but it does not hold good for the doctrine of the five groups, as this is in flagrant opposition to the Mahāyāna affirmation concerning the nature of Buddha which is within everyone. Therefore it is obvious that practical reasons would rather have brought him to this form of syncretism. Here we can only guess. It does not appear improbable that in this doctrine he wished to preserve the Buddhism of his sect for the Chinese intelligentsia and for a small group he wished to exclude the syncretic popular masses. The fact that to this end he had to make some concessions to the orthodox doctrine of the Vijñānavādin was no problem to him as an East Asian with syncretism in his blood."

[1] Cf. Yoshioka Yoshitoyo, *Dōkyō to Bukkyō*, vol. I, p. 464. This was particularly expressed in Chinese poetry of that time, in which Buddhist and Taoist expressions are used indiscriminately. Hermits of both persuasions enjoyed, according to this writer, the same respect amongst the people. Many poems mention Taoist and Buddhist monks, who lived together and helped each other.

ed here and there to appease the souls of the dead. But here too the concern was not to help the dead, but to improve oneself.[1]

All of these theories were examined in many discussions from every angle in Chinese salons, according to a special technique [2] in a search for points of contact with Mahāyāna. Such discussions probably aided the origination of later Buddhist schools. Before the South of China attained a similar school activity owing to a few fruitful efforts by monks from the North, the Buddhism which had been developed here had already burst through to the common people in the North. In the North were located especially those who were to carry it further, into Japan.

Now, how did it become a genuine popular movement in the North? We believe that three monks in particular, namely Fo-t'u-teng (+349), Tao-an (312-385) and Hui-yüan (334-416), further provided for Buddhism's loss of its Indian trappings. However, they were not solely responsible, but were not a little assisted by entirely new trends which gave them an entirely new orientation.

Before investigating the preparatory work of these monks, we should first consider the developments in which they were involved. These processes were of various types and were independent of the political, geographical and new religious situation in North China.

From a political point of view, vast changes had come about here. China, which had been divided until the year 265 into three realms, was plundered and ransacked by the Five Hu from that date on. These invasions, however, had not only catastrophic consequences, they also brought China's northern territories into contact with the religions of the peoples and tribes who encircled the Chinese realm. Owing to this, entirely new prospects were opened up for the Chinese religions as well and totally new processes commenced. Thus a trend of ideas and cultures was brought into circulation

---

[1] Cf. Tsuda Sōkichi, op. cit., pp. 238-262. As a typical example he mentions the *Urabon*, 盂蘭盆, a sacrifice to the dead still alive in Japan today in the annual Bon feasts and Bon dances in July and August. This sacrifice originated in the old Chinese ancestor worship and was 'legitimized' in China by Buddhism with its own *Urabon sūtra*. In this it was expounded that the gifts for the dead should be sacrificed to Buddhist monks. At a later stage this sacrifice became a gift to Buddha himself, for the benefit of the dead. In this he had become more of a deity than a scholar. Cf. the development of this belief in a soul, E. Zürcher, op. cit., p. 11.

[2] Such assemblies were called *ch'ing-t'an*, 清談, 'pure conversation'. Cf. E. Zürcher, op. cit., p. 93.

whose origins might be found in the huge geographic areas which is bordered by such lands as Korea, Kashmir and Turkestan. This was principally the case during the reign of the Hun ruler, Liu Yüan (-310) [1] and the Tibetan Fu Chien (-383).[2] The latter especially had, up to 376, built up an extensive domain, which bordered on North Korea and Turkestan.[3]

This political situation was not the only favourable condition for life for the new and unknown flowering of Buddhism in North China. There were also other conditions. Thus the geographical expanse of the realms of both rulers made it possible for merchants from Iran and Turkestan to arrive in the two capitals of this area: Loyang, 洛陽, and Ch'ang-an, 長安. Turkestan especially was of great importance at that time because here Indian, Iranian and Hellenistic influences met each other.[4] These merchants also imported, along with their merchandise, their own opinions. Amongst these opinions the doctrine of the future Buddhist saviour, Maitreya, belonged. Although he is mentioned in the oldest Buddhist *sūtras* and therefore the Maitreya theory was basically Indian,[5] according

---

[1] It is interesting that the ambitions of Liu Yüan did not differ greatly from those of the Fu-yü rulers in Korea and Japan. However, that which succeeded there was doomed to failure in China. W. Eberhard says of this:

"The Hun Liu Yüan was the ruler of a league of feudal tribes, which was expected to take its place as an upper class above the unchanged Chinese agricultural population with its system of officials and gentry." *The History of China*, p. 139.

[2] Fu Chien did not work with an 'upper class' made up from his own tribe. His organisation was based on various groups, to which the Chinese, Hsien-pi and Hsiung-nu (= Huns) belonged.
Cf. W. Eberhard, loc. cit.

[3] Cf. E. Zürcher, op. cit., pp. 111, 112; O. Franke, op. cit., vol. II, p. 88: "Fu Kien trieb eine weit ausgreifende Politik nach Turkestan." O. Franke designates the Turkestan of that period as: "Ein Sammelbecken der indischen, iranischen und hellenistischen Kulturströme", op. cit., vol. II, p. 287.

[4] O. Franke, op. cit., p. 63. Further on Franke calls him: "Ein Mann der den Beruf und auch die Fähigkeit zum Universalherrscher bewusst in sich trug." See op. cit., p. 116.

[5] Various traces may be found in the oldest Indian manuscripts which indicate his Indian origin.

1. The oldest traces of a deliverer similar to Maitreya may be found in the figure of Kanda. He was born of the immense ascetism of Shīva. When the 'daughter of the mountains', Pârvatî, succeeded, after many reincarnations, in attracting Shīva's attention, he ignited, and nothing could contain his burning sperm. Through the fire and the Ganges, it came to rest in a bundle of

of arrows. From this the deliverer or Kanda (which means jet of sperm) was born. Hence he was born without being in a womb. Also, he never married. He was also called Kumāra (=chaste youth). He became famous as a god of war as he came to earth in order to command the army of the gods. As such he was not so much the son, but rather a new incarnation of Shīva himself. His invincibility and superhuman power—as illustrated in the *Mahābhārata* —was based on this fact. His history is to be found in manuscripts such as the *Maitrāyani Samhīta* and the *Chandōgya Upanishad.* In this latter work he is called Sanat Kumāra (=eternal youth). His relationship to Maitreya is apparent from his cosmology. Here he is identified with the energy of the sun. Hence he rules in the highest regions above the earth, and causes the creation of the year. It was to these points in particular that Maitreyanism could later link itself. His celestial dwelling place was the first impulse for the idea of the Tuṣita heaven. As the sun god he was sure of popularity amongst many peoples, such as those of Korea and Japan, which already had their own sun cult. His capacity as future Buddha who, after many centuries would be reborn as saviour of the world, can be reconciled with Kumāra's function as deliverer and the fact that the creation of the world dated back to him. For all these data see Alain Daniélou, *Le Polythéisme Hindou,* Paris 1960, pp. 452-456.

2. Another trace can be found in the six sons (Kumāras) of Brahman, who will be born after the destruction of the old world, and will exhaust his energy in creating a new world. Their role is specially described in the *Viṣnu-puraṇa,* cap. V. As creators of a new world of the future, they refer even more fully than does Kanda to Maitreya as Buddha of the future. Cf. L. Renou, J. Filliozat, *L'Inde Classique,* tome I, Paris 1947, p. 450 (paragraph 1026); Étienne Lamotte, *Histoire du Bouddhisme Indien,* Louvain 1958, p. 435.

3. There is also mention of him in the oldest Buddhist sources.

a. The theme of the Eternal Youth is incorporated in various places into the *Majjhimanikāyo.* The most important reference is probably the *Sekhapatipadāsuttam.* Cf. Karl E. Neumann, *Die Reden Gotamo Buddhas,* Munich 1922, part 2, pp. 31-42. In this all the good attributes of the eternal youth (=Sanan-kumāro) are mentioned. Cf. K. Neumann, op. cit., part 1, p. 778, no. 20. He is described as: "der Erhabene, der Heilige, vollkommen Erwachte, der Wissens- und Wandelsbewährte, der Willkommene, der Weltkenner, der unvergleichliche Leiter der Männerherde, der Meister der Götter und Menschen, der Erwachte, der Erhabene". (op. cit., p. 36.) Actually Brahma himself has revealed the specific nature of this eternal youth, op. cit., p. 41:

> "Auch Brahma hat da, der ewige Jüngling, den Spruch gesagt:
> Der Krieger ist der höchste Herr
> Von Allen, die von Adel sind;
> Der wissend, wandel'nd ist bewährt
> Ist höchster Herr bei Gott und Mensch."

This *sūtra* depicts the process which everyone will have to experience if he wishes to reach the highest levels of Buddhism in the *bodhi.* Nevertheless, the concrete, divine figure of Sanat Kumāra (as we have become acquainted with it in Hinduism above) has certainly contributed, in the background, to this illustration. Therefore this illustration is not merely one of a well-intentioned Buddhist who aspires to the highest levels, but also one of the Buddha of the future, who is later to be called Maitreya. This eternal youth then becomes no one less than the anonymous Maitreya.

b. The belief in a future Buddha existed as early as the third century B.C. It is represented on the *stūpa* of Bhārkut. On the gateway of Sânchî this belief has been expressed in the form of (still) empty seats of Buddhas under bodhitrees. See Emil Abegg's extremely good article, "Der Buddha Maitreya", *M.S.G.*, VII, 1945, pp. 7-37; here pp. 8, 9.

c. In other Buddhist sources, however, Maitreya is explicitly mentioned.

i. The *Pārāyaṇa,* one of the few sources of the *Nikāya* and the *Āgama,* mentions Maitreya and Ajīta as two of the sixteen pupils of Bavari, who were converted to Buddha. Cf. É. Lamotte, op. cit., p. 775.

ii. The *Nikāya* and the *Āgama* themselves mention him as the future Buddha. In the *Mahāparanibbana-suttam* of the *Dīgha-Nikāya,* Buddha suggests to his pupil Sāriputta the existence of Buddhas of the past and of the future. He does likewise in his parting speech. In other places he mentions Maitreya by name. Cf. E. Abegg, op. cit., pp. 10, 11. Furthermore, there is also a close connection with the Kāśyapa legend, who, even as a skeleton manifested his superfluity of virtues. Namely, Maitreya was to render these virtues recognisable once again.

Originally the Maitreya proclamation limited itself to these data from the oldest Buddhist canon.

iii. These original data were continually enhanced in later manuscripts. For instance, in the Tibetan and Chinese translations of the now lost *Divyāvadāna,* there was an accurate description of Maitreya's return. He will be born as son of a Brahmin under the rule of King Sankha, one of the three rulers which the world will still recognise then. At first he will instruct 80.000 pupils in the *mantras* of the Brahmin. Hereafter the two rulers of the world will come to King Sankha and give him two miraculous columns, Mahāpranāda. King Sankha will hand these on to Maitreya. Thereupon the Brahmin will break them into pieces. For Maitreya this will be the means by which he achieves the recognition of the transcience of wordliness. Therefore he retreats in a wood. Even that same day he will reach the *bodhi*. Hereafter he will be called the Samyak-sambuddha, 'the wholly enlightened'. At the moment of his *bodhi* the seven indications of the regal worthiness of Sankha will vanish, i.e.: the wheel, the state elephant, his horse, crown jewel, queen, representative and commander of the army. Hereupon the king will search for Maitreya in his wood and become his pupil. Then Maitreya will go to the Gusupada mountain, together with many monks, not far from Bodh-gaya, where the earthly remains of Kāśyapa are buried. The mountain will open of its own accord and relinquish Kāśyapa's skeleton. Maitreya will take it into his hand and announce the virtues of Kāśyapa. Hereupon Kāśyapa will hand over his monks' robes. As a sign of his power, Maitreya will then ascend and display to all the spiritual changes which have taken place in him.

iv. According to Abegg, op. cit., p. 17, these data were incorporated and

to some, it was strengthened by the Iranian ideal of *saošyant*.[1] Probably they also imported the cult of the Buddha of Light, Amitābha,[2] who was practically unknown in India and who was, according to others, a Buddhist pendant of the Iranian god of light, Mithra, or of the Manichean Father of Light.[3] Naturally the Iranian origin of these two characters cannot be proved, but ideals can be ascertained which are closely related to those of Maitreyanism and Amidism. All of this probably supported these two cults in the

---

extended at a later stage in the *Anāgatavaṃsa*: "die ausführlichste Darstellung des Maitreya-Lebens". Here his life is described by analogy with the biographies of the Buddhas of the past, the *Buddhavaṃsa*. In the *Anāgatavaṃsa* the details given above are considerably elaborated. Even the size of his body was indicative of his holiness and power: its length was 28 ells and the breadth of his chest was 25 ells. The tree, under which he achieved the *bodhi* without any exertion was supposed to be a Nāga tree, 120 ells broad, with 2.000 branches. The wreath of rays belonging to Maitreya was supposed to reach as far as 20 miles. Abegg designates the latter as "ein Zug . . . , der ihn in dem Zusammenhang der iranischen Lichtgottheiten insbesondere Mithras rückt." Op. cit., p. 21.

Besides this *Anāgatavaṃsa* there were also Burmese manuscripts about him. One of them describes his previous existences. Thus he was supposed to have been born at the time of Buddha as king Ajâtasattu of Magadha's son, and have met Gotama. Cf. E. Abegg, op. cit., pp. 22, 23.

v. The later Tibetan and Chinese versions of the life of Maitreya elaborate these already fantastic data of the *Anāgatavaṃsa* even further. Thus lives of Maitreya appeared in languages such as Kucha and Uigur. There is even known to be a poem in Sakian (Middle-Iranian), which strongly emphasizes the sun and light characteristics in Maitreya. Cf. E. Abegg, op. cit., pp. 30, 31. This latter is surely proof that the Maitreya cult lay in the same direction as that of Mithra even if they can not be identified. See E. Abegg, op. cit., p. 32. For all of this Maitreya literature, see L. Abegg, op. cit., pp. 8-31. See also É. Lamotte's list, op. cit., pp. 780 ff.

[1] Hence his special title *ajīta* could revert to Mithra as 'sol invictus', and his character as saviour to the Iranian saviour Saošyant, cf. J. Filliozat, op. cit., p. 539 (paragraph 2281). Filliozat is of the opinion that the supposition of an Iranian origin is unnecessary. Cf. op. cit., p. 573 (paragraph 2337). We believe that we have indicated that lack of necessity adequately in the previous footnote.

[2] Cf. É. Lamotte, op. cit., pp. 550, 551, and the very extensive literature mentioned elsewhere.

[3] Thus the transcendency principle of the Mahāyāna, from which all Buddha-hood arises, the *ādibuddha*, was especially connected with the five *tathāgatas* which emanated from it and could be compared to the Manichean 'Father of Light' and the five aeons. Cf. H. Hoffmann, *Die Religionen Tibets*, Freiburg 1956, pp. 40-42.

background, just as some hesitant translations acted similarly in China. Perhaps the Western paradise of Amitābha indicates a truly Western origin of Amidism itself. In any case, it can be said of the contact with the merchants that it brought East and West a great deal nearer to each other. The extent of Maitreyanism at that time, from the borders of North Korea to those of Iran and Turkestan still bears witness to this.[1]

Two other favourable conditions which contributed to the success of the above mentioned three monks lay in the field of religion. The first is certainly to be found in the terrific enthusiasm for translation which had characterised Chinese Buddhism up to this point. As a result of this, even at that time, almost all of the Buddhist canons had been translated. Thereby the monks had gained access to a superfluity of material. We shall point out later that some of these were not chosen for their specifically Buddhist content, but rather those translations which reflected more of the Shamanist mentality of the Chinese northern frontier peoples. The Buddhist *sūtras* were not important to these peoples as genealogies of Indian Buddhism, but as improved formulations of their own opinions.

Tsui Chi[2] points out yet another condition. Owing to all the treachery and wars of the 'barbarians', the deeply rooted '*diesseits*' belief (belief in the present) of the North Chinese had become fairly blunted. Happiness and peace were no longer achievable for the Chinese, to whom this life on earth meant everything. Here only a new theory could bring salvation and compensation. This consisted in their gradual looking forward to an 'earthly' life, which must be possible somewhere, and which lay beyond the reach of barbarian despots. Thus these Chinese were actually prepared for the Maitreyanistic and Amidist belief in heaven.

All the tendencies, of which we have indicated a few, demanded people who could inplement them from a religious point of view. The one who had done the most is undoubtedly Fo-t'u-teng, 仏圖澄,[3] the teacher of Tao-an. He especially owed his popularity and wide

---

[1] Cf. W. Baruch, "Maitreya d'après les sources de Sérinde", *R.H.R.*, vol. 132, 1946, pp. 67-90.

[2] Cf. Tsui Chi, *Histoire de la Chine et de la Civilisation Chinoise*, Paris 1949, p. 111.

[3] For his biography see Arthur Wright, "Fo-t'u-teng", *H.J.A.S.*, vol. 11, 1948, pp. 312-371; E. Zürcher, op. cit., pp. 181 ff.

influence to his very close contacts with the Central Asian merchants who came to North China. This was not too difficult for him, as he—in contrast to the two other monks Tao-an and Hui-Yüan—was not a Chinese but a Central Asian and Sogdian. Distant travels had already carried him to Kashmir in his youth. Amongst the common people he was known as a great worker of miracles.[1] This 'miracle-worker', who was not a Shaman but a soothsayer, incorporated from the year 310 until his death in 349 everything concerning Buddhism which might be found in the North.

We do not know much more about this Fo-t'u-teng, who resided from 310 on at the court of the Hsiung-nu rulers Shih Lo, 石勒, and Shih Hu, 石虎, than the general description by Zürcher, who sees in him "one of the most interesting and bizarre personalities of early Chinese Buddhism." [2] Nevertheless, we believe that many of those interesting and bizarre occurrences have been provided merely by the pens of his biographers. Many of the miracles ascribed to him describe his position in popular belief rather than his own reality. His pecularity was mythologised in these miracles.

The rapid conversion of the North to Buddhism is to be ascribed to his practical magic, whereby he foresaw even military occurrences, such as the coming of the Hsiung-nu enemies, the Hsien-pi.[3] Many authors are inclined to belittle his importance for Buddhism, as though he had been merely a mass converter, with little penetration. These authors, however, do not do him justice by viewing him only from their scriptural and dogmatic Buddhism.[4] Actually, he was a person who had a greater interest in the practical experience and the devotional aspects than in the exegesis of the *sūtras*, even of the Mahāyāna *Prajñāpāramitās*.[5] His influence on North Chinese popular Buddhism was not comparable to that of exegetes and translators. He was more prophetic and charismatic. It is here, therefore, that the explanation of his success lies. Another consequence was that more than ten thousand pupils followed him from all parts of Central Asia and even from India. As a result he con-

---

[1] For these miracles see Arthur Wright, op. cit., pp. 337, 338, 339, 353.

[2] Op. cit., p. 181.

[3] Cf. A. Wright, op. cit., p. 361.

[4] Cf. A. Wright, op. cit., p. 325: "had he reached there at a less disturbed time, he would no doubt have become a great translator and exegete".

[5] E. Zürcher, op. cit., p. 183.

verted the entire province of Chung-chou, 中州,[1] to Buddhism and 893 temples founded by him could be found. However, one should not ascribe all of these successes entirely to him. We have already pointed out that, in Fo-t'u-teng's time, under the oppression of the Huns and other Hu, a kind of Messianism had arisen amongst the Chinese people of the northern territories. This explains how various rebelling Chinese leaders put themselves at the head of the opposition against the Hsiung-nu under the title 'Crown-prince of Buddha'. They contended that they, by themselves, had come from the great West (litt.: the great Ch'in) in order to save China (litt.: the little Ch'in).[2] Later such leaders were to say of themselves that they were Maitreya, the genuine Crown-prince of Buddha.[3] These Messianic slogans, inspired by their own nationalism, certainly drew many to Buddhism. Such conversions therefore also contributed a great deal to the final victory of these Maitreyas over the Hsiung-nu who, as a result of this religious fanaticism, were revengefully exterminated. The mass conversions ascribed to Fo-t'u-teng certainly had something to do with this nationalistic Messianism, although precisely what can no longer be traced.

Whether this Fo-t'u-teng was a genuine Shaman is hard to tell, as too few definite facts are known about him from which this might be deduced. Nevertheless, he did interact as a kind of Shaman on the Chinese and non-Chinese, because very many of them recognised his spiritual leadership. That Chinese followed him can only be explained by the fact that he—himself a foreigner—nevertheless had absorbed the Chinese ideology concerning the holy and the good of this life. The non-Chinese recognised their own North Asiatic religious opinions in him. For them he certainly counted as a Shaman. If one does not accept this, then the extensive support he received remains inexplicable.

Now it is hard to reconcile with this some opinions which hold that Fo-t'u-teng was specialised in the *Prajñāpāramitā* literature.[4] The actual hub of the *Prajñāpāramitā sūtras* is formed by the

---

[1] Ibid.

[2] Ibid.

[3] See previous chapter, p. 140.

[4] E. Link, "Biography of Shih Tao-an", *T.P.* XLVI, 1958, p. 7, note 6, writes: "Judging from the studies pursued by the disciples of Fo-t'u-teng, it would seem that the latter's specialisation lay in the Prajñā-pāramitā literature".

thesis which is unacceptable to most Chinese, namely that of the unreality of (earthly) phenomena.[1] We do not wish to deny that he was aware of these works, but nevertheless believe that he must have found these incompatible with the spirit of the peoples amongst whom he laboured. His own mentality was—vide his success—too closely interwoven with that of China. Though he might be a monk, he was equally a North Asian. It is therefore obvious that a sorcerer such as he chose from the entire arsenal of Buddhist literature only that in which he recognised his own North Asiatic mentality. He used the Buddhist writings in a way very similar to that in which most of our Western theologians utilise Holy Scripture. Just as little as we can nowadays expect it from our theologians, could it be expected of Fo-t'u-teng that he would get madly excited about something that lay entirely outside the framework of the opinions of those whom he encountered daily. As our own theologians render theology up-to-date and actual, French or German, he similarly made Buddhism East Asiatic. At the same time he felt no need to return continually to the old *sūtras* or to the original. Buddhists are inevitably not Protestants or Roman Catholics, who continually have to conform to Holy Writ. Additionally, they recognise no supreme authority which would compel them to do so. The real service Fo-t'u-teng did to Buddhism did not, therefore, lie in the fact that he was a great scholar, but that he, as a link between Buddhism and other North Asiatic philosophies, was the first to release a hitherto unknown mass reaction of the people towards Buddhism.

Fo-t'u-teng's work was continued after his death in 349 by his pupil Tao-an, 道安, (317-385). He has a vast reputation as a translator, compiler and commentator on various Hīnayāna and Mahāyāna *sūtras*.[2] He did not, however, stop at that, but even attempted to reconcile the doctrine of *hsüan-hsüeh* and of the *Prajñāpāramitās*.[3] He was extremely suited to this, because he, also as a Buddhist, had never kept himself apart from Taoist works. Nevertheless,

---

[1] For the doctrine of the *Prajñā-pāramitā*, see Erich Frauwallner, *Philosophie des Buddhismus*, Berlin 1956, pp. 149, 150; H. Zimmer, op. cit., p. 324.

[2] Cf. Genjun Sasaki, op. cit., pp. 503-504; E. Zürcher, op. cit., pp. 186-187; O. Franke, op. cit., p. 293, calls him one of the first, perhaps the first Chinese monk to be tutored by Indian teachers.

[3] Cf. E. Zürcher, op. cit., pp. 190-194.

he did not get much further than an attempt. Zürcher says of this: [1] "Tao-an's concept seems to be a mixture of the Taoist idealised *tohu-va-bohu* . . . and the Mahāyāna concept of the true nature of all Dharmas, which is empty by its own nature. He still contrasts 'fundamental non-being' with 'final being',[2] and seeks to reach the one, by excluding the other form in mind and in this he still fails to realise the absolute identity of emptiness and phenomena, of *nirvāṇa* and *saṁsāra*, a truth which only dawned on the Chinese exegetes after the introduction of the Mādhyamika treatises by Kumārajīva and his school." He did not, therefore, succeed in finding a suitable link between Buddhism and Chinese ideology, or in making this in any way saleable to the Chinese intelligentsia.

Nevertheless there is one aspect in which he differed genuinely from other predecessors. Owing to this he became a key figure in East Asiatic Buddhism. His personal Buddhist convictions were namely not dependent on the solution of the above mentioned incompatibilities but much more on his Maitreya beliefs. This was expressed in 370 when he, together with many other pupils, made the vow before the image of Maitreya to enter the Maitreya heaven, inhabited by the Tuṣita gods. Some opinions are inclined to connect this vow with his translation activity.[3] This is, however, but one of the many aspects of this vow, which contains far more. It is impossible to separate the actual contents from Maitreyanism. In the centre Maitreya stands, not as an exegete, but as Buddha of the future. With this we do not doubt that in many *sūtras* he is accounted primarily as an exegete [4] and secondarily as the inspirer of the Mahāyāna authors Maitreyanātha and Asaṅga.[5] On the

[1] Op. cit., p. 192.

[2] Cf. p. 157.

[3] Cf. E. Zürcher, op. cit., p. 194; Genjun Sasaki, op. cit., pp. 503, 504.

[4] For instance, compare his role in the *Lotus sūtra*, Dover Edition, New York 1963, its introduction by Max Müller, pp. 4 ff., further pp. 286 ff.; pp. 328 ff.

[5] Cf. Jean Filliozat, op. cit., pp. 379 and 573; E. Abegg, op. cit., p. 33. Other famous monks and authors who saw him were Buddhabhadra, Dharmadatta, Vasumitra, et al. Cf. P. Démiéville, 'La Yogācāra-bhūmi de Saṃgharakṣa", *B.E.F.E.O.*, XLIV, 1947-1950, Paris-Hanoi 1951,pp. 378-383. Asaṇga describes how he saw Maitreya in, i.a., his *Prakaraṇāryaśāsana-śāstra*, op. cit., p. 384. These relations between Asaṅga and Maitreya were further described by Paramārtha, Sthiramati and K'uei-ki, op. cit., pp. 385 ff. The reorganizer of the Hossō-*shū*, Hsüan-tsang, had great respect for

basis of this, this vow certainly had something to do with Tao-an's translations. However, this does not exhaust the contents of his vow. It was primarily directed towards the saviour Maitreya. This is shown by the fact that Tao-an made the vow to achieve the Tuṣita heaven himself, where Maitreya sits between the Tuṣita gods.[1]

This doctrine of salvation of Maitreya is described in various Maitreya *sūtras* [2] of which Tao-an certainly knew the oldest trans-

---

Maitreya, op. cit., p. 388. He also, moreover, was reborn in the Tuṣita heaven. Cf. E. Abegg, op.cit., p. 32.

[1] The Tuṣita heaven was originally one of the heavenly realms over which the ruler Saṃtuṣita reigned. Moreover, it became a kind of limbo from which future Buddhas descended to earth. Cf. Willibald Kirfel, *Symbolik des Buddhismus*, Stuttgart 1959, p. 26. Kirfel has described the place of this heaven in the *devaloka* more circumstantially, op. cit., pp. 25 ff. É. Lamotte gives a clear diagrammatical survey of this, op. cit., p. 35.

There is a great difference between the Tuṣita heaven and Sukhāvatī. The former is an earthly heaven, accessible to all. The *devaputra* form Maitreya's following, gods from the *kāmadhātu*, the lowest level of the *devaloka*. Cf. É. Lamotte, op. cit., p. 35. These are to accompany Maitreya on his arrival on earth. Cf. P. Démiéville, op. cit., p. 394. On the other hand, Sukhāvatī is not a heaven for everyone. Hsüan-tsang named this a genuine: 淨土, *tsing-t'u*, 'Pure Land'. It is destined only for the bodhisattvas of the highest *bhūmi*. Cf. P. Démiéville, op. cit., p. 389. Therefore Sukhāvatī is of a very different order to the Chinese heavens and the heaven of the Tuṣitas. Hsüan-tsang considered the latter merely as: 穢土, *hui-t'u*, 'Impure Land'. Sukhāvatī exists in a genuinely heavenly Paradise, "qui rompt le cadre de cosmologie normale". Cf. P. Démiéville, op. cit., p. 395. Marc Aurel Stein discovered a picture of the Tuṣita heaven, which apparently consisted of nothing other than a distant place on earth, therefore a Chinese heaven. Cf. E. Abegg, op. cit., pp. 35, 36. Many Chinese authors later placed Sukhāvatī on the same level as the heaven of the Tuṣitas. Cf. P. Démiéville, op. cit., p. 393. This was to cause its expansion in East Asia into a heaven for all.

In the Greek and Roman religions too, similar concepts are to be found concerning a horizontal, earthly, or subterranean Hades and a vertical astral heaven. The soul reached the astral heaven in stages—varying from 3 to 7 or 8—by ridding itself in each planetary sphere of the powers and forces which it had borrowed from, for example, the moon, Venus, and Mars sphere. Cf. F. Cumont, *Lux Perpetua*, Paris 1949, pp. 185-188. The hereafter was seen horizontally in: "notre terre parce qu'elle est le plus bas des cercles cosmiques". Cf. F. Cumont, op. cit., p. 204. This horizontal belief in Hell comprised both the fields of the Blessed as well as the place where the wicked were punished. Cf. F. Cumont, op. cit., pp. 189-234.

[2] For all of these Maitreya manuscripts and the five *Maitreyavyākaraṇa* see É. Lamotte, op. cit., pp. 778 ff.

lation, namely the *Mi-lo-hsia-shêng ching,* 彌勒下生経. Namely, this *sūtra* was translated in 308 by the Indo-Scythian Dharmarakṣa (±230-308), who came from Tunhuang, 敦煌.[1] That happened in the same Ch'ang-an where Tao-an had resided since 379. In this town this translator, later praised by Tao-an as the greatest translator of Mahāyāna, had founded a school with several thousand pupils who came from all parts of Asia and even from India. The *sūtra* translated by him describes Maitreya's advent on earth, his *bodhi* under the *bodhi* tree and the salvation of humanity by means of the threefold preaching. All of that could only happen in the era after ours. That is in the tenth period of the second of the (in total three) *kalpas,*[2] which cover the entire happenings of the world. Therefore that event would take place approximately 56 milliard years after Śākyamuni's *nirvāṇa*. From other *sūtras* also the translator Tao-an learnt to know that Maitreya was the Buddha of the future, because he is to be found as such in the *Āgama* and the *Nikāya.*[3]

[1] This was situated at the entrance of the Tarim basis, and was renowned for its old library. Cf. H. Hoffmann, op. cit., p. 4.

[2] The Buddhist cosmic outlook, in which Maitreya takes his place as future Buddha, covers many *kalpas,* which, as his time draws nearer, become continually shorter. *Kalpa*—originally a compromise solution between the tales of creation of the *Upanishads* and the infinity of the *saṁsāra*—encompasses the existence of the entire universe, including the gods. This can also be found, i.a., in the *Bhagavadgīta*; cf. S. Radakrishnan, *Indian Philosophy,* London 1929, vol. 1, pp. 513, 514. This system of the *kalpas* was adopted by Buddhism. Cf. J. Filliozat, op. cit., p. 528 (paragraph 2265). Originally it constituted the cosmic chronology of Brahmanism. Cf. Alain Daniélou, op. cit., p. 383. The duration of these *kalpas* in Chinese and Japanese Maitreyanism is described by Harper H. Coates and Ryugaku Ishizuka, *Honen, The Buddhist Saint,* Tōkyō, 1930, p. 308.

Concerning his date of birth— in this text we have indicated the mahāyānistic chronology—the various manuscripts do not agree. It is said in the *Nikāya* and the *Āgama* concerning this: "When the lives of man have reached a length of 80.000 years, the Lord Maitreya will be born into the world as a saint and one who is wholly enlightened". Cf. É. Lamotte, op. cit., p. 777. According to these sources his advent was none too close. A Singalese calculation contrives the year 4457 A.D. for this. According to the *Anāgatavaṃsa,* mentioned in footnote 5 on p. 163, this advent will only take place after millions of years have passed. Cf. E. Abegg, op. cit., p. 32.

Concerning the number of Buddhas which, just as Maitreya, are still to appear during our *kalpa,* the sources also disagree. According to later Mahāyāna texts, our present-day *kalpa* should have, after Maitreya, not five other Buddhas, but 996. Cf. E. Abegg, op. cit., pp. 31, 32.

[3] See our comments in footnote 5 on p. 162. Maitreyanism belongs to the Hī-

However private the circle in which Tao-an made his vow, it is nevertheless apparent that he admitted of that Messianism which Maitreya had already incorporated in India and Ceylon [1] and which, at Tao-an's time, already embraced all of the frontier territories of China. Thus many survivals of an earlier Maitreya cult have been found in Central Asia.[2] Perhaps here he had become the Buddhist answer to a cult of the Iranian god Mithra and responded to Messianic expectations which were very much alive in Iran and India.[3]

---

nayāna Buddhism not only by virtue of these texts but also in its origin. This is also one of the reasons why it was ousted by Amidism, which is Mahāyāna Buddhism. Maitreyanism enjoyed great popularity amongst the Hīnayāna school of the Sarvāstivādin, who were narrowly concerned with the origin of the later Mahāyāna Yogācāra school. Cf. E. Conze, op. cit., p. 116. According to W. Baruch, op. cit., p. 67, both, Maitreyanism and the school of the Sarvāstivādin, had a mutual cradle in Kashmir. This Hīnayāna origin clarifies their mutual opposition to Amidism. P. Démiéville, op. cit., p. 397, says of these two:

"Les conceptions relatives à Maitreya, attestées à la même époque et pour la même région, réflètent le même stade d'évolution doctrinale: elles sont, elles aussi, à chéval sur les deux Véhicules". Despite this, Maitreya continued to take a prominent place, also amongst other Mahāyāna Buddhas. Cf. W. Kirfel, op. cit., pp. 31, 47, and 52.

[1] Cf. É. Lamotte, op. cit., pp. 786, 787.

[2] As far as this cult is concerned, according to various Chinese monks there were several Maitreya images in India at the beginning of our era, which were highly respected. According to Fa-hien there was a Maitreya image in the area of Darel or Darda on the Indus, which was more than 80 ells high. On *uposatha* days this gave forth a light which was visible far abroad. Hsüan-tsang also mentions a Maitreya image on the banks of the Indus which seems to date from the third century B.C. and the days of king Aśoka. It was made, just as the other one, by an artist who had first himself ascended to the Tuṣita heaven in order to discover Maitreya's appearance. According to him, when the erection of this statue was started, the doctrine of Buddhism also began to flow towards Central Asia and China. Buddhist missionaries also carried Maitreya images. The conversion of a country or a district was begun by erecting such a Maitreya image.

Though these images were scarcely distinguishable from those of other Buddhas, Śākyamuni for instance, despite all of the foregoing and the trips to the Tuṣita heaven, nevertheless a specific type of Maitreya image originated in the art of Gandhāra. This reached its peak in the second and third centuries A.D. Data from Chinese pilgrims show that the Maitreya cult had achieved full development in the fifth century. In it standard exclamations to Maitreya were also used. Cf. E. Abegg, op. cit., pp. 33-36.

[3] We have already indicated in footnote 5 on pp. 160 ff. that the starting point of the Maitreya doctrine was in India. It is therefore improbable that

In this he had, as a kind of supreme deity, far exceeded his original function of exegete. At the time of Tao-an this devotion did not appear to dwell only among the common people, but also in monkish circles. The latter could not in this deny their Chinese nature. Their own religious aspirations demanded such a Maitreya cult rather than any other abstruse speculations. Hence, in Tao-an's case, this cult can just as easily be considered as a fruition of his earlier (Shaman's) practice in Yeh.[1]

After Hsiang-yang, 襄陽, was conquered in 379 by Fu Chien, Tao-an accompanied this ruler to his capital Ch'ang-an. Just as had been the case previously with other rulers, here too he became Fu Chien's principal adviser as well as the adviser of all the others who were ordered by this ruler to consult him. Tao-an succeeded in making Fu Chien an eastern Constantine who disseminated Tao-an's doctrine to the borders of his realm. This Buddhism must have been little other than Maitreyanism which was equally widespread at that time; or at least they were very closely interconnected. We

---

it underwent Persian influences in its eschatological aspects. (J. Filliozat, op. cit., p. 537, opposes E. Conze, op. cit., p. 111 in this.) E. Abegg, op. cit., p. 32, says: "Wenn dem gegenüber schon vermutet worden ist, dass im Namen Maitreya der iranische Licht-und Freundschaftsgott Mithra stecke, so könnte dies nur im Sinne eines sekundären Angleichung verstanden werden, aus der Zeit, da auf persichem Gebiet tatsächlich Berührungen der buddhistischen Messiasvorstellungen mit Gedanken der iranischen Lichtreligion und der zarathustrischen Eschatologie bestanden; aber eine ursprüngliche Ableitung des Namens Maitreya von Mithra verbietet schon sein Vorkommen im Dîgha-Nikâya, der zu den ältesten und im wesentlichen schon in die Zeit des Buddha zurückgehenden Schriften des Kanons gehört."

Though its origin is therefore Indian, Maitreyanism nevertheless was incorporated together with Persian and other influences in the religous developments of Central Asia at the beginning of our era. This led to several kinds of syncretism. Thus, in Manichean texts, "Mithras invictus" is mentioned together with "Jesus, Son of God" and 'Maitreya Ajīta", who were all fused into each other. Cf. É. Lamotte, op. cit., pp. 784, 785. Also the Maitreyan confessions of sins served as a model for the Manichean confessions in the caves of Tunhuang. Here Maitreya was replaced by the "Emissary of Light, Mani". On the other hand, these texts continued calling Mani a *dhyānibuddha*, from whom Maitreya emanated. Cf. W. Baruch, op. cit., p. 77. It is not probable that there was also a process in the opposite direction, as Manicheism reached China fairly late. Cf. Geo Widengren, *Mani und Manichäismus*, Stuttgart 1961, p. 134. In any case, this is a good example of the way in which the great religious trends on the Asian continent fructified each other.

[1] Cf. E. Zürcher, op. cit., p. 181.

have already pointed out that here especially the necessity of visualising Buddhist doctrine in images was pronounced. Tao-an saw a means of facilitating his *dhyāna*, which was aimed at Maitreya, in such images.[1] Such images could far more easily popularise Buddhism for the masses than any kind of *sūtra* reading. With regard to native religions these images gave the beliefs of the masses a firm grip. Now it was Fu Chien in particular who often donated such images. Thus not only Tao-an [2] but also the ruler of Koguryŏ, Sosurim (Chin.: Hsiao-shou-lin, 小獸林, 371-384) received images from him in 372. These images were probably closely connected with Maitreyanism, which continually increased its influence on Tao-an's life. This is particularly shown at the end of his life. For instance on the 22nd. of February 385 he was supposed to have seen Maitreya himself in the Tuṣita heaven. It is known of his pupil Chu Sêng-fu, 竺僧輔, that he spread the Maitreya belief in Hupei, 河北.[3] In all of this Tao-an had taken care that Maitreyanism was built on the initial foundation of a vague and anonymous Buddhism.

The third monk in whom the Northern Chinese reaction of Buddhism on the mentality of the Northern Chinese people manifested itself was Hui-yüan, 慧遠, (334-416).[4] Although he, just as did Tao-an, respected the Tibetan dynasty of Fu Chien, he did not, however, wish to dwell in proximity to these rulers. Therefore he withdrew to the mountain Lu-shan, 盧山. In 386 he founded his own community of monks there. Thus the temples and monasteries of the Lu-shan became a counterpart for many Taoist monasteries. Moreover, many Chinese intellectuals sought sanctuary here from the excesses of the barbarian domination. As a result of this all kinds of non-Buddhist opinions, Taoism amongst them, also penetrated the monasteries of this mountain. Thus the Lu-shan expanded into a focal point for laymen and monks, Buddhists and those of other opinions. This certainly hastened the formation of the Buddhism born from Chinese and Hu mentality.

In 402 Hui-yüan made a vow, together with 123 monks and lay-

---

[1] For this veneration of images, see footnote 2 on p. 171, E. Zürcher, op. cit., pp. 223 ff.

[2] Cf. E. Zürcher, op. cit., p. 188.

[3] Cf. E. Zürcher, op. cit., p. 204.

[4] Cf. E. Zürcher, loc. cit.

men, amongst whom were various learned Confucians,[1] in front of the statue of Amitābha,[2] to attain the Western Paradise or Sukhāvatī. This devotion was an extension of Tao-an's Maitreyanism. It was indeed a fairly similar answer to the same Messianic expectations which was given according to a similar procedure. Only Amitābha, with his own heaven, had taken the place of Maitreya, with his Tuṣita heaven. Only it was even more Chinese and Central Asiatic in character. According to some Amitābha, 'eternal glory',[3] was merely the Hindu and Buddhist replica of an Iranian sun god.[4] Others consider him to be the Buddhist answer to Manicheism; hence the five *tathāgatas*, to which Amitābha belonged, and those which emanated from *ādibuddha*, the arch-Buddha,[5] were supposedly connected with the Manichean Father of Light and his five aeons.[6] However, all these opinions cannot give a satisfactory explanation of the actual origin of the Light Buddha Amitābha; therefore his origin remains just as misty. We can only say of him that in fact he was the answer to the same Messianic expectations as Maitreya. Moreover, as Amitābha, he had much in common with the sun and light deities which were to be of great support especially amongst the North Asiatic, Korean and Japanese peoples. Here especially belief in him was not considered separately from his other name, Amitāyus, possessor of eternal life. It would not surprise us if, in Japan, he was considered as a kind of Buddhist *musubi*. In any case the Japanese Amida stands for both terms.[7]

The idea of Sukhāvatī was really the idealisation of the ten stages, the *daśabhūmika* which the bodhisattva himself had to follow on his path to the *bodhi*. Hence it lay on a higher level and was also

---

[1] Cf. O. Franke, op. cit., p. 298.

[2] According to an old tradition, this occurred before the images of the three saints of the 'West'. Those 'saints' were: Amitābha, Avalokiteśvara and Mahāsthāmaprāpta. See O. Franke, loc. cit.

[3] Cf. J. Filliozat, op. cit., pp. 569, 570.

[4] Cf. É. Lamotte, op. cit., p. 551.

[5] This relationship between *ādibuddha* and *tathāgatas* may be found as described by H. von Glasenapp, *Buddhismus und Gottesidee*, pp. 478, 479.

[6] Cf. H. Hoffmann, op. cit., p. 4.

[7] For this see the extensive article by Matsumae Takeshi, "Taiyō no fune to tokoyo-shinkō" (The Sun Ship and the *tokoyo* Belief), *K.G.Z.*, vol. LXII, February, March, 1961, nos. 2, 3, pp. 23-43.

For the two properties of Amida here mentioned, see W. Gundert, *Japanische Religionsgeschichte*, pp. 83 ff.

more respected than the more 'vulgar' [1] heaven of the Tuṣitas of Maitreyanism. The latter removed itself, moreover, too far into a very distant future. Furthermore, the theory of the Western Paradise could also more easily be brought into conjunction with the belief in paradise already extant in China. This is proved by the repeated mention in China's oldest tales of the immortality gardens of the queen Hsi wang-mu, 西王母. This word Hsi wang-mu means little else than 'Queen of the West'. Later Liu An, 劉安, even extended this theory of the Western Paradise with his assurance that, above the K'un-lun mountain, in Paradise, immortal and divine beings dwelt who were ruled by the T'ai-ti, i.e. the Great Emperor.[2] This is further confirmed in one of the nine Shaman songs, translated by A. Waley. Namely in the eighth song there is a mention of this same K'un-lun, 崑崙, mountain. This mountain particularly gained its mythical significance from the fact that the Yellow River rises on its slopes. The Shamans who climbed it symbolically said, amongst other things: [3]

"With you I wandered down the nine rivers;
A whirlwind rose and the waters barred us with their waves.
We rode in a water-chariot with a wing of lotus leaf
Drawn by two dragons, with griffins to pull at the sides.
I climb K'un-lun and look in all directions."

---

[1] Cf. L. Wieger, *Amidisme chinois et japonais*, 1928, p. 23; H. de Lubac, *Amida*, Paris 1955, pp. 42 ff.

One can search in vain the doctrine of *daśabhūmi*, or the ten degrees, for the paradise character which so specifically belonged to the heaven of the Tuṣitas or Sukhāvatī. Compare, for instance, the *Lotus sūtra* description of the Tuṣita heaven (Dover Edition, p. 436: "He who writes the Dharma-paryâya of the Lotus of the True Law with undistracted attention shall be supported by the hands of a thousand Buddhas from face to face. He shall not sink down into a state of wredchedness, and after disappearing from this world he shall enter into the company of the Tuṣita-gods, where the Bodhisattva Mahâsattva Maitreya is residing, and where, marked by the thirty-two sublime characteristics, surrounded by a host of Bodhisattvas, and waited upon by hundred thousands of myriads of *kotis* of heavenly nymphs he is preaching the law.") to that of the ten *bhūmi* by N. Dutt, "The Fundamental Principles of Mahāyāna", *Pr. de B.*, pp. 324-327, or by Filliozat, op cit., pp. 571, 572. As far as the 'orthodoxy' of Sukhāvatī is concerned, see the Buddhist parallels to this in H. de Lubac, op. cit., pp. 40 ff.

[2] Cf. J. J. M. de Groot, *Universismus*, Berlin 1918, pp. 124, 126.

[3] A. Waley, op. cit., p. 47.

It is clearly apparent from this passage that K'un-lun, and hence the Western Paradise, was connected with Shamanism. It is interesting that in this mountain the latter was connected with the old, pre-Shaman Chinese symbols of the religious world: mountain, source and water, which, in Chinese art, often form the definitive elements of the scene.[1] In these three a kind of sacred marriage of the earth with the heaven was achieved. They are, moreover, the three symbols of the Tao, which was born of the marriage of *yin* and *yang*.[2] The scaling of this mountain smacked of the ascension of the Old Testament Shaman Elijah, who also drove in a heavenly chariot.[3] This text illustrates the extent to which Shamanism and belief in heaven encountered each other as two successive phases of development, of which, much later, Amidism was to be the last stage. Indeed, the latter's Western Paradise lay in the same line as the K'un-lun. For this latter reason Maitreya's less Chinese heaven of the Tuṣitas eventually had to give way to Sukhāvatī. These backgrounds illustrate that the devotion, which Hui-yüan vouchsafed, formed the conclusion of religious opinions which had long existed in China outside Buddhism.

Hui-yüan's practice was much more suited to laymen than that of Tao-an. It could be practised while remaining at home.[4] In the prescribed ceremonial *dhyāna* exercises occurred which did not demand vast exertions. As a result of the mercy, or *bhakti*, of Amitābha all lengthy procedures were put aside which had been required until then, in order to achieve one of the *daśabhūmika*. In this, Amitābha's *bhakti*, more so than in Maitreya's case, took the place of intercession for mercy by the Shaman. Thus the intermediary's function of the Shaman was set aside. It was supplanted by Amitābha himself and by the collective exertions of all those with whom

---

[1] This has even been emphasized very highly in the build and structure of the celestial altar at Peking. Cf. J.J.M. de Groot, op. cit., pp. 190, 192 ff.

[2] Cf. J. J. M. de Groot, op. cit., pp. 7 ff.

[3] Cf. 2 Kings 2.11.

[4] The actual basic principle of this cult is the *nien-fu*, 念仏, Jap.: *nenbutsu*. This *nien-fu* is based on the *Pan-chou-san-wei*, 般舟三昧, Jap.: *Han-ya-sammai*, which had already been consulted by Hui-yüan, and consisted of recalling Amitābha while meditating, as if he were present. This led to the necessity of an Amitābha image. This *nenbutsu* was later simplified to a single exclamation: Namu Amida-Butsu. Cf. E. Zürcher, op. cit., pp. 219-221.

the vow had been taken. Thus a circle of friends came into being who, together, wished to realise the path of Sukhāvatī.

This Amidism, propagated since 402 as the Chinese sublimation of Maitreyanism by Hui-yüan, resulted that same year in the first Chinese Buddhist school, the Pê-lien-shê, 白蓮社, the White Lotus Society.[1] Later 'Pure Land Schools' all contended that they descended from this.[2] Since Hui-yüan Amidism began to develop in the steps of Maitreyanism to "the popular devotion directed to Amitābha and his sensual paradise."[3] Both in China and in Japan it succeeded in exceeding and forcing aside Maitreyanism. More than any other Buddhist group it continued from that time on until the present day to maintain the greatest power of expansion. This huge expansion is owing only to its great similarity of formulation to the religious opinions of the Chinese border peoples.

Until now we have approached Maitreyanism and Amidism from the popular beliefs. Nevertheless, from the point of view of Buddhism, one question remains unanswered. This concerns the concurrence of these two Buddhist opinions with the individual Amitābha and Maitreya *sūtras*. These two groups of basic data indeed formed the constitution for both. They alone permit us to investigate the extent to which the East Asiatic conversions were also truly 'orthodox'. We have already indicated above how even Chinese translators and exegetes warped basic Buddhist concepts to their own Chinese way of thought. This was certainly even more the case amongst the ordinary people with regard to our two Buddhist groups. Therefore, on the basis of all we have said concerning the Chinese and North Asian mentality, all of those texts merely formed the framework around which in both cases individual forms of experience were to grow, in which specific national character and religious thought were amalgamated. This latter growth process must not be left unconsidered by maintaining a certain contempt for all kinds of 'unorthodox' syncretism. Immediately the popular mentality, which was still foreign to the genuine Buddhist, decided for (or against) Maitreyanism or Amidism it did not mean to say that these two were then experienced in accordance with the classic Maitreya and Amitābha texts. One must also

[1] Cf. E. Zürcher, op. cit., p. 219.

[2] For further details on this, cf. O. Franke, op. cit., p. 298.

[3] Cf. Léon Wieger S.J., *Vinaya, Monachisme et Discipline*, Leiden 1951, p. 101.

bear in mind that the old religions continued to exist as before. Maitreyanism and Amidism were not given a place in these as independent *systems* but as *elements* which, depending on the local situation, had contrived to capture a place *together* with these religions in the vision of East Asian and Shaman beliefs. Of the Indian cosmology, into which Śākyamuni projected his doctrine, little was preserved or remained. Though, indeed, the Buddhist foundation of the Four Noble Truths did not disappear, it was pushed into the background. Hence this doctrine became something which, according to von Glasenapp: "eine Form des Buddhismus darstellt, die dogmatisch, philosophisch, wie seinem Gefühlsgehalt nach von der alten Lehre völlig verschieden ist".[1]

Must one now go even further and say that this was no longer Buddhism? [2] It is certainly incorrect just to take certain Buddhist *sūtras*—analogous to Christianity—as a kind of scales on which all other later Buddhist developments must be weighed in order to be accounted at least as still being true Buddhism. Nevertheless this frequently happened. It is impossible to mention all of the names, often of Western Buddhologists, of those who have so immersed themselves in this literal Indian Buddhism that they were involuntarily inclined to measure any Buddhist group whatever only against the Indian and scriptural original. In addition, the individual capacity and mentality of the peoples who accepted this were not taken into account. Thus there was great danger that all kinds of Buddhism which existed only in books were projected onto those peoples.

This risk was great specifically in China and Japan as in these countries there was no inclination whatsoever to accord with the original.[3] The above mentioned 'scriptural mentality'—as we call it—has led to the repudiation, as being syncretisms and bastardisations, of various Buddhist sects which had so entirely integrated with the popular character that they had deviated noticeably from

[1] H. von Glasenapp, *Buddhismus und Gottesidee*, Wiesbaden 1954, p. 472. Cf. also L. Wieger, op. cit., p. 101: "Quant à l'Amidisme et au Tantrisme ils n'ont rien de commun avec le bouddhisme qu'ils ont supplanté".

[2] Cf. O. Franke, op. cit., p. 298.

[3] For instance, if one compares the so-called *kyōhan*, 教判, or the Buddhist criteria, with each other, with which later schools and sects attempted to outdo each other in Buddhism, then it becomes clearly apparent that a Mahāyāna Buddhist is more inclined to evolutionary thought and attaches more value to the latest developments than to the first link of a chain.

the original. In this it was not realised that no Buddhist—bearing in mind Tao-an and Hui-yüan—maintained such puritanical thoughts. The vast expansion of Buddhism, which has become the collecting centre of all kinds of religious forms and religions, does prove that in each integration of popular elements it sees an enrichment as well as an approach to new, as yet often undiscovered, human values. Hence one can only gain a proper approach to this Buddhism if one recalls the words of Fenollosa, which he wrote more than fifty years ago: [1]

"It is enough for scholars, who sometimes have a missionary bias, that Southern Buddhism, the 'Lesser Vehicle', being the older (and the easier to refute), must lie nearer to the original source, Śākyamuni himself and is therefore the only form that we need seriously study or consider, Northern Buddhism, they think, being derivative, revolutionary and corrupt, need be studied only as a perverse curiosity. The great truth which they forget is that Buddhism, like Christianity—and unlike Mohammedanism—has been an evolutionary religion, never content with old formalisms, but, filled with spiritual ardour, continually re-adapting itself to the needs of the human nature with which it finds itself in contact. Thus becoming Northern or positive Buddhism with the more vigorous Northern races in the North-West of India, it became still more positive, social and human with the great practical home-loving races of China and Japan."

3 *Buddhism of the North Chinese society*

In Fo-t'u-teng, Tao-an and Hui-yüan Buddhism of China's northern territories lost much of its anonymity. However, this did not owe its character solely to monks. Others have also contributed to this. In gaining its definitive form it owed just as much to laymen. As far as this is concerned the course of events in the North differed from that in the South, as in the North it did succeed in gaining a place in Chinese society. This occurred especially under the government of the T'opa rulers (386-581). Since this T'opa Buddhism was carried further, into Korea and Japan, it is important to know how it penetrated the various layers of T'opa society.

How did this take place? After its North Asiatic assimilation

[1] Ernest Fenollosa, *Epochs of Chinese and Japanese Art*, New York 1912, vol. I, p. 29.

process it here encountered the still latent Chinese Wu-ism as well as what Eberhard calls 'folk-Taoism'.[1] This latter was actually not much more than a continuation of the old rural fertility cult which encompassed magic, Shamanism and polytheism. To this the Shamanism of the non-Chinese must also be added. Here we must point out that this growth process was not achieved in the same way on the various levels of the population. This becomes comprehensible on considering the social structure of the T'opa realm. Namely, nobility and commonalty lived separate from each other. This division was widened owing to the racial differences between Chinese and non-Chinese aristocracy as well as the difference in the way of life between Chinese farmers and non-Chinese nomads. Therefore in the following pages we shall investigate the integration of Buddhism specifically in these individual groups.

a North Chinese aristocracy

We must say that the T'opa nobility was not very homogeneous. It was sub-divided into Chinese nobility and non-Chinese nobility. Among the latter one could encounter representatives of all of the tribes who had ever ruled the northern territories of China.[2] Shamanism was highly respected amongst them. It was very different among the Chinese aristocracy who demonstrated the same contempt towards it as did the writers of the *Wei chih* towards Himiko Shamanism. Therefore it preferred to attach itself to a kind of state Confucianism which was made up of a tangle of rules and regulations which were inclined more towards ethics than to religion. Here only the scrupulous 'rubricist' could find his way; and counted as a 'finished man'. He, however, who could not cope with it, "gehörte nicht zur Schicht".[3] As a purely legalistic brew this state Confucianism was poor in specific ideology. As a reaction, those who had been excluded and passed over were to reach out for another ideology which was the only one to counter it: Buddhism. The most attractive aspect of this was, for the latter group, in particular the (un-Chinese) fact that it terminated all inequality of race and social class. As a larger organisation it could sublimate

[1] Cf. W. Eberhard, *Das Toba-Reich Nord Chinas*, p. 237. See also the typification of this northern Buddhism in Zürcher, op. cit., p. 146.

[2] Cf. W. Eberhard, op.cit., p. 30.

[3] For the exposition which follows here, cf. W. Eberhard, op. cit., pp. 236 ff.

and compensate all kinds of inferiority complexes which resulted from this discrimination. Thus it could neutralise the '*Schichten-moral*' of the Confucianists.

Thus it can be understood that various non-Chinese rulers, as a reaction against the narrow-mindedness of their Chinese aristocratic subjects, gratefully accepted Buddhism, since philosophically this could still offer the most opposition to their legalistic Confucianism. As a means of political warfare it was more easily used than their own primitive Shamanism. This explains the fact that Buddhism during the first period of the T'opa reign, that is to say until the reign of the T'opa emperor Ming Yüan-ti, 明元帝 (409-423), could be used to render T'opa Shamanism fit for the salon at the courts of these rulers. In this court-Shamanism it was given a place beside Taoist and Wu-ist sorcery. Thus initially the Shamanism of these rulers, which was given individual shape in each tribe, was levelled up by Northern Buddhism. As a result of that the minor differences in mentality among other North Asiatics was so sublimated that a great mutual exchange of ideas became possible.

This was terminated by the chancellorship of the fiercely anti-Buddhist Chinese Ts'ui Hao (417-450).[1] At this time the T'opa rulers had already amalgamated with the Chinese groups in their realm to such an extent that they also were beginning to value belonging to the Confucian elite. Having achieved a higher social level they discovered that their Shamanism could no longer be presented in Chinese salons under a Buddhist garb.[2] From that time Buddhism once again began to separate itself from all kinds of T'opa additives. In the T'opa emperors it began to co-exist with Confucianism.

In this co-existence both began to take on an individual appearance. They became two modalities, supplementing each other, in the T'opa state. In this Buddhism formulated the religious and charismatic aspects of emperor and people, while Confucianism dealt more with the hierarchical and institutional aspects common to both. To this court etiquette also belonged. The fact that Confucianism at the T'opa court had succeeded in co-operating with Buddhism was mainly owing to the economic development of the T'opa realm. Namely, the Chinese farmer had taken up a definitively

[1] Cf. Lin Tsiu Sen, *China und Japan*, part I, pp. 137 ff.
[2] W. Eberhard, op. cit., p. 237.

privileged position over and above the T'opa steppe hunters. Hence Confucianism could no longer be ignored. However, it had gradually developed into a bureaucrats' morality. Therefore it was no longer an extensively worked out religious system. As a result of this mutual confrontation both began to lose their philosophical sharpness and depth.[1] Hence Eberhard could say of it: [2] "Der officielle Buddhismus wird eine harmlose Form der staatlichen Repräsentation." This last development in the T'opa realm is reminiscent of similar parallels in Japan. The two modalities of Buddhism and Confucianism were embodied in Japan by the Soga and the Nakatomi. There the emperors, desirous of incorporating the ideals of both, also attempted to make them into allies, which considerably undermined Buddhism.

The leaders of T'opa society, the rulers themselves, possessed, between Buddhism and Confucianism, just as did the Japanese emperors, a vast spiritual authority. This became specifically apparent when the 'chief monk' Tao-kao, 道高 (died after 416), arrived with the solemn declaration, obviously founded on the Buddhism of that time, that the T'opa ruler of his period was the living Maitreya. After this declaration he threw himself to the ground before him "as before a god".[3] It is clear that here we are not dealing with a procedure founded on the *sūtras* of Maitreya, as these *sūtras* promised his advent only after many millions of years. Rather, the monk Tao-kao behaved in accordance with the traditions which were alive in the T'opa popular beliefs themselves. As the tribal head he originally had high Shamanistic spiritual authority. In this one can find another proof of the fact that the northern peoples, just as the Chinese themselves, attempted to integrate Buddhism with their own religious world, without losing the latter.

Though these emperors called themselves Maitreya, it did not mean that they had entirely accepted Buddhism. Thus the idea of *saṁsāra* was inevitably lacking in their conceptions. This is proved by the Buddhist temples which the T'opa rulers had built from 398

---

[1] W. Eberhard, op. cit., pp. 238, 239.

[2] W. Eberhard, op. cit., p. 237.

[3] W. Eberhard, op. cit., p. 229. See Chapter II footnote 2 on p. 140. Also Empress Wu (684-705) of the T'ang dynasty called herself Maitreya. Cf. E. Abegg, op. cit., p. 36.

on in Yung-kang and four other places.[1] Their building put the people under severe pressure.[2] Amongst all of these temples those of Yung-kang took the first place. The unusual quality of these Buddhist temples is that they were built by the emperor "for himself and his ancestors".[3] All of these temples were hewn in caves just because the T'opa, as did the Turks, believed that their ancestors dwelt there.[4] Here all important decisions were discussed with the ancestors. It is known of Hsiao Wên-ti that he removed his capital to Loyang only after he had consulted them in the same year, namely 499. Hence these strikingly built monuments bear witness equally to Buddhism and to ancestor worship, which had pushed aside the idea of *saṁsāra*. This can also be seen in the many commemorative plaques which were hung as ex-votos everywhere in these temples. Here one can read the motives as to why not only the temples but also often statues higher than sixty foot of Maitreya, for instance, were hewn in the rocks. Amongst them there is the 40 foot, 60 ton Buddha image, in which more than 750 lbs. of gold had been melted, which Hsien Wên-ti, 獻文帝 (465-471), had cast in 470 and which must have required vast sums.[5] One of these commemorative plaques unveils why those monuments arose:[6] "We respectfully make and present this holy image in honour of the Buddhas, Bodhisattvas, and pray that all living creatures may obtain salvation, and particularly that the souls of our ancestors and relatives (names given) may find repose and release."

It is apparent from this text that Buddhas and Bodhisattvas were not so esteemed as those who had something to do with *bodhi*. Far rather they were considered as a kind of divinity who, in their mercy, were capable of guaranteeing the future of the believers in one of their heavens. This is also clear from a later funerary service such as the Urabon sacrifice for death which is respected in China and Japan even at the present day. According to Tsuda,[7] in the T'ang period (618-907) especially, particular sacrifices were made

---

[1] Cf. René Grousset, *Les Civilisations de l'Orient*, Tome III, *La Chine*, Paris 1930, pp. 180-190.

[2] W. Eberhard, op. cit., pp. 169-170.

[3] W. Eberhard, op. cit., p. 288.

[4] René Grousset, *La Face de l'Asie*, Paris 1955, p. 269.

[5] Lin Tsiu Sen, op. cit., p. 144.

[6] Arthur J. Wright, *Buddhism in Chinese History*, p. 59.

[7] Op. cit., p. 249, cf. footnote 1 on p. 159.

to Buddha himself, who, as a kind of deity, had to ensure the happiness of the dead in the hereafter.

Other motives also, which caused the emperors to build these temples, were not all the product of Buddhism. To these certainly belonged the desire to balance their own emperorship against that of the *T'ien-tzŭ*, the Sons of Heaven of the Southern Chinese realm. This was not expressed in a careless or arbitrary fashion. We have seen in the foregoing that they found the definition for this in the religious world of the T'opa themselves. There Shamanism, ancestor worship and Maitreyan Buddhism had their place. Thus one can visualise a contemporary, new interpretation of the originally Shamanistic role of leader in such T'opa rulers as Maitreya, which interpretation he enacted at the head of his tribe.

b The people of North China

We have seen in the foregoing how the imperial and aristocratic members of society gave Buddhism a North Asiatic appearance. Was this the case amongst the lower classes as well? It is difficult to trace all that happened here. It can be partially reconstructed from the history of the monasteries. We know of these that the social changes realised by the T'opa rulers also concerned the monastic population to a high degree. This was the case especially since the beginning of the fifth century when Buddhism became the official state religion. Though at first they had counted as a kind of preparation for the hereafter, since that time they became centres where courtiers and councillors were created. As the monasteries were initially open to everyone they gave many farmers the chance to advance themselves to becoming high statesmen. Hence monks of lowly descent could become a new elite. It is self-evident that this made the old nobility most uneasy. In various ways they gradually succeeded in blocking entry to the monasteries for the ordinary person and in gaining control of the most important offices within the monastery walls for themselves. This resulted in an undermining of the religious ideals of the monasteries. Finally nothing remained of the Buddhist ideal but hollow externals. In the famous Wei sculptures of the above mentioned cave-temples this was expressed in the rich drapery of the robes: "Le manteau monastique adoré en tant que tel." [1] Gradually celibacy was also

[1] René Grousset, *Les Civilisations de l'Orient*, Tome III, *La Chine*, p. 186.

abandoned as women were secretly smuggled into the monasteries and even secret chambers were reserved for them.[1] Thus the nobility contrived to continue their old way of life within the monastery walls. Particularly under the ruler Wên-ch'êng-ti, 文成帝 (452-465), they began to extend the power of the monasteries by incorporating the farmers' land as well. Instead of being serfs to the nobility these farmers became tenants of the monasteries. On the basis of their religious convictions they could be even more exploited than they were previously by their worldly leaders. This exploitation merely strengthened among the farmers the belief in release after death. Eberhard writes[2] that these lower Buddhist levels of society actually only began to fight back against the nobility when they no longer wanted to wait for their release until their future births and Messianic thoughts arose amongst them. We, however, are inclined to doubt whether this Buddhist theory of rebirth ever actually lived among this commonalty. Their Buddhism was too elementary. This theory only barely existed among most Chinese Buddhists.

Now what should we understand by those Messianic thoughts? We believe that they certainly had something to do with the ideas of later protagonists of Maitreyanism who, in the Sui, 隋 (581-618), and T'ang (618-907) periods, wished to realise the Tuṣita heaven on earth by means of rebellions.[3] Hence this Messianism must have been similar to the elevation of the T'opa rulers to Maitreya. Pronouncing the Chinese rebel leaders 'Crown Prince of Buddha' under the rule of Hsiung-nu tyrants indicates the same perspective. Hence we again arrive at Maitreyanism.

This development in the T'opa realm, which bordered on North Korea, illustrates that Buddhism in the fourth and fifth centuries there gained an entirely specific form, especially in the shape of Maitreyanism. At that time there was scarcely any mention of Amidism. Only after and during this East Asiatic 'incubation' could Buddhism continue its pilgrimage to Japan over the bridge

---

Involuntarily one is reminded of the Japanese *musubi* belief, which incorporated the spirits in the clothing. Cf. Chapter II, footnote of p. 107.

[1] Lin Tsiu Sen, op. cit., pp. 142 ff.

[2] Op. cit., p. 235.

[3] Cf. A. Wright, op. cit., p. 89: "The North in the period of disunion had seen numerous popular uprisings centered on this cult".

of the Korean peoples. We shall look at this more closely in the second part of this chapter.

Part Two

B KOREA, BRIDGE FROM CHINA TO JAPAN

At the beginning of this chapter we have already pointed out [1] that Japanese Buddhism followed the same path as did the 'imperial tribe' when invading Japan.[2] Namely, it did not arrive directly in Japan by sea from China. This appears from the fact that both Chinese and Japanese chronicles of the period of the arrival of Buddhism in Japan, i.e. the period between 503 and 600, register no single diplomatic contact between the two countries.[3] As the *Nihonshoki* of the sixth century expressly mentions 'the beginning of Buddhism' and other circumstances which indicate its commencement,[4] it is impossible that Buddhism should have arrived with the embassies prior to 503, mentioned by the Sung chronicles. Moreover, no single text of, or about, Japan, written before that date, mentions Buddhism. Furthermore, here the language and writing difficulties must not be lost sight of, which might have brought about such a contact on a religious level. Unavoidably, the Chinese were not always available to the Japanese, as was the case, for instance, in the northern territories of China, in order to elucidate the Buddhist manuscripts, which were already difficult and scarcely intelligible in their Chinese translations. These objections could only be cleared up by the activities of the Korean immigrants. However,

---

[1] Cf. pp. 143, 144.

[2] See Dr. E. Zürcher, *Het Boeddhisme*, Amsterdam 1961, map no. 9.

[3] The following dates may be found in the Chinese manuscripts concerning that period:
57 A.D.; 107 A.D.; 238 A.D.; 243 A.D.; 247 A.D.; 421 A.D.; 425 A.D.; 443 A.D.; 478 A.D.; 600 A.D.
Cf. Ryūsaku Tsunoda, op. cit., pp. 2-24 and Suematsu Yasukazu, op. cit., pp. 64-65 and p. 224. The dates 249, 266, 413, 426, 432, 451, 471, 480 and 503 A.D. of the Japanese sources (especially the *Nihonshoki*) are unreliable owing to the impossibility of dating data from these various periods. Hence authors do not agree. Compare, for instance, A. Wedemeyer, *Japanische Frühgeschichte*, pp. 90-98, Lin Tsui Sen, *China und Japan*, part I, pp. 174-176, and further Suematsu Yasukazu, loc. cit.

[4] For these texts see in particular the following chapter.

at that time these conditions for a dialogue with the Chinese had yet to be created by them.

Hence the path of Japan's oldest Buddhism first ran through Korea. Here it had entered from the Chinese frontier provinces. Hence on its arrival in Japan, Buddhism not only bore all the characteristics of the Chinese and northern Buddhism, but had, moreover, become Korean. Hence we shall also have to examine, after that of China, the further growth of Buddhism in the Korean peninsula. In this we must not stop at Buddhism. As Korean Buddhism is concerned here, we shall also have to take into account other characteristics as well.

A glance at the map is sufficient to convince us that Korea, as an offshoot of the East Asian continent—even more so than Kamchatka with the Kurile Islands—forms a natural bridge from China's northern territories to Japan's island realm. That which is indicated by Korean geography is also valid with regard to racial, political and religious aspects. In all of these aspects this country appears as a bridge, with a typical one-way traffic, which runs from north to south, from China to Japan. This is even apparent in Korean, where, according to Ch'oe Hyŏnbae, words such as front (*ap'*) equals south, and back (*twi*), north. That is indicative of the southern migration direction of these peoples.[1] The Korean bridge had one other characteristic: the differences with China and the northern peoples decrease towards the north, those with Japan are most limited in the southern part of Korea. All of this made Korea particularly suited to serve also as a bridge for Japanese Buddhism.

[1] The philologist Ch'oe Hyŏnbae compared the words 'before', 'behind', 'south' and 'north' to each other in Mongolian, Manchurian and Korean and reached the conclusion that here we are dealing with words which, at first sight, scarcely cause one to suspect a relationship between these languages. Now it is of interest that in all of these languages the concepts 'south' and 'before' were indicated by one and the same word. This is also the case with the concepts for 'north' and 'behind'. Thus these words betray the direction of travel of these peoples, which was towards the south.

Concepts	Mongolian	Manchurian	Korean
Before—south:	*ŏmunŏ*	*julŏrki*	*ap'* or *arp*
Behind—north:	*hoitu*	*amarki*	*tü*

Cf. Tschö Hyonbä (= Ch'oe Hyŏnbae), "Beziehungen zwischen Korea und Japan in alter Zeit", *Koreanica*, (Festschrift für Dr. A. Eckardt), Baden Baden 1960, p. 23. Cf. also on this subject Suematsu Yasukazu, op. cit., pp. 121, 143.

Therefore we shall examine more closely the aspects just mentioned, which prepared Japan's oldest Buddhism. Because the Korean immigrants conveyed this to Japan, we shall close this chapter with an appraisal of these immigrants.

a Korea: ethnologically and archaeologically

Considering its races and peoples, Korea formed a real connection between the continent and Japan. In the south particularly, the same—though not southern—pre-mongolian components formed, just as in pre-imperial Japan, the oldest foundations of the population. Remnants of this race had amalgamated, especially in the areas along the south and south-east coasts, with northern Tungusian elements from later periods. These Tungusian components of the Korean population in particular must have had a numerically vast predominance over this ancient population group. These newer components were mostly provided by Manchurian and Tungusian tribes which must originally have fanned out from the north over the entire peninsula. As a result, the Tungusian element became strongest towards the north.[1]

The oldest Korean tribes known to us must have originated in the second century A.D.[2] Of the thirteen major tribes and peoples [3] we shall mention only the most important here. In the north-eastern frontier territory the Fu-yü, (Kor.: Puyŏ) [4] and the Wu-chü, 沃沮, (Kor.: Okchŏ) dwelt, partially on Korean and partially on Manchurian territory. Of these two, the Puyŏ—according to the legends—had provided most of the royal families for the later Korean states, and possibly also that of Japan. In addition, in the north there also dwelt the Ch'ao-hsien (Kor.: Chosŏn), 朝鮮, and the Kao-chü-li (Kor.: Koguryŏ), 高句麗, who were later to form the nucleus of the state of Koguryŏ and were supposed to have originated from the Puyŏ. On the south coast the so-called Han tribes in particular had settled, in whom the afore-mentioned pre-Mongolian

---

[1] W. Gundert, *Japanische Religionsgeschichte*, Stuttgart 1935, p. 187. See also O. Graf, "Ein Abriss der Religionsgeschichte Koreas", in *C.u.R.*, vol. III, p. 380.

[2] Cf. Wolfram Eberhard, "Kultur und Siedlung der Randvölker Chinas", Leiden 1942, supplement of *T.P.*, vol. XXXVI, p. 28.

[3] Cf. W. Eberhard, op. cit., pp. 15-28.

[4] Cf. Ikeuchi Hiroshi, "A Study on the Fu-yü", *T.B.*, no. VI, 1932, pp. 23-60.

characteristics were found most extensively. They united into three tribal unions. These were, at first, the Chin-han (辰韓) in the south-east, the basis for the later kingdom of Silla; then in the southwest corner the Ma-han (馬韓), the actual nucleus for the later kingdom of Paekche. Wedged in between on the south coast was the third and weakest tribul union: the Pyŏn-han (弁韓). These latter were later, under the pressure of their neighbour states, to call in the aid of the Japanese, who were to seize this opportunity in order to make an attacking base of their small territory, which they called Mimana, 任那. The Tungusian and North Asiatic predominance in all of these tribes ensured that in other fields also they would manifest their strong relationship to the North Asians. Examples of this can be found in their language [1] and their Shamanism. We shall return in particular to the latter.

This brief sketch of Korea's significance as a bridge for various racial developments is also confirmed by various archaeological finds. Here we shall examine three of the total of five grave cultures because it is just they which bear this 'bridge' characteristic.

In the first place, the so-called stone coffins which have been found in various places in Korea. Of these, the most important to us are those which were built of grave chambers dug in the ground, of which the walls and top were covered with thin stone slabs. These graves occurred mostly in North Korea and South Manchuria. However, they became more rare towards South Korea.[2] Of these 'house of cards' graves many have been discovered on Tsushima and Ik, 壱岐. They were less numerous in North Kyūshū and the southern point of Honshū.[3] They date from the earlier Yayoi period (prior to 100 B.C.).

Objects found in these graves prove that the second series of graves also was not entirely independent, namely: they coexisted.[4] This second series involves an entirely different way of burial. Here the dead were buried in jars of 5 to 6 feet in length, or in two jars

[1] Cf. footnote 1 on p. 187 and footnote 1 on p. 198.

[2] See Umehara Sueji, "Kodai nissenkan no bunbutsu no kōryū" (the Cultural Exchange between Japan and Korea in Antiquity), in *C.G.*, no. 11, 1957, March, pp. 1-19. For the description of a cist, namely that in Naman, 咸安, cf. p. 9. For the South Manchurian graves see p. 3.

[3] Cf. J. E. Kidder, *Japan before Buddhism*, pp. 105-106.

[4] Cf. Umehara Sueji, op. cit., p. 6. The same was the case in Japan. Cf. J. E. Kidder, loc. cit.

with the openings of the jars connecting. In general, these graves (found, for instance, in Kimhae, 金海, and Tongnae, 東莱, (Silla)) showed great similarity to those of Lo-lang, 楽浪, in the north and in China.[1] The sarcophagus pithoi especially, which were found in 1934 in the shell-mounds of Kimhae—linked to each other in pairs—display in their shape and points of connection a great resemblance to similar pithoi of the Japanese Middle Yayoi period which were found in North Kyūshū, specifically at Karatsu, 唐津, and in the vicinity of Fukuoka, 福岡. This resemblance was not only limited to these pithoi; the ritual objects discovered round the grave, such as swords and mirrors, displayed an identical similarity to those of the above-mentioned Kyūshū sites. Furthermore, the Kimhae grave proved, on closer examination, to be older than these Japanese graves. What was not to be expected in this was the confirmation that these Kimhae finds bore a greater resemblance to those of the North Kyūshū sites than to other Korean locations, such as, for instance, that of the not far distant Tongnae.[2]

All of this is an indication of the fact that these Kimhae sarcophagi, just as those of North Kyūshū, derive from the same tribe, which dwelt on either side of the Strait of Korea. Hence this Kimhae find can serve as an archaeological argument for the relationship of the later Silla population to that of the Japanese Izumo, as Kimhae was situated in Silla. According to the similar and older pithoi graves of Manchuria and China, this tribe must have been preponderantly continental and North Asiatic.[3] Nevertheless this 'Kimhae tribe' differed from most tribes of North Korea. Other objects, found round the Kimhae graves, indicate this. Thus the half-moon shaped stones—called *magatama*, 勾玉, in Japan —only occur in the south of Korea. Some similar *magatama* have

---

[1] Umehara Sueji, op. cit., pp. 3, 4; J. E. Kidder, op. cit., p. 107.

[2] Cf. Umehara Sueji, op. cit., p. 6; Kidder, loc. cit. Kidder attempts to clarify the mutual differences and similarities between the Chinese, Korean and Japanese pithoi graves by the supposition that this method of burial reached Japan directly from China, and worked back to Korea from there. Umehara is also inclined towards a similar theory and links this to the Japanese dominion of South Korea, op. cit., pp. 18, 19. The archeological data, namely, that the *pithos* sarcophagus found in Kimhae after 1934 is older than the Japanese of the same type, is, however, contradictory to this. Cf. Umehara Sueji, op. cit., pp. 5, 6.

[3] J. E. Kidder, op. cit., p. 107 mentions Lo-lang and Manchuria here.

also been met with in the Kyūshū graves.[1] However, these southern tribes were not wholly independent of northern influences, because some of the mirrors of pure Korean make and design were also discovered in the old kings' graves of the northern state Koguryŏ.[2]

With regard to the afore-mentioned burial methods, we agree with Umehara Sueji that all of these graves bear a specifically continental character. Because the northern graves are older than the southern ones the north-south direction can be defined in which this continental funerary cult developed.[3]

Other excavations brought to light that at a later stage this old agrarian culture, which was coeval with that of the Japanese Early Yayoi period, was driven out by North Asiatic warriors. Their new weapon was the horse, and it was owing to this that they succeeded in Korea and Japan. The artifacts of the 'burial mound culture' indubitably indicate this radical change. With this an entirely new cultural layer spread over Korea and Japan in the fourth century and earlier.[4]

b The new nomad tribe

These archaeological indications of the nomadic invasion in the Korean territories which had been inhabited by agrarian tribes are also confirmed by myths, sociology and linguistics.

From the Korean myths especially, it appears that these nomads achieved more or less the same as the Norsemen in Europe a few centuries later. Of the latter we know that they, with only small numbers, contrived to establish themselves at the head of various European realms. One need only think of Rollo in Normandy, the Dane Canute the Great and the Norman William the Conqueror in England, Rorik in Russia and Robert Guiscard in Apulia in South Italy.[5] According to the myths, the nomad tribe with which we are concerned did precisely the same in Korea. Here too various leaders

---

[1] Most *magatama* were found in the Silla kings' graves of Kyŏngju, 慶州. In Japan many green *magatama* in particular were found, whereas *magatama* with specially old characteristics were lacking, such as those, for example, which were found in the Korean Naju, 羅州, district. Cf. Umehara Sueji, op. cit., pp. 11, 12; J. E. Kidder, op. cit., p. 181.

[2] Umehara Sueji, op. cit., p. 13.

[3] Umehara Sueji, op. cit., p. 2.

[4] Cf. F. Vos, *Volken van één stam?*, The Hague 1959, pp. 11, 12.

[5] Cf. F. Vos, op. cit., pp. 22, 23. See E. Sloots, "Noormannen" in *K.E.*, vol. 18, pp. 836, 837.

of just a few clans contrived to extend their power into becoming kings of entire Korean areas. We saw in the first chapter that in Yamato one of them managed to originate the royal dynasty.[1]

The indications in the myths of this tribe can be found especially in the royal tales of the Korean states Koguryŏ, Paekche and the later Japanese protectorate Mimana. In the first of the two oldest Korean historical works, the *Samguk yusa*, 三國遺事, and the *Samguk sagi*, 三國史記, compiled from older—now lost—material by, respectively, the monk Ilyŏn (1206-1289) [2] and Kim Pusik (1057-1151),[3] Tan-gun, 檀君, is named as the actual founder and patriarch of all the Korean royal families. In the first chapter we already saw him as the grandson of the Celestial Emperor Hwan'in, 檀因, and the son of Hwan'ung, 檀雄.[4] Takahashi Tōru [5] has shown that

---

[1] See Chapter I, pp. 39 ff.

[2] Takahashi Tōru has treated of various problems surrounding the antiquity of the *Samguk yusa* in his article (Japanese): "The Commentaries of the *Samguk yusa* and the Development of the Legend of Dangun", (this title in English by *C.G.*), in *C.G.*, no. 7, 1955, March, pp. 63-90; especially pp. 63-74.

[3] Cf. F. Vos, "Kim Yusin, Persönlichkeit und Mythos", *O.E.*, Jahrg. I, 1954, p. 32; for the classification of the *Samguk sagi* see op. cit., footnote 17.

[4] W. Gundert, op. cit. p. 188 sees in this word a translation of the two Chinese concepts 天: *t'ien*, Korean: *hanŭl*, heaven, and 帝: *ti*, Korean, *nim*, lord, emperor. See also F. Vos, op. cit., p. 36, footnote 47. This derivation betrays the Chinese origin of this word, although the Korean Hananim or Hwan'in, in contradistinction to the Chinese t'ien, also maintained direct relations with ordinary mortals, also those who were not emperors. The Chinese 上帝, Shang-ti, is also often used for Hwan'in.

The Chinese characters which indicate the names Hwan'in, Hwan'ung and Tan-gun also in the *Samguk yusa* and the *Samguk sagi* imply yet another meaning. Accordingly Hwan'in: 檀因, Tan'in (Chin.: T'an-yin) is called: the soil of existence of the sandalwood tree. The Tan, 檀, of Tan'in has the meaning of sandalwood tree, a tree of the family of the *Santalaceae*, *Santalum album*. This tree had in China, and especially in Buddhism, a sacred meaning owing to the incense which was obtained from it. Concerning this tree see *K.E.*, vol. 21, under *Sandelhout*, p. 451, col. 1. The character: 檀 means *mayumi* in Japanese, spindle tree (*euonymus*). This translation is, however, not very probable.

F. Vos, *Volken van één Stam ?*, p. 20, on the basis of the Korean pronunciation, considers this tree to be the *paktal* tree, a birchlike tree (*Betula Schmidtii*). The tree under discussion here is also written as, 栴檀, *chan-t'an*, in some texts, which also means sandalwood tree. On this basis we prefer this translation of sandalwood tree. Hence the meaning of the afore mentioned names is as follows: Hwan'ung: 檀雄, Sino-Kor.: Tan'ung (Chin.: T'an-this figure, descended from Koguryŏ, was especially used in the *Samguk yusa* to accentuate and symbolise the unity of Chosŏn (=Korea).[1] Furthermore, Koguryŏ was supposed to be the country to which all other Korean territories could be traced.[2] They even wanted to depict him as the patriarch of all of the East Asiatic peoples, and for this end some elevated him into being Hwan'ung or Hwan'in in person.[3] These nationalistic intentions brought about without any textual criticism, made the *Samguk sagi* and the *Samguk yusa* conflict with each other as well as with other, older texts from which the Tan-gun myth had been drawn.[4] Thus it was intended to create the impression that the Tan-gun tale was Korea's oldest myth.[5] Nevertheless these royal tales were certainly as old and

---

hsiung): the hero of the sandalwood tree; Tan-gun: 檀君, Sino-Kor.: Tan-gun (Chin.: T'an-chün): lord of the sandalwood tree. The descent of Hwan'ung took place under the: 檀樹, Sino-Kor.: *tansu* (Chin.: *t'an-shu*), sandalwood tree. According to the *Koguryŏ-pongi* part of the *Samguk sagi*, Tan-gun was born of a marriage between a granddaughter of Hwan'in (according to F. Vos, *Volken van één Stam* ?, p. 20, a she-bear) to the god of the sandalwood tree: 檀樹神, Sino-Kor.: Tansu-sin, (Chin.: T'an-shu-shên). Prior to the wedding Hwan'in provided a potion which changed her into a human. Cf. Takahashi Tōru, op. cit., p. 78. This reference to a tree is, moreover, a reference to the sun worship of the Koreans, to whom the tree was a sun symbol. Hence Hwan'in, as the heart of the sandalwood tree, was considered to be a sun god.

[5] Takahashi Tōru, "The Commentary of Samguk-yusa and the Development of the Legend of Tan-gun", especially in the second part: "Tan-gun densetsu no hatten", (The Growth of the Tan-gun Tales), *C.G.*, no. 7 (1955), pp. 74-80.

[1] Takahashi Tōru, op. cit., pp. 75, 76.

[2] Takahashi Tōru, op. cit., p. 80.

[3] Especially in the *Tan-gun-pongi* for instance, current in Koryŏ (= Korea from 918 to 1392), Tan-gun was equated with Hwan'ung = 天王. Cf. Takahashi Tōru, op. cit., p. 79.

[4] According to the *Samguk sagi*, the son of Tan-gun, King Tongmyŏng, (Chin.: Tung-ming, 東明) was also called Chumŏng (Chin.: Chu-mêng, 朱蒙). Now in the Manchurian Fu-yü, it was opined that this latter Chu-mêng was a son of the ancient and parentless ruler Chieh-fu-lu, 解夫婁. Now this Chieh-fu-lu (Sino-Kor.: Haeburu) was simply called a son of Tan-gun in the *Samguk yusa*. This is a clear example of the fact that, without paying any attention to existing traditions, the royal houses of Korea were accommodated in Tan-gun's genealogy. Thus the same Tan-gun could simultaneously become father and grandfather to Chumŏng. Cf. Takahashi Tōru, op. cit., p. 76.

[5] Therefore Takahashi Tōru concludes as follows: "The Tan-gun myth

as important as that of Tan-gun himself. Though later all the Korean rulers were placed in the genealogy of Tan-gun as his sons or grandchildren, the actual original genealogies of these rulers differed. They far more probably went directly back to the tribe of the Fu-yü which is illustrated by the very oldest royal myths, especially those of Koguryŏ, Paekche and the later Mimana.

1. According to the *Koguryŏ-pongi*, 高句麗本紀, part of the *Samguk sagi*, Tan-gun's son Tongmyŏng (Chin.: Tung-ming, 東明) was Koguryŏ's first king. At the time when Emperor the Great Yü (2205-2197 B.C.) called together in China the leaders of the peoples from all parts to the T'u-shan, 塗山,[1] Tongmyŏng arrived there to represent all the people of Korea.[2] In this Koguryŏ myth he, just as was Tan-gun, was given a pan-Korean character.

Nevertheless this Tongmyŏng was probably none other than a mythical Puyŏ ruler originally. This ruler is mentioned in a considerably older manuscript than the *Samguk sagi*. In the *Fu-yü-chuan*, 扶餘伝, of the well-known *Wei chih*, a note has been incorporated which was supposedly quoted by a certain P'ei Sung-chih (裴松之) of the Liu-Sung period (420-479) from the *Wei-lioh*, 魏略, a historical work now lost, which was supposed to have been written by Yü Huan, 魚豢, from the time of Ming-ti, 明帝 (227-240). In this the first Fu-yü king is mentioned. It is a fairly lengthy tale, which we can therefore only briefly recount.[3] In it the life story of the first king of the Fu-yü is told. His mother was a chambermaid of the king of Kao-chü-li (Koguryŏ). When she suddenly became pregnant the king wanted to kill her. However, she contrived to save herself from death by announcing: "Gas in the shape of a hen's egg descended upon me, and then I found myself with a child."[4] Some time later she had a son. The king attempted to kill him by casting him before the swine and horses. When, however, nothing happened to him, the mother was given permission to rear

---

was simultaneously linked to that concerning the foundation of Koguryŏ and the Fu-yü realm, without any attention being paid to the actual historical development." Cf. op. cit., p. 79, under footnote 2.

[1] For more data concerning this legendary emperor, see Tsui Chi, *Histoire de la Chine et de la Civilisation Chinoise*, Paris 1949, pp. 15, 16; see also E. Zürcher, op. cit., p. 286.

[2] Cf. Takahashi Tōru, op. cit., p. 76.

[3] The literal English translation of this may be found in Ikeuchi Hiroshi op. cit., pp. 23, 24. See also W. Eberhard, op. cit., p. 16.

[4] Ikeuchi Hiroshi, op. cit., p. 23.

him. He was given the name Tung-ming (東明). He was especially charged with the care of the horses. However, because the king feared he would steal his realm, he again attempted to destroy him. During his flight to the south, however, Tung-ming managed to cross a bridge of fish and tortoises over the river Shih-yen-shui, 施掩水, thus escaping his pursuers. Here he founded the capital of the Fu-yü realm.

In the foregoing tale the Fu-yü realm appears to evolve from that of Kao-chü-li (= Koguryŏ). It appears, however, that this is an error and that a different country was probably meant by Kao-chü-li, as it is a fact that the Fu-yü did not dwell to the south but to the north of Koguryŏ, as far as the depths of Manchuria.[1] The southern flight of Tung-ming (or Sino-Kor.: Tongmyŏng) therefore indicates a different realm. The particular which is of interest to us here is that the first Fu-yü king bore the same name as the king of Koguryŏ. It is obvious that later compilers of the *Samguk sagi* inserted the Fu-yü material from this 'old tale' [2] in the *Koguryŏ-pongi* of this work. Other myths confirm this supposition because in these the Koguryŏ Tongmyŏng is named as a Fu-yü descendent.[3] In other tales Tan-gun immediately became a Fu-yü figure, owing to his being equated with one or other Fu-yü ruler.[4] This makes it clear that the Fu-yü kings certainly had something to do with the first rulers of Koguryŏ.

2. The Fu-yü relations with Paekche follow immediately from the fact that the ruling house of this land prided itself on its descent from that of Koguryŏ.[5]

3. The Pyŏn-han federation, which later expanded into Japan's

[1] This becomes comprehensible from the fact that the Chinese only initially came into contact with the Fu-yü after the beginning of our era. See Ikeuchi Hiroshi, op. cit., p. 25.

[2] Ikeuchi Hiroshi suspects that this tale originated as early as the early Han period, as a certain Wang Ch'ung, 王充, (born 27 A.D.) also related this in his work *Lun-hêng*, 論衡. Cf. Ikeuchi Hiroshi, op. cit., p. 24.

[3] Thus it is related in the Korean manuscript, 遺事記異篇, *Yusagi ip'yong*, how Tung-ming-*wang* founded the realm of the northern Fu-yü. This whole history ends with the comment: "Thus it is said Koguryŏ came into being", 即高句麗之始云々. Cf. Takahashi Tōru, op. cit., p. 76.

[4] This happened indirectly, owing to the fact that gradually Tongmyŏng, his son, was equated with the Puyŏ ruler (Hae) Buru: Chieh-fu-lu. They were both called brother by different mothers. On this see Takahashi Tōru, op. cit., pp. 75-80.

[5] Cf. Bruno Lewin, *Aya und Hata*, p. 7.

beachhead in Korea, also had its own royal myth, which equally indicates a similar Fu-yü myth. It can be found in the *Karak-kukki*, 駕洛國記, the Pyŏn-han part of the *Samguk yusa*.[1] This describes how the population of this area, in the year 44 A.D., was severely plagued by a drought. Of the nine groups into which this population was divided, two or three hundred people assembled to hold ritual purifications. Suddenly from somewhere they heard a human voice. This voice announced itself as belonging to the founder of a new land: "I have received from the gods in heaven the command to become king of this land." Hereupon the population was summoned to dance and to sing. Then the tale continues: "When they looked at the skies, a purple thread suddenly descended from the heavens, which twisted towards the earth which was shimmering in the glow (of the sun). When they went to the place where this thread reached the earth, a golden box, wrapped in red and green cloths, was found. On opening it, it was found to contain six golden eggs. They glowed like the disc of the sun. The people who saw this rejoiced and came to worship it repeatedly." When the box was re-opened after twelve days, the eggs had changed into children. They grew at a great speed. "Their face was lovely as that of an ancestor from the Han period." Each came to be head of one of the small states, which they called Kaya lands.[2]

Something similar may also be found in the myths of the Fu-yü. Here it is not only of interest that the Fu-yü ruler Tung-ming also owed his birth to: 'Gas in the shape of a hen's egg',[3] but also that more or less the same myth was to be found amongst the Fu-yü. According to an old Fu-yü legend namely, their matriarch was supposed to have found a box containing six eggs, from which six boys were similarly born.[4] It would have been very coincidental if these two myths were to have originated independently. Here too an identical Fu-yü influence is obvious. The friendly relations which this Pyŏn-han federation established with Japan may be an indication of the fact that the Fu-yü ,who, together with their clans,

---

[1] These data have been taken mainly from the Japanese translation of this by Mishina Shōei, "Sankoku-iji-koshō" (Research into the *Samguk yusa*), *C.G.*, no. 29, 1963, Oct., pp. 148-170. This myth can be found on pp. 150-152.

[2] For the quotations in this text, see Mishina Shōei, op. cit., p. 151.

[3] Cf. this Chapter p. 194.

[4] Cf. W. Eberhard, op. cit., p. 16.

were beginning to form the top people in various Korean states, did not stop at the Straits of Korea, but in Yamato also laid the foundation of the Japanese imperial house.

In the Korean peninsula, this Fu-yü element might have formed the contrast to the only state which had not known a Fu-yü summit, i.e. Silla. Here the tradition was alive that Maro, in 42 A.D., climbed the mountain Kut, situated not far from Kimhae, and viewed the land of Kaya or Kara [1] and then founded the Kaya realm there under the name of K'ungi-guk. Neither in his case, nor in the royal tales of Silla which was founded after him, was there mention of Fu-yü descent. He was considered to be a distant descendent of the Chinese primeval emperor Shao-hao, 少昊, (2597-2513). This also indicates that this area (the future Silla) equated Izumo in Japan, just as Yamato (in its Puyŏ descent) had much in common with the remaining Korean states.[2]

All of this is also confirmed from a sociological point of view. We have already pointed out in our first chapter the five-fold clan structure which characterised the imperial tribe.[3] This was also to be found to an important degree in old Korea. Both the *Wei chih* and the *Tung-i chuan* of the *Hou Han-shu* give a definite summary of these five clans [4] with regard to Koguryŏ. There was a similar clan structure in Paekche.[5] All of these structures probably lead back to the five-fold clans, named after totems, of the Fu-yü.[6]

Linguistically an immediate Fu-yü influence is hard to prove as the Fu-yü language disappeared from history together with the Fu-yü themselves. Nevertheless, both in Korean and Japanese many similarities can be found to Manchurian, which also had a place in the formation of the Fu-yü language. In the field of syntax and morphology especially such similarities may be found. These

---

[1] See further on p. 203, footnote 3.

[2] Brief mention of this tradition can be found in F. Vos, "Kim Yusin, Persönlichkeit und Mythos", *O.E.*, 1954, p. 33 and the footnotes 26, 27 and 28. These Silla data especially have a strong Chinese tendency. For the relationship of these districts, see F. Vos, *Volken van Eén Stam*?, p. 24.

[3] Cf. Chapter II, pp. 114 ff.

[4] Cf. Mishina Shōei, "Kokuryō no gozoku ni tsuite", (The five Clans of Koguryŏ), *C.G.*, no. 6, 1954, Aug., pp. 13-57. Mishina also attempts to trace in this article the influences of this clan structure on later structures in Koguryŏ.

[5] F. Vos, op. cit., p. 23.

[6] Cf. Chapter II, pp. 114, 115, footnote 4.

cannot only be explained as pure coincidence.[1] They might go back to an earlier Fu-yü invasion. The fact that, for instance, in Japan various religious terms and names of deities prove to be of Manchurian origin [2] can only be ascribed to such an invasion, which would have brought about the entirely new religious and social structures which we have described in the previous chapters.

All of these data indicate a trend to the south by the Fu-yü, which only halted in Japan.[3] It is, however, noteworthy, that the Chinese sources do not describe this Fu-yü invasion anywhere. This is, however, not surprising as the Chinese themselves only became acquainted with the Fu-yü at the beginning of our era. The sources only recorded anything which had to do directly or indirectly with the history of China itself. The trend to the south by the Fu-yü lay entirely beyond the scope of the Chinese. It coincided with the same migration which involved the entire Eurasian continent. The Chinese had their hands full dealing with the Five Hu and could scarcely become involved with migrations which, at that time, did not touch China. The fact that the Fu-yü suddenly disappeared entirely from history merely indicates that they had then become inaccessible to Chinese chroniclers.[4] In any case, after 497

---

[1] For further details of the similarities between Korean and Manchurian, see footnote 1 on p. 187. For the similarity to Japanese see J. Romieux, "Mythes du Japon ancien vus à la Lumière de la Linguistique Comparative", *M.S.G.*, VIII, 1946, pp. 63-93. Here the syntactic and morphologic similarities to Korean are to be found on pp. 70-72. The word comparison of Japanese to Manchurian has already been indicated in Chapter I, pp. 41 ff.

In this chapter we have not investigated more closely the relationship between Japanese and Korean as we know too little of the latter to be able to compare it to Japanese. We can only refer to more competent specialists for this. F. Vos has summarily described the Japanese-Korean relationship in his *Volken van Één Stam?*, pp. 12-18. Furthermore there are also the various word comparisons by Mishina Shōei and Kanazawa Shōzaburō, to which we shall return at different points in this chapter.

[2] This is valid for terms such as *matsuri*: divine sacrifice; *harai*: ritual libation; *imi*: abstinence; *idzu*: holy; *mikoto*: spirit, and *ame*: heaven; furthermore names of deities such as Susa *no* O, Ame *no* Uzume *no mikoto* and Ninigi *no mikoto*. Cf. Romieux, op. cit., pp. 75-90. In this it is interesting that a word such as *musubi*, fundamental to the Japanese concept of god, belongs here. Romieux, op. cit., p. 67. Cf. Chapter II, footnote 3 on pp. 105 ff.

[3] See also F. Vos, op. cit., p. 23.

[4] According to W. Eberhard, op. cit., p. 17, they disappeared from history after 285 A.D. This is not entirely correct as the official T'opa chronicles, the *Wei-shu*, relates of them, that they sent delegations in 457

nothing more is heard of them. They continued to dwell anonymously in the realms which they themselves had founded. After them the T'opa especially were to contribute culturally and religiously—via the Korean one-way traffic—to the further development of the peninsula and southern Japanese islands.

The Korean aspects discussed here of the so-called horse-riding tribe naturally form an important argument for the hypotheses of Egami [1] and Kida [2] concerning this tribe. They illustrate that the processes of which there is mention in these hypotheses were possible because unavoidably an extensive relationship existed in many aspects between the Korean and Japanese populations.[3]

c The political bridge: Korea

The bridging position of Korea is also confirmed by its political history. In this aspect this land, during the fifth and sixth centuries as well as throughout its entire later history, may be compared to Poland which also always remained wedged as a buffer-state between two powerful countries. Korea also was continually attacked or occupied, sometimes from the north, by China, or from the south, by Japan. This was noticeably furthered right from the beginning by the internal division of this territory into a few large states and many minor states. In the following pages we shall only consider such political developments as in particular opened up this land for Buddhism.[4]

The first to contrive to benefit from this buffer character of Korea was China. Since 108 B.C. its emperors had managed to retain various of its central and northern areas under their own occupation. Originally four Chinese prefectures were even founded on the remains of the old North Korean state Chosŏn (Chin.: Ch'ao-hsien). At the beginning of our era, however, only the pre-

---

and 494 to the T'opa court, the first time to pay their tribute, the last time for their total submission. Also the memorial pillar of Kwanggaet'o, which we have already encountered in connection with the Japanese campaigns in Korea, records a conquest of the Fu-yü at the end of the fourth century. See Ikeuchi Hiroshi, op. cit., pp. 55-59.

[1] Egami Namio in "Nihon-minzoku-bunka no genryū . . . .", *M.G.K.*, vol. 13, no. 3 (1948), p. 239-240.

[2] F. Vos, op. cit., p. 7.

[3] See also our comments on this in Chapter I, pp. 35 ff.

[4] Here we are relying in particular on Bruno Lewin's data, op. cit., pp. 5 ff. For further literature, we refer to this source.

fecture of Lo-lang remained of all the central and western Korean areas. At that time especially many Chinese settled in these Chinese colonies. They in particular knew how to elevate this country culturally, politically and economically. Most of the areas in the north, however, were gradually lost from then on to the increasingly powerful North Korean state Koguryŏ. At the beginning of the third century Koguryŏ had succeeded also in gaining the western Chinese areas and in cutting off the remaining Chinese territories in Central Korea from the motherland. All that remained of the old prefecture Lo-lang was reorganised at that time by the energetic Chinese duke Kung-sun K'ang, 公孫康, into the new, Central Korean, Chinese colony Tai-fang, 帶方.

This very oldest 'Chinese' history does show that in Korea, despite all initial Chinese superiority, there were nevertheless sufficient opposing powers present to terminate all Chinese rule. The first Korean state to succeed in this was Koguryŏ, 高句麗. This was moreover the largest of all the Korean states which had developed after the Han period. On the north it bordered on the Manchurian territories of the Fu-yü and the Wu-chü, in the south on the areas inhabited by the tribes of the Wei and Mai. Its nucleus lay in a part of the Chinese prefecture Lo-lang and the dwelling area of the Fu-yü. It is therefore understandable that the Koguryŏ royal family descended from the Fu-yü. Hence this was the first Korean territory to manage to liberate itself from all original Chinese rule. Right from the beginning it made a dangerous neighbour for the remaining Chinese areas. Initially it still left the western passage from China to the Chinese colonies in Central and South Korea open. However, in 313 Koguryŏ was strong enough to capture these northern areas and the western territories along the Korean west coast. With this Koguryŏ became the cork in the bottle of the Korean peninsula, which kept further immediate Chinese influence and government outside the Korean borders. This date, 313, had far-reaching consequences for Korean nationalism and also for Japanese Korea politics. Simultaneously it contrived to incorporate the Wu-chü in the north-east as well as the Wei, 濊, and the Mai, 貊, on the Korean east coast. The pressure exercised by the Hsien-pi on its northern frontiers in the fourth century necessitated the removal of its capital from the Yalu, 鴨綠, river to the more southern P'yŏngyang, 平壤. Changing its centre of gravity to the south caused all kinds of shifts among the other Korean states. In antiquity also these took place not far from the 38th. parallel, especially after Paekche had annexed the prefecture Tai-fang.[1]

The part of the peninsula which Koguryŏ had left untouched was rapidly occupied by three separate states. This too was preceded by a highly specific development. Towards the end of the Han period, therefore at the beginning of our era, three minuscule states—tribal unions rather—were situated squeezed up to the Korean south coast. These were: the Ma-han federation, consisting of 54 tribes, in the west; the Chin-han federation, made up of 12 tribes, in the east; and between these two the Kaya federation of Pyŏn-han, composed of six states, was wedged.[2]

Partially under the influence of the afore-mentioned royal leaders of the Fu-yü, entirely new realms resulted from this in the third century. The Ma-han federation developed, partially owing to the initiative of the Paekche tribe, into the kingdom of Paekche, 百済. Of all the Korean states, this country maintained the best relations with Japan during the fifth and sixth centuries.[3] This can still be seen from the *Nihonshoki* which, in its reports about Korea, leans exclusively on the chronicles of Paekche or Kudara.[4] Kudara is the Japanese word for Paekche. These so-called Kudara chronicles first originated in Japan, made by Paekche immigrants living there, who offered these sheafs to the Japanese government. Hence the names of these sheafs are known to us only from the *Nihonshoki* and not, for instance, from Korean history.[5] They are especially quoted in the *Nihonshoki* for the period covering from the 47th year of Jingū to the 17th year of Emperor Kimmei.[6] These sound relations between Paekche and Japan were

[1] Bruno Lewin, op. cit., p. 8.

[2] Cf. F. Vos, op. cit., p. 10.

[3] F. Vos, op. cit., pp. 22, 23.

[4] Those are the *Kudara-ki*, 百済記, the *Kudara-shinshen*, 百済新撰, and the *Kudara-hongi*, 百済本記. Cf. Itamoto Tarō, "A Critical Study of the Sources of the Keitai-Section of the Nihonshoki" (Japanese, English title by *N.K.Z.*), *N.K.Z.*, vol. 62, 1961, no. 9, pp. 43-54.

[5] Cf. Itamoto Tarō, op. cit., pp. 53-54

[6] They occur as follows in this period: the *Kudara-ki* in Jingū's 47th, 62nd year, Ōjin's 8th, 25th year and Yūryaku's 20th year; the *Kudara-shinsen* in Yūryaku's 2nd, 5th and Buretsu's 4th year; finally the *Kudara-hongi* in Keitai's 3rd, 7th, 9th, 25th year, Kimmei's 2nd, 5th (8 times), 6th, 7th, 11th (24 times) and 17th year. Cf. Mishina Shōei, "On *Kudara-ki*, *Kudara-shinsen* and *Kudara-hongi*" (Japanese), in *C.G.*, no. 24, 1962, July, pp. 1-18. He is of the opinion that the *Kudara-ki* and the *Kudara-hongi*

also reflected in the vast numbers of Paekche immigrants in Japan,[1] the many names of places in Yamato made up of Kudara (= Paekche) [2] and finally in the Kudara gods who had become integrated in Yamato.[3] Among those gods King Sŏng of Paekche was also counted, to whom the very first growth of Buddhism in Japan is actually owed. It is hoped to show this in the following chapters. These amicable relations with Japan were largely also the result of the political situation in the peninsula. In 131, when Koguryŏ annexed the remainder of the prefecture Lo-lang, Paekche occupied the prefecture Tai-fang. This combined the borders of Paekche and Koguryŏ. From then on Paekche was disturbed by all kinds of border incidents by Koguryŏ, which also wanted to annex Tai-fang. Paekche needed its friendship with Japan in order to be free to fight Koguryŏ, and later Silla.[4]

Opposite Paekche, in the south-west of Korea, on the other side in the south-east a new state was also growing from the Chin-han federation when the Saro tribe put itself at the head of the federation. Originally this state was also called Saro, 斯盧, after this tribe.[5] From the beginning of the sixth century it was called Silla,

especially served to show Paekche's superiority in the Mimana district. Cf. English summaries, pp. 2, 3.

[1] Cf. B. Lewin, op. cit., pp. 8, 9.

[2] It is said in the *Kojiki*, middlemost *maki*; Kuroita Katsumi, Maruyama Jirō, *Kokushitaikei Kojiki*, p. 10, first line, of Takeuchi: Kudara no ike o tsukuriki: he built the Kudara (= Paekche) paddy.

Emperor Bidatsu (572-585) established his residence in Kudara no Ōi, as did Kōgyoku (641-654) after him. Cf. Chapter V, footnote 100. Yōmei moved to the Kudara *no miya*, the Kudara palace, which was situated on the Kudara-*kawa*, the Paekche river. Not far from here the Kudara *no tera* was built, the Paekche temple. During the reign of Temmu (672-686) the Kudara house is mentioned. Cf. Kanazawa Shōzaburō, "Chōsen-kenkyū to *Nihonshoki*", *C.G.*, no. 1, May 1951, pp. 85, 86 ff.

[3] Thus King Sŏng (523-554), Jap.: Seimei, of Paekche, who introduced Buddhism officially into Japan, became venerated as the god of Imaki in Yamato-Takaichi. This Imaki is not only the name of a village in Yamato, but *imaki*, 新来, meaning 'recent arrivals', is moreover another name for the Korean immigrants of that period. Thus it is understandable that both the Emperors Kōnin (770-781) and Kammu (781-806) made a pilgrimage to that village Imaki in Yamato. Moreover the god of Hirano, 平野, was originally a Paekche ancestor of a famous immigrant lineage. Cf. Kanazawa Shōzaburō, op. cit., p. 89.

[4] Cf., for instance, Suematsu Yasukazu, op. cit., pp. 169 ff.; pp. 408 ff.

[5] Cf. F. Vos, "Kim Yusin, ...", *O.E.*, 1954, p. 13, footnote 16; Bruno Lewin, op. cit., p. 7.

新羅, (Jap.: Shiragi).[1] Partially as a result of the reigning non-Fu-yü influences there, it was not on a very good footing with countries of different outlook, such as Koguryŏ, Paekche and the more distant Yamato. Though, according to Lewin [2] Chinese immigrants must have dwelt in this area from an early date, it was only in the sixth century that it was to begin integrating with Chinese culture, so that it was capable only far later than its neighbours of improving its own political situation. From that time on it was to keep South Korea in a state of continual unrest. It first tried out its power on Mimana, which was incorporated definitely in 562 after years of raids. In 663 and 668 it also contrived to occupy Koguryŏ and Paekche respectively. Hence it was Silla particularly which, at the time of the advent of Buddhism in Japan, formed a continual threat to Mimana and Paekche.

We have already briefly indicated that the third federation, namely that of Pyŏn-han or Kaya [3] was repeatedly in conflict with Silla. At first the six small states of this area could not achieve unity. Under the threat of both of her powerful neighbours and on the initiative of Taegaya, 大伽耶, one of the six small states, the aid of the Japanese was finally called in, who, as we shall see in the next chapter, had been in Korea before. In the middle of the fourth century they made their own bridge-head of this. At about that time it also received the status of protectorate, although in the *Nihonshoki* it is called: Yamato *no mikotomochi*, 'property of the emperor of Yamato'.[4] This area was given the name of Imna, 任那, (Jap.: Mimana) which really means 'the country of the lords'.[5]

---

[1] Ibid.

[2] Loc. cit.

[3] According to F. Vos, op. cit., p. 33, footnote 23, this word should far rather be Kara.

[4] Mimana and Paekche are both called *miyake*, 官家, twice, in the *Nihonshoki*. Silla also was indirectly considered as *miyake*. Cf. Chapter IV, pp. 227 ff. After Empress Jingū's campaigns, when Mimana was given a governor, it was indicated by: *uchi-tsu-miyake*, 内官, '*miyake* of the interior'. Cf. Suematsu Yasukazu, op. cit., p. 253. The word Yamato *no mikotomochi*, first written as: 宰國司, 國守, and later as 日本府, originally meant nothing other than 'deputy for the emperor'. Cf. Suematsu Yasukazu, op. cit., p. 259. This word was written in total three times phonetically as 彌移居, *miyake*. Cf. A. Wedemeyer, op. cit., p. 132 and especially p. 298, footnote 109.

[5] For the derivation of this word Mimana see Mishina Shōei, "*Nihonshoki*

Both the wars between Silla and the other Korean states as well as the Japanese campaigns on Korean territory provided a great mass of refugees who sought peace in this country; many of whom emigrated from it to Japan. We must accept that the first Buddhists also reached Japan in this way. However small, Imna was nevertheless a last opening to them, through which they might reach the Japanese islands. The importance of this area is described as follows by Bruno Lewin: [1]

"Die Gründung des Protektorates Mimana an der koreanischen Südküste und die konsequente Bündnispolitik mit Paekche bildeten die Tragpfeiler für das Eindringen der Festlandkultur nach Japan. Mimana wurde das Sammelbecken der aus Korea kommenden Emigranten, und dies ist mit die wichtigste historische Rolle, die das japanische Protektorat seit seines Bestehens spielte."

Korea also became accessible to Japan owing to the foundation of this protectorate. That the Japanese benefitted from this is proved by the old historical evidence concerning Japanese activities in the Korean peninsula: the Kwanggaet'o monument erected in South Manchuria, which records these activities for the years between 391 and 414.[2] These distant raids also partially explain the vast number of refugees, who probably landed in Japan via Mimana, fleeing before the Japanese armies. In connection with the chronological difficulties associated with the *Nihonshoki* and the specific nature of its composition it appears, however, too daring to date other invasions in Korea, described in the *Nihonshoki*, by the use of this monument.[3] During the entire fifth century as well as the

---

Nissen-kankei kiji kōshō" (Research of the chronicles of the *Nihonshoki*, concerning the relations between Japan and Korea), *C.G.*, vol. 14, 1959, Oct., p. 507. The translation here is based on the Korean roots *nim* (= lord (Suematsu) or divine place of encounter (Mishina)) and *ya* (= country) which grew together into Mimana. So Mimana would have two meanings: the country of the lords and the country of the rendezvous with the gods. Cfr. Suematsu Yasukazu, op. cit. p. 36. The name Mimana occurs on the Kwanggaet'o monument of 414 as 任那加羅. Later it occurred only sporadically in Korean. In 438 Mimana was mentioned in the *Sung-shu*, together with Paekche and Silla. This is the only Chinese source where Mimana is mentioned. Cf. Suematsu Yasukazu, op. cit., p. 34.

[1] Op. cit., p. 8.

[2] Cf. for this Chapter I, pp. 37 ff.

[3] B. Szcześniak's attempts to accord the chronology of this pillar with that of the *Nihonshoki* can scarcely open many new perspectives when considering specifically the chronological difficulties of the *Nihonshoki* and

beginning of the sixth the Japanese were to occupy this bridgehead in Korea. They did provide that the door to the south remained open.

Approximately 50 years before Korea was burst open from the south by the 'Wajin' it was also 'opened' from the North. This fact was of the greatest importance to religious development in Korea, especially for Buddhism. Namely, in the year 340, the Hsien-pi ruler of the Yen, 燕, realms—situated to the west of Koguryŏ—who was named Mu-jung Han, declared to his brother Mu-jung Huang concerning the importance of this opening: [1] "After the defeat of the Kao-kou-li (= Koguryŏ) we could destroy the Yüwen. The conquest of these two countries will be of the utmost advantage for our country." They did not stop at these words. In 342/343 Koguryŏ was radically vanquished [2] and the Hsien-pi carried off 50,000 Koguryŏ men and women. These same Hsien-pi were, in their turn, similarly vanquished in 370 by the Ch'in ruler Fu Chien. Together with their leader Mu-jung Wei, 40,000 Hsien-pi were forced to dwell in Ch'ang-an, the capital of Fu Chien's realm. One of their leaders, Mu-jung P'ung, escaped to Koguryŏ, but was extradited by this state back to Fu Chien.[3] This certainly contributed to the friendly relations between Fu Chien and the North Korean ruler Sosurim. With this Korea also stood open to the vast Asiatic expanse which Fu Chien had contrived to gain dominion over and which stretched from Korea up to Kansu and Turkestan.[4] In any case, this tie of friendship resulted in Koguryŏ's first contact with the Buddhism now common at the court of Fu Chien, in its own characteristics noticed at the beginning of this chapter. From this moment it began its march to the Japanese islands together with the stream of one-way traffic over the Korean bridge. This bridge had been opened up from two sides for this march by the political developments of the fourth century and later.

---

its entirely individual composition. Cf. B. Szcześniak, "Japanese-Korean Wars in A.D. 391-407 and their chronology", *J.R.A.S.*, 1946, parts 1 and 2, pp. 54-66, especially pp. 63 ff. Emile Gaspardone in "La Chronologie Ancienne du Japon", *J.A.*, tome CCXXX, Avril-Juin 1938, p. 266, also warns against such attempts.

[1] Cf. G. Schreiber, op. cit., p. 466.

[2] Cf. G. Schreiber, op. cit., p. 467.

[3] Cf. O. Franke, *Geschichte des Chinesischen Reiches*, Band II, p. 83.

[4] Ibid.

d KOREA: BRIDGE OF THE RELIGIONS

From a religious point of view also, Korea was a natural bridge from Asia's northern territories to Japan. Here we find, i.a., typical North Asiatic religious phenomena such as Shamanism and Sun-worship, and also such religions as Confucianism, Taoism and Buddhism.

1 *Korean Shamanism*

In the previous chapter we mentioned the Japanese Shamanism as practised by women, and at the beginning of this chapter we encountered Tungusian Shamanism, which was practised from Central Asia to the borders of Koguryŏ, in the T'opa realm, for instance, preferably by men. These forms of Shamanism, practised by both men and women, had not halted at the northern and southern boundaries of Korea. It is noteworthy that specifically in the northern districts male Shamans, named *paksu*, 覡, were more prominent, while in the central and southern areas female Shamans, named *mu* or *mudang*, 巫堂, held sway.[1] These forms of 'Japanese' and 'Siberian' Shamanism [2] encountered each other in the intermediary zone, namely the province of Hangyŏ-namdo, 咸鏡南道, where this Shamanism was practised by both sexes.[3] Concerning the origin of Korean Shamanism, Eliade says: [4]

"It is difficult to determine the 'origin' of Korean Shamanism; it may include southern elements, but the presence of staghorns on the Shaman's headdress of the Han period indicates relations with the stag cult characteristic of the ancient Turks . . . In addition the cult of the stag is typical of hunter and nomad cultures, in which Shamanesses do not appear to play much of a role."

Hence, according to Eberhard, the male Shamans of antiquity were much in the majority, in contradistinction to the present-day

---

[1] Cf. J. M. Martin, *Le Shintoïsme*, tome II, pp. 263-268.

[2] Hence the *miko* and the *mudang* had the same attributes as the Shamans of Siberia. Cf. F. Vos, *Volken van Één Stam*?, p. 22. Moreover, their dance had much in common with that of the Tungusians. Cf. W. Gundert, op.cit., p. 190; O. Graf, op. cit., p. 380.

[3] See J. M. Martin, op. cit., p. 267; W. Gundert, op. cit., pp. 190, 191.

[4] Cf. M. Eliade, "Recent Works on Shamanism", *H.o.R.*, vol. 1, 1961, p. 180. Here his opinion seems to rely particularly on W. Eberhard, *Lokalkulturen im alten China*, Peking 1942, Band II, pp. 313 ff.

female preponderance in Korean Shamanism.[1] In later centuries all of these Shamans were to form their own organisation. After the thirteenth century they were not too highly respected.[2] We do know that, in antiquity, the *mudang* in particular had great influence at the courts of Koguryŏ and Silla.[3] This roughly described Korean Shamanism too indicates the typical bridge situation of Korea, where the actual threshold lay between the North Asiatic and southern Shamanism. Now if, together with this Korean link, we look at the entire complex of Asiatic Shamanism and include all those forms of Shamanism which in reality constitute that complex, then it appears—from a geographical point of view—to cover an area which spanned from Hungary [4] over Siberia, North and South China and Korea to the farthest corners of the Japanese islands.

---

[1] W. Eberhard, loc. cit. Others also ascribe an important influence to the *mudang* in antiquity. Cf. O. Graf, op. cit., p. 381. All of these suspicions rest on the scant details available in the *Samguk yusa* and the *Samguk sagi* concerning this Shamanism. In a manuscript entitled: "Die Religionen Koreas", which Prof. Dr. F. Vos of Leiden kindly lent, we found the following *Samguk yusa* and *Samguk sagi* details on p. 32: "Das *Samguk yusa* enthält u.a. folgende Angabe in bezug auf den alten Königstitel *ch'ach'aung*: "Was *ch'auch'aung* oder *chach'ung* anbetrifft, so sagt Kim Taemun (Ende des 7. und erste Hälfte des 8. Jahrhunderts): "Vulgo sagt man *mu*(*dang*). Die Menschen respektieren die *mu*, weil sie den Geistern dienen und ihnen Opfer darbringen". Im vorigen Abschnitt sahen wir schon, dass die Schriftzeichen für *ch'ach'aung* wahrscheinlich *chung* (Schamane) gelesen werden müssen.

"Im *Samguk sagi* lesen wir, dass König Yuri (trad. Daten 29 v. Chr.—18 n. Chr.) von Koguryŏ im 9. Monat seines 19. Regierungsjahres durch eine Schamanin von einer Krankheit geheilt wurde. Unter der Regierung von König Ch'adae (trad. Daten: 146-165) und König Sansang (trad. Daten 197-227) desselben Landes machten Schamaninnen wichtige Voraussagen. König Ŭija (645-660) von Paekche berief Schamaninnen zu sich und fragte sie um Prophezeiungen über das Schicksal des Landes. Aus diesen wenigen Beispielen ist ersichtlich, dass das Schamanentum in der Zeit der Drei Reiche von grosser Bedeutung war".

[2] Cf. W. Gundert, op. cit., p. 190.

According to Martin this was also not the case previously. Thus they were supposed to have made up the seventh class of the eight non-noble classes at the time of the Three Kingdoms (IV-IXth. century), between the sixth caste of the farmers and the eighth of the pariahs. Danseuses (4th) and merchants (5th) were classified at a higher level. Cf. Martin, op. cit., p. 264.

[3] See W. Gundert, loc. cit.

[4] Cf. a recently published Hungarian work on this: Wilmos Dioszegi.

2 *Korean Sun-worship*

The Korean sun-worship also links this country with North Asia and Japan. Japanese mythology contains enough indications of this Korean belief in heaven. Empress Jingū's ancestor, for instance, was named 'Heavenly Spear of the Sun', Ama *no* Hiboko. According to the *Kojiki* and the *Nihonshoki* he came originally from Silla.[1] In this one can see the symbol for the Korean immigrants who had either brought this sun-worship to Japan or strengthened it there. Thus the oldest sun calendars or *hijiri* were supposed to have found their way to Japan.[2]

Hence one can ask oneself whether Amaterasu, as a sun goddess, might not also have been of Korean descent, as was Ama *no* Hiboko. Various Japanese folklorists opine that she supplanted either Takamimusubi [3] or Hachiman,[4] who reached Japan far later, in order to take their place and function amongst the Japanese people. I believe that, when considering Amaterasu, we should only link the aspect of sun-worship with the possibility of Korean

---

Die Elemente des Schamanismus in der hungarischen Volkskultur, Budapest 1958. Cf. for a discussion of this: *Anthr.* vol. 55, 1960, p. 253: "Ein lückenloses Vergleichsmaterial über einen Zeitraum von mehr als Tausend Jahren". See also M. Eliade, op. cit., p. 171; according to Eliade, Dioszegi considers Shamanism in his Hungarian work as: "a constitutive magical-religious element of the original culture of the Magyars".

Tibetan Shamanism, which also belongs here, is known only from a more recent date. Refer to Charles Eliot, *Hinduism and Buddhism,* London 1921, vol. III, pp. 383-385. Helmut Hoffmann, *Die Religionen Tibets,* pp. 2-3, writes about this Tibetan Shamanism: "dass das urtümliche Bon die nationaltibetische Ausprägung jener alten animistisch-schamanistischen Religiosität gewesen ist, welche einst nicht nur die Weiten Sibiriens beherrschte, sondern auch ganz Innenasien, Ost- und West-turkestan, die Mongolei, Manschurei, das tibetische Hochland und sogar China. Es hat sich ferner eine gewichtige Stimme gemeldet, die auch Iran, zumindest seinen Osten, miteinbeziehen und die Verkündigung des Propheten Zarathustra als schamanistisch erweisen wollte, doch hat sich diese Ansicht nicht allgemein durchsetzen können".

See further: H. Hoffmann, op. cit., pp. 7-13 and p. 190.

[1] Cf. Chapter I, footnote 2 on p. 45.

[2] Udō Masamoto, "Kodai Nihon no Taiyō-shinkō to sono bungakuhyōgen", *K.G.Z.*, vol. 59, nos. 10, 11, Oct., Nov. 1958, pp. 125-131, considers the sun calendars or *hijiri* to be expressions of the most ancient sun worship. They were due to immigrants of Chinese or Korean origin.

[3] Cf. Matsukawa Jirō, op. cit., p. 115.

[4] Cf. Matsukawa Jirō, op. cit., pp. 86 ff.

descent. She herself was indeed a Shaman of the first phase of Japan's society. It appears probable to me that she, just as Amateru *no mitama no kami*, 天照御魂神, came as a deity from the island of Tsushima, situated between Kyūshū and Korea, to Yamato in antiquity.[1] In that case it becomes hard to explain how, right from the beginning, she was regarded as part of the Yamato pantheon.[2]

Actual sun-worship dwelt in Korea in the same form as in Japan. Ch'oe Namsŏn has given a reconstruction of that over the period 1,000 B.C. to 500 A.D. In that, Palk was the Korean counterpart of Amaterasu and Kud of Susa *no* O. Graf, who mentions this reconstruction, notes here that no mythology exists in Korea about this which one might compare to that of the *Kojiki*.[3] Hence this sun-worship can be more readily deduced from the afore-mentioned Japanese 'Korean' figures. Of the northern inhabitants of Korea, Eberhard says: [4]

"Die Stammesmythen von Fu-yü und Kao-chü-li zeigen starke solare Motive und die ganze Religion mit ihren Himmelsopfern, ihrem Sternkult und vor allem dem Sonnenkult ist überwiegend astral und solar."

Korean sun-worship had much in common with that of Japan. It was practised with more or less the same symbols. The most important sun symbols were the ship, the tree and the mountain.

As far as the ship is concerned, the *Kojiki* [5] represents the patriarch of the Funa-ki, 舟木, (litt.: ship's timber)-*muraji*, the sun god (Hi *no kami*, 日の神) as sailing to Japan by ship. As a reminder of this emperors were later buried with a ship among their grave goods. This idea of the sun ship can also be encountered in the ships of the sun gods: Amateru *no mitama* in the *Harima-Fudoki*, [6] Nigihaya-bi *no mikoto*, 饒速日命, and Ho-akari *no mikoto*,

---

[1] Matsumae Takeshi, "Amateru-mitama no kami kō" (Research into Amateru-mitama no kami), *K.G.Z.*, vol. 62, 1961, Oct., pp. 49-50.

[2] As J. Romieux contends, op. cit., p. 91. Cf. footnote 6 of this page.

[3] Cf. Olaf Graf, *C.u.R.*, III. Band, p. 381.

[4] W. Eberhard, *Kultur und Siedlung der Randvölker Chinas*, p. 27.

[5] These and the following examples are to be found in Matsumae Takeshi, "Taiyō no fune to tokoyo shinkō", (Sunship and Tokoyo Belief), *K.G.Z.*, vol. 62, 1961, nos. 2, 3, Feb., March, pp. 23-43.

[6] This also mentions a ship sailed by Amaterasu; cf. *Harima-fudoki*, 山田の里, Yamada no sato, 猪飼野, Ikaino, Takeda Iukichi, op. cit., pp. 222-223. This reference to the ship is probably also connected with Amaterasu's voyage from Tsushima to Yamato.

火明命. Various paintings of such sun ships have been found in the burial mounds of Fukuoka in North Kyūshū.[1] Also the souls of the dead there were despatched in small boats to the land of the sun.[2] In southern parts of Korea such as Silla and Imna Japan was not only considered to be the land of the sun, but the belief in the sun ship dwelt here also.[3] Interconnected with this belief in the sun ship there was also the opinion in both districts that only that piece of land, house or grave might be considered good if it was shone upon by both the morning and the evening sun.[4] Nevertheless this belief in ships dwelt more strongly in maritime Japan than in Korea.

It was entirely different with the more continental sun symbol: the tree. We have already indicated the connection between Hwan'in, Hwan'ung and Tan-gun with the *paktal* or sandalwood tree.[5] The tree, with its sun-made shadow, had, in timeless Korean antiquity, the specific function of sun dial and sun calendar for the seasons.[6] Gigantic trees especially formerly dictated not only the work schedule for the farmers but also, for instance, right and left, and the place for important buildings and monuments. An indication of this function can still be found in the name of Silla: the holy wood (Korean: *kyerim*) of the Korean '*matsurigoto*'.[7] Hence the trees of antiquity were greatly respected and had their own cult. In some parts of China it was believed that there were trees which reached to the sun.[8]

Hence trees and forests were considered to be the habitations of gods and spirits in Korea and Japan. For instance, Japanese

---

[1] Matsumae Takeshi, op. cit., p. 38.

[2] Cf. Nishida Chōnan, "*Nihonshoki* no rekishi-shisō" (The Historical Ideology of the *Nihonshoki*), *K.G.Z.*, vol. 57, no. 7, 1956, Feb., pp. 54-55.

[3] Cf. Matsumae Takeshi, "Amateru-mitama no kami kō", *K.G.Z.*, vol. 62, 1961, Oct., no. 10, pp. 54-55.

[4] Nishida Chōnan, op. cit., p. 39.

[5] See footnote 4 on pp. 192, 193.

[6] Cf. Udō Masamoto, op. cit., p. 125 and also J.J.M. de Groot, *Universismus*, pp. 23 ff.

[7] This is written, i.a., as follows 雞林 in the *Samguk yusa*. The second character: 林, '*sup*', wood, is according to Mishina Shōei also read as 邑, *sup'ul*, village, but also means 'holy wood' or 'royal residence'. Here also it was the place of the '*matsurigoto*' of government and divine worship. Cf. Mishina Shōei, "*Nihonshoki* Nissenkankei kiji koshō", (Japan-Korean Relations of the *Nihonshoki*), *C.G.*, vol. XIV, 1959, Oct., p. 511.

[8] Cf. Udō Masamoto, op. cit., p. 128.

synonyms for temple, such as *yashiro, mori, himorogi,* all had something to do with tree or forest.[1] *Nami* of the Japanese word *kaminami*—much used in the Yamato area—derives from the Korean *namu, namo* or *namg-ki*: (Sino.-Kor.: *mok*), tree. Hence *kaminami* indicated tree-god.[2]

The Korean mountain belief was also extensively associated with this sun worship. Among the Fu-yü there was the following myth which is, perhaps, the foundation of the Korean Tan-gun and the Japanese *Tenson-kōrin* myths. It can be found in a Korean work [3] and is as follows: "According to the old chronicles of the northern Fu-yü, in the third year, *jên mao,* 壬戌, fourth month, eighth day of *Shên-chüeh,* 神爵, (61-57 B.C.; honorific name under Emperor Hsüan-ti 宣帝, (74-49 B.C.)), of which there is mention in the Han manuscripts, T'ien-ti, 天帝, (Hwan'in) supposedly descended on the Chi-shêng-ku, 紇升骨, in the area of Ta-liao-i chou-chieh, 大遼醫州界, (lit.: the very far distant province of healing). He set out in a chariot drawn by five dragons, founded a capital and appointed a king there. He gave the land the name of North Fu-yü. The king was called Haemosu, 解慕漱. He begot a son, who was named (Hae) buru, 夫婁." [4] According to the *Samguk yusa* Hwan-'ung was sent by Hwan'in to the mountain T'aebaek, 太白山, in order to found the Korean realm. The first contact with earth took place especially via these mountains, as they were shone on from all sides by the sun. Hence, in China, the T'u-shan, 塗山,—probably the model for the Japanese Takachiho—was considered specifically to be a special place for the sun cult.[5] Moreover, those who descended on the Japanese Takachiho mountain were all personifications of the sun symbol: the tree.[6] The *paktal* tree, under which Hwan'ung came to earth, also indicates this. It is clearly apparent from all of these examples that the Koreans formed a bridge between the North Chinese and the Japanese sun worship. Hence its inhabitants

---

[1] Cf. Kanazawa Shōzaburō, "Nissengo hikaku zakkō" (Various Thoughts on the Comparison between Japanese and Korean), *C.G.*, vol. VIII, 1955, Oct., pp. 25 ff.

[2] Cf. Kanazawa Shōzaburō, op. cit., pp. 26-27.

[3] Namely the *Yusagi ip'yŏn*; cf. Takahashi Tōru, op. cit., p. 76.

[4] Although *Hae* is given in the text as clan name, and one therefore reads Hae Mosu and Hae Puru, this *hae* can undoubtedly be identified with the Korean word for 'sun'.

[5] Udō Masamoto, op. cit., pp. 127, 128.

[6] Matsumae Takeshi, op. cit., pp. 50, 51.

could justifiably call themselves *Il-cha*, 日者,[1] sons of the sun. Later Buddhism of the sun and light Buddha Amitābha could, in particular, link up with this. Therefore Buddhism could be carried from the north, through these forms of local religiosity, further into Japan.

3 *Confucianism and Taoism*

Besides the afore-mentioned forms, Confucianism and Taoism also came to Korea from the north. Although not too much is known about the earliest history of this,[2] it appears that, at first, they did not meet with great success in Korea. According to some, Confucianism arrived in Korea as early as the Han period,[3] whereas others [4] contend it arrived only in the fourth century A.D. Until the beginning of the sixth century it was scarcely capable of exercising any influence on the state whatsoever. It should also not be compared to metaphysic Confucianism, which had reigned supreme so long in China. The only aspect of this which met with any popularity was ancestor worship.[5] In the kingdoms of Paekche, Silla and Koryŏ, 高麗, (918-1392) it had only occasionally to serve as counterweight to the —according to Gundert [6]—powerful spread of Buddhism.

Taoism was known in antiquity only under the name of Togyo, 道教, commonly Taoism. This only encompassed all kinds of odd religious usages,[7] but was, however, not strong enough to withstand Buddhism. Therefore, until the beginning of the sixth century, it was probably much the same as the T'opa Taoism.

4 *Buddhism*

Just as amongst the T'opa, Buddhism enjoyed general popularity in Korea right from the beginning. Moreover, Korea was also of great importance to Buddhism itself. During the first fifty years

---

[1] O. Graf, op. cit., p. 383.
[2] August K. Reischauer, *Studies in Japanese Buddhism*, p. 77.
[3] Cf. O. Graf, loc. cit.,
[4] Cf. W. Gundert, op. cit., pp. 191, 192.
[5] O. Graf, loc. cit.
[6] Op. cit., p. 192.
[7] Cf. W. Gundert, op. cit., p. 191.

after the advent of Buddhism in Japan, Korea—as we have seen [1] —formed the only 'conduit pipe between China and Japan'.[2] We have already pointed out at the beginning of this chapter that Buddhism going to Japan followed more or less the same route as the Fu-yü tribe, which founded the imperial rule there, did. Moreover, Korea only knew of contact with China by land.[3]

Now the Japanese chronicles concerning the sixth century repeatedly mention two Korean states, which were closely concerned in this, i.e. Koguryŏ and Paekche. At a later stage there was also to be mention of monks from Silla. However, this latter state was first to become acquainted with Buddhism itself in the sixth century, in contradistinction to the other two states, where Buddhism had already entered some time earlier. Of all these states, the very first contact with Japan was to be Paekche's.

These data from the Japanese sources, which will be further discussed in the following chapters, accord amazingly well with the actual growth of Buddhism in all of these lands. Indeed, in Paekche and Koguryŏ Buddhism had been accepted since the fourth century. Thus, in Paekche a legendary figure, the monk Maranant'a, 摩羅難陀, (Malananda?), was supposed to have brought Buddhism from the Chinese Eastern Tsin, 晉, state (317-420) (to be distinguished from the Ch'in, 秦, realm in which, amongst others, Fu Chien reigned) to Paekche. No more is known of him.[4] Of the Buddhism in this eastern Tsin state we know that it originated from the great communities of Hsiang-yang and the Lu-shan which, as we noted in the first part of this chapter, were under the leadership of the famous Chinese monks Tao-an and Hui-yüan, the same who, especially in North China under Fu Chien, pushed such new forms of experience as Maitreyanism and Amidism. Possibly the influence of these two also spread out to Maranant'a, if he ever really existed. It is, however, pointless to render the entire development of Buddhism in the Eastern Tsin realm dependent on this unknown figure, in order to explain that of Paekche. This Buddhism is inescapably too multi-sided to define accurately which of its aspects represented Maranant'a.[5]

---

[1] See footnote 3 on p. 186.

[2] Cf. Christmas Humphrey, *Buddhism*, p. 68.

[3] This is apparent from the entire political development of this country.

[4] Cf. W. Gundert, op. cit., pp. 193, 194.

[5] See E. Zürcher, *The Buddhist Conquest of China*, pp. 86-159; pp. 180-239.

Besides the Maranant'a legend there was also another popular tradition in Paekche, which contended that Buddhism arrived directly from India by sea.[1] This tale probably served to give Paekche Buddhism a certain independence, which would free it from the Chinese and Koguryŏ Buddhism. This direct arrival from India is a fantasy because the Indians were certainly not sailors. These legends in Paekche were actually intended to veil the true original advent of Buddhism from Koguryŏ.[2] The origin of Korean Buddhism therefore really lay in this country.

We have already pointed out repeatedly in this chapter that between Koguryŏ and the Chinese borderlands in the north there was a relationship in many ways. It is also owing to this that Buddhism came from these districts to Koguryŏ. According to Pratt [3] a Buddhist monk, Sundo, 順道, must have crossed the Yalu river as early as 369. Zürcher [4] points out an even earlier Buddhism in Koguryŏ, which must have been there when the monk Chih Tun, 支遁, (314-366) wrote a letter to a 'monk of Koguryŏ'. Most authors, however, opine, that 372 must be considered as the first year.[5] In that year Fu Chien sent to the address of the Koguryŏ king Sosurim (371-384) not only some active monks but also images and *sūtras*. It is not of great importance to us to know exactly when Buddhism reached this country. Moreover, the scarcity of data makes research into this extremely difficult. The only thing which should interest us in all this is the figure of Fu Chien. It is in him that the origin and the specific nature of Koguryŏ and Paekche Buddhism can be traced. We have already described this in the first part of this chapter. The developments at his court and those of the later T'opa automatically 'pushed on' to Koguryŏ

---

[1] W. E. Griffis, *Corea, The Hermit Nation*, London 1905, p. 35, is of the opinion that Buddhism existed in Paekche long before 372. H. von Glasenapp, *Der Buddhismus in Indien und im fernen Osten*, Berlin 1936, p. 239, has a different opinion.

[2] The relationships between these two countries offer adequate motives for this attitude. Consider, for example, the struggle of both countries for the old Chinese prefecture Tai-fang.

[3] James Bisset Pratt, *The Pilgrimage of Buddhism*, New York 1928, p. 417.

[4] Op. cit., p. 140 and p. 77, at the bottom.

[5] Cf. W. Gundert, *Japanische Religionsgeschichte*, p. 193; H. von Glasenapp, loc. cit.

and Paekche. Therefore the monks Sundo (Chin.: Shun-tao),[1] Ado, 阿道, (Chin.: A-tao)and Tamsi, 曇徵, (Chin.: T'an-shih) who had been sent by him took care that in 375 a monastery was founded in P'yŏngyang. With this Fu Chien's influence on Korean Buddhism was incontrovertible. This also solves a great part of the question as to what kind of Buddhism was brought with them to Korea.

Hence I am not inclined towards Gundert's opinion [2] that these monks maintained close relations with Kumārajīva, the great translator of Mahāyāna Buddhism. He settled only in 402, that is to say 30 years later, in Ch'ang-an, the capital of the realm of Fu Chien.[3] Therefore these monks exported the northern Buddhism which just at that time, especially in the realm of Fu Chien, was beginning to get under way and which had ripened as Maitreyanism for its encounter with Korea and Japan.

We do not know how Koguryŏ Buddhism otherwise reached Paekche. If Maranant'a really brought it in 385, then it was not much younger than that of Koguryŏ. As the Buddhism of Maranant'a, like that of Fu Chien, went back to that of Tao-an and Hui-yüan, Paekche Buddhism can not have been very different to that of Koguryŏ. Therefore the Buddhism which crossed to Japan under the Paekche kings Sŏng (Jap.: Seimei, 523-554) and Widŏk, 威德, (554-598) from this district had the same character as that of the realm of Fu Chien and had gained only a few Korean characteristics.

As far as those characteristics are concerned, we cannot agree with Eliot, who says of Korean Buddhism: [4] "The Buddhism of Korea cannot be sharply distinguished from the Buddhism of China and Japan . . . there is little originality in art: in literature and doctrine none at all." We must add, however, that Eliot was particularly concerned with the Buddhist schools which originated in the seventh century. The Buddhism, however, which was to be found in Korea before the origin of these schools, gives the lie to Eliot's contentions. In the course of time it did indeed gain a Korean exterior. This is proved by Korean Maitreyanism and Amidism.

---

[1] This Shun-tao (Kor.: Sundo) is the same as Pratt's Shindo, pronounced with a Japanese accent.

[2] Loc. cit., p. 193.

[3] Cf. O. Franke, op. cit., p. 293. He did, however, maintain close contact with Tao-an, p. 292.

[4] Charles Eliot, op. cit., p. 336.

The meaning of Maitreya in Korean popular belief may be seen from the following description by Pratt:[1] "Korea abounds in large stones of odd contour, that have been roughly shaped into Buddha-images of Miryok (=Maitreya). In fact the word Miryok or Miriok has come to the common noun, which denotes these stones. Besides there are many gigantic bas reliefs of Miryok graven upon the face of the cliffs in various parts of the land."

Other forms of syncretism have also been preserved in Korea, which indicate that Buddhism did not remain wholly colourless there. One of them is the identification of raw rice with Bodhisattva. This is mainly the result of a none too extensive knowledge of the Buddhist doctrines (can one expect otherwise in a popular belief?) and of the phonetic similarity of the Korean words for unboiled rice (*ssăl*), Bodhisattva *Posal* and the old abbreviation *Sasa* which was previously frequently used in copying *sūtras* to replace the long ideogram required for Bodhisattva.[2] Of more interest is the place which was eventually given to Tan-gun in Buddhism. This was done by identifying Hwan'in with the Indian *deva* Indra, 帝釈天, Sino-Kor.: Chesŏk-ch'on.[3] This happened owing to the special intervention of the Zen monk Ilche, 一祭.[4] Tan-gun himself became the Korean *avatāra* of Śrī-mahā-devi, 吉祥天, Sino-Kor.: Kilsang-ch'ŏn, just as Amaterasu became that of Vairocāna Buddha.[5] This Buddhism developed in the direction of Maitreyanism and Amidism. That is apparent from the fact established by Pratt, that even now Śākyamuni, Maitreya, Amitābha and Avalokiteśvara (Sino.-Kor.: Kwanseum) are still accounted the most popular Buddhas and Bodhisattvas.

Thus Korea served as a bridge for quite separate forms of Buddhism. We have seen in this chapter how, under the influence of the quite peculiar national character of the Chinese and the Koreans,

[1] In *Pilgrimage of Buddhism*, p. 424. The correct Sino-Korean reading of the Chinese characters: 彌勒 for Maitreya is: Mirŭk. The Mirŭk stones, which are mentioned here, replaced the stone columns which even today enrich every Korean village and which were viewed as protective spirits which, i.a., had to protect the roads. Cf. W. Gundert, op. cit., pp. 188-189.

[2] Cf. Kanazawa Shōzaburō, "Sammai to bosatsu", (Rice and the Boddhisattva), *C.G.*, no. 11, 1957, March, pp. 36-38.

[3] Cf. Takahashi Tōru, op. cit., p. 79.

[4] Ibid.

[5] Takahashi Tōru, op. cit., pp. 79-80.

this Buddhism against the background of its—originally Indian—view of life, was difficult to understand and to translate and had to surrender much of this in exchange for many religious values, experiences and interpretations which were favoured in these territories bordering on Japan. This whole complex of East-Asian Buddhism was to be carried from Paekche on to Japan mainly by the:

e The Korean immigrants

Those who contributed most to the origin of Japanese Buddhism were the Korean immigrants, named *kikajin*, 帰化人, in Japan, who, up to the sixth century, crossed in large numbers from Mimana to Japan. They introduced very many reforms and innovations. Thus, in 645 they were the prime movers behind the scene who brought about the fall of the antiquated, degenerate structure of Japanese society and made room for the bureaucracy inspired by China. This finally broke the power of the omnipotent *shizoku* permanently. I hope to show in the following chapters that their specific place in Japanese society guaranteed the first flowering of Buddhism on Japanese soil. Hence we must take a closer look at the particular nature and historical growth of this group.

According to the oldest Japanese sources the first immigrants Achiki and Wani came to Japan as early as during the reign of emperor Ōjin. Wani was even supposed to have brought the first Chinese classical works to Japan. The *Kojiki* specifically mentions the book *Lun-yü*, 論語, the Analects of Confucius, and the book named *Ch'ien-tzŭ-wên*, 千字文.[1] The doubtfulness of these data appears from the fact that this latter work, *Ch'ien-tzŭ-wên*, was only accomplished during the Liang, 梁, dynasty (502-557).[2] Hence

[1] *Kojiki*, 2nd. *maki*, Kuroita Katsumi, Maruyama Jirō, *Kokushitaikei Kojiki*, p. 104: "The ruler of Paekche, Shōko, 照古, sent a stallion and a mare and entrusted these to master Achiki. Further, he gave to Wani the *Lun-yü* in 10 *maki* and the *Ch'ien-tzŭ-wên*."

[2] This work of Chou Hsing-szŭ originated at the time of Emperor Wu, 武, (502-549). It could therefore certainly not have reached Japan before Buddhism. According to A. Wedemeyer, op. cit., p. 57, footnote 82, an older work was indicated by the same title. Arai Hakuseki and Tanigawa Kotosuga see yet another work in this, but their solutions do not satisfy either. It is better to bring this work into context with the compilation of the *Kojiki* at the beginning of the 7th. century: this work, popular at that time, was simply inserted into the *Kojiki* text, without anyone being aware that by

its mention during Ōjin's reign is an anachronism. This also makes it doubtful whether the *Lun-yü* also really reached Japan in Ōjin's time. Moreover, at that time there was no one who could read it. Hence we are of the opinion that this passage has been inserted into Ōjin's chronicles with Confucianist intentions.[1] This probably occurred after the 645 reformation, because from then on especially State Confucianism was supreme at court.

Just like so many 'ancestors' in these Ōjin chronicles, Achiki and Wani are therefore constructions of a few prominent immigrant-officials of the seventh century who, just like the other nobles of this period, wanted a genealogy in the state chronicles. Tsuda [2] believes that until Suiko's period (therefore up to the end of the sixth century) such Confucian scholars certainly did not come to Japan. Moreover, until that time this country was far too torn apart by various civil wars to appear as an Eldorado to such scholars. Therefore Confucianism did not begin in Japan much more swiftly than Buddhism.

This does not mean to say that the phenomenon of the Korean immigration must therefore also be dated equally recently. There are various references in the Ōjin chronicles to Korean ponds, built by Koreans.[3] Whether they were indeed built as early as this also becomes doubtful in the light of the foregoing remarks. However, probably one of the oldest group of immigrants must have worked on this. Now when did they come to Japan?

We believe that, to a great extent, Japan owed these immigrants to the political shifts in Korea itself mentioned in this chapter.[4] The first prompting to these immigrations must have been Taegaya's appeal of 369, on behalf of the other participant states of the Pyŏn-han federation, to Japan for aid against Paekche and Silla. Thus the Japanese fairly easily established their own bridgehead on Korean

---

so doing an anachronism was caused. Cf. B. Lewin, op. cit., p. 13, footnote 4. See further: Paul Pelliot, "Le Ts'ien Tseu Wen ou 'Livre des mille mots' ", *T.P.*, XXIV (1926), p. 209.

[1] For example, in order to give Confucianism in Japan an older history than Buddhism. This was very closely connected with the *Lun-yü*. B. Lewin, loc. cit., opines: "Es lässt sich nicht beweisen, ob die *Einführung des Rongo* (= *Lun-yü*) und *Senjimon* (= *Ch'ien-tzû-wên*) auf Wani zurückgeht".

[2] Tsuda Sōkichi, *Nihon Jōdaishi no Kenkyū*, pp. 492 ff.

[3] Cf. footnote 1 on p. 129.

[4] Pp. 199-205.

soil, which was highly suitable as a reception centre for Korean refugees from other states. This was where the immigrants, particularly from the Mimana area, entered Japan.

According to Lewin [1] the first wave of *kikajin* arrived circa 400 A.D. Japanese scholars have worked out that at that time the inhabitants of 127 villages crossed to Japan.[2] When reading the Japanese sources one might not suspect this. However, when reading the names in the chronicles one must consider that these are only the Korean leaders of entire groups. Lewin also sees these names as designating whole groups of people.[3]

The second wave of immigrants followed Silla's conquest of Mimana in 562. Of this Ch'oe Hyŏnbae says that it raised the number of Korean settlements in Japan to 7,500 with a population of at least 37,500 people.[4] The third and last wave occurred after the arrival of Buddhism. In 663 and 668 Paekche and Koguryŏ were overrun by Silla. This brought "whole swarms of the defeated to Japan in order to find a new home there".[5] The *Shinsen-shōjiroku*, 新撰姓氏錄, of 815, the genealogical register, records that of the 1,182 noble families 327 came from Korea.[6]

However exaggerated this may sound, nevertheless, these groups of Koreans in Japan brought about a vast revolution in the fields of technology and philosophy. This was largely owing to the fact that many of them were of Chinese origin. Their ancestors had come to Korea some hundreds of years previously from China during the period of Chinese dominion there. According to the group they belonged to, these Chinese were called the Aya, 漢, and Hata, 秦.[7] Most of them had come to Japan on their own initiative, inde-

---

[1] Bruno Lewin, op. cit., p. 190; further Ch'oe Hyŏnbae in "Korea von Japan aus gesehen", *Koreanica*, p. 33, 34.

[2] Ch'oe Hyŏnbae, loc. cit.

[3] B. Lewin, op. cit., p. 9, footnote 20.

[4] Cf. Ch'oe Hyŏnbae, loc. cit.

[5] Ibid.

[6] B. Lewin, op. cit., p. 192. More or less the same numbers are to be found in F. Vos, *Volken van Één Stam* ?, p. 7. From the numbers given by both authors the important contribution from Paekche to all of these immigrants becomes apparent, namely, almost double that of all the immigrants together from other areas.

[7] B. Lewin wrote in particular the excellent work concerning them which we have quoted repeatedly here: *Aya und Hata*, Wiesbaden 1962.

pendent of the mass migration.[1] This can certainly not be said of the mass immigrations. These had taken place on both sides owing to necessity rather than to free will. This necessity lay not only in the political complications on the Korean peninsula, but also on the Japanese side. The Japanese were driven to bringing immigrants to Yamato owing to their own ignorance and the necessity, for example, of draining the Yamato marshes [2] and irrigation of entire areas for the cultivation of rice.[3] To these ends they risked large parts of their Korean campaigns. Just as the T'opa, they needed not only dyke-builders but also farmers.[4] Therefore even prisoners from Silla and even whole villages were taken to Japan [5] and added to the domains of the *shizoku*.

As a result of the fact that great population masses shifted across the bridge of nations to Japan, this land became even more closely linked to everything vital on the Eurasian continent. This added somewhat to the continental outlook of the Japanese population. It is, however, very hard to dissect the new amalgam which had thus come about so that the components which distinguish the individuality of these two groups stand out clearly. This is because both had much in common from the earliest stages. Indeed, the imperial tribe on its way through Korea to Japan had not remained foreign to Korea. Additionally, both had Tungusian blood.

---

[1] Nevertheless their numbers dwindle against the vast masses of Koreans who spread from the peninsula to Japan. Cf. B. Lewin, op. cit., p. 10.

[2] Cf. concerning the dates of that drainage the highly interesting though unconvincing article by Higuchi Kiyoyuki, "Jōdai gūshi-densetsu no kenkyū", *K.G.Z.*, vol. 62, 1961, no. 9, Sept., pp. 33-43. By use of the geography of the old palaces and the archeological finds in the Yamato plain, he attempts to establish the height of the water during several centuries in this plain. By this he hopes to establish the historicity of a figure such as Jimmu and other old emperors. His arguments are not too convincing because the imperial palaces did not sink very noticeably along with the water which sank owing to dyking. Thus the palaces of Senka, Kimmei and Bidatsu stood on an average higher than those of the so-called first Emperors, Jimmu, Suizei and Annei.

[3] The discovery of rice in the graves of Kimhae and round Lo-lang is a strong argument for the fact that the rice cultivation of the Han period came via Korea to Japan. Cf. Igata Sadachi, "Chōsen ni okeru tōzaibo no kigen", (Origin of Rice Cultivation in Korea), *C.G.*, no. 18, Jan. 1961, pp. 1-31. Cf. J. E. Kidder, op. cit., pp. 95 ff.

[4] Cf. W. Eberhard, *Das Toba-Reich Nord Chinas*, pp. 201, 202.

[5] B. Lewin, op. cit., p. 193, footnote 24.

This relationship was also expressed in their mutual religions. These cannot be analysed too clearly. Everything which is known derives from the seventh century, at which time the assimilation between both groups was already fully active. Also, at the time of the Korean immigrations, almost nothing is known about these individually. Moreover, most of the data on Japanese religions has been recorded and edited by descendants of immigrants. The first writing experts were indeed produced from their ranks.[1] Hence their descriptions of Japanese religions are likely to have a Korean tinge. Therefore, if similarities can be discovered between both of them, this is not only owing to the fact that here we are already dealing with a Japanese-Korean amalgamation of both, but rather that much of this should be ascribed to Korean editors and reporters. Hence we cannot simply conclude, as does Ch'oe Hyŏnbae,[2] from the pre-history of the sources with, for instance, regard to the tales of the emperors' descent, that Japan's imperial ancestors migrated from Kamapol (= Korea) to Japan. Here indeed we are dealing with a rendition of the origin of Japan's imperial house which is extremely inspired by Korea.

In Japanese mythology there are various elements of which it is hard to define whether they are purely Japanese. Similar elements can also certainly be found in Shintō. Nevertheless there are also a few cults which probably relate to the contribution of the *kikajin*. Those are the Inari cult, still very popular and closely connected with rice production, and that of Matsuno-o, 松尾.[3] These devotions were originally propagated only by the *kikajin*. This was also the case with the Hachiman cult, as prominent immigrant families occupied various important functions in his main temple of Usa, 宇佐, on Kyūshū.[4] Some of these Korean devotions, even today, enjoy extreme popularity in Japan. Thus, for example, the country is covered from the north to the south with small Inari, 稲荷, temples.

---

[1] Cf. B. Lewin, op. cit., pp. 177-183.

[2] Cf. *Koreanica*, p. 27.

[3] Cf. Bruno Lewin, op. cit., pp. 172-175. For the Inari cult, see M. Eder, "Die Reisseele in Japan und Korea", *Folk. St.*, vol. XIV, 1955, pp. 237 ff.

[4] Cf. B. Lewin, op. cit., pp. 171, 172, footnote 36. See also U.A. Casal, *Hachiman der Kriegsgott*, Tōkyō 1962. Here an implication may be found of the Chinese origin of this god (cf. op. cit., p. 1). However, he gives no further history of this.

However small, they can be found on every street corner and in every family.[1]

Japan's situation was noticeably influenced not only religiously but also culturally and politically by these immigrants. Nearly all cultural and technical achievements of that time were their work: the construction of paddy fields, building of palaces for the emperors and the leaders of the great *shizoku*, temple building, town planning, even chronicle writing. We have already pointed out that in the field of politics they prepared the revolution of 645, which made Japan a bureaucracy and gave it its first constitution. All of this put the Japanese in a position of great dependence towards them. Many among them eventually found this hard to endure. All the more so because all attempts up till then had failed to keep the Imna bridgehead in Japanese hands. All of this resulted in these achievements by immigrants being allowed to disappear from history, a process which began early in the ninth century and was achieved by burning [2] the manuscripts concerning this, or by forgery.[3] This happened in particular under the reign of Emperor Kammu (782-806).[4] The fear of Koreans gaining a place somewhere

---

[1] Cf. B. Lewin, op. cit., p. 171, bottom, p. 172.

[2] A pronunciation on this may be found in the *Jinnōshōtōki*, 神皇正統記 a work written in 1343 by Kitabatake Chikafusa, 北畠新房, (1292-1354). This work contains mostly a consideration of the imperial tribe originated from the south, and its principle errors and successes since the days of Jimmu. It states: "The documents which contended that Japan belonged in antiquity to the three Han states (Ma-han, Chin-han and Pyŏn-han) were committed to the flames under the reign of Kammu. After the 'opening' of the heavens and earth, Susa *no* O *no mikoto* also went to the land of Kara, etc. Hence their lands also should belong to the heritage of our gods. Was this not altogether painful?" Cf. Kanazawa Shōzaburō, "Chōsen-kenkyū to *Nihonshoki*" (Korea Study and the *Nihonshoki*), *C.G.*, no. 1, 1951, May, pp. 86, 87.

[3] Thus the *Shinsen-shōjiroku*, 新撰姓氏録, the register of the noble families which was composed in 815 by Manda Shinō and others, was supposed to be a fairly arbitrary choice from the *Shōjiroku* dating from 659. According to Kanazawa, the term *Shinsen*, 新撰, in the title *Shinsen-shōjiroku*, which means 'new choice' is indicative of falsifications of a later date; op. cit., p. 88. Furthermore, he quotes decrees from 799 and 809, from which not only investigations, but also reprisals, and measures of confiscation of the immigrant registers are laid down; op. cit., p. 88.

[4] Cf. Kanazawa Shōzaburō, op. cit., p. 89: "In order to avoid the disunion amongst the *shizoku*, the Korean registers were burnt during the reign of Emperor Kammu."

in the imperial genealogy especially led to this purge of the manuscripts.[1]

All of this also reflected on the writing of history prior to that time, of which it must be accepted that it was rewritten in many aspects. With regard to Buddhism it was made to seem as if it owed its existence in Japan to Emperor Kimmei's approval. No longer was attention paid to the fact that it was originally matured in a Korean immigrant society in preparation for its encounter with the entire Japanese society, in which the imperial house also participated. This resulted in the necessity of creating a figure such as Shōtoku Taishi in order to suggest that this initiative had always lain in Japanese hands. We hope to show this course of events in the following chapters. This is the only way to discover how Buddhism actually met Japan and became an integral part of it.

---

[1] Cf. Kanazawa Shōzaburō, op. cit., p. 89: "As a result of the fact that close relationship existed between the imperial house and the Paekche immigrants, the chronicles which applied to these Korea relations were all committed to the flames under Kammu, in order to eradicate difficulties with the *shōji* (= *uji*).

The *Jinnōshōtōki* says of this: Then the *banjin* (i.e. the groups of immigrants with their own genealogy, which expressed that relationship to the emperor) came. They increased the unrest by calling themselves descendants of the emperors and the gods. In order to prove this, they wrote their genealogies, the *Shōjiroku*. These genealogies were abrogated in 799 and later." Cf. also W.G. Aston, op. cit., vol. II, p. 77, footnote 3.

CHAPTER FOUR

THE ORIGIN OF BUDDHISM IN JAPAN

In the previous chapters we have observed two processes which, as yet, have little to do with each other: that of the (social) growth of the Japanese people and that of East Asian Buddhism. We have followed these processes up to the moment of meeting, namely the moment at which East Asiatic Buddhism had more or less crossed the Korean bridge and was on the point of crossing over to and finally reaching Japan.

The following chapters will consider especially the actual meeting of these two, from which Japanese Buddhism originated. We believe that this meeting took place in three stages. These stages are:

1) The arrival of Buddhism in Japan,
2) The adaptation to personal and Japanese Buddhism, and finally
3) The origination of state Buddhism.

We have set forth these three stages in three different chapters in the rest of this book.

Hence this chapter is particularly concerned with the origin of Buddhism in Japan. However, before considering this encounter face to face, we must first look at the political situation at the time of this origination, all the more so because it is this which made the advent of Buddhism in Japan possible.

1 THE POLITICAL DEVELOPMENTS PRIOR TO AND DURING THE ADVENT OF BUDDHISM IN JAPAN

We pointed out in the second chapter that the emperor was the apex of a society divided into *shizoku*. This was the case until the Taika reformation of 645, at which time this society was entirely altered in structure. Hence the Buddhism which arrived in Japan in the sixth century was also associated with this ancient social structure.

At that time in particular the emperor's task was dual. First and foremost he had to preserve the balance between the *shizoku*, which were each highly susceptible to favouritism. Simultaneously he had to exhort all of these *shizoku* towards the wars in Korea. Thus the political situation of the sixth century was more or less defined by these two conditions: the political tensions in Korea and the differences and frictions between the *shizoku* amongst themselves.

a The Japanese Korean policy [1]

In the previous chapter we have very briefly described Mimana, Japan's bridgehead in Korea. In order to comprehend Japan's Korean policy we must go into this more extensively here. It is a generally recognised fact that the main Japanese foreign relations and difficulties of that period can only be understood from the problems surrounding this area.[2] Hence Mimana formed the real starting point for Japan's Korean policy.

Mimana had already played a part in Japan's relations with China. In Chapter I we pointed out that these relations went back to 57 A.D., as the roads to China passed through Korea. Initially they even ended in the Chinese provinces of Lo-lang and Tai-fang in Korea. When the Japanese emissaries later actually managed to reach China their road still led through the Korean districts of Chŏlla Namdo, 全羅南道, and Kyŏngsang-namdo, 慶尙南道.[3]

Hence Japan was already confronted, through its embassies, by the Korean relationships. We believe that Japan, therefore, for various reasons, maintained a small occupied district on the Korean

---

[1] This Korea exposition is not intended to be a duplication of the second part of the previous chapter, as it only concerns the relations between Japan and Korea. Here we have been particularly supported by the extensive work by Suematsu Yasukazu, *Mimana Kōbōshi*, (History of the Rise and Fall of Mimana), Tōkyō 1949. Here the author has collected the points of view of many Japanese authors concerning Mimana, such as Tsuda Sōkichi, Naka Michiyo, and others and arranged them. For this Mimana literature see his work, pp. 1-20.

Cf. also his summarizing article: "Japan's Relations with the Asian Continent and the Korean Peninsula", *J.o. W.H.*, IV, no. 3, pp. 671-683.

[2] Cf. Suematsu Yasukazu, op. cit., p. 245: "Japan's relations with Korea from 350 up to 640, therefore a period of 300 years, encompass the period of Mimana's existence. Japan's relations to Paekche, Silla, Koguryŏ and China can be reduced to Mimana problems."

[3] For further details of this route, see Suematsu Yasukazu, op. cit., p. 65.

south coast even in early times, which was initially intended as a post for provisions and as a staging post for the embassies which travelled up and down from China to Japan. There were also other reasons for the existence of this Japanese enclave. In the first chapter we saw that the *Tenson* or *kiba* tribe crossed to Japan from Korea and there began the unification of this country under the hegemony of its tribal leaders. The Japanese enclave on the south coast of Korea could very easily be the last scrap of the districts which this tribe had passed through and occupied in Korea. Although also at this time Korea, seen from the cultural point of view, remained a bridge with one-way traffic towards Japan, politically speaking this was no more the case because, owing to the advent of the Japanese, developments in the northward direction were also beginning to take place. As a result of the lack of genuine Korean unity the Japanese influence could make itself felt fairly widely from this area. That this supposition is not based on fantasy can be concluded, for instance, from the tribute which lands such as Paekche and even Silla had to pay to Japan.[1] This tribute is inconceivable if Japan had not had some kind of claim in these districts. Therefore it probably had something to do with ancient Japanese ascendency in the Korean peninsula, or even with the *kiba* tribe. This tribute formed a completely specific problem even in later centuries. We shall return to this later.

The actual turning-point in this Chinese-Japanese domination was reached with the fall of Lo-lang in 313. This terminated contact with China by land. However, this fall had further consequences, as it marked the rise of Koguryŏ as well as of other Korean states which began to utilise for their own ends the political organisation imported by China. We have seen, in the previous chapter, how all of this took place. Despite these new developments Japan did not abandon Korea but began to enter into relations with the new states. What did Japan intend by this? We can deduce these intentions from the historical developments which followed the year 313.

---

[1] These occurred particularly in the 46th, 47th, 49th, 51st and 52nd years of reign of Empress Jingū. Here mainly *mitsugi* (= levies) from Paekche were concerned.

At the same time Silla also committed itself to annual contributions, which consisted especially of horses and slaves. Cf. W. G. Aston, *Nihongi I*, pp. 246-251; Suematsu Yasukazu, op. cit., pp. 255 and 256.

In 367 Paekche is supposed to have sent emissaries to Japan for the first time, with the special assignment of obtaining military reinforcements against Silla. This is recorded both in Japanese and Korean sources.[1] Here Paekche gained its objective. According to the *Nihonshoki*, it contrived, with the help of Japanese troops, to regain a large number of districts in Imna.[2] Later also it appeared that Paekche felt itself a great deal stronger with this Japanese support. In 371 it even dared to campaign against Koguryŏ. It destroyed the capital, P'yŏngyang, and killed the king of this realm. The result of these military achievements was that the old Chinese territory of Tai-fang came under the rule of Paekche. A year later, in 372, an emissary was even sent to China, who was supposed to obtain high-level Chinese recognition of the occupation of previously Chinese districts. It is clear that Paekche owed all of these large extensions of territory to Japan.

Now this Japanese support was unthinkable without the presence of a wholly Japanese bridgehead in Korea. Hence this must have been there prior to 370. The data in the Japanese and Korean sources scarcely admit of doubt, all the more so because this area held a wholly specific place in the Japanese Korea strategy. The Japanese occupation of Mimana, confirmed as an historical reality some twenty years later on the previously mentioned commemorative column of King Kwanggaet'o, not only took place, incidentally, in order to help Paekche, but must also have been part of the Japanese plans for Korea. There are various signs which indicate that Japan not only coveted the hegemony over Korea which China had permitted itself to be robbed of in 313, but even demanded this. These indications are clearly obvious in the Japanese sources.[3] It appears from the *Kojiki* that in Japanese antiquity, i.e. the period at which this work was compiled, the idea of Paekche and Silla as two imperial districts, *miyake*, was enthusiastically toyed with. Thus Jingū was allowed to conquer Silla and make it

---

[1] Cf. *Nihonshoki*, 9th *maki*, Jingū kōgō, 49th year; Kuroita Katsumi, Maruyama Jirō, *Kokushitaikei Nihonshoki*, part 1, pp. 260, 261; W.G. Aston, *Nihongi* I, pp. 248, 249. From Korean sources and geography, Suematsu Yasukazu proved the historical reality of this text, op. cit., pp. 46-63.

[2] *Nihonshoki*, 9th *maki*, Jingū kōgō, 49th year; Kuroita Katsumi, Maruyama Jirō, op. cit., p. 260; W. G. Aston, *Nihongi* I, p. 249.

[3] For this presentation of proof, see Suematsu Yasukazu, op. cit., pp. 253-257.

into '*Mimakai*', that is to say 'groom to the imperial horses'.[1] On that same occasion Paekche was given the title of '*Wata no miyake*', '*miyake* of the crossing'.[2] These two names had quite clearly expressed Japan's never fully realised ambitions.

Therefore Mimana, often branded in the Japanese sources as *miyake*, was, as Japanese territory, merely the initial move in a large-scale plan which aimed at hegemony over the whole of Korea.

Another indication of this Japanese purpose was the aforementioned tribute—the *mitsugi*, 調,—from almost all the Korean states to Japan. Officials were even appointed by Japan at the Korean courts in order to supervise the payment of the *mitsugi*.

The presumed presence of Japanese on their own bridgehead, and their part as leaders which was keenly emulated, are confirmed as historical reality in early Korean history by the Kwanggaet'o monument. As we have seen in the first and third chapters, various Japanese activities between the years 391 and 405 are registered on this although they terminate in a total victory for Koguryŏ. The historical development which the 203 characters of this inscription—largely mutilated—bring to light was not too satisfactory for Japan, even though it did not end—as the *Samguk sagi* triumphantly claims—in an invasion of all the Korean states in Japan itself.[3] It was of importance to the further relations of the Japanese with Korea that, according to this monument, Paekche was crushingly defeated together with Japan in 405. This double defeat may have meant the end of Japan's high aspirations in Korea. It did make Japan and Paekche even more closely bound together by fellow-suffering. The close tie between these two lands was to exist throughout the whole of the fifth century and thereafter.

Nevertheless Japanese troops also acted in other Korean states as preservers of the mutual balance between these states. Thus the Japanese soldiery intervened in 464 [4] in order to terminate the more than 50 years occupation of Silla by Koguryŏ troops.

---

[1] *Kojiki*, 2nd *maki*; Kuroita Katsumi, Maruyama Jirō, *Kokushitaikei Kojiki*, p. 96.

K. Florenz calls this "Fütterer der erlauchten Rosse", op. cit., p. 110. It is written phonetically in the *Kojiki* as: 御馬甘.

[2] Ibid., written as: 渡屯家.

[3] For further details concerning the contents of this inscription we refer to Matsukawa Jirō, "Tennōshijō no Bōten", *Tennō no Rekishi*, pp. 65-67; Suematsu Yasukazu, op. cit., pp. 71-78. See further Chapter I, footnote 3 on p. 38.

[4] See *Nihonshoki*, 14th *maki*, Yūryaku, 8th year; Kuroita Katsumi,

Despite this aid to Silla, Japan continued to feel itself more closely tied to Paekche from Mimana. This does not mean to say, however, that Paekche had actually become a kind of *miyake* or province of Mimana. Proof of this may be found in the *Sung-shu*. Here Paekche is mentioned in the year 451, in contrast to many Mimana states and even to Silla, as not being a vassal to Japan; it was not under the command of a Wa (= Japan) general[1] recognised by China. Moreover, these Chinese chronicles also bear witness to Japan's ambitions in Korea.

Seen from the point of view of these ambitions, the diplomatic activity between Paekche and China must have been hard for Japan to bear. However, Paekche had paid tribute from 372 to Eastern Tsin. In contrast to Koguryŏ and Silla, it had intended, throughout the years 438, 451 and 458, to be recognised directly by the *T'ien-tzŭ*. Not only the kings but also the lower rulers and nobles of Paekche strove after Chinese titles of nobility[2] in the years 472, 490 and 495.

Against foreign enemies such as Koguryŏ it also attempted to get Chinese support. Thus, in 472, it appealed—without much success however—to the T'opa of North Wei to give aid against the intruding Koguryŏ. The troops of Koguryŏ were not intimidated by these spasmodic diplomatic essays by Paekche. They marched on the south, and in 476 captured the so-called Paekche fort, the royal castle.[3]

The increase in power of lands such as Koguryŏ and Silla and the political tensions which grew steadily between the three Korean realms at this time made it obvious to the Japanese that they would never succeed in realising the unification of Korea under

---

Maruyama Jirō, op. cit., part 1, pp. 272-274; W. G. Aston, *Nihongi* I, pp. 351, 352; for an opinion of these facts see Suematsu Yasukazu, op. cit., pp. 81-86.

[1] Under the year 451 there is mention of: "the additional title was granted of General Who Maintains Peace in the East Commanding with Battle-Ax All Military Affairs in the Six Countries of Wa, Silla, Imna, Kala, Chin-han and Mok-han." In the same *Sung-shu* the same formula also occurs under the year 478. Here however there is mention of: "Seven Countries of Wa, Paekche, Silla, Imna, Kala, Chin-han and Mok-han, . . ." Cf. Ryūsaku Tsunoda, *Japan in the Chinese Dynastic Histories*, pp. 22 and 23.

See also Suematsu Yasukazu, op. cit., p. 98.

[2] Cf. Suematsu Yasukazu, op. cit., pp. 108-110.

[3] Cf. *Nihonshoki*, 14th *maki*, Yūryaku, 20th year; Kuroita Katsumi, Maruyama Jirō, op. cit., pp. 387, 388; W. G. Aston, *Nihongi* I, pp. 366, 367.

the *ō-kimi*. This revelation noticeably weakened Japan's interest in Korea. The Korean lands also, especially the states of Paekche and Silla, situated closer to Mimana, felt the Japanese grip loosening.

Therefore Paekche and Silla began to benefit from Japan's lack of interest by forcing various territorial expansions at the expense of Korea's weakest territory, Mimana. This occurred especially at the beginning of the sixth century, the time at which Buddhism gained a permanent footing in Japan. In this respect Paekche took the initiative by capturing the island of Tonra, situated on the coast of Mimana. According to the *Samguk yusa*, Tonra, 耽羅, had already begun paying tribute to Paekche in 476, and was occupied by Paekche in 498. The *Nihonshoki* places this occupation in 508. Although we cannot say too much about this occupation, it is nevertheless certain that it happened at the beginning of the sixth century.[1]

In 509, the third year of the reign of Emperor Keitai, all people of Paekche descent were thrown out of Mimana as a reprisal.[2] The areas thus depopulated were filled by Koreans from the northern districts. Thus it was attempted to minimise the Paekche majority in Mimana. Paekche, however, did not allow itself to be distracted by this, and in 512 demanded the incorporation of four Mimana districts near Paekche: Upper Tari, 上哆唎; Lower Tari, 下哆唎; Sata, 娑陀; and Muro. 牟婁.[3] These four districts form part of the present-day Chŏlla Namdo.[4] According to the *Nihonshoki*

---

[1] Itamoto Tarō sees in Tonra the island Cheju (= Quelpart). According to him the composition of the Keitai chronicles in the *Nihonshoki* is of such a nature that no value can be attributed to its dates. Hence, according to him, Paekche could have occupied the island Tonra even prior to 508.

Cf. Itamoto Tarō, "Keitaiki Shijitsu?" *K.G.Z.*, vol. LXII, 1962, Sept., no. 9, pp. 47, 48.

See also Suematsu Yasukazu, op. cit., p. 115, who holds the same opinion.

For the texts see *Nihonshoki*, 17th *maki*, Keitai, 2nd year; Kuroita Katsumi, Maruyama Jirō, op. cit., part 2, p. 16. See also W. G. Aston, *Nihongi* II, pp. 6 and 7. Here, in contrast to Suematsu and Kuroita Katsumi, Maruyama Jirō, op. cit., he gives Tonra its Korean name Tamna. Moreover, in footnote 3 he equals it to Cheju.

[2] See *Nihonshoki*, 17th *maki*, Keitai 3rd year, 2nd month; Kuroita Katsumi, Maruyama Jirō, op. cit., part 2, p. 17; W. G. Aston, *Nihongi* II, p. 7.

[3] See *Nihonshoki*, 17th *maki*, Keitai 5th year, 12th month; Kuroita Katsumi, Maruyama Jirō, op. cit., part 2, p. 17; W. G. Aston, loc. cit.

[4] They formed the southern half of Chŏlla Namdo. Suematsu has here

this request was submitted that same year to the emperor for approval by the *mikotomochi*, that is to say, the imperial representative of Mimana, Ōtomo *no* Kanamura, 大伴金村. Hereafter Mononobe *no ōmuraji* Arakao, 麁鹿火, was appointed as imperial ambassador in order to convey the imperial approval to the Paekche delegation. This happened despite the dramatic and interesting protestations by his wife, which are as follows: [1]

"Long ago the (great) god of Sumiyoshi, 住吉, entrusted the gold and silver countries on the side of the sea, Koguryŏ, Paekche, Silla and Imna, to the emperor of Homuda, 譽田, (= Ōjin) while he was yet within the womb. Hereafter the Empress Okinaga Tarashi *hime no mikoto*, 氣長足姫命, (= Jingū) and the *ō-omi* Takeuchi *no sukune* turned these districts one by one into *miyake*, withdrawn from the eye by the surface of the sea. There were certainly reasons for this development. If now we are to divide this territory and give it to others, then we oppose our own country. How shall we then for a long time remain free from the criticism and reproach which will be voiced against us!"

These words, referring to an earlier oracle—as probably previously uttered by a woman (could she have been a Shaman ?) — could not, however, move Arakao to rescind the imperial concession. As a result of this almost all of Chŏlla Namdo belonged to Paekche. The transfer of these four districts also had other implications later. Therefore we must consider it briefly. Namely, it is inconceivable that the concessions made here did not include some obligations on Paekche. Without these, the facility with which Paekche got what it wanted at the Japanese court cannot be imagined.

Now what were these obligations ? We believe that they were not to be found in military guarantees. Paekche could only offer its own culture as an equivalent exchange. Paekche did not owe this culture to its own efforts, but to the afore-mentioned contacts with China. We have already mentioned that since 372 it had maintained direct relations with China. These diplomatic contacts also lasted throughout the Sung, Ch'i, 齊, and Liang periods (420-557). They indubitably went hand in hand with cultural and religious influences from China which, particularly in these respects,

---

attempted to localize these areas more definitively, op. cit., pp. 118-123.

[1] Cf. for this text: *Nihonshoki*, 17th *maki*, Keitai, 6th year, 12th month; Kuroita Katsumi, Maruyama Jirō, op. cit., part 2, p. 18. See further W. G. Aston, *Nihongi* II, p. 8.

greatly outshone Paekche. The most important reason for Paekche's cultural superiority over Japan lay in the fact that it had, for long, incorporated the old Chinese prefecture of Tai-fang within its borders. Thus many Chinese living in Tai-fang had had the opportunity of reorganising Paekche economically and culturally according to the Chinese model.

Now Japan also wanted to benefit from this cultural and religious renovation—consider, for instance, Buddhism—which was progressing steadily in Paekche. Hence Japan considered the cession of the afore-mentioned four districts a welcome opportunity for demanding the advent of cultural and religious experts from Paekche. Now that Japan no longer aspired to territorial expansion in Korea, the importation of this Chinese and, in many aspects, still superior Paekche culture represented the only genuine gain which the centuries-long Korea policies could still offer.

Although there is no mention of an official cultural contract between Japan and Paekche, it appears that such an agreement was certainly made. Otherwise the large numbers of specifically cultural and religious experts who entered, particularly since 512, from Paekche cannot be explained. Even in 513, a year after the transfer of the afore-mentioned four districts, Paekche had already sent a scholar of the Five Classics, who is called Tanyōni, 段楊爾,[1] in the *Nihonshoki*. There is no agreement as to what precisely should be understood by these Five Chinese Classics, as they varied according to each period.[2] This scholar of the Five Classics was exchanged in

---

[1] Cf. *Nihonshoki*, 17th *maki*, Keitai, 7th year, 6th month; Kuroita Katsumi, Maruyama Jirō, op. cit., part 2, p. 19:

"Paekche sent General Sami Monkui, 姐彌文貴, and General Suri Soni, 洲利即爾, with the *omi* of Hotsumi Oshiyama, 穗積臣押山. As tribute they offered a scholar of the Five Classics, Tanyōni."

W. G. Aston, op. cit., p. 9, gives in his translation the Korean names of all of these gentlemen, respectively General Chyami Mun-kwi, General Chyu-ri Cheung-ni and the scholar Tan Yang-ni. Here we prefer the Japanese pronunciation of these names, as these Korean names have been reproduced in the Japanese sources as they sounded in Japanese ears. The original Korean pronunciation is therefore difficult to reconstruct from the *Nihonshoki* only. Where possible we shall reproduce the Korean names (according to the old reading by Aston).

[2] Suematsu Yasukazu, op. cit., p. 267, considers it probable that they existed in the following works and collections:

1. The *Li-shu*, 礼書, the 'Book of Rites'. Cf. for the contents and history

516 for Aya *no* Kōanmo, 高安茂.[1] A noteworthy particular of this exchange is that on the same occasion as this exchange, the Paekche ambassador came to thank the emperor for a new territorial concession to Paekche which the emperor had made the previous year by which the Paekche district of Chŏlla Namdo was extended even further.[1] This more or less systematic exchange was later enlarged on a far greater scale so that even entire teams of experts replaced each other regularly. We shall return to this in the following chapter.[2]

Therefore the good relations which existed between Japan and Paekche and between their ruling houses must be ascribed particularly to this cultural and—in our opinion—religious ascendency of Paekche over Japan. Later sympathy for Paekche was extensively aroused by these experts in Japan. Hence it is not surprising that no foreign ruler enjoyed greater popularity in Japan at that time than the king of Paekche and especially the ruler under whom this cultural exchange reached extremes, King Sŏng (Sino.-Jap.: Seimei, 聖明, 523-554). This popularity is also apparent in the many lines devoted to him in the *Nihonshoki*. This is extremely odd as Paekche otherwise remained just as dangerous to Japanese territory in Korea as the far more militant Silla. Both indeed sought after territorial expansion at the expense of Mimana. Therefore Paekche

---

of this: Nagasawa Kikuya, Eugen Feifel, *Geschichte der Chinesischen Literatur*, p. 107.

2. The *Yüeh-shu*, 楽書, the 'Book of Songs' which also comes from the Han period, see Nagasawa-Feifel, op. cit., pp. 137 ff.
3. The *Lun-yü*, 論語, by Confucius, cf. Nagasawa-Feifel, op. cit., pp. 29 ff.
4. The classic work on childish piety, *Hsiao-ching*, 孝経, which, together with no. 3 formed the text book for the education of the wealthy classes in the Han and T'ang periods. Cf. Nagasawa-Feifel, pp. 110, 111.
5. The prose work from the Chou period: the *Shang-shu*, 尙書. See Nagasawa-Feifel on this, op. cit. p. 87 and further pp. 105 ff.

[1] Cf. *Nihonshoki*, 17th *maki*, Keitai, 10th year, 5th month; Kuroita Katsumi, Maruyama Jirō, op. cit., part 2, p. 23.

"Paekche sent General Suri Soshi, 州利即次, (W. G. Aston, op. cit., p. 14: Chyuri cheuk-chhă) along with Mononobe *no muraji* in order to return thanks for the cession (litt.: gift) of the territory of Imon, 己汶, (Aston, loc. cit.: I-mun).

As tribute he presented moreover the scholar of the Five Classics, *Aya no* Kōan-mo (W. G. Aston, loc. cit.: Ko An-mu of Han) with the request to exchange him for Tanyōni. That happened in accordance with this request."

[2] See pp. 317 and ff.

could never have counted on the various Japanese concessions if it had not, in contrast to Silla, been capable of a reasonable cultural exchange.

It is obvious that the various concessions made by Japan to Paekche for its own benefit did not render the leaders and population of the remaining scraps of Mimana particularly well-disposed towards Japan. As a result of everything they felt Japan had betrayed and deserted them. It is therefore—psychologically—very understandable that here there was a growing sympathy with Silla. This is already apparent in the marriage of a minor ruler of one of these states, the little land of Hahi, 伴跛, to a princess of Silla in 522. By this marriage he attempted to impede Paekche's campaign in Mimana. As, however, the ruler of Hahi preferred his own national robes over and above the raiment given him by Silla, this marriage was dissolved a year later and the bride was taken back to Silla. Possibly a considerable amount of *musubi* belief was hidden in this quarrel of the robes, as this belief considered the arraying in robes rather as being an endowment with the god who dwelt in them. Hence the anger of the Silla king Pŏphŭng, 法興, (514-540) becomes comprehensible in the insult offered to the god within the Silla robes.

In 524 the king of Silla went "on an inspection to the southern border".[1] During the next eight years following, Silla was gradually to conquer the actual nucleus of Mimana, Kŭmgwan, 金官, (this is the later Kimhae). Despite various attempts by Mimana it fell in 532.[2] These Silla conquests were even more facilitated owing to the Japanese expeditionary force being held up in Kyūshū in order to subdue the Iwai, 磐井, rebellion which had broken out

[1] Cf. Suematsu Yasukazu, op. cit., p. 133.

[2] The sympathy of Silla for the inhabitants of this district does appear from the fact that the petty king of Kŭmgwan received the highest distinction (上大等). Moreover, he was permitted to remain in his own country. This can be read in the *Silla pongi* of the *Samguk sagi* under the 19th year of Pophŭng. Cf. Suematsu Yasukazu, op. cit., pp. 135-140. Afterwards this area, situated in the neighbourhood of Kimhae and Pusan, was of great importance to the further cultural development of Silla. It was probably also the cradle of the Kim dynasty. Cf. Suematsu Yasukazu, op. cit., pp. 232-236. As far as the relationship in the myths of both countries is concerned, they probably went back to a communal source. Suematsu Yasukazu, op. cit., p. 232. The kings of Silla were related to those of Kŭmgwan, see Suematsu Yasukazu, op. cit., pp. 233, 234.

with the help of Silla sympathisers. We shall return to this. Therefore Japan had to stand by powerless in Mimana.

It is clear that these Silla successes—together with the expressed sympathy for Silla of the remaining Mimana districts—began to get Paekche on its nerves with its similar Mimana plots; this all the more so as it was more than ever threatened from the north by Koguryŏ. As a first measure it moved its capital from Kumanari, 熊津, to the south in 538. According to Suematsu[1] this removal first and foremost achieved a renewal of Korean culture, as the new capital, Puyŏ, 扶餘, had better connections with most areas of Mimana than the old. Also it was better protected than the old from all kinds of attacks by Koguryŏ.

The second of Paekche's measures consisted of a peace treaty with Silla in 541. Thus it hoped to gain adequate peace for its struggle against Koguryŏ. By this treaty Paekche reached an odd situation as, simultaneously, Japan considered it as the only nation which could and might regain the territories of Mimana lost to Silla. Japan also expected that if Paekche rather than Silla occupied Mimana, Japan itself would, moreover, gain all kinds of additional cultural exchanges. Owing to this manoeuvre by Paekche with Silla, Paekche found itself forced into various double, often contrary, diplomacies; on the one hand it had to unite with Silla against Koguryŏ, while on the other hand it had to move Japan into opposing the Silla strategy with regard to Mimana. In this latter Paekche intended outstripping Silla in the conquest of Mimana. This explains the Japanese hesitancy during those years, which repeatedly comes to light in the *Nihonshoki* and expresses itself in very many words with a minimum of actual aid.[2] Nevertheless, Paekche had not taken its precautions for nothing.

In 547 Koguryŏ invaded Paekche territory. However, three thousand soldiers from Silla ensured that Koguryŏ was defeated. In 551 Paekche and Silla together succeeded in reconquering their

---

[1] Op. cit., p. 149.

[2] Thus the *Nihonshoki* chronicles of the years 544 (Kimmei, 3rd year), 545 (Kimmei, 4th year) and 546 (Kimmei, 5th year) only mention in this last year some small aid. The same obtains in 547 (Kimmei, 6th year), when only 70 horses and 10 'ships' were sent. Cf. *Nihonshoki*, 19th *maki*; Kuroita Katsumi, Maruyama Jirō, op. cit., part 2, pp. 54-72.

Cf. W. G. Aston, *Nihongi* II, pp. 47-60. Cf. Suematsu Yasukazu, op. cit., pp. 156-168.

old territories from Koguryŏ. Thereby Paekche recovered the Seoul district, occupied in 475 by Koguryŏ, which was approximately half of the present-day Kyŏnggi-do, 京畿道. Silla took the eastern part of this for itself. However, hereafter Silla, to the detriment of Paekche, went even further and, in 552, also annexed the northern territories regained by Paekche. In this emergency, in 552 and 553, Paekche asked Japan for reinforcements. In exchange for this Japan was given a great number of scholars, who arrived a year after the request by Paekche. The number of scholars and multiple requests which occur in the *Nihonshoki* serve to illustrate the state of emergency at which Mimana especially had arrived.[1]

At that time it became apparent that, although Koguryŏ had not been conquered, Silla, nevertheless, with its southern aspirations, had become a far more dangerous rival to Paekche. In 554 the eldest son of King Sŏng of Paekche, Ch'ang, 昌, entered Silla territory with fresh Japanese troops, which had come to Korea as a result of the previous years' requests, and mounted an attack. On the border of Silla they succeeded in capturing a Silla fort. In order to aid his son, King Sŏng also campaigned against Silla. However, he was cut off from his country by Silla troops and killed. This defeat meant the end of all her Mimana dreams for Paekche.

For Silla it was now no longer difficult to occupy what remained of the Mimana district. It started its last attack on this area in 561, when King Chinhŭng, 眞興, (540-576) had a stone erected on the border of Mimana on which he claimed the territory of Mimana. In 562 the entire region of Mimana was in Silla's power. This occupation of Mimana by Silla was not too difficult for Silla as Mimana itself considered it as a kind of liberation.[2] It meant the end of Japanese rule in Korea. Of all the high Korean aspirations which Japan had ever fostered little remained other than a regular tribute paid by both Silla and Paekche to Japan.[3] Furthermore,

[1] Cf. *Nihonshoki*, 19th *maki*, Kimmei, 13th and 14th year; Kuroita Katsumi, Maruyama Jirō, op. cit., part 2, pp. 76-80; W. G. Aston, op. cit., pp. 65-70. We shall return to a part of these texts.

[2] Cf. Suematsu Yasukazu, op. cit., p. 188.

[3] According to Suematsu, the fact of this tribute by both countries is unalterable. There is not, however, a united opinion concerning the question what precisely represented these tributes. This tribute also continued after the unification of Silla, hence after the fall of Koguryŏ and Paekche, although eventually it changed into a mutual trade agreement. Cf. Suematsu Yasukazu, op. cit., pp. 254-257.

Japan also regularly received hereafter a separate tribute from Mimana itself which, in agreement with the actual occupier of these districts, was presented at the Japanese court either via Silla [1] or via Paekche.[2] This *mitsugi* or tribute was more important to the Japanese economy in antiquity than one might now think.[3] Hençe one can imagine how contented Japan was when, after the fall of Mimana, these tributes continued to arrive. Thus the unfortunate termination of Japanese military activities in Korea did not end the cultural and religious development of this country itself by Koreans of Chinese or pure Korean blood. Against this background of Japanese relations with Korea Buddhism also came to Japan with its images, *sūtras* and monks, as a kind of exchange which paid off the military aid to Paekche. It is hoped to show here that this Buddhism came as an exchange between Japan and Paekche, an exchange which at an early stage had been prepared almost exclusively by Korean immigrants and not by Japanese returning from Mimana. This, in other words, would mean that Japan's oldest Buddhism came from Paekche and not from Mimana.

b Japan's home policy

As the state chronicles concerning this period are far more likely to have come from the various *shizoku*, little is known to us about those at the head of the sixth century Japanese nation, whether they were *ō-kimi* or emperors. We have seen in the second chapter that the *shizoku* often used these *ō-kimi* to typify themselves. Nevertheless we hope to bring out specific characteristics of these figures on the basis of the various texts about Buddhism in this and the following chapters.

[1] The first Mimana tribute was only paid for the first time 40 years after the fall of this territory, by Silla, namely in 600, 610, 611, 623, 638 and in 645. From a Silla tribute of the year 575 (3rd year of Emperor Bidatsu), which mentions a tribute from Silla *and* four villages, Suematsu deduces that also the Mimana tributes of after 600 concerned these four villages, which were situated in the area of Pusan and Kimhae. Cf. Suematsu Yasukazu, op. cit., pp. 191-195.

[2] Namely, Mimana had again come into Paekche's possession from 642 on. At that time many voices were raised in Japan in order to have this occupation by Paekche recognised. Cf. Suematsu Yasukazu, op. cit., pp. 211, 212. Paekche paid the Mimana tribute up to the moment when it too was forced under Silla's yoke, that is to say, until 663.

[3] At least, Suematsu tries to prove this, as the whole diplomatic commerce occupied itself with this problem after the fall of Mimana. Cf. op. cit., p. 254.

The first emperor of the sixth century was apparently a fairly powerful figure. His original name was O-odo, 袁本杼. However, he is better known by the name of Keitai, 繼体. His reign lasted from 507-531. The *Kojiki* allows him to become 43 years old.[1] Thus he would have ascended the throne at a fairly early age. His length of reign was occupied, abroad, by the Mimana problem, at home especially by the Iwai rebellion. These were two series of developments which both took up many years and were also both highly conditioned by each other.

The struggle for Mimana was not fought out entirely under Keitai, although at the end of his reign it was more or less decided. The Iwai rebellion contributed to it to an important extent. Because just at the moment when Silla began to capture one fortification after another in Mimana this same Silla, by means of intrigues managed to draw out this rebellion in Kyūshū for many years. The Japanese armies which in 527 for instance marched south in order to participate in the struggle in Korea were detained by this Iwai rebellion. It is possible that this rebellion, although described only under the reign of Keitai, lasted until the fall of Mimana in 562 before it was radically suppressed.[2] In any case, the expeditionary force which was first to suppress this rebellion could no longer beneficially affect the situation in favour of Japan in Korea, when it finally arrived there.

The suppression of the rebellion also slowly led to the decline of the *shizoku* then ruling, i.e. the Ōtomo and the Kose, 巨勢. The Mononobe gradually replaced them. After the death of Keitai in

---

[1] Cf. *Kojiki*, 3rd *maki*; Kuroita Katsumi, Maruyama Jirō, *Kokushitaikei Kojiki*, p. 146.

[2] This would be a good explanation of the fact why Japan could do so little for the relief of Mimana and had to disappoint Paekche continually with large promises which always remained unfulfilled. This too could be a good reason why Paekche simultaneously had its territorial demands on Mimana territories granted. Itamoto Tarō, who, as we saw in footnote 1 on p. 230, does not have too much faith in the historical reality of the Keitai chronicles, opines that this Iwai rebellion belongs to the few genuinely historical hubs of these chronicles; op. cit., pp. 46, 47. He too does not consider it impossible that it lasted longer than the *Nihonshoki* suggests, op. cit., p. 45. According to the *Nihonshoki* it was large enough to prevent an army of 60.000 men 'for years' from crossing to Korea. Cf. *Nihonshoki*, 19th *maki*, Keitai, 21st year (527); Kuroita Katsumi, Maruyama Jirō, *Kokushitaikei Nihonshoki*, part 2, p. 24; W. G. Aston, *Nihongi* II, p. 15, translates by "several years".

531 the court became split into two parties. This did not, however, result in a bisection of the Japanese realm as this division remained merely personal. The three sons of Keitai could not agree about the succession. This led to an eight-year period of opposing emperors. On the one side there was Ankan, 安閑, (531-536) and Senka, 宣化, (536-539); and on the other Kimmei, 金明, (531-571). The latter managed, as he was the stronger, to survive both opponents. As a result of this struggle—mostly veiled—the institution of the emperorship, or, if one so desires, the *ō-kimi*ship, lost immeasurably in respect and power.

The leaders of the two most powerful *shizoku* especially benefitted from this: those of the Mononobe and the Soga. They had contrived to reach the top of the *muraji* and of the *omi* respectively. It is understandable that, after Keitai's death and amongst all the brotherly disaffection of the *ō-kimi*, they had noticeably increased their position and influence. However, their influence had not increased only owing to the imperial quarrels. As a result of Japan's policy towards Korea it was they who considerably strengthened their ranks with Korean immigrants. Of this Suematsu Yasukazu says:[1]

"The arrival of the immigrants was an immediate result of the foundation of Mimana. It was they who contributed much to the actual development of Japan's history. We must reconsider this point. Most of them had settled in Yamato. Thereby they exercised a great political and economic influence on the court of Yamato. This is a suspicion which can scarcely be doubted.

"In fact all of this meant a vast flowering of the *be*, who belonged immediately to the court or the large *shizoku*. Probably as a result of this, these *be*-supported *shizoku* became somewhat problematical. The problems surrounding the origin of the *be* vastly affected the well-being of the country, the fierce strife between the great *shizoku* with each other and the imperial house, and other important historical events of the fifth and sixth centuries."

Hence it was these great *shizoku*, supported by immigrants, and not so much the emperors themselves in the sixth century that were to decide politics. The *ō-kimi* had nothing to fear if they were left to their own devices. In this situation the ō-*kimi* were forced, after the death of Keitai, rather to preserve the balance between the *shizoku* than to govern and direct them. Emperor Kimmei

[1] Cf. Suematsu Yasukazu, op. cit., pp. 264, 265.

(531-572) and his son Bidatsu, 敏達, (572-585) succeeded admirably in this. During the greater portion of the sixth century they managed to play off these two totally opposed groups against each other. Under their reigns Buddhism was to be able considerably to strengthen its position in Japan. This too, however, as we shall see repeatedly in the coming chapters, had to take place under the *shizoku* yoke.

This tense situation eventually had to result in a decisive battle between the two *shizoku*. In the course of years the balance had lain sometimes with the Mononobe, at other times with the Soga. This was often accompanied by mutual revenge. Finally the Soga succeeded in gaining control of both the districts beyond Yamato belonging to the emperor, as well as of the finance.

In 585 Yōmei became emperor. He was a very outstanding figure as he was not only Kimmei's son but also a grandson of Iname, the Soga leader under Kimmei. He illustrates in his person that in his reign the power of the Soga was strong enough for a showdown with the Mononobe. This did indeed happen in 587. In that year the Soga, supported by many Korean immigrants, contrived to inflict a crushing defeat on Moriya, 守屋, the leader of the Mononobe. From that moment on all influence at court was monopolised by and radiated only from the Soga.

Hereafter the Soga were omnipotent. They more or less had full control of the emperor. Yōmei's successor, Sushun, 崇峻, who came to power in 588, experienced this. He had a hearty dislike of the Soga leader of that time, Umako, 馬子. Therefore he attempted to go his own way by circumventing Umako. In 592 this cost him his life, when he was stabbed to death by the Soga confederate, the immigrant Aya *no atae* Koma, 漢直駒. After this Soga *no* Umako took precautions that no other independent *ō-kimi* should come to power again. His niece was given the emperorship: Empress Suiko, 推古, (593-629). Under her rule the Soga reached the peak of its power. During her reign this power was divided between Umako and Shōtoku Taishi, also of Soga origin. The latter has already been referred to in this work as 'Father of the Fatherland'. His political achievements and those of his aunt, the empress, will be subjected to closer investigation in our last chapter. Hence we can suffice with the foregoing rough outline. Against the background of foreign and internal affairs here depicted, the oldest form of Buddhism began to grow in Japan.

2 THE ORIGIN OF JAPANESE BUDDHISM

The question of the initial meeting between Buddhism and Japan is not too simple. Namely, there is only one of the oldest sources, the *Nihonshoki*, which informs us of it. Despite this fairly one-sided information various opinions exist concerning the time and the nature of that meeting. It is obvious that these opinions are closely connected with the interpretations of the *Nihonshoki* texts about this.

Most of these opinions centre round the—so-called—'oldest' *Nihonshoki* text about Buddhism. It occurs under the thirteenth year of the reign of Emperor Kimmei and is dated as the year *mizunoe-saru*. According to the *kanshi* system this equals 552. Before examining these opinions more closely, we must first look at this text. It is as follows: [1]

"Winter, tenth month. The king of Paekche, Sŏng-myŏng, 聖明, (Jap.: Seimei = Sŏng, governed from 523 to 554) [2] sent the Tassotsu, 達率,[3] of the clan of princesses of Habe, 部, in the West,[4] namely To(or Nu)ri Shichikei, 怒唎斯致契,[5] and others.[6]

---

[1] Cf. *Nihonshoki*, 19th *maki*, Kimmei, 13th year, 10th month; Kuroita Katsumi, Maruyama Jirō, op. cit., part 2, pp. 76-78; see also W. G. Aston, *Nihongi* II, pp. 65-67; K. Florenz, op. cit., pp. 306-309.

[2] A commentary adds to this: "or King Sei, 聖". Sŏng is his own and generally used name. The added myŏng probably derives from the name Myŏng-nŏng, under which he appears, for instance, in the Korean sources. This Myŏng-nŏng, 明農, (= the bright and flowering one) can be encountered for instance in the report on his last battle and death in the *Samguk sagi, Silla pongi*, 15th year of King Chinhŭng, 7th month.

Cf. Suematsu Yasukazu, op. cit., p. 182.

The term Seimei, 聖明, used by the Japanese, means: the holy and bright one.

[3] Kor.: *tal-sol*, cf. W. G. Aston, op. cit., p. 65. This was the second rank of a total of 16 official ranks which Paekche recognised at that time and, in its turn, had borrowed from the rank system of Koguryŏ. Ranks made up with this '*sol*' (in Paekche that was a total of six, namely from the 2nd to and including the 7th rank) occurred only in Paekche, not in the other Korean lands.

Cf. Miyazaki Ichijō, "Sankanjidai no ikaisei ni tsuite", *C.G.*, vol. XIV, Oct. 1959, pp. 272-274.

[4] Jap.: Seihō Kishi (Kor.: Kwisi, cf. W. G. Aston, loc. cit.) Here we translate by *Habe* in the West, because further on in our text he is called 'the servant of Habe'.

[5] Kor.: Nuri sachhi-hyé, cf. W.G. Aston, loc. cit.

[6] The text gives: 等, others. Neither Aston nor Florenz have translated this.

"They donated a gilt-copper image of Buddha Śākyamuni, very many banners, silken screens[1] and very many book-scrolls of *sūtras*.[2] In a separate letter he praised their services for the dissemination of religious respect everywhere amongst men. He said:

" 'This teaching is the very best of all existing doctrines. Nevertheless it is hard to explain or understand. Neither the duke of Chou, 周, [3] nor Confucius could comprehend it.[4] This teaching is capable of producing happiness and reward in unlimited quantities and without boundaries. It leads indeed to distinguishing the sublime *bodhi*.[5] It can be compared to a man who has every treasure he could wish and which he can use as he pleases. The riches of this amazing teaching are similar. Each prayer and desire is fulfilled without there being anything lacking.[6] Moreover, it came from

---

[1] It is apparent that here silken screens were intended from the *furigana* text: *kinukasa*.

[2] Here the word *kyōron*, 経論, used for *sūtra*'s can also be translated by: *sūtra*'s and commentaries, cf. Kanda Ichikyōsuke, *Jikai*, Tōkyō 1957, p. 481, column I.

[3] He was a younger brother of Wu wang, 武王, the founder of the Chou, 周, dynasty in China (1122-255 B.C.). He is known as a legendary Chinese scholar of the second half of the 12th century B.C., who was supposed to have codified the state institutions of the Chou.

Cf. E. Zürcher, *The Buddhist Conquest of China*, p. 317.

[4] In this text the name of Laotzŭ is lacking. Especially also because in China it was simultaneously attempted to suggest on all kinds of apologetic grounds, that these three scholars were merely pupils or even *avatāras* of Buddha. That appears, for instance, from the words which Emperor Wu wrote about the Liang dynasty some time previously: "Although Lao-tzu, the Duke of Chou and Confucius were disciples of the Buddha, yet the outward manifestations of their doctrines are not correct, since they are limited to what is good in this world." Cf. E. Zürcher, op. cit., pp. 317, 318.

[5] Jap.: 菩提, *podai*. This also means the way to the *bodhi*. Kando Ichikyōsuke, op. cit., p. 987, column III.

[6] The contents of this letter is borrowed up to 'lacking' according to Renondeau and Tsuda Sōkichi from the (*Konkōmyō*) *Saishō-ō-kyō*, the translation of the *Suvarṇaprabhāsa*, also called the *Suvarṇaprabhā-sottama* (*rāja*)—or *Suvarṇabhāsottama sūtra*.

See J. Filliozat, *L'Inde Classique*, tome II, p. 370; É. Lamotte, *Histoire du Bouddhisme Indien*, p. 637; H. Coates and R. Ishizuka, *Honen, The Buddhist Saint*, p. 454, footnote 1. This passage occurs in the chapter *Nyōrai Juryōbon*, which treats of the length of life of the *tathagata*. According to Renondeau only a few words are altered in this. In the text of this *sūtra*, instead of the usual introduction 'This teaching' the entire title of the *sūtra* is mentioned and 'Neither the Duke of Chou nor Confucius' has replaced 'The listeners

distant India to our three Han [1] where it was accepted as it was preached and where scarcely anyone is found who does not respect it. Therefore your servant, the king of Paekche, Mei, 明 (= Sŏng),[2] has sent in all humility his own servant of Habe, Tori Shichikei, in order to make known in the land of the emperor and to fulfil throughout the entire district of Kinai, 畿内, (= the Yamato area) [3] the words of Buddha, which are: 'My teaching will spread to the East'.

"On that day, when the emperor heard this, he danced with delight. Thereupon he gave the ambassadors (various) commands and said: 'Never since my long-gone days of youth was I permitted to hear anything comparable to this wondrous teaching. Nevertheless, I cannot decide on this.' Therefore he questioned his ministers [4] and said: 'The visage of the Buddha, which our westerly neighbours have offered us, is so blinding that we have never experienced the like before. Must I now worship this or not?' The *ō-omi* of the Soga, Iname *no sukune*, 稲目宿禰, answered this: 'All countries of the West, each one, worship it. Should Yamato, with its purple autumn [5] then alone resist this?'

"The *ō-muraji* of the Mononobe, Okoshi, 尾輿, and the *muraji* of the Nakatomi, Kamako, 鎌子, said, as if with the same mouth:

---

and the *Pratyeka* Buddhas (that is to say, the Buddhas for themselves)'. The remainder up to 'lacking' is identical in both letter and *sūtra*.

Cf. W. Renondeau, "L'Introduction du Bouddhisme au Japon," *T.P.*, XLVIII, 1 and 2 (1959), pp. 21, 22. Tsuda Sōkichi reaches the same conclusion. Cf. *Nihon Koten no Kenkyū*, part II, pp. 86-87.

[1] This expression 'three *Han*', 三韓, was, as we have observed in the previous chapter, really an indication for South Korea (Ma-han, Chin-han and Pyŏn-han), but is also used for Paekche, Silla and Koguryŏ.

Cf. W. G. Aston and K. Florenz, loc. cit.

[2] According to W. G. Aston, op. cit., p. 66, footnote 6, Myŏng was his real name. We do not agree with this. Cf. footnote 2 on p. 241.

[3] According to the *furigana*: '*uchi no kuni*', 'in our land'. Actually Kinai covers the following districts: Yamashiro (present-day Kyōto), Yamato (present-day Nara prefecture), Kawachi (partially Nara prefecture and Ōsaka prefecture), Izumi (Ōsaka prefecture) and Settsu (Ōsaka prefecture).

[4] This can also be translated by servants as it uses the same character as in Sŏng's letter a few lines earlier.

[5] Just before the word Yamato the characters 豊秋 are used, which have been 'Japanesed' in *furigana* to '*toyo akitsu*': (the Yamato) of the purple autumn.

Aston leaves this untranslated. Cf. W. G. Aston, op. cit., p. 66.

'Those who govern our land have always made the worshipping of the 180 [1] gods of heaven and earth, of provinces and houses,[2] in spring, summer, autumn and winter, their task. If at this point we follow another way and begin worshipping the deities of the neighbouring countries, then we must fear the revenge of our national gods.'

"Hereupon the emperor said: 'It is right to give it (= the statue) to him who has asked, Iname *no sukune*. As an experiment let it be worshipped by him.' Thereupon the *ō-omi* knelt down and received it gladly. He gave it a place in his dwelling in Owarida, 小墾田.[3] Whole-heartedly he carried out (the rites of) foresaking the world. He made this the source of his activities. Furthermore, he spring-cleaned his house in Mukuhara and made it into a temple.

"Hereafter an epidemic broke out in the land, which killed the population rapidly. The longer it lasted, the greater it became. It was incurable. The *ō-muraji* of the Mononobe, Okoshi, and the *muraji* of the Nakatomi, Kamako, said together (to the emperor): 'Because you did not before give heed to the advice of us, your servants, it has now reached the stage that people die of this disease. If now, before it has gone too far, you return to your ways, then certainly happiness will return. It would be right to throw this (= this god) away and to start striving whole-heartedly after our future happiness.'

"To this the emperor answered: 'Let us adhere to your advice.' The officials [4] cast away the Buddha image into the canal of Naniwa, 難波.[5] Also they set fire to the temple. This burnt down entirely, so that nothing was left of it. Hereafter a catastrophic fire during cloudless and windless weather turned the great hall of the (imperial) palace into ashes." [6]

---

[1] This does not mean to say that at that time there were only 180 gods. In *furigana* it is written here: '*momo yaso*' which has the meaning of 'very many'.

[2] In *furigana* the character 稷, '*ie*', 'house' is written beside it. This character itself rather indicates grain gods. In this context we prefer the term house-gods to that of grain-gods. Cf. W. G. Aston, op. cit., p. 67; K. Florenz, op. cit., p. 308.

[3] This lies in the district of Takaichi, which belongs to the Yamato area.

[4] Here already 有司, is mentioned, '*tsukasa tsukasa*', officials. At this time it was still naturally an anachronism, as the bureaucracy was only established in 645 with the Taika reformation.

[5] This runs through Ōsaka.

[6] 'Catastrophic fire' is the translation of the *furigana*: '*no wazawai ari*'.

For many this text has been the starting point from which to date and define the specific nature of Japan's oldest Buddhism. Hence, on the basis of this text, 552 is considered to be the year it began, both by Japan's oldest authors as well as by most western authors.[1]

More modern Japanese authors and one or other western author [2] believe that this date should be put forward to 538. Others again believe that Japanese Buddhism started when, in 522, it was brought from Korea to Japan by Shiba Tattō, 司馬達等, (Chin.: Szŭ-ma Ta-teng; Sino-Kor.: Sama Taltŭng).[3] This Shiba Tattō, as we shall see later, was an immigrant of Chinese descent. He counted as one of the leaders (very specially named *suguri*, 村主,) of the *be* of the saddlers (鞍作, *kuratsukuri*, or saddle-*be*, 鞍部, named *kura-be*). We shall investigate later the fact that his leader's title, *suguri*, betrayed his Korean descent. Those who connect their opinion of Japan's oldest Buddhism particularly with Shiba Tattō rely especially on sources other than the *Nihonshoki*.

Cf. K. Florenz, op. cit., p. 309, footnote 20. This chronicle is followed here by a report concerning the war in Korea, i.a., the cession of Hansyŏng, 漢城, and P'yŏngyang by Paekche to Silla. After that, under the fourteenth year of Kimmei, the narrative continues with a story about the miraculous origination of a Buddha image. This has obviously been inserted by a monk, in order to provide an existing image of his time with adequate antiquity. According to this chronicle this image is still supposed to be available in the Yoshino temple. As this story of more recent insertion is of no further importance to us, we shall not return to it.

For this text see *Nihonshoki*, 19th *maki*; Kuroita Katsumi, Maruyama Jirō, op. cit., pp. 78, 79; cf. W. G. Aston, op. cit., p. 68.

[1] Cf. W. Gundert, *Japanische Religionsgeschichte*, p. 194; E. Naberfeld, *Grundriss der Japanischen Geschichte*, Tōkyō 1940, p. 26; A.U. Reischauer, *Studies in Japanese Buddhism*, p. 91; H. de Lubac, *Amida*, p. 133; H. Coates and R. Ishizuka, *Honen, The Buddhist Saint*, p. 4; E. Zürcher, *Het Boeddhisme*, p. 69; E. Conze, *Buddhism*, p. 214; C. Humphrey, *Buddhism*, p. 69, et al.

[2] Ōno Tatsunosuke, *Nihon Bukkyō-shisō-shi*, Tōkyō 1958, p. 37 maintains 538 as the year of the Kimmei text which we quoted above. Naoki Kojirō does the same in *Daigaku Nihon-shi*, part 1, p. 47. Of the non-Japanese authors we mention W. Renondeau, op. cit., p. 25 ff. Bruno Lewin is based entirely on him, cf. op. cit., p. 147, footnote 13.

[3] Ui Hakuju writes in *Nihon Bukkyō-gaishi*, Tōkyō 1958, p. 1: "Buddhism was certainly present in the Keitai period". He considers 538 as the thirteenth year of Kimmei and therefore surmises an origin of Buddhism long before this date.

In the afore-mentioned first two opinions only the dating is given. For this the interpretation of the foregoing *Nihonshoki* text is relied upon. The last and third opinion implies a totally different start of Buddhism. According to this it would have arisen from the Korean immigrant milieu.

These three opinions express to a great extent the various origins of Buddhism. Namely, the question arises here, whether it was imposed upon the people from above by a semi-imperial intervention or whether it began at the bottom and worked up. Therefore the question of date, which arises in all of these opinions, is very closely connected with the question concerning the kind of environment in which Buddhism settled and germinated. Hence we are not only concerned with a search for one or other arbitrary date, but also especially for a deeper insight into the origin and early growth of Japanese Buddhism.

We believe that this did indeed begin with Shiba Tattō and gained a more official character only later, by the recognition of the emperor. In the following pages we shall motivate our opinion more thoroughly, without, however, by-passing the foregoing opinions. We hope to prove this opinion by studying a development which took place in two phases.

First phase: The origin of Buddhism in Japan

The beginnings of Japanese Buddhism lay probably in the early sixth century, around the year 522. In that year Shiba Tattō crossed to Japan and founded a Buddhist community there. This is handed down to us in a manuscript which is less authentic than the *Nihonshoki*, namely the *Fusō ryakki*, 扶桑略記. This is supposed to have been edited and compiled in 30 book-scrolls between 1094 and 1169 by the Tendai monk Kōen, 皇圓, who belonged to the famous Fujiwara lineage and died in 1169.[1] Only sixteen of these scrolls have been preserved. Its contents consist mostly of reports about Japanese history from the reign of Emperor Jimmu until the year 1094. One of those reports is dated in the sixteenth year of Emperor Keitai (522) and is as follows: [2]

[1] This Kōen was, amongst other things, the teacher of Hōnen; cf. H. Coates and R. Ishizuka, op. cit., pp. 131 ff.; pp. 535-537.

[2] The text mentioned here can also not be found in the *Fusō ryakki* under the 16th year of Keitai. Various other traditions of Buddhism of that time have been added to the text about the introduction of Buddhism to

"The master of the law, Yakutan, 薬恒,[1] of the mountain Hiei, 比叡, (near Kyōtō) says in (the manuscript) *Hokke Kenki*, 法華験記: 'A document of the monk Zenshin, 禅岑,[2] of the Enryakuji, 延暦寺,[3] reads: "Sixteenth year of the twenty-seventh emperor, Keitai, *mizunoe-tora*. The *Ayabito*, 漢人, of China (lit.: the great T'ang) and the *suguri* of Abe, 安部,[4] Shiba Tattō came to Japan, spring, second month. Of grass he made (lit.: wove) a temple in Sakatabara, 坂田原, in the district of Takaichi, 高市, situated in the province of Yamato, and installed therein an image which he worshipped. He turned to it and worshipped it. All the people of that time said: 'This is the god of China (lit.: the great T'ang)'."

In this text an appeal to the monk Zenshin, who lived in the ninth century, establishes the beginning of Buddhism in the year *mizunoe tora*, which here equals 522.

This same text can also be met with in another manuscript, dating from the fourteenth century, the *Genkō shakusho*, 元享釈書, which consists of 30 scrolls and was intended as a history of Japanese Buddhism up to the Kamakura period (1185-1333).[5]

---

the Japanese court of the 13th year of Kimmei. One of them is our text. For this cf.: *Fusō ryakki*, 3rd *maki*, Kimmei, 13th year; *Kokushitaikei* (Edition of *Keizai Zasshi*), part VI, Tōkyō 1906, pp. 483-484.

[1] This monk also belonged to the Tendai-*shū* and lived under Emperor Sujaku, 朱雀, (913-946).

[2] He lived in the ninth century. Not much is known of him.

[3] The Enryakuji is the main temple of the Tendai-shū. In 788, three years after the founder of the Japanese Tendai Saichō had built a small temple of grass at the age of nineteen, he built a temple on the mountain Hiei near Kyōto, which he named Hieisanji (temple of the mountain Hiei). Later it was given another name: Ichijō-shikanin, 一乗止觀院. In 823 it was called after the period in which it was founded: Enryakuji. Thereafter it formed i.a. the centre of the struggle of the Tendai monks against those of the monasteries of the town Nara. In 1571 it was burnt down, but rebuilt some 70 years later, where it stands up to today.

[4] According to this text Shiba Tattō also had something to do with the Abe tribe, which later received the honorific of *asomi*. Cf. Bruno Lewin, *Aya und Hata*, p. 143, footnote 163.

[5] This text is as follows: "Shiba Tattō was a person from south Liang (= China under the dynasty of that name. Here he has obviously been confused with the Ssŭ-ma Ts'ao-ta, mentioned in the *Sung-shu*. Cf. Ryūsaku Tsunoda, *Japan in the Chinese Dynastic Histories*, p. 21, p. 25, footnote 5). In the 16th year of Keitai he came to Japan. At that time there was as yet no Buddhism in these districts. In Yamato, Takaichi, Sakatabara, Tattō made a temple of grass and served Buddha. At that time Buddha was

One should not let one's arguments rest too greatly on these texts as earlier supporters of the Shiba Tattō opinion have done. Just as so many works have derived from the Enryakuji on Mount Hiei since the ninth century and later, these two can also have been forged in many ways for the benefit of the ambitions of the Tendai-*shū*. We shall comment on such forgeries in our final chapter.

The great value of these texts is therefore particularly that they refer to historical realities which can, moreover, be found in the *Nihonshoki*, more than four hundred years older. On this specifically we have based our opinion and summarised in the following three points:

1) Japan's oldest Buddhism was closely connected with Shiba Tattō.
2) With him, the chief of the saddlers, this came in the beginning of the sixth century (522) from Paekche to Takaichi in Yamato.
3) From the group of saddlers it began to infiltrate Japanese society.

1 *Japan's Buddhism and Shiba Tattō*

We do not need the *Fusō ryakki* and the *Genkō shakusho* in order to meet the person Shiba Tattō; the *Nihonshoki* also mentions him in the long story which this old manuscript registers under the thirteenth year of Bidatsu (572-585). Hence it would date from 584, sixty-two years after Shiba Tattō would have brought Buddhism to Japan according to the foregoing data. This text is as follows: [1]

"Autumn, ninth month. From Paekche the *omi* of Kafuka, 鹿深, came with a stone image of Maitreya, and the *muraji* of Saeki, 佐伯, with a Buddha image. That same year Soga Umako *no sukune* asked for these two images. He sent the head of the 'saddlers guild',[2] Shiba Tattō, and Ikebe *no atae* Hida, 池邊直水田,[3] every-

---

unknown, and was called a foreign god. This Buddhism belonged to the district of Umako."

Cf. *Genkō Shakusho*, 17th *maki*, *Kokushitaikei* (Edition *Keizai Zasshi*), part XIV, Tōkyō 1897, pp. 912-913.

[1] Cf. *Nihonshoki*, 20th *maki*, Bidatsu, 13th year, 9th month, Kuroita Katsumi, Maruyama Jirō, op. cit., part 2, pp. 112, 113; see also W. G. Aston, op. cit., p. 101; K. Florenz, op. cit., pp. 312-314.

[2] Here: *Kura-be*, the *be* of the saddle. See also B. Lewin, op. cit., p. 118.

[3] Concerning him, see B. Lewin, op. cit., pp. 147, 148.

where to seek practitioners of Buddhism. During this they discovered that in the district of Harima, 播磨,[1] a monk had returned to lay status. He was called Ebin, 惠便,[2] of Koguryŏ. The *ō-omi* (= Soga Umako) made him a 'Master of Teaching'. Shiba Tattō ordered his daughter Shima, 嶋, to enter a nunnery (11 years old)[3]. She was called the nun Zenshin, 善信.[4] Two pupils of the nun Zenshin also entered. One of them was Toyome, 豊女, the wife of the *Ayabito* Yayabo, 漢人夜菩. She was given the name of nun Zenzō, 禅藏.[5] The second was Ishime, 石女,[6] of the brocade-weaver Tsuoga, 壺.[7] She received the name Ezen, 惠善.[8]

"Only Umako respected, in accordance with Buddha's laws, the three nuns. He ordered Hida *no atae* and Shiba Tattō to give them food and clothing. East of his own dwelling he built a hall of Buddha. Here he installed the stone image of Maitreya. He asked the three nuns urgently to hold a large religious gathering there.[9]

"At that time Tattō discovered a relic of Buddha upon the foods for fasting. He gave this *shari*, 舎利, (= relic) to Umako *no sukune*. As an experiment Umako *no sukune* laid it on a block of iron and hit it with an iron hammer. Both the iron block and the hammer were shattered. It was, however, impossible to pulverise the relic. When he hurled the *shari* into water it floated or sank as desired. From then on Umako *no sukune*, Ikebe *no* Hida and Shiba Tattō believed deeply in Buddhism and experienced it without shortcomings. Thereafter Soga Umako furnished a hall for Buddha in

---

[1] Harima encompasses almost the same area as the present-day Hyōgo prefecture.

[2] Sino-Kor.: Hyép'yŏn. Cf. W. G. Aston, loc. cit.

[3] This is a commentary added to the text.

[4] Meaning: Belief of Virtue.

[5] This means: Treasury of Dhyāna.

[6] *Ishime*, literally: stone woman, is another word for childless woman.

[7] Brocade weaver, *nishikori*, 錦織, was a permanent title just as *kuratsukuri*.

[8] This means: Blessing of Virtue.

[9] Cf. De Visser, *Ancient Buddhism in Japan*, p. 29. He translates this by "worship of a great meeting". Kanda Kyōichisuke, op. cit., p. 232, column II, gives the term *ogamisu* the *furigana* added here, not the meaning of "worship".

Ogamisu: 設斎, has the same meaning as: 斎会: to invite monks to one for a great gathering with a meal and *sūtra* reading. Cf. also Kanda Kyōichisuke, op. cit., p. 716, column I. In the text 大会設斎 is used: the '*ogamisu*' of a great gathering.

his Ishikawa, 石川, house. Here the origin of Buddhism began.[1]"

This text is very closely interrelated. Tsuda [2] considers it a Buddhist insertion. Hence it would not originally have been entered in the state chronicles, but have been inserted at a later date initially, together with other Buddhist texts. In any case, this tale about the relic does indeed lie somewhat outside the limits of a state chronicle, which is what the *Nihonshoki* intends to be, especially in the 'younger' and later texts such as these.

The opening phrase 'at that time' occurs twice in the original text. It lent itself satisfactorily to stringing together various tales without any transition. Hence the foregoing chronicle is made up of three separate pieces which were linked to each other in this way. Therefore this text forms a series of tales which were smuggled into the state chronicles as a 'Buddhist chronicle'. The starting point of this tale was therefore the short report concerning the coming of the Maitreya image. Of the entire series of happenings recounted under this thirteenth year of Bidatsu, this fact was probably the only one which had anything to do with that date. This is apparent from further analysis of the text. Events are mentioned which could only have happened after the arrival of the Maitreya image, such as the building of a temple for it. On the other hand many facts of an earlier time are mentioned. Amongst these, Shiba Tattō's daughter's entry into the convent can definitely be counted. It is indeed stated that her 'pupils' also entered. Obviously, at the time of Shiba's daughter's entry, they could never have been her pupils as she was only eleven years old.

Here one can ask oneself how to associate the appointment of Shiba Tattō and Ikebe *no atae* Hida as Buddhist inspectors with the 'origin of Buddhism' mentioned at the end of this long text. Here it is of less importance whether the trial of strength with the relic or Soga's building of the temple near his Ishikawa house is considered as the origin. Therefore all that which has been appended to one date actually took place over a fairly long time. The chronicle of the Maitreya image forms a ready excuse for a monk chronicler to describe the origin of Buddhism and its further history up to the arrival of the image. The 'origin of Buddhism' mentioned here therefore had nothing to do with the thirteenth year of Bidatsu

[1] The Japanese text of this sentence which is important to us is: "*Hotoke no minori no hajimete kore yori mata okoreri*: 仏法之初自玆而作".

[2] Tsuda Sōkichi, *Nihon Koten no Kenkyū*, part II, p. 180.

(= 584), but lay further back in antiquity. In this, according to the text, not only Soga and Ikebe *no atae* Hida were concerned, but also particularly Shiba Tattō. This appears from the tale of the relic. In it, Shiba Tattō offered this relic to Soga Umako. This ceremony indicates that the origin of Buddhism must first be sought in this Shiba Tattō. Therefore the occurrences at the end of this chronicle concern only the very first stage of Buddhism in Japan.

It is interesting that in this disjointed history of Buddhism there is absolutely no mention of the text, always considered so important, of the thirteenth year of Emperor Kimmei (552) which also indeed mentions the origin of Buddhism. Nevertheless, these texts, despite the lack of inner connection, did have something to do with each other. We shall return to this.[1] This Bidatsu text shows that the patriarchal figure Shiba Tattō was closely linked to Japan's oldest Buddhism. This can also be seen in yet another text of the *Nihon-shoki*.

This text is to be found under the fourteenth year of Empress Suiko's reign (606). We have already pointed out that the *Nihon-shoki* becomes more believable as its chronicles come closer to the year of its final recension. This also applies to the following text:[2]

"Fifth month, fifth day. The empress said to Tori, 鳥,[3] the grandson of Shiba Tattō of the saddlers: 'I wish to bring the teaching of Buddha into flower. When I was on the point of building a Buddha temple I searched for relics for the first time. At that time it was your grandfather, Shiba Tattō, who offered them to me. Then there were no monks or nuns in this land yet; then your father Tasuna, 多須那, for the sake of the Emperor Tachibana *no* Toyohi, 橘豊日, (Yōmei, 586-587) entered a monastery and rever-

---

[1] Cf. p. 269 ff.

[2] Cf. *Nihonshoki*, 22nd *maki*, Suiko, 14th year; Kuroita Katsumi, Maruyama Jirō, op. cit., part 2, p. 147; W. G. Aston, op. cit., p. 134; K. Florenz, op. cit., p. 324.

[3] According to his title, Tori was a 'saddler', also a sculptor, or, even better a woodcarver, as most images of that period were made of wood. They demanded more or less the same degree of skill as making saddles, which, at that time, were usually wooden and had to be carved out of wood.

The extraordinary gratitude which Tori receives here from the empress is mainly concerned with the fact that he, without demaging the doors of the great temple hall of the Gangōji, contrived to place a large Buddha image inside it.

enced the teaching of Buddha. Your aunt Shimame, 嶋女, (called Shima elsewhere) was the first who entered as a nun, took upon herself the guidance of other nuns and caused them to practise the teaching of Buddha.' "

In this Suiko definitely bears witness to the patriarchal part played by Shiba Tattō with regard to Japanese Buddhism. His son and daughter were indeed the first who started the monastic life in Japan.

From the fact that Suiko knew Shiba Tattō some deduce that it would be impossible for him to have lived at the beginning of the sixth century. The reason for this was supposedly that Suiko's reign occurred only at the beginning of the seventh century.[1] Here they lose sight of the fact that Suiko was already fifty-three years old when, in 606, she bore witness to her close relationship with Shiba Tattō. Suiko and Shiba Tattō knew each other for some time, even if Shiba Tattō lived in the first half of the sixth century. Actually the birth date of Shiba Tattō is unknown. Therefore we do not know how old he was when, about 522, he brought Buddhism to Japan. If, however, one presupposes that he did this when he was about thirty years old and that his meeting with Suiko occurred when she was about twenty years old, then that meeting would have taken place in 573. In that case Shiba Tattō would have been in his eighties. Therefore Suiko could have continued knowing him for some years. Therefore there is no need to strain credulity in order to show that Suiko and Shiba Tattō were contemporaries for some time.

Seeing that Shiba Tattō holds such an important place in the foregoing two texts, one must also ask oneself why he is not mentioned at all in the 'oldest' Buddhist text of Kimmei quoted at the beginning of this chapter. We believe that this can be ascribed to the fact that Shiba Tattō had nothing to do with the political intentions which lay behind the occurrences of the Kimmei text. Namely, this latter text was on an entirely different level from that of the saddlers and Buddhist believers such as Shiba Tattō. It is the description of a political move by the king of Paekche, who hoped to extract some military aid by it. He would be more likely to succeed at the Japanese court if he could convert the

[1] Cf. W. Renondeau, op. cit., p. 19. Owing to these words by Suiko, he wrongly draws the conclusion that Shiba Tattō lived at the end of the sixth century, and not at its beginning.

Japanese emperor to his own belief, Buddhism. Hence this was a matter which would have to be dealt with by the emperor and his most important councillors, the leaders of the three supreme *shizoku*. Therefore the Soga had an important part in it.

The Bidatsu and Suiko texts quoted above do indeed bear witness to an extremely friendly relationship between Soga and saddlers. This was also to become apparent from the further history of the Soga. For instance this was the case in 645, the year of the Soga downfall. Then it was a descendent of Shiba Tattō who stood up for the Soga, died and was buried together with them.[1] We therefore believe that Shiba Tattō—though unrecorded—had an important influence behind the scenes on this introduction of Buddhism.

2 *The beginning of Japanese Buddhism in 522 in Takaichi*

The *Nihonshoki* establishes only negatively and not explicitly that the origin of Buddhism occurred in the year 522, under the reign of Emperor Keitai, with the coming of Shiba Tattō to Japan. Namely, when looking at the chronicles of Keitai in the *Nihonshoki*, it is noteworthy that two periods of his reign, namely that of his first to his tenth and of his twenty-first to his twenty-fifth and last year of government, are described year by year, covering more than 20 pages, or 180 lines of the Kuroita-Maruyama edition of the *Nihonshoki*. The intervening period, between the tenth and twenty-first years of his reign, covered more than a third of his entire rule. It is, however, dealt with in the *Nihonshoki* in five half lines. Of these, two are devoted to Korea and commemorate the death and succession of one of the kings of Paekche. Two other half lines mention changes of house of the emperor himself. According to the foregoing text of the *Fusō ryakki* the coming of Shiba Tattō occurred in this latter period, namely in Keitai's sixteenth year. In the chronicles of Keitai nothing can be found concerning this year, as is also the case for the 11th, 13th, 14th, 15th, 19th and 20th years

---

[1] Cf. for this long narrative: *Nihonshoki*, 24th *maki*, Kōgyoku, 4th year, 6th month; Kuroita Katsumi, Maruyama Jirō, op. cit., part 2, pp. 209-210; W. G. Aston, op. cit., pp. 192-193. Even after the death of the *kuratsukuri*, his body was used to force the then leader of the Soga, Emishi, to capitulate. The narrative about the communal struggle between the saddlers and Soga is terminated with the report: "That day permission was granted for the burial of the bodies of Soga *no omi*, Emishi and of the *kuratsukuri*, in one grave." B. Lewin also points out this close tie, op. cit., p. 170, footnote 29.

of his reign. One gains the impression that here one or other compiler has cut out entire parts of the chronicles, so that only a few half-lines comments remain as page fillers. Thus a Shiba Tattō text could also have disappeared from the chronicles.

That indeed a passage about Buddhism must have disappeared here is apparent from the nature of the short notes on the 17th and 18th years.[1] They merely mention, as stated, the death and succession of a Paekche king. This implicitly admits that at that time there were relations between Keitai and Paekche. That is also apparent from the political situation at that time. Were not the emperor and Paekche together involved in the struggle against advancing Silla? From earlier chronicles of the *Nihonshoki*[2] it furthermore becomes apparent that all saddlers specifically came from this Paekche. Shiba Tattō was one of their prominent members. From the afore-mentioned Bidatsu chronicles it is clear that the oldest Buddhism in Japan is closely interwoven with his person. According to the context of these Keitai chronicles the contents of the *Fusō ryakki* text should also have been given here. It has been removed at a later date.[3]

---

[1] Cf. *Nihonshoki*, 17th *maki*; Kuroita Katsumi, Maruyama Jirō, op. cit., part 2, p. 23:
"17th year, summer 5th month. The King of Paekche, Muryŏng, 武寧, died." "18th year, spring 1st month. The crown prince of Paekche Mei (= Sŏng) became king."
See also W. G. Aston, op. cit., pp. 13, 14. Muryŏng governed altogether 23 years.

[2] This is mentioned in the 7th year of Emperor Yūryaku, which, according to the official count would have equalled 463. For this text see footnote 1 on next pages.

[3] These 'Korean' chronicles of King Muryŏng and Sŏng themselves form another argument for the removal of the Shiba Tattō passage. These accord fairly closely with the *Samguk yusa* as far as dating is concerned. Only, in this latter work the year of Muryŏng's death was also the first year of Sŏng's reign. Hence there must have been just at this time extremely good contacts with Paekche. The Paekche sources also bear witness to this, which are frequently referred to herein. We pointed this out in Chapter III, footnotes 4 and 6 on p. 201. These Keitai chronicles in particular are moreover fairly corrupted. Some of them are pure inventions in order to supplement certain gaps. The entire system of dates is highly problematical as at that time no such system existed. Furthermore, various insertions in these Keitai chronicles were intended to add an official air. They consisted of, for instance, the ceremony of the ascension to the throne, which was borrowed from the Chinese Han manuscripts, the appointing of an empress (1st year), of a crown prince (7th year), etc. Cf. Itamoto Tarō, op. cit., pp. 44-47.

Now what were the motives which could have induced the disappearance of this text? We believe that these were certainly not anti-Buddhist, as in other places in the *Nihonshoki* much space has been devoted to it. There is only one motive for this disappearance, namely that at the time of the compilation of the *Nihonshoki* it was not very popular to admit that the origin of Buddhism in Japan was owing to Korean immigrants—moreover, without any Japanese initiative. Therefore the actual origin of Japanese Buddhism disappeared from the chronicles. The path which it followed is indicated not only by textual criticism of the *Nihonshoki* itself but also by an accurate interpretation of the mentality which brought about the compilation. On the other hand, the official importation of the Buddhism of the Kimmei chronicles is overemphasised as its actual origination. Did not this leave the initiative for this importation completely in Japanese hands? For the same reason Shiba Tattō remains unmentioned in the Kimmei text. Thus the absence of the *Fusō ryakki* text from the *Nihonshoki* can still bring to light the true origination of Buddhism in Japan.

From all of this it is clear that Shiba Tattō's Buddhism had something to do with Paekche. We know from Korean history that this could not possibly have come from Silla, for instance, to Japan, as this country was not yet ready for Buddhism around the twentieth year of Keitai's reign. Paekche, however, knew of it at the end of the fourth century. Under Emperor Keitai, moreover, the only reports came from here. Furthermore, the saddlers, of whom Shiba Tattō was a leader, all came from Paekche according to the *Nihonshoki*.[1] Also, the leaders' title, *suguri*, which Shiba Tattō

[1] The chronicles of Yūryaku's 7th year are ended in the *Nihonshoki* by a narrative concerning a certain Tasa, 田狹, whose goodlooking wife was taken by the emperor for himself. Therefore he went over to Silla, the great enemy. In this narrative, which we can not reproduce in its entirety, Paekche is mentioned as the land of provenance of various immigrants. (For the complete text cf. W. G. Aston, *Nihongi*, I, pp. 348-351). The principle places in it are as follows: (cf. *Nihonshoki*, 14th *maki*; Kuroita Katsumi, Maruyama Jirō, op. cit., part I, p. 371). "At that time an expert came from West Han Kanin Chiri, 歡因知利, who went and stood at the emperor's side. He came forward and spoke (to the emperor): 'In the land of Han (=Korea) there are many craftsmen, more skilled than slaves. They must be brought into your service.' Hereupon the emperor commanded his ministers: 'It would be advisable to add Kanin Chiri to Otokuni, 弟君, and the others. They must set out for Paekche.' Simultaneously an imperial rescript was issued which gave the order to hand over craftsmen".

held, was not Japanese but an old Korean word which means village chief or, even better, guild master. It was used exclusively in connexion with certain crafts. It can be explained etymologically only from the Korean.[1] It is therefore obvious that this word could

---

A little further on the text says: "He (=Otokuni) collected on a large island the recently arrived (W. G. Aston, op. cit., p. 149, leaves '*Imaki*', 今来, untranslated here and refers to Imaki in Yamato. The '*Imaki*' here simply means 'recently arrived'.) artisans, whom Paekche had offered as tribute". At the end of this long narrative, in which Otokuni is also killed, because of his infidelity to the emperor, by his own wife and buried in her room, it is further said of her and the craftsmen: (Kuroita Katsumi, Maruyama Jirō, op. cit., p. 372; W. G. Aston, op. cit., p. 351).

"Together with Amabe *no atae*, Akao, 海部直赤尾, she tended the experienced craftsmen whose Paekche had offered and they remained on the large island. When the emperor learnt that Otokuni was no longer there, he sent Hitaka *no* Kishi, Katashiwa, 日鷹吉士堅磐, and Koansen, 固安錢. He sent them an order to return (all) together. They (the craftsmen) finally settled in the village Ato *no* Hirokitsu, 吾礪廣津, in the Yamato district. Here many of them became ill and died. Therefore the emperor commanded the *ō-muraji* of the Ōtomo, Moriya, to give Yamato *no* Aya *no atae*, Tsuka, 掬, the order to move with the Imaki (新, or 'new comers'; here 'Imaki' has become an established term) *no* Aya, namely Kōki, 高貴, (W. G. Aston, loc. cit.: Ko-kwi) of the *Sue-tsukuri be* (the potters), Keiki, 堅貴 (W. G. Aston: Kyön-kwi) of the *Kuratsukuri be* (the saddlers), Inshi Raga, 因斯羅我, of the *Egaki be* (the painters), Chōan Nakomu, 定安那錦, of the *Nishikori be* (the brocade weavers), Bō Anna, 卯安那, of the translators and others to the three places: Upper Momohara, 桃原, Lower Momohara and Magami *no* Hara, 眞神原.

[1] It is typical that just the Japanese transcription of the word *suguri*, namely: 勝, (*suguru* = surpass, *suguri*) is to be found in the oldest chronicles about the immigrants, for instance, those of Yūryaku; *Nihonshoki*, 14th *maki*, Yūryaku, 15th year; Kuroita Katsumi, Maruyama Jirō, op. cit., part I, p. 385, last line. This 勝 is also read as *katsu*, *kachi*, *masabe*; cf. Bruno Lewin, op. cit., p. 133 and footnotes 122 and 123. In later chronicles, such as those of Bidatsu for example, 13th year, 20th *maki*; Kuroita Katsumi, Maruyama Jirō, op. cit., part 2, p. 112, last line, the characters 村主 are used for '*sukuri*'. According to Lewin this was still the Korean script. The use of this Korean and older script for *suguri* is an indication of the fact that, for example, the chronicles of Bidatsu concerning the Korean immigrants are probably older than those of Yūryaku and Ōjin. Cf. B. Lewin, op. cit., p. 149, footnote 3. For the term 村主, see B. Lewin, op. cit., p. 118. The word *suguri* can easily be traced back to the Korean *sup'ul* or *su-kur* which means village. Cf. Suematsu Yasukazu, op. cit., p. 86. The Korean derivation of this word is indubitable. Considering the close relations with Paekche, we believe, with Lewin, that: "Tatsächlich hat es den Anschein, dass die

integrate in Japan only from a Korean environment. When someone entered Japan from Korea and was addressed right from the beginning as *suguri,* then this can only be explained by the fact that he already held that title in Korea. Now that was the case with Shiba Tattō. His title of *suguri* was not yet hereditary. Therefore it only expressed his own true position with regard to the saddlers.[1] In other words Shiba Tattō was their leader.

One can further query why a Korean such as Shiba Tattō was called a Chinese in the *Fusō ryakki* text. This was because he belonged to the Aya and Hata who, just as he, had come from Korea to Japan and were all of Chinese origin. Thus Shiba Tattō could, with a Korean title, nevertheless reach Japan as a Chinese. Our *Fusō ryakki* text does not mention anywhere that he came directly from China to Japan.[2] Therefore he was called Chinese in the same sense as is done nowadays with regard to descendents of Chinese who have come to Europe from China many generations

---

Dorfvorsteher in Paekche mit einem entsprechenden Wort (als Sukuri) bezeichnet wurden". Bruno Lewin, loc. cit.

[1] Cf. Bruno Lewin, op. cit., pp. 118, 119. For the sake of his *Aya* and *Hata,* Lewin can hardly accept a de-mythologising of the chronicles before 500 A.D. See, for instance, his point of view on p. 20 and footnote 38 of his work. Hence he will accept the establishment of this title in Japanese society of before that date. Hence *suguri* would count as a generally recognised Japanese title even at the time of Shiba Tattō. This explains his surprise about the fact that neither the granting of this *kabane* (or title) nor Tattō's immigration were included in the chronicles. Cf. B. Lewin, op. cit., p. 148, footnote 16. We believe that at that time *kabane* were scarcely in Japan, and that Shiba Tattō already held the title of *suguri* in Korea and maintained it in Japan. This title was not inherited by his son or grandson, respectively, Tasuna and Tori. Hence it will not be found in any of their chronicles, as we have discovered.

[2] The Chinese manuscripts about Japan even mention Shiba Tattō. Thus we can read in the *Sung-shu*: "In the second year of Yüan-chia (425) during the reign of T'ai-tsu, Ts'an (cf. Chapter I, p. 32) sent Ssu-ma (or better Szŭ-ma) Ts'ao-ta to the Court with a memorial and offered native products." Cf. Ryūsaku Tsunoda, *Japan in the Chinese Dynastic Histories,* p. 21. This Szŭ-ma Ts'ao-ta should not be identified, as does Ryūsaku Tsunoda, op. cit., p. 25, footnote 5, with our Shiba Tattō, as he lived at least a hundred years earlier. Nevertheless it is not impossible that our Shiba Tattō was related to him, and might even have descended from the Chinese, who, as a result of the disturbances in China had taken refuge in Paekche particularly between 400 and 500 A.D.; Suematsu Yasukazu, op. cit., p. 266, considers this possibility.

ago. Moreover, in the Japan of that time the word Chinese also had the meaning of person of position and culture. It is possible, but hard to prove,[1] that Shiba Tattō belonged to the group of Aya.

From all the foregoing facts it is clear that Japan owed its very oldest Buddhism to the immigration. This immigration caused so many population groups to shift to Japan that by chance the small Buddhist group which Shiba Tattō led was also to be found amongst them. Namely, I believe that the group which Shiba Tattō led was also Buddhist. This is apparent from the strong collective conscience alive in this group (as is also the case in the related Japanese *uji*): the communal interests in it were far superior to those of the individual member. Just as today in the Japanese countryside and in each conservative group, moreover, deviating philosophies were not allowed. The opinions of the group were established by the leader of the whole group both in material and in philosophical aspects. This is also somewhat confirmed by the naming of whole groups of immigrants after their leaders.[2] It is therefore obvious that the other saddlers, just as was their leader Shiba Tattō, were Buddhists.

This Buddhist group which accompanied him to Japan was not spread throughout various districts after its arrival. They were all given their own district where, in relative independence, they could continue in their old Korean communities. According to the *Fusō ryakki* text that district was to be found in Takaichi, situated to the south-east of Ōsaka. The *Nihonshoki* also confirms this, as here Takaichi is also mentioned as the dwelling place of the other saddlers.[3] This Takaichi district was part of the province of Yamato. On the north-east it bordered on the Sakurai, 櫻井, district, where Emperor Keitai was to reside at the end of his days. According to the Yūryaku chronicles of the *Nihonshoki* the saddlers were given the following districts to dwell in: Kami, 上, and Shimo, 下, Momohara, 桃原, and Magami *no* Hara, 眞神原, in the eastern corner of this

[1] A. Wedemeyer, *Japanische Frühgeschichte*, attempts to show that his name Ts'ao-ta was partially a Chinese writing error of *tomo* as *Ts'ao* and *atae*, *miyatsuko* as *ta*. The word *Szŭ-ma* = 'Rosswart' (groom) might indicate that he had something to do with the horsebreeder Achi *no omi*, the ancestor of the Aya (according to Ōjin, 20th year). Cf. A. Wedemeyer, op. cit., pp. 67-70, 108 ff.

[2] Cf. Chapter III, p. 219.

[3] The new settlements mentioned in footnote 1 on p. 256 were all in Takaichi.

district. In the neighbourhood of these settlements Shiba Tattō built his temple of grass at Sakatabara. Thus we can conclude that from out of these hamlets Buddhism began to spread in Japanese society as an oil stain spreads on water.

3 *The Buddhism of the saddlers and Japanese society*

There still remains a last question concerning Japan's oldest Buddhism about the grafting of this primeval immigrants' Buddhism on Japanese society. We believe that right from the beginning it was known to all layers: *ō-kimi, shizoku* and other immigrants. This follows particularly from an analysis of the situation of the imperial residences. We shall show this for each of these groups.

a The ō-kimi

Now what was the position of the emperors, as seen from the Buddhist nucleus district of Takaichi? This can best be deduced from the geographical location of their residences. Of all the emperors of the sixth century, Keitai was the greatest traveller. This betrayed his East-Asiatic nomad nature. From the first year of his reign (507) until the twelfth (518) he resided at Kusuha,[1] situated on the line Ōsaka-Kyōto, about twenty-eight miles from Kyōto. In his twelfth year he moved to Otokuni,[2] situated about thirteen miles from Kyōto. This Otokuni was just about as far from his first residence as from Kyōto. At the time of his residence there Shiba Tattō came to Japan. As the emperor dwelt more than sixty miles to the north of the Takaichi district he knew nothing about this. Moreover, his 'emperorship' was founded rather on a religious primacy of state than on a thoroughly organised state and bureaucratic apparatus which would have been able to make the imperial autonomy felt immediately to the furthest corners of the realm or, alternatively, would have informed him of everything which occurred throughout the entire country. The autonomy of the

---

[1] Cf. *Nihonshoki*, 17th *maki*, Keitai 1st year, 1st month, 12th day; Kuroita Katsumi, Maruyama Jirō, op. cit., part 2, p. 13: "The emperor arrived in the Kusuha, 樟葉, palace". Cf. W. G. Aston, *Nihongi*, vol. II, p. 3. *Kusuha* means camphor leaf.

[2] Cf. *Nihonshoki*, 17th *maki*, Keitai 21st year, 3rd month, 9th day; Kuroita Katsumi, Maruyama Jirō, op. cit., part 2, p. 23: "The Miyako (= imperial residence) was moved to Otokuni, 弟國". Cf. W. G. Aston, op. cit., p. 14. *Otokuni* means brother land.

shizoku was far too great for any of this. Therefore it is almost certain that Shiba Tattō's arrival was unnoticed by the emperor.

The situation changed entirely when Keitai, at the end of his life, that is to say in the twentieth year of his reign (527), again changed his residence. This time he moved from his Otokuni residence, as the crow flies more than sixty miles, to the south. If one considers the bad and winding roads of that period, this must have been a trip of more than ninety miles. During it he followed the banks of the river Kizugawa, 木津川, partly, and further other rivers in the delta area of the Yamato river. He settled in the historical Iware,[1] the place which was later to be personified by the 'founder' of the Japanese realm, Jimmu. Before Keitai the Emperors Richū (400-406) and Seinei (480-485) had lived there. Several decades later Emperor Yōmei (586-588) was also to live there. With this move Emperor Keitai found himself in an area which was densely inhabited at that time.

This Iware itself is situated in the southern suburbs of the present day town of Sakurai in the district of Tochi, 十市, (now Sakurai district) in the centre of what was the Yamato province at that time (now Nara prefecture). His palace was given the name Tama-ho. He continued living there until his death in 531.[2] This Tochi district bordered in the west on the north-east edge of the Takaichi district of the saddlers. Thus he came to live on the same mountain slope on which, three miles further on, the saddlers lived. Buddhism, planted by Shiba Tattō around 522 in the saddlers community on this mountain slope, could no longer remain unnoticed by the court

[1] Cf. *Nihonshoki*, 17th *maki*, Keitai, 20th year, 9th month, 13th day; Kuroita Katsumi, Maruyama Jirō, op. cit., part 2, p. 24: "The Miyako was moved to Tamaho, 玉穗, of Iware." Cf. W. G. Aston, op. cit., p. 15. *Tamaho* means valuable ear (of corn).

[2] Cf. *Nihonshoki*, 17th *maki*, Keitai, 25th year, 2nd month, 7th day; Kuroita Katsumi, Maruyama Jirō, op. cit., part 2, p. 33: "The emperor died in Iware, Tamaho *no miya* (Tamaho palace). He was 82 years old." Cf. W.G. Aston, op. cit., p. 24.

This palace was 228 feet above sea level. It lay in the present-day town of Sakurai, namely in 'Abe *no* Ike *no* naka', 阿部池中. Close to it there have been large finds of all kinds of artefacts from the Jōmon and Yayoi periods. To the east of it lay the mountain Abe, 阿部, and to the north the river Teragawa, 寺川. From here there was a good view of the whole Asuka area. It was a typically old district with very good access. Cf. Higuchi Kiyoyuki, "Jōdai gushi-densetsu-chi no kenkyū," *K.G.Z.*, vol. LXII, 1961 Sept., no. 9, pp. 37, 42.

from the time that Keitai also settled there. Perhaps it was from this time on that it began to become a subject of controversy in Japanese society. This was not owing to Keitai deciding either for or against this Buddhism, but because of the typical *shizoku* structure of that period.

b The shizoku

In the second chapter we established the location of the dwelling areas of the most important *shizoku* and mapped them.[1] From this it is apparent that the *shizoku* who undertook the daily government lived too far away from this immigrant mountain edge to be touched by the new doctrine. The Ōtomo, Mononobe and the Kose dwelt 5, 10 and 10½ miles respectively away from here, the Nakatomi approximately 6 miles away. The situation was entirely different for the Soga as this oldest Buddhist settlement bordered on their own home territory. Although the Ōtomo lived relatively close they nevertheless had to cross the country of the Soga, who were inimical to them, to reach the Takaichi settlement. Therefore the new religion remained a stranger to them also.

Additionally, the interest of both of these groups was focussed more on the *ō-kimi* and, as a result, upon his residences. At the time of Shiba Tattō's arrival in Japan this was at Otokuni. At that time the leaders of the Ōtomo and the Mononobe counted as *ōmuraji*. The Kose leader was *ō-omi*. It was they in particular who were the great councillors and actual governors at court. Considering the lines of communication which linked the imperial Otokuni residence with their dwelling areas, Takaichi lay ex-centrically. This also placed it outside the tension area of interior politics. This all changed, however, when Keitai came to live at Iware. The entire power complex of the aforementioned *shizoku* relations was also radically changed by this. The Ōtomo and Kose leaders had to go past the mountain slope of the saddlers, whether they wanted to or not, in order to reach their own tribal areas from the imperial residence. Whether they did in fact pass through this area is none too certain as this mountain slope was also under the control of the Soga. They could easily close off this mountain slope and render Iware inaccessible for the Ōtomo and Kose. In that way their relations to the imperial house were also severed. This did indeed

[1] See Chapter II, pp. 121 ff.

happen soon after the moving of the imperial residence.[1] Only the Nakatomi and the Mononobe, who lived on the other side of Iware, could reach it without passing through Takaichi. As a result of the satisfactory location of their territory they alone had an adequate chance of becoming rivals to the Soga, who were soon to supplant the Ōtomo and Kose in their court duties.

Therefore the previously described geographical situation at the time of Emperor Keitai typified the historical situation: no necessity existed for either the Mononobe or the Nakatomi to 'infect' themselves with the 'foreign' doctrine. On the other hand, the leaders of the other *shizoku* all first had to pass the saddlers' Buddha in order to reach the emperor. The Soga also, who benefitted most from the change of imperial residence, were not an exception. The growth of their power was particularly ascribable to the fact that they lived so close to the emperor. They did not need to cross the Hasekawa, 初瀬川, first, as did the Mononobe, in order to reach him. This increase of the power of the Soga especially benefitted the Korean Buddhists of Takaichi.

As the saddlers dwelt so close to the Soga, when the Soga power began to expand they became a part of the Soga jurisdiction area. Therefore it is amongst these Soga that the first Japanese are to be found who did not feel themselves drawn to the new religion owing to their purely material dependence on the immigrants. We must accept that such contacts took place during the reign of Emperor Keitai. The saddlers formed indeed no independent group, but resorted to the community of interests which the progressive and open-minded Soga had built up in and around their own territories.

---

[1] It is of interest to see how these leaders gradually disappear from the chronicles of the *Nihonshoki*. For instance, Kose *no omi* no longer occurs in the Ankan chronicles. Cf. *Nihonshoki*, 18th *maki*, year before his ascent to the throne; Kuroita Katsumi, Maruyama Jirō, op. cit., part 2, pp. 37, 38: "That month (the second month). The Ōtomo *no ōmuraji* Kanamura, 金村, and the Mononobe *no ōmuraji* Arakao (or: Sokao), 麁鹿火, were made *ō-muraji*, as used to be the case." Cf. W. G. Aston, op. cit., p. 26. Under Emperor Senka, according to the *Nihonshoki*, Ōtomo had not yet disappeared but nevertheless a Soga had contrived to have himself appointed to *ō-omi*. Cf. *Nihonshoki*, 18th *maki*, Senka, 1st year, 2nd month, 1st day; Kuroita Katsumi, Maruyama Jirō, op. cit., part 2, p. 44: "Ōtomo *no* Kanamura *no ōmuraji* and Mononobe *no* Arakao *no ōmuraji* were appointed to *ōmuraji*, as they had already previously been. To *ō-omi* was appointed Soga *no* Iname *no sukune* and to *matsurigoto no machikimi*, 大夫, (a kind of minister) Abe *no* Ōmaro, 阿倍火麻呂." Cf. W. G. Aston, op. cit., p. 33.

They had developed this into the nucleus of all Korean immigrants,[1] to whom they owed their ascendency.

c The other immigrants

Yet others belonged to those communities who, just as were the saddlers, were settled in the Takaichi area. No one in our Western literature has investigated this more thoroughly than Bruno Lewin by use of Japanese sources of the eighth century and later. In this research he has accurately established the territories of the various immigrants. Of all the Yamato districts, that of Takaichi and the neighbouring Katsuraki *no kami*, 葛城上, district were the most densely populated. Here there were respectively six and four settlements of the so-called Yamato *no* Aya, 倭漢.[2] By these Yamato *no* Aya are meant the Han Chinese, who were related to the saddlers and immigrants from Korea. The *Ayabito* also, related to them, had their only settlement throughout the entire Yamato province[3] in Takaichi. The Ch'in Chinese emigrants from Korea, the so-called Hata, 秦, numbered amongst their six Yamato settlements one in Takaichi.[4] The presence of so many Koreans of Chinese extraction in Takaichi makes one suspect that here almost all—also pure Korean—groups were represented. This made the Takaichi district —more so than any other part of Japan—a replica of the diversity (on religious grounds also) of Korea itself.

Additionally, all these people with their different opinions and philosophies, who lived in Korea several miles away from each other, were suddenly forced in this small area to encounter and become acquainted with each other's mental attitudes. As a Korean minority they were more dependent on each other than before, because the average distances in this area, from north to west and from east to south, were not more than six to seven miles. This area can therefore not have been much bigger than the Dutch island of Walcheren, in the province of Zeeland.

Thus the map on p. 470 illustrates that the Hata were not even 2½ miles from the habitations of the saddlers. This proximity had

---

[1] From out of this central area they spread themselves over other parts of Yamato and the other districts and provinces of Kinai. Cf. B. Lewin, op. cit., p. 64.

[2] Cf. Bruno Lewin, op. cit., p. 63.

[3] Cf. Bruno Lewin, op. cit., p. 65.

[4] Cf. Bruno Lewin, op. cit., p. 83.

important consequences for Buddhism as, owing to this, it immediately encountered other philosophies such as those which, for example, were alive amongst the Hata. Owing to this, Buddhism, as well as other religions such as Korean Shamanism, Taoism and Confucianism, was given more than enough chances for dialogue in these various Korean settlements. Possibly one can ascribe to this the fact that the idea of the 'Pure Land', for instance, in which Shōtoku Taishi was thought to be after his death, was tinted just as much by Buddhism as by Taoism. We shall confirm this in the last chapter.

That the oldest Buddhism could only later take root and grow further in the Japanese mentality is owing to the fact that the Korean group of saddlers could remain, even after its arrival in Japan, as a unit and was not abruptly torn asunder. Initially living among Koreans of Chinese family, it could become acclimatised to the new situation before it encountered Japanese society itself.

This inward process of ripening was also greatly facilitated by the protection and sympathy of the Soga, who protected their relative independence. The fierce civil war which followed upon the death of Emperor Keitai in 531 between his three sons Ankan, Senka and Kimmei for the time being at least withdrew all attention from the religion of the 'Chinese deity' of Shiba Tattō. Thus Buddhism was given the chance, on the edge of the Soga district, to stabilise itself and gradually to become Japanese Buddhism.

This latter especially must have been a very slow process. The fact that most Takaichi immigrants came from Paekche and reached Japan as part of the political intentions of this country does not exclude the possibility that the king of Paekche himself anonymously supported Buddhism via leaders such as Shiba Tattō. In any case, for the first decade it remained Korean Buddhism transplanted to Japan. It became more Japanese only with the occurrences of the second phase, which are described in the chronicles of the thirteenth year of Emperor Kimmei.

Second phase: The origin of Japanese Buddhism

In the initial stage of Japanese Buddhism described above we established that this was already alive in the immigrants' community of saddlers and that it could not, situated as it was only a short distance from the imperial residence, remain hidden for long. Nevertheless, a more open beginning of it came to light only in the

Nihonshoki chronicles of Emperor Kimmei. This emperor bore the richly symbolic Japanese name of *Ame kuni oshi-hiraki hiro niwa*, 天國排開廣庭, which can be translated as: the broad garden (the imperial court with the courts of the imperial women) which thrusts open the land of heaven.[1] How it thrust open this heaven is demonstrated in the elementary text at the beginning of this chapter.[2]

There we already pointed out that this text used to be considered by many Japanese authors, and even now by some Western authors, as the very earliest description of the actual introduction of Buddhism to Japan. According to them, the thirteenth year of Kimmei could be equated to 552 here. This was because they uncritically respected the *Nihonshoki* as a genuine state chronicle, built up and tended with great care year by year. From the first chapter we know that nothing was less true. Nowadays the conviction has been established that the facts related deserve less and less reliance as they become situated further back in antiquity, and thus further from the date of compilation. This has been the reason for which many authors no longer take the *Nihonshoki* date of 552 seriously and, supported by other data, date this chronicle of the thirteenth year of Kimmei as 538.[3]

However, the protagonists of this latter date realise too little that the objections to these *Nihonshoki* texts with regard to the date 552 are equally valid for the 'old Japanese data' to which they appeal.[4] This is because these data also have been dated according to the same process as the *Nihonshoki* itself, namely with dates which, at the earliest, may have been added at the beginning of the seventh century to existing texts and chronicles. Moreover, it must be added, that none of the texts which they introduce as proof, in opposition to the *Nihonshoki* dates, boasts greater histori-

---

[1] Cf. W. G. Aston, op. cit., p. 36.

[2] Cf. pp. 241 ff.

[3] Tsuda Sōkichi, *Nihon Koten no Kenkyū*, part II, p. 87, points out that these texts were not in the least written with the intention of giving dates.

[4] It is also difficult to construe proof by use of Korean works such as the *Samguk yusa* and the *Samguk sagi* as they too do not agree on various dates of this period. Thus, according to the *Samguk yusa*, King Sŏng was supposed to have started his reign in 513, according to the *Samguk sagi* in 523 and according to yet other Korean sources in 524 or 527. Cf. Kasai Wajin, "*Sankoku iji* Kudara-ōreki to *Nihonshoki*" (The calendars of the kings of Paekche in the *Samguk yusa* and the *Nihonshoki*), *C.G.*, no. 24 (1962), July, pp. 100, 102.

cal reliability than the *Nihonshoki* itself. They are equally valueless for the verification or earlier dating of the date of the public introduction of Buddhism to Japan. Therefore the value of these texts can only be considered in so far as they indicate relatedness to each other.

Hence all of these texts are of value only in so far as they can confirm the contents of the *Nihonshoki* text quoted above. They can co-operate in finding a context in the *Nihonshoki* itself in which the actual facts concerning the importation of Buddhism are revealed. Thus they can become a good stimulus for initial doubts and consequential dissection of the *Nihonshoki* texts, by which an entirely new picture of Buddhism can be evolved.

The question of dates remains just as insoluble.[1] Therefore it is of secondary importance in our argument.[2] It can only help to

---

[1] In our last chapter Japanese data will be mentioned on pp. 375 ff. which are older than the *Nihonshoki*. Here only more recent data, concerning, for instance, the death of Shōtoku Taishi, are recorded. Our Kimmei text however can neither be verified nor dated in conjunction with these texts because they do not mention it. Furthermore an inscription must also be mentioned which is indicated in the *Gangōji-garan engi* (mentioned below) by *Gangōji torobanmyō*, 元興寺塔露盤銘, *stūpa* inscription of the Gangōji. It says: "At the time of the emperor (Jap.: *tennō*) of Yamato, Shikishima (name of the imperial residence which was also used for the emperor himself), who was called *Ame kuni oshi-hiraki hiro niwa mikoto*, when the Soga called Iname served him, the King of Paekche, Seimei (here written: 正明) offered —it is said—him the law of Buddha, which is the highest of all laws."

For the *Kambun* text, cf. Kasai Wajin, op. cit., p. 101. According to Kasai Wajin this text derives from 593. Owing to the use of the word *tennō* in it, which became used at the earliest after 625, we should not date this text earlier than 625. In this text it merely states that the advent of Buddhism derives from the time of Emperor Kimmei, not that by so doing it was also directly linked with this emperor.

[2] Kasai Wajin tries to equate the text of the thirteenth year of Kimmei with the 26th year of King Sŏng of Paekche. Thus he attempts to reduce the discrepancies in the dates of the Japanese sources, 538 or 553, to those in various Korean sources. Cf. footnote 1. Nevertheless, this 'fortunate' coincidence does not solve the question of dating. They are merely reduced to the 'undatability' of the Korean data. His reference to the *Liang-shu* does indeed create the possibility of equating this 26th year with 549. Here however the open question remains as to whether, in the first place, this specifically Japanese historical fact *may* be placed under the 26th year of Sŏng, thus rendering it rather as a datum of the Korean sources than of the Japanese, all the more so as it does not occur at all in the Korean sources. Cf. Kasai Wajin, op. cit., pp. 100-103.

discover the actual motives which have played a part in the origination of Japan's oldest Buddhism. All of these texts which fall outside the scope of the *Nihonshoki* therefore have more value as illustrative material rather than as proof, because they are too tendentious for the latter.

Now which are these texts? In total there are supposedly four which would correct the *Nihonshoki*. The first is to be found in a manuscript which bears the long title of *Gangōji-garan engi hei ryū ki shizaichō*, 元興寺伽藍緣起幷梳記資財帳, inventory (or list of goods) of the chronicles concerning the origin and development of the Gangōji (name of temple) monastery (Jap.: *garan* = Sanskrit: *saṃghārāma*, monastery). We shall refer to it hereafter as: *Gangōji-garan engi*. It was composed after 747 as the result of an imperial command to inventory all temple treasure. It is certainly of a far later date. In it the following is written: [1]

"The Buddhism of the Yamato area dates from the time of Emperor *Ame kuni oshi-hiraki iro niwa* (= Kimmei), who resided in the palace of Shikishima and reigned over the people and the celestial country, when Soga Iname *sukune* served him. In the seventh year of his reign, the year *tsuchinoe-uma*, the twelfth month, during the reign of King Seimei (Sŏng) in Paekche, the image of the Prince (Śākyamuni), the ritual objects for the *kanjō* [2] and an explanatory writing concerning the origin of Buddha were offered."

The year *tsuchinoe-uma*, 538, is here supposed to be the seventh year of Kimmei. However, if one checks the *Nihonshoki* for this year of Kimmei's reign, one may search in vain. This year corresponds to the third year of Kimmei's predecessor, Senka. This same fact can also be encountered in a more authentic source than the foregoing, namely the life history of Shōtoku Taishi, *Kamitsumiya Shōtoku Hōōteisetsu*, 上宮聖德法王帝說, or briefly *Hōōteisetsu*.[3] This collection of all kinds of data concerning Shōtoku Taishi was made at the beginning of the Heian period (794-1185). It was therefore

[1] This text is to be found here amongst data on the Daigo temple of Yamashiro in Yamato, the *Yamashiro Daigoji-hon*. Cf. *Daigaku Nihon-shi*, part 1, pp. 78-79.

[2] *Kanjō* 灌頂: *Sanskrit*: *abhiṣeka*, ceremonial acceptance of the *vinaya*. Cf. Inoue Tetsujirō, *et al.*, *Bukkyō Jiten*, Tōkyō 1938, p. 162, column II.

[3] Kida Teikichi and other, especially modern, authors all agree on the greater antiquity of this text over and above that of the other sources mentioned here. Cf. Kasai Wajin, op. cit., p. 100.

certainly younger than the *Nihonshoki*. Hence many of its facts are frequently expansions of those of the *Nihonshoki*. It did, however, use older and more succinct sources here and there. This depicts the origination of Japanese Buddhism as follows:[1]

"When Emperor Shikishima (= Kimmei) [2] reigned, King Seimei (= Sŏng) of Paekche sent on the twelfth day of the tenth month of the year *tsuchinoe-uma* for the first time an image of Buddha, manuscripts and monks."

In the controversial pamphlet (written in 821 by Saichō, 最澄, founder of the Tendai-*shū*), called *Kenkairon*, 顕戒論,[3] Saichō makes the following objection to the contention of the monk Gomyō, 護命,[4] of the Hossō-*shū*, 法相宗, that Buddhism had reached Japan in the year *tsuchinoe-uma*:

"The arrival of the emperor took place in the year *kanoe-saru* (= 540). His reign lasted 32 years as a whole. During this the year *tsuchinoe-uma* did not occur. By starting from this date the *Gangōji engi* (= *Gangōji-garan engi*) is contrary to the true annals (= the *Nihonshoki*)."

Thus, in this text, the founder of the Japanese Tendai-*shū*, Saichō, attributed greater value to the *Nihonshoki* than to the *Gangōji-garan engi*. Hence he remained true to the traditional opinion.

The same is also to be found in the fourth work. The medieval monk Gyōnen, 凝然, (1240-1321) [5] reveals in his *Sangoku buppō dentsū engi*, 三國仏法伝通縁起, (the history of the origination of Buddhism in the three lands, i.e. India, China and Japan) the eighth century monk Shinshō, 審祥,[6] who was supposed to have written the following in his own work, *Daianji Shinshō Daitokki*, 大安寺審

[1] Cf. Sakaino Kōyō, *Shōtoku Taishiden*, Tōkyō 1917, p. 110. W. Renondeau, op. cit., p. 26.

[2] See page 266, footnote 1.

[3] For this text cf. W. Renondeau, op. cit., p. 27.

[4] He lived from 749 to 834. He stayed, *i.a.*, in the Gangōji and wrote several *sūtra* commentaries. Cf. Inoue Tetsujirō, op. cit., p. 339, column III.

[5] Gyōnen was a very many-sided personality, who was not only at home with the doctrines of nearly all the Buddhist sects of that period, but also with those of Lao-tzŭ and Confucius. Cf. Inoue Tetsujirō, op. cit., p. 194, column III; p. 195, column I.

[6] Shinshō came from Silla. He was honoured by imperial order to hold *sūtra* readings from 740 until the year of his death, 742, in the Daianji. Cf. Inoue Tetsujirō, op. cit., p. 609, columns I, II.

祥大徳記, (chronicle of the Daitokki (= official honorific) Shinshō of the Daianji):[1]

"The twelfth day of the twelfth month of the third year of Emperor Senka, namely *tsuchinoe-uma*, Buddhism came from Paekche."

Therefore all of these texts point to 538 as being the year in which Buddhism was officially imported. Nevertheless, one should not yet be satisfied with this date. The texts themselves are not sufficiently historically reliable for that. Therefore they will also have to be tested, especially according to their contents, by the data of the *Nihonshoki*.

The foregoing texts certainly do establish that there has always been uncertainty regarding the date of the Kimmei text.[2] They can, however, also aid the demythologisation of all of these facts related in this Kimmei chronicle. Thus they have brought us to the following conclusions, which we shall describe in the coming pages:

1) Kimmei's government was anti-Buddhist rather than Buddhist. Therefore the importation of Buddhism could never have taken place during his reign. The text about this has arrived in the Kimmei chronicles arbitrarily.
2) Therefore the official importation of Buddhism took place under Emperor Senka, who sympathised with it. It had been prepared to a great extent by the immigrants.
3) The Buddhism of the sixth century was born of contrasts between immigrants, *shizoku* and emperors.

1 *The impossibility of official introduction under Kimmei*

The year 552 which, until recently, was generally thought to be the (official) date of the origin of Buddhism in Japan should not be doubted only on the basis of external criticism of the *Nihonshoki*. The exegesis of the *Nihonshoki* text itself also evokes all kinds of doubts. An example of that consists in the comparison of the Buddhist chronicles of Kimmei with those of Bidatsu. Namely, between the two of them a certain parallelism exists which cannot

---

[1] Cf. W. Renondeau, op. cit., p. 27; Kasai Wajin, op. cit., p. 100.

[2] Concerning this, see the various studies mentioned by Kasai Wajin, op. cit., pp. 100, 101.

be described as purely accidental. The texts themselves force one to recognise this, as both pretend to describe the origin of Buddhism.[1] This parallelism consists of the fact that both collections of chronicles describe the Buddhist chronicles during the sixth, thirteenth and fourteenth years of the two emperors. In both, the chronicles of the sixth year refer to the influences of Paekche Buddhism in Japan. They are very brief. Those of the thirteenth year describe the origin of Buddhism as dependent on both emperors. Compared to other Buddhist chronicles they take up most space. Those of the fourteenth year relate a miraculous occurrence common to both: with Kimmei it was the origin of the Buddha image of the Yoshino, 吉野, temple; with Bidatsu it was the miraculous conversion of Ikebe *no atae* Hida, Soga *no* Umako and Shiba Tattō. Furthermore, in the thirteenth year of Kimmei and the fourteenth year of Bidatsu an epidemic is mentioned, which caused a persecution of Buddhism. Tsuda says of this double persecution that, originally, in the chronicler's mind, there was only one.[2] This also confirms the foregoing parallelism as it gives a very synthetic impression. It causes one to suspect that the dates of these texts have been fitted in according to some system, because no one really knew what their sequence should have been. Hence the tales related here could equally well have belonged elsewhere.

Analysis of the Kimmei text itself leads to the same conclusion. Namely, it shows that it is impossible to link all of the facts related there to the year 552.

If one compares the Buddhist formulations of these Kimmei chronicles to the remaining state chronicles of that period, then these Buddhist texts continue to disagree in style, as the state chronicles are characterised by a far briefer and more business-like approach than those of Buddhism. The difference in style indicates not only a different purpose but also a different author from that of the other chronicles. We therefore believe that the religious texts—including those about Buddhism—were only later inserted amongst the existing state chronicles.

---

[1] The Kimmei texts of the sixth, thirteenth and fourteenth year are to be found in this work on pp. 275, 241 ff. respectively; and footnote 6 on p. 245 of this chapter. Those of the sixth, thirteenth and fourteenth of Bidatsu are in this work in footnote 5 on p. 291 and pp. 248 ff. and 302 ff. respectively.

[2] Tsuda Sōkichi, *Nihon Koten no Kenkyū*, part II, pp. 95-96.

Furthermore, one expects that a chronicle will describe the occurrences or series of events of one day or of a fairly circumscribed period. It should never encompass a tale of many years. In that case we are indeed dealing not with a chronicle but with a history. The larger part of the Kimmei chronicles, such as that concerning the Korean war for instance, answers to that condition. The text we are discussing, however, is an exception to this. It conveys a tale that was spread over many years. It related facts which could not possibly have happened in the short space of time required by a chronicle.

Comparison of the most important facts in it proves this. The offer of the image and other gifts by the emissaries of King Sŏng, the mutual consultation, the erection of the Mukuhara temple and the like could have happened in a fairly short time. This becomes more difficult with the epidemic which, according to the text, lasted 'a long time'. Its duration even aroused the dissatisfaction of the Mononobe and Nakatomi and finally led to the destruction of the Mukuhara temple. These latter facts could have occupied many months and years. A tale with so many various stages could have been inserted in the imperial chronicles at different places. Now why was it given a place specifically in the thirteenth year of Emperor Kimmei? The reason is that one or other fact of the entire series had something to do with this date, or rather with Kimmei himself. Otherwise it is hard to explain why the 'interpolator' should have added this specifically to the Kimmei chronicles. It is therefore of importance to know which fact, in a lengthy series such as this, caused the entire tale to be placed here. Then the date concerns only this occurrence most important to the chronicler, not any of the other particulars.

Now how can one discover this fact? In order to discover this, it is necessary to find out the main intention of the writer of the entire history. Was he concerned only with the advent of Buddhism to Japan, or was it just the persecution and destruction of it which held his interest? Usually such an intention can be discovered from the warmth and enthusiasm with which various details are described. Now in the Kimmei-thirteen-text little of this is noticeable. The only pericope in which more knowledge of and sympathy for Buddhism is apparent is the contents of the letter from King Sŏng. Now just this letter is certainly an anachronism, inserted a few centuries later by a monk. It is indeed a literal quotation from the *Suvarṇaprabhāsa-sūtra*. This *sūtra* was initially translated into Chinese between 700 and 712 by Yi-tsing and reached Japan only after 734, nearly 100 years after the death of King Sŏng.[1] At that time the recension of the *Nihonshoki* had been completed for nearly forty years. Therefore this passage—obviously inserted later—had nothing to do with the intentions of the author of the remainder of the text.

In tracing this intention the context can be of the greatest importance. Now the context of our passage is rather more anti-Buddhist. This appears from the following texts. Under the fourth month of the same year, the Japanese emperor sent an address to the Korean rulers who had come to him for military aid, which is as follows:[2]

"Now the kings of Paekche, of Kara, 加羅, of Ara, 安羅, and our minister (servant) of Yamato *no mikotomochi* (= Mimana)[3] have together sent us emissaries, and finally enlightened us regarding the situation. Now it is right that in future they will be one with Mimana in heart and power, as was the case until now. Then they will certainly gain the good fortune and blessing of the protection from the high heavens. Further you must rely on the souls of the noble emperors." This 'good fortune and blessing of the protection from the high heavens' and the 'reliance on the souls of the noble emperors' were actually intended towards the Korean rulers as a delicate nudge to conversion to the belief of the emperors. The same can also be noted in the chronicles after the thirteenth year of Kimmei.

In the sixteenth year of Kimmei, the Korean prince Kei (Kor.: Hye), the same prince who a few years previously had invited the emperor in King Sŏng's name to become a Buddhist, recorded the death of this king of Paekche. On hearing this, the Soga addressed him. It could be expected of the Soga that his Buddhist sympathies, as known from the chronicles, would be apparent in his words. This was, however, not the case. He said to Hye:[4]

"King Sŏng possessed an admirable knowledge of the ways of

---

[1] Cf. footnote 6 on p. 242.
Cf. also W. Renondeau, op. cit., pp. 21, 22.

[2] Cf. *Nihonshoki*, 19th *maki*; Kuroita Katsumi, Maruyama Jirō, op. cit., dart 2, p. 76. See also W. G. Aston, op. cit., p. 65.

[3] Cf. p. 203, footnote 4.

[4] Cf. *Nihonshoki*, 19th *maki*; Kuroita Katsumi, Maruyama Jirō, op. cit., part 2, pp. 86, 87. Cf. also W. G. Aston, op. cit., p. 76.

heaven and the principles of earth. His fame has spread everywhere.[1] We hoped that he would preserve the peace for a long time, that he would govern the neighbouring lands west of the sea and would always [2] serve our emperor. To our surprise he has suddenly been removed far from us.[3] Just as running water he will never return, but has gone to rest in a dark place. Oh, what a hideous grief this is! What a sorrow, which truly causes pain! Who has any feeling, without suffering from this? Moreover, on what should we blame this disaster? However, what means must we now adopt in order to restore your country to peace again?"

Here it is conspicuous that the Buddhist Soga, when describing Sŏng's significance, does not mention his Buddhism. Nowhere does he praise Sŏng as a promoter of Buddhism, neither can he find the words in which to express what this ruler achieved for Japanese Buddhism. In his address to Hye, Soga even went further: [4]

"Previously, under the reign of Emperor Ōhatsuse, 大泊瀬, (Yūryaku) your country was threatened by Koguryŏ. Even more so than for a pile of eggs (of the silkworm) [5] it was very dangerous at that time. Then the emperor ordered the priests of the earth and heaven gods [6] to gain the council of the gods of heaven and earth with all due respect. The priests [7] were granted a divine revelation and answered: 'If you humbly request the god and founder of the country, then you will deliver your master, who stands on the point of destruction. Your country will then certainly return to peace

---

[1] Lit.: after the four *hyō*, 表, our compass points: north, south, east and west, and after the eight *hō*, 方: north, north-east, east, south-east, south, south-west, west, north-west.

[2] Lit.: 1,000 years, even 10,000 years. In *furigana* it is followed by: *itsu made mo*: always.

[3] Thus the *furigana* text. Literally it says: 'Now he has arisen suddenly on a morning and departed from us'.

[4] Cf. *Nihonshoki*, 19th *maki*; Kuroita Katsumi, Maruyama Jirō, op. cit., part 2, p. 87; W. G. Aston, op. cit., pp. 76, 77.

[5] According to the *furigana*.

[6] It says literally: to the *kamu-tsukasa*, 神祇伯, the officials of the heaven and earth gods (according to the *furigana*). This was an office introduced only after 645.

[7] The expression used here: *hafuri*, 祝者, represented a certain kind of *kannushi*, 神主, priest. Usually this word is reserved for priests of the Sumiyoshi temples. As rank, the *hafuri* stood below the *sukune*. Cf. Shimonaka Yasaburō, *Shintō Daijiten*, Tōkyō 1940, part 3, p. 168, columns I, II. Cf. also the special meaning of this word in the *tsuchigumo*, chapter II, p. 95.

and the people will dwell in tranquility.' Therefore the god was beseeched hereafter for deliverance. Thus country and houses [1] once again returned to peace. Now the god who founded your country in the beginning was the god who, at the time of the division between heaven and earth, when plants and trees could still speak, descended from the heavens and created our land.

"Recently I have heard that your country has deserted him and no longer honours him. If, however, you now once again repent of your faults of the past, build a temple for the god and bring this divine spirit sacrifices and worship him, then your land will once again return to great prosperity. Here you must not forget this!"

In this text we find no trace of Soga's Buddhism. Nearly every sentence is directed towards impressing on Hye respect for the Japanese gods. This form of propaganda is to be expected from the afore-mentioned Soga opponents, the Mononobe and the Nakatomi. In the mouth of a Soga it is unimaginable. Probably it was put in his mouth by a later editor.

All of these texts together arouse the incontrovertible impression that they were written from a mentality which wished to ignore Buddhism. They clearly chose the side of those who, in the text of the thirteenth year of Kimmei concerning the origin of Buddhism, opposed Buddhism.

Let us return from this context to the tale of the introduction of Buddhism at the court of Kimmei. Then we must also establish from the foregoing that it was not a triumphant Buddhist tale of conquest. Indeed it terminates in stalemate: the disastrous fire of the Mukuhara temple and the casting away of the Buddha image into the Naniwa canal. An eulogy on Buddhism would never end in a defeat which was not simultaneously set right again.

In these very last facts the actual intention of the chronicler comes to light, which consisted of the destruction of Buddhism. For him therefore this fact was of the greatest importance. His entire tale is directed towards this. Therefore it has also been dated from this. This means that the dates of the other occurrences in this tale must be placed from these very last facts. They must have taken place before the thirteenth year of Kimmei, as they all precede it. Hence the year 552 was most likely a black year for Japanese

---

[1] In *furigana* 稷, is added, millet: houses. Cf. also footnote 2 on p. 244.

Buddhism. It is therefore not surprising that specifically Buddhist manuscripts such as the *Gangōji-garan engi* and others mentioned on pp. 267 ff. prefer to leave this date unmentioned.

If the destruction of the Mukuhara temple happened according to the *Nihonshoki* in the year 552, then in which year must the invitation to Buddhism by the Paekche emissaries be sought? An answer to this is only possible if one or other text somewhere in the *Nihonshoki* refers us to such an occurrence. Now in the *Nihonshoki* there is one passage, even before the thirteenth year of Kimmei, which mentions Buddhism. It is given under the sixth year, ninth month of Kimmei: [1]

"That month Paekche had made an image of Buddha of 1 *chō* 丈, 6 (*shaku* 尺) [2] (= 15.76 feet). Moreover, a prayer text was composed which was: 'As you have heard, the making of an image of Buddha of 1 *chō*, 6 *shaku* is a work of great merit. Now that we have accomplished this meritorious work respectfully, we pray that the emperor may achieve the highest virtue. May also the land of the *Miyake*, which stands under the rule of the emperor (i.e. Mimana), receive, together with him, blessing. Also we pray for the people under heaven, that they may all receive deliverance. Because it is for that that we have made this image.' "

The foregoing text is the very first to mention Buddhism in the *Nihonshoki*. It could be a good start for the Buddhist facts of the thirteenth year of Emperor Kimmei, and allow these to begin here as a result of this special prayer for the emperor. Thus the Korean ruler would be behaving towards the Japanese *ō-kimi* in the same spirit as Fu Chien had done 150 years previously towards Sosurim.

The erection of an image almost 16 feet high was, for the king of Paekche, a fact of national importance. It is comparable to the construction of a similar image in Japan under Empress Kōken, 孝謙, in 752: the *dai-butsu*, 大仏, or Great Buddha, of Nara, famous even today. According to the chronicles of that period this was considered the most important religious event of the century. Moreover, Shintō—mainly in its chief gods Amaterasu and Hachiman—was abundantly involved.[3] Now in the religious history of

---

[1] Cf. *Nihonshoki*, 19th *maki*; Kuroita Katsumi, Maruyama Jirō, op. cit., part 2, p. 71; W. G. Aston, op. cit., p. 59; Karl Florenz, op. cit., p. 306.

[2] One *chō*, 丈, equals 3,03 metres, one *shaku*, 尺, equals 0.303 metres. Hence the image was approximately 4.85 metres high, or nearly 16 feet.

[3] Cf. M. W. de Visser, *Ancient Buddhism in Japan*, vol. II, pp. 643-644.

Paekche there is no better opportunity imaginable in the sixth century for the introduction of Buddhism to the Japanese court than the creation of the Paekche image.

Before these emissaries from Paekche could reach the Yamato court of the emperor many months must have passed since the festivities in Paekche. Therefore they could complete their errand only in the following year, that is to say the seventh year of Kimmei. Therefore this seventh year is mentioned in the *Gangōji-garan engi* for instance. According to the *Nihonshoki* this year was equal to *hinoe-tora*: 546. Nevertheless this still remains a partial solution, as not all the difficulties have yet been removed. The main one still exists. In the light of what we have established above it is unthinkable that this image should be offered to someone like Emperor Kimmei. His chronicles unavoidably indicate all too clearly his preference for the *ujigami* beliefs, which did not admit, under any pretext, a foreign religion. Kimmei and his court therefore had nothing to do with the origin of Buddhism.

2 *The introduction of Buddhism at the Senka court*

If this introduction did not take place under Kimmei, under whom then did it happen? We believe that this was the case under the reign of Emperor Senka, the second anti-emperor to Kimmei. The *Nihonshoki* affords proof of this supposition. In the thirty-second year of the reign of Empress Suiko (624) a letter from the famous monk Kanroku to Suiko can be found which can aid us. This letter was a result of an investigation Suiko commanded into various malpractices by Buddhist nuns and monks. Namely, one of them was supposed to have hit his grandfather with a pan. Kanroku's intention in this letter was to obtain clemency by showing that their Buddhism was still very young and therefore none too deep-rooted. A passage states: [1]

"Buddha's teaching was handed down through the lands of the West, came to China after 300 years and was brought from there to Paekche. Scarcely a hundred years ago our king (= Sŏng) heard of the wisdom of the Japanese emperor. Therefore he pre-

---

Amaterasu was concerned in this as the Japanese *avatāra* of Vairocāna Buddha.

[1] Cf. *Nihonshoki*, 22nd *maki*, Suiko, 32nd year, 4th month; Kuroita Katsumi, Maruyama Jirō, op. cit., part 2, pp. 164, 165. This text has not been translated by W. G. Aston, but by K. Florenz, op. cit., pp. 330, 331.

sented an image of Buddha, and *sūtras,* not a hundred years ago. Hence, at the moment, nuns and monks do not yet know the prescriptions of the teaching very well and they easily turn to all kinds of misdeeds."

This passage is very important owing to its greater historical reliability. It dates indeed from the year 624. Therefore it is actually more valuable according to its contents and date than the Kimmei chronicles. The value of this text is also considerably enhanced by the authority of the 'bridging' figure, Suiko, who was also closely concerned with the origin of Buddhism. This letter must have reminded her of events, the leading participants in which she must have met repeatedly. Namely, when she received this letter she was already seventy years old. She had known her own father, Kimmei, very well; he died when she was eighteen. We have already pointed out that she was very friendly to those who had brought Buddhism to Japan, especially to Shiba Tattō.[1] Therefore, if she received a letter concerning the last hundred years, then it must have actually been a hundred. Thus the introduction by Sŏng must have lain rather in the neighbourhood of the year 538 than in that of 552, all the more so because this latter date occurred precisely two years prior to her birth. In the latter case, Kanroku could scarcely have written of Buddhism that it was nearly a hundred years old. He probably rounded off the actual age of Buddhism. Her own age forced him to do this fairly accurately. Therefore the date 538 lies just on the border of a century in round figures. Now according to the *Nihonshoki* Kimmei came to the throne in 540. Therefore the seventh year of his reign occurred in 546 according to the Japanese count. However, in that year Buddhism could not possibly have been introduced in harmony with Kanroku's letter.

We hope to show that this happened far more probably in 538. At the beginning of this chapter [2] we have pointed out the nowadays [3] generally accepted supposition that after the disputed

---

[1] Cf. pp. 251 ff.

[2] Cf. pp. 237 ff.

[3] Cf. Naoki Kojirō in *Daigaku Nihon-shi,* part 1, p. 43, This opinion is based on the article by Hayashiya Shintarō: "Keitai Kimmei-chō nairan no shiteki bunseki" (Historical analysis of the disputes between the Keitai and Kimmei courts), *Ritsumeikan Bungaku,* p. 88.

death [1] of Emperor Keitai, his sons Ankan, Senka and Kimmei became divided between themselves and exercised the emperorship simultaneously. Thus it happened that, for instance, first Ankan (531-536) and later Senka (536-539) were the anti-emperors to Kimmei who, in contradiction to the *Nihonshoki* reports, came to power as early as 532 and not in 540. Only after the death of Senka in 539 did the unity of the Japanese realm return. Seen from this angle the seventh year of Kimmei, the year of the official introduction of Buddhism into Japan, could also be the third year of Senka: the year 538.

In contrast to this the chronicler of the *Nihonshoki* gave a wholly different picture. To him, apparently, the termination of the fraternal strife by Senka's death was so important that he only permitted Kimmei's reign to begin after Senka, in 540. Thus he made room after Keitai's death in the *Nihonshoki* for Ankan and Senka and, after them, for Kimmei. He also counted the *kanshi* system consecutively by these means. As a result of this the first eight years of Kimmei's reign disappeared and the first fifteen years of his reign had to be compressed into the first six or seven years of the *Nihonshoki* chronicles. We have clarified this involved situation in the table on page 281. In any case, from this it is apparent that Senka too had some connection with the introduction of Buddhism.

---

[1] Cf. *Nihonshoki,* 17th *maki,* Keitai, 25th year, 2nd month; Kuroita Katsumi, Maruyama Jirō, op. cit., part 2, p. 33; W. G. Aston, op. cit., pp. 24, 25.

No agreement has yet been reached concerning this death. According to the *Nihonshoki,* Keitai died in his 25th year of government, namely the year *kanoto-i,* 531. Ankan succeeded him in the year *kinoe-tora,* 534. Absolutely nothing is said about either of the years in between, *mizunoe-ne,* 532 and *mizunoto-ushi,* 533. What happened during that interval? A commentary at the end of the Keitai chronicles of the *Nihonshoki* notes that he died, according to a certain book, in the year *kinoe-tora,* 534, the 28th year of government. That was the same year in which Ankan took up the government. With a reference to another source, namely the *Kudara-ki,* this commentary also records that not only Keitai, but also the crown prince and other princes died. Hence the writer of this latter source prefers the 25th (= 531) rather than the 28th (= 534) year of reign as the year of his death. This commentary refers to older—probably Korean—sources than the *Nihonshoki.* Discrepancies concerning the dates in these sources are thus reflected in the *Nihonshoki.* The *Kojiki* names the year *hinoto-hitsuji,* 527 as Keitai's year of death. All of this proves that Keitai's year of death was simply unknown. Concerning this, cf. Itamoto Tarō, op. cit., pp. 43-45.

The latter is also confirmed by the geographical situation of the courts of the three emperors mentioned here. Thus Ankan dwelt in the Makarikane *no hashi*, 勾金橋, palace.[1] This lay on the border of the Furuchi, 古市, district of the Kawachi province with the Yamato province (See the map p. 470). Here Ankan died and was buried, also according to the *Kojiki*,[2] in the same district. As he lived to the west of the territory of the Ōtomo he had to pass through their land to reach that of the Soga. Living as he did at a distance of more than fifty miles from the Buddhist Takaichi mountain slopes he probably did not know Buddhism.

This was entirely changed in the case of his successor Senka. According to the *Kojiki* and the *Nihonshoki* [3] he lived in Iwoiri *no hara*, 廬入野, in Hinokuma, 檜隈. This Hinokuma is to be found in the Takaichi district already known to us. The most important personalities of the immigrants of this district had settled here. This is apparent from their titles.[4] For instance the Omiashi, 於美阿志, temple of Achi *no omi*, who was one of the most important leaders amongst the Korean immigrants, was built at Hinokuma. About three miles from here lay the habitations of the saddlers in Kamitsu- and Shimo-Momohara. Thus the original area of Buddhism was not too far from Senka. Moreover, his residence lay on the edge of the jurisdictionary area of the Soga. Soga Iname, who had been appointed *ō-omi* [5] by Senka, maintained his residence in Owarida Mukuhara, on the northern border of the Takaichi district. This was situated 3 miles from Hinokuma, $2\frac{1}{3}$ miles from the saddlers' settlement of Magami *no hara* and $3\frac{1}{2}$ miles from a similar settlement at Momohara. According to the Kimmei chronicle

---

[1] Cf. *Nihonshoki*, 18th *maki*, 1st year, 1st month and 2nd year, 2nd month; Kuroita Katsumi, Maruyama Jirō, op. cit., part 2, pp. 38 and 43 respectively; W. G. Aston, op. cit., pp. 26 and 32 respectively.

[2] Cf. *Kojiki*, 3rd *maki;* Kuroita Katsumi, Maruyama Jirō, *Kokushitaikei Kojiki*, p. 146.

[3] Cf. *Nihonshoki*, 18th *maki*, 1st year, 1st month and 4th year, 2nd month; Kuroita Katsumi, Maruyama Jirō, *Kokushitaikei Nihonshoki*, part 2, pp. 44 and 46 respectively; W. G. Aston, op. cit., pp. 33 and 35 respectively; *Kojiki*, loc. cit.

[4] Amongst them were counted, i.a.: a *tsukitsukai*, 調使, tax collector of the Aya, cf. B. Lewin, op. cit., pp. 59, 116; a *suguri*, cf. B. Lewin, op. cit., p. 23, also footnote 1 on page 256 of the present work; a *sukune*, cf. B. Lewin, op. cit., p. 141 and an *imiki*, 忌寸, cf. B. Lewin, op. cit., p. 64.

[5] Cf. *Nihonshoki*, 18th *maki*, Senka, 1st year, 2nd month; Kuroita Katsumi, Maruyama Jirō, op. cit., part 2, p. 44; W. G. Aston, op. cit., p. 33.

this house was furnished as a temple and later destroyed. Therefore we do not know what the original appearance of the temple was like. It can be deduced from examination of the building methods used on temples some decades later that this must have stood in the middle of a plain on a hillock. Thus it could easily be seen throughout the countryside.[1] Owing to all of this, Emperor Senka could make regular contact—far more easily than the other two emperors—with the immigrants and the Soga. They were indeed his close neighbours. All of this goes to prove that he alone could have received the image of Buddha 'dancing with joy' from Paekche.

It is also highly probable that the violent discussion after the offering of the Buddha image took place with him. The *Nihonshoki* makes it fairly clear—with whatever reservations—that Senka stood on the side of the Soga. For the latter it was not difficult to find space for all of King Sŏng's gifts in his house, which had been converted into a temple. It lay only a few miles from the Senka court.

The situation in Kimmei's case was totally different. He lived in Kanasashi, 金刺, to the north of Iware, in the jurisdictionary area of the Mononobe.[2] This lay far distant from the habitations of all of the other *shizoku*, and there was moreover a dividing river. This local situation proves that Kimmei, far from Takaichi, was certainly no Buddhist sympathiser.

The foregoing geography makes it clear that the occurrence described at the beginning of the Kimmei thirteen chronicle actually took place at Senka's court.

Now can this also be deduced from the chronicles of Emperor Senka himself? These mention three of the four years of his reign.

---

[1] Cf. Naitō Masatsune, "Azuka-jidai no Ji-in," *Shūkyō kōron*, vol. XXV (1955), no. 4, p. 37, in which the position of these oldest temples in this landscape is described. Apparently Tsuda Sōkichi does not know of these Kimmei-Senka problems in his *Nihon Koten no Kenkyū*. He only points out the Korean origin of those chronicles which record anything about Korea; op. cit., pp. 80, 81.

[2] Cf. *Nihonshoki*, 19th *maki*, Kimmei, 1st year, 7th month, 13th day; Kuroita Katsumi, Maruyama Jirō, op. cit., part 2, p. 51: "The residence was removed to Shikishima in the Shiki district of the Yamato province. It was called the Kanasashi palace of Shikishima." Cf. W. G. Aston, op. cit., p. 38. Previously we have noted that Emperor Kimmei was also called Shikishima, 磯城嶋, after this palace. See, for instance, p. 268.

They are: the first (536: *hinoe-tatsu*), the second (537: *hinoto-mi*) and the fourth (539: *tsuchinoto-hitsuji*). The third, *tsuchinoe-uma* (538) cannot be found. Now this third year of Senka coincided precisely with the seventh year of the opposing Emperor Kimmei. As a result of the erection of the Paekche image in the sixth year of Kimmei, the introduction of Buddhism by Sŏng could therefore have taken place in this third year of Senka. We have clarified this calendar aspect in the following table.

Kanshi	*A.D.*	*Nihonshoki*	*Modern Historians*
Kanoto-i	531	Keitai (25)	
Mizunoe-ne	532		Kimmei (1)
Mizunoto-ushi	533		Kimmei (2)
Kinoe-tora	534	Ankan (1)	Kimmei (3)
Kinoto-u	535	Ankan (2)	Kimmei (4)
Hinoe-tatsu	536	Senka (1)	Kimmei (5)
Hinoto-mi	537	Senka (2)	Kimmei (6)
Tsuchinoe-uma	538	Senka (3)	Kimmei (7)
Tsuchinoto-hitsuji	539	Senka (4)	Kimmei (8)
Kanoe-saru	540	Kimmei (1)	Kimmei (9)

According to this table, this introduction could have occurred in the third year of Senka and the seventh of Kimmei. For both this year was the same as the calendar year mentioned in the other sources: *tsuchinoe-uma*: 538. This is therefore suitable for the reconciling of all texts concerned with the official beginning of Buddhism. It can mainly be ascribed to the double rendition of the years of Kimmei's reign: that of the *Nihonshoki* and that of modern historians. The latter rendition was in advance of the former in this.

Although on the basis of the late institution of the *kanshi* system even this dating remains dubious, it nevertheless forms a remarkable strengthening of the supposition which we have already accepted on the grounds of other arguments, namely that the official introduction of Buddhism took place during the reign of Emperor Senka. Thus he appears not only as the political, but also as the religious antagonist of Kimmei. From all of this it is comprehensible that, in the chronicle of the thirteenth year of Kimmei, one emperor is mentioned who 'danced for joy' because of the arrival of Buddhism in Japan: Senka, and one emperor who signed the decree for its destruction: Kimmei. This again entails a new parallelism between the Kimmei and the Bidatsu chronicles, as both give a version of the very first history of Buddhism. In the Bidatsu thirteen chronicle the 'origin' of it remained during Keitai's reign. In that of Kimmei this tale began with the third year of Senka. The terminal points of both tales must have coincided with the respective dates of the chronicles under which they were written. Therefore in the later Bidatsu chronicles a revival of Buddhism could already be mentioned in the building of temples and monasteries after the persecution by Kimmei.

Finally, there remains one more question: why did the official introduction of Buddhism arrive in Kimmei's chronicles and not in those of Senka? There are various reasons for this. Firstly, Kimmei held a far more important position in the history of the sixth century than Senka. In his personal struggle against Senka he had been the ultimate victor. Moreover, as opposed to the four years of his rival's reign he had scored forty. It is obvious that gradually such an important occurrence would more readily be ascribed to him than to Senka, with whom he had also simultaneously ruled. Other motives also played a part in this. The nationalistic compilers of these chronicles attributed little value to a form of Buddhism which was the symbol of the cultural and religious independence of Korea. They made this adequately clear in the refusal of Sŏng's gifts by the emperor who, indeed, had handed these gifts on to the Buddhist sympathiser, Soga. Kimmei's unwillingness to accept and integrate Buddhism, which is so clearly apparent in other Kimmei chronicles, also illustrates this.

That was probably the reason why the introduction was first written under the third year of Senka but disappeared later, just as the Shiba Tattō chronicle of 522 was eradicated from the Keitai chronicles. Later, however, it was once again considered as suitable material, which would serve as introductory matter for the Kimmei tale of the destruction of Buddhism. This was intended to air the vast displeasure at the time of the compilation of the *Nihonshoki* concerning various irregularities in the Buddhist monasteries of that period.[1] An editor could more easily link that disapproval to the old

[1] That displeasure is clearly apparent in the *Shoku-Nihongi*. Under the second year of Empress Genshō (715-724), 5th month, 15th day, a very long narrative is recorded which clearly shows the dissatisfaction of the empress about the neglect of Buddhism. Under her third year (717), 4th

texts, which allowed more space, than to the younger Buddhist chronicles. These latter texts did indeed describe facts which were too easily remembered.

Research into the origin of Buddhism in Japan has not been facilitated by calendar problems, the matter of the anti-emperors and the preconceived compilation of the *Nihonshoki*. By extracting the *Nihonshoki* text of Kimmei thirteen from all these distortions the Buddhism of the Kimmei texts in Senka also appears more related to that of the immigrant community in the district of Takaichi. This also bridges the gap between these two 'points of origination' of Buddhism in Japan.

3 *The Buddhism of the sixth century as born of the contrasts between immigrants, shizoku and emperors*

In the foregoing we have shown how Buddhism made contact with Japanese society in two ways: on the one hand by simply being there as the profession of the Korean saddlers' faith, who arrived in Japan together with other compatriots; on the other hand by the Fu Chien procedure: the sending of an image with flags and *sūtras* by the king of Paekche to the *ō-kimi* of Japan. This latter was a gesture which politically and religiously had the same characteristics as that made by Fu Chien to Sosurim. Moreover, the offer of the image by Sŏng had certainly been prepared by the Takaichi immigrants. They lived close enough to the residence to do this, where the encounter with the emissaries from Sŏng took place. On the other hand they were very much in favour of maintaining the connection with their previous motherland, Paekche. It is therefore quite possible that the initiative for presenting the image and the *sūtras* initially originated from them. That would

month, 23rd day, once again complaints are mentioned regarding the begging practices of monks. That same year again, in the eleventh month the fact is regretted that highly talented monks waste their valuable time in the streets. Under the fourth year (718), 10th month, 10th day, the materialism of the monks is objected to. Cf. *Shoku-Nihongi*, 8th *maki*; Kuroita Katsumi, Maruyama Jirō, *Kokushitaikei Shoku-Nihongi*, part 1 (no. 3), pp. 65-78.

Here it is noteworthy, that all of this was noted at the same time as the final recension of the *Nihonshoki*. However, in these sombre data on Buddhism of that period, one must not forget that the most ancient documents on this, together with other Soga data, were burnt in 645. These chronicles, edited by Soga supporters, certainly gave a more favourable verdict on the Buddhism of that period.

have occurred in the form of reports to the king of Paekche. From this starting point Buddhism has gone its own way in Japan. This was the result of various contrasts which existed mutually amongst the immigrants as well as the local *shizoku* society of Japan.

a Immigrant contrasts

Now how did the contrasts between the immigrants contribute to the growth of Buddhism in Japan? It is known of the Korean immigrants that they bore an important part in the political and religious contrasts of the beginning of the sixth century. Thus, for instance, Kimmei received power over the whole realm after Senka's rebellion owing to the economic support of the Hata.[1] One of them he rewarded for this by giving him what Lewin describes as the '*Schatzkanzleramt*'.[2] It cannot be geographically traced whether these Hata lived in the vicinity of Kimmei's residence or in the Shiki district at all.[3] It is, however, known of them that they usually dwelt in the neighbourhood of the imperial residences. This was certainly the case under Emperor Kimmei, as the Hata had great influence on him at the beginning of his reign.[4] Their political influence also afforded them the opportunity to influence Kimmei on religious grounds. Now it is a fact that some of them were convinced Buddhists. The oldest Hata Buddhist occurs in the *Nihonshoki* chronicles of Empress Suiko under the year 603 by the name of Kawakatsu, as the builder of the Hachioka temple.[5] Later other Hata Buddhists also became prominent.[6] Most Hata, however, were fervent protagonists of what was later to be called Shintō. In this respect they differed from many other Korean immigrants, who were not so 'Shintō-minded'. Of this Lewin says: [7] "Im Gegensatz zu den übrigen alten Kikajin verfügten die Hata über grössere Ahnenschreine, die sich vermutlich an all ihren Siedlungsplätzen befanden." Hence the Hata who served Emperor Kimmei must

[1] Cf. Bruno Lewin, op. cit., p. 146.

[2] Ibid. W. G. Aston, op. cit., p. 39, speaks of 'Director of the Treasury'. Cf. also *Nihonshoki*, 19th *maki*, Kimmei, 1st year, 8th month; Kuroita Katsumi, Maruyama Jirō, *Kokushitaikei Nihonshoki*, part 2, p. 51.

[3] Cf. B. Lewin, op. cit., p. 75: "Die Ermittlung der Wohnplätze der Hata ist schwieriger zu bewerkstelligen als die der Aya . . ."

[4] Cf. B. Lewin, op. cit., p. 146.

[5] Cf. the next chapter, p. 311; Bruno Lewin, op. cit., pp. 167, 168.

[6] Cf. B. Lewin, loc. cit.

[7] Op. cit., p. 171.

therefore also for the greater part have been such ancestor worshippers. Possibly this too brought them to choosing the side of the traditionalistic Mononobe, in contrast to the Aya, who preferred to support the Soga. We therefore believe that the mutual philosophical contrasts amongst the immigrants waxed until they became the great tensions and conflicts which were arising throughout the whole of Japanese society, starting with the feud between Ankan, Senka and Kimmei.[1] Actually they accompanied the beginning of the dissolution of the *uji* society, which was to cease to exist entirely in 645 with the Taika reformation.

Now the actual starting point of all of those immigrant tensions lay in their land of origin, Paekche. Differences of opinion and contrasts which existed there began to extend throughout Japan owing to the immigrants. The conflicts grew fiercer because this society also began to display—also philosophically—greater and more penetrating aspects than ever before.

As a result of this, Buddhism on Senka's side and the *ujigami* belief on Kimmei's became in increasingly great measure systems which sharpened themselves on each other like knives. The ideologists in the background throughout all of this were mainly immigrants. All of those mutual points of difference produced appetising fodder for the *shizoku*, who burdened each other's feuds with these ideological variances. The Soga and the Mononobe excelled at this.

Now none of this must be considered as friction between the immigrants of the Soga area and Buddhism, or between those of the Mononobe area and the *ujigami* belief. Both religions were to be found in almost every settlement where they dwelt. The presence of these religions was connected with the fact as to whether they gave Buddhism or ancestor worship their preference. In this it was also of importance as to whether they acknowledged Senka or Kimmei. Probably the Buddhist ideologists were in the majority only in the Soga area, while in the Mononobe area the 'Shintō' ideologists predominated. Thus we consider that Korean contrasts —via the immigrants—participated, behind the facade of the *shizoku* relationships. This therefore is additional proof of the fact that in the sixth century these immigrants were to be reckoned, in regard to religion, politics[2] and culture, as more the 'makers of Japan' than were the Japanese themselves.

[1] See also the quotation from Suematsu Yasukazu on p. 239.

[2] That this also happened with regard to politics is proved not only by

b Shizoku contrasts

In the foregoing the appearance may have been created that Ankan, Senka and Kimmei reigned as rulers of two different realms beside each other. In the Europe of the Middle Ages a royal feud automatically resulted in such partition. In the Japanese society of those days it was, however, all quite different. It has already been pointed out in the second chapter that the Japanese emperor had a greater moral, and spiritual preponderance than might be deduced from the size of his domain. The residences which they inhabited until and including Kimmei, and the facility with which they transferred these certainly show that they did not consider themselves specifically linked to a personal tribal area, as did, for instance, the *shizoku*. Nevertheless, they counted as the highest offices and authorities. Now the eruption of imperial disunity after Keitai's death splits this into two. This moreover completed a kind of division of spirit throughout the entire realm. The *shizoku* contrived to benefit from this in order to increase and strengthen their own influence and jurisdictionary areas. Thus the purely personal differences between the emperors mutually explain why the Mononobe were *ōmuraji* under Ankan, Senka and Kimmei, and the Soga were *ō-omi* under Senka and Kimmei.

The personal vendettas between the emperors mutually and their expressed sympathies with the Soga and the Mononobe sharpened the contrasts between the latter all the more. As a result of this, in the time of Ankan, Senka and Kimmei, as well as long afterwards, throughout the entire period of the struggle for power between the Soga and the Mononobe, two ideologies were built up which were to define the specific character of the *shizoku* in years to come. They were clearly apparent in the Kimmei thirteen chronicle. The ideology of the Mononobe inveighed against the 'foreign' deity and, from obstinate nationalism, kept to the national deities, although many of these were also originally importations from Korea. That of the Soga, on the contrary, considered the acceptance of the 'foreign god, worshipped throughout all of the West' as no danger. Thus the two philosophies clashed. Here open and internationally orientated progress opposed traditional conservatism.

Kimmei's victory over Senka with the aid of the Hata, but also by the regular support which the Soga experienced from the Aya in their struggle against, for instance the Mononobe and Emperor Sushun. We shall return to this in our fifth chapter.

The Mononobe group was prepared to be internationally-minded in so far as it itself should benefit. That is apparent from the aid given by the Hata in the conquest of Senka. The Soga protection of all the various immigrants tacitly implied the recognition of all the Buddhist, Taoist, Confucian and Shamanistic philosophies current amongst them.

The Emperors Senka and Kimmei did not join in this ideological struggle amongst the *shizoku,* even if they occasionally felt themselves more indebted to the most powerful party. Therefore Senka—in the Kimmei thirteen chronicle—left the decision regarding the acceptance of Buddhism to the leaders of these *shizoku.* The latter seized this as a suitable opportunity to demonstrate and enlarge mutual dislike and schism, because Buddhism also restored their enmity to the ideological plane as well. Nevertheless, throughout all of this, both parties were to remain faithful to the old *ujigami* belief. The fact that the Mononobe opposed Buddhism strengthened the desire to accept it among the Soga. For that reason Buddhism had plenty of opportunity to expand throughout the Soga area from the time of Shiba Tattō's arrival in 522 until the defeat of the last Mononobe leader, Moriya, in 585. As a result of this the king of Paekche could send monks unquestioned to this area, without running the risk of their being deported.[1]

On the other hand this Buddhism was to fluctuate in accordance with the political successes of the Soga. The destruction of the Mukuhara temple in 552 (the thirteenth year of Kimmei) happened at a moment of Mononobe superiority. Only at such times could the Mononobe work their will with Buddhism. Climbing along the *shizoku* contrasts Buddhism could penetrate in a fairly short space of time to the peak of the Soga nobility. There it was given the chance of expanding from a foreign religion into a national religion. The more it became a token of opposition to the Mononobe, the more it could count on the Soga identifying themselves with it. Just as later, in the Japanese history of Christianity for instance, fanatical reactions from the conservatives were essential to ensure its success. Such contrasts brought Buddhism into the *shizoku.* When this was finally a fact, it could begin to play

[1] The possibility for this became available owing to —forgive the expression—the vast necessity for genuine development assistance, which Japan had made clearly apparent especially in the early sixth century in its relations with Paekche. Cf. pp. 232 and 233 of this chapter.

a part in the family relations of the *shizoku* with the emperors.

Until now we have grown to know Kimmei as someone who felt more at home among the Mononobe. Nevertheless he, as supreme *uji no kami* of the nation, must have felt very deeply about maintaining the balance between the most prominent *shizoku*. Possibly this caused him to start a family tie with the Soga. The *Kojiki* namely shows that, of his five wives, two were Soga. These two Soga ladies gave him 18 of his 25 children.[1] The more eminent of these two was called Kitashi *hime*, 岐多斯比賣. She was a daughter of the Soga leader of that time, Iname. She became the mother of the future Emperor Yōmei and Empress Suiko. His other Soga wife, Oehime, 小兄比賣, gave him another successor in Emperor Sushun. This does go to show that the Soga at the court of Kimmei had succeeded in penetrating the family scene [2] of the emperor. By so doing this *shizoku* had become the 'purveyor' of the imperial women. As a result the emperor, residing in the Mononobe district, was nevertheless strongly enough tied to the Soga to maintain the balance of power in the Yamato area.

These marriages of Kimmei also smoothed the path of Buddhism at the imperial court by way of the Soga *shizoku*. During Kimmei's reign or that of his son Bidatsu [3] this was not yet the case. Of this latter emperor the *Nihonshoki* [4] expressly states:

"The emperor did not accept the teaching of Buddha, but gave patronage to the literature."

On the other hand, the *Nihonshoki* itself admits to the great personal interest in Buddhism expressed by Yōmei and Suiko, although we know nothing regarding Sushun. Yōmei and Suiko

---

[1] Cf. *Kojiki*, 3rd *maki*; Kuroita Katsumi, Maruyama Jirō, *Kokushitaikei*, *Kojiki*, p. 147: "Furthermore, he was married to Kitashi *hime*, the daughter of Soga Iname *no sukune*. She brought forth: Tachibana *no* Toyohi *no mikoto*, 橘豊日命, and also the Prince Imo-iwa-kuma *no mikoto*, 妹石埛王, the Prince of Atori, 足取, further Toyomike Kashikiya *hime no mikoto*, 豊御気炊屋賣命." Nine other children are also briefly mentioned here. Of those mentioned here, Tachibana was later the Emperor Yōmei and Toyomike Kashikiya the later Empress Suiko.

[2] All kinds of genealogies and distinctions were later appended to this relationship with the imperial house. Cf. Nagano Tadashi, "*Tennō taii no rekishi*", *Tennō no Rekishi*, p. 276.

[3] This was Ishihime, 石比賣, namely. Cf. *Kojiki*, 3rd *maki*; Kuroita Katsumi, Maruyama Jirō, op. cit., p. 147.

[4] Cf. *Nihonshoki*, 20th *maki*; Kuroita Katsumi, Maruyama Jirō, *Kokushitaikei Nihonshoki*, part 2, p. 101; cf. W. G. Aston, op. cit., p. 90.

only owed that sympathy to their ties with the Soga, that is to say, to their Soga mothers and, via those mothers, to their 'membership' of the Soga *shizoku*.[1] These mothers could interest their children in these matters as they, just as did all the other empresses, presided over their own courts. This was one of the few remains of the earlier matriarchy. At the courts of their father Kimmei and their mother Kitashi *hime* both Yōmei and Suiko became acquainted with Buddhism and *ujigami* belief, two philosophical trends which had little in common. As a result of this double contact these future rulers were faced by an entirely new task. This consisted of the fact that they had to integrate both religions and their future emperorship in their own persons.

This task was especially facilitated by the specific nature of Buddhism of that period. As it came from Korea, it certainly shared similarities with Central Asiatic and North Chinese Maitreyanism. The Bidatsu chronicle of the thirteenth year already points that out.[2] Although this was not total Maitreyanism, nevertheless it had already been defined prior to its encounter with Japanese *ujigami* belief which, in its turn, still required much of the systematism of Buddhism (owing to its rawness) in order to become a corresponding partner to this.

From here on this imperial task can be found mirrored in every imperial chronicle concerning Japan's origin. It gave the emperors a double aspect: one for Buddhism and one for the *ujigami* belief. It is to be found expressed most clearly in the *Nihonshoki* description of Emperor Yōmei: [3] "*Tennō Hotoke no minori o uketamae, kami no michi o totobitamau*"—which is to say: "The emperor believed in the law of Buddha and moreover respected the way of the gods."

Both the double court structure and the schism between the Soga and the Mononobe had prepared the encounter between Buddhism and Shintō. For the time being this Buddhism preserved most of its vitality within the dwelling communities of the immigrants. This was to remain like this until it could naturally say that it had become Japanese Buddhism.

---

[1] We shall return to these two figures in detail in the following and last chapters.

[2] Cf. the text on p. 248, where the arrival in Japan of a Maitreya image is mentioned, as well as the erection of a temple for this image.

[3] Cf. *Nihonshoki*, 21st *maki*, Yōmei; Kuroita Katsumi, Maruyama Jirō, op. cit., part 2, p. 119; cf. W. G. Aston, op. cit., p. 106.

CHAPTER FIVE

THE FORMATION OF JAPANESE BUDDHISM UP TO THE TIME OF SHŌTOKU TAISHI

(up to 592)

In the previous chapter not only the double start of Buddhism—namely the growth from above and below—came to light. Simultaneously it became apparent that in both cases the land of its genesis, Paekche, was always the same. Thus the developments of North Chinese Buddhism had created an entry into Japan for themselves via the arrowhead Paekche. The Buddhism which had thus reached Japan therefore also bore more or less the same characteristics as that in North China, for instance, under the T'opa. Thus it is difficult to define it right from the beginning as being a monkish ideal, experienced only in monasteries, which sought after a link with more 'orthodox' and Indian forms of Buddhism which were far removed from the local East Asian popular mentality. It was also characterised to a great extent by the contributions of the non-monks, the laity. We believe that it was the Buddhism accepted by these people which grew into the national Japanese Buddhism, that is to say, into Buddhism in which the *ujigami* belief was also integrated.

This growth into Japanese Buddhism is the theme of this chapter. We shall further analyse this growth into two aspects, namely as seen from the nature of Japan's first monasteries and from the mentality of its first laymen.

1 The Monasteries

In the previous chapter we have seen that the *Nihonshoki* clearly mentions the origin of Buddhism. Nevertheless it is unclear whether this origin was accompanied by the foundation of monasteries and the organisation of monastic communities. The existence of these is hard to deduce from the various texts previously quoted. There is, however, mention of temples, which may also have been monasteries. Thus the *Fusō ryakki* [1] mentions together with Shiba

[1] Cf. previous chapter, p. 247.

Tattō the temple of Sakatabara. The *Nihonshoki* [1] permits Soga Iname to turn his Mukuhara house into a temple in order to house his recently received Buddha image, while the son of Iname, Soga Umako, is also said to have built a temple near his Ishikawa house.[2] All of these temples were probably lost in the 552 persecution, as nothing has been recovered of them.[3] Therefore it can be discovered of none of them whether they where only houses of prayer or also actually served as monasteries. The presence of monasteries can initially be deduced only from the advent of monks and nuns from Korea.

The only text in the *Nihonshoki* which speaks of *first* monks and nuns is given under the fourteenth year of the reign of Empress Suiko and has already been quoted in the previous chapter.[4] Here Suiko thanks the artist Tori for everything he and his family have done for Japanese Buddhism. Besides Shiba Tattō she mentions by name his father Tasuna and his aunt Shimame, who entered a monastery "when there were not, as yet, monks and nuns in this land (= Japan)". It is hard to decide from this text at what time the first monk and nun entered his or her cloister. It is also uncertain whether the relic-worship by Shiba Tattō, mentioned in this same text, coincided with Shimame's entry. If these two events happened at different dates, then Shimame could have bidden farewell to this world before the birth of Suiko in 542. That entry did in any case take place prior to 577, because in that year the king of Paekche gave his emissary Ōwake, 大別, a nun to take back with him to Japan.[5] Thus Simame's entry lies somewhere between the years 526 and 577.

Now when did Tasuna become a monk? If he was the first monk

---

[1] Cf. previous chapter, p. 244.

[2] Cf. previous chapter, pp. 249, 250.

[3] Cf. Naitō Masatsune, "Asuka-jidai no Jiin", *Shūkyō Kōron*, vol. 25, no. 4, p. 36.

[4] Cf. pp. 251, 252.

[5] Cf. *Nihonshoki*, 20th *maki*, Bidatsu, 6th year; Kuroita Katsumi, Maruyama Jirō, *Kokushitakei Nihonshoki*, part 2, p. 107: "11th month, 1st day. The king of the land of Paekche gave, by means of the returning emissary, Ōwake, 大別, and others presents: many book rolls of *sūtras* (or: and commentaries), a *vinaya* (= discipline) master, a meditation master, a nun, a *dhārāni* master, an artist and (wood) carver of Buddha images and a temple architect. All in all six people. They were all lodged in the monastery of the *omi* Ōwake in Naniwa." Cf. W. G. Aston, *Nihongi* II, p. 96.

known to Japan, it must have happened some time before 555. In that year the monk Dōshin, 道深, and his 7 companions who had come to Japan earlier were relieved by the monk Unkei, 雲惠, and his nine companions.[1] Now how could Tasuna be Japan's first monk on the basis of his vow made in 587 to Yōmei, if there were already monks in Japan before 555? He promised this namely, according to the *Nihonshoki*, in 587. His vow is to be found under the second year of Emperor Yōmei: [2]

"The pains of the emperor gradually increased in severity, so that he began to long for the end at that time. Therefore Tasuna of the saddlers' guild (a son of Shiba Tattō) [3] spoke to him: 'Your servant offers for you, the emperor, to leave his house and to go and live the life of an ascetic. Furthermore I offer you an image of Buddha of 1 *chō*, 6 *shaku* (nearly 17 feet; 4.85 metres) [4] and the erection of a temple.' This greatly impressed the emperor." The fulfilment of this promise followed three years later, in 590, under the third year of Emperor Sushun: [5] "... The son of Shiba Tattō also entered and took the name of 'master of the doctrine (law), Tokusai, 德齊'." In the year in which this happened various

[1] Cf. *Nihonshoki*, 19th *maki*, Kimmei, 14th year, 6th month; Kuroita Katsumi, Maruyama Jirō, op. cit., part 2, p. 79: "An imperial instruction (for the king of Paekche) was: 'the army, which you requested, is already at your disposal'. A special imperial charge was: 'Scholars of medicine, soothsaying and calendrics would have to travel up and down (between Paekche and Japan). Now is the right time (lit.: month and year) to relieve the first group of people. Let them return with the emissaries and alternate with each other. Send us also books on soothsaying, calendrics and various kinds of medicinal remedies". Cf. W. G. Aston, op. cit., p. 68. This request was granted eight months later, under the eighth day, second month of the following year. On that date there is also mention of: "the master of the law Unkei, 雲惠", (Aston, op. cit., p. 72: Tamhyé) who "with nine companions came to relieve the master of the law Dōshin (W.G. Aston: To-sim, ibid.) with his seven companions". Cf. W. G. Aston, op. cit., p. 72; see also Suematsu Yasukazu, *Mimana Kōbōshi*, pp. 267, 268.

[2] Cf. *Nihonshoki*, 21st *maki*, Yōmei, 2nd year, 4th month, 2nd day; Kuroita Katsumi, Maruyama Jirō, op. cit., part 2, pp. 123, 124; W. G. Aston, op. cit., p. 111.

[3] This is a commentary inserted into the text.

[4] Cf. Chapter IV, footnote 2 on p. 275.

[5] Cf. *Nihonshoki*, 21st *maki*, Sushun, 3rd year; Kuroita Katsumi, Maruyama Jirō, op. cit., part 2, pp. 130, 131; W. G. Aston, op. cit., p. 118. The title 'master of the law', Japanese *hōshi*, 法師, is a permanently established Buddhist honorific for monks.

monks had long dwelt in Japan. According to the *Nihonshoki* they had already come to Japan in 555 and 577.[1] How could Tasuna nevertheless be the first monk? The declaration is insufficient that he could have been the first immigrant to accept the monastic life in Japan itself, because that had already been done before him by Ebin of Koguryŏ [2] who had since then returned to the laity. There is only one motivation for the fact that he was Japan's first monk, namely, that he was regarded as the first monk whose life was given an official status in the service and by order of, the emperor and the state. In later years, that is to say, some time after the compilation of the *Nihonshoki*, he has been projected as the first monk and forerunner of an institution which already existed at that time, namely that of the *nenbundosha*, 年分度者. These were monks who, on the orders of and for the benefit of the state, took on monastic life. Thus Tasuna was the first *nenbundosha*.[3] Although

---

[1] For the year 555 see footnote 1 on p. 292; for 577 see footnote 5 on p. 291.

[2] See the Bidatsu text on p. 249.

[3] The Japanese government of later ages tried to tie the monks to itself by the inauguration of the institution of the so-called *nenbundosha*. This word might be transliterated by: "an annual number '*pāramitā* practitioners' ". These '*pāramitā* practitioners' must be seen as monks of which a fixed number were assigned annually to the various Buddhist groups, with the special charge to practise the '*tokudo*', 得度, in the name of the government. This *tokudo* involves the *sad-pāramitā*, the six levels of Boddhisattva asceticism, which must be undergone in order to attain the *bodhi*. Actually this meant the acceptance of monasterial life in service of and for the salvation of the nation. The origin of this system probably goes back to various decrees by Aśoka (273-232 B.C.), the grandson of Chandragupta, who, after the death of Alexander the Great overcame the Greek armies and founded a realm which knew its greatest flowering under Aśoka. He ordered several of his officials to "advance *Dharma*". He also provided that monks and nuns regularly read texts about the *Dharma* and meditated on them.

Cf. N. A. Nikam and Richard MacKeon, *The Edicts of Asoka*, Chicago 1959, p. 52 (rock decree no. XII), p. 58 (rock decree no. V) and pp. 66 ff. It would be worth the trouble to trace how the institution of the *nenbundosha* grew over the course of time from the rock decrees of Aśoka. This institution was inaugurated in Japan in 803. In that year both the Sanron- and the Hossō-*shū* were each assigned five persons as *nenbundosha*. Later this number was extended to twelve and the Hossō and Sanron schools each received three, the Ritsu- Tendai- and Kegon-*shū* each received two *nenbundosha*.

The various excercises were divided in accordance with the six *pāramitā* amongst the representatives of the afore-mentioned schools. Every morning two of them had to recite the most important *sūtras* of their own school.

prior to this point other monks had come to Japan, he was the first whose ascetic life became a state office. In addition, it could also have easily been possible that Tasuna, just as his sister, had entered a monastery even before Unkei. Thus one can imagine that under Yōmei he became the first state monk because he was Japan's first monk. Summarising, it must therefore be said that the Buddhism of the monasteries in its very first stage also went back, without any doubt, to him who brought Buddhism to Japan: Shiba Tattō, father of Tasuna and Shimame.

Thus it can be said that Japan's oldest monastic Buddhism was to a great extent dependent upon Paekche, and even that the monastic life of Paekche found its continuation here. That is apparent not only from the population of Japan's first monasteries, but also from the establishment of those monasteries themselves. We shall throw more light on this in the following pages.

As far as the first is concerned it must be said that all monks and nuns who came to Japan from Korea prior to 595 came from Paekche. They were:

1. In 555: Unkei, who, together with nine other monks, came to relieve Dōshin and his seven companions, also from Paekche.[1]
2. In 577: A "master of discipline and meditation and a nun" whom the emissary Ōwake brought from Paekche and housed in his Naniwa monastery.[2]
3. The monks Esō, 惠捻, Ryōkon, 令斤, Eshoku, 惠寔, Ryōshō, 聆照, Ryōi, 令威, Eshu, 惠衆, Eshuku, 惠宿, Dōgon, 道厳, and Ryōke, 令開, who accompanied Paekche emissaries in 589.[3]

This was called the *baramitsu* (波羅密, derived from *pāramitā*) of the whole nation. This does make it apparent that a *nenbundosha* represented the interests of the state in his own person. His task gave him an entry to the highest offices. It is obvious that the way to this function was not available to everyone. The novice *nenbundosha* had certain demands made upon him by the monastery he entered and by the government. An examination was one of them. If he completed this with good results, he was given a testimonial. Then followed a six-year study. The Tendai-*shū* even stretched this study to twelve years. Only after this were they divided amongst all the regional state temples, the *kokubunji*, 國分寺.

[1] Cf. footnote 1 on p. 292.

[2] Cf. footnote 5 on p. 291.

[3] Cf. *Nihonshoki*, 21st *maki*, Sushun, 1st year, 3rd month; Kuroita Kat-

Only after 595 were monks from other areas to join them. Thus in the year 595 not only the monk Esō of Paekche came to Japan, but also from Koguryŏ Eji, 惠慈, the later teacher of Shōtoku Taishi.[1] In 602 the famous Paekche monk Kanroku also followed, bringing with him many other manuscripts.[2] That same month he was followed by the monks Sōryū, 僧隆, and Unsō, 雲聰, from

---

sumi, Maruyama Jirō, op. cit., part 2, p. 129: "That year the land of Paekche sent emissaries and together with them the monks Esō (W. G. Aston, op. cit., p. 117: Hyé-song), Ryōkon (Aston, loc. cit.: Nyŏng-Keun) and Eshoku (Aston, loc cit.: Hyé-sik). They presented a relic of Buddha. Furthermore the land of Paekche sent the *onsotsu* Shushin, 思率首信, (Aston, loc. cit.: Eun-sol, Syu-sin; Eun-sol, 恩率, Tök-sol, 徳率, and Na-sol, 那率, with the following names were the 3rd, 4th and 6th rank of Paekche's 16 ranks, fashionable at that time; cf. p. 241, footnote 3), the *tokusotsu* Emon, 徳率蓋文, (Aston, loc. cit.: Tök-sol, Ké-mun) and the *nasotsu* Fukufu Mishin, 那率福富味身, (Aston, loc. cit.: Na-sol, Pok-pu-mè-sin), who presented the tribute. Besides relics they took the following monks with them: the discipline master Ryōshō (Aston, loc. cit.: Nyŏng-chyo), further Ryōi (Aston, loc. cit.: Nyŏng-wi), Eshu (Aston, loc. cit.: Hyé-chyung), Eshuku (Aston, loc. cit.: Hyé-syuk), Dōgon (Aston, loc. cit.: To-öm) and Ryōke (omitted in Aston, loc. cit.); furthermore the temple builders Tarō Mita, 太良未田, (Aston, loc. cit.: Ta-nyang Mi-ta), and Monke Koshi, 文賈古子, (Aston, loc. cit.: Mun-ko-ko-chă); the mastersmith *shōtoku* (= 7th Paekche rank, 將徳 which was also written *shōsotsu*, 將率), Haku-mai-shun, 白昧淳, (Aston, loc. cit.: the Chyang-tök Pèng-mè-syun); the roofing tile expert Mana Monnu, 麻奈文奴, (Aston, loc. cit.: Mana Puno), Yō-i-mon, 陽貴文, (Aston, loc. cit.: Yang Kwi-mun), Ryō-i-mon, 陵貴文, (Aston, loc. cit.: Neung Kwi-mun), Sekima Teimi, 昔麻帝彌, (Aston, loc. cit.: Syök-ma Tyé-mi) and the painter Hakka, 白加, (Aston, loc. cit.: Pèk-ka)." Cf. W. G. Aston, op. cit., p. 117.

[1] Cf. *Nihonshoki*, 22nd *maki*, Suiko, 3rd year, 5th month, 10th day; Kuroita Katsumi, Maruyama Jirō, op. cit., part 2, p. 137: "5th month, 10th day. The monk Eji of Koguryŏ came to Japan and became teacher to (Shōtoku) Taishi. That year the Paekche monk Esō came. These two monks propagated the teaching of Buddha. They were together the supporting beam (lit.: 棟梁 *mune-uji-hari* or *munagido*: supporting beam of the roof) of the three treasures (= Buddhism)." Cf. W. G. Aston, op. cit., p. 123.

From 596 Eji and Esō established themselves in the newly completed Hōkōji, 法興寺. Cf. *Nihonshoki*, loc. cit.: "Fourth year, winter, 11th month. The building of the Hōkōji is completed. A son of the *ō-omi* (therefore of Umako), Zentoku *no omi*, 善徳臣, was appointed as temple official. That day the monks Eji and Esō moved in for the first time into the Hōkōji." Cf. W. G. Aston, op. cit., p. 124.

[2] Cf. Chapter I, footnote 2 on p. 60.

Koguryŏ.[1] The last Korean monk to cross to Japan during the reign of Empress Suiko was Ekan, 惠灌.[2]

That this strong Korean influence until the end of the sixth century was due to the direct influence from Paekche is apparent not only from the descent of those who entered Japan at that time, but also from the names of those who entered cloisters as monks or nuns in Japan itself. It is a fact that until 590 only descendents of immigrants were to be found. This is clearly apparent in the *Nihonshoki*. Various data concerning this are provided by the Bidatsu thirteen chronicle quoted in the fourth chapter about the 'origin of Buddhism'.[3] This mentions various immigrants who entered monasteries. The first among them was the previously mentioned Ebin of Koguryŏ. He came from Harima. His name indicates that he, or someone in his ancestry, descended from Koguryŏ. The three nuns of this chronicle were also immigrants' daughters. With regard to Shima, Shiba Tattō's daughter, no doubt is possible. The members of her community were also of Korean origin. The first of the two, Toyome, the nun Zenzō, is described as the wife of the Aya Yayabo here. She was also probably closely connected to the environment of this Aya. That is also valid for the second nun, Ishime, the nun Ezen, wife of the brocade weaver Tsuoga. We do indeed know of the brocade weavers that they, according to the *Nihonshoki*, came from Paekche to Japan together with the saddlers.[4]

Not only the descent and environment of these nuns, but also their further history illustrates that their own Buddhism was related to that of Paekche. Dissatisfied with their own inadequate experience of convent prescriptions, they addressed the following request to Soga Umako in 587:[5]

---

[1] Cf. *Nihonshoki*, 22nd *maki*, Suiko, 10th year; Kuroita Katsumi, Maruyama Jirō, op. cit., part 2, p. 140: "Intercalary day, 10th month, 15th day. The Koguryŏ monks Sōryū and Unsō came together to Japan." Cf. W. G. Aston, op. cit., p. 126.

[2] Cf. *Nihonshoki*, 22nd *maki*; Kuroita Katsumi, Maruyama Jirō, op. cit., part 2, p. 166: "33rd year, spring, first month, 7th day. The king of Koguryŏ gave the monk Ekan as a tribute." According to W. G. Aston, op. cit., p. 154, this occurred in Suiko's 32nd year.

[3] Cf. Chapter IV, p. 249.

[4] Cf. Chapter IV, footnote 1 on p. 256.

[5] Cf. *Nihonshoki*, 21st *maki*, Sushun, year before the ascension to the throne, 6th month, 9th day; Kuroita Katsumi, Maruyama Jirō, op. cit., part 2, p. 125. See also W. G. Aston, op. cit., p. 113.

"The real core of monastic life (lit.: the way of 'house-leaving'—leaving the house is a technical term for the acceptance of the monastic state) lies in complying with the discipline. Therefore we request you for permission to go to Paekche there to be instructed in the *vinaya* . . ." This request was granted by Soga Umako. After some hesitation the Paekche delegates took them back to their country.[1] They returned in the summer of 590 and settled in the monastery of Sakurai.[2] This tale of travelling goes to show that they considered Paekche as the true fatherland of their Buddhism. This Korean character was also preserved in the later development of this community. Namely, in that same year of 590, this inwardly strengthened monastic community was considerably enlarged by a considerable group of fresh candidates. The *Nihonshoki* mentions them in the following scarcely translateable text, under the third year of Emperor Sushun:[3]

"That year the following persons entered: the daughter of Ōtomo *no* Sadehiko *no muraji*, 大伴狹手彥連, Zentoku, 善德; the wives of (Ōtomo *no*) Koma, 狛;[4] the noble lady of Silla, Zenmyō, 善妙, and those from Paekche: Myōkō, 妙光;[5] also the Ayabito Zensō,

[1] Cf. *Nihonshoki*, loc. cit.: "That same month the emissaries for the tribute from Paekche came to the court. The *ō-omi* (= Umako) said to them: 'Take these nuns with you, cross with them to your land and let them there learn the *vinaya* (teaching on discipline). When they are ready, let them then go back'.

The emissaries answered hereupon: 'Before your servants return to the neighbouring country, they should first discuss it with the king of their country. It will not last too long, afterwards to let them depart'. Cf. W. G. Aston, loc. cit.

[2] Their return from Korea is reported under the third year of Sushun in the *Nihonshoki*, cf. Kuroita Katsumi, Maruyama Jirō, op. cit., part 2, p. 130: "The third year, summer, third month. The nuns Zenshin and others who had increased their knowledge, returned from Paekche and settled themselves in the temple of Sakurai". Hence they did not live far from Iware. For this text see also W. G. Aston, op. cit., p. 118.

[3] Cf. *Nihonshoki*, 21st *maki*, Sushun, 3rd year; Kuroita Katsumi, Maruyama Jirō, op. cit., part 2, p. 130. Cf. also W. G. Aston, op. cit., p. 118; K. Florenz, op. cit., pp. 320, 321.

[4] W. G. Aston, loc. cit., here translates by "and his Koma wives". K. Florenz, op. cit., p. 320, does similarly. Koma is written 狛 here and not as 高麗 = Koguryŏ. The edition of Kuroita Katsumi and Maruyama Jirō has added to this Koma: 大伴 = Ōtomo here. Hence obviously another Ōtomo was intended.

[5] This can also, however, be translated as a kind of summary. It is not

善聰, Zentsū, 善通, Myōtoku, 妙徳,[1] Hōjō, 法定, Shōzen, 照善, Chisō, 智聰,[2] Zenchie, 善智惠, and Zenkō, 善光. Also the son of Shiba Tattō of the *Kurabe*, Tasuna, entered at the same time and took the name of master of the law, Tokusai." Except for the one Ōtomo daughter, all the persons named here were either Koreans, such as the two noble ladies for instance, or Korean immigrants: the Ayabito who, just as Tasuna, were descended from Korean immigrants.

The appointment of inspectors who were to search after Buddhists confirms this Korean predominance in the monasteries. In the foregoing Bidatsu text, Shiba Tattō and Ikebe *no atae* Hida were "sent everywhere to search for practitioners of Buddhism"[3] by Soga Umako. Not only Shiba Tattō but also Ikebe *no atae* Hida was an immigrant and he descended from the immigrant Niwaki *no atae*, 爾波木直, and belonged to the tribe of the Fumi *no* Ikebe *no imiki*, 文池邊忌寸.[4] The appointment of these two 'foreigners' by Soga Umako, who was himself a Japanese, can only be explained if one accepts that in all the monasteries of that time the majority of the inmates were Koreans and descendents of Koreans. It must be considered out of the question that Japanese belonged amongst them at that time.

Moreover, it was to be a long time before Japanese entered these communities, as later also Koreans or immigrants were always considered for such functions. For instance, in 624 Empress Suiko issued the following decree as a result of various irregularities in the monasteries: [5]

"An imperial decree was as follows: 'If even monks no longer

---

clear from the text. Thus the text could also be: the wives of (Ōtomo *no*) Koma, the noble lady of Silla, Zenmyō, the noble lady of Paekche, Myōkō, also the . . .

[1] This name is omitted by Aston, loc. cit.

[2] Here our translation follows from the punctuation of Kuroita Katsumi and Maruyama Jirō: 法定°照善°智聰°. These three names result from this. Others punctuate as follows: 法定照°善智聰. From this only two names follow: Hōjōshō and Zenchisō. This is the basis for the translations by Aston and Florenz, loc. cit.

[3] Cf. pp. 248, 249.

[4] Cf. B. Lewin, *Aya und Hata*, p. 148.

[5] Cf. *Nihonshoki*, 22nd *maki*, 32nd year, 4th month, 13th day; Kuroita Katsumi, Maruyama Jirō, op. cit., part 2, p. 165. Cf. K. Florenz, op. cit., p. 331. The text can not be found in Aston.

keep to the laws, how are they to teach them to ordinary people? Therefore *sōjō*, 僧正,[1] and *sōzu*, 僧頭,[2] will be appointed in the future, who will supervise monks and nuns'."

Under the seventeenth day the *Nihonshoki* follows this with:[3] "The monk Kanroku was appointed to *sōjō*, the saddler Tokushaku, 徳積, to *sōzu*." Now the Paekche descent of Kanroku has already been established, as we have previously pointed out. Here it is also interesting that Tokushaku again was an immigrant. Had there been an adequate Japanese participation in the monasteries, this would never have been possible.

The predominantly Korean population of the monasteries is also apparent from the four monk-students which Suiko sent to China in 608. They were all sons of immigrants. As far as that is concerned, the text speaks for itself:[4]

"At that time the following students were sent to T'ang (= China): the Yamato *no* Aya *no atae*, Fukuin, 倭漢直福因, Nara *no* Osa *no* Emyō, 奈羅譯語惠明, the Takamuku *no* Aya (*no*) *bito*, Kuromasa, 高向漢人玄理, the Imaki *no* Ayabito, Ōkuni, 新漢人大國, and, as student-monks: the Imaki *no* Ayabito, Nichimon, 新漢人日文, the Minabuchi *no* Ayabito, Shōan, 南淵漢人請安, the Shiga *no* Ayabito, Eon, 志賀漢人惠隠, the (Imaki *no*) Ayabito Kōsai, (新)漢人廣齊; all together eight people. That year many came from Silla to Japan."

Not one of the texts quoted in the foregoing pages allows any

---

[1] The *sōjō* was appointed by the court. He held the highest official function in a monastery. His task consisted of "self-improvement and correction of others". He is comparable to an abbot. Later this function was divided into three hierarchically: the *taisōjō*, 大僧正, the *jōsōjō*, 正僧正, and the *gonsōjō*, 權僧正. Now this is no longer a rank. Cf. Inoue Tetsujirō, e.a., *Bukkyō Jiten*, Tōkyō 1938, p. 666, col. I.

[2] This function came under that of the *sōjō*. The *sōzu* was also appointed by the court. This function was later extended into four different posts, subordinated to each other: *daisōzu* 大僧都, *gondaisōzu*, 權大僧都, *shōsōzu*, 少僧都, *gonshōsōzu*, 權少僧都. Besides these two officesof *sōjō* and *sōzu*, yet another office, that of *risshi*, 聿師, was also sub-divided into three, and determined by the court. Cf. Inoue Tetsujirō, op. cit., p. 667, column II. In Suiko's chronicles there is also mention of the office of *hōtō*, 法頭, a kind of censor. This was not a monk but a layman.

[3] Cf. *Nihonshoki*, loc. cit.

[4] Cf. *Nihonshoki*, 22nd *maki*, Suiko, 16th year, 9th month; Kuroita Katsumi, Maruyama Jirō, op. cit., part 2, p. 151. Cf. W. G. Aston, op. cit., p. 139; these names are slightly different in K. Florenz, op. cit., pp. 325, 326.

doubt to remain about the fact that Japan's very oldest monasteries were populated by Koreans and immigrants. Hence they formed islands of Korean Buddhism in Japanese society. As a result of their isolation and their close links with Paekche an actual encounter with the differently orientated Japanese society could scarcely be achieved either within them or from out of them. This was particularly difficult when one remembers that these monasteries were there not to disseminate Buddhism but to experience it.

In the foregoing pages we have established the Korean character of Japan's first monastery population. The same is proved by the buildings which housed these monks and nuns. What do we know of this?

Not too much is known about the very first Buddhist temples or monasteries. According to the *Nihonshoki*, five are supposed to have existed before the building of the great temple institutions. They were:

1. The Mukuhara temple, destroyed *ca.* 552 by the Mononobe; [1]
2. The Ishikawa house temple of Umako, from which Buddhism started; [2]
3. The Buddha hall for the Maitreya image built to the east of Umako's house; [3]
4. The pagoda built for the relic of Buddha to the north of the Ōhara hill; [4]
5. The convent of the persecuted nuns. [5]

All of these edifices were lost owing to the persecutions which the Mononobe unleashed because of the obstinate epidemic. This is to be found under the thirteenth and fourteenth years of the Bidatsu chronicles (584 and 585). In this latter chronicle there is a commentary as follows: [6]

"It is said in a manuscript: Mononobe *no* Yuke *no* Moriya *no ōmuraji*, 物部弓削守屋大連, Ōmiwa *no* Sakae *no kimi*, 大三輪逆君,

[1] For the building and devastation of the Mukuhara temple, cf. Chapter IV, p. 244.

[2] For the Ishikawa and Maitreya temple, cf. Chapter IV, p. 249, 250.

[3] Cf. p. 249.

[4] Cf. p. 323.

[5] Cf. p. 324 ff.

[6] Cf. *Nihonshoki*, 20th *maki*, Bidatsu, 14th year, 6th month; Kuroita Katsumi, Maruyama Jirō, op. cit., part 2, p. 104. Cf. W. G. Aston, op. cit., p. 104.

Nakatomi *no* Iware *no muraji*, 中臣磐余連, conspired to destroy Buddhism. They intended the burning of *tera* (temples) [1] and pagodas and the casting down of Buddha images. Umako *no sukune* objected to this and did not give in." The destruction of these buildings was the result of this. Hence it is only with difficulty that one can trace the specific nature of these tiny monasteries or small houses of prayer. One does not get much further than the confirmation that they were not very large and were usually merely rebuilt dwelling houses. They were therefore just large enough for the Buddha images and various banners.

Only in 578 (the sixth year of Bidatsu) is a monastery in the true sense mentioned for the first time. Then the Japanese emissary Ōwake came from Korea accompanied by various monks and temple experts, amongst whom there was a temple architect. They all received lodging in his monastery buildings of Naniwa.[2] This Naniwa monastery must have been situated approximately in the centre of present-day Ōsaka. Here it was beyond reach of the persecuting Mononobe and Nakatomi. Therefore it has not suffered in the least from their persecutions. Thus, until 585, it made a safe retreat for monks and technicians arriving from Korea.

The special feature of this Naniwa settlement was that it housed the first Korean temple builders. If Japan at that time had been capable of building its own temples and monasteries, Ōwake need not have brought them from Korea. However, this is not admitted too clearly in the *Nihonshoki*. Thus, for instance, Soga *no* Umako is named as the builder of the Mukuhara, Ishikawa and Maitreya temples. He also built the pagoda for the relic which he had received from Shiba Tattō. Nevertheless, Umako was little more than the Maecenas who provided the material for the edifice. The real builders of all these temples and small prayer houses were, however, all to be found amongst the immigrants of the Takaichi district, who lived only a few miles away from all the little temple projects Soga had. The building of the genuine temples, however, began only with the arrival of the building experts brought by Ōwake

[1] *Tera*. 寺, does not only indicate temple or sanctuary here, but also an entire complex of buildings, amongst which the quarters for monks and nuns must also be counted. For the Korean derivation of this word, cf. W. Gundert, op. cit., pp. 28, 29.

[2] Cf. footnote 5 on p. 291.

in 578. They therefore probably also built the Sakurai convent in 590 for the nuns who had meanwhile returned from Paekche.[1]

The remaining temples recorded up to the death of Empress Suiko by name in the *Nihonshoki* were certainly built by Koreans. In our day and age it has been established that they were modelled after temples in Korea, the remains of which were discovered chiefly during the years prior to the last world war.[2] They bear traces of Korean society of that period, not of Japanese. Now which were these edifices? The main temples of that time were the following three: the Shitennōji, 四天王寺, the Hōkōji, 法興寺, and the Hōryūji, 法隆寺.

1. The *Shitennōji* was the oldest of the three. The *Nihonshoki* relates the foundation of this temple in a tale of miracles, in which it is described as a monument to the conquering of the Mononobe. Its origin has been linked to the battle in which the Soga defeated the Mononobe. Thus this struggle was idealised into a triumphant religious war, which involuntarily calls to mind a similar battle in the West between Constantine and Maxentius. All the more so because here Buddhism, just as Christianity in 312 and 313, made its first public appearance by building this vast, spectacular temple edifice. This tale of miracles is to be found under the year preceding Sushun's acceptance of the emperorship, 587, and is as follows: [3]

"Autumn, seventh month. Soga *no* Umako *no sukune no ō-omi* incited all the princes and all the *omi* to combine to destroy the Mononobe *no* Moriya *no ōmuraji*. The princes of Hatsusebe, 泊瀬部,[4] Takeda, 竹田, Umayado, 廐戸, (= Shōtoku Taishi), Naniwa, Kasuga, 春日, Soga *no* Umako *no sukune ō-omi*, Ki *no* Omaro *no*

---

[1] Cf. p. 297.

[2] Ishida Mōsaku in particular has shown this in his excavations in Japan and Korea and in his reports on it. Cf. the description of his excavations: "Kudara-jiin to Hōryūji", (The Paekche monasteries and the Hōryūji), *C.G.* 1953, no. 5, Oct., pp. 77-86. See also Okabe Nagaaki, "Shōwa no Horyūji-mondai to Taishi-shinkō", (Modern Hōryūji problems and the belief in Shōtoku Taishi), *Shūkyo Kōron*, vol. 25 (1955), no. 4, pp. 26, 27. Ishida Mōsaku concludes from his comparison of the Shitennōji to the Paekche temples, that here also, with some differences, dependence is apparent on Paekche Buddhism. Cf. Ishida Mōsaku, op. cit., pp. 83, 84.

[3] Cf. *Nihonshoki*, 21st *maki*, Sushun, year before the ascension to the throne, 7th month; Kuroita Katsumi, Maruyama Jirō, op. cit., part 2, pp. 125-127; W. G. Aston, op. cit., pp. 113-115.

[4] This prince is the same as Emperor Sushun.

sukune, 紀男麻呂宿禰, the Kose *no omi*, Hirofu, 巨勢臣比良夫, the Kashihade *no omi*, Katafu, 膳臣賀拖夫, the Katsuraki *no omi*, Onara, 葛城臣烏那羅, set out with their armies and advanced to attack the *ōmuraji*. The Ōtomo *no muraji*, Kurabu, 大伴連嚙, the Abe *no omi*, Hito, 阿倍臣人, the Heguri *no omi*, Kamite, 平群臣神手, the Sakamoto *no omi*, Arate, 坂本臣糠手, and the Kasuga *no omi* followed them with their armies to the land of Shiki and thus reached his house in Shibugawa, 澁河. The *ōmuraji* himself, with his followers and an army of slaves, had thrown up a protective ramp and fought there. Here the *ōmuraji* climbed into the branches of a Chinese nettletree.[1] From there he shot down arrows like rain. His armies were strong and well-manned, they filled his house and flooded the plain. The armies of the princes and the soldiers of all the *omi* were very frightened and retreated thrice.

"Then Prince Umayado tied up his hair on to his forehead.[2] He followed the rearguard, considered by himself and said: 'We must contrive that we are not beaten. If we do not pray it will grow hazardous for us.' Then he snatched a piece of lac wood and rapidly began to carve four small images of the four heavenly kings (the four *devas*) from it. He placed them on his bunch of hair. Then he pronounced the following vow: 'If now you permit us to conquer our enemies, we shall build a temple and a pagoda for the four kings, the protectors of our lives'. Thereupon Soga *no ō-omi* prayed: 'All heavenly kings and great king of gods,[3] protect us and let us win this advantage. If our prayer is granted, we shall erect a temple and a pagoda for all the heavenly kings and the great divine king, and disseminate the Three Treasures (Buddhism).' After having

[1] Jap.: *enoki*, 榎, nettle tree, Celtis sinensis. This species cannot have been anything but Celtis Davidiana (synonym Bungeana) nowadays also called Celtis koraiensis. The height of this species was 15 to 30 feet, another species even 50 to 70 feet. This tree is between a nettle and an elm. Formerly it was said to belong to the Urticaceae. In 1956 it was preferred to include it in the family of the Ulmaceae.

[2] A commentary adds to this: "This was an old custom. Youths tie up their hair from their 15th and 16th year above their foreheads (according to W. G. Aston, op. cit., p. 114, the temples). In their 17th and 18th (year) they make a central parting."

[3] 大神王. This is the same as Mahākalā. Even today he enjoys great popularity in Japan as Daikokusama, 大黒様. Cf. K. Florenz, op. cit., p. 309, footnote 4; see for Daikoku, 'der grosse Schwarze', U. A. Casal, *Die Sieben Glücksgötter*, Tōkyō 1958, pp. 10 ff.

made this vow, they threw every kind of troops forward, into the attack. Amongst them was also Tomi *no obito,* Ichii, 迹見首赤檮. He shot the *ōmuraji* from his branch. He killed the *ōmuraji* together with his children. Thus the army of the *ōmuraji* was devastated of its own accord in a wink. The armies were assembled together, all wore black clothes. In the plain of Hirose *no* Makari, 廣瀬勾, they were pursued and dispersed. In this battle some of the family and some followers of the *ōmuraji* ran away or hid themselves in the plain of Ashihara, 葦原. They changed their *kabane* (titles) and names. Others moved far away and were forgotten as if they had gone to unknown places.

"At that time the people said to each other: 'The wife of Soga *no ō-omi* is a younger sister of Mononobe *no* Moriya *no ōmuraji*. The *ō-omi* made bad use of his wife's advice and killed the *ōmuraji*.' After the disturbances it became peaceful again. In the district of Settsu, 攝津, (present-day Ōsaka) the Shitennōji was built. Half the slaves and houses of the *ōmuraji* were made over to be the slaves and property of the great temple. Tomi *no obito,* Ichii received about 10,000 rice fields. Furthermore Soga *no ō-omi* founded, according to his vow, the Hōkōji in the district of Asuka, 飛鳥."

We shall return later to the Mononobe struggle described here.[1] The temple history of the Shitennōji begins with the part played by Umayado in this struggle, described above. Tsuda Sōkichi [2] calls this an invention, as it is unbelievable that this Umayado—only fourteen years old—could take a vow on which victory or defeat depended. He believes that a later Buddhist author used the war between the Soga and the Mononobe in order to sustain the Umayado story by it. According to him this is also supposed to be a passage from the *Suvarṇabhāsottama-sūtra*.[3] Hence in this text the same procedure has been followed as in the Sŏng letter of the Kimmei thirteen chronicle, which was indeed also a quotation from the same *sūtra*.[4] As this *sūtra* reached Japan only after 677, this passage too has been constructed some time after the final recension of the *Nihonshoki* and inserted into the Sushun chronicles. We have already pointed out that various Buddhist tendencies led to correcting earlier anti-Buddhist editorial trends. This has also happened

[1] Cf. pp. 367 ff.
[2] Tsuda Sōkichi, *Nihon Koten no Kenkyū*, part 2, p. 106.
[3] Tsuda Sōkichi, loc. cit.
[4] Cf. Chapter IV, pp. 271, 272.

here. Nevertheless, traces of the anti-Buddhism of the final recension can still be found in the gossip—so clearly contrary to the businesslike tone of a state chronicle—concerning the fervent Japanese Buddhist Soga *no* Umako, in which he, despite the communal share of many princes and nobles, was made responsible for the death of the Mononobe, Moriya. Moreover, other places in the Sushun chronicle indicate that the chronicler had little sympathy for Soga *no* Umako. Thus he was indicted, together with the immigrant, the Yamato *no* Aya *no atae*, Koma, 東漢直駒, by the chronicler as the murderer of Emperor Sushun.[1]

In the foregoing tale the chronicler tried to mitigate the bad name of Umako and his immigrants by linking them to the figure of Empress Suiko's prince chancellor: Shōtoku Taishi. Thus he rendered the initiator of the erection of the Shitennōji temple as an incontrovertible Japanese. We, however, agree with Tsuda in thinking him too young for this.

Then who did undertake the building of this temple? We have already noted that just in the area where the Shitennōji temple was built, temple builders had settled from 577 in Ōwake's monastery. They must have been responsible for the building of the Shitennōji temple. Indeed, in various communities Japanese could scarcely be found capable of building this edifice, otherwise later chronicles would have recorded them generously. Another reason why Koreans such as these would have built the Shitennōji can be found in their interest in the devotion to the four heavenly kings. Wedged in and threatened by the *shizoku* society of that period they required the international support of the four *devas* more than anyone else.

The real origin of these four heavenly kings, the *Caturmahārājikadevas*, Jap.: *shitennō*, 四天王, in Indian Buddhism was of less importance to them.[2] Hence it will have meant little to them that

[1] Cf. *Nihonshoki*, 21st *maki*, Sushun, 5th year (592); Kuroita Katsumi, Maruyama Jirō, op. cit., part 2, p. 132: "11th month, 3rd day. Umako *no sukune* deceived all the notables by saying: 'Today I have paid the tax from the northern provinces to the emperor". He sent the Yamato *no* Aya *no atae*, Koma, who killed the emperor." Cf. also W. G. Aston, op. cit., p. 119.

[2] Cf. É. Lamotte, *Histoire du Bouddhisme Indien*, pp. 34, 35. W. Kirfel, *Symbolik des Buddhismus*, p. 25.

Vaiśravaṇa in particular was later to enjoy great popularity in Japan under the name of Bishamon, 毘沙門, as one of the seven gods of fortune. Cf. U. A. Casal, *Die Sieben Glücksgötter*, Tōkyō 1958, pp. 20, 21.

initially these kings were part of the first of the six groups of *devas* in the *devaloka*, the heaven of the *devas*.[1] For them this significance lay in the fact that these four rulers, namely, Dhṛtarāṣṭra, Virūḍhaka, Virūpākṣa, and Vaiśravaṇa had, however, as representatives of the Indo-Aryan and barbarian linguistic areas, been converted by Buddha himself in their own language and were given the order to protect Buddhism everywhere:[2] Dhṛtarāṣṭra the lord of the Gandharva[3] was to protect the east; Virūḍhaka the lord of the Kumbhāṇḍa[4] the south; Virūpākṣa the lord of the Naga[5] the west; and Vaiśravaṇa the lord of the Yakṣa[6] the north. As rulers of the four points of the compass they counted as the protectors of Buddhist expansion. As we have seen, Buddhism of that time dwelt almost solely in the immigrant communities and amongst a few sympathetic Japanese. This explains that the thought of building a temple under the patronage of these four heavenly kings was considerably more alive amongst these immigrants than amongst others. This is also implicitly admitted by the *Nihonshoki*. It is significant that the *Nihonshoki* does not record the building of the temple under the name of Soga *no* Umako, although it does name him as the builder of the Hōkōji. Later editors—fostered by various nationalistic tendencies of their period—were to transmute this Korean temple into a nationalistic bulwark. To this end they sought a variety of tricks, amongst which were a quotation from the *Suvarṇabhāsottama-sūtra* and the figure of Shōtoku Taishi, whom they summoned to their aid. This was all to eradicate the last reminders of the true founders.

We do not wish to deny with this that the foundation of the *Shitennōji* had nothing whatsoever to do with the struggle of the Soga against the Mononobe. The immigrants also had an interest in a Soga victory. Therefore they probably built the Shitennōji as a result of this struggle. It is hard to believe that this temple was built spontaneously by the Japanese people who, at that time, still considered Buddhism a religion belonging to foreigners.

Furthermore, it is apparent that the building of the Shitennōji

---

[1] For their position in Indian cosmology, see É. Lamotte, op. cit., p. 35.

[2] For this cf. É. Lamotte, op. cit., pp. 608, 609.

[3] Cf. É. Lamotte, op. cit., p. 760.

[4] Ibid.

[5] Ibid.

[6] Ibid.

was originally done outside Japanese society, from the fact that even chroniclers of the *Nihonshoki* could not say precisely when it was built. This is stated in two separate chronicles which are five years apart. The first records the building immediately after the afore-mentioned Mononobe struggle in the year 588. This report actually forms the termination and crowning of the story about this struggle. The second report permits the building of it to start only in 593, the first year of the reign of Empress Suiko. It is noteworthy that it is this 'youngest' text which speaks of the *beginning* of that building.[1] Obviously no one knew quite what to do about the initial date of the building. This could never have been the case if the Shitennōji, in accordance with the *Nihonshoki* tale, had genuinely been erected as a victory monument. We therefore believe that its erection was achieved without the attention of the Japanese public and outside the sphere of national interest. When examining the context of these chronicles more closely, it appears that their authors never knew the real initiators of the building work. Two different names are mentioned: Umako in 588 and Shōtoku Taishi in 593. This latter fact appears from the context as here the building report is linked to a tale concerning his childhood.[2] This indicates that the chroniclers had no data available from which the origin of the temple became apparent. This can only be explained by the fact that it was built by non-Japanese. Moreover, the inaccuracy of these premature datings and the Korean origin of this temple are confirmed by the most recent excavations and research.[3]

---

[1] For the first report see p. 304.

The second can be found in the *Nihonshoki*, 22nd *maki*, Suiko, 1st year, 9th month; Kuroita Katsumi, Maruyama Jirō, op. cit., part 2, p. 136.

"That year the building of the Shitennōji in Arahaka, 荒陵, in Naniwa was started on."

[2] That was his Mononobe battle, in which he was scarcely 14 years old. Cf. p. 303.

[3] Until now the various temple styles have been categorised according to the dates of the *Nihonshoki*. Thus the Shitennōji was supposed to be the oldest, followed only afterwards by the Hōkōji and the Hōryūji. On the basis of his excavations and new discoveries made during them, however, Ishida Mōsaku believes that this order should be reversed. Thus one arrives at the following scale: 1. Hōryūji style; 2. Hōkōji style; 3. Shitennōji style; 4. Yakushiji style; 5. Tōdaiji style, etc. The rise of the Shitennōji style was thought to be at the end of the Asuka (522-645), early Hakuhō, 白鳳, period (645-710). (According to others—particulary Western authors, such as J. E.

2. Many of the foregoing remarks are equally applicable to the building of the *Hōkōji*. Its construction was also linked to the afore-mentioned Mononobe struggle. Its building was the result of a vow made by Umako in this struggle.[1] This vow had nothing to do with the one made by Tasuna, at Yōmei's deathbed, to build a temple. Indeed, Umako had not been present there.[2] Now this Hōkōji was built in the same district where Buddhism had started with Shiba Tattō. It rose, however, in far grander style than the small temples which the Soga had already built there. That is clearly apparent from the vast number of construction workers who came to Japan the following year from Paekche: temple builders, smiths, roofing-tile makers and painters.[3] The initial building

---

Kidder, op. cit., p. 156—this latter period ran from 673-686). The Shitennōji style, namely, had much in common with some of the temples of Paekche and Silla and reverted directly to a more continental pattern. Cf. *Asuka-ji-hakkutsu Chōsahōkoku* (*Asukadera Temple Site*, archeological survey carried out in 1956-57) published by: Nara National Institute of Cultural Properties, Nara 1958 (Japanese), p. 38.

Also the temples which Ishida Mōsaku excavated in Paekche were of the same Shitennōji type. He arrives at this conclusion particularly by comparison of the various ground plans, although there were also minor similarities in these Paekche temples to the older Hōryūji type. Ishida Mōsaku estimates that the temples examined by him some thirty years ago (1936-37; 1939), situated slightly south of the old Paekche capital Puyŏ, derive from the period shortly before the destruction of Paekche by the T'ang armies in 663. Older temples from the beginning of the sixth century have, to my knowledge, not been dug up. As good as nothing remains of them as a result of Paekche's total ruin by the allied T'ang armies. It is therefore hard to discover whether types older than the Shitennōji were also modelled on Paekche temples. Ishida Mōsaku says of this: "Therefore we must excavate the remains of the present-day Paekche temples. It is sad that this is not more strived after. As the study of Korea certainly involves Japanese culture, this too should be investigated. It remains my desire and prayer that this day may soon dawn." Cf. Ishida Mōsaku, op. cit., pp. 80-86.

[1] Cf. p. 303.

[2] See also text on p. 292

[3] Cf. footnote 3 on pp. 295 ff.

It is noteworthy that in the remains of the Hōkōji excavated some years ago, traces have been discovered of this Paekche craftsmanship. The site records record: "Korean influence was also noticeable in the tiles used in the temple, as if to endorse the recorded statements that they were made under the guidance of Paekche craftsmen. The majority of the round tiles for eaves discovered from the site have a tenpetaled lotus flower pattern whose parallels are found in Paekche. Also the construction of the kiln where the tiles were fired bears marked resemblance to that which was

activities are recorded in the same chronicle a few lines further on:[1]

"The house of Konoba, 樹葉, who was the ancestor of the *miyatsuko* of Kinunui, 衣縫, in Asuka, was broken down and the construction of the Hōkōji started. That place was called Asuka *no* Magami *no hara*, 飛鳥眞神原, or Asuka *no* Tomata, 飛鳥苫田."

This chronicle also has been written at a later date. The owner of the house which had to make way for the temple was an ancestor of Kinunui, a contemporary of the writer of this chronicle. Hence this text primarily had to prove the antiquity of the Kinunui family, just as so many immigrant chronicles under Ōjin had to. Therefore this text also was derived from a far later date and had been connected to the Sushun chronicle purely accidentally. In this chronicle the building of the Hōkōji temple—just as was the case for the Shitennōji—was recorded for the second time, and once again in a different year. The fact that these passages do not agree can only be ascribed to no one knowing the actual origin of this temple. That was because it was built by immigrants, not by Japanese. This can also be deduced, even now, from recent excavations. In 1956-57 the remnants of the 'Great Hall', permanently destroyed by fire in 1196, and the pagoda of the Hōkōji were examined and the same conclusion was reached. The remains clearly indicate a strong relationship to temples in the neighbourhood of the old Koguryŏ capital P'yŏngyang.[2] The only definite date the *Nihonshoki* has to offer is the year of its completion: 596.[3] But in the light of all the other date questions, even this date does not offer much hold, all the more so as this temple was also completed by immigrants.

---

used in Paekche. The excavation revealed how deeply indebted was the building of this temple to the technicians who came from Korea." *Asukadera Temple Site*, (English summary), pp. X, XI.

[1] Cf. *Nihonshoki*, 21st *maki*, Sushun, 1st year; Kuroita Katsumi, Maruyama Jirō, op. cit., part 2, p. 130; cf. K. Florenz, op. cit., p. 320; W. G. Aston, op. cit., p. 118.

[2] This was specifically valid for the stone layer which served as foundation for the various buildings. Here a striking similarity can be established to similar temple foundations in the old capitals of Koguryŏ and Paekche. Also the flat stones, used for the foundation of the Western *kondō* and the covered circumambulatory, display great similarity to those used in various old Koguryŏ temples. Cf. *Asukadera Temple Site*, p. 47.

[3] Cf. *Nihonshoki*, 22nd *maki*, Suiko, 4th year, 1st month; Kuroita Katsumi, Maruyama Jirō, op. cit., part 2, p. 137: "Fourth year, winter, 11th month. The erection of the Hōkōji was completed." Cf. W. G. Aston, op. cit., p. 124.

This temple was not only Korean by origin; it was also largely populated by Koreans or immigrants. Were not the first monks to live here Koreans? In 596, the year of its completion, a Koguryŏ and a Paekche monk settled here: Eji and Esō.[1] In 608 eleven Paekche monks were added.[2] Shiba Tattō's grandson, the wood-carver Tori, carved a Buddha image in 606 which was given a place in the Kondō, 金堂, or 'Golden Hall' of this temple.[3] This completed the building and equipping of this temple. The immigrants, living in every direction around this temple, considered this temple built, as it was, according to a Korean ground-plan,[4] to be the symbol

[1] Cf. footnote 1 on p. 295.

[2] For the eleven other Paekche monks, cf. *Nihonshoki*, 22nd *maki*, Suiko, 17th year, 5th month, 16th day; Kuroita Katsumi, Maruyama Jirō, op. cit., part 2, p. 152: "Fifth month, 16th day, Tokumaro, 徳麻呂, and the others reported (to the empress) their return (from China). Tokumaro and Tatsu, 龍, were both sent back. Together with them persons from Paekche were sent back to their own country. When they arrived in Tsushima, the eleven monks (lit.: practitioners of the way) all expressed their desire to stay (in Japan). After this had been communicated (to the court) they were permitted to stay. Hereupon they received the command to establish themselves in the Gangōji." Cf. W. G. Aston, op. cit., p. 140.

[3] Cf. *Nihonshoki*, 22nd *maki*, Suiko, 14th year, 4th month, 8th day; Kuroita Katsumi, Maruyama Jirō, op. cit., part 2, pp. 146, 147: "14th year, spring, 4th month, 8th day. The copper and embroidered representation of 1 *chō*, 6 *shaku* (approximately 17 feet) were both completed. On the same day the copper image of 1 *chō*, 6 *shaku* was installed in the Golden Hall of the Gangōji." Cf. W. G. Aston, op. cit., p. 134. One may ask onself in how far a wood-carver and saddle-maker such as Tori would be competent to make a copper statue. This image must therefore—like most of those images which have survived from that period—have been a gilded or copper-plated wooden statue. Taking this into account the wood-carver Tori may indeed have been the maker.

[4] This had a completely different appearance from that of the Shitennōji and the Hōryūji. In the Hōkōji the pagoda lay centrally with a relic laid in a hollow in the foundation stone which was deeply buried in the ground. To the east, west and north of this pagoda three *kondō* were built. These four buildings were surrounded by a covered circumambulatory, which started at the main portal. Outside the rectangle of this circumambulatory lay the hall for the recitation of the *sūtras* (the *kōdō*, 講堂). In the report on the excavations of this temple the discovery of this groundplan is called a discovery which "exceeds all imagination". *The Asukadera Temple Site*, p. 47. The Shitenn-ji plan was entirely different. It neither had three different *kondō* and the circumambulatory was also considerably smaller. Now a striking similarity does exist between this plan and that of the temple of Ch'ŏng'am-ni, 清岩里, situated not far from P'yŏngyang. This plan has not

of their land of origin. Later, however, it received more publicity. It was sometimes called Gangōji, 元興寺, Hōmanji, 法滿寺, or, after its location, Asuka-*dera*, 飛鳥寺. Later it also became the court house of prayer. When the court moved to Nara, the temple too had to go with it. Thus, in 718, a temple was built in Nara which was called Shin-, 新, (= new) Gangōji, while the original edifice was called Hon-, 本, (= real) Gangōji from then on.[1] The name of Gangōji was also closely connected to the Nara schools of the Sanron, 三論, and the Hossō who, from this temple edifice in Nara, launched their own views of Buddhism. The origin, however, of this famous temple lay with the Korean immigrants also called *kikajin*.

In passing, we must also mention the origin of the smaller temple, the Hachioka-ji, 蜂岡寺. Its erection was also traced back to Shōtoku Taishi in the *Nihonshoki*. Nevertheless, only in the tale about this temple does an immigrant appear as the real temple builder. Possibly this also brings to light the genuine facts surrounding the building of the 'great' temples. According to the *Nihonshoki* it was built in 603: [2]

"Eleventh month. The *kōtaishi* (= Shōtoku Taishi) spoke to all the officials: 'I have a Buddha image with me worthy of honour. Who will receive it and worship it?' The Hata *no miyatsuko*, Kawakatsu, 秦造河勝, thereupon came forward and said: 'Your servant will worship it.' Thereupon he received the image and built the Hachioka-ji for it."

Besides this Hata leader there was also another immigrant temple builder, who enjoyed great popularity, especially in Suiko's time. This was Tori. This saddler and woodcarver (both trades

---

yet been discovered in Paekche, but this is merely due to the fact that there the finding and excavation of temples of that same period has not yet been done. Cf. footnote 2 on pp. 307 and 308.

Moreover this similarity in ground plans marks the way which Buddhism followed across Korea to Japan.

[1] Cf. *Shoku-Nihongi*, 8th *maki*, Yōrō, 2nd year, 9th month, 23rd day; Kuroita Katsumi, Maruyama Jirō, *Kokushitaikei Shoku-Nihongi*, part 1, (no. 3), p. 74: "The Hōkōji was removed to the new capital (= Nara)".

For the further history of the Hōkōji see Inoue Tetsujirō, op. cit., p. 10, column III, under *Asukadera*.

[2] Cf. *Nihonshoki*, 22nd *maki*, Suiko, 11th year; Kuroita Katsumi, Maruyama Jirō, *Kokushitaikei Nihonshoki*, part 2, p. 141; cf. K. Florenz, op. cit., p. 324; W. G. Aston, op. cit., vol. II, p. 127.

were in the same field as saddles were also carved from thin wood) is also mentioned by the *Nihonshoki* as a temple builder. This records in 606 (fourteenth year of Suiko) an eulogy from the empress addressed to him, which he owed to the skillful installation of an image, carved by himself, of approximately 7 feet, in the Golden Hall of the Hōkōji: [1]

"'When the image was completed, it could not get into the hall. Many builders could not evolve a plan and wanted to break away the entrance to the hall. You, however, have succeeded in getting it in, without breaking down the door. All of that is your achievement'. Therefore she gave him the rank of *dainin*, 大仁, (one of the ranks instituted by Shōtoku Taishi). In the Province of Ōmi, 近江, the district of Sakata, 坂田, she gave him 20 *chō*, 町, (nearly 50 acres) in rice fields. For the sake of the empress and from the proceeds of these fields, he built the Kongōji, 金剛寺. Nowadays this is called the convent of Sakata in Minabuchi, 南淵." Thus this temple also could be traced to an immigrant's son.

3. The oldest and most respected edifice of that period is the *Hōryūji*. This temple was for some time the main seat of the Hossō school. It is situated a few minutes from Nara by bus. From olden times it was a point of pride that from the beginning of the seventh century up to the present day it has stood without ever suffering a fire. Most of the 'old' Japanese temples have been burnt down at least once or twice in their history. The Shitennōji had burnt down twice, up to the Second World War. What remained of it at that time dated from 1812.[2] In the middle ages Gangōji burnt down entirely. Only a section of its monks' quarters remained. Besides these quarters nothing of it was ever rebuilt. The Hōryūji, however, amongst all of the Japanese temples, was considered as the only monument which has stood unchanged from its foundation up to our time.[3] Now this temple was particularly ascribed to Shōtoku Taishi because, according to the *Nihonshoki*, he dwelt close to it.[4] However, one can search the *Nihonshoki* in vain to find

---

[1] Cf. *Nihonshoki*, 22nd *maki*, Suiko, 14th year, 5th month, 5th day; Kuroita Katsumi, Maruyama Jirō, op. cit., part 2, p. 147; see also W. G. Aston, op. cit., pp. 134-135.

[2] Cf. H. Coates and R. Ishizuka, *Honen, the Buddhist Saint*, p. 306.

[3] This building is still well known under the name of Gokurakubō, 極楽坊, Heaven's Convent.

[4] Cf. *Nihonshoki*, 22nd *maki*, Suiko, 13th year (605), 10th month; Kuroita

a chronicle which establishes him as its builder. The *Nihonshoki* can only record a number of rice fields which he had received as a reward for his *sūtra* reading and which he is supposed to have allotted to the temple of Ikaruka, 斑鳩, = Hōryūji.[1] That he was its builder has been attributed to him at a later date. Hence he was later wrongly considered to be the guardian deity of builders.

Then who did build this temple? The excavations of Dr. Ishida Mōsaku especially have shown that this was the work of Koreans.[2] Owing to these excavations two points have been established.

Firstly, the present-day Hōryūji should not be identified with the temple edifice which was erected in Shōtoku Taishi's time. Ishida found the remains of this original complex in 1939. This oldest temple foundation is now generally known as Wakakusa-*garan*, 若草伽藍, (lit.: the *saṃghārāma*—monastery—of the fresh grass). It was sited between the West Hall of the present-day Hōryūji and the East Hall or Yumedono, 夢殿, (dream Hall) of Shōtoku Taishi, under which the temple remains of his afore-mentioned palace are situated.[3] During the excavations burnt earth and charred wood were also found. Obviously this was still a remnant of the Hōryūji fire which destroyed this old complex in 670.[4] By determining this point the Hōryūji dispute was settled concerning the double question whether the present-day Hōryūji was that of Shōtoku Taishi and whether—assuming it was burnt down—the present-day Hōryūji is nothing more than a faithful reconstruction of the old Hōryūji. The Wakakusa-*garan* has proved that one should deduce nothing from the buildings of the Hōryūji still existing concerning the very first builders of the pre-670 Hōryūji.

Katsumi, Maruyama Jirō, op. cit., part 2, p. 146: "Winter, 10th month. The *kōtaishi* established himself in the Ikaruka palace." Cf. W. G. Aston, op. cit., p. 134. This palace lay only a few dozen yards away from the present-day Hōryūji.

[1] Cf. p. 393.

[2] Cf. Okabe Nagaaki, op. cit., pp. 25, 26.

[3] See the description of this by Ishida Mōsaku, the researcher himself: op. cit., pp. 81 ff.

[4] Cf. *Nihonshoki*, 27th *maki*, Tenchi, 9th year, 4th month, 30th day; Kuroita Katsumi, Maruyama Jirō, op. cit., part 2, p. 297: "Summer, fourth month, 30th day. After midnight a fire broke out in the Hōryūji. Not a single room of it remained. It rained heavily and thundered." Cf. W. G. Aston, op. cit., p. 293.

Furthermore, it has appeared from the location of these remains that they must have been closer to the palace of Shōtoku Taishi, in contrast to the present-day temple complex. The main discovery was, however, that the ground-plan differed entirely from that of the present-day Hōryūji and is also to be found in Paekche temples.[1] In building the Shitennōji a similar ground-plan has been used.[2] This was supported partially by the village structure of old Korea [3] and partially by the temple forms known to the North-east Asian continent.[4] Therefore this ground-plan points to an old Korean society. Also, the comparison of the lotus motifs on the roofing-tiles of the Wakakusa-*garan* with those of Paekche proves that they have much in common. There were but minor discrepancies between this complex and the temples of Paekche, also discovered by Ishida. These small differences can, however, be explained by the fact that the Paekche temples are of a far later date [5] than the Wakakusa-*garan*.

---

[1] Up to the time of the excavation, it was generally believed that the groundplan of the Hōryūji had nothing in common with that of the Paekche temples. Furthermore, it was believed that therefore this differed entirely from that of the Shitennōji. Now the excavated Wakakusa-*garan* showed that the most ancient Hōryūji was similar qua groundplan to that of the Shitennōji and therefore also to the temples discovered by Ishida Mōsaku in Paekche. See the more detailed description by Ishida Mōsaku, op. cit., pp. 81 ff.

[2] Cf. Ishida Mōsaku, op. cit., p. 83.

[3] This would depend on a division of the area into nine parts. In this the temple had a specific place. Cf. Okabe Nagaaki, op. cit., p. 26.

[4] See the report on the excavations of the Asukadera, *The Asukadera Temple Site*, p. 38.

[5] These discrepancies are the following:
1. The central stone in the foundation of the pagoda contained—in contrast to the Paekche and Asukadera pagodas—no cavity in which the small wooden ship with the relics was kept. Also, this stone was found on the surface and not deeply buried. It is apparent from fire stains that this stone was also fairly close to the surface in the first Hōryūji temple. The lack of the hollow can be explained by the fact that the relic was preserved in a separate post in the pagoda. Cf. for instance the *Nihonshoki* description of this method on p. 323.
2. The supporting stones of the present-day Hōryūji contain traces of a fire (in total there were thirteen stones). Apparently they have therefore also been used for the Wakakusa-*garan*. What is typical about these stones is that they are all circular in shape, in contrast to the square stones used in Paekche for this purpose.

All these fairly recent finds therefore give us the right to say that the actual architects and executors of these temple projects were not Japanese such as Shōtoku Taishi and Soga *no* Umako, but Koreans and immigrants. The title of guardian deity of the builders which was later conferred on Shōtoku Taishi is therefore a wrongly aimed mystification of the extraordinary skillfulness of these Koreans. These excavations prove that the Japanese were simply not ready for the technical capacity and professional skill which the wooden constructions of the later Hōryūji demanded, which command respect even to this day. On the other hand, they were also not entirely interested. Were not temples and monasteries concerned here which were intended for foreigners and foreign deities?

This does not detract from the fact that the number of all of these predominantly Korean monks, nuns and monasteries increased considerably over the course of years. This is apparent from the statistics established by the inspectors appointed by Suiko in 624.[1] In that same year there were supposed to be 46 temples, populated by 816 monks and 569 nuns. Dr. Ishida Mōsaku has proved by the number of roofing-tiles he found that this number of temples was not an exaggeration.[2] Calculated per cloister, there

---

3. The proportions in breadth and length are different in the *kondō* of the Hōryūji to those in the two Paekche temples investigated by Ishida Mōsaku. These differences can, however, be ascribed to the fact that these Paekche temples were completed some fifty years after the Hōryūji. These differences will perhaps only be fully explained when temples are discovered in Paekche of the same period as the Hōryūji. Cf. for further details, Ishida Mōsaku, op. cit., pp. 84, 85.

[1] Cf. *Nihonshoki*, 22nd *maki*, Suiko, 23rd year; Kuroita Katsumi, Maruyama Jirō, op. cit., part 2, p. 165: "Autumn, ninth month, 3rd day. An investigation was instituted into the monasteries (*tera*), monks and nuns. Furthermore a precise report was made up concerning the data on the erection of the temples, of the circumstances under which monks and nuns accepted Buddhism and also of the year, month and day on which they began the monasterial life (= the *pāramitā*). At that time there were 46 *tera*, 816 monks and 569 nuns. In total that was 1385 people." Cf. W. G. Aston, op. cit., pp. 153, 154.

[2] Thus there were 28 temples in the province of Yamato, 5 in that of Kawachi, 4 in that of Izumi, 4 in that of Yamashiro, 3 in that of Settsu, and also one in Iga and one in Iyo. Therefore most of these temples lay in Yamato and along the coasts of the Japanese inland sea, the Setonaikai. Cf. Takatori Masaō: "Kodai Minshū no Shūkyō", *N.S.K.*, p. 16.

must have been approximately 30 monks or nuns to each. Such communities were large enough to guarantee a continuation of the 'Korea' Buddhism. In such groups isolation with regard to the outside world was easily preserved.

All these monasteries were therefore little other than non-Japanese islands in the culturally still primitive Japanese landscape. As centres of culture they contrasted sharply with the poverty of the Japanese farmer and fisherman, who were even forced frequently to part with their own rice fields to increase the wealth of the monasteries. This is apparent from many chronicles of the *Nihonshoki* as well as from its sequel, the *Shoku-Nihongi* [1]. Moreover, they were often forced to help, under the supervision of Korean experts, in building temples technically almost impossible to them. Of this Kadowaki says: [2]

"The villagers of Yamato who, with their primitive beliefs, still dwelt in caves at that time, were most surprised at these majestically built temples and Buddha images. Not only that, they were also forced to build the Hōkōji for instance, just as the inhabitants of the Kawachi plain had to build the Shitennōji." Coming from these rich monasteries, a genuine dialogue with the Japanese 'man in the street' could not be expected. The attention of the monks and nuns was too much centred on Korea and, beyond Korea, on China, for this to be possible.

Their isolation forced them to follow and transplant to their own monasteries every new development in these two countries. Therefore new schools, which had come into existence in China as a result of the improved translation of Hīnayāna and Mahāyāna literature, were to find warm promoters shortly afterwards in Japan. Thus at the end of Suiko's life, the Gangōji was already the first institute where the doctrine of the Korean Sanron school was applied. The Hossō-*shū* was forty years later, in its turn, to drive the Sanron protagonists out of this *tera*. Thus one school succeeded another. None of those Nara schools were to concern themselves expressly with 'folk Buddhism'. Therefore ideologically all of these

[1] See for instance the text on p. 312, which mentions Tori, who received such gifts of land property. These gifts were still relatively small compared to those of later dates. In 749 Empress Kōken defined the lands of the monasteries. Cf. M. W. de Visser, *Ancient Buddhism in Japan*, part 1, pp. 638, 639.

[2] Cf. *Jimmu Tennō* p. 176.

schools remained fairly sterile in Japan and were doomed to extinction.

This growth of the rich monasteries in the impoverished Japan of that time was made possible on the one hand by the king of Paekche, who supplied monks and nuns in exchange for new Korean territories, and on the other hand by the emperors and the *shizoku*, who requested and needed them for the cultivation of the Japanese countryside. So both were bound hand and foot to these development centres. Technicians, palace builders, scholars, governors and also the later officialdom were all produced from it. Therefore not only Buddhism, but also the still young state, benefited from the building of monasteries and temples.

Little can be said of the nature of Buddhism in these monasteries. There was certainly not the depth of the later schools, which attempted to introduce a return to the orthodoxy of Indian trends and a conscious rebuttal of the national East Asiatic mentality. Prior to this 'school Buddhism', the '*vinaya* and meditation masters', so often mentioned in the *Nihonshoki*, probably brought about some improvement. Thus amongst such nuns as Shiba Tattō's daughter there was sufficient diligence to attain an improved experience of *vinaya*, if necessary by means of a trip to Paekche. Despite that, it must still be said that in the fairly easily surveyed and controlled group of 1385 monks and nuns present in Japan at the beginning of the seventh century the genuine experience of Buddhism was not yet very deeply rooted. We have seen how the Paekche monk Kanroku noted this in his letter to Empress Suiko in 623.[1] For, he reduced many of the misdemeanours of the monks and nuns in the communities to innocence and inexperience. His letter was clearly not only a reaction to the monk's crime (who had hit his grandfather with a pan) but rather an excuse for the innocence amongst all monks, which had come to light in the outside world also, owing to this offence.

Later chroniclers must also have felt that lack of genuine penetration in cloister Buddhism of the first century, otherwise they would not have repeatedly peppered the chronicles of the *Nihonshoki* with tales which obviously were intended to suggest greater depth in the monastic life of that period. In this they succeeded only partially, so that these tales actually betrayed the true poverty

---

[1] See pp, 276, 277.

of the religious situation of that time by anachronisms. In the following chapter we shall encounter some such examples. We have twice met with an example of this in the words of Sŏng or Shōtoku Taishi, inserted into the text, which, however forceful they might be as evidence, were nothing other than pericopes copied from the *Suvarṇabhāsottama-sūtra* which was introduced much later.

The indirect relations with these T'opa monasteries, which were not deeply spiritual and were more interested in material prosperity and politics, left the Japanese monasteries at a low ebb. In this, owing to its exclusively Korean character, it had become too isolated to be able to achieve a dialogue with the Japanese mentality. Actually this dialogue never took place within the monasteries. Buddhism first achieved its own Japanese shape in:

2 The lay Buddhism

Although Buddhism originally did not gain an individual Japanese aspect in the monasteries, its part was not ended with this. Meanwhile, it had contrived to become significant to the layman as well. In the previous chapters we have already pointed out that, in contrast to its beginnings in China, it had meanwhile managed to integrate the religious convictions of the North Asiatic tribes. In this stereotype North Asiatic form it not only presented itself to Japanese society, but also began a dialogue.

The main central event in this dialogue was the conversion of the two *uji no kami* of the Soga: Iname and Umako. This two-fold fact turned this 'foreigners' religion' into one of the pillars of Japanese religious mentality. The process of mental change brought about by this dialogue followed the structure of Japanese society. Therefore major alterations and decisions were achieved amongst the *uji no kami* themselves, not amongst the lower orders of the *uji*. This process is understandable because, unavoidably, all the members of the *uji* were 'adjusted' in their religious convictions to those of their leaders. The *uji* organisation which, among the lower ranks, limited individual liberty, tolerated no conversions here. Conversion was possible only at the highest level of the *uji no kami* as it meant a breakthrough of the religious structure of the entire *uji*. Even today, in some places in the Japanese countryside, the mentality of the whole society can be changed only via its leaders. It is therefore also not surprising that so few came forth from the lower ranks of *uji* society with a vocation for the monasteries in the sixth century. Those could be expected only after the *uji* had turned to Buddhism in the upper layers. Therefore lay Buddhism of the sixth century dealt with the top figures of the *shizoku*, in particular those of the Soga.

This is characterised by a three-fold development. This centred on the conversion of the Soga. It did not remain limited to the Soga because the imperial house was also closely concerned. In the first stage of this development Buddhism was flatly rejected by the *ujigami* belief. Integration of Buddhism with this *ujigami* belief was achieved only in the second stage by the conversion of the Soga and was completed in the third stage by the 'conversion' of the emperor himself. This conversion became a fact after the destruction of the Mononobe who, until then, had been the symbol of all who disagreed with this development.

a *First stage: the resistance by the* ujigami *belief*

This resistance to Buddhism occurred particularly during the reigns of the emperors Kimmei and Bidatsu. This is not surprising as it emanated from these emperors themselves. In the previous chapter [1] we have already pointed out how definitely Emperor Kimmei was opposed to Buddhism. He did not yet see it as something which should be integrated with his function of supreme *uji no kami*. It did not yet raise any questions of conscience for him. This same Buddhism, however, did raise a question of conscience for his successor Bidatsu. His solution to it was a determined and explicit denial of that Buddhism. This is readily deduced from the chronicles of the *Nihonshoki*. His personal attitude was so decided that even his chronicler, as we have seen, typified him as one who "did not accept Buddhism, but gave his preference to literature". [2]

This less sphinx-like and hesitant attitude towards this new religion is confirmed by the geography of his residences. Just as was Kimmei's court, Bidatsu's was the 'Rome' of the *ujigami* belief. According to the *Nihonshoki*, he resided from the first to the fourth year of his reign (572-575) in the palace of Kudara *no* Ōi, 百濟大井.[3] This lay in the Yamato province, on the border of the

---

[1] Cf. Chapter IV, pp. 269-276.

[2] See p. 288.

[3] Cf. *Nihonshoki*, 19th *maki*, Bidatsu, 1st year; Kuroita Katsumi,

districts of North Katsuraki and Shiki, where Kimmei had resided before him. It was situated at an almost equal distance from the central areas of the Soga, Mononobe and Nakatomi *shizoku*. The situation of this palace indicates that the emperor was concerned with preserving the balance between these three *shizoku* which, during Kimmei's reign, had also been each other's opponents in their views of life. The Buddhist core of the saddlers was at an even greater distance. The distance to this area was too great to assume Buddhist influence on the emperor from it. Thus he continued to move amongst the different parties.

This situation was maintained until the emperor, in the fourth year of his reign, moved his residence to Osada, 譯語田,[1] in the neighbourhood of present-day Miwa, 三輪, which was at that time considered as the actual centre of the Mononobe area. This brought him considerably closer to the Mononobe than to the other *shizoku*. His residence lay somewhat to the south of the Mononobe area.[2] This is apparent from the map on p. 470. According to the *Kojiki* [3] he was supposed to have dwelt here quite from the beginning for fourteen years. The *Nihonshoki* adds that the name of this residence was Sakitama. Now Sakitama has various meanings. According to the characters used in the *Nihonshoki*: 幸玉, it can be translated by the neutral term 'Lucky Jewel'. This name was quite applicable to the palace of Emperor Bidatsu who, according to his long Japanese name, was called, i.a., *tamashiki*, 珠敷, that is, Jewel Strewer. If, however, one ignores these Chinese characters, which often fulfil a purely phonetic function in the *Kojiki* and the *Nihonshoki*, this Japanese word, *sakitama*, also had another meaning. *Sakitama*, or the more general *sakimitama*, 幸魂, was also

---

Maruyama Jirō, op. cit., part 2, p. 101: "That month he built his palace in Kudara *no* Ōi," Cf. W. G. Aston, op. cit., p. 90.

[1] Cf. *Nihonshoki*, 20th *maki*, Bidatsu, 4th year; Kuroita Katsumi, Maruyama Jirō, op. cit., part 2, p. 106: "That year. He caused soothsayers to establish the ground for a house of the ruler of Amabe, 海部, and the ruler of Itoi, 絲井, by soothsaying. The soothsaying turned out favourably. Finally he built a house in Osada. It was called the palace of Sakitama." Cf. W. G. Aston, op. cit., p. 95.

[2] This lay in the district of Shiki no Kami. Cf. B. Lewin, op. cit., p. 61.

[3] Cf. *Kojiki*, 3rd *maki*; Kuroita Katsumi, Maruyama Jirō, *Kokushi-taikei Kojiki*, p. 148, line 3: "His son was Nunakura Futotamashiki *no mikoto*, 沼名倉太玉敷命 (= Bidatsu), he resided in the palace of Osada, where he ruled the people fourteen years."

the indication of one of the two souls which everyone owns.[1] The *Nihonshoki* also mentions such a *sakimitama*—contracted to *kami*[2]—which is represented here as the spirit of peace and harmony which, even better than the god Ōnamuchi, 大己貴, himself, contrived to subject the wild territory of Izumo. He was given his own temple on the Mimoro, 三諸, mountain of Yamato [3] and was worshipped there under the name of Ōmiwa, 大三輪. Moreover, *sakimitama* was also one of the *ujigami* of the Mononobe. Thus the name of this palace also became a symbol of its sympathy with the *ujigami* belief of the Mononobe. It is hard to discover whether dislike of Buddhism was also present in this. If, however, he aligned his belief with the Mononobe, then this seems obvious.

This dislike certainly became stronger as, one year after his move to Osada, he married the lady who was later to succeed him as empress,[4] known under her posthumous name of Suiko. This hap-

[1] The *Nihonshoki* relates of Ōnamuchi that everywhere where there was disturbance and disorder he brought peace and tranquillity. Thus he also came to Izumo, the most desolate of all the territories that he had encountered until now. However, here too he succeeded in creating order. He was very proud of this achievement and began to ask himself as to who other than himself was capable of such prowess. Then someone came over the sea towards him who claimed the peace and harmony in Izumo entirely for himself, as the subjection of Izumo was impossible without him. When Ōnamuchi asked him who he was, he received the answer: "I am your Sakimitama, your Kushimitama". Cf. *Nihonshoki*, 1st *maki*; Kuroita Katsumi, Maruyama Jirō, *Kokushitaikei Nihonshoki*, part 1, pp. 48, 49. See also K. Florenz, op. cit., pp. 172, 173.

This *kushimitama*, 奇魂, and *sakimitama*, 幸魂, are respectively the miraculous and felicitous aspects of one and the same soul: the *nigimitama*, 和魂, the soul of peace and harmony, which, together with the *aramitama*, 荒魂, the soul of disorder, is to be found in every human in a certain relative polarity. These two, *nigimitama* and *aramitama* were balanced in more or less the same sense as that which we call the good and the evil spirit in a person. For all of these spirits cf. K. Florenz, op. cit., p. 173, footnote 4; Kiyohara Sadao, *Shintōshi*, pp. 13, 14. Shimonaka Yasaburō, *Shintō Daijiten*, part 2, p. 101, column III, describes this *sakimitama* as also being the spirit of felicity of humanity. Otherwise this work gives the same picture of these spirits and souls as does Florenz.

[2] Cf. *Nihonshoki*, 1st *maki;* Kuroita Katsumi, Maruyama Jirō, op. cit., part 1, p. 49; W. G. Aston, op. cit., vol. I, p. 61, translates *sakimitama* and *kushimitama* respectively by 'guardian spirit, the wondrous spirit'.

[3] This is the present-day mountain of Miwa or Ōmiwa-san and lies in East Yamato in the Shiki district, also in the Mononobe district.

[4] Cf. *Nihonshoki*, 20th *maki*, Bidatsu, 5th year, third month; Kuroita

pened four months after the previous empress had died.[1] Suiko was a granddaughter of Soga *no* Iname and, just as Yōmei, born of the marriage between Kimmei and Iname's daughter Kitashi *hime*. In her testimony to Tori, Shiba Tattō's grandson, she declared that she had believed in Buddhism from early childhood.[2] In her person, Bidatsu also encountered Buddhism. On the other hand at her own court Suiko was enabled to maintain close relations with the Buddhism of that period, independently of Bidatsu. This court was far more important at that time for the influence of Buddhism on Bidatsu and many others than were the saddler Buddhists in the Takaichi district. Every meeting with his Buddhist wife placed him before the dilemma whether or not to accept the new doctrine. She forced him to take sides with regard to religious matters. She did not succeed, however, as he could not reconcile Buddhism with his own *ujigami* belief. He has made that clearly apparent in his attitude, because otherwise his chronicler would never have said, at the beginning of his chronicles, that he did not accept Buddhism.

The Buddhist preponderance at his wife's court forced him to a reaction which consisted of an even stronger affirmation of the *ujigami* belief. In this he fell back even more greatly on the Mononobe's support. This in nowise forced Bidatsu to live in celibacy because, according to the *Nihonshoki* and the *Kojiki*, he also had various other wives,[3] to whom he could resort when his relations with his Buddhist wife had cooled.

Katsumi, Maruyama Jirō, op. cit., part 2, p. 106: "Fifth year, spring, third month, 10th day. The officials (Jap.: *tsukasa tsukasa*—this is an anachronism because there were no officials yet at that time) addressed the request to him to appoint an empress. Thereupon he had Toyomike Kashikiya *hime no mikoto* proclaimed empress. She brought two boys and five girls into the world. The first of them was called Uchi *no* Kaitako *no kōjō*, 菟道貝鮹皇女. She married Shōtoku of the eastern palace (= Shōtoku Taishi)." Cf. W. G. Aston, op. cit., vol. II, p. 95.

[1] Cf. *Nihonshoki*, 20th *maki*, Bidatsu, fourth year; Kuroita Katsumi, Maruyama Jirō, loc. cit.: "Eleventh month. Empress Hirohime, 廣姫, died". Cf. W. G. Aston, op. cit., p. 95.

[2] See previous chapter, pp. 251, 252.

[3] The *Kojiki*, 3rd *maki*; Kuroita Katsumi, Maruyama Jirō, *Kokushitaikei Kojiki*, p. 148, mentions a total of four women: Toyomike Kashikiya *hime no mikoto*, Ogumako *no* Iratsume, 小熊子郎女, Hirohime *no mikoto*, 比呂比賣命, Ominako *no* Iratsume, 老女子郎女. The *Nihonshoki* mentions only the first and third of them. Cf. footnotes 4 on p. 321 and 1 on this page.

At the end of his reign he could not visit her as often as before, as her court lay in the Soga territory, namely in Toyora, 豊浦. The fight against Buddhism had become too serious for this.[1] Hence the persecution of Buddhism, described in the last year of Bidatsu's reign, follows the pattern of Bidatsu's aversion to it. Many of the details of this persecution are dubious. It is, however, certain that it took place under his government; all the more so as during this time the political tensions between the chief *shizoku* of that period began to be more sharply defined. The tales of those persecutions make it clear that Bidatsu maintained a far firmer standpoint towards the new doctrine than his predecessor Kimmei. It can be seen in the following *Nihonshoki* tale of the fourteenth year of his reign:[2]

"Fourteenth year, spring, second month, fifteenth day. The Soga *no ō-omi* Umako *no sukune* built a pagoda to the north of the Ōhara, 大原, hill. Here he held a large religious meeting with a meal.[3] The religious relic which Tattō had received he installed in the middle of a niche in the column of the pagoda.[4]

---

[1] This Toyora lay only a few hundred yards from the Mukuhara house of Soga Iname and at a similar distance from the Hōkōji. A few miles to the south-east of this Suiko residence the Momohara settlement of the saddlers lay. As a result it lay entirely within the sphere of Soga influence. (See map on p. 470) It is reported at the beginning of the Suiko chronicles that she accepted the imperial dignity in the palace of Toyora. (Cf. *Nihonshoki*, 22nd *maki*, Suiko chronicles for the ascension to the throne; Kuroita Katsumi, Maruyama Jirō, *Kokushitaikei Nihonshoki*, part 2, p. 135: "Winter, 12th month, 8th day. The empress assumed the imperial dignity in the Toyora palace." Cf. W. G. Aston, op. cit., p. 121.)

Here there is no question whatever of a move, as was the case with previous emperors. Hence she must already have been living there. The assumption of the imperial dignity did not also cause her the necessity of moving the imperial residence. It is therefore probable that she already dwelt here when, at the end of Emperor Bidatsu's reign, eight years before she became empress, the persecution of Buddhism broke out.

[2] Cf. *Nihonshoki*, 20th *maki*, Bidatsu, 14th year, 3rd month, 1st day; Kuroita Katsumi, Maruyama Jirō, op. cit., part 2, pp. 114, 115. See also W. G. Aston, op. cit., pp. 103-104.

[3] See Chapter IV, footnote 9 on p. 249.

[4] The pagoda was built round a wooden, separate pillar. In the core of this pillar (lit.: 柱頭, *hashiragami*; Kanda Ichikyōsuke, *Jikai*, p. 1477, column II, translates this word by 'core of the pillar'. We follow this translation, and not that of M. W. de Visser, op. cit., p. 28: 'on the top of the pillar', because the excavations of the Hōryūji for instance, point in this

"Twenty-fourth day. Soga *no ō-omi* grew ill. Therefore he consulted a soothsayer. This (soothsayer) told him: 'This curse depends on the disposition of the 'Buddha god'[1] who was worshipped in your father's time.' The *ō-omi* sent his servants to make known this oracle (to the emperor). Thereupon the following command came from the emperor: 'We decree that in accordance with the soothsayer's oracle, the god of your father shall be worshipped.' In accordance with that order the *ō-omi* worshipped the stone image of Buddha and prayed for prolongation of his life. At that time an epidemic occurred, of which very many people died.

"Third month, first day. The *ōmuraji* of the Mononobe, Yuke *no* Moriya, and the *daibu* (or *taifu*, 大夫)[2] of the Nakatomi, Katsumi, 勝海, said (to the emperor): 'Why do you not act according to our words? Since the previous emperor, and in your reign, the epidemic has spread more and more, so that the population will perish. The cause of this is entirely based on the fact that Soga *no ō-omi* has taken the initiative in practising Buddhism.' Hereupon the emperor decreed: 'It is clear. Let us stop the Buddhism.'

"Thirtieth day. The *ōmuraji* of the Mononobe, Yuke *no* Moriya, went of his own accord to the temple. He placed himself on a 'prayer stool',[3] knocked down the pagoda and set it on fire. He also burnt the Buddha image and the hall of the pagoda. He had the charred remains of the Buddha image collected and cast into the canal of Nahiwa. That day there were no clouds, but there was rain and wind. However, the *ōmuraji* had rainwear on. He ordered that Umako *no sukune* and those who had followed him in practising Buddhism should be severely humiliated and abased. Hereafter

---

direction) the relic was present. Cf. K. Florenz, op. cit., p. 314, footnote 12. See further concerning this pagoda footnote 4 on p. 310 and especially footnote 5 on p. 314 under 1 of this chapter.

[1] Lit.: 佛神之心, the heart of the Buddha god.

[2] The word *taifu* or *daibu* used here was a high official rank.

[3] Lit.: *agura*, 古䏶. According to some this word was derived from *a* = *ashi*, 足, foot, and *kura* = saddle and would therefore mean footsaddle; others derive this word from *a* of *age*, 上, = stand up, raise oneself, and *kura*, 座 = seat (cf. Shimonaka Yasaburō, op. cit., part 1, p. 14, column III; p. 15, column I). In any case it was a kind of upright chair with a fairly low seat, comparable to the prayer stools frequently used in Belgian and French churches. This was used in various ritual ceremonies in the temples. In modern Japanese it has the neutral meaning of stool, in old Japanese however it was a ritual pew. Cf. Kanda Ichikyōsuke, op. cit., p. 907, column II.

he had the *miyatsuko* Saeki Mimuro, 佐伯造御室, Zenshin and the other nuns who were provided for by Umako *no sukune* summoned. Umako *no sukune* could not find the courage to object to this order. Deeply grieved he summoned the nuns and handed them over to (Saeki) Mimuro. The officials [1] removed the (Buddhist) robes from the three nuns. In an inn of the town of Tsubakii, 海石榴, they were shut up and beaten."

A little further on this tale is interrupted by a few sentences concerning Mimana:

"The emperor was considering rebuilding Mimana. For this he appointed the prince Mimiko of Sakata, 坂田耳子, as his emissary. Just at that time both the emperor and the *ōmuraji* were suddenly troubled by disease. Therefore he was not sent. He (= the emperor) therefore invited Prince Tachibana *no* Toyohi (= the later Emperor Yōmei) to come to him and said to him: 'We must not oppose the decisions of our previous emperor. Therefore we must have an eye to restoring the government in Mimana.' The entire country was filled with people who once again were troubled with the sores, and with the dead. Those who were covered with them said: 'It is just as if our bodies were being burnt, beaten and pummelled.' They died in tears. Both young and old said secretly to each other: 'Is this the punishment for burning the Buddha image?'

"Summer, sixth month. Umako *no sukune* spoke to the emperor: 'The sickness of your servant is not yet healed. If we do not receive the power of the three treasures (= Buddhism), no healing or liberation is possible.' Thereupon the emperor gave Umako *no sukune* an order as follows: 'Thou alone must practice Buddhism. Others, however, must cease from it.' Hereupon he also returned the three nuns to Umako *no sukune*. He received them joyously. He grieved about their unforeseen adventures and treated them with respect. He built them a new *tera*, led them within and provided them with means.

"Autumn, eighth month, fifteenth day. The disease of the emperor increased in severity. He died in the 'Great Hall'."

This entire pericope from the Bidatsu chronicles provides various reasons for consideration. In the first place, the hand of a Buddhist propagandist is clearly recognisable, who incorporated an original

---

[1] Japanese: 有司 *tsukasa*. For this anachronism, see Chapter IV, footnote 4 on p. 244.

chronicle concerning the resistance of the emperor and the *shizoku* against Buddhism, in order to tie in a tale of foundation and a moral. The foundation tale already begins in the thirteenth year of Bidatsu.[1] It consists of the narration of the foundation and initial difficulties of Japan's oldest convent of nuns. This account has been cut up and peppered over the Buddhist pericopes of the thirteenth and fourteenth years which, interestingly enough, occupy almost half of all the Bidatsu chronicles put together. The devout monk, who inserted his history here, betrayed, however, that he himself was not thoroughly acquainted with the situation of that time. He permits the nuns to be robbed even of their Buddhist robes, by officials moreover. He did not take into account that those officials came only after 645. Therefore his interpolations derive from a far later period.

The foregoing description also had its own moral. The same, or some other, Buddhist propagandist has used the same original data of this chronicle as a lesson on the healing power of Buddhism and on the punishments which await those who refuse to accept this. That this is probably a different author is apparent from the fact that the nuns' tale is separate from the history concerning the epidemic. This moral lesson is badly given because, while it is clear from the narration that the enemies of Buddhism did not escape their punishment, as they died of the disease, it is not related whether Soga's promotor was healed. Nevertheless he survived Bidatsu and both his successors and also served many years under Empress Suiko.

A comparison of this text to that of Kimmei thirteen raises even more doubts. Here too a persecution is mentioned.[2] Various data there coincide surprisingly with those of these chronicles. Indeed, both mention an epidemic, the destruction and firing of a temple and an image, and finally the casting away of the fragments of this image in the Naniwa canal. Perhaps this latter was indeed intended as a disguised explanation for the building of the Shitennōji in the vicinity of this canal. It is also remarkable that in both the account is terminated with an unusual weather report about a cloudless sky which, in the Bidatsu chronicle, is moreover given a more miraculous character by storm and rain. That a relationship

---

[1] Cf. Chapter IV, pp. 248 ff.

[2] Cf. Chapter IV, p. 244.

between both persecutions existed is apparent from the words of Mononobe in the foregoing Bidatsu chronicle about the epidemic: "Since the previous emperor, and in your reign, the epidemic has spread more and more". The words "in that time an epidemic occurred", which is reported in the Bidatsu chronicle a few lines earlier, must therefore be interpreted in the wider sense of: in the time of Emperor Kimmei. The epidemic mentioned in both chronicles was one and the same. Only, a later Buddhist sympathiser warped the detail concerning the sores a little further for the benefit of Buddhism.

Here, together with Tsuda,[1] one can ask oneself whether not only this epidemic, but also the persecution, was one and the same in both chronicles. No answer can be given. Buddhism of that time was very strongly tied to the Soga. In the foregoing account, these close ties are even admitted by the emperor. Therefore Buddhist persecutions were linked to political defeats of the Soga themselves. Considering the tense relations between the *shizoku*, one may assume that in the period between 552 (Kimmei thirteen) and 585 (Bidatsu fourteen) various such explosions occurred. Owing to the apparent ineradicability of the epidemic, they continually led to revenge by the Mononobe and emperors sympathetic to them on Buddhism, which was considered responsible for this. The number of such revengeful exercises is, however, hard to establish.

The Bidatsu chronicles allow many doubts to persist. Despite this, the emperor's antipathy to Buddhism is clearly established. It is adequately and succinctly expressed in his words concerning the 'stopping' of it. In him this antipathy was not only the result of his dependence on the Mononobe, but had also grown from the encounters with his wife, the future Empress Suiko. Apart from these two factors, Buddhism was, moreover, hard to reconcile with Bidatsu's status of supreme *uji no kami* of the nation. This too stimulated him to revolt against it. Hence public and conscious opposition to Buddhism characterised him to his death. This was self-evident to later Buddhist interpolators. Therefore they left him as he was: the one who refused to accept Buddhism. Until his death Buddhism had no hope of a real 'Japanese' expansion, with the exception of the courts of the Soga, who withdrew from this influence.

---

[1] Cf. Chapter IV, p. 270.

b *Second stage: the conversion of the Soga*

The initial contacts of Buddhism with the imperial courts of Kimmei and Bidatsu had been fruitless. Simultaneously, however, at the 'courts' of the two Soga leaders, Iname and his son Umako, it was actively becoming Japanese Buddhism. They were the first laymen to find a place for Buddhism in their own religious function of *uji no kami*. Though they may have been the most important, they were not, however, the only lay Buddhists of that period. More are known. As most of them were Korean immigrants, they could not succeed in integrating Buddhism with Japanese society. These immigrants are of interest in as far as the course of Buddhist expansion under the emperors Kimmei and Bidatsu can be mapped by use of data concerning them in the *Nihonshoki*.

Now who were these laymen? Amongst all of them, the first place undoubtedly belongs to Shiba Tattō. Together with his son Tasuna he occupied the first place in immigrant Buddhism in the *Nihonshoki*, as we have already pointed out at some length.

However, besides him, there is yet another figure mentioned, who was certainly his match in importance. This was the Ikebe *no atae*, Hida. According to the chronicles of Bidatsu thirteen [1] he, together with Shiba Tattō and Soga *no* Umako, was one of the three who strengthened their belief as a result of the trial of strength with the relic of Buddha. We also meet him as an inspector of Buddhism and as the one who, together with Shiba Tattō, received the order to provide for the nuns Zenshin *cum suis* in their upkeep. From all of this it is clearly apparent that in the oldest Japanese Buddhism he was Shiba Tattō's compeer. We have seen that he descended from the immigrant Niwaki *no atae* and therefore also belonged to the vast immigrant tribe of the Fumi *no* Ikebe *no* Imiki.[2] The dwelling area of this immigrant tribe was to be found in Ikebe or Ikenobe in the Iware district, which represented the southern part of the present-day city of Sakurai. From this he derived his name: the *atae*(= title) Hida of Ikebe.[3] Just as was Shiba Tattō in Takaichi, he must have been the principle Buddhist layman in the district of the Iware residences. From his functions, which

---

[1] Cf. pp. 248 ff.

[2] Cf. p. 298.

[3] The word *atae*, which is used here, is not a proper name, but a title (Cf Bruno Lewin, op. cit., p. 107, footnote 10).

parallel those of Shiba Tattō, it can be deduced that he fulfilled a similar leading role towards his clan as did Shiba Tattō towards the saddlers.

Another layman, Ōwake, has already been mentioned. He also is named in the Bidatsu chronicles.[1] He is supposed to have represented the Japanese emperor as an emissary at the court of the king of Paekche.[2] In his own house or monastery he lodged all the monks, nuns and other experts whom he brought from Korea. It is not known whether Ōwake was himself an immigrant. It is, however, probable, that, as the Japanese representative in Korea, he must have been in frequent contact with the immigrants. In any case, he was no Aya or Hata.

The *omi* of Kafuka and the *muraji* of Saeki, who in 584 imported a Maitreya image and a Buddha image from Korea, were merely envoys. They had no religious ties with the images which they carried as, according to the chronicles, they handed them on to Soga *no* Umako.[3] It appears in the chronicles of a year later that Saeki, in the service of the Mononobe, had to imprison the nuns. Hence they were not Buddhists.

Further, we can only localise the lay Buddhism of that period by reference to the descent of the ex-monk Ebin of Koguryŏ and the nuns. It is said of this Ebin that he came from Harima. Possibly there was also a small settlement of Buddhists there. Besides Shima, Shiba Tattō's daughter, there were two other nuns who followed her into the convent. They were the wife of the Aya, Yayabo, who was called Toyome (= flowering daughter) and Sshime (lit.: the stone = childless woman), who was the wife of the *Nishikori* (= brocade weaver) Tsuoga. Toyome cannot be localised as her husband is mentioned only in connection with her entry in the Bidatsu thirteen chronicle. This is not the case with Sshime. According to the *Nihonshoki* the brocade weavers had come to Japan together with the saddlers.[4] It is almost certain that they lived in the Ōmi area in the Shiga district to the west of the Biwa lake. This area lay approximately fifty miles to the north of Takaichi.

All these details make it possible for us to map the expansion of

---

[1] See p. 291.

[2] See footnote 5 on p. 291.

[3] Cf p. 248

[4] Cf. Chapter IV, footnote o on p. 256.

Buddhism during the first sixty years after its arrival in the Takaichi district in 522. Some of these data are recorded on the map on p. 470.

In view of the names of all of these laymen, Buddhism had remained during all of that time the Buddhism of the immigrants. This was owing to its remaining too strongly tied to the major dwelling areas of the virulently rival *shizoku*. Hence Buddhist propaganda outside these places must have been impossible. Buddhism only reached all of those places accompanying the immigrants as they arrived from Korea. Nothing more. Therefore the initiative for the origination of this immigrants' Buddhism was in the hands of the Paekche king Sŏng, by means of the immigrants living in Japan. By sending images, monks and nuns he strengthened and ensured the Buddhist bridgeheads in Japan. Hence the Buddhism which was also to be met with in districts other than Yamato, such as Naniwa, Harima and Shiga, did not owe its origin so much to the missionary activities of Shiba Tattō. These conversions continued to be limited to the Takaichi area only. Therefore he was perhaps, chronologically, Japan's first Buddhist, but not the actual founder. Not all trends of Buddhism of the sixth century converged in him. These trends merely indicate the home districts of the Korean immigrants in Korea itself. There, at the most, they converged in the person of King Sŏng of Paekche. These immediate foreign links between the immigrants and their ruler in Korea gave the Japanese the feeling that they were encountering a religion of the neighbouring country.[1] None of them even considered a general religion. For them there was only one, which served the Paekche concerns.

For that reason it was possible in the *Fusō ryakki* [2] to call the Buddha image of Shiba Tattō a Chinese deity. For the same reason the Mononobe and Nakatomi reaction in the Kimmei thirteen dialogue [3] was aimed against the 'foreign' gods. Emperor Bidatsu's command to Soga in 584: [4] "We decree that in accordance with the soothsayer's oracle, the god of your father shall be worshipped" was a product of the same fear of foreign gods. To all of the Japanese, including the emperor, Buddhism was little other than a

---

[1] Cf. Chapter IV, p. 244.

[2] Cf. p. 247.

[3] Cf. pp. 243, 244.

[4] Cf. p. 324.

Korean *ujigami* belief. Hence they could not easily accept this Paekche offshoot. Moreover, until the conversion of the Soga, Buddhism itself was not even directed towards the Japanese people. It was merely considered to be the personal religion of the immigrant communities. Moreover, it lived there in introversion, without the inclination to come forth dynamically.

This was all entirely different in the conversion of the Soga, however, as in them, for the first time, the encounter between Buddhism and Japanese mentality became a fact.

The actual conversion of the first Soga

Two figures are mentioned in particular in the *Nihonshoki* who, as the first Japanese, 'turned' towards Buddhism. Moreover, the analysis of the specific nature of this conversion offers the best opportunity for gaining some insight into Japan's oldest Buddhism.

On the whole, only few Japanese are known of in the sixth century whose conversions are recorded. The most famous amongst them was undoubtedly the Japanese 'Father of the Fatherland', Shōtoku Taishi. The history of his conversion, however, has been so warped and exaggerated by later myth constructions about his person, that it can scarcely be counted as an unveiling of the religious mentality of his era. In the following chapter we shall try to extract his real significance to the Buddhism of that time from the mists of later myths.

Less 'burdened' by later historical appendages are the histories of conversion of the two Soga leaders, Soga Iname and Umako. Their acceptance of Buddhism meant, moreover, the transition of the entire Soga *shizoku*, of which they were *uji no kami*. This also brought Buddhism, via them, into the imperial house. Imperial figures such as Yōmei, Suiko and Shōtoku Taishi owed their own Buddhist convictions to this Soga initiative.

1 *Soga* no *Iname*

The older of the two was Soga (*no*) Iname. In Japan's oldest sources not too many personal details are known of him. In the *Kojiki* [1] he is mentioned only as the father of Kitashi *hime*. According to the *Nihonshoki* he had great influence at the imperial court.

[1] *Kojiki*, 3rd *maki;* Kuroita Katsumi, Maruyama Jirō, *Kokushitaikei Kojiki*, p. 147: "Furthermore, he was married to Kitashi *hime*, the daughter of Soga *no* Iname *no sukune*".

Nevertheless there is no mention anywhere of his birth or age. As *ō-omi* he served under Emperor Senka (536-540) together with his rivals the Mononobe Sokao and the Ōtomo Kanamura.[1] He also served under Kimmei (531-571) [2] with the two *ōmuraji*, the Mononobe Okoshi and the Nakatomi Kamako. He died in the thirty-first year of Kimmei (562). He was the first Japanese whose positive attitude towards Buddhism became apparent when its introduction was decreed in 538.

This fact of his priority is apparent on closer consideration of the Kimmei thirteen text. Namely, when the Buddha image with the flags and the dubious letter from Sŏng were offered to Emperor Senka, Iname spoke as follows: [3] "All countries of the West, each one, worship him (= Buddha). Should Yamato with its purple autumn there alone resist this?" This inducement to belief in Buddhism, extended by Iname to the emperor, aggravated the leaders of the other *shizoku* into a revolt which they motivated as follows: "Those who govern our land always made the worshipping of the 180 gods of heaven and earth, of provinces and houses, in spring, summer, autumn and winter, their task. If at this point we follow another way and begin worshipping the deities of the neighbouring countries, then we must fear the revenge of our national gods." For the emperor, this argument by the Soga's opponents was adequately decisive for him to refuse Buddhism and pass the invitation on to the Soga. As we have seen, he did this in the following words: 'It is right to give the statue to the one who has asked, Iname *no sukune*. Let it be worshipped by him as an experiment.' Thereupon the *ō-omi* knelt down and received it with delight. He gave it a place in his dwelling in Owarida. For the emperor this was a deft political manoeuvre, which did not make trouble for him among the other leaders of the *shizoku*. On the other hand, this gesture to Soga gained him credit amongst the important group of immigrants, on whom he too depended. Indeed, among

---

[1] Cf. Chapter IV, footnote on p. 262.

[2] Cf. *Nihonshoki*, 19th *maki*, year before the ascension of the throne, 12th month, 5th day; Kuroita Katsumi, Maruyama Jirō, *Kokushitaikei Nihonshoki*, part 2, p. 50: "The *ōmuraji* of the Ōtomo Kanamura and the *ōmuraji* of the Mononobe Okoshi became *ōmuraji*; the *ō-omi* of the Soga Iname became *ō-omi*. As had been the case previously." Cf. W. G. Aston, op. cit., pp. 37, 38.

[3] For the context see Chapter IV, pp. 243, 244.

them there were various Buddhists for whom Soga functioned as a mouthpiece. Refusing this image would have been a naked insult to those immigrants of the Soga's territory. By giving the Soga this command he left it to them.

An indication of the fact that here we are dealing with a political move can be found in the letter which accompanied the image. It has already been noted that this letter was inserted later. In the *Nihonshoki*, however, yet another letter from King Sŏng is mentioned, which was written on the occasion of the erection of a Buddha image in Korea.[1] This mentions the motives for erecting it. One of them concerned the power of the Japanese emperor. Also the actual letter by King Sŏng to the Japanese emperor in 538 on the occasion of the presentation of the Buddha image must have been more or less similar to this, all the more so as it is apparent from the date problem surrounding this letter that it was written not much later than the first letter, that concerning the Buddha image in Korea. Neither the Soga nor the emperor could have comprehended a term such as *mokṣa* for all people. However, Sŏng's prayer for the supreme power of the emperor in this letter must have convinced both the emperor and the Soga of the woundrous power which emanated from this image. This resulted in their declaring for it in a political formula.

Therefore political motives also played a part in the conversion of Iname, just as they did in Sŏng's gesture. Sŏng was concerned in getting Japanese aid and freedom of action in Korea, whatever the cost. The 'conversion' of Iname to Buddhism was also not free from similar motives. His conversion also had little to do with the acceptance of Buddhism as a way to enlightenment or the *bodhi*, as an awareness of the four noble truths, or the possibility of liberating oneself from the doom of rebirth. All this was excluded. No Japanese such as a Soga nor a Korean such as Sŏng was very upset by the idea of the necessity of rebirth. Their ideological relationship to everything alive in the north-east corner of Asia did not lead to such a consideration of life and death. This is illustrated by the *Nihonshoki* where, indeed, it is posited that after death one was not reborn but merely went to a 'dark place', as is apparent from the previously quoted text.[2]

---

[1] See p. 275.
[2] See p. 273.

The issue at stake for the Soga and the Mononobe was not the Way which Buddha preached but the acceptance or refusal of an image. Indeed, nowhere is it apparent from the *Nihonshoki* context that the Soga, the leaders of the *shizoku* or the emperor considered this image a pointer towards Buddha's doctrine or as a symbol of it. Here they were concerned only with a foreign deity, a Korean god. For reticent conservatives such as the Mononobe the acceptance of this deity meant a rebuff to their own nationalism. For the 'available' Soga the acceptance of it counted as an enlargement and strengthening of their own arsenal of spiritual powers. Indeed, Sŏng's letter named this image a guarantee of the emperor's might. As a nation Japan had found itself in the fact that the emperor, as the *uji no kami* of all *uji no kami*, became the one in whom all the *ujigami* of the various *shizoku* met each other as in one symbol. Now by taking over the *ujigami* of Paekche he could also be accounted the true *uji no kami* of Paekche. With this—interpreted by the Japanese as—Paekche concession, this country could get what it willed from Japan, even territorial extensions. Thus it is also understandable that these texts were so closely linked with what was happening in Korea.[1]

From this it appears that this image enlarged the spiritual reserves of the Soga group over and above those of the Mononobe. The Soga controlled not only the power of all the *ujigami* but also that which is described in the *Nihonshoki* as the Korean 'Buddha deity'[2]. The persecution which arose against this Buddha image lay therefore at a level of a struggle between Japan's gods against a foreign god, not—one need only refer to Kimmei thirteen [3]—against a new religion or its propagators. Otherwise the Soga would have been murdered and no one would have stopped at the burning of the image. It was a struggle for the strongest: the *ujigami* or the Buddha deity.

What Soga Iname saw in Buddhism is illustrated by his words to the Korean prince Kei (or Kor.: Hye) of the year 557. This prince had come to Japan in order to report King Sŏng's murder. Previously the same Kei had served as an envoy from Sŏng for the introduction of Buddhism in Japan. It is obvious that Iname, on

[1] See also what we said on this matter on p. 232 of Chapter IV.

[2] For this *Nihonshoki* formulation used by a soothsayer of Soga, see p. 324 and footnote 1 of this page.

[3] Cf. pp. 243, 244.

hearing of the death of Sŏng, should praise him particularly for his services to Japanese Buddhism. He did not, however, do so. Rather, he depicted him as a Chinese sage. Namely, this Soga called him someone "who had an admirable knowledge of the ways of heaven and the principles of the earth" and went "to rest in a dark place".[1]

The image that the Soga here reveals of Sŏng is not that of a Buddhist Sŏng (as he is known to history) but far rather his own projection of Sŏng, an image of this ruler derived from the Soga himself. Firstly, he was depicted according to the meaning of his name. Sŏng, written 聖, should be translated into Japanese by *hijiri*.[2] A *hijiri*, sometimes also written 日知り, is someone who knows the sun. Only he, as 'knower' of the sun, is capable of laying down the sun calendar. In a broader sense he was also someone who, just as the sun communicates its light, communicates knowledge to others: the sage. Iname's expression of his admirable knowledge of heaven (= the sun) and earth was therefore also an explanation of Sŏng's name. This name is actually symbolic of the Korean sun worship which, made concrete in the calendars, reached Japan at that time via the Korean immigrants.[3] In the sixth year of Bidatsu even a *be* was instituted which was given the special task of sun worship and probably also of the laying down and calculation of the calendar.[4] It need not be discussed that members of this *be*,

---

[1] See pp. 272, 273.

[2] This word is very closely connected with the sun and the sun cult. A *hijiri* was originally a sun priest, who determined and appointed the years, months and days. The fact that in Japan and China for instance the years are counted according to the reigns of the emperors goes back to the activities of these *hijiri*. Naturally he gradually came to be seen in the same perspective as the sun, with which he was so closely linked. Thus the *hijiri* was looked upon as the one, who, just as the sun, let the light of his knowledge shine over others: the sage. It is interesting that particularly diligent monks of the sun Buddha Amida were called Amida-*hijiri*, 阿彌陀聖, in Japan: a monk who, by multiple invocations of Amida, wished to bring the people to convert to Amida. Cf. Udō Masamoto, "Kodai-Nihon no Taiyō-shinkō to sono bungaku-hyōgen", *K.G.Z.*, vol. 59 (1958), nos. 10 and 11, Oct., Nov., pp. 129-131; Inoue Tetsujirō e.a., op. cit., p. 20, col. I.

[3] For instance, that happened during the fourteenth and fifteenth year of Kimmei (554, 555), see footnote 1 on p. 292. Udō Masamoto, op. cit., p. 131, writes of this: "It is clear that the *hijiri* of solar calendars was obtained from the immigrants of Chinese or Korean origin."

[4] Cf. *Nihonshoki*, 20th *maki*, Bidatsu, 6th year, 2nd month, 1st day;

as was the case in so many new *be*,[1] were either immigrants or people closely connected with them. Thus this expression of Soga Iname was confirmation of the fact that the Korean sun worship also had a place beside the *ujigami* belief of that time.

Also the words: "He has gone to rest in a dark place" betray Iname's projection of himself into the person of Sŏng. In this he bore witness to his own ancestor worship and his opinion of existence after death: in a dark place! It is not hard to recognise Chinese or Korean thought processes in this remark. With these words he more or less displayed the mentality which confronted Buddhism of the sixth century. Nevertheless, here one must also take into account the opinions of the compilers and editors of the *Nihonshoki*, who also could have put any words whatever into his mouth. This ancestor and soul belief was so important at that time—according to Takatori Masao—that *shizoku* society was based on it. As a result this belief began to rule the entire society and allowed no further free development to the idea of the deity. The basis of this belief was the 'divine human', as embodied in the head of the old tribe and his successors.[2] The Soga's remarks about the dead Sŏng were both rather Chinese than Buddhist. Here one might even doubt whether Sŏng was a Buddhist at all.

Why did Iname, supposedly himself a Buddhist sympathiser, devote no word to Sŏng's contributions to Paekche and Japanese Buddhism? Various explanations for this are possible. One might say that later *Nihonshoki* compilers did not consider it worthwhile to make much of Sŏng's Buddhism. We believe that the explanation of this problem lies in the nature of Iname's Buddhism. Namely, had Iname succeeded in indicating Sŏng's contributions to Buddhism in specific Buddhist categories, then it would have been impossible for a later interpolator to twist his words into the aforementioned sense. This would have been quite different if one accepts that Iname simply lacked these elementary Buddhist concepts. To him Buddhism was merely the image of the Buddha god. His conversion consisted of accepting this image as a new *ujigami*. Therefore

---

Kuroita Katsumi, Maruyama Jirō, op. cit., part 2, p. 107: "Sixth year, 2nd month, 1st day. According to an imperial command, a *be* of the *hi no matsuri*, 日祀部, (sun worship) and of the Kisaichi, 私部, were instituted." Cf. W. G. Aston, op. cit., p. 95.

[1] Cf. pp. 232 ff.

[2] Cf. Takatori Masao, op. cit., p. 55.

his *ujigami* belief was not shaken by this conversion. We have even seen in the foregoing lines that he could project this on to Sŏng.

The proof of this can be found in the continuation of his address to Prince Kei. Iname went even further in this: [1]

"Long ago, under the reign of Emperor Ōhatsuse (Yūryaku) your land was threatened by Koguryŏ. Even more than for a pile of eggs, it was very dangerous then. Then the emperor ordered the priests of the gods of the heavens and earth to gain, with all due respect, the council of the heaven and earth gods. The priests received a divine revelation and answered: If you humbly request the god and founder of the country, then you will rescue your lord, who stands on the point of destruction . . . Therefore the god was beseeched for liberation hereafter . . . Now the god who, in the beginning, constructed your country, was the god who, at the time of the division of heaven and earth, when trees and plants still spoke, descended from heaven and created our country. Recently I have heard that your country has deserted him and does not honour him. If, however, you now repent anew of your faults in the past, build a temple for the god and sacrifice to this divine spirit and worship him, then your land will return to prosperity. This you must not forget here!"

With these words, which we have already encountered in the previous chapter in a different connection, Iname bounced back the Korean Buddhist initiative of three years previously with a Japanese *ujigami* parcel (which was, moreover, mostly derived from Korea!). Could he have taken such steps if he had renounced this *ujigami* belief by accepting the Buddha image three years previously? Thus, if Iname's conversion is mentioned, then it consisted only of the addition of the Buddha image as *ujigami* to the other *ujigami*. His attitude towards Buddha did not differ greatly from that of his contemporaries, who called Shiba Tattō's image a Chinese deity.[2]

Towards this conversion, which was consequently rather an extension of his *ujigami* belief than the acceptance of an entirely new doctrine, the immigrants fulfilled a very specific task, as only they could add depth to his belief. Just as is the case with his son, we do not know whether Iname, for instance, maintained relations

[1] See Chapter IV, pp. 273, 274.
[2] Cf. p. 247.

with Shiba Tattō at that time. This would certainly not have been easy as divergences of language and mentality would not have facilitated an encounter between the two. Even if one supposes that there was some contact, then this could not easily have led to a general change of outlook. Indeed, it is nowhere apparent that Buddhism was very deep-seated even amongst these immigrants. Therefore in Iname's ideas a kind of amalgamation must have taken place of this Buddha image with the existing *ujigami*. Despite merely external discrepancies, the inherent function of the image as a pointer towards the *bodhi* was not yet recognised. It remained no more than a new *ujigami* in which the abstract and impersonal powers of the *ujigami* had been reduced to more human proportions in the human shape of the image.

This mentality produced Iname's admonition to remain faithful to the *ujigami*. Therefore it did not as yet imply any renunciation of Buddhism. It merely shows that he had not yet recognised the real function of the image given to him. There can have been no question of his reading the *sūtras*, as they were in Chinese, unintelligible to him. Thus Iname's entire innovation consisted of little else than an open mind towards Buddhism which was still wholly rooted in the Japanese *ujigami* belief.

He handed on this open-mindedness to his descendents. However limited his knowledge of Buddhism may have been, he certainly gave his children and grandchildren, later the three emperors, something of his toleration with regard to the religions of the non-Japanese, together with his *ujigami* belief. His 'Buddhism' was more an open mind to foreign influences than Buddhism itself. This was an adequate basis for bearing in mind, primarily, the communal basis of Buddhism and *ujigami* belief even in later differentiations of these.

However scanty, nevertheless this Buddhism of Iname was important as he could authoritatively impose this basic attitude on his following. He owed this to his authority as *uji no kami* of the Soga *shizoku*; indeed it was he who not only embodied the religious mentality of the Soga group, but could also impose it on all members of that group. Those who were later to assume the emperorship but, as yet, were still a part of the *shizoku*, also belonged to this category. The Buddhism which his grandson Tachibana, born in 519 and later known as Emperor Yōmei (585-588), professed was therefore also probably more similar to that of Iname than that of

Yōmei's sister, not born until 554, the later Empress Suiko. She was indeed but eight years old when, in 562, Iname died. Tachibana, however, already experienced the 'conversion' of his grandfather when he was nineteen.

This conversion of Iname spread even further, to all the subjects and serfs of the Soga *shizoku*. That followed unavoidably from the structure of *shizoku* society of that time. Therefore the temple which Iname built was not only a private sanctuary, but was destined equally for the use of all the other members of the *shizoku*. Not only for the Mononobe or the Nakatomi, but also for the Soga, with their scant knowledge of Buddhism, it was accounted the place where the foreign deity dwelt. Therefore all the Soga subjects were closely concerned in the temples of Mukuhara, Owarida or Ishikawa. This makes the aggravation of the Mononobe comprehensible: these temples did indeed attract an important part of Japanese society to them. Additionally, it was equally unbearable to the Mononobe that Iname, as *uji no kami*, felt himself stronger than the Nakatomi or the Mononobe owing to this god, while they had to manage without this god. Not only Iname, but many others after him have not seen much more in such Buddha images than 'stone' or 'wooden' gods. This has been confirmed in so many words in the *Fudoki* of Harima which mentions a "stone divine image, which resembles Buddha".[1]

---

[1] Cf. *Fudoki*, Takeda Iukichi, *Fudoki*, p. 200: "The reason why Kamishima, 神島, Itoshima, 伊刀島, were called god's island is to be found in the fact that on the west side of the island there is a stone image of a god which resembles Buddha. Hence that name was given. In the visage of this god there was a five-coloured gem and tears which fell on his breast. These too were five-coloured. The reason of his tears lay in the fact that in the time of Emperor Honda, 品田, (= Ōjin) a strange kind of people from Silla had come to him. When they saw the miraculousness of this divinity and that it had caused this uncommon gem, they hollowed out his visage and put out one eye. Therefore the divinity wept. He grew dreadfully angry, raised a tempest and destroyed the ship of these people. The ship sank at the level of the southern shore of Takashima. They all met their deaths there and were buried on this shore. This was called the Kara shore hereafter."

Other texts of the *Fudoki* also show how little Buddhism as genuine Buddhism reached the circles of the commonalty, from which the *Fudoki*, in contrast to other old Japanese sources, originated. The *Fudoki* of Shima, 志摩, the west point of the present-day Mie prefecture (now called Shimagun) gives a story about the legendary monk Gyōgi, 行基, (670-749), Hossō monk of the temple Yakushiji. This story also does not give us a less syncretic

All of this shows that originally Buddhism was considered by the Japanese population and its Soga sympathisers as a new form of *ujigami* belief. This is comparable to a somewhat similar development in Japan some twelve hundred years later. At that time many Japanese—after their conversion to Christianity—began to see Western Shintō gods in Christ and Mary. To many Mary became a Portuguese replica of Kannon, 觀音, the East Asian goddess of compassion who, in her turn, was a distorted replica of the Indian Bodhisattva Avalokiteśvara.[1] In the sixth century Buddhism could present itself as Buddhism just as little as Christianity could do this as Christianity because the stock terminology and the precisely paralleling and wholly corresponding categories were simply not available for this. The Chinese, and corrupted Sanskrit, terms were just as foreign to the Japanese with their *ujigami* belief as the Latin terms in which Francis Xavier wrapped up and presented the Christian truths. Those who were converted to both religions did this as something new, which came into existence at the same time as their 'conversion' and which resorted for 90% to the old *ujigami* belief, as originally the convert continued to think in terms borrowed from this.

In this too the Japanese remained himself. Hence his conversion could only gain more access as the new belief was presented to him in more adequate terms of his own religious mentality. This was due to his conversion being far more an acceptance of something new, not as something different but rather as something which already belonged to him: it was a new and fresh return of what

---

impression: "In the middle of the Shintō temple area, at the place where the *matsuri* of the gods were celebrated, there is an ancient oak tree. This oak tree has outgrown all the trees of the mountains of the islands Kitsu, 吉津, and Toku, 土貢. In the *Fudoki* of the island Kitsu it is said that long ago the Brahman and monk of Southern India, the *Bodhisattva* Gyōgi planted the three oak trees and that thus the garden of the Daijingū, 大神宮, (the great Shintō temple) came about. The 17th day of the twelfth month of the ninth year of Tempyō (737) its feast was celebrated." Cf. Takeda Iukichi, op. cit., p. 363.

All other passages in the *Fudoki* concerning Buddhism are not more than casual explanations of names. It is clearly apparent however, from these two passages how closely Buddhism and *ujigami* belief were interwoven.

[1] Cf. the studies on this subject by Dr. Tagita Kōya, *Shōwajidai no senpuku Kirishitan* (The crypto-Kirishitan (=Christianity) of our time), Tōkyō 1958; further his publication "Nōtoshin to sono Yurai", (Nōtoshin and his origin), *Shūkyō Kenkyū*, no. 135, (date unknown), pp. 27-108.

was once his own. Thus the conversion of Iname and his family contained in an equal degree the birth of a totally new religion. Basically it was rooted in the old *ujigami* belief which, moreover, lent it its authority. This simultaneously exposed it to the new doctrine of Buddhism, however inadequately it presented itself. A radical conversion to Buddhism demanded a clean break with the old *ujigami* belief. Now this scarcely occurred during the first centuries of Japanese lay Buddhism.

What then was the attitude of these 'Iname' Buddhists towards the religion of the Korean immigrants? The latter indeed, with its continuity of the age-old Paekche Buddhism and the ancient Chinese traditions, lay far closer to the original purpose of Buddha. This was due to this continuity being maintained by the monks from Paekche itself. This Korean Buddhism was certainly not visualised without specific Korean categories. In this immigrants' Buddhism the Chinese and Korean characteristics had also been taken into account. In the following chapter we shall return to this. Compared to Japanese Buddhism of that time it contained more Buddhism and less *ujigami* distortion. Nevertheless both—however faintly—contained elements in common. Originally that consisted only of an openness which drove them towards each other, from which a mutual expansion of each other's thought material resulted.

The extent of this mutual fertilisation and enriching is to be deduced from the persecution which broke shortly after the conversion of Soga Iname between the years 538 and 554. On that occasion the divine image and the Mukuhara temple were burnt. More important than these external facts is the change in mentality which accompanied such a persecution.

A religious persecution is always the logical consequence of a clash between different mentalities. The stronger party persecutes, the weaker is persecuted. Despite this external difference in strength, both are equally determined not to align with each other's opinions. Simultaneously, each of the two groups clings convulsively to its 'being different' to the opponent. This can be so strong that, under pressure of a stronger opponent, even old and well-established antitheses grow indeterminate, at least for the time being.

Examples of this are plentifully known in our environment: the antithesis between Roman Catholic and Protestant forced the losing Catholics in the Netherlands a hundred years ago to unreal and bombastic dithyrambics on the 19th century 'holy' Rome. The power of the Nazis, however, forced them to unite again on one front. Recent years, however, produced too strict measures from Rome's conservative Curia, which again awakened in the Dutch consciousness an awareness of the national Dutch character of their Catholicism. This made them more inclined towards Protestantism. This non-acceptance of the 'being different' of the opponent, and even of co-religionists, led on the one hand to a 'purification' of one's own religious convictions, but also to a greater unity. In the other person only the foreign element was recognised: a kind of inhuman caricature of his religious conviction. Thus in Christianity purity, but also intolerance towards its opponents, resulted from the Roman persecutions. This intolerance was also to remain alive in confrontations with other forms of paganism and with 'heretical' Christianity. In these to and fro movements, as a result of persecutions and opposition, Christianity could not avoid that it was itself made into a caricature of itself by its opponents as well as something which it was not originally. This happened often just by a refusal to do the same as its opponents. The Counter Reformation and the Reformation were thus suspended directly opposite each other and were maintained for centuries by the fact that both parties wished to be the denial of each other. This was apparent not only in an institution such as the Inquisition, but also in the new formulations of the ecclesiastical doctrine which, as expressions of frozen narrowness, were no longer to be called Christian. All of this provides adequate proof for the theory that persecutions in the broadest sense of the word not only work purgatively but may also frequently radically mutilate and change the original concept of a religion. These mutilations can be neutralised only by quiet and phenomenological consideration of everything positive which has been forced out or changed into the opponents' camp owing to age-old antitheses.

There is yet another aspect which has a part in every persecution, namely that its success becomes all the greater according to the degree in which it encompasses the totality of the mentality of those persecuted. The more phenomenological its purpose, the deeper and more basic its knowledge of the opponents' being 'different', and the adaptation of the method of persecution to this, the greater will be the success of the persecution as the extermination of an unfavourably viewed mentality. In other words: according to the success of the 'persecutors' in more than bodily harm, but in changing the psychic and mental constitution of the 'persecuted', their conversion will also be guaranteed. The scope of the mentality one desires to change is in this of great importance: is an entire system concerned here, or merely a superficial datum such as belief in an image? The greater the scope of someone's religious mentality, the harder it will be to bring about a change in it. The history of Christianity is available to confirm all these laws.

These laws will be encountered continuously, both within and outside Christianity, as they are unavoidable data in every human situation. One need only think of the Islamic projection of the 'Christian dog', on which it whetted its fanaticism; a projection which the crusaders proved in many respects. Similar tendencies were also at work in the very oldest persecutions of Japanese Buddhism.

The persecution which the Kimmei chronicles describe could have forced Iname and his following to grasp more firmly what they considered to be Buddhism. This persecution made it considerably easier for them to repudiate those elements within their own mentality which they had in common with their opponents. Here, however, one must ask oneself what such a persecution achieved in Iname, with his primitive ideas about Buddhism. The result of the original persecution can be understood only in the face of his Buddhism. As we have seen, it had a place somewhere amongst his *ujigami* belief. The persecution which he underwent did not separate it from this. With the destruction of the Buddha image, Iname's belief in its power was also lost. Destruction of the image and the temple, moreover, meant to him the end of Buddhism. These two had not yet achieved the function of signpost to Buddha's teaching in his mentality. His Buddhism was still too little interiorised to provoke a determined inner resistance. The new doctrine had differed too little in him from his *ujigami* belief to separate from it as a result of this persecution.

Buddhism itself too could not be separated as such from this *ujigami* belief. The openness, which until now it had shown in China and Korea with regard to religions extant there, did not demand a radical purge of the *ujigami* belief as a condition for conversion. The persecution of Japan's first Buddhists such as Iname did not therefore mean a radical change of mentality from *ujigami* belief to exclusive Buddhism. It merely led to a disillusionment with the Sŏng image. With this the introduction of Buddhism via the court came to nothing. Its presentation had been too meagre and the persecution had made it into a bitter disillusion. Indeed, the image had not made its alleged power come true.

2 *Soga* no *Umako*

The contact Shiba Tattō had with Iname's son, Umako, led to a far more lasting success. Very little is known of the birth or age of Soga Umako. With his appointment as *ō-omi* in the first year of Bidatsu in 572 [1] he entered into the rights and responsibilities of his father. At that time he was already the *uji no kami* of the Soga *shizoku*. Despite his disillusionment with the Buddha image, his father is likely to have given him his sympathy for Buddhism. Iname's Buddhism, which did not exceed the cadre of his *ujigami* belief, therefore certainly prepared the conversion of his son Umako. He had not, however, been converted to Buddhism. This conversion is first recorded in Bidatsu thirteen (= 584). As this chronicle—as we have seen—offers a more historical retrospect, his conversion will have taken place considerably before 584, but it cannot be dated with any certainty.

Now if one compares the history of his conversion to that of his father, some differences can be noted. Soga Iname acted on his own initiative when he accepted the Buddha image and built a temple for it. In the case of Umako it was the immigrants Shiba Tattō and Ikebe *no atae* Hida who were the two figures who passed on Buddhism to Umako, albeit in the form of a relic. Hence here there is explicit mention of the encounter between immigrants' Buddhism and the Soga. This implicitly admits that Soga Buddhism was actually the continuation of that of the immigrants.

Both chronicles also mention a persecution. In the Kimmei chronicle this entailed the destruction of everything which counted as Buddhism. It lay more on the material plane: the destruction of an image and a temple. At that time it did not yet have any penetrating philosophical antitheses. This was entirely different in the persecution of the Bidatsu chronicle: here not an image, but an ideology was concerned. The persecution was arranged as a

[1] Cf. *Nihonshoki*, 20th *maki*, Bidatsu, 1st year, 4th month; Kuroita Katsumi, Maruyama Jirō, op. cit., part 2, p. 101: "(That month) . . . He made the *ōmuraji* Mononobe *no* Yuke *no* Moriya an *ōmuraji*, as he had been before. The Soga *no* Umako *no sukune* became *ō-omi*." Cf. W. G. Aston, op. cit., p. 90.

chastisement of ideas and therefore had entirely different consequences to those of the Kimmei chronicle. This more recent persecution also resulted from the same cause, an incurable epidemic. From this it becomes apparent, however, that Buddhism had meanwhile gained a wholly different content. A relic, a pagoda, a Maitreya image and nuns are mentioned. With this Buddhism was already dependent upon far more points than the image Buddhism of Iname. Thereby it could also differentiate more strongly from the old *ujigami* belief. In the second persecution of the Mononobe it had developed something inherent on which it could fall back. Now the Mononobe resistance brought—in contrast to that under Iname—Buddhism to an even more determined self-affirmation, owing to which it began to distinguish itself more and more from the old *ujigami* belief. The history of Soga Umako's conversion is a symbolic confirmation of this.

The text which relates this has preserved the opinions of his contemporaries for us, concerning what they now actually saw in Buddhism. His conversion was not, just as little as was Iname's, achieved under Buddha's tree, the bodhidendron, as the result of lengthy contemplation of human existence. It was just as little the fruit of consideration of the Four Noble Truths with the eightfold path. From this point of view, Soga Umako, had not, by his conversion, become a Buddhist who put liberation from this earthly wheel of life above all else. His conversion had a different beginning, which we noted in the previous chapter.[1] It was the result of a trial of strength which showed that Buddha's relic could withstand the severest physical force of an iron hammer and could therefore take up the cudgels against the *ujigami*. The *ujigami*, however, in contrast to the persecution of the Kimmei chronicles, are not mentioned at all here. However mythical the entire story of his conversion may be, it did not consist, as did his father's, of a blind acceptance of Buddhism. The disillusionment which followed the first persecution had not passed him over. Nevertheless, according to the text, his belief in Buddhism was not wholly dead. Because, even before his conversion, he was very set on the two images which the *omi* of Kafuka and the *muraji* of Saeki had brought to Japan coming into his possession.

For him the relic had to justify itself, not so much as a relic but

---

[1] See Chapter IV, pp. 248, 249.

as a centre of power, before he would concede. This was owing to his conversion being at the same level as that of his father, who considered only the *strength* of the deity as decisive. The relic convinced him that the power of Buddhism symbolised by it was greater than that of his own *ujigami*. Whether mythical or not, this story served to illustrate the Buddhist preponderance at the level of the *ujigami* belief. "Therefore" it is said in the text "Umako *no sukune*, Ikebe *no* Hida and Shiba Tattō believed deeply in Buddhism and experienced it without shortcomings." [1]

In the foregoing text *shin*, 信, is mentioned, = believe. The Japanese reading in *furigana* of this *shin* is: *tamachi-ukete*. This means preserve and receive. This cannot be translated by *kaeshin*, 回心, conversion or change of mentality. Therefore the conversion of Soga Umako did not mean the termination of his *ujigami* belief or of the *ujigami* itself and the spiritual preponderance which he possessed in his function of *uji no kami*. For him it was important just because of that preponderance to remain, also from the spiritual point of view, the *uji no kami* of his *shizoku*. Hence his conversion contained an hierarchical shift within the limits of the *ujigami* belief itself. Everything connected with Buddhism was involved with this belief, but also rose higher in value with regard to the other *ujigami*. His Buddhism, like his father's, was still defined fairly extensively by the image. This is why Soga Umako took care that the two images which the *omi* of Kafuka and the *muraji* of Saeki brought from Paekche to Japan came into his possession.[2]

One of these two images was a Maitreya image. For this specifically he built a temple, to the east of his own house. Probably the Maitreya cult points the way to the specific nature of Soga Umako's Buddhism and, moreover, to that of the sixth century. Did he put this image close to his home because he himself expected a lot from it? Or had it become a kind of *ujigami* deity to him, a protective god more efficient than the old *ujigami*? We do not know. In any case, he certainly did not put aside the old *ujigami* as otherwise it remains inexplicable how his niece and nephew, Suiko and Yōmei, and his grandson Umayado (Shōtoku Taishi) continued to honour this *ujigami* belief despite a far deeper knowledge of Buddhism. Hence we must accept both in their case and in

---

[1] Cf. p. 249.
[2] Cf. p. 248.

Soga Umako's that in their 'conversion' rather a kind of co-existence came about between Buddhism and the *ujigami* belief. In this great care will have to be taken with the use of words which might indicate a widely set up system such as Buddhism and Shintō, as the systematics of both *were entirely absent* in these 'converts'.

Soga Umako knew only the Buddhism which was brought to him. This occurred in a shape which was very unsuitable because the basic Japanese formulation for various Buddhist terms, which might have excluded every misunderstanding, was simply not available. Umako and many others after him had the same kind of *ujigami* belief as Iname, which offered concepts with which they had to accept Buddhism. These were aimed mainly at the '*diesseitige*'. This can be explained from the Japanese incapacity even today for abstract speculations concerning metaphysical problems.[1]

The persecution which Umako experienced was aimed, according to the Bidatsu chronicle, far more at the three nuns. It was far more intensive than that against Iname's Buddha image because it touched a much larger area of live Buddhism.

It was no longer aimed merely at an image or a temple, but against those who at that time embodied Buddhism: the three nuns. That in this story there is no mention of the persecution of monks can be explained only if one accepts that at that time there were no monks at all. Hence this persecution raged before the advent of the first Korean monks in Japan. It reached a dead-end as the exertions of the Mononobe were not concentrated on the nucleus of Buddhism which dwelt in the three nuns. Neither did they attempt to twist this into *ujigami* belief, but limited themselves merely to hard external measures. Hence it had the result that benefited the nuns that, more so than ever before, Umako undertook the protection of them and was therefore forced more towards relations with the three nuns and their communities.

As the Mononobe made no effort on their side to seize the Buddhism of Umako and his following at its ideological root, no purge was engendered amongst these very first Buddhists as a result of the persecution of their personally experienced *ujigami* belief and what they saw as Buddhism. Moreover, such a purge was very diffi-

[1] See our remarks on this in "Katholieke Theologie en Oosters Denken" (Catholic Theology and Eastern Thought), *H.M.*, vol. 44 (1965), 2nd issue, pp. 120, 121.

cult particularly in Umako as his function of *uji no kami* of the Soga *shizoku*, his position at court and even his resistance against the Mononobe was largely supported by his *ujigami* belief.

The persecution did, however, sharpen his resistance against the Mononobe and their allies. This was strengthened by the ideological contrasts between the three most prominent *shizoku*. One must not see these as contrasts between on the one hand *ujigami* belief and on the other Buddhism, but between open *ujigami* belief which accepted Buddhism, or rather could accept (of the Soga), an open *ujigami* belief which did not wish to progress with its openness further than, for instance, Confucianism (of the Nakatomi), and a completely closed nationalistic and to foreigners inaccessible *ujigami* belief (of the Mononobe). At this level not only personal differences between one *ō-omi* and two *ōmuraji* were concerned but between the *shizoku* themselves of which they were *uji no kami*.

Hence Soga Umako's 'conversion' equally concerned his closest collaborators, family members and his own *shizoku*. The trial of strength with the relic, however unhistorical and mythical it may have been, was the 'primeval occurrence' which was to explain the turning of the mentality of the *shizoku* of Soga towards Buddhism. This brought it into his family. Hence his niece, the later Empress Suiko was afterwards,[1] in the tale of her own conversion history, to mention just the relic which she had received from Shiba Tattō. Whether or not intended, the 'conversion' as belief in the relic's power betrays the nature of Umako's Buddhism which was still a long way away from the path defined by Buddha himself.

Not the persecution, but contact with the groups of Buddhist immigrants such as Shiba Tattō and Ikebe *no atae* Hida gradually changed this still very 'Shintoistic' Buddhism to other and newer forms which more resembled true Buddhism. The nieces and nephews of Umako in particular were to support more 'orthodox' Buddhism under such influences. Nevertheless, one must not presuppose too much from the latter, because at that time—however strange that may seem to us in the West—no orthodox Buddhism was known. East Asian Buddhism formulated itself continuously anew, not, as is the case in Christianity, by new light being continually shed on and by fresh exegeses of the basic event of its origination, but

---

[1] See Chapter IV, p. 251.

by continually adapting to the changing situations. This has been especially apparent in the third chapter.

After Umako's conversion has been described in the foregoing lines, and also the state of his Buddhism with regard to, or rather in, his *ujigami* belief has been established, it still remains to define the specific nature of this Buddhism.

I believe that this is very closely connected with Maitreyanism. It has already been pointed out [1] that all the Buddhist facts described in the *Nihonshoki* under the thirteenth year of Bidatsu actually took place over a period which spread from the beginning of Buddhism in Japan (522) until 585, the thirteenth year of Bidatsu. Individually most of these facts cannot be dated. Nevertheless, as we presupposed before, the entire Bidatsu thirteen chronicle was dated according to the most important fact in it. That was the erection of a *tera* by Umako, east of his house. Therefore this temple was built in 585. It was intended for the Maitreya image which the *omi* of Kafuka had brought from Paekche.[2]

This image is an indication of the fact that the Maitreya cult may have begun in Japan even at that time. This must not be supposed without more ado. It cannot be deduced from the presence of a Maitreya image that the connective Buddhology and eschatology was known down to the last detail. The best proof of this supposition is to be found in Japan's oldest plastic Buddhist arts. The images of that time had so much in common that it was difficult to differentiate the various Buddhas.[3]

In any case the *Nihonshoki* confirms with this datum that the Maitreya cult, started by Tao-an in 385 and propagated by his imperial protector Fu Chien as far as North Korea, had certainly reached Japan in 585 via Paekche. The vast success which this cult enjoyed in Korea makes it highly probable that the image offered to Senka in 538 had more to do with Maitreya than with Śākyamuni. All the more so as the images, as we have seen, were at that time so impersonal that they could represent both Śākyamuni and Maitreya simultaneously. In addition, the presentation of this

---

[1] See Chapter IV, pp. 250, 251.

[2] See Chapter IV, p. 248.

[3] That was the case for instance in the Hōryūji with the image of Amitābha (Amida) in the *kondō* of the West Hall (Saiin) and the images of Bhaiṣajyaguru Vaidūrya (Jap.: Yakushi) and Śākyamuni of the great Golden Hall. See Okabe Nagaaki, op. cit., p. 27.

image recalls the ceremony with which Tao-an surrounded his Maitreya cult: "with a display of streamers and banners".[1] Thus the line of the origin of Korean and Japanese Buddhism points to him who embodied the Maitreya cult in China: Tao-an. By building a temple for Maitreya close to his house Soga Umako made it apparent how much he and his followers approved of the belief in Maitreya, which also to a great extent fitted in with the Messianic and political aspirations of the T'opa emperors. This belief demanded of Soga and his following no great changes as it was nothing other than a Buddhist concession to the Shaman and ancestor beliefs of Central and East Asia, of which Japan was also a part.

It could easily take its place beside the old *ujigami* belief without making too sharp a contrast to it: on the one hand it added glitter to the *uji no kami* with a kind of saviour figure, but, on the other hand, left the ancestor belief and that of the heaven and earth deities intact. This explains the success which awaited Buddhism amongst the emperors and the princes, to whose education Iname's and Umako's conversion had contributed vastly.

c *Third stage: completion of the Soga conversion in the conversion of the emperors*

We have already pointed out that the conversion of the two Soga also had an immediate influence on the imperial house. This happened because various Soga daughters had married Japanese emperors. The new doctrine which had been accepted by the Soga leaders was also imposed on them as subjects of the Soga *uji no kami*. By the institution of the double courts a syncretic process

---

[1] Cf. E. Zürcher, *The Buddhist Conquest of China*, p. 188. H. de Lubac, *Amida*, p. 133, sees the image which Sŏng presented to the Japanese emperor as an image of Amitābha: "Il n'est même pas impossible que le Bouddha doré offert par le Seimei de Kudara, en 552, à l'empereur Kimmei fût un Amida, et non simplement un Sakyamouni." For this opinion de Lubac appeals to A. K. Reischauer, *Studies in Japanese Buddhism*, pp. 80 and 105: "probably an image of the Buddha Amitābha and not of Gautama." Reischauer does not attempt to justify his opinion. Nonetheless here he has overlooked that Maitreyanism, according to the *Nihonshoki*, was not only in Japan (where Amida was first mentioned in 602) but throughout all of East Asia the first step towards Amidism. Furthermore, when considering the oldest Japanese Buddhism as being principally Korean Buddhism, the immense popularity of Maitreyanism in Korea at that time must not be ignored. Concerning this, see p. 216.

had already, as we have seen,[1] been unleashed which initially created the sixth century *ujigami* belief and after this, via the Soga daughters, realised the possibility of a syncretic coalition between Buddhism and *ujigami* belief. In this last phase of syncretism the Soga *shizoku* had the largest share. Towards the end of the sixth century the Soga had linked themselves in many ways to the imperial house by means of marriages thanks to the polygamous system of the imperial marriages. This reached its apex in the imperial figures of Yōmei and Suiko. We have already pointed out that the mother of these two, Kitashi *hime*, was the daughter of Soga Iname and the sister of Umako. Yōmei himself also married two other daughters of Iname. The later crown prince Umayado, better known under the name of Shōtoku Taishi, was descended from one of these marriages. Therefore he was related to the Soga both on his mother's and on his father's side. The first three rulers who succeeded Bidatsu, the Emperors Yōmei and Sushun and Empress Suiko were all brought up at the court of their Soga mother and became acquainted to a greater or lesser degree with Buddhism there. The nature of this Buddhist influence was very closely connected with the entirely specific nature of the Buddhism of the two *uji no kami* Iname and Umako.

The common destiny of all these future emperors with the *shizoku* of the Soga signified for them all the acceptance of Buddhism. This did not happen from free choice but was due to their social ties with the Soga community. The marriages of the Emperors Kimmei and Bidatsu to Soga daughters, and also the remnants of matriarchy, gave to the conversions of Iname and Umako a national significance. Owing to this Buddhism could become the state religion in Japan. How close these ties between the imperial house and the Soga were can be seen from the following table: [2]

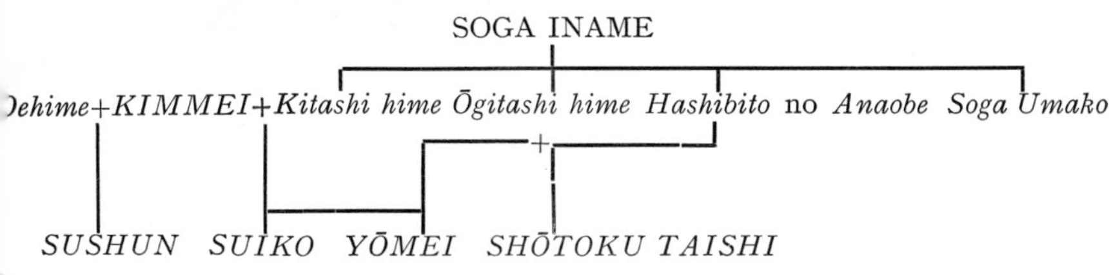

N.B. Oehime was an aunt of Kitashi *hime*
+ : married to

[1] See Chapter II, p. 117.

[2] This diagram is based on the *Kojiki*, which limits itself as far as

In the *Kojiki* Oehime is called an aunt of Kitashi *hime*. Therefore she must have been a sister or sister-in-law of Iname. Marriages with aunts frequently occurred. Thus Yōmei married two of his aunts: Ōgitashi *hime*, 意意芸多志姫, and Hashibito *no* Anaobe, 間人穴太部. This table shows that the two leaders had immeasurable preponderance in the field of religion and politics with regard to the emperors and successors of Bidatsu as their *uji no kami*. Hence their conversion also penetrated to the emperors who were already related to them. That appears from the chronicles of Yōmei and Sushun, in a positive sense for the former, in a negative sense for the latter. We shall take a clear look at this in the coming pages. Further, we hope to make it apparent in the next chapter that the Buddhism of Suiko and Shōtoku Taishi was wholly similar to that of these two Soga leaders.

1 Emperor Yōmei (586-588)

Now how did this Buddhism live in these two emperors? The first, Yōmei, called in Japanese Tachibana (= camphor tree) was the half-brother of his predecessor Bidatsu. He was also grandson and son-in-law of Iname and nephew to Umako.[1] He was born in 519 and succeeded his half-brother only at the age of sixty-five. After assuming the emperorship he settled in Ikenobe *no miya*, 池邊宮,[2] according to the *Kojiki*. The *Nihonshoki* can specify this residence even more accurately:[3] "He resided in Iware, his palace was called Ikenobe *no* Namitsuki *no miya*, 池邊雙槻宮." Therefore Yōmei too resided in the famous Iware.

Just as Keitai, he did not live too far from Takaichi, the first Buddhist breeding ground. On either side he knew himself to be protected by the Soga on the West and the Nakatomi on the East. These were two *shizoku* which, even during his reign, did not have too much in common. For instance, the Nakatomi had sided with

---

Kimmei, Bidatsu, Yōmei, Sushun and Suiko are concerned to a few "pedigree" data. Cf. Kuroita Katsumi, Maruyama Jirō, *Kokushitaikei Kojiki*, 3rd *maki*, pp. 147 up to 149 inclusive.

[1] See note 2 on page 351.

[2] Cf. *Kojiki*, 3rd *maki*; Kuroita Katsumi, Maruyama Jirō, op. cit., p. 149: "His younger brother Tachibana *no* Toyohi *no mikoto* established himself in Ikenobe *no miya*."

[3] Cf. *Nihonshoki*, chronicles for the ascension to the throne, 9th month; Kuroita Katsumi, Maruyama Jirō, *Kokushitaikei Nihonshoki*, part 2, p. 119; cf. W. G. Aston, op. cit., p. 106.

the same degree of violence as the Mononobe against all Buddhist successes.[1] Hence it appears from the location of this residence that Yōmei, albeit of Soga family, nevertheless, as supreme *uji no kami*, preferred a mediator's position between these inimical *shizoku*. Thus his court was available not only to the Soga but also to the Nakatomi.

This latter was rather extraordinary for a Soga descendent such as Yōmei. All the more so as he too was impregnated by the new doctrine. When his grandfather was converted he was nineteen. From that time on he too certainly became more closely acquainted with Buddhism. Just as his sister Suiko and his uncle Umako, he also certainly met Shiba Tattō. Similar contacts are known of with certainty, from the *Nihonshoki*, of Yōmei with Shiba Tattō's son, Tasuna. His interest in Buddhism indubitably had something to do with his Soga sympathies. This sympathy surely existed as he never rebelled against the powerful Soga policy. It is all the more remarkable that he did not choose the Soga side without more ado but, as emperor, strove to maintain a centrally balanced position.

The latter is apparent moreover from his measures with regard to the *ujigami* belief. These measures prove that he did not ignore this policy. Thus he began his reign with an imperial decree which appointed Princess Nukate, 酢香手, a priestess in Ise, where she was to remain for thirty-seven years.[2] This decree proves our comment in the second chapter, that the cult of the Sun goddess was reserved for the female branch of the imperial house.[3] The extent to which his personal Buddhism accorded with this decree

---

[1] Cf. p. 244 for instance.

[2] Cf. *Nihonshoki*, 21st *maki*, year before the ascension to the throne, 9th month; Kuroita Katsumi, Maruyama Jirō, op. cit., part 2, p. 120: "(9th month) 19th day. An imperial command came containing, i.a., the following: 'Princess Nukate will go to the temple of Ise and will offer her services to the *matsuri* of the Sun god(dess) (lit.: 日之神, Hi *no kami*, Sun god)'".

That here an appointment for many years was concerned and not merely an incidental visit is apparent from the commentary which follows: "From the time of the reign of this emperor (Yōmei) this female ruler withdrew there. She remained there until during the reign of Princess Kashikiya (=Suiko) and served in the feasts for the Sun god. She resigned voluntarily, withdrew to Katsuraki and died there. All of this may be found in the chronicles of Kashikiya. Another work says of her: she served the Sun god 37 years. Then she retired and died." Cf. W. G. Aston, op. cit., pp. 106, 107.

[3] Cf. Chapter II, p. 135.

is unknown. It illustrates that the fact of his Buddhism did not mean this prevented him being *uji no kami* of the nation. It follows from this decree that he was equally conscious of his responsibility towards the *ujigami* belief. Moreover, he was the first emperor of the sixth century to appoint such a priestess of Ise. That proves that the *ujigami* meant just as much to him as it did to his predecessor.

There is yet another measure which shows how much he was concerned with Japan's national religion. It is recorded in the following *Nihonshoki* chronicle: [1] "In the fourth month of the second year (587) the *niwanai*, 新嘗, (feast) was celebrated in Kawakami, 河上, of Iware." [2] This feast of *niwanai* was closely connected in its initial origin with both the Japanese *musubi* belief and the harvest.[3] This latter is also expressed in the name, because *niwanai* or *niiname* means: the tasting of the new harvest. Originally it had something to do with the descent of the divinity into the harvest community. It was considered a cult repetition of the sacrifice which Ama-waka *hiko*, 天稚彦, brought to Amaterasu after her grandson had descended to earth to found the Japanese realm.[4] Not only as a harvest festival but also as an enthronement feast of the emperor this celebration had a special lustre. On this occasion the emperor clothed himself in a room especially reserved for this within the palace, the Iwaido, 齊戸, hall,[5] with the old ritual robe, the *matoko*

---

[1] Cf. *Nihonshoki*, 21st *maki*, Yōmei, 2nd year, 4th month, 2nd day; Kuroita Katsumi, Maruyama Jirō, op. cit., part 2, p. 122. W. G. Aston, op. cit., p. 109, translates this by: "tasting the new rice" according to the actual sense of '*niwanai*'.

[2] There were various names for this feast, which are more or less similar in sound, such as *niwanai*, *niwanae*, *niwa no ai*, *niinai*, *niinae*, *niiname*. The word *ōni'e* was also used. For all these names see Shimonaka Yasaburō, op. cit., part 1, p. 240, column III.

[3] For the link with Japanese *musubi* belief, see Chapter II, footnote 3 on p. 107 under subheading 3. Further see the extremely good article by Sasaya Ryōzō: "Musubi-gami no shinkō", *K.G.Z.*, vol. 64 (1963), nos. 8, 9 (Aug., Sept.), especially pp. 91-100.

[4] Cf. Yanagita Kunio, *Nihon no Matsuri*, Tōkyō 1956, pp. 41, ff.; see also Arai Tsuneyasu, *Nihon no Matsuri to Geinō*, Tōkyō 1956, pp. 54 ff.

[5] This Iwaido hall was probably a holy place within the imperial palace in antiquity, although we do not know where that place was precisely located. It was the place where the partite soul of Amaterasu and Takamimusubi was 'put away'. In the Middle Ages it was even officially defined. Cf. Sasaya Ryōzō, op. cit., p. 100.

ou no fusuma, 真床覆衾, which means 'blanket of the true bed'. It was believed that this robe was the real seat of the divine holiness. Thus Sasaya at least translates this name.[1] It was believed that in this *matoko ou no fusuma* the *musubi* dwelt which united the new emperor with the partite soul of Amaterasu. By clothing himself in it, the divine power penetrated to him. Thus the actual heaven of Amaterasu became tangible here on earth and concrete in the emperor thus clothed in this robe. This too was a cult repetition of a primeval occurrence which is described in the *Nihonshoki*. Namely, before the imperial patriarch and grandson of Amaterasu, Ninigi *no mikoto*, descended on the earth he was covered by the *musubi* of Amaterasu, namely Takamimusubi with a 'divine' *matoko ou no fusuma*.[2] Thus the very first *niiname* feast celebrated by the new emperor was not only a ritual descent of the *musubi* of the grain or rice but also of the gods to whom Japan owed its existence.

It is self-evident that in the annually recurring *niiname* feast the emperor was accounted the chief personage in all the ceremonies.[3] Representatives from all groups of imperial officials were present there. Naturally the whole ceremony, as the name indicates, was terminated by a meal. It was thought that the deity, for whom the seat of honour was often left vacant, shared this. From the reign of Empress Kōgyoku (642-645) on this feast was celebrated annually on the twenty-second of November. The character of thank-offering for the harvest was strengthened even more later. At it 304 gods were remembered and thanked. Its original meaning of feast of encountering the divinity has been preserved even today in some parts of Kyūshū for instance. Thus, in these parts, young people will disguise themselves as the visiting deity and partake of the communal meal.[4]

---

[1] Sasaya Ryōzō, op. cit., p. 91.

[2] This primeval event is described in the *Nihonshoki* as follows: "At that time Takamimusubi covered the imperial grandson and the divine Prince Ninigi *no mikoto* with the *matoko ou no fusuma* and let him descend (to earth)". Cf. *Nihonshoki*, 2nd *maki*; Kuroita Katsumi, Maruyama Jirō, op. cit., part 1, p. 64; W.G. Aston, op. cit., vol. I, p. 70, translates *matoko ou no fusuma* by: "coverlet which was on his true couch".

[3] For these ceremonies see: Shimonaka Yasaburō, op. cit., part 3, p. 71, column III; p. 72, column I, under *niiname-matsuri* (Japanese).

[4] Cf. Arai Tsuneyasu, op. cit., pp. 53 ff. According to the *Fudoki* of Hitachi (the present-day prefecture Ibaraki) the tribal deity visited his younger sister on the night of the *niiname*, who afforded him 'shelter', after

The institution of this *niiname* feast by Yōmei illustrates that he too saw himself as the one who incorporated the *ujigami* belief of the nation in himself. This can be explained only if Buddhism and *ujigami* belief were not getting in each other's way.

His function of *uji no kami* did not present an obstacle to Yōmei for a more open acceptance of Buddhism, because the *niiname* feast, for instance, was, according to the chronicles, part of his first step towards his conversion. Indeed, immediately after this feast he introduced his change to Buddhism to his councillors of the Mononobe, Nakatomi and Soga as follows: [1]

"Second year, summer, fourth month, second day. In Kawakami in Iware the *niiname* was celebrated. On that day the emperor became ill. He returned again to his palace. There all the notables stood at his service. The emperor made a declaration, which was: 'I feel drawn to the three treasures (Buddhism). Consider this!' Hereupon all the notables took council. The *ōmuraji* Mononobe *no* Moriya and the *muraji* of the Nakatomi Katsumi did not agree to the imperial decision and said: 'Why do we turn our backs on the gods of our country and respect foreign gods? Such things were unknown of old!' Hereupon the *ō-omi* of the Soga, Umako *no sukune*, said: 'Let us, in accordance with the imperial command, support him. Who will appear with contrary plans?' The prince and younger brother of the emperor hereupon brought the monk Toyokuni, 豐國, to the court.[2] Mononobe *no* Moriya stared at him and became dreadfully angry."

The foregoing text describes yet another phase in the genesis of Japanese Buddhism. Namely, in contrast to the 'changes' of the

---

he had been refused by his elder sister. Cf. *Fudoki*; Takeda Iukichi, op. cit., p. 49.

During this night all girls and women had to fast and abstain. Other examples of similar divine visits can also be found in the article by Takatori Masaō, op. cit., p. 46: "In East Japan the custom existed of chasing all the permanent household members from the house on this night. Only the lady of the house or a young girl remained. As the divinity visited her specifically, she was not allowed to maintain any relations with the household members." Similar customs still exist on Okinawa.

[1] Cf. *Nihonshoki*, 21st *maki*, Yōmei, 2nd year, 4th month, 2nd day; Kuroita Katsumi, Maruyama Jirō, op. cit., part 2, pp. 122, 123; W. G. Aston, op. cit., vol. II, pp. 109, 110.

[2] An additional commentary on this says: "The prince and the younger brother was called Anaobe. He was a half-brother to the emperor and born of a concubine."

two Soga, Iname and Umako, this text mentions a conversion for the first time. Yōmei has expressed his attitude to Buddhism in the concept: 帰, which has the sense of: being drawn to, inclined towards. The *furigana* text is: "*Ore Sanbō ni moto yori matsuramu to omou*: I have intended from earlier times on to worship the three treasures."[1] The reactions of the two *muraji* are more compatible with this *furigana* text than with the above, which follows the Chinese characters. Hence here a genuine change of mind was concerned. Despite this, we do not believe that this conversion was really accompanied by a total desertion of the *ujigami*. Here a change of mental outlook was in the balance which was directed to a religion of the same structure as Japan's own *ujigami* belief: a foreign but national religion, not three treasures, Buddha, *dharma*, *saṅgha*, as a later editor wanted to suggest. The stake here was therefore not the *ujigami* belief but the question as to whether it should be a closed door or open. Whether or not an association of *ujigami* belief with Buddhism was permissible was at stake. As a true Soga supporter, he considered Buddhism a better way to the *ujigami* and a welcome addition to what was at that time a fairly meagre *ujigami* belief.

Both *muraji*, however, saw Buddhism as the Korean duplicate of their own *ujigami* belief, which would render the emperor as supreme *uji no kami* superfluous. Their own bigotry prevented them seeing Buddhism differently. Emperor and Soga also probably interpreted this Buddhism in the categories of their own *ujigami* belief, but their availability allowed them sufficient latitude gradually to weaken and reshape these nationalistic concepts under the influence of Korean monks and immigrants. Thus one can imagine that Umako and the two *muraji* talked entirely at cross purposes. For the *muraji* a 'converted' emperor could no longer possibly count as the incorporation of his own *ujigami* at the *niiname* feast. By this his task of supreme *uji no kami* became highly dubious. On the other hand Soga Umako contended that only the supreme *uji no kami* had the right to decide whether Buddhism could or could not be united with his emperorship. He certainly did not believe that the emperor would no longer be the *uji no kami* of the nation by this step, just as little as Soga Umako himself ceased

---

[1] Cf. *Nihonshoki*, loc. cit.; Kuroita Katsumi, Maruyama Jirō, op. cit., part 2, p. 122.

to be the *uji no kami* of the Soga *shizoku* by his conversion under the rule of Bidatsu. For the Soga the decree concerning the imperial conversion was perfectly adequate to demand complete obedience from the two *muraji*. For these latter, however, the emperor had lost any right to their obedience. Therefore immediately after this they revolted against the imperial authority.

Whether the emperor was actually converted as a result of this discussion is not stated in so many words. His younger brother Anaobe did indeed fetch a monk to the court. This, in fact, implied the conversion of the emperor. The imperial court had certainly always had a strict '*ujigami*' character. Now the arrival of this monk made a break in the existing traditions of this court. It could only be the result of an imperial conversion. The advent of this monk could also avail the court of a greater openness towards Buddhism in the future. This now began to play a more active part in the *ujigami* belief via the emperor's person.

Now how can this conversion be reconciled with that of his childhood? As Yōmei, owing to his typical Soga education, was already orientated towards Buddhism, this entire dispute concerned not his conversion as a private person but as an emperor. This education was the obvious extension of that of Iname and Umako, as the Soga member Tachibana also had to follow the convictions of his *uji no kami*. Here, however, it was not Tachibana but Emperor Yōmei who was converted. The emperorship itself was being 'baptised'. Here an official repudiation of the Mononobe's bigoted *ujigami* belief was concerned. By taking this last step, Yōmei had entirely identified himself with the Soga opinion on Buddhism. It also meant that his part as *uji no kami* of the nation was completely ended for the Mononobe. Therefore the Mononobe Moriya felt himself compelled to disassociate himself from Yōmei and to give the emperorship to someone else.[1] The struggle which broke out owing to this opinion is therefore related in the *Nihonshoki* in one breath after the report of the arrival of the monk Toyokuni at Yōmei's court. Thus the conversion of Yōmei formed the starting

---

[1] Cf. the article by Matsukawa Jirō, "Tennō-taii no rekishi" (history of the abdications of the emperors), *Tennō no Rekishi*, p. 276. Here he is of the opinion that the Mononobe undertook a serious attempt to establish Anaobe, Yōmei's younger brother on the throne. He however terminated these plots by suicide.

point for the 'show-down' between the conservative Mononobe leaders and those of the Soga.

Meanwhile the emperor's sickness increased. This resulted in two measures in his circle which betray the specific nature of his Buddhism, and that of his successors, even more clearly. It is interesting that both measures had something to do with Tasuna, the son of the bearer of Buddhism, Shiba Tattō.

Firstly Tasuna was brought, by his illness, to "leave his house for the sake of the emperor and to begin leading an ascetic life." [1] We have already noted that this gave a more official cachet to the monastic life of this monk,[2] as he became the forerunner of the later institution of the *nenbundosha*.[3] With this measure, which certainly partially emanated from Yōmei, as only he could appoint such 'state monks', Yōmei became the first emperor to utilise Buddhism for his own benefit. Here the emperor—as the *uji no kami* of the nation—managed every form of religion within his reach and under his authority for his own well-being. That personal well-being benefited by sacrifices in Shintō temples, as well as by the building of Buddhist monasteries and the admittance of Buddhist monks. This trait especially found expression when situations arose which were critical for the Emperor, such as epidemics or famines. Here it is not clearly apparent whether this policy also served to realize the *bodhi* or that it arose from some understanding of the *saṃsāra*. Formerly this idea was quite detached. Otherwise it is not comprehensible why this specifically Buddhist background is nowhere pointed out in this text. In later chronicles of the *Nihonshoki* and of the *Shoku-Nihongi* we find this applied *ad absurdum*. It became a specific characteristic of Japanese Buddhism.

Thus Emperor Tenchi, 天智, (661-671), during his last illness, caused his own crown prince to enter a monastery for the sake of the Emperor's healing.[4] His successor Temmu (673-686) on his deathbed not only summoned all the monks but also had sacrifices made in the Shintō temples.[5] Jitō (687-697), at the end of her life,

---

[1] See p. 292.

[2] Cf. p. 293.

[3] Cf. this chapter, footnote 3 on pp. 293, 294.

[4] Cf. *Nihonshoki*, 27th *maki*, Tenchi, 10th year, 10th month, 17th day; Kuroita Katsumi, Maruyama Jirō, op. cit., part 2, p. 300; see also W. G. Aston, op. cit., p. 297.

[5] Cf. *Nihonshoki*, 29th *maki*, the first year of Akamitori, 朱鳥, (686),

had *sūtras* read in all temples of the capital and in the Kinki district. All officials above the fifth grade were moreover caused by her, for the same ends, to scrub Buddhist temples. Simultaneously, for the sake of a happy issue out of her affliction "sacrifices had to be made to all the heaven and earth gods".[1] During the malady of Emperor Mommu (701-706) Buddhist meetings were held for his health [2] but sacrifices were also made to all the gods of heaven and earth.[3] Under Empress Genshō (715-723) in 722, for the healing of the *dajō tennō* (that is to say, an emperor who has withdrawn from court life into a monastery but, despite the presence of another emperor at court, still undertook the government), [4] the following was decreed: [5] the copying of 400 rolls of six principle *sūtras* of that time,[6] the making of eight votive flags, 1.000 temple flags, 36 ivory inlaid small elbow rests, 168 copper pots and 82 willowwood small chests. A little later 2,638 monks and nuns had

6th month, 16th day; Kuroita Katsumi, Maruyama Jirō, op. cit., part 2, p. 384: "He sent the ruler of Ise and officials to the Asuka-dera. An imperial decree to all monks was: 'all is none too well with me physically of late. I beseech you to appeal to the power of the three treasures, to gain repose for my body.'" Cf. W. G. Aston, op. cit., p. 377.

In this illness however, Shintō was also called in to aid. This appears from the following text a few lines further on. Kuroita Katsumi, Maruyama Jirō, op. cit., part 2, p. 386: "8th month, 6th day. Because all was not well with the emperor, the gods of heaven and earth were prayed to. The Hata *no* Imiki received an order to offer *mitekura* (sacrifices) to the gods of Dosa, 土左."

[1] Cf. *Nihonshoki*, 30th *maki*, Jitō, 11th year, 6th month; Kuroita Katsumi, Maruyama Jirō, op. cit., part 2, p. 428.

[2] Cf. *Shoku-Nihongi*, 3rd *maki*, Mommu, Keiun third year, 1st month, 5th day; Kuroita Katsumi, Maruyama Jirō, *Kokushitaikei Shoku-Nihongi*, part 1 (no. 3), p. 24. Cf. J. B. Snellen, op. cit., Ist Series, vol. XI, 1934, p. 208.

[3] Cf. *Shoku-Nihongi*, 3rd *maki*, Mommu, Keiun 4th year, 4th month, 25th day; Kuroita Katsumi, Maruyama Jirō, op. cit., part 1 (no. 3), p. 28. "The people were sick and starving; in all Shintō temples the emperor offered *heihaku* (= *mitekura*, sacrifices), in all the *tera* of the capital and the Kinki district he had *sūtras* read." Cf. J. B. Snellen, op. cit., p. 238.

[4] For this *dajō-tennō*, see Kichimura Shigeki, "Inseijidai no tennō" (emperors of the period of the 'monastery' government), *Tennō no Rekishi*, pp. 197 ff.

[5] Cf. *Shoku-Nihongi*, 9th *maki*, Yōrō 6th year, 12th month, 13th day; Kuroita Katsumi, Maruyama Jirō, op. cit., part 1 (no. 3), p. 95.

[6] Those were the *Kegon-kyō*, 華嚴経, Sanskrit: *Buddhāvataṃsaka-(Mahāvaipulya-) sūtra*;

to do penance. All of this reached a climax under Emperor Shōmu, 聖武, (724-748). When he became ill in 745 he decreed that all hawks and cormorants were to be freed and penances [1] should be performed everywhere. Moreover, he caused 3,800 persons to enter (monasteries) in order to perform ascetic exercises for the sick Emperor.[2]

Not only in the case of sickness but also in other situations, imperilling the country, monkish ascetics, *sūtra* readings, penances, entry into monasteries by many laymen, feasts of lights but simultaneously also sacrifices to the *ujigami* had to bring salvation. Without any differentiation, simultaneously, an appeal was launched using Buddhist, Shintō and Taoist rites impartially. They were simply brought into practice next to each other and intermingled. It would be necessary to print the continuation of the *Nihonshoki*, namely the *Shoku-Nihongi*, almost in its entirety to illustrate this. Of the Buddhism which appears from this work, for instance, we must say that as *Japanese* Buddhism alone it is incomprehensible unless taken in its co-existence with the Japanese *ujigami* belief and other religious forms derived from China. Hence if one only desired to describe Buddhism by use of purely 'Buddhist' chronicles, without also involving the non-Buddhist data as well, then one would achieve merely a skit and caricature of the true aspect of Japanese Buddhism.

One might also question that the emperor, in the foregoing chronicle, appealed to every kind of religion in which he himself did not believe. This is also just as little the case because Buddhism, from the time of Emperor Yōmei on, had been made co-existent with the *ujigami* belief. Therefore for him Buddhism was a powerful means to which one could resort in all kinds of difficult situations, such as disease or the threat of various disasters. For that purpose it was just as useful as *ujigami* belief. Here one must bear in mind that the emperor himself was too much *uji no kami* and focal point

the *Daishū-kyō*, 大集経, Sanskrit: the *Mahāvaipulya* and the *Mahāsannipata-sūtra*;
the *Nehan-gyō* 涅槃経, Sanskrit: *Mahāparinirvāṇa-sūtra*;
the *Daibosatsuzō-kyō*, 大菩薩藏経, Sanskrit: *Bodhisattva-piṭaka*;
Kanzeon-gyō, 觀世音経, Sanskrit: *Avalokiteśvara-sūtra*.

For further details see: M. W. de Visser, op. cit., p. 424.

[1] Cf. for this M. W. de Visser, op. cit., pp. 294 ff.

[2] Cf. *Shoku-Nihongi*, 17th *maki*, Shōmu, 17th year, 9th month, 19th day; Kuroita Katsumi, Maruyama Jirō, op. cit., part 1 (no. 3), p. 184.

of all Japanese religiosity to comprehend the true sense of Buddha's Way or his *sūtras*, incomprehensibly set out in Chinese. All of this was merely a magic means to him, which only he, as distributor of the nation's spiritual reserves, could put into motion. A better knowledge of Buddhism therefore, for the time being, meant no more than a greater variety of means at his disposal besides the *ujigami* belief.

The conversion of the Japanese emperor to the new religion therefore actually meant merely a welcome reinforcement of his *uji no kami* position. The 'Japanising' of Buddhism at that time consisted only in this, that this latter was seen merely as a means and nothing else which, together with *ujigami* belief, was to guarantee good fortune against death. Thus it really had very little to do with what Buddhism actually was. Furthermore, the Japanese character of it consisted of the fact that it began to co-exist with the *ujigami* belief. By this it became wholly '*diesseitig*'. The development described here had its starting point in Yōmei's conversion, which lay on the same plane as that of the Soga.

A second measure in which Yōmei was closely concerned during his final illness consisted of Tasuna's vow to make a Buddha image approximately 16 feet tall.[1] This vow indubitably answered to Yōmei's religious aspirations. Hence this vow slightly reveals Yōmei's attitude towards Buddhism. It makes it clear that he certainly did not seek an abstract path or a system. Moreover, it is far from certain whether the Korean immigrants knew anything of Buddhism as a specific system, considering the development which Buddhism had experienced after its advent in Korea. But even then, had that been the case, it is still doubtful whether at this time they were capable of adequately translating all of this into Japanese terms. Just at that time Japanese needed these immigrants to produce from the Chinese the abstract concepts which it lacked itself. At this beginning stage it was out of the question that scarcely arrived immigrants could clearly and sharply define the most essential notions of Buddhism in Japanese, all the more so as these Buddhist concepts—as we saw in the third chapter—had not yet reached perfect clarity in China itself. Moreover, for the Japanese, always so based on reality, these notions were hard to find a market for.

---

[1] Cf. p. 292.

This is still apparent in our own time. Possibly the failure of Christianity in Japan can also be blamed on the fact that it presented itself too abstractly, too universally and too unrealistically and impersonally to make any impression on a Japanese. A system only appeals to him after it has been made concrete in some fascinating personality. A Japanese is not readily attracted by metaphysics which remain far from concrete reality. This is valid for the oldest Buddhism. It had a chance of success only after it had contrived to present itself realistically. Now this had taken place in images and various personalities such as Shiba Tattō, Sŏng and now Tasuna. By these means, Buddhism not only reached the Japanese, but also the East Asian mentality. Now a symbol of this was Tasuna's image.

To all of this some other, specifically Japanese characteristics must be added. Thus Tasuna's Buddha, made on the model of other Korean images, also became a symbol of power as a completely new *ujigami*. Namely, this image also began to incorporate a piece of *ujigami* belief. Hence it enjoyed much respect not only in Buddhist but also in Shintō circles. Its dimensions therefore symbolised equally the spiritual superiority of Buddhism and that of the emperors, the supreme representatives of the *ujigami*. History proves this.

It is an incontrovertible fact established by the chronicles that the initiative for the erection of such images, from Yōmei on, lay more or less with every emperor. Thus Yōmei's desire formed the starting point of a fairly strongly syncretically coloured historical development. Approximately twenty years after Yōmei, in 605, Empress Suiko gave Tori, son of Tasuna, the order to make two depictions of Buddha, one in copper and one embroidered, both in identical dimensions of almost nine feet high.[1] In 686 Emperor Temmu ordered that Buddha images should be placed in every house.[2] In 737 Shōmu caused one image of Śākyamuni and two

---

[1] Cf. *Nihonshoki*, 22nd *maki*, Suiko, 13th year, 4th month, 1st day; Kuroita Katsumi, Maruyama Jirō, *Kokushitaikei Nihonshoki*, part 2, p. 146: "13th year, spring, 4th month, 1st day. The empress summoned the imperial prince (= Shōtoku), the *ō-omi*, all the princes and notables together, to take a communal vow to begin the making of a red copper and an embroidered depiction of Buddha, both the size of 1 *chō*, 6 *shaku* (= 4.85 metres). The saddler Tori was commissioned with its construction." Cf. W. G. Aston, op. cit., pp. 133, 134.

[2] Cf. *Nihonshoki*, 29th *maki*, Temmu 14th year, 3rd month, 27th day;

images of Bodhisattvas to be made for every province.[1] Furthermore, he also had 177 images of Kannon made in 727 for the benefit of the recovery of the crown prince.[2] In 746 his idolatry reached its apex. The *Shoku-Nihongi* says of this: [3]

"(Tenth month), sixth day. The emperor, the *dajo* emperor and the empress went to the Konshuji, 金鍾寺, in order to light lamps and sacrifice before the image of Vairocāna-Buddha. In front of and behind this image more than 15,700 lamps stood. In the evening, at about eight o'clock, the empress gave the order to several thousand monks to sacrifice these candles. Till 12 o'clock they proceeded thrice round the Buddha image while offering prayers of thanksgiving."

All of these facts, as well as others not mentioned, are no more than sober notations of fact by the chroniclers. In them there is no mention of ascribing a syncretic sense to the idolatry itself. It could be considered just as much proof for the conversion of the emperors to Buddhism if, besides these chronicles, there were not others which show that the same emperors continued to honour the old *ujigami* belief equally. Thus the chronicles of Empress Suiko for instance are continuously evidence for Buddhism. The following chapter, however, will show that neither she nor her prince Shōtoku had neglected the *ujigami* belief. In the chronicles of Temmu and Shōmu the Shintō pericopes even predominate. These interchange so frequently with other Buddhist deeds of the emperors that here there can no longer be any question of a repeated conversion of these emperors to Buddhism or the *ujigami* belief, but of a syncretic attitude. Therefore Buddhist and 'Shintō' practices and ideas were equally integrated in the mentality of these emperors. To them, each inclination to the one did not mean a dislike of the other. Both religions co-existed. They did even more than that: they influenced and changed each other. This too was naturally a growth process, which required many years. At its starting point stood a kind of

Kuroita Katsumi, Maruyama Jirō, op. cit., part 2, p. 376. Cf. W. G. Aston, op. cit., p. 369.

[1] Cf. *Shoku-Nihongi*, 12th *maki*, 9th year of Tempyō, 3rd month, 5th day; Kuroita Katsumi, Maruyama Jirō, *Kokushitaikei Shoku-Nihongi*, part 1 (no. 3), p. 143.

[2] Cf. *Shoku-Nihongi*, 10th *maki*, Shinun 5th year, 8th month, 21st day; Kuroita Katsumi, Maruyama Jirō, op. cit., part 1 (no. 3), p. 114.

[3] Cf. *Shoku-Nihongi*, 16th *maki*, Tempyō 18th year, 10th month, 6th day; Kuroita Katsumi, Maruyama Jirō, op. cit., part 1 (no. 3), p. 189.

co-existence between these very different religions. Owing to the lack of any conscious metaphysical foundation and the openness of Buddhism towards any form of religiousness this co-existence was possible.

In the chronicles various places can be found which indicate the syncretic growing together process of both religions. One passage is to be found in the chronicles of Emperor Shōmu (724-748). After gold had been found in the northern province of Mutsu, the emperor published the following proclamation:[1]

"In the land of Mutsu and in the district of Oda, 小田, gold has been found and given to me as a present. I believe that our country is protected in accordance with the word of Buddha and I proclaim to you that this now excels above all other lands. In every province of our land the *Saishō-ō-kyō*, 最勝王經,[2] is present. We pray to the gods of heaven and earth for Rusana-butsu, 盧舍那佛, (= Vairocāna-Buddha)." In the same proclamation, now directed towards this Rusana-butsu, the emperor continued: "At all the temples of the gods, beginning with that of Ise, we have celebrated the gods' feasts."

With these words the emperor himself established between a Buddha image such as that of Vairocāna and the *ujigami* a kind of hierarchical arrangement, whereby the latter became the protectors of the former. Proceeding from the same train of thought, the Shintō god Hachiman could lay down, even later, what kind of gold was to be used for the moulding of an image for Rusana-butsu, now better known by the name of Nara Daibutsu, the great Buddha of Nara which was completed in 746. This is made very clear in an address which one of Empress Kōken's (749-758) ministers, Tachibana *no sukune*, 橘宿祢, directed in the name of the empress to, i.a., Hachiman:[3]

"Our emperor declares: 'When I had not yet thought of making an image, I worshipped Rusana-butsu of the Chishiki-*dera*, 智識寺, in the Ōagata, 大縣, district of the province of Kawachi. Now I turn very particularly to the great god Hirohata Yawata, 廣幡人幡, (= Hachiman) of the Usa district in the province of Buzen. Divinity,

[1] Cf. *Shoku-Nihongi*, 17th *maki*, Tempyō Shōō 1st year, 4th month; Kuroita Katsumi, Maruyama Jirō, op. cit., part 1 (no. 3), p. 198.

[2] See Chapter IV, footnote 6 on p. 242.

[3] Cf. *Shoku-Nihongi*, 17th *maki*, Tempyō Shōō 1st year, 12th month, 27th day; Kuroita Katsumi, Maruyama Jirō, op. cit., part 1 (no. 3), p. 206.

do call the heaven and earth gods here. Cause that the copper casting of the image mixes without difficulty with my body (= blood), plants, wood and earth.'"

It appears from this text that Kōken saw in the Vairocāna image of the Chishiki temple a kind of deity: she worshipped it. In this newly to be cast image the entire cosmos was to be absorbed,[1] namely the human body, plants, wood and earth. With the co-operation of all the gods of heaven and earth it was supposed to be charged with cosmic power. Thereby it became more powerful and mightier than all the other images. The relation of this Buddha image to the Shintō god Hachiman was thought to be so close that the most prominent Hachiman priestess came from Usa to Nara in order to pray before this image. Thus from Yōmei's time on, the images served not only as the embodiment of the Buddhist truths, but also as signs of relationship with the old *ujigami* belief.

All of this confirms what the chronicle writer wrote down 125 years after Yōmei's death in a sentence at the beginning of his chronicles as a summary of his religious mentality: [2]

"*Tennō Hotoke no minori o uketamae, kami no michi o tōtobitamau*", which means "the emperor had accepted the teaching of Buddha and had moreover respect for the ways of the gods". This typified him as the first Japanese emperor in whom the co-existence of Buddhism and *ujigami* belief was a fact.

With all of this we do not wish to contend that in him Buddhism and *ujigami* belief already existed as two separate systems. Both were still too primitive for this and too much tied to an image or an object. In him Buddhism and *ujigami* belief did not stand as two extremes opposite each other; but there was, as yet, no real meeting between these two, at which both showed and maintained their own faces. For him they were merely two means which made it possible for him to realise more fully his own need for religious forms. Owing to the greater depth of his Buddhism, his conversion had become, to an even greater extent than that of Iname, a discovery of a new formulation of his own *ujigami* belief, borrowed from Buddhism. This was a rediscovery of something which he had

---

[1] Just as the casting itself, this cosmic process also comes from China. Cf. M. Granet, *Danses et Légendes de la Chine Ancienne*, tome II, p. 497 ff.

[2] Cf. *Nihonshoki*, 21st *maki*, Yōmei, year before the ascension to the throne; Kuroita Katsumi, Maruyama Jirō, *Kokushitaikei Nihonshoki*, part 2, p. 119; cf. W. G. Aston, op. cit., p. 106.

already always believed in. In contrast to the Mononobe, no single dogma hindered him in accepting wholeheartedly everything he thought useful in the new doctrine. Therefore he must have had great personal equilibrium to be able to endure in his own person the linking of two such extremes. Hence the retrospection of his chronicler might equally well be translated by: He remained himself even in the acceptance of that which he thought to be Buddhism.

2 Emperor Sushun (588-593)

The second 'Soga' emperor was Sushun. He was an entirely different figure to Yōmei. Nowhere in the *Nihonshoki* can an indication be found that he was a Buddhist. Nevertheless his government and his death throw just as much light on the Buddhism of his time as that of his predecessor.

Now who was this Sushun? He was the twelfth son of Kimmei and a nephew of Soga Umako. His Japanese name was Hatsusebe *no* Wakasaki, 長谷部若雀. According to the *Kojiki*[1] he dwelt in Kurahashi *no shiba no gaki*, 倉椅柴垣, which lay approximately six miles to the east of Iware. Although he was therefore of Soga family, he resided as far away as possible from the Soga district, at only a few miles distance from the tribal areas of the Mononobe and the Nakatomi.[2] When he began his reign he was already sixty-eight. However, before he reached this stage, the Mononobe Moriya (and his supporters) were first shatteringly defeated. This struggle covers more than half of his *Nihonshoki* chronicles. The battle is depicted here as a religious event in which the fourteen-year-old Shōtoku Taishi plays the main part. We have already indicated[3] that its miraculous character and the consequent victory had to serve to disguise the actual course of events. They consisted of the following: the final result, the downfall of the Mononobe, was due to a great extent to the technical capacities of the immigrants. The horses, and consequently also the saddlers, played an important part in this. The Buddhism which conquered here was rather that of the saddlers than that of Shōtoku Taishi.

This victory, however, did not remove all the enemies of the Soga. Some of them, such as the Nakatomi for instance, even maintained

---

[1] Cf. *Kojiki*, 3rd *maki*; Kuroita Katsumi, Maruyama Jirō, *Kokushitaikei Kojiki*, p. 149.

[2] Cf. the map on p. 470.

[3] Cf. the narative concerning this struggle on pp. 302 ff.

their powerful position of earlier days. One of them was also Sushun. He was not Soga Umako's best friend. Not for nothing did he reside as far away as possible from the tribal area of the Soga. What he thought of the Soga is clearly apparent in the *Nihonshoki*. Once, when he was presented with a bear's head, he said: [1]

"When shall I, in the same manner as this bear has been beheaded, make an end of those whom I despise?" Sushun did not leave at this, because the text continues: "He collected an unusually large army. Tenth day. When Soga *no* Umako *no sukune* heard of the imperial decision and further how he was despised and feared by him, he called together his followers in order to put in hand the death of the emperor."

Hereupon it came to a genuine 'show-down' between him and the emperor. In it, the chronicler blames the Soga for the history, by ascribing the plot to him, in which the Korean immigrant Yamato *no* Aya *no atae*, Koma murdered the emperor. Afterwards Soga is supposed to have made the latter pay for his murder of the emperor by death. As a pretext for this he used the fact that the immigrant maintained certain relations with his wife.

This imperial murder was, up till then, the second in Japan's history. Emperor Ankō had been the first emperor, in the second half of the fifth century, to die a violent death. Sushun's death had not only a political but also a religious character, as the emperor was still the supreme spiritual leader of the nation. He was the go-between between the *ujigami* and all the *shizoku*. Therefore his murder was also a kind of sacrilege. No greater crime was possible at that time. Umako and his Korean immigrants can therefore not be discriminated against in the forum of later generations more thoroughly than by connecting him with this murder.

It is, however, another matter as to whether this murder should really be ascribed to Umako. For Umako, whose Buddhism lay so deeply rooted in his *ujigami* belief and with his high opinion of the function of *uji no kami* on which his entire existence depended, such an imperial murder was out of the question. Seen from the structure of society of that time, it was impossible. Indeed, it would automatically have undermined the Soga's spiritual authority in his own *shizoku*. Also, with this murder in mind, his high

---

[1] Cf. *Nihonshoki*, 21st *maki*, 5th year, 10th month; Kuroita Katsumi, Maruyama Jirō, *Kokushitaikei Nihonshoki*, part 2, p. 131; cf. W. G. Aston, op. cit., p. 119.

position under Empress Suiko and beside Shōtoku Taishi is unthinkable.

With this murder Japanese history certainly achieved that the significance of Umako to Japanese Buddhism is completely veiled. The real cause can be found amongst the nationalistic politicians of the eighth century. They wished at all costs to prevent that the succeeding generations should gain the impression that, for the construction of Japanese culture, statesmanship and religion, it had been dependent on non-Japanese.

This explains why Soga Umako, who actually brought Buddhism forth from its hiding places in the immigrant colonies and took it to the imperial court, has been forgotten as the actual first *Japanese* pioneer of Buddhism. Later historiography even intended separating its origin as much as possible from the Soga. This was achieved by, i.a., putting forward the Kimmei thirteen text as Japan's oldest chronicle concerning its Buddhism. On the other hand the text concerning the factual origination was maimed and put at a far later date (Bidatsu thirteen). Hence Soga Umako's figure was tarnished in order to be able to elevate his blameless nephew Shōtoku as the actual founder of Japanese Buddhism.

The foregoing murder is certainly an illustration of the extreme tensions which existed mutually between the Japanese leaders at that time. They manifest a similarly uncertain era as that in which we ourselves are living. The arrival of many qualified immigrants to Japan with entirely new techniques and ideologies deeply shocked many of the Japanese who were tied to the old traditional society. Also old values were radically replaced throughout society by new ones. The destruction of the Mononobe and the death of Sushun belonged just as much to the crisis of this interim period as did the newly planted Buddhism.

What Sushun's own attitude was to Buddhism is not known, but may be surmised. Owing to his dislike of Umako he probably stood philosophically closer to the Mononobe. Seen from this point, his death was a last convulsion of the Mononobe struggle. Just as little as the leaders of this *shizoku* can he have relished an *ujigami* belief peppered with Buddhism. Thus Sushun is actually a negative illustration of sixth century Buddhism.

What may be said at the end of this chapter about Japanese lay-Buddhism of that time? The two Soga and Yōmei demonstrate positively, and Sushun negatively, that at that time the most prominent laymen harboured it as a wholly new and third religion. It had its starting point in a fairly primitive *ujigami* belief, which was just busy freeing itself from the individual *uji*, and in a form of Hīnayāna or Mahāyāna which was misunderstood as Buddhism. This latter was only accepted by the Japanese layman and comprehended in its unlimited openness. He saw it as a new mirror and a more modern translation of his *ujigami* belief. What that translation was, is best detailed in the figure of Shōtoku Taishi. If at least one has the courage to see him also in the perspective of the *ujigami* belief of his era.

CHAPTER SIX

THE GROWTH TOWARDS JAPANESE BUDDHISM SHŌTOKU TAISHI (574-622)

In the previous chapter mention was made only of people who played an historic part in Japanese Buddhism but who in our time have lost their significance. We diagnosed that their historical function with regard to Japanese Buddhism afterwards shrank and was depreciated because of their un-Japanese descent or because of their being narrowly connected with Chinese-Koreans who had emigrated to Japan. The approach to their religiosity in the previous chapters attempted to give them back their rightful place in the religious development at the commencement of Japanese history.

Quite a different part had been reserved in Japanese history for Umayado, the son of Emperor Yōmei, who, after his death, was given the honorary title of Shōtoku Taishi, 聖德太子, i.e. 'great prince of holy merit.' According to tradition he was a Japanese who had understood and examined Buddhism better and more thoroughly than any one of his contemporaries whatever. It was even allowed to appear as if this study had been first begun by him. This picture of Shōtoku is still always to be found in all Western and in nearly all Japanese authors as well.[1] The exceptional position, however, of Shōtoku Taishi in Japanese Buddhism calls up a whole series of questions which all go back to the hub of the matter as to how it was possible that in him Buddhism could suddenly take on completely different, and then indeed more 'orthodox', properties, while nevertheless at the end of the sixth century it had developed into no more than a more modern version of the *ujigami* faith. This chapter, therefore, is devoted to this question. Here the dissection of all the data concerning Shōtoku forces us to the conclusion that at the beginning of the seventh century there were not two kinds of Buddhism: Soga Buddhism and an opposing Shōtoku Buddhism. For, in this author's opinion, this latter form was on the same lines as that of the Soga. Furthermore, it seems probable that the opponents of Soga, owing to Shōtoku's integrity,

---

[1] See e.g. E. D. Saunders, *Buddhism in Japan*, pp. 99-100; Naoki Kojirō in *Daigaku Nihon-shi*, vol. I, p. 47.

came to employ him as the one who should take over and sublimate the part played by the Empress Suiko, the Soga and the Korean immigrants. In doing so they showed no hesitation in falsifying history.

This is the explanation of the fact that year after year in each succeeding century the importance of Shōtoku's place in history became more and more heavily underlined. Gradually people began to attribute all the achievements of his fellow-workers and contemporaries to him. Thus people asserted that he was the builder of all the Buddhist temples of his time. He it was who gave Japan a completely new constitution. In him Buddhism commenced completely anew.

Thus it was not difficult to make him into the forerunner of later Buddhist sects. His figure waxed to the Japanese version of Śākyamuni. In Shintō he became one of the gods who descended to earth for a while in order to start the Japanese Empire. In Japan's later history popular religion made him appear repeatedly anew in other shapes and in times of change to be born again as various important personages. This continued up to the present day. Of his significance in Japanese education, for example, Gundert writes:[1]

"Der Buddhismus erfreut sich darum in der neuen Ära Shôwa (seit 1926) auch beim Staate eines Ansehens, das zur Meijizeit nicht denkbar gewesen wäre. Zwar ist die staatliche Schule nach wie vor religionslos, erteilt also keinen Religions-, sondern nur Moral-unterricht. Aber es wird neuerdings darauf gesehen, dass im Geschichtsunterricht die religiösen Führer Japans und die Bedeutung des Buddhismus für die japanische Kultur besser zu ihrem Recht kommen als es früher der Fall war. Dies gilt besonders von dem geistigen Vater der ganzen buddhistischen Entwicklung Japans, von dem kronprinzlichen Regenten Shôtoku, dessen Bild in allen grossen Sektenstiftern lebendig gewesen, von den geistigen Führern der Tokugawa-zeit dagegen um so unfreundlicher beleuchtet worden war, aber nun heute wieder, namentlich durch die 'Gesellschaft zur Ehrung des Gedächtnisses von Shôtoku Taishi' (Shôtoku Taishi Hôsankwai, seit 1918) geflissentlich hervorgeholt wird, um an ihm die unauflösliche Verbindung zwischen Buddhismus und japanischer Staatskultur darzutun."

Gundert wrote this before 1935. We shall see, however, that

---

[1] W. Gundert, *Japanische Religionsgeschichte*, pp. 177-178.

also in these days this 'Shōtoku Taishi' belief has by no means faded with many people. Although an historical figure Shōtoku has been so much mythologised in the course of time and has become so much a part of folklore that his original traits are difficult to recognise.

Therefore a de-mythologising will be necessary. The intention of this debunking is not to lay aside a specified conviction which immortalises him as 'the eternal Japanese' but to obtain a just estimate of the historic reality of Shōtoku and his religion. It is a question of the keystone necessary for the reconstruction of Japan's oldest Buddhism. This Buddhism appears rather less hazy and anonymous in Shōtoku Taishi than in Soga Iname or Umako. The devaluation of Shōtoku, which is the natural result of this de-mythologising, will at the same time restore the Empress Suiko to her original function as Shaman, administrator and spiritual leader. Thus Suiko is raised above Shōtoku.

Nevertheless it seemed imperative to head this chapter with Shōtoku's name. For Suiko's role only becomes apparent after the analysis of the Shōtoku-figure. Little is known of her personally. Another reason for this is that it is precisely in approaching the original shape of Shōtoku that the Buddhism of his era becomes clearer. This is effected in three ways in this chapter. Only after an attempt has been made to capture the very first germination of his myth can one check what his real stature was. His real faith, which also represented that of his people, only emerges in the events and works of art which came about at the time of his death.

1 Growth of the popular image of Shōtoku Taishi

How did the popular image of Shōtoku arise? Before enquiring as to its origin it is perhaps as well just to look at the whole extent of the picture of him which is projected on to the screen of modern Japanese history. Kaneko Taiei [1] writes in 1940: "Taishi was the

---

[1] Kaneko Taiei, *Nihon Bukkyō Shikan*, Tōkyō 1940, p. 36. How strongly this projection is believed in even at present is also evident from Masaharu Anesaki's article: "The Foundation of Buddhist Culture in Japan, the Buddhist Ideals as conceived and carried out by the Prince Regent Shōtoku", *M.N.*, no. VI, 1943, pp. 1-12. In it special attention is paid to the three *sūtra* commentaries, but also many other facts, such as the promulgation of his law in 17 articles, are dealt with. Unfortunately this author did not take a critical consideration of the *Nihonshoki* texts as his starting point.

descendent of the gods. Against this background one cannot object to all his words and deeds being divine", and: "Buddhism was introduced according to the divine intentions of the gods. It goes without saying that we must worship the will of the gods expressed in his commentaries on the *sūtras.*" These words illustrate the fact that in Japanese popular religion up to 1945 Taishi took a place which far exceeded his historical importance. From the following quotation, however, it is evident that also after 1945 this belief lived on just as powerfully.

In 1955 Asano Motohiro wrote in an article:[1] "The god, that Taishi was, could develop only the Mahāyāna; in other words, the people, who knew not what to do with the primitive Hīnayāna faith, were led by him to a deep insight. This was possible because Taishi was a god. This Buddhist flowering was, through him, the work of our celestial and earth gods . . . His ideal was harmony.[2] Basing himself on *shizoku* society he wished to establish the unity of the state centred round the emperor. For that purpose the 17 articles were framed.[3] Thus he delivered the greatest blow to the leading Soga *shizoku.* Taishi was really the god of peace. His ideal was contained in the elevation of harmony above friendship in all things . . . As god he was steeped in this, the above mentioned articles. This frame of mind runs parallel to the benevolence of Confucius, the *jên,*[4] the *mahākaruṇa* of Buddha and the love of Christ . . ." With this equalisation of Shōtoku with Confucius, Buddha and Christ the apex is about reached of the whole development of the Taishi-faith through the centuries. What is interesting in this quotation is that the writer of it is of the opinion that between the Buddhism of Shōtoku and that of his time there was such a deep gulf that only a 'god' such as Shōtoku could bridge it. We believe that, as long as there is another way to bridge this gulf, Shōtoku as godhead has served his turn and not only as '*deus ex machina.*' I have endeavoured to discover the other way. This, then, consists of retrieving his real shape from under all these projections, despite the strong involvement of Shōtoku

---

[1] Asano Motohiro: "Waga Taishi shinkō" (My belief in Shōtoku Taishi), *Shūkyō Kōron,* vol. 25, 1955, no. 4, June, p. 41.

[2] This harmony is based on the first article of Shōtoku's law in 17 articles. See footnote 4 on p. 390.

[3] See p. 389.

[4] Jap.: *jin.*

Taishi in popular belief. Such a procedure carries certain risks with it, viz. that it might disclose that the greatness and divinity of Shōtoku Taishi is more the work of later centuries than his own merit. Such a discovery would naturally not be very exhilarating. However unsympathetic this method may be, nevertheless, an honest reconstruction of Japan's oldest Buddhism demands this unveiling of Shōtoku.

This reconstruction has been planned as follows. First the determination of the various phases in which Shōtoku became a myth. These phases run right through to the present day. As this work is not concerned with the Shōtoku myth as it has survived until today, but only in as far as this can help us to a correct picture of sixth and seventh century Buddhism, it is not necessary to go through all the historical phases and developments in the formation of this myth. The very oldest data about Shōtoku are the most important for this purpose. They formed, moreover, the first impetus for all further and later myth-making. By means of a critical exposition of this material we shall endeavour to break through into the innermost core of the Buddhism of Shōtoku and his contemporaries. The data to be discussed here may be divided into two groups: viz. data from the periods before and from those after the compilation of the *Nihonshoki* and the *Kojiki*.

a *The period before the compilation of the oldest Japanese sources* (Kojiki *and* Nihonshoki) (*to 712*)

From the period up to 712, that is to say the first hundred years after the death of Shōtoku, no writings have come down to us which give anything about the personality of Shōtoku or his life, for the oldest manuscripts are those of the *Kojiki* and the *Nihonshoki*. Nevertheless much of the material, in the *Nihonshoki* for example, must stem from this period. Because, however, it became mixed up with data of the time of the compilation this material is not sufficient to give a picture of Shōtoku as people thought of him in the first years after his death.

Nevertheless there are yet other particulars. For these we must thank the inscriptions on several works of art which have remained preserved to us. However scanty, it is exactly these which are the most trustworthy of all historical Shōtoku data, because they date from his own time. For our attempts to recover Shōtoku

Taishi's own religious convictions and those of his contemporaries they will prove to be of the utmost importance.

What, then, are these inscriptions? After the death of Shōtoku orders were given for the creation of two works of art, both still extant. The first is the famous Shaka-*sanzon*, 釈迦三尊, a kind of Buddhist trinity. This consists of a large archaic statue of Shaka (= Śākyamuni) flanked on both sides by two smaller statues of Bodhisattvas, viz. Bhaiṣajyarāja (Jap.: Yakuō, 薬王) and Bhaiṣajyarājamudgata (Jap.: Yakujō, 薬上).[1] The second is Japan's oldest embroidery, Tenjukoku-*mandara*, 天壽國曼陀羅, called: 'the *maṇḍala*[2] of the land of long life in heaven'. This latter is a depiction of the hereafter wherein Shōtoku's existence after his death is imagined. On both of them there is an inscription regarding Shōtoku Taishi. Less well-known are some inscriptions of later date: one on a statue of Yakushi (Bhaiṣajyaguru-vaidūrya), 薬師, and one on a memorial stone in the little town of Iyo, 伊豫.

In the following pages these will be examined in detail.

1) The Shaka statue [3] owed its origin to the last illness of Shōtoku Taishi. It was made between 621 and 630. As the *honzon*, 本尊, i.e. the most respected object of the Hōryūji,[4] it was given the chief

[1] For Yakuō and Yakujō see M. W. de Visser, *Ancient Buddhism of Japan*, vol. II, p. 633. With regard to their function he refers to the places in the *Saddharma-puṇḍarīka-sūtra* where they are mentioned. Because of their ties with medicine they had an evil magic significance in Shōtoku's time.

[2] A *maṇḍala* may be compared with a ground plan, a plan. At one glance it gives a complete picture of the whole and the real core of Buddhism. Thus it may be said that "le *maṇḍala* se compose de la réunion de toutes les images des divinités qui sont chacune le symbole d'une des innombrables vertus du Buddha". Cf. Ryūjun Tajima, *Les deux Grands* Maṇḍalas *et la doctrine de l'Esotérisme Shingon*, Tōkyō 1959, p. 35. For this concept see further op. cit. pp. 33-44. There is, however, yet another element which belongs equally to the nature of the *maṇḍala*: viz. that all the divine symbols of Buddha depicted on the *maṇḍala* are arranged in a close and organised connection with the centre, the *axis mundi*. This centre is Buddha himself. The *maṇḍala* thus comprises, as in a microcosm, all the beings which participate in the nature of the Buddha which is symbolically placed in the centre of the picture. Cf. Ryūjun Tajima, op. cit., p. 34. Thus it may be said that the Tenjukoku-*mandara* was a cross-section or a ground plan of the faith of Shōtoku Taishi's time.

[3] Shaka, 釈加, is the abbreviated Japanese transcription of the Sanskrit: Sākyamuni. This is written in full as Shakamuni: 釈迦牟尼.

[4] The *honzon*, 本尊, is the object most worthy of reverence to be found

place in the 'golden hall' of this temple. Some maintain that the original statue was lost in the temple fire of 670 and that the one now present is only a reconstruction of the old one. But it is now agreed that this Shaka-*sanzon* was not lost in this fire. A comparison with reconstructions of art treasures which were certainly lost at that time brought this to light. One of these lost treasures was certainly a statue of the Buddhist divine physician Yakushi,[1] already mentioned here. This is supposed to owe its origin to the illness of Emperor Yōmei and accordingly was made by Tori in 607.[2] According to the *Nihonshoki* this was the first statue made in Japan proper. This statue, however, is not identical with the present-day Yakushi statue which was reconstructed only after the temple fire. This appears from the discovery of the remains of the Hōryūji fire and from fresh insight gained by art historians such as Machida Kōichi[3] who have detected a later style in various features of this statue. According to these views the Shaka-*sanzon* now qualifies as the very oldest work of art from the Asuka period (592-697). This is simply owing to the fact that it was not burnt to ashes in 670. Its age became apparent from the traces of fire which were chiefly found on the upper half of the great Buddhist nimbus behind this statue which is called the *kōhai*, 光背, or *gokō*, 後光, in Japanese.[4] Later on an attempt was made to restore this fire damage. The lower part of this *kōhai* was not touched by the fire so that this did not require restoration after the conflagration.

Now exactly on this part of the *kōhai* there is an inscription about Shōtoku. Now that the greater age of this statue and its inscription with regard to the Yakushi statue has been established it is possible to point out two stages in the making of the Shōtoku myth. It then appears that the inscription on the Shaka-*sanzon* is older than that of the Yakushi statue. We shall see, however, that nevertheless it

---

in the temple and to which such a temple owes its fame. It could consist of a depiction of a Buddha, Bodhisattva, but also a *maṇḍala*.

[1] For Yakushi see Inoue Tetsujirō, op. cit., p. 1050, col. III; p. 1051, col. I.

[2] See p. 362.

[3] Cf. Okabe Nagaaki, "Shōwa no Hōryūjimondai to Taishi-shinkō", *Shūkyō Kōron*, vol. 25, 1955, no. 4, June number, pp. 28 and 29.

[4] Both words already express almost the same function as our saint's halo. For they mean: beam of light on the back.

is not the oldest evidence about Shōtoku Taishi. This inscription runs as follows:[1]

"In the thirty-first year of Hōkōgen, 法興元,[2] in the year *kanoto-mi*[3] (621), in the twelfth month the former empress died (= Empress Anaobe *no* Hashibito, the mother of Shōtoku). The next year, the first month, twenty-second day, Kamitsumiya (lit.: (the dweller) in the upper palace), the *hōō*, 法王, (*dharmarāja*, king of *dharma*, a title of Buddha)[4] became ill. He took a dislike to his food. The Empress too was very distressed about this. At this time the Empress, princes and all dignitaries came to his bedside. In deep grief they together swore a solemn oath before the three treasures to have a statue of princely size made for Shaka. Might Buddha in compliance with this prayer bring about a change in the illness, prolong his life and give him a peaceful life. Should this really be at variance with the world's destiny might he then go to live in *jōdo*, 浄土, the Pure Land[5] and quickly ascend to receive the reward of his deeds. The second month, twenty-first day, of the year *mizunoto-tori* (613) the Empress died. The following day the *hōō* (= Shōtoku) died. In the year *mizunoto-hitsuji* (623), in the middle of the third month, the statue of Śākyamuni, together with the two flanking statues, was ceremoniously completed in accordance with the promise. It became a symbol of happiness which not only brought knowledge of the way to belief, but also rest and certainty. Mankind goes to meet life and death in obedience to these three masters. The blossoming

---

[1] For the Japanese text see Sakaino Kōyō, *Shōtoku Taishi-den*, Tōkyō 1931, p. 144.

[2] This is a Buddhist name of the period or *nengō*, 年号. The first year of *Hōkōgen* is identical with the 4th year (591) of Sushun. The translation of this period name is: 'Origin of Buddhist *dharma*'. For what reasons this period began in exactly 591 is not clear, since the *Nihonshoki* does not produce a single important Buddhist occurrence to which this title might refer.

[3] In the text it says *kanoto-mi*: 621. This, however, will have to be the year *mizunoe-saru* = 612, because otherwise this whole text loses its meaning. This error in this inscription is a clear illustration of the great uncertainty with regard to the calendar which existed at the beginning of the sixth century and long after. In any case this error is clear proof of the great age of this inscription.

[4] This title served especially as an honorific one for Buddha himself. In the Nara period it also came to indicate a high monastic rank.

[5] This expression, as also the whole terminology of this text, indicates that it was written in a monastic milieu. Tori, the maker of this statue, was himself the son of a monk: Tasuna.

of Buddhism will hereby be exalted to the highest point, and people will together with them achieve *higan*, 彼岸, the hereafter.[1] Further, this symbol diffuses the *hokkai*, 法界, (= *dharma-dhātu*: the Buddhist reality present in everything) [2] over the six paths (i.e. everywhere).[3] It loosens the bonds of suffering and directs endeavour to the *bodhi*. They had this made by Tori, the *obito*, 首, (= a title) of the saddlemaker Shiba."

However old this text may be, in reading it one is struck by the first signs of Shōtoku-worship. Here he is not only given the title of prince, *ōshi*, 王子, but also the title which is specially reserved for Buddha, *dharmarāja*. The expression 'six paths' and the Buddhist terms *jōdo* and *hokkai* betray a later editing which was certainly after the year 645.[4] This inscription, although incised before the fire but still fairly late, at any rate belongs to a time in which the Shōtoku-worship already overstepped the bounds of the normal respect which is usual to have for a princely and deserving person.

2) There is yet another text which—as we believe—is even older. This is to be found on the Tenjukoku-*mandara*, the piece of embroidery which Shōtoku's widow had made after his death. It was intended as a lasting memorial of the Taishi's stay in the land of the heavenly life. At the end of this chapter we shall return to this concept of heaven. Round this representation—even now preserved in the Chūgūji, 中宮寺, which lies behind the palace of Shōtoku, which equally forms part of the Hōryūji complex—are the 400 characters of the inscription placed on the backs of 100 tortoises. Thus four characters on each tortoiseshell. This text appears to stem from Suiko's time because various later manuscripts refer

---

[1] Literally: the other side of the river.

[2] Literally: *hokkai*, 法界, Sanskrit: *dharma-dhātu*. Buddhism knows various classifications of phenomena. According to one of these classifications phenomena may be divided up into eighteen elements (*dhātu*). The twelfth *dhātu* is that of *dharma*. This comprises all phenomena inasfar as they are the object of our thought. Cf. É. Lamotte, *Histoire du Bouddhisme Indien*, pp. 32, 33. Proceeding from this basic idea this concept achieved a separate meaning in Japan's own schools such as those of the Kusha, Kegon, and Tendai. Cf. Taya and others, *Bukkyō-gaku Jiten*, Tōkyō 1957, pp. 397, 398.

[3] This expression 'six paths' reveals that this text is of a later date. The system of the six paths, according to which the Japanese provinces were grouped, was only established after 645.

[4] See footnotes 5 on p. 378 and footnotes 2 and 3 on this page.

to it.[1] It was last restored in 1274.[2] This text runs as follows: [3]

"The Emperor, whose name was Amekuni-oshiharuki Hironiwa *no mikoto* (= Kimmei) and who reigned in his Shikishima palace, took Kitashi *hime no mikoto*, the daughter of the *ō-omi* of the Soga, Iname *no sukune*, to wife. He gave her the title of Empress. She gave birth to Tachibana Toyohi *no mikoto* (= Yōmei) and his younger sister named Toyomike Kashikiya *hime no mikoto* (=Suiko). Furthermore he married a younger sister of Kitashi *hime*, viz. Ōane *no mikoto*, 乎阿尼. She gave birth to a princess who received the name of Anaobe *no* Hashibito. A son of the Shikishima Emperor (= Kimmei), viz. Nunakura *no* Futotamashiki *no mikoto* (Bidatsu) married his younger sister (= half-sister) viz. Toyomike Kashikiya *hime no mikoto* and gave her the title of Empress. She resided at Osada *no miya*. She produced a prince called Owari, 尾治. Tachibana Toyohi *no mikoto* married his half sister Anaobe *no* Hashibito and made her Empress. She resided in Ikebe *no miya* (in Iware) and gave birth to a prince named Toyotomimi, 等己刀彌彌, (with the beaming ears = Shōtoku). He married a daughter of the prince of Owari, who was called Tachibana *no* Ōiratsume, 大女郎. In the year *kanato-mi*, the twelfth month, twentieth day, the year *mizunoto-tori* (613),[4] his mother, Anaobe *no* Hashibito, died at daybreak. The next year, the second month, twenty-second day of the year *kinoe-inu* (= 614) the Taishi (= Shōtoku) died at midnight. Then Tachibana *no* Ōiratsume was deeply grieved and sobbed with grief. She spoke to the reverend Empress: 'I cannot put my sorrow into words. That my prince and my mother should die one after the other has grieved me so much that my throat is choked. My *ō-kimi* always said: This world is only vain and passing; the real truth, however, is Buddha. He toyed with this truth. As reward my

---

[1] In the work *Hōōteisetsu*, 法王帝說, which, after the *Kojiki* and the *Nihonshoki*, is the oldest text on Shōtoku Taishi, it says: "This is to be found in the treasure house of the Hōryūji. It consists of two tapestries sewn together, in which there is a text inscribed on the backs of tortoises." Cf. Sakaino Kōyō, op. cit., p. 194.

[2] Cf. Sakaino Kōyō, loc. cit.

[3] The present author found this text, according to that on the backs of the tortoises, printed in Sakaino Kōyō's: *Shōtoku Taishi-den*, in rows of four characters each on pp. 191-192.

[4] The compiler of this text reveals here his own doubts regarding the correct dating by mentioning both years. The dating problems here are therefore of the same nature as those of the Shaka-*sanzon* inscription.

prince is therefore reborn in the land of the long heavenly life (= *tenjukoku*). Now I cannot see with my own eyes the actual shape of that land. Therefore I beg you for a representation of it. I long to see the great prince in the way he lives there and is reborn.' The Empress agreed to this request, for she too was grieved. Therefore she spoke: 'Only one was really my son. Therefore I give the order to all women to make two tapestries.' They were designed by the Yamato *no* Aya, Matsuken, 末賢, Kasei, 加西, of Koguryŏ and Aya *no* Nukakori, 奴加己利. The order for this was given to the Kurabe *no* Hata, Kuma, 久麻."

In contradistinction to the preceding inscription this text speaks nowhere of a special worship of Shōtoku. Here there is only a sorrowful widow speaking who has lost her beloved husband, nothing more. The Tenjukoku-*mandara* itself is not a representation of her deified or sainted husband, but of the place where he, together with many others, remained. We shall return to this. This text and the Tenjukoku-*mandara* both derive from the time when the Shōtoku cult had not yet begun. Both can be dated as being even before 645 when the Japanese realm was reconstructed on the Chinese model. Various data in the text do not yet show the slightest sing of this Chinese reformation. One of these is the exclusive use of the original Japanese imperial names of Kimmei and Bidatsu. Neither the word *tennō* [1] nor later Chinese appellations appear here. There are also other indications such as the old Japanese title *ō-kimi* for Taishi, the calendar uncertainty and the sober evidence of Taishi's faith.

This inscription is older than that on the Shaka-*sanzon* statue. This is evident from a comparison with each other. For the Shaka inscription evidences a more detailed knowledge of Buddhism. Moreover in it Shōtoku is already especially called *dharmarāja*. Shōtoku-worship rings clearly in this appellation. In the inscription of the Tenjukoku-*mandara* no words appear which point to an author of the period after the Taika reformation. In contradistinction to the Shaka inscription the text of this *mandara* did not originate from a monkish milieu. Its composer has obviously only listened to the widow and has been, in his depiction of the hereafter, the interpreter of the people.

3) Still another inscription is known, viz. that of the Yakushi

---

[1] For the late origin of the word *tennō* see Chapter I, pp. 65 ff.

statue already mentioned. When comparing this statue with that of the Shaka-*sanzon* it appears that, for example, the draping of the chairs, the fall and the folds of clothing, the *kōhai*- (nimbus) motives and the gestures of the hands (*mudrā*) are identical in both statues. Apparently the one statue was the model for the other. They even resemble each other so much that without a special inscription it is not possible to determine which of the two represents Śākyamuni and which Bhaiṣajyaguru. These almost identical figures demonstrate, despite all the technical perfection of that time, how little was yet known of the difference between Śākyamuni and Bhaiṣajyaguru.[1] Again, if indeed both statues were modelled after each other, nevertheless there appears in the features of both an equally undeniable dependence on the sculptures of the T'opa, the so-called Northern Wei sculptures. This also is now generally acknowledged in Japan.[2] Both statues thus witness at the same time to the influence of the Buddhism from the T'opa kingdom. In contradistinction to the statue of the Shaka-*sanzon* this Yakushi statue was created after the great temple fire of 670. The inscription on it must therefore also be ascribed to the last decades of the seventh century. This inscription runs: [3]

"In this time the Emperor who ruled over the people from the Ikenobe palace (Yōmei) had much pain. That year—it was the year *hinoe-uma* (586)—he called the Empress Ō-kimi (Suiko) and the Taishi to him. They swore a solemn oath: 'In accordance with our burning desire that the illness shall cease we order a temple to be built and a statue of Yakushi to be placed there.' Then he died. He was never able to build the temple himself. The Empress Ōkimi, however, who reigns over the people from the Owarida palace, and the holy prince, *Higashi-miya*, 東宮, (Eastern palace: Shōtoku) obeyed this command in the year *hinoto-u* (607) with this religion."

This inscription confirms the opinion of those who think that this Kakushi statue was only reconstructed after the fire. There are

[1] Of this Takatori Masaō says: "If in the gold hall of the Hōryūji the *kōhai* were not standing behind the statues of Yakushi and Shaka we should not know that these were really statues of Yakushi and Shaka." Cf. "Kodai Minshu no shūkyō", *N.S.K.*, vol. 2, p. 55.

[2] Statues with similar Wei characteristics are indeed indicated as such in the Hōryūji catalogues, as observed by the present author on a visit. Via the Wei sculptures they were still related to those of Gandhāra and Greece. Cf. O. Franke, *Geschichte des Chinesischen Reiches*, vol. II, p. 288.

[3] For the Japanese text see Sakaino Kōyō, op. cit., pp. 129-130.

The Shaka-*sanzon*

The Hōryūji Yakushi

in this text various elements which indicate that it is later than both the afore mentioned inscriptions. Actually this inscription consists of two parts. The first runs as far as the death of the Emperor Yōmei inclusive. It might have been from the same time as the Tenjukoku-*mandara*. Shōtoku Taishi is here called Taishi: the great prince. This word is not an exaggeration when one considers that he was prince-chancellor under Suiko. It is otherwise, however, with the second part in which Shōtoku is called the 'holy' prince from the Eastern palace. With this title Shōtoku had, here too, come to stand above the ordinary ruck. In the period between the composition of the Shaka-*sanzon* inscription and that of the Yakushi statue Shōtoku had, in the meantime, taken a more than ordinary place in popular belief. To express this in Catholic terms he had become a 'servant of God.' This latter part is therefore certainly younger than the inscriptions of the Shaka-*sanzon* and the Tenjukoku-*mandara*.

Finally there is another inscription about Shōtoku which falls somewhat outside the framework of the above mentioned three Hōryūji inscriptions. This was to be found on a memorial stone of an *onsen*, 温泉, or hot spring, of which there is mention in the *Fudoki* of Iyo. This *onsen* was situated on the island of Shikoku in the present-day prefecture of Ehime. It lies to the west of the modern town of Matsuyama. In this stone, together with the inscriptions already mentioned, Tsuda Sōkichi [1] sees the most ancient evidence of Shōtoku Taishi. It is supposed to have been erected later by monks in memory of a meeting between Shōtoku Taishi, the Paekche monk Esō and Soga Umako at this spring. According to some [2] their conversation on this occasion was concerned with the reconquest of Mimana by Japan on Silla. After describing how in former times the gods asked to bathe here the *Fudoki* continues: [3]

"In our times, too, it (the spring) meant to the diseased the healing force which cured maladies and revived the body. Five times emperors came here to bathe in it. Emperor Ōtarashihiko (Keikō) and Empress Sakairi *hime no mikoto* (his wife) came here once. Emperor Tarashi Nakatsuhiko (Chūai) and Empress Ōkinaga

[1] Tsuda Sokichi, *Nihon Koten no Kenkyū,* vol. 1, p. 157.

[2] Cf. Igarashi Sukehiro, "Taishisokkin no hitobito" (People of the *cercle* of Shōtoku), *Shūkyō Kōron,* vol. 25, 1955, n. 4, June number, p. 47.

[3] Cf. Takeda Iukichi, *Fudoki*, p. 322.

Tarashi *hime* (his wife, the later Jingū) also came here once. Then there also came here the prince Kamitsumiya Shōtoku. With him came the Koguryŏ monk Esō and the *omi* of Katsuraki (= Umako). At that time a memorial stone was placed on the hill near the hot spring with the following inscription:

'The sixth year and the tenth month of Hōkō,[1] viz. the year *hinoe-tatsu* (596) our great ruler and *Hōō* [2] (Taishi), the teacher of Buddhism Esō and the *omi* from Katsuraki walked to the village of Iyo. When they looked at the divine spring they rejoiced over the good things of this life. Together they spoke about its meaning and composed the inscription on this stone. It is a good thing to consider how the light of sun and moon from above does not conceal anything and how here below the miraculous spring keeps bubbling up. In everything one experiences Buddha himself, but one can also go unobtrusively among the people. One may enjoy it without becoming known at once. Would it be different here from what it is in the land of long life? [3] As the pistil of the lotus flower discloses or conceals itself, even so does one plunge into this wonderful spring and thus are diseases cured. Would one not become unconscious on coming out of the pond, where it rains flowers? Seeing the steep mountain walls one could live there like Tsu-ping.[4] The shadows of the camphor trees form curved arches as if they were five hundred silk umbrellas. In the morning the birds sing and play and twitter. What discordant sounds or noise could one hear there? Red leaves and flowers sparkle everywhere. The spring makes the water rise mixed with pearls of fruit and flowers. It runs and plays amongst them. Here one obtains a taste of the heavenly garden of abundance. Intelligence and talent bow respectfully before the *shichi-bo* (a plant). May also the sons of the nobility not be bereft of happiness.''' [5]

This inscription shows several signs which make it much later than all the above mentioned ones. The name Tsu-ping, which

[1] This is the same *nengo* as the above mentioned Hōkōgen, see footnote 17.

[2] See footnote 2 on p. 378.

[3] Literally: *jukoku*, 壽國, the land of long life.

[4] Tsu-ping, a person mentioned in the *Hou Han-shu*.

[5] In other texts of the *Fudoki* Shōtoku is only mentioned *obiter*. Thus the *Fudoki* of Harima; Takeda Iukichi, p. 179, mentions "a stone called Ōishi, 大石, which, from Shōtoku's time, comes from Yuke *ōmuraji* (= the Mononobe Moriya)." Then a hunting region of Shōtoku's is mentioned, op. cit., p. 377.

occurs in the *Hou Han-shu*, a work which arrived late in Japan, proves this. Otherwise this text is not without value as a description of the land of long life.

In all these texts and inscriptions Shōtoku Taishi is described as a respected, though not as a deified, being. Yet, when looking at the historical sequence of these texts, a gradually growing worship of Shōtoku Taishi may be observed. Via words such as *dharmarāja* in the Shaka and Iyo inscription its climax is reached in the Yakushi inscription: holy prince. This greatly changed in the second period:

b *The period of the compilation of the* Nihonshoki *and* Kojiki

The *Kojiki* is the first authentic text mentioning the name of Shōtoku Taishi. This reference, however, is very brief. In it only the following is to be found on Shōtoku amongst the Suiko chronicles: [1]

"Furthermore he (= Yōmei) was married to a younger sister (of Ōgitashi *hime*, the daughter of Soga Iname) Hashibito *no* Anaobe *no mikoto*. She gave birth to Umayado *no* Toyotomimi *no mikoto*."

This long name of Shōtoku in the *Kojiki* means when translated: the prince of the horses' stable of the radiant ears. This was an allusion to his birth in the neighbourhood of the horses' stable, which is narrated more fully in the *Nihonshoki*.

On account of this nomenclature a brief remark should be appended to this *Kojiki* text on the various names which Shōtoku was given. For each name often indicated a new phase in the development of Shōtoku-worship. This becomes evident in the *Kojiki*. For here the legend of his birth had already found expression in his name. The *Nihonshoki*, too, often uses this name, but moreover adds the word 'holy.' We observed that he is also called after his palace. The name now generally accepted, Shōtoku Taishi, 聖徳太子: the man holy by merit, only came into vogue a few centuries after his death, attended by his increasing popularity.[2]

[1] Cf. *Kojiki*, 3rd *maki*; Kuroita Katsumi, Maruyama Jirō, *Kokushitaikei Kojiki*, p. 149.

[2] The first writing to use this name was the *Hōryūji-garan engi* from the Kamakura period (1192-1333). This work may be compared with the *Gangōji-garan engi*, mentioned on p. 267. In it he is called: Higashimiya, Kamitsumiya Shōtoku-*hōō*, 東宮上ツ宮聖徳法王, the *dharmarāja* Shōtoku of the eastern upper palace. The appellation usual up to then was: Umayado

The above brief narration of the *Kojiki* especially points to Shōtoku's ancestry. It is very similar to the beginning of the Tenjukoku-*mandara* inscription. Both texts may be considered as utterances from a period in which there was not yet any question of a Taishi cult proper. Both narrate without any hesitancy his origin and his relationship with the Soga. Later this was more and more obscured. It was preferred to make it appear that Japan's history began with him. It is, therefore, hardly likely that in publications about his origin his relationship with the Soga-*shizoku* would be emphasised.[1] The reason for this is that it would hinder his glorification. History simply begins with him. Thus it was attempted to raise an artificial dividing wall between him and his relations.

Nevertheless, a complete valuation of Shōtoku begins right at the beginning, that is to say, with his ancestry. This was as follows. His paternal grandmother was a daughter of Iname, just as was his own mother. From this we must deduce that he too, therefore, in accordance with the customs of the time, was brought up in the company of his mother, i.e. of the Soga. It is to this, therefore, that he owed his Buddhism and his progressiveness. Viewed from these close ties with the Soga it is very improbable that Shōtoku was a kind of antithesis of them, as some have represented him.[2] It is more probable that Shōtoku followed the guidance of Umako who, be it remembered, was his *uji no kami*. We would rather think, therefore, with Matsukawa Jirō,[3] that there were no discrep-

kōshi and Kamitsu *kōshi*, Jap. 馬屋戸皇子 and 上ツ宮皇子 respectively: prince of the horses' stable and prince of the upper palace. Cf. Okabe Nagaaki, op. cit., p. 29.

[1] Cf. Sakaino Kōyō, op. cit., pp. 14 and 15. In it a pedigree is indeed given from the time of Emperor Kimmei. Since the author, however, limits himself to the male line: Kimmei—Yōmei—Umayado, he avoids the necessity of mentioning the name Soga. If he had, however, also mentioned their wives and the children of these wives, only then would the influence of the Soga have become evident, as each of the emperors mentioned here had married Soga women. Then the Soga ancestry of Yōmei and Shōtoku would also have been apparent.

[2] Cf. Kadowaki Teiji, *Jimmu Tennō*, p. 178. Similarly he considers the establishment of the 'cap degrees' of 603 a measure intended to neutralize the influence of the Soga.

[3] Cf. Matsukawa Jirō, "Soga Tennō no Rekishi" (History of the Soga emperors)', *Tennō no Rekishi*, p. 247: "Shōtoku was a nephew of Suiko's and Umako's son-in-law. Both were not only in affairs of state but also in

ancies between Shōtoku and Umako. Clearly Shōtoku, just as much as other members of the Soga-*shizoku*, respected Umako's important position.

In contradistinction to the above sparse data of the *Kojiki* the *Nihonshoki* contains an abundance of information about him. From this it repeatedly appears that there existed a positive worship of Shōtoku among its compilers. In the various tales related here this growth of myths can be observed. In the preceding chapters one of them, from the Sushun chronicles, was mentioned in which Shōtoku, as a kind of Constantine, also defeated Moriya of the Mononobe.[1] It was pointed out, in agreement with Tsuda, that all this is a falsification intended to deprive Umako of his wreath of victory.

Most data on Shōtoku, however, are to be found in the Suiko chronicles. From this most later additions were developed, many of them unreliable. All the development of the Shōtoku myth will therefore have to be approached and explained on the basis of these *Nihonshoki* data. These are amply sufficient for a Shōtoku biography. But one will have to bear in mind that in all these data truth and unbridled imagination are already closely interwoven. The true Shōtoku will have to be reconstructed exactly from this. It is, therefore, not enough to produce a summary reproduction of the *Nihonshoki* texts, the more so since they form the basis for further investigation.

Shōtoku's biography from the Nihonshoki

All the facts and stories belonging to Shōtoku's biography will be grouped in the following into two parts, according to their connection with either his birth and upbringing or his period of rule:

1) The whole chronicle from the first year of Suiko (593)[2] is concerned with his birth and upbringing:

---

their Buddhism closely connected with each other. Umako is likely to have had great respect for Taishi's knowledge. With regard to his father-in-law the latter probably had no ambitions of his own. That Suiko's court was a peaceful one is mainly to be attributed to the fact that these two got on well with each other."

[1] Cf. Chapter V, pp. 302 ff.

[2] Cf. *Nihonshoki*, 22nd *maki*, Suiko, 1st year, 4th month; Kuroita Katsumi, Maruyama Jirō, *Kokushitaikei Nihonshoki*, part 2, p. 136. Cf. W. G. Aston, op. cit., pp. 122-123.

"That summer, fourth month, tenth day, Umayado *no* Toyotomimi *no mikoto* [1] was appointed *kōtaishi* (= prince-chancellor).[2] He then undertook the *matsurigoto* (government). The whole administration (lit.: the 10,000 *matsurigoto*) was entrusted to him. He was the second son of Emperor Tachibana *no* Toyohi (Yōmei). His mother, the Empress, was called princess Anaobe *no* Hashibito. On the day on which the Empress was to bear him she walked about in the forbidden palace grounds in order to visit all the officials.[3] Thus she happened to approach the horses' stables. Exactly at their door she suddenly gave birth to him without any travail.[4] At birth he could already speak and possessed the knowledge of wisdom. He was quite capable of listening to the complaints of ten persons at the same time and of giving a verdict without making a mistake. Furthermore, he knew what was going to happen in the future. He was instructed in Buddha's doctrine [5] by the Koguryŏ monk Eji and in the non-Buddhist sciences by the scholar Kakuka. He had mastered both down to the smallest details. His father, the Emperor, loved him and allowed him to live in the upper hall of the southern palace. That is why he is called: Kamitsumiya, Umayado *no* Toyotomimi *no taishi* (the great prince of the radiant and quick(ly understanding) ears of the upper palace hall and the door of the horses' stable)."

In the account given above all kinds of things about Shōtoku have been brought together which in reality lay many years apart. Thus it is difficult to place his masters Eji and Kakuka in his youth. Both only came to Japan in 595. Shōtoku was then already 23 to 24 years of age and entrusted with the government of the

---

[1] Or *kōshi*, 皇子, imperial prince. The *furigana* text reads *miko*.

[2] He was the first in Japanese history to exercise this special function of *kōtaishi*. While Soga *no* Umako as *ō-omi* represented more directly the interests of his *shizoku*, Shōtoku as *kōtaishi* especially looked after the government affairs of the empress. As regards their interests they were both on the same level.

[3] Cf. what has already been noticed on this, Chapter V, footnote 4 on p. 322.

[4] According to some this Shōtoku story derives from the Bible. That is why Sakaino Kōyō considers that he ought to oppose this with no less interesting contention that "both the story of his miraculous birth and that of his 'Solomon's' judgement originate from India as the Biblical parallels do". Op. cit., pp. 13-14.

[5] Literally: the inner sciences: Buddhism. This is in contradistinction to 'outer sciences' = non-Buddhist sciences, also used here.

country.[1] The only fact belonging to his years of adolescence is his fight with the Mononobe which—as has been seen—is described in the Sushun chronicles.

2) Many political and religious occurrences belong to Shōtoku's period of government. Amongst the political ones those of importance were: his appointment as *kōtaishi* in 593 (see above); the building of his palace in Ikaruka in 610, which is situated in the present-day Hōryūji area;[2] the institution of the degrees of the caps in 603;[3] the promulgation of the 'constitution' in seventeen articles in 604;[4] and the order to keep up the state chronicles in

---

[1] Cf. Chapter V, footnote 1 on p. 295.

[2] Cf. *Nihonshoki*, 22nd. *maki*, Suiko, 9th year, 12th month; Kuroita Katsumi, Maruyama Jirō, op. cit., part 2, p. 139: "9th year, spring, 2nd month. The *kōtaishi* starts the building of a palace in Ikaruka." Cf. W. G. Aston, op. cit., p. 125.

[3] Cf. *Nihonshoki*, 22nd *maki*, Suiko, 11th year, 12th month; Kuroita Katsumi, Maruyama Jirō, op. cit., vol. 2, p. 141: "12th month, 5th day. The cap degrees are promulgated, viz.: *daitoku*, 大徳 (great merit), and *shōtoku*, 小徳 (small merit); *dainin*, 大仁 (great benevolence), and *shōnin*, 小仁 (small benevolence); *dairai*, 大礼 (great gratitude), and *shōrai*, 小礼 (small gratitude); *daishin*, 大信 (great confidence), and *shōshin*, 小信 (small confidence); *daigi*, 大義 (great deliberation), and *shōgi*, 小義(small deliberation); *daichi*, 小智 (great knowledge), and *shōchi*, 大智 (small knowledge); in all therefore twelve distinctions." Cf. W. G. Aston, op. cit., pp. 127-128.

The differences between these ranks appeared from the colour of the caps which were carried by those favoured. Hence they were called cap degrees: *kan'i*, 冠位. These cap degrees do not go back to direct Chinese influence, but to Korean. In those days a twelve-rank system, originating from Koguryŏ, was used in all three Koreas.

The distinction: 大小, *dai-shō*, was even then applied in this country. This system was unsuitable to Japanese circumstances; it had been borrowed heedlessly from abroad. Later, when contact was made with the Chinese ranks, this system was abandoned as boorish. Cf. Miyazaki Ichijō, "Sankanjidai no ikaisei ni tsuite" (The rank system of the three Koreas), *C.G.*, vol. XIV, 1959, Oct., p. 277.

[4] Since the present work is not aimed at Shōtoku Taishi's political activities, the purely political ones have been omitted from the articles here following, the more so as further on this law is discussed more as a whole than article by article. Because the first four are of a more general and religious purport attention has been concentrated on them. For the remaining articles see: W. G. Aston, op. cit., pp. 310-133. For the present text see: *Nihonshoki*, 22nd *maki*, Suiko, 12th year; Kuroita Katsumi, Maruyama Jirō, op. cit., vol. 2, pp. 142 ff.: "Summer, 4th month, 3rd day. The *kōtaishi* was the first to write a (constitutional) law in seventeen articles." Here the word *kenpō*, 憲法, is used for *law*, which means both regulation, law and

620.[1] By his appointment as *kōtaishi* he became, for all practical purposes, the executor of imperial policy. But of all the occurrences in his political career the promulgation of the seventeen articles was by far the most important, since by it the whole social structure of those days was overturned and a state run by officials came about with the Emperor as its centre.

The chronicles of his religious activities are further to be subdivided into religious occurrences with which Shōtoku is concerned as a result of his office of *kōtaishi*, and those where his own

---

constitution. If any reality is to be attributed to this law, then it was no more than a general norm for the society of those days, which itself was not yet ready to receive a constitution. Cf. K. Florenz, *Japanische Annalen*, pp. 13-20. It is intended to prove below that this law was an attribution to Shōtoku which took place at a time when Japan had an entirely different and reformed society. With it Shōtoku was to be made the designer of a true constitution.

The first article runs: "There must be respect for the *yawaragi*, 和, (i.e. harmonious mildness or 'moderation'). Also there must be the will not to oppose anything. All people are each other's friends. Only a few are aware of this. That is why it happens that they either do not obey their masters and parents, or live in discord with their neighbouring villages. When, however, the higher ranks live in harmony and the lower ones in friendship, when further, in the discussion of problems, concord is achieved, then insight will be obtained into the connection of all things. How much will then not be brought about?" For the second article see p. 391.

The third article runs: "The commands (of the emperor) must be accepted with deep respect. The master is heaven. The servant is earth. Heaven covers; earth, however, carries. According to the order of the four times very many signs penetrate them. If, however, earth attempts to dominate heaven this will lead to the very greatest catastrophe. (Aston, op. cit., p. 129, translates: 'Heaven would simply fall in ruin', but according to the punctuation 'heaven' belongs to the preceding sentence.) That is why, when the master speaks, his servants listen. When those of higher rank act, the subjects bow. If, therefore, you receive the emperor's orders with reverence, you must accept them with reverence. He who lacks that reverence is doomed to perdition of his own accord."

The fourth article runs: "Notabilities and officials (*tsukasa tsukasa*, 百寮, see Chapter V, footnote 4 on p. 322), the basis of your conduct must be reverence. The foundation of the government of the people lies in reverence. If there is no reverence amongst the higher ranks then there is most certainly all sorts of criminality. If, therefore, you, gentlemen, possess that reverence then there will be no disorder at any of the levels (of the population). If this reverence is found among the people then the country's government is carried on of its own accord." Cf. W. G. Aston, op. cit., pp. 129-130.

[1] Cf. first chapter, pp. 55, 56.

convictions and philosophy are involved. Among the former four must be accounted:

a. The decree concerning the spread of Buddhism in 594 which runs as follows: [1]

"Second year, spring, second month, first day. An imperial decree for the *kōtaishi* and the *ō-omi* (= Umako) to make the three treasures (= Buddhism) flower. All the *omi* and *muraji* vied to build houses for Buddha for the sake of the benediction of their ancestors. They called them *tera*." [2]

According to this chronicle the initiative clearly lay with Suiko and not with Shōtoku. Thus she proclaimed Buddhism as the state religion.

b. The second comprises the article on Buddhism in Shōtoku's law in seventeen articles. This may be found under the twelfth year (604), the fourth month, the third day: [3]

"The second article says: Respect the three treasures. These three treasures are: Buddha, Dharma and Saṇgha. They signify the total reversion at the end of the four kinds of life.[4] For all countries they form the highest aim. Which generation and which people would not respect this law? Of totally bad people there are only few, but even they, on the basis of this doctrine, can again become tractable. How can one, however, bend straight what was crooked if they do not convert themselves to the three treasures?"

Here it is interesting that in none of the seventeen articles was the *ujigami* faith mentioned or recommended.

c. The casting of a Buddha statue in 605 was the third religious fact which, again, took place on the initiative of the Empress rather than on that of Shōtoku. This appears from the text of the *Nihonshoki*: [5]

---

[1] Cf. *Nihonshoki*, 22nd *maki*, Suiko, 2nd year; Kuroita Katsumi, Maruyama Jirō, op. cit., vol. 2, pp. 136-137; cf. W. G. Aston, op. cit., pp. 122-123.

[2] See Chapter V, footnote 1 on p. 301.

[3] Cf. *Nihonshoki*, 22nd *maki*, Suiko, 12th year, 4th month, 3rd day; Kuroita Katsumi, Maruyama Jirō, op. cit., vol. 2, p. 142; W. G. Aston, op. cit., p. 129.

[4] These four kinds of life derive their distinction from birth: birth from eggs, from the womb, from fluid, or by means of a metamorphosis, in the way a butterfly evolves from a caterpillar. Cf. W. G. Aston, op. cit., p. 129, footnote 2.

[5] Cf. *Nihonshoki*, 22nd *maki*, Suiko, 13th year, 4th month, 1st day;

"Thirteenth year, summer, fourth month, first day. The Empress called together the *kōtaishi*, the *ō-omi* and all the notabilities in order to take a common oath, viz. to start the making of a copper and an embroidered image of Buddha of the size of 1 *chō*, 6 *shaku* (= 17 feet, 6 inches). The making of the Buddha was entrusted to the saddler Tori. At that time the King of Koguryŏ, Daikō, 大興, (Kor.: Te-phŭng),[1] heard that the Japanese emperor had ordered an image of Buddha. He sent a tribute of 300 *ryō* in metal (gold)."

d. The last was the sacrifice to all the gods of heaven and earth in 607. In this case too, according to the text, the initiative lay with the Empress: [2]

"(Fifteenth year, spring, second month,) ninth day. An imperial decree runs as follows: 'I have heard how formerly my imperial predecessors in their government, when they bowed before heaven or moved over the earth, manifested deep respect to the gods of heaven and earth.[3] Everywhere they worshipped mountains and rivers, and they were in a mysterious contact with the forces of nature. Thus *yin* and *yang* disclosed themselves and everything was brought into perspective and harmony. How then do we celebrate in our world the festivals of the gods of heaven and earth? Is there really room here for neglect? Let therefore all princes and notables respect with all their hearts the gods of heaven and earth.'" With this order of Suiko was also connected the special celebration for the gods following next and described under the fifteenth day: "The *kōtaishi*, the *ō-omi*, in the company of all officials, worshipped the gods both of heaven and of earth."

Of the four official acts of government mentioned here three were instigated by the Empress Suiko. Only the article on Buddhism stood in Shōtoku's name. From this it appears that, notwithstanding

---

Kuroita Katsumi, Maruyama Jirō, op. cit., vol. 2, p. 146. Cf. W. G. Aston, op. cit., p. 133.

[1] At that time in Koguryŏ a king of another name ruled, viz. Sansang (197-227).

[2] Cf. *Nihonshoki*, 22nd *maki*, Suiko, 15th year, 2nd month, 9th day; Kuroita Katsumi, Maruyama Jirō, op. cit., vol. 2, p. 146. Cf. W. G. Aston, op. cit., p. 135.

[3] Literally: *jingi*, 神祇. *Jin*, 神, has the meaning of celestial gods; *gi*, 祇, of terrestrial gods. Cf. Shimonaka Yasaburō, *Shintō Daijiten*, vol. 2, p. 208, col. III.

all the power exercised by Shōtoku, religious authority, concerning both Buddhism and the *ujigami* faith, rested practically entirely with Suiko. One may deduce from this that, even at the time of Shōtoku, Suiko was still considered the highest *uji no kami*. As such she embodied everything there was in the way of religion in the country. Her declaration that the *ujigami* faith was the object of special government care is the best proof of this. It is remarkable that exactly in these chronicles nothing is to be found of a special worship of Shōtoku.

The same cannot be said of the second group of facts. For these are concerned with Shōtoku's own religious mentality. In the preceding chapter two of them have been referredto, viz. Shōtoku's share in the foundation of the Shitennōji [1] and the allotment by him of a statue of Buddha to the Hata Kawakatsu.[2] As regards the former, doubt has already been expressed concerning the real role played by Shōtoku in the construction of this temple. It is impossible to establish in how far in the Kawakatsu story there is a question of truth or imagination.

Apart from these two, however, other occurrences may also be found in the *Nihonshoki* which indicate an already far advanced formation of Buddhist myth. In all there are three different occurrences, viz. his *sūtra* lecture, his relationship with the beggar of Kataoka, and what happened in connection with his death. Let us observe these facts in the *Nihonshoki* itself.

1) His *sūtra* reading and explanation took place in the year 606 (the fourteenth year of Suiko). The *Nihonshoki* describes this as follows: [3]

"Autumn, seventh month. The Empress ordered the *kōtaishi* to lecture on the *Shōman-gyō*, 勝鬘経, (Sanskr.: *Śrīmālā-devī-siṃha-nāda-sūtra*). After three days he finished his lecture. That year the *kōtaishi* lectured on the *Hokke-kyō*, 法華経, (Sanskr.: *Saddharma-puṇḍarīka-sūtra*) in the palace of Okamoto, 岡本. The Empress was greatly delighted. She gave the *kōtaishi* 100 *chō* of ricefields in the land of Harima. He added them to the lands of the Ikaruka temple (the Hōryūji)."

---

[1] Cf. Chapter V, pp. 302 ff.

[2] See p. 311.

[3] Cf. *Nihonshoki*, 22nd *maki*, Suiko, 14th year; Kuroita Katsumi, Maruyama Jirō, op. cit., vol. 2, p. 148; cf. W. G. Aston, op. cit., p. 135.

When one is acquainted with the primitive phase of the *ujigami* Buddhism of the Soga it is clear that with these *sūtra* explanations the exegete Shōtoku went immensely far beyond this stage. That such a sharp division was made between his Buddhism and that of, for example, the Soga is mainly based on these facts related in the *Nihonshoki*. It is rather interesting that, together with this *sūtra* reading, also the two *sūtras* referred to here are mentioned for the first time in the *Nihonshoki*. On account of this it will have to be investigated whether Shōtoku was not purposely connected with these *sūtras* to enhance his glory. In any case these two readings form an excellent basis for a later Buddhist idealisation of Shōtoku Taishi.

2) Then the moving story of the beggar of Kataoka, 片岡, is to be found in the *Nihonshoki*. In contrast with the preceding more matter-of-fact chronicles this story was intended as a downright sanctification of Shōtoku. It is supposed to have taken place in 613 (the twenty-first year of Suiko):[1]

"Twenty-first year, twelfth month, first day. The *kōtaishi* left for Kataoka. At that time a starving man was sitting by the road. He (= Shōtoku) asked him his name, but obtained no answer. The *kōtaishi* interested himself in his fate and gave him food and drink. He took his own *miso*, 衣裳, (or *mikeshi*: an ancient word for attire) off and with it dressed the starving man. Then he said: 'Now sit down comfortably'. Thereupon a song was made which runs as follows:

'Radiant sun,
On the mountain of Kataoka there is a starving and emaciated man,
Pitiful for the traveller to see!
Have you no parents and no master, as is the case with
Sprouting bamboo?
It is a starving and emaciated being
Pitiful for the traveller to see!'

"Second day. The *kōtaishi* had enquiries made about the starving man. When his messenger returned he said: 'The starving man has already died.' Then the *kōtaishi* became very sad and caused him to be buried on the spot. The grave was strongly sealed.[2] A long

[1] Cf. *Nihonshoki*, 22nd *maki*, Suiko, 1st year; Kuroita Katsumi, Maruyama Jirō, op. cit., vol. 2, pp. 156, 157. Cf. W. G. Aston, op. cit., pp. 144-145.

[2] This closing or sealing up consisted of placing a substantial quantity

time afterwards he (= Shōtoku) called the servants of his entourage together and said to them: 'The starving man who was lying by the side of the road some time ago was not an ordinary human being. He must have been a sage.'[1] He sent someone to look for him. When this person returned to him he said: 'When I arrived at the grave and looked at it, nobody had touched the heavily sealed grave. When, however, I opened it and looked in, the bones were not there any more. Only the clothes lay, folded, in the coffin.' Thereupon the *kōtaishi* sent him back and ordered him to fetch the clothes. Then he wore them again as he was used to do. His contemporaries greatly marvelled at this and said: 'It is verily thus that the one *hijiri* knows the other'. And he became more and more respected."

In this story about Shōtoku who, as an East Asian St. Martin, gave away his own clothes to a beggar, clearly trouble has been taken to illustrate Shōtoku's sanctity. Later it was to be further enhanced by the addition that the starving man was none less than one of China's most revered Tendai monks, just as also St. Martin's beggar was none less than Christ. This detail, too, formed the excellent basis for later, even greater mythologising. In the *Nihonshoki* itself this mythologising found its strongest expression in:

3) The *Nihonshoki* chronicles concerning Shōtoku's death. This is no longer related in a factual manner, such as is customary in the country's chronicles and has been, so far, the case with other prominent Japanese. His death is described as that of a god. It is related as having happened in 621 (the twenty-ninth year of Suiko):[2]

"Twenty-ninth year, spring, second month, fifth day. In the middle of the night the imperial prince Umayado Toyotomimi died in the Ikaruka palace. At that time all princes and subjects who live beneath heaven, all, one by one, felt as old people who had lost a loved son or who did not taste any more in their mouths the taste of salt and vinegar. Youths felt as if in him they had lost their

---

of earth on the tomb itself. The beggar is unlikely to have achieved a tomb, such as in those days was usual for persons of rank, with many grave chambers, such as, e.g., the tomb of Soga Umako. Cf. first chapter, footnote 3 on p. 34. Cf. W. G. Aston, op. cit., p. 145, footnote 2.

[1] Literally: he was an upright man. The text in *furigana* calls him a *hijiri*, cf. Chapter V, footnote 2 on p. 335.

[2] Cf. *Nihonshoki*, 22nd *maki*, Suiko, 29th year; Kuroita Katsumi, Maruyama Jirō, op. cit., vol. 2, pp. 159-161. Cf. W. G. Aston, op. cit., pp. 148-149.

beloved father. The streets were filled with lamentation. Men working on the land left their spades. Women no longer moved their pestles up and down in their mortars. Everyone said: sun and moon have lost their light. Suddenly heaven and earth have died. On whom shall we rely in future? That month prince Kamitsumiya was buried in the grave-mound of Shinaga. At that time, too, the monk of Koguryŏ, Eji, heard of the death of the *kōtaishi* Kamitsumiya. He then began to grieve deeply. For the sake of the *kōtaishi* he called all the monks to himself and held a communal exercise.[1] That day he himself expounded the *sūtras*. Then he swore the following oath: 'In the land of Japan there is a *hijiri* called Kamitsumiya Toyotomimi. Verily by virtue of heavenly consent he was born in the land of Japan possessing the virtues of a *hijiri*. He was entirely steeped in the three fundamental principles [2] and he followed the prescripts of former *hijiri*. He cherished a deep respect for the three treasures and delivered the people from their danger. He really was a great *hijiri*! Now the imperial prince has died! Even though I was an alien, yet we were good friends. What use is it to me if I should remain alive by myself? On the fifth day of the second month of next year I shall surely die. Therefore I shall meet the great prince Kamitsumiya in the Pure Land. Together we shall then undergo the changes of all people.' Eji then died when the day had come which he himself had fixed. Therefore his contemporaries said: 'Not only the great prince Kamitsumiya is a *hijiri*, Eji, too, is a sage.' "

When comparing these last occurrences related in the *Nihonshoki* with one another it is evident that just in these the glorification and mythologisation of Shōtoku find their strongest expression. And in each of the five chronicles mentioned above there is an underlying intention to elevate Shōtoku's Buddhism above that of his contemporaries.

Let us, however, look back not only at this last group of occurrences but also at all the other above mentioned particulars concerning Shōtoku. When investigating which of all these facts have played a decisive part in the later mythologisations of Shōtoku, it appears that several groups of facts may be left out of account for this purpose. In the first place his political achievements. By

[1] See Chapter IV, footnote 9 on p. 249.

[2] Which consist of heaven, earth and man. He was therefore a philosopher. Cf. W. G. Aston, op. cit., p. 149.

this it is not intended to contend that no part of this achievement was an enlargement of Shōtoku's real role, but only that it has not inspired later generations, after the final redaction of the *Nihonshoki*, to further expression of these data. Also, everything he did at the Empress Suiko's order left too little material on which to build a special worship of him, since he acted only as an executive in this. The fact that afterwards Shintōists, for example, harked back to Shōtoku's *Shintō* sacrifice of 607 occurred more because they were challenged by Buddhist idealisation to turn Shōtoku into an equally great Shintō figure. That is why they relied on this text as the only Shintō witness relating to Shōtoku.

Equally, the texts concerned with his relationship to the Shitennōji and the Hachioka temple were not only intended for the glorification of Shōtoku, but also to make the history of these temples commence as early as possible with the figure of Shōtoku. At the most some connection between him and the building of these temples will become discernable. This, too, became a separate development which contributed to his glorification.

That the above texts have been, with some reservations, cut loose from the further development of the Shōtoku myth does not necessarily mean that, in their relationship to Shōtoku, they would not require critical examination. They, too, may be helpful in the discovery of Shōtoku's true figure. For, though they themselves were subsequently no further mythologized, it is yet not impossible that they too were the reflection of a certain myth formation around Shōtoku which, however, had come to a stop before the final editing of the *Nihonshoki*. For this reason it cannot be permissible to regard these texts, without more ado, as the only Shōtoku material which reveals to us the true situation of his time. We shall revert to this.

Thus eventually another three groups of texts in the *Nihonshoki* remain which later, during the further growth of the Shōtoku faith, kept on playing a part. These were first of all the occurrences around Shōtoku's birth. The *Nihonshoki* chronicle which here suddenly loses all its sober factual character offered ample material for such glorification.

The same applies to the occurrences around his premature death. This death, viewed by the people as a punishment and experienced as a shock, in some way had to be glossed over. The Eji story clearly has such a tendency: Shōtoku was even holier than Eji and merited death as a punishment less than he. Both had to die to save the people. Later on even better explanations of his death were going to be found.

In between these two there were three other occurrences. These were the exposition of the *Shōman-gyō* and *Hokke-kyō*, the story of the Kataoka beggar and his attitude towards the building of the temples. The Kataoka story as well as the Eji one was illustrative of Shōtoku's holiness, but both were also concerned with his death as symbolised by that of the beggar. Birth, *sūtra* readings, the building of the temples and death thus form the 'topics' of groups of facts which illustrate how much Shōtoku was idealised even as early as the beginning of the eighth century. His further mythologisation was to take place on the basis of these topics. It arrived at its zenith in this that in Japan Shōtoku became the incarnate Buddha and the *avatāra* of Kannon. In Shintō he was turned into the god of the building trade [1] and of easy birth. The starting points of these developments lie in the *Nihonshoki*. But they are also at the same time of the greatest importance for the delineation of Japanese Buddhism in Shōtoku's time. On the basis of these data it is therefore that the attempt will be made to repair the image of:

2 The true figure of Shōtoku Taishi

So far the Shōtoku myth has been observed in its growth through various stages up to the time of the compilation of the chronicles. Resisting this mythological growth the very earliest data concerning his personality will have to be weighed in order to be able at least to approach his real figure. Only thus will a possibility open up of revealing the religious situation of his times. In order to arrive at this goal it will not be necessary to pull down phase by phase the image of Shōtoku as it has grown until the present day. The present investigation is not directed against the mythol-

[1] This occurred especially at the beginning of the fifteenth century. Beside Sugiwara Michisane, 菅原道真, (845-903), famous Chinese ambassador and minister, who was idealised into *Tenjinsama*, 天神様, celestial god and guardian of the sciences, Shōtoku Taishi became the building trade's own god. He even obtained a temple of his own, where he was worshipped in a Taishi hall. Here, too, discourses on him were given regularly. In popular art this was reflected in the shape of statues and poems. Cf. Ishida Mōsaku, "Ibutsu kara mita Taishiden no hensen" (Changes in the Shōtoku tales, as they may be observed in the remains), *Shūkyō Kōron*, vol. 25, 1955, no. 4, p. 32.

ogisation resulting from the Shōtoku faith. Our only interest is to retrieve the basic historical data, in which the myths concerning Shōtoku had their beginnings. That is why the revaluation of the Shōtoku figure is greatly dependent on the historical value of the above mentioned *Nihonshoki* data.

These, therefore, form the starting point for further examination of Shōtoku's figure. It goes without saying that this will have to cover facts from which, in the course of centuries, many Shōtoku myths derive. But also those activities have to be covered which have not occasioned later myth formation. These appear especially, as has been seen, in the field of politics. Thus one will have to ask oneself whether all the political reforms of Shōtoku, related in the *Nihonshoki,* such as the 'constitution' in seventeen articles and the institution of the cap degrees of rank, really did take place. If here we are dealing with historical reality, then Shōtoku, with his 'seventeen article constitution', had in fact cast aside the old *shizoku* society. His cap degrees of rank, furthermore, had undermined the real significance of the *uji no kami* of the *shizoku.* They would also have had religious implications. The present investigation, of Shōtoku's real figure, therefore does not only cover his Buddhist 'activities' but also his political ones. It is, for this reason, divided into a critical consideration of his political and Buddhist activities and the various occurrences around his death.

a *Examination of Shōtoku's political activities*

Although Shōtoku's politics are on the perimeter of the present investigation they were yet linked, in many aspects, with Japan's religious structure. Religion and politics as the two extremities of *matsurigoto* happen to be too close together. Thus some political success was often crowned with the building of a temple. The 'constitution' in seventeen articles contained a paragraph of its own on Buddhism and the cap degree system derived from Confucian philosophy. The seventeen articles put an end, it was thought, to the social structure of those days and thus, too, to the religious conditions on which that structure was mainly based. It is evident that in consequence of such radical changes all spiritual authority came to rest with Shōtoku Taishi, who thereby must have given his contemporaries the impression of a modern *uji no kami.* But was all this really the case?

In *Tennō no Rekishi* [1] Matsukawa Jirō gives a warning against exaggerating Shōtoku Taishi's political power. He is of the opinion that the centre of gravity of political influence in those days was to be looked for with the Soga Umako rather than with Shōtoku, who "with regard to his father-in-law did not aim at a disturbance of his peaceful relationship with him." According to him the ascendancy of Umako is convincingly apparent in a *Nihonshoki* chronicle of 607 which circumstantially describes how ambassadors from Korea presented their letters of credence to Umako. Shōtoku Taishi's name does not occur in this narrative.[2]

When viewing the factual political performance of the statesman Shōtoku Matsukawa considers it an open question whether Shōtoku is really the author of his most important deed, the law in seventeen articles. In contemporary Japan, too, this doubt is unusual since Shōtoku is generally acknowledged as the draftsman of this piece of legislation. One need but look up any historical work in order to establish this fact.[3] Matsukawa, however, does not trouble to motivate this doubt. But that does not imply that this doubt is so far-fetched. For it seems that in this law itself enough arguments can

---

[1] Matsukawa Jirō, "Soga Tennō", *Tennō no Rekishi*, pp. 246-247.

[2] Cf. *Nihonshoki*, 22nd *maki*, Suiko, 18th year, 10th month; Kuroita Katsumi, Maruyama Jirō, op. cit., vol. 2, p. 153: "9th day. The guests paid a visit to the court. On that occasion the order was given to make the Hata *no miyatsuko*, Kawakatsu, 秦造河勝, and Dobu *no muraji*, Usagi, 土部連菟, into guides for Silla. The Hashibito *no muraji*, Shiofuto, 間人連鹽蓋 and Abe *no omi*, Ōko, 阿閇臣大籠, were to accompany them to Mimana. From the southern gate the guests were taken along and given a place within the palace precincts. At that moment the Ōtomo, Kurafu *no muraji*, 大伴咋連, Soga *no* Toyora *no* Emishi *no omi*, 蘇我豊浦蝦夷臣, Sakamoto *no* Nukate *no omi*, 坂本糠手臣, and Abe Toriko *no omi*, 阿倍鳥子臣, rose from their places, went forward and kneeled before the court. After this the guests from both countries uttered a new salutation and declared the aim of their mission. The four *daibu* (cf. Chapter V, footnote 2 on p. 324) went to report this to the *ō-omi*. The *ō-omi* rose from his seat, stood in front of the palace hall and listened to them. Thereupon gifts were offered to all the guests, each according to his rank." Cf. W. G. Aston, op. cit., p. 141. This argument of Matsukawa's on the power of Umako is rather important when considering that we are dealing here with chronicles from which, after the fall of the Soga in 645, the great sympathy with the Soga and their domination was carefully eradicated.

[3] This opinion may be seen reflected in *Daigaku Nihon-shi*, vol. 1, p. 45 (Naoki Kōjirō) and e.g., in several articles of vol. 25, no. 4 of *Shūkyō Kōron* (Jubilee number of Shōtoku).

be found to support this doubt and seriously to question Shōtoku's authorship. It is Tsuda Sōkichi in particular who has pointed out several of these arguments.[1] These are the following:

1) The 'constitution' in seventeen articles is conceived on the basis of a state run by officials. The frequent use of the word: *tsukasa*, official,[2] points to this in the first place. It is remarkable that the system of officials is clearly assumed in this 'constitution' as existing, whereas it appears nowhere either from the law itself or from the *Nihonshoki* context that this system was established. Nor is there anywhere, for instance, a clause abrogating the old *shizoku* system.[3] Not only the frequent use of the word *tsukasa* presupposes this system, but also the tenor and the contents of all the articles aim at a definition of the morals and duties of the state official. All these articles, with the exception of that on Buddhism, form a group of regulations which apply in any state run by officials, independent of the question whether it is a Japanese, a Chinese or a Western one. They did not, however, apply to the Japanese *uji* society of those days. Thus these articles presuppose a social and political structure then not yet in existence. For the state run by officials was only to be established in 645 by the Taika reforms.

---

[1] Cf. Tsuda Sōkichi in *Nihon Jōdaishi no Kenkyū* and *Nihon Koten no Kenkyū*.

[2] The term *tsukasa*, official, occurs four times in the seventh article, twice in the thirteenth, and once in the fourth, eighth and fourteenth in the plural form. Cf. *Nihonshoki*; Kuroita Katsumi, Maruyama Jirō, op. cit., vol. 2, pp. 142 ff.; Tsuda Sōkichi, *Nihon Koten no Kenkyū*, vol. 2, p. 123. Then, in article twelve, *kuni no tsukasa*, 國司, is mentioned. Tsuda Sōkichi points out that both *kuni* and *tsukasa* are anachronisms. Cf. *Nihon Jōdaishi no Kenkyū*, pp. 290-291. According to him the *kuni no tsukasa* was an imperial tax-gatherer who, however, was not allowed, as was the *kuni no miyatsuko* or the *tomo no miyatsuko*, to keep this tax. This function of *kuni no tsukasa* presupposes a central administration and did not fit in with the social structure of those days in which the leaders of the *shizoku* enjoyed fiscal independence. Cf. Tsuda Sōkichi, *Nihon Koten no Kenkyū*, vol. 2, p. 122.

[3] Another argument for the late origin of this 'construction' is to be found in this, that the term *tomo no miyatsuko* is not mentioned in any of the articles whereas this function was only to disappear under Empress Kōtoku (645-655). Under Tenchi (third year) this title occurred only as a domestic one without significance, as if from days long gone by. Cf. Tsuda Sōkichi, *Nihon Jōdaishi no Kenkyū*, pp. 218-219.

2) Very closely connected with the preceding argument is the second. This is based on the fact that the law was not adapted to the actual situation of Japan at that time.

Socially Japanese society was, as has been repeatedly observed, delimited by the system of the *uji*. Now in this 'constitution' there is nowhere any mention of the special relationship which ought to exist between the *uji no kami* mutually and with their subjects.[1] Also the problem of the large *shizoku*, widely spread throughout various *be*, has not even been touched on. Yet this problem was much greater than that of the officials who did not even exist then. One may be reminded, for instance, of the fierce fight between the Soga and the Mononobe. The only problem the first article concerns itself with is merely the quarrel between neighbouring villages.[2]

From the religious point of view it is very strange that no mention whatever is made of the faith of Japanese society, the *ujigami* faith, although it was on this faith that the regime of those days rested to a great extent. Buddhism did indeed get an article of its own,[3] but this article does not witness to either a Buddhism such as we have come to know in, for instance, the preceding chapters. For here Buddha was no longer a new *ujigami*. Already people had even made themselves familiar with the notion of *saṁsāra*, notwithstanding the fact that in China — as has been seen in the third chapter—this had required a few centuries. This makes it clear

---

[1] The only word here recalling the old *uji* society is *kuni no* (*miya*)*tsuko*, which is used in the twelfth article together with *kuni no tsukasa* (*furigana*: *mikotomochi*) mentioned in footnote 2 on p. 401. On the basis of this word the present argument might perhaps be inverted by pointing out that it is exactly this word which refers to the ancient *uji* society. Now just this word, *kuni no miyatsuko*, is one of the few concepts remaining from the *uji* system which outlived it for a long time. Thus mention is made, e.g., in the *Nihonshoki* under the twelfth year of Temmu (684) and the first year of Jitō (690) of a *kuni no miyatsuko*. Here is it interesting that in the same connection also the word *kuni no tsukasa* is mentioned. Does this not raise the possibility of dating the twelfth article in the period of Temmu and Jitō? Cf. *Nihonshoki*, 29th *maki*, Temmu, 12th year, 1st month, 18th day; Kuroita Katsumi, Maruyama Jirō, op. cit., vol. 2, p. 367; cf. W. G. Aston, op. cit., p. 359; cf. *Nihonshoki*, 30th *maki*, Jitō, 1st year, 10th month, 22nd day; Kuroita Katsumi, Maruyama Jirō, op. cit., vol. 2, p. 396; cf. W. G. Aston, op. cit., p. 387; cf. Tsuda Sōkichi, loc. cit.

[2] Cf. footnote 4 on p. 390.

[3] Cf. p. 391.

that the whole wording of this article was not inspired by popular belief. It betrays the agency of a monk who, judged by his knowledge of Buddhism, belongs at the earliest to the end of the seventh century.

According to some this latter article was especially directed against the dictatorial influence of Soga Umako, even though he is not explicitly mentioned in it.[1] If, however, this article is a protest against Soga Umako's influence, how is it then to be explained that it could appear under his omnipotent and dictatorial government?

3) According to Tsuda [2] one law of five and another of six articles were mentioned in the *Tsin-shu*, 晋書, the collection of chronicles of the Chinese Tsin dynasty (265-420) under the Emperor Wu, 武, (265-290). These may have been the model for that of Shōtoku. Tsuda moreover draws attention to the fact that so many "imperial decrees of the *Nihonshoki* in reality were written by the redactors themselves". Thus the compilers of the *Nihonshoki* used the country's chronicles to demonstrate their own knowledge of Chinese law and the Chinese situation. They preferred to project their knowledge into a period of Japanese history which was just sufficiently remote for such an experiment. Various Chinese technical terms in the 'constitution' reveal that something similar has happened to that too.[3] In Shōtoku's time relations with China had

[1] Cf. *Nihonshoki*, 22nd *maki*, Suiko, 12th year; Kuroita Katsumi, Maruyama Jirō, op. cit., vol. 2, p. 146: "The seventeenth article runs: One should not decide upon important things alone. One should assuredly discuss them with many. Affairs of small weight need not be taken so seriously. For them (advice from) many is not required. If, however, in discussing important matters one doubts whether one is going to commit an error, one will only obtain the correct conclusion after consulting many." Cf. W.G. Aston, op. cit., pp. 132-133.

[2] Tsuda Sōkichi, *Nihon Koten no Kenkyū*, vol. 1, p. 126.

[3] Cf. Tsuda Sōkichi, op. cit., p. 126. He says: "In the constitution characters such as 君 (master), 臣 (minister), and 民 (people) are used. These witness to Confucian influence. This occurs especially in articles 3, 4 and 16. In other articles, too, abstract doctrines are found with a strongly Confucian bias. The fifth article uses as an adjunct of time the concept: 頃 (about) and article 11 the word: 時 (at that time). These are rather vague terms which occurred frequently in juridical language especially after the Taika reformation (645)." For this Confucian influence, especially with regard to the *yawaragi* (和) and the *rai* (礼), such as these are to be found in the book *Lun-yü* of Confucius, see also: Dr. Nakayama Kyūshirō, "Taishi-kenpō to Jūkyū" (The constitution of Taishi and Confucianism), *Shūkyō Kōron*, no. 25, 1955, vol. 4, pp. 6 and 7.

hardly started. They were then still too recent to have resulted immediately in a 'constitution' such as this.

On the basis of these three arguments it appears to the present author that this 'constitution' came into being only after the Taika reforms, probably at the time of the Emperor Temmu (673-687).[1]

Another regulation of Shōtoku's consisted of the institution of the cap degrees of rank. It has already been pointed out that this originated from Koguryŏ. It is not clear what he intended to do with these cap degrees, for the *uji* society of those days could hardly be expected to put up with these degrees of rank since it had its own hierarchical organisation. It should be remembered that there were not yet officials who had merited a special reward. These have, therefore, been transferred from Koguryŏ without realising what use they could be in Japan's totally different society. Thus, in Suiko's chronicles, there is only one place where people are mentioned with such a rank.[2] Here, therefore, we have another institution which was as little adapted to that time as the above-mentioned 'constitution'. Although one can neither prove nor deny its existence in Shōtoku's time, as in the case of Shōtoku's 'constitution', since Japan had been in regular contact with Korea for a considerable time, yet it may be considered as certain that at that time people did not know what to do with it. Hence, also, Tsuda's difficulty in motivating its place in Shōtoku's period.[3]

Whatever may have been Shōtoku's significance for Japan as a politician, it is certain that he neither upset the ancient *shizoku* society nor intended to depose the Soga who was too closely connected with him. The other chronicles concerned with his political activities

---

[1] Relying on what was established in footnote 3 on p. 401 and footnote 1 on p. 402 the present author considers it probable that the law in 17 articles came about after Empress Kōtoku (i.e. after 655) and before the disappearance of the word *kuni no miyatsuko* (at the latest 690). Cf. also Tsuda Sōkichi, op. cit., p. 136. Tsuda Sōkichi concludes, from the imperial title used in this text (which displays a great similarity to that of Emperor Temmu's period), that: "Summarising, we must say that the 'constitution' in 17 articles was written at the time of Temmu, or even after this." Cf. Tsuda Sōkichi, *Nihon Jōdaishi no Kenkyū*, pp. 293-294.

[2] A few years later, namely in 611, the dressing of the hair of bearers of this rank is described. Cf. *Nihonshoki*, 22nd *maki*, Suiko, 19th year, summer, 5th month, 5th day; Kuroita Katsumi, Maruyama Jirō, op. cit., pp. 153-154.

[3] Cf. Tsuda Sōkichi, op. cit., pp. 291-292.

leave him in a position which was certainly not higher than that of Umako; as *kōtaishi* he was at the most his equal. Of the remaining chronicles only the decree ordering the maintenance of the state chronicles is in his name. For his remaining official actions he was always co-responsible with Umako. On the basis of these established facts one can hardly continue to consider Shōtoku Taishi as the real founder of the Japanese nation.

Now that it has been established that Shōtoku was not himself the draftsman of the seventeen articles long 'constitution', one should ask oneself why it has been attached to his name. As regards its formulation and contents it can certainly not have been written by a Japanese. Otherwise one can hardly visualize why the *ujigami* faith was not given an article of its own in it. Confucian abstraction and details from Chinese constitutional law in it rather point to a Chinese author. Probably this was an Aya or a Hata. In ascribing it to Shōtoku the obvious intention was to hide this Chinese authorship and to attribute the achievement to Shōtoku. This role he can only have been given by the same nationalists of the time of the Emperors Temmu and Kammu who, for instance, burnt the records of the Korean immigrants.[1]

It is regrettable that Tsuda, too, omits to point out these underlying motives of the Shōtoku myth; thus he only took away from the person concerned that which he was not entitled to without rehabilitating the injured party.

b *Examination of the Buddhist Shōtoku Taishi*

If the seventeen articles of the 'constitution' do not belong to Shōtoku's biography, and if it was difficult to motivate the place of the cap degrees of rank in it, what should we then think of the mainly Buddhist data about him?

In the first part of this chapter it was established that these were chiefly concerned with his birth, the building of temples, the *sūtra* expositions and his death.

The chronicles dealing with his birth and the story of the Kataoka beggar were already mythology when they were incorporated in the *Nihonshoki*. His painless birth, the fact that he could already speak at birth and possessed great knowledge would not be dissonant in a hagiography from our own Middle Ages. They derive from a time

[1] Cf. Chapter III, footnote 3 on p. 222 and footnote 1 on p. 223.

when Shōtoku had already grown into superman; faith and piety had already overlaid the original facts. Probably the compilers of the *Nihonshoki* themselves, or their contemporaries, recorded these pious products of popular belief. These improbable occurrences also raise all sorts of doubt with regard to other, less spectacular, qualities of Shōtoku, such as his ability to give a Solomon's judgement and to predict the future. Since his intelligence was well above that of his surroundings these characteristics were indeed within the compass of human possibilities.

In how far Eji was his master has been indicated above.[1] This was the case when Shōtoku was 23 or 24 years of age and had had the country's government in his hands for two years. The Buddhism of his childhood, i.e. up to the time of his first meeting with the monk Eji, must therefore have been that of his own family. Thus it was a Buddhist-directed *ujigami* faith. It has already been pointed out that another occurrence in his youth, his miraculous role in the fight against the Mononobe Moriya, is historically untenable.[2] In the *Nihonshoki* all these mythologisings have overshadowed the genuine qualities of Shōtoku and made them dubious. Viewed historically, Shōtoku's youth has only been made more nebulous by them than it would have been, in any case, without them. All the later stories and developments in the Shōtoku myth have made these mists even denser.

The same may also be said about the story of the starving man of Kataoka. This, too, is obviously written as an illustration of his holiness. This is emphasised in the last sentence of the story: "And he became more and more respected." It is from this admiration that this story took its origin. Together with the story of the death of Shōtoku's master Eji it is, according to Tsuda, borrowed from a Chinese original, viz. the *Shên-hsien shuo*, 神仙說, i.e. 'Stories about Taoist immortals'.[3] Neither story, therefore, enables us to approach a single step nearer Shōtoku's figure.

As regards the building of several monasteries, it has already been shown in the preceding chapter[4] that at the most Shōtoku has been their Maecenas. He has therefore later been made, if mistakenly, the god of the building trade. This myth only came

[1] Cf. p. 388.
[2] Cf. pp. 304 and 305.
[3] Cf. *Nihon Koten no Kenkyū*, vol. 2, p. 118.
[4] Cf. pp. 302—315.

about because people did not wish to put the building of the Hōryūji in the name of the real builders, the Korean immigrants.

The most important data, however, for Shōtoku's Buddhism are the reports of his *sūtra* readings. On account of this a Buddhism entirely his own has been ascribed to him which made him tower far above his contemporaries. Yet he has had no share in this either.

In the first place it is out of the question that he should have been the author of some written commentary. For genuine written *sūtra* commentaries have been attributed to him, probably because of his *sūtra* readings mentioned in the *Nihonshoki*. Thus he is supposed to have written not only a commentary of his own on the *Hokke-kyō* and *Shōman-gyō*, but also on the *Yuima-kyō*, 維摩経, (Sanskr.: *Vimalakīrti-sūtra*). These commentaries are supposed to have been handed down to the present day.[1] So then, his commentaries on the *Shoman-gyō* and *Yuima-kyō* have been attributed to him only in the twelfth or thirteenth century. They are mentioned for the first time in the work belonging to that period, called *Hōryūji-garan engi*.[2] His commentary on the *Hokke-kyō* was put under his name in the *Kamitsumiya Shōtoku Hōōteisetsu* [3] which was edited more than a hundred years later than the *Nihonshoki*.[4] In the *Nihonshoki* itself no single written commentary is mentioned.

Yet a really very old *Hokke-kyō* commentary has been preserved up to the present day, which is attributed by many to Shōtoku. It was discovered in 1920 in the Imperial Library in Tōkyō. At the beginning of the text of this repeatedly corrected document there is the following superscription: "From Kamitsumiya's own collection, ruler of the land of Yamato. This work did not originate overseas." On the basis of this superscription it could of course be contended—as is done by many—that it is authentic. One should, however, differentiate between the age of the work itself and that of the superscription. Its last clause especially, "This work did not originate overseas", gives the impression of having been added at

---

[1] See the review of this, Sakaino Kōyō, op. cit., pp. 174-179.

[2] For this work see footnote 2 on page 385. According to it he is supposed to have written a commentary on the *Hokke-kyō* in three volumes and, in all, four *maki*; and a commentary on the *Yuima-kyō* in one volume and three *maki*; and a commentary on the *Shōman-gyō* in one volume and also in one *maki*. For the literal text see : Sakaino Kōyō, op. cit., p. 167.

[3] Cf. Chapter IV, p. 267, 268.

[4] The *Hōōteisetsu* for instance says of him: "He wrote a commentary on the *Hokke-kyō* in seven *maki*." Cf. Sakaino Kōyō, op. cit., p. 134.

a later date from anti-Chinese or anti-Korean resentment. This explicit denial of the foreign origin of the work might well signify its confirmation.

Suji especially has exhaustively studied the authenticity of this work.[1] From a comparison with Chinese works from Kansu it became evident to him that it certainly dates from the period of Shōtoku. For this reason Suji calls it Japan's oldest work, but he does not consider it proven that it comes from the hand of Shōtoku himself, even should one be convinced of its Japanese origin. Despite the fact that the characters, 御製, i.e. work worthy of veneration (because it is Shōtoku's), have been inscribed on the whalebones to which the work has been affixed, Shōtoku's authorship remains unthinkable. Of this Tsuda says:[2]

"We should not forget here that Taishi did not study the *sūtras* as an expert and a monk. Burdened with the heavy national task, his duties did not release him. The deeply scholarly explanations had little in common with the religious experience and the day-to-day life of the period, the more so since the former did not signify much more than praying for one's happiness here on earth and in the hereafter."

Another argument is to be found in the fact that Shōtoku was only instructed for a short period by Eji in Buddhism after he had taken on himself the government of the country. Thus he must have had little time for the study required for the writing of such a commentary. For this assumes a deep knowledge of the *Hokke-kyō* which in itself is already difficult of comprehension and especially for a Japanese such as him, written in unintelligible Chinese. If this commentary was conceived in Shōtoku's surroundings it is more likely that it was written by a monk such as Eji, if need be to the order of his master and 'disciple' Shōtoku.[3] The present author, however, agrees with Tsuda [4] that all this was the work of a *Hokke-kyō* group *par excellence*, the Tendai-*shū*.[5] For this group wished

[1] Cf. Suji Zennosuke, *Nihon Bunka-shi*, Tōkyō 1953, vol. 1, pp. 25-27.

[2] *Nihon Koten no Kenkyū*, vol. 2, p. 137.

[3] Especially Suji, op. cit., p. 26, strongly inclines towards this view.

[4] Cf. Tsuda Sōkichi, loc. cit.

[5] This group was thus called after the mountain T'ien-t'ai, in Tse Kiang, where its founder Chih k'ai, 智顗, spent the greater part of his life. Influenced especially by the Sanron and Dhyāna schools in China, he drafted its doctrine without turning it into a religious organisation. He was especially fascinated by the harmony enclosed in all things which keeps them to-

to make use of this and other Shōtoku data in order to prove that Shōtoku had really been its pioneer. Of this Tsuda says:[1] "The

gether in the Buddha nature (*buddhattva*) common to all. One becomes conscious of this harmony in all things in deep contemplation. The foundation of this doctrine was laid down by Buddha himself in the *Hokke-kyō*. He considered this work, above all, the most perfect writing on Buddha. His activity was mainly concerned with the writing of several commentaries on this *sūtra* and on the *Mahāprajñā-pāramitā-śāstra* of Nāgārjuna and the *Mahāparinirvāṇa-sūtra*. It was only when he had reached the age of 55 that Chih k'ai (538-597) became convinced that he really should form a group of his own in order best to preserve his doctrine for posterity. However, he never got as far as that. It was his disciples especially who formed such a group. This group developed well up to the year 845 when, as a result of anti-Buddhist laws, it had to leave China and make room for Taoism. On this the Japanese Tendai continued to build. It was especially Saichō, 最澄 (767-822), who afterwards obtained the honorific title of Dengyō Daishi, 伝教大師, who called upon it as a militant group against the Nara sects. He attempted to prove with his doctrine of perfect harmony that all these Nara sects were already antiquated and thus had lost their raison d'être within the Buddhism of those days. In 804 he travelled together with Kūkai, 空海 (774-835), the founder of the tantristic Shingon, 真言, school to China. There he found confirmation of what he had learnt in Japan about the Tendai. After nine months he returned to Japan. On January 3rd, 806, the Tendai was officially acknowledged by the Japanese state. Just as the Japanese Emperor Kammu moved the seat of his empire's government to Kyōto, even so Saichō accompanied him from Nara to the sacred mountain Hiei, near Kyōto. Here he went on to expand his new school.

Meanwhile he had to make a stand here against his former travelling companion Kūkai, who began to use the same methods with regard to the Tendai that Saichō had used against the Nara sects, by proving with his tantrism that the Tendai, too, did not appeal any longer to the mentality of the Japanese people, whose syncretism fell in good soil in the tantrism of Shingon. This was too much for Saichō. His last years are, as a result, marked by an embittered fight against Kūkai, who completely ignored him and his school. This fight was continued by his successors Enzai, 円澄 (772-837), Ennin, 円仁 (794-864), and Annen, 安然 (end of the 9th century) and others. It is exactly in this period that, on behalf of this struggle, many new 'ancient' sourcers were discovered which were to prove the veracity of the Tendai. In one of these sources, for instance, Shōtoku became, in one of his former lives, one of the co-founders of the Tendai. His *Hokke-kyō* commentary was an invitation to the Tendai to render him one of the predecessors of the Japanese Tendai. For further data see Fukuda Tadashi, *Tendaigaku-gairon*, Tōkyō 1954, pp. 1-61.

On this Tendai influence upon the mythologisation of Shōtoku Taishi see my article: "Oorsprong en groei van een mythe" (Origin and growth of a myth), *H.M.*, XXXXVI, 1967, no. 2, May, p. 98-113.

[1] Cf. Tsuda Sōkichi, op. cit., p. 136.

relationship which bound Taishi (= Shōtoku) to the *Hokke-kyō* had only been thought up, just as the story about Eji (after Taishi's death), after the entrance of the Tendai ideology into our country." It appears, therefore, that the *Hokke-kyō* commentary originally comes from China; at the beginning of the ninth century, however, when the battle between the Tendai sect and the other Nara schools was at its fiercest, this work of the Tendai was ascribed to Shōtoku.

What applies to these written commentaries equally applies to Shōtoku's *sūtra* lectures, even though in the *Nihonshoki* itself a *Shōman*- and a *Hokke-kyō* lecture are described.[1] It is remarkable that, in the text of the *Nihonshoki* dealing with these readings, there is question of a reward of rice fields situated in Harima which were to be allotted to the Hōryūji. Because of this latter detail it may be assumed that the compilers of the *Nihonshoki* have derived it from the traditions of the temple. These were the same sources from which, later, the afore-mentioned *Hōryūji-garan engi* originated. It is, therefore, rather interesting that in the latter work too Shōtoku's *sūtra* explanation is mentioned.[2] Apart from a few extensions which were evidently added later, this text is found again in a much older work which has been mentioned before, the *Kamitsumiya Shōtoku Hōōteisetsu*.[3] When comparing the one with the other it appears that these texts are closely related. They indicate two cross-sections in a direct development in which that of the *Hōōteisetsu* is apparently the older.[4] With regard to the real wording of the *sūtra*

---

[1] Cf. p. 393.

[2] The translation of this text runs: "The empress who resides in Owarida (Suiko) invited in the year *tsuchinoe-uma* (6th year of Suiko), 4th month, 15th day, the prince Kamitsumiya Shōtoku and ordered him to lecture on the *Hokke*- and *Shōman-gyō*." Cf. Sakaino Kōyō, op. cit., p. 164.

[3] The translation of this *Hōōteisetsu* text runs: "The year *tsuchinoe-uma*, 4th month, 15th day. The empress of Owarida sent for the prince Kamitsumiya and let him lecture on the *Shōman-gyō*." Cf. Sakaino Kōnō, op. cit., p. 157.

[4] The two texts in footnotes 2 and 3 above may for instance be compared. Here the Shōtoku data contained in this relatively ancient *Hōōteisetsu* will have to be considered, even though briefly because of lack of space. Apart from a few details this material does not differ in essentials from that of the *Nihonshoki*. The latter work does not mention, for instance, a birth or a death date for Shōtoku. The *Hōōteisetsu*, on the other hand, calls the year *kinoe-uma* (574) the year of his birth. It also mentions other wives of Shōtoku. Especially on two points it has expanded the original *Nihonshoki* data. The first was the building of temples. It calls him the builder of several temples: the Shitennōji, the Hōryūji, the Chūgūji, the Tachi-

lecture of the *Hōōteisetsu*, the *Hōryūji-garan engi* introduced an extension with three characters. On the other hand the *Nihonshoki* left the *Hōōteisetsu* text as it stood, but gave the *Hōryūji-garan engi* extension concerning the *Hokke-kyō* lecture in a separate clause, composed according to a divergent formula. This situation has been clarified in the following diagram:

HŌŌTEISETSU: 令講 勝鬘経 trans.: She ordered (him) to lecture on the *Shoman-gyō*.
NIHONSHOKI (1): 令講 勝鬘経 trans.: She ordered (him) to lecture on the *Shoman-gyō*.
HŌRYŪJI-G. ENGI: 令講 法華 勝鬘経等 trans.: She ordered (him) to lecture on the *Hokke-kyō* and *Shoman-gyō*.
NIHONSHOKI (2): ×講 法華 ××経× trans.: He lectured on the *Hokke-kyō*.

From a comparison of the *Hōryūji-garan engi* with the first two texts it appears that of the three additional characters two signify *Hokke*. The third character, *tō*, 等, is still used with a double meaning. Attached to the word *kyō*, 経, *sūtra*, to form *kyōtō*, 経等, it might be its plural form. Now in Japanese there is usually no audible difference between singular and plural. These have usually, therefore, to be deduced from the context. Thus *kyō* without this *tō* may be equally well singular or plural. Moreover the word *tō* also has the meaning of *et cetera*. In this latter meaning the possibility arises of including other *sūtras* not yet mentioned. With the addition of this last character in the above diagram the text of the *Hōryūji-*

---

banaji, the Hachiokaji, the Ikebeji and the Katsurakiji. Cf. Sakaino Kōyō, op. cit., p. 127. In the *Nihonshoki*, however, only the Shitennōji is mentioned. Of the Hachiokaji the text explicitly relates that the Hata Kawakatsu was its builder. The Hōryūji was built in Ikaruka, where Shōtoku resided. This must have been the Ikarukaji of the *Nihonshoki*. There, however, it is nowhere stated that Shōtoku was also the builder of this temple, as we saw (cf. p. 313). But even if this last temple be granted to Shōtoku he can, then, according to the most liberal interpretation of the *Nihonshoki* texts, only be accepted as the founder and builder of two temples. Thus the *Hōōteisetsu* has added five, although of one of these five, the Hachiokaji, it is known for certain that Shōtoku was not its builder.

The second extension is concerned with the *sūtra* commentaries. Admittedly Shōtoku, according to the *Hōōteisetsu*, gave only one reading, but at the same time he became the author of several *sūtra* commentaries. Cf. Sakaino Kōyō, op. cit., pp. 156-157.

garan engi offers the possibility of inserting further *sūtras* apart from the two already mentioned.

When further comparing the *Nihonshoki* texts of this diagram with one another and with the two others two further things leap to the eye.

First of all the wording of the *Hokke-kyō* lecture differs completely from that of the other ones. This also appears elsewhere. In the *Nihonshoki* this paragraph on the *Hokke-kyō* has been attached rather loosely to that on the *Shōman-gyō*. That was done without any date and in the rather vague words: 'That year etc..' There is no question of an invitation by Suiko. Tsuda [1] further points out his reward of land for his reading of the *Hokke-kyō* "as if he were a monk". To a person of Shōtoku's authority such an action on the part of the Empress meant a humiliation rather than a reward. By this, too, the chronicle reveals that it was written at a time when the position of the emperor was entirely different. It may be concluded from this that, if the lecture on this text did take place in Shōtoku's time, it was done not by Shōtoku but by a monk who, therefore, was rewarded as a monk. It appears that this *Nihonshoki* text is an even later extension of what the *Hōryūji-garan engi* attempted to relate in one form of wording. This loose addition to the *Shōman-gyō* chronicle may well be connected with the attribution of the *Hokke-kyō* commentary to Shōtoku by Tendai monks. Thus it may be explained that no indication of a *Hokke-kyō* lecture is to be found in the 'older' text of the *Hōōteisetsu*. This absence and the lack of unity in the wording concerning the *Hokke-kyō* lecture reveal the arbitrariness with which it was inserted in the *Nihonshoki*.

The second point which attracts attention in this comparison is the fact that the *Shōman-gyō* lecture in all the works mentioned here is described in the same standard wording. Moreover, this mutual dependence appears not only from the comparison of the characters in the above diagram but also from the wording of the whole chronicle from which these characters are taken. This mutual similarity implies a source which has also been used by the compilers of the *Hōōteisetsu* and the *Nihonshoki*. In its sober brevity the material of the *Hōōteisetsu*—at least as regards this detail—appears to be closer to that source than the *Nihonshoki*. This stamps the wording of the *Hōōteisetsu* as the most original particular. Later it was

[1] Cf. Tsuda Sōkichi, op. cit., p. 129.

expanded and mythologised into the reading of the *Hokke-kyō* and later still into Shōtoku's authorship of the three commentaries. That is why Shōtoku is supposed originally to have read or explained the *Shōman-gyō* only. We shall now have to investigate whether he has really done so.

It is, in itself, not impossible that Shōtoku was acquainted with this *sūtra*. The *Shōman-gyō*, namely, as well as the *Hokke-* and *Yuima-kyō* had been translated into Chinese between 402 and 453,[1] There is therefore a possibility that in Shōtoku's time these had already arrived in Japan via Korea. At the time of the *sūtra* reading there was not yet any direct contact with China. This was only the case after 607 and 608.

To this, however, should be added that, starting from Shōtoku himself, it was impossible for him, an illiterate, to become in three years time a person able to read *sūtras* even translated into Chinese. In China itself these latter, because of the many Sanskrit corruptions, are accounted the most difficult literature. Added to this the translators had only imperfectly succeeded in reproducing various Buddhist basic concepts in good Chinese. This has already been emphasised in the first part of the third chapter.[2] It is, therefore, out of the question that a beginner in Chinese such as Shōtoku Taishi could read them. Anyone who realises the great linguistic differences between Chinese and Japanese and the limited opportunities for the study of language at that time will admit this. At the present day nine years schooling are set aside in Japan for the study of the Chinese characters, drastically reduced to 1,800. In the short period of three years Shōtoku—however intelligent and however much a genius he may have been—could not possibly learn to read, between all the distractions of his office, any *sūtra* at all, let alone explain it.

However unimportant these reports of Shōtoku's *sūtra* lectures may be for the formation of a judgement of his time, they yet afford some insight into that form of Buddhism which later one would have liked to see realised in Shōtoku as Japanese Buddhism *par excellence*, lay Buddhism. The circumstance that he was supposed to have lectured exactly on these writings was, according to

---

[1] Cf. W. M. de Visser, op. cit., vol. I, pp. 3-6.

[2] Cf. Chapter III, pp. 153 ff.

Dr. Nakamura Moto,[1] brought about by Japan's own nature. Thus the *Hokke-kyō* was chosen because this dealt with the problem of the redemption of the common man. The *Yuima-kyō*[2] defined the position of the lay Buddhist in the world and the *Shōman-gyō* that of women in Buddhism. Here it should not be forgotten that this trend of thought was also that of the Tendai-*shū*. In sharp rivalry with the Shingon-*shū*, the first group of tantric Buddhism in Japan, and no less from a reaction to the aristocratically exclusive Nara schools, the Tendai-*shū* tried in every way to win over the layman. It is therefore from Tendai-*shū* proselytism that Shōtoku, as a Buddhist layman, was elevated well above his contemporaries such as Soga Umako and the Empress Suiko. Nevertheless he originally had had nothing to do with the *sūtra* readings attributed to him.

The above explanation of Nakamura's, however acceptable, does not satisfy as an explanation of the question why Shōtoku, according to the oldest data, read the *Shōman-gyō* rather than a much more influential *sūtra* such as the *Hokke-kyō*. Viewed historically, the reading of the *Shōman-gyō* afforded the Tendai groups a welcome occasion to attach to it a reading of the *Hokke-kyō* as well. Why was this occasioned by a reading of the *Shōman-gyō*?

In the present author's opinion the reason for this is to be found in the fact that this *sūtra* refers to the person who, in Shōtoku's time, actually possessed all spiritual authority, the Empress Suiko. This appears from the special character of this *sūtra*. For the *Shōman-gyō*, i.e. the *Śrīmālā-devī-siṃha-nāda-sūtra*, is nothing but a personal testimony of the princess Śrīmālā concerning her faith in Śākyamuni.[3] This was to give woman a place in Buddhism, which originally she had never had. In Shōtoku's time there was need of this as the country happened to be governed by a woman, the Empress Suiko. The connection between her and this *sūtra* is also unmistakeably present in the *Nihonshoki*. For it was the Empress Suiko herself who invited Shōtoku to explain this *sūtra*. It is further said that she was very pleased with his explanation. In the minds of

---

[1] In his article: "Fuhenteki kokka no risō" (The ideals of a universal nation), *Shūkyō Kōron*, vol. 29, 1959, no. 9, p. 12.

[2] Dengyō Daishi (= Saichō) himself wrote a commentary on this *sūtra*, viz. the *Yuima Kaihatsu*, 維摩開発. Cf. de Visser, op. cit., vol. II, p. 601. Cf. Jakob Fischer and Yokota Takezō, *Das sūtra Vimalakirti*, Tōkyō 1944.

[3] Cf. Inoue Tetsujirō, op. cit., p. 582, col. II.

the later chroniclers this *sūtra* lecture had to give her position as an empress and a Buddhist the required support. In her, Japanese Buddhism was forced to give up its discrimination against women. This was caused by the Empress Suiko's powerful support, greater than that of her predecessors. This is witnessed too by her decree about the expansion of Buddhism in 594, the order for a statue to be executed by Tori and his reward for this in 605 and 606. Finally the exposition of the *sūtras* by Shōtoku was equally on her initiative.

There were, however, other reasons as well why Shōtoku was made to explain the prominent place of Suiko. One of them is that she, as a woman, was able to become empress at all. In the Japan of the last thousand years that would have been impossible.[1] For, in contrast to Japanese antiquity, women played no role whatever in public life. In Shōtoku's Japan this was still possible, for which there were several reasons. According to Higo Kazuo one of them was that the men of her surroundings projected on to her a kind of deity.[2] This reason may better be formulated otherwise: in Suiko, unmarried like Himiko, there was still present something of the old Shamanism. Her Japanese name, Toyomike Kashikiya, has the meaning: she who prepares the sacrifice for the gods.[3] That is why there was a relationship between her and the gods which was so close that she could still be accounted one of the last really influential Shamans, of whom Japan had known so many in antiquity. All this explains why in the *Nihonshoki* she made her religious influence felt. That is apparent in the decree of 594 concerning its expansion with regard to Buddhism. The old *ujigami* faith witnessed her special influence in the imperial decree of 607 on the making of sacrifices to Japan's own celestial and terrestrial gods. As a religious leader she comes more to the fore in the demythologised *Nihonshoki* than Shōtoku himself. In that sense the Empress Genshō's characterisation (who lived a century after her)

---

[1] Cf. Higo Kazuo, art. "Jōteiki" (Chronicles of the empresses), *Tennō no Rekishi*, p. 232.

[2] Ibid. He compares this with the great reverence for Mary customary in the Middle Ages in Western Europe.

[3] Literally: princess of the cooking place of the abundant and sublime food. Cf. W. G. Aston, op. cit., p. 121. According to Higo Kazuo, op. cit., p. 231, she is supposed especially in her youth to have exercised this function of preparer of sacrifices.

equally applies to her: "The empress possessed a thorough knowledge of the gods."

In the old *shizoku* society of those days she was the person in whom the old Shaman faith strongly revived. This faith must have been so deeply rooted in the people that Buddhism would have been injured by disturbing her position on the basis of Buddhism itself. That even here she had such a powerful influence is at the same time a proof of the fact that this, too, was still along the same lines as the *ujigami* faith and had been rendered subject to Suiko's Shamanism. Her proclamation on its expansion was, therefore, able to bring the people, who believed in her as a Shaman, nearer to Buddhism in great numbers. For this was an instruction from its highest *uji no kami*. She did not cease to be this by her decree.

After all the preceding demythologising one gains a strong impression that the place at first taken by Suiko was handed over to Shōtoku in a later more Buddhist and patriarchal society. Thus he became, to many, a kind of superman. In the *Nihonshoki* the main fact which is emphasised is that he took upon himself the whole government (= *matsurigoto*). Thus the historic Shōtoku came to be politically and in matters of religion strongly exaggerated at the expense of the Empress. The story of the *Shōman-gyō* reading thus appears as a clever attempt of a later date to conceal Suiko's Shamanism by motivating her predominance on Buddhist grounds. Perhaps it is exactly this point from which the whole mythologising of Shōtoku started. It is to be regretted that open-minded and honest authors such as Suji and Tsuda in their analysis of the *sūtra* commentaries hesitatingly avoid these last logical conclusions.

The preceding pages may have given the impression that it is the present author's aim to demolish the aureole with which Shōtoku had come to be adorned in the course of centuries. That was, however, not intended. It was intended rather to discover his real personality. Even so, little has remained of the picture presented to us by the *Nihonshoki*. His position in antiquity has been pushed back by this examination behind that of Suiko and Umako. At the same time, however, those who for the sake of Shōtoku's myth had to be 'debunked', recovered their true place in history. This means in fact that a kind of Taika reform did not begin with Shōtoku's 'constitution' of 604, but only after 645. Japan's social and religious pattern continued as before. Another consequence was that popular and monkish Buddhism also under Shōtoku remained on either side of a Japanese-Korean linguistic frontier, since it was impossible that Shōtoku had explained the *sūtras*. Thus Shōtoku's balloon, which was blown up in the course of centuries, was pricked, chiefly by Tsuda and Suji. After a long journey we are now faced with a new Shōtoku figure, even more veiled in mists.

This new Shōtoku figure reveals at the same time the nationalist tendency which caused everything not properly Japanese, though valuable, in the very earliest Buddhist development simply to disappear from history behind Shōtoku's broad back. These were the dependence on Korean immigrants and their cultural, political and religious achievements. To this also belongs everything which compromised the Japanese as such, such as Suiko's matriarchy and the enormous open-mindedness of that protector of immigrants, Soga *no* Umako.

However valuable the discovery of this tendency may be for a correct insight into Japanese history, this investigation has yet not rendered Shōtoku's figure entirely superfluous. For there are some other sources which give us the opportunity of approaching positively this so far 'debunked' Shōtoku. These enable us to obtain some insight into his own religious views in so far as they reflected those of his Japanese contemporaries. This insight, then, into his own religious world has become possible by this 'debunking.' We owe this insight chiefly to various chronicles, inscriptions and works of art preserved up to the present day, all of which are connected with his death. Through them it is possible to reveal:

c *The Buddhist faith of Shōtoku and his contemporaries*

When examining the *Nihonshoki* texts remaining after Shōtoku's demythologisation it appears that while, on the one hand, as a Buddhist he continued the traditions of his Soga family, on the other hand he also equally clung to the old *ujigami* faith. This latter is evident from his sacrifice to the gods in 607.[1] It appears from this, just as from the still-remaining Buddhist chronicles about him, that as a Buddhist or as a 'Shintoist' he always acted on the instructions of a higher spiritual authority, viz. Suiko. From this it appears that the figure of the emperor or empress still continued,

[1] Cf. p. 392.

in his time, to determine the religious mentality of the people. Now the interesting fact emerges under Suiko that that imperial authority covered not only the *ujigami* faith but also Buddhism.

How strongly people were convinced of this in those days appears from the letter which Silla, together with Mimana, sent to the Empress in 600:[1] "In heaven is the *kami* and on the earth the emperor. Whom would one have to fear but these two *kami*?" In this text, then, the Empress is implicitly called a *kami* who is on the same level as the *kami* in heaven. This text, too, might serve as a starting point for de-mythologising Shōtoku. For Suiko could only be called *kami* here because people saw in her a Shaman or *uji no kami* connected with the gods. This defined her whole value for the people as well as for Shōtoku. That is why her orders were carried out without demur and why she possessed an authority which did not distinguish her from her predecessors. Only herein not only the *ujigami* faith but also Buddhism had found a place and thus—willy nilly—came to be part of the *ujigami* faith. That is why Buddhism was viewed as a new possibility of transmuting the old rather than as a system introduced to upset it.

This characterisation of imperial Buddhism also applies to popular Buddhism. This, too, was understood by the people in terms of the *ujigami* faith. In this 'primitive' Buddhism, then, only one thing could be found which gave it an advantage over the *ujigami* faith. These were the Buddhist illustrations. This can be proved from the *Nihonshoki* and plastic art of that period. With these means it is possible to reconstruct the true nature of the Buddhism of Shōtoku's time. It will be attempted to render this reconstruction possible by examining how the sayings of the *Nihonshoki* can be verified by the plastic arts of that period.

Apart from the Suiko texts already dealt with there is mention only of statues in the remaining *Nihonshoki* texts on Buddhism. In the fifth chapter it has already been indicated how important a part statues—and later whole temples—played in the Buddhism of that period.[2] Under Suiko these statues were not unconnected with non-Buddhist ancestor worship. Linked up with the decree of 594

---

[1] Cf. *Nihonshoki*, 22nd *maki*, Suiko, 8th year, 2nd month; Kuroita Katsumi, Maruyama Jirō, op. cit., vol. 2, p. 139; cf. W. G. Aston, op. cit., p. 125.

[2] Cf. pp. 362 ff.

on the expansion of Buddhism one may find, as already quoted,[1] the passage on *omi* and *muraji* who, for the sake of the benediction of their ancestors, rivalled each other in building houses for Buddha which they called *tera*. It is in this passage that the popular faith is clearly typified. The explanation of the word *tera*—so often used in the *Nihonshoki*—was intended to give this text a somewhat archaic character. The great age of this text, however, affects one as being rather exaggerated, since, according to the *Nihonshoki*, there were already in those days several *tera*, such as the Shitennōji and the Hōkōji. This text, therefore, is probably not old. The 'new element' in it, then, is the fact that it establishes for the first time a connection between ancestor worship and Buddhism. Thus it illuminates the fact that the traditions existing in the Buddhism of the T'opa had also reached Japan. The same indeed appears from other monuments of the sixth and seventh centuries. Thus we know that Buddhist temples, statues and even copies of *sūtras* were made for the sake of the memory of the ancestors. Usually this was indicated by the term, originally Chinese: 七世父每, the parents of seven generations.[2] By this one should not only understand seven generations of ancestors, but also the great family collective which covered all the ancestors of a certain family. The third chapter deals fully with this Chinese view of the hereafter.[3] There the expression fits perfectly. It has also been seen in that chapter how indigestible to Indian Buddhism was the Chinese belief in souls. It has been observed that Chinese popular belief accepted all Buddhism had to offer in so far as it could assist towards the clarification or better expression of its own mentality. At the same time it remained far removed from such concepts as, for example, *saṁsāra* and *nirvāṇa*. In China—one should think, for instance, of the T'opa—the presence of a temple, a statue or a *sūtra* copy, which had the value of a magic object, kept at a distance the souls of the dead, which menaced this life. Here the inscriptions and the ex-votos in the temples speak their own language. Thus it came about that monasteries, where lived monks with the Indian view of life, were built owing to this Chinese ancestor worship. And thus they were not only schools for exercising Indian thought

[1] Cf. p. 391.

[2] On this see Takatori Masao, "Kodai minshū no shūkyō" (Popular belief in antiquity), *N.S.K.*, vol. 2, p. 20.

[3] Cf. Chapter III, pp. 153 ff.

but also places which were to inflict fear on, or give happiness to, the souls of the ancestors. In this way Buddhism and ancestor worship were brought into contact there. Is it possible to meet with these two in Japan also?

It will probably remain an insoluble question whether this ancestor worship was already connected with Buddhism when it came to Japan or underwent its own development only on Japanese soil. It appears from the building of *tera* for the benediction of the ancestors mentioned in the *Nihonshoki*, that at the beginning of the seventh century here, too, ancestor worship and Buddhism were already related to each other, though it can hardly be established on the basis of this single text how this came about. When relating the imperfect manner of both their introductions to this [1] one can only accept that Shōtoku's contemporaries saw no more in either than two elements of one and the same religion, the religion of the aliens. Yet there is not only the *Nihonshoki* quotation mentioned here to illustrate both their places in the *ujigami* belief. Still other proofs of this at that time can be found, namely:

1. A statue of Amida, now lost.[2] The *Sairinji-garan engi*, 西林寺伽藍縁起, which originated in the same manner as the *Gangōji-garan engi*,[3] calls this statue an ex-voto. For there was an inscription added to it which wished ten thousand years to members of the family mentioned by name, benefactors and the 'parents of seven generations'. This statue then was made in the year 659. Thus it was not much younger (and perhaps even older) than our 'ancestor text' from the *Nihonshoki*. Further, it is interesting that the Sairinji, in which this statue was to be found, was called an *uji no tera* in 1063, i.e. the real 'habitation' of the *ujigami* of a certain *uji*. In this *uji* the statue had taken the place of *ujigami*. If, here, a Buddha became *ujigami* it would be equally possible to imagine that, under the influence of ancestor worship, the *ujigami* could gradually change from, initially, protectors of the *uji* into its ancestors. It is, however, unknown when this new, adapted *ujigami* belief began to exist. Takatori is of the opinion that the erector of this statue was an immigrant who had very quickly become a

---

[1] One need only think of the linguistic difficulties; cf. Takatori Masao, op. cit., pp. 61 ff.

[2] Cf. Takatori Masao, op. cit., p. 22.

[3] Cf. p. 267.

Buddhist.[1] It appears rather that here we are dealing with a phase of development in Japan's religious history in which Chinese ancestor worship, Buddhism and *ujigami* belief had met each other in a non-existential manner, i.e. without being aware of each other's 'otherness', so that they came to identify with each other mutually.

2. A memorial stone of the year 726. This ranks as one of the three famous stones of the area of Kozuke, 上野, the region of the present-day Gumma prefecture.[2] The stone is to be found in the hamlet of Takata, 高田. Erected by a certain Miyake, 三家, it, too, has the same stereotyped dedication: 'To the parents of the seven generations and the present parents'. On this stone, then, there is no mention of Buddhism, but of an oath made to heaven and earth.

Taken together these two examples illustrate how, at that time, ancestor worship joined on to *ujigami* belief and Buddhism indiscriminately. Buddhism, therefore, which was to be expanded by Suiko's decree, was really viewed as a kind of ancestor and *ujigami* belief. It is understandable that such a form of Buddhism could easily contribute to defining Suiko's function as *uji no kami* and as a Shaman. For the greater part it was identical herewith. Developments of a still later period are similar. Thus the *Gangōji-garan engi* was able to treat Buddhism and *ujigami* belief alike by saying: "*Hotoke, kami wa osoremono ni arikeri*", i.e. Buddha and *kami* were awe-inspiring beings.[3] That the Buddhism of that time described here was not really very profound is also proved, apart from the inscriptions mentioned above, by the statues of the period. It has already been pointed out that they looked so much alike that labels were required to establish whom they really represented.[4] They were practically identical as regards expression of face, posture, the fall of the folds of the robes, and the *mūdra* (gestures of the hands). Thus Takatori Masao compared for instance the Shaka-*sanzon* and the statue of Yakushi of the Golden Hall of the Hōryūji and the Kannon of the Kanshinji, 観心寺, of Kawachi with one another. He came to the following conclusion: [5] "These inconsistencies (the mutual identity of the statues which is incompatible with the nature of Buddha and the Bodhisattvas) indicate that

---

[1] Op. cit., p. 25.
[2] Ibid.
[3] Cf. Takatori Masao, op. cit., p. 49.
[4] Cf. p. 349, footnote 3.
[5] Cf. Takatori Masao, op. cit., p. 55.

Buddhism was then not yet very deeply rooted and that there was no interest in Buddha's own nature." Evidently people were satisfied that the statue derived some magic power or other from the person represented. Of this Takatori says:[1] "This magic mysterious significance occupied the centre of interest." The impersonal expression of all these statues stamps them as the true representatives of an as yet anonymous Buddhism. This was but a Buddhism which only comprised a few notions from the marginal area of Indian and Chinese Buddhism: it was really image worship rather than Buddhism.

May one then identify Shōtoku Taishi's Buddhism with this? According to the *Nihonshoki* his must have been more profound as he maintained a regular contact with the monks Eji and Esō. In his knowledge of Buddhism he must clearly have been greatly dependent on these monks. Since their Buddhism came from Korea and thus from China his Buddhism cannot have been, as a mirror of theirs, anything but very Korean and Chinese. Consequently it may be assumed that it had but little to do with 'orthodox', i.e. Indian, Buddhism or that of the schools. This may not only be concluded from the nature of Japanese Buddhism of the period as a continuation of that of Korea and the T'opa realm, but a few texts and monuments still survive to prove this. Those texts and monuments especially have revealed that which originated in connection with his death. They equally show how Buddhism was experienced in his own circle. The share of Shōtoku's contemporaries was as great as his own. It may therefore be stated that with Shōtoku's death began the real witnessing to Buddhism of Shōtoku and his time.

Here again the starting point for this witnessing was formed by the *Nihonshoki* data concerning Shōtoku's death. It has been shown that the *Nihonshoki* description of the occurrences after his death were nothing but later myths woven around him which gave no idea of Shōtoku's own faith.[2] Since even in the descriptions of the famous emperors no passages are found such as, for example, the lyrical description of the people's grief on the occasion of Shōtoku's death, it must be admitted that these myths concerning his death

---

[1] Ibid.
[2] See pp. 395 ff.

do impair the sober style of the *Nihonshoki*. The same may be said of the immediately following report on the death of his instructor Eji.[1] In both descriptions the sanctification, or rather the proclamations as a *hijiri* or a *kami*, of Shōtoku is already an accepted fact. Yet it is mentioned so positively in these texts that one comes to be inclined rather to believe in the opposite. That inclination grows stronger when one brings into the discussion Chinese ideas on premature death: in China premature death was, and still is, considered a punishment. Shōtoku's relatives too, and especially Aya and Hata who had gathered round him are certain to have experienced his early death as a kind of punishment. Both stories were thus intended to take away this irrational feeling of punishment.

Let us look more closely at these two descriptions. It rather appears as if the story of Eji is the younger one, for it impresses one as being more artificial than that of the people's grief. This follows not only from the main trend of both stories, but also from several details. This may be stated chiefly on account of two remarks which are outside the normal framework of Buddhist linguistic usage employed in the *Nihonshoki*. Both expressions reveal the time in which the Eji text originated, for in his oath to die just like Shōtoku, Eji says of Shōtoku: *Makoto ni ten ni yurusaretari*, 固天攸縱, that is to say 'he was truly admitted to heaven'. What is meant by 'heaven' remains unclear from this formulation. The Chinese *t'ien* need not only imply our Western concept of heaven as a place of bliss somewhere beyond the earth. *T'ien* may just as easily be the soul's abode somewhere in the vicinity of the body. We shall investigate the latter more fully in the following pages. In any case, it is particularly striking that this teacher of Shōtoku was here allowed the use of an entirely Chinese and non-Buddhist terminology. This is further apparent from the fact that here he does not call Shōtoku a Bodhisattva, but that Eji says of him repeatedly and in various wordings that he was a sage, a *hijiri*. The impression is even gained that the whole piece was written in order to emphasise strongly the fact that he was a *hijiri*. Contrary to Chinese logic one wished to prove that, notwithstanding his short life, Shōtoku was nevertheless a sage. Where arguments were ineffective, repetition was invoked. Hence the author of this text makes the monk

[1] Ibid.

Eji say four times that Shōtoku *was* a *hijiri*. The third time he uses the word, Eji even cries: 'He was verily a great *hijiri*!' It does not require proof that this way of stating the same thing again and again does not constitute the strongest argument, though psychologically it may yet convince.

From this somewhat forced argument which was intended to gloss over his—according to Chinese conceptions—unhappy, because brief, life, later myths about Shōtoku also grew up. Then even crasser arguments were added. Thus he was supposed to have lived another seven lives in China, even before his birth in Japan. His last Chinese life would then have been that of the Tendai precursor Hui-szŭ (Jap.: Eshi), 慧思 (515-577). Also his great knowledge of the *Hokke-kyō*, for instance, he owed to his former incarnations, especially that of Eshi.[1] This last argument admittedly disproves itself, for this Chinese monk could not possibly have been a former incarnation of Shōtoku, who was already four years old when Eshi died. Even after his 'Japanese' incarnation Shōtoku Taishi was made to be repeatedly reborn in Japan, i.a. as Kannon.[2] The real starting point for all these mythical arguments was formed by his early death, which was difficult to accept. It is the present author's opinion that on the same basis attempts were made to fill in his short life in Japan. Thus he became the framer of the 'constitution', gave his *sūtra* lectures, wrote commentaries on them, and became the builder of temples. In this way his life could easily be made to equal the richly well-spent life of even an aged, highly esteemed Chinese.

The mention of the Chinese heaven—not the *kami*—which had given him wisdom and the whole of Eji's argument reveal at least how Chinese must have been the compiler of this text. In Shōtoku's time there could not have been such a Chinese influence, since contact with China had hardly been re-established. That is why in this text we are dealing with the ideas of some *Nihonshoki*

---

[1] For this see Suji Zennosuke, *Nihon Bukkyō-shi no Kenkyū*, Tōkyō 1930, continuing vol., pp. 3 ff.

[2] For this see Suji Zennosuke, op. cit., pp. 13-14; Sakaino Kōyō, op. cit., p. 197. Thus according to the *Fusō ryakki*, prince Asa, 阿佐, and according to the *Genkō shakusho*, prince Nichira, 日羅, both from Paekche, are supposed to have recognised him as Kannon even during his stay on earth. Cf. *Fusō ryakki*, 3rd *maki; Kokushitaikei*, vol. VI, p. 497; *Genkō shakusho*, 15th *maki Kokushitaikei*, vol. XIV, p. 879.

compiler of the beginning of the eighth century, not with those of Shōtoku or his contemporaries.

A second remarkable expression in this text of Eji (see p. 396) is to be found in his prophecy: "Therefore I shall meet the great prince Kamitsumiya in the *Pure Land.*" On the basis of the word 'Pure Land', Jap.: *jōdo,* 浄土, one might come to believe that Shōtoku's contemporaries had known the Tuṣita heaven or Sukhāvatī, that is to say that Maitreyanism and Amidism were known even at that date. Could this really be established then the veil of anonymity spread over the Buddhism of that period would be lifted. Could this word, then, have had that meaning, at that time?

Viewed by itself the *jōdo* need not have this meaning. It has only a neutral meaning and need not necessarily refer to the Tuṣita heaven or Sukhāvatī.[1] Sometimes it is used in contrast to the unclean earth. Here there is no question of such a contrast. *Jōdo,* however, is used not only for a heaven or a hereafter, but also for this world. In this latter sense it was later thought that Shōtoku was active in the 'Pure Land' of Japan like Kannon. Like Kannon he carried the Pure Land with him. Until the present day Japanese nationalists call Japan a *jōdo.*[2] In this way the purity of race and country, in the widest sense of the word, is made to contrast with the impurity of foreign countries. Naturally in modern Japan this conception is adhered to only by a few. It may be said that the word *jōdo* in Eji's mouth probably had not this latter meaning; it was understood as a kind of hereafter, a meeting-place after death.

Now, apart from this text in the *Nihonshoki,* it is known that in Shōtoku's times there certainly existed some conception of a hereafter. This is known by both the inscriptions on the Shaka-*sanzon* and the Tenjukoku-*mandara* and no less by the picture of heaven on the Tenjukoku-*mandara* itself. In the inscription of the Shaka-*sanzon,* translated above pp. 378, 379, the Pure Land is also mentioned in the following sentence: "It became a symbol of happiness . . . The blossoming of Buddhism will hereby be exalted to its highest point and people will together with them achieve the hereafter." In the Japanese text this thereafter is called *higan,* i.e.

[1] For the significance of the Pure Land see: Inoue Tetsujirō, op. cit., p. 571, col. II.

[2] Thus the ideologists of the Sōka-gakkai attempt to bend the Buddhist eschatology on the *jōdo* towards this world. Cf. Werner Kohler, *Die Lotus-Lehre,* p. 282.

(land on the) other side. In Buddhism this word has the specific meaning of *nirvāṇa*.[1] It is to be found outside the world of pain and grief, of life and death. *Higan* is also used in the sense of *pāramitā*, one of the degrees of Buddhist perfection on the way to the *bodhi*.[2] Here *higan* has certainly not this latter meaning. Since, a few words earlier, death is mentioned it is here identical with the hereafter. It is, therefore, not difficult to see in this inscription a kind of witness to the belief in the hereafter. Yet this does not bring us much further forward.

We possess a better and more detailed picture of this belief in a hereafter in the embroidered heaven which Suiko had had designed at the request of Shōtoku's widow. In it she wished—according to the inscription belonging to it—to see her husband as he "lives there and is reborn".[3] It is to this that the Tenjukoku-*mandara* owes its origin. What then should we understand by the "land of the long life heaven" depicted here? It appears to the present author that this is not only a view of the immigrant designers on human existence after death. It is also an expression of the faith of the widow herself and hence also of Shōtoku. If in her faith Shōtoku took up such a central place it must be supposed that she also adapted herself as much as possible to his religious views. On the basis of the Shōtoku demythologisation dealt with above it is not so

---

[1] Cf. Inoue Tetsujirō, op. cit., p. 891, col. I. *Higan* in this sense is preserved in the festival *higan-e*, 彼岸会, which was celebrated in the early days of spring and autumn. It was thought that exactly on these days the invisible *dharma-kaya* (Buddha's spiritual body present in everything) would become visible. It seems to owe its origin to a decree of 806, when monks of all districts were ordered to read twice annually, viz. in the middle of spring and autumn, during seven days, the *sūtra* celebrated in Japan, *Kongō-hannya-kyō*, 金剛般若経, Sanskrit: *Vajracchedikā-prajñāpāramitā-sūtra*. De Visser and others, however, do not ascribe the origin of this festival to this decree, but to an inscription on the western gate of the Shitennōji, which is supposed to derive from Shōtoku himself. In connection with the fire of the Shitennōji which took place later this has, of course, become doubtful. We do not know, therefore, when this 'other side festival' was celebrated for the first time. It was a purely Japanese festival, without either Chinese or Korean parallels. It clearly indicates the strong need of that time also to see the other bank of the stream of this life. For details and its background see: M.W. de Visser, op. cit., vol. I, pp. 366-373; Inoue Tetsujirō, op. cit., p. 891, cols. I, II.

[2] Cf. footnote 3 on p. 293.

[3] Cf. the inscription of the Tenjukoku-*mandara*, pp. 380-381.

difficult to understand this. We are, therefore, not entitled to the assumption that her faith was so much more primitive than that of Shōtoku himself. Some people like to suggest this latter idea on the basis of their Shōtoku myth.[1] Her faith is indeed not likely to have been identical with that of Shōtoku in every respect. Some individual differences and gradations could in all likelihood always be found. But since it was exactly a heaven she wanted to see, in which her Shōtoku lived, her conception of it is not likely to have been very different from that of Shōtoku himself. The artists and designers of the Tenjukoku-*mandara* presumably executed their order in a form borrowed from Korea. Nevertheless, even they must have taken care that this work of art did really answer to the expectations of Shōtoku's wife Ōiratsume.

Of what then did this heaven of Shōtoku and Ōiratsume consist which was depicted in it? This question is not quite easily answered as opinions are rather divided. Influenced by the above passage on the *jōdo* in the *Nihonshoki* some have come to see Sukhāvatī in this picture. De Visser [1] even wants to prove with it that in Shōtoku's time there was already Amidism in Japan. In the years before the war this opinion was even generally accepted.[3] It was based on several arguments, usually borrowed from Eji's words in the *Nihonshoki* and the Shōtoku commentary on the *Yuima-kyō*. As regards the former it has already been shown above that Eji's words cannot be used as an argument, as they are of a much later date. With regard to the *Yuima* commentary Suji points out that in it there is nowhere mention of a promise by Shōtoku to be reborn in Sukhāvati.[4] Because, however, the commentary itself has also been ascribed to him there is no sense in deriving arguments from it either for or against. Thus it is impossible to prove in this manner that Shōtoku could have been acquainted with Amidism.

Another argument in its favour has been attempted by connecting

---

[1] There are even now those who would wish to differentiate between the hereafter belief of Shōtoku and that of his widow. Cf. Kanaji Isamu, "Shōtoku Taishi no jōdokan" (The vision of Shōtoku Taishi of the Pure Land), *Shūkyō Kōron*, vol. 29, 1959, no. 9, p. 3.

[2] Op. cit., p. 323.

[3] These opinions may be found in Suji Zennosuke, "Shōtoku Taishi" in *Nihon Bunka-shi*, pp. 28 ff..

[4] Cf. Suji Zennosuke, op. cit., p. 30.

the word *tenjukoku* with Shōtoku's beloved adage, quoted by his widow: "This world is only vain and passing; the real truth, however, is Buddha." [1] For these words are supposed to refer to the 'Amidistic' double concept: pure land and unclean land. This, however, is too far-fetched. For Shōtoku's beloved adage is not an Amidistic text but a general formula which is applicable to any form of Buddhism and not only to Amidism. We know, for that matter, from other inscriptions of the period of the Tenjukoku-*mandara* that the development towards Amidism was still to come; moreover, in the history of the Buddhism of that time there is no evidence to be found of the existence of Amidism. It appears that many followers of Amidism, under the spell of over-institutionalist thought, committed the error of supposing the presence of a whole system behind a statue found somewhere, or a *sūtra*. In this case that error was compounded since such an Amida statue or Amidistic *sūtra* does not occur in Shōtoku's time. It has earlier been pointed out that in these matters it is only too often forgotten that in Japan, Korea and China these things acquired, in the popular belief as well as amongst the intelligentsia, an appreciation and a place in people's lives which is outside the existing systems. Western dogmatism and 'systematic thought' may in this way attach a completely distorted and untrue situation to one simple historic fact.

If we are not dealing with Amidism in the picture of the Tenjukoku *mandara* it should not for that reason be thought that it is a picture of the Tuṣita heaven.[2] Those defending this opinion rely on the fact that in that period there was already Maitreyanism in Korea. They find another argument in the stone Maitreya statue which had come to Japan in 584, and the temple which Soga Umako built for it.[3] It has already been pointed out that these two things may imply some forms of a Maitreya cult.[4] Yet there was equally no question of a Tuṣita heaven in those days.[5] This heaven was mentioned for the first time in 669 in a funeral oration for the Nakatomi Kamatarō, 中臣鎌足, who, in 645, had defeated the Soga for good.[6] Soon after this Maitreyanism was ousted, especially

[1] Cf. p. 380.
[2] Cf. M. W. de Visser, op. cit., p. 323.
[3] Cf. p. 249.
[4] Cf. p. 289.
[5] For these proofs see Suji Zennosuke, op. cit., p. 33.
[6] Cf. Suji Zennosuke, loc. cit.

since, some ten years later, the Amidist monks Chikō, 智光, and Reikō, 礼光, had arrived in Japan.[1] The defenders of the Tuṣita heaven draw their main argument from the Japanese 'great age' of Maitreyanism with regard to Amidism. For this reason, according to them, the Tenjukoku-*mandara* was a picture of the Tuṣita heaven. All this, however, cannot be proved by external arguments without examining the Tenjukoku-*mandara* itself, since eventually this will have to supply the main evidence.

Of this Dr. Maeda Eiun, one of the defenders of the Tuṣita heaven view, says: "We are here dealing with a very difficult problem. Since this is a most extraordinary picture it is audacious to arrive at any conclusions on this basis."[2] Suji, the foremost expert on Japanese Buddhism of antiquity, himself went to see this *maṇḍala* in 1901. Of it he says: [3] "It is an error to see a picture of the heaven of the Tuṣita gods in this Tenjukoku-*mandara*. It resembles neither the Tuṣita heaven nor Sukhāvatī. It is a representation of its own." Even so it would appear that, this opinion notwithstanding, Buddhism was really connected with this embroidery. The figures seated on lotuses prove this. Only one may not without further ado call this '*maṇḍala*' after some Buddhist grouping or other. Saying this does not suddenly make this Tenjukoku-*mandara* valueless for our understanding of Shōtoku's Buddhism. On the contrary we owe it exactly to this that the vision of Buddhism and the hereafter of that period has been preserved.

On closer inspection of this work of art it appears that the hereafter was not dominated by some central figure such as Amitābha or Maitreya, flanked by two Bodhisattvas, as is the case in pictures of the Tuṣita heaven or Sukhāvatī. Nor was their place taken by Shōtoku Taishi but by several figures. Most of them are seated on a lotus; others, however, appear to be walking about. It looks rather like a meeting place of anonymous Buddhas. Thus the work is a good representation of the Buddhism of the time. For it proves the same anonymity as do the statues of the period. The capriciousness and indefiniteness, characteristic of this Tenjukoku-*mandara*, do not, however, entirely derive from Buddhism. They also come from Japan's own *ujigami* belief into which, be it remembered, Buddhism had penetrated. As a witness of Shōtoku's

---

[1] Ibid.

[2] Cf. Suji Zennosuke, op. cit., p. 32.

[3] Cf. Suji Zennosuke, op. cit., p. 28.

faith, therefore, the Tenjukoku-*mandara* provides the evidence that in him, too, Buddhism and the *ujigami* belief were co-existent.

Another proof of this latter thesis is also to be found in the text of the tortoise-backs which border the Tenjukoku-*mandara*. In it Shōtoku's widow says: "As reward my prince is therefore reborn in the land of the long heavenly life." De Visser would like to translate this 'land of the long heavenly life', Jap.: *tenjukoku*, by Sukhāvatī.[1] On closer inspection, however, this appears a Chinese rather than a Buddhist formula. The components of this term: *ten*, 天, *ju*, 壽, and *koku*, 國, are ancient Chinese concepts. We have seen in the third chapter how it was exactly these concepts which considerably altered the Buddhist idea of *bodhi* and *saṃsāra*.[2] Thus in this respect *tenjukoku* may be called a Japanese-Chinese pendant of *shêng-t'ien*, which in China, be it remembered, was the Buddhist reception centre of the souls of the dead.[3] It was a place somewhere on earth, predestined as the abode of the dead. *tenjukoku*, therefore, was rather a second level of land (= *kuni*) somewhere on earth than a heavenly land 'on the other side' of the earth. There cannot be any question here of a Pure Land, with the implied contrast with the unclean earth—such as Amidism taught.[4]

In the same sense should also be understood Umako's, Shōtoku's and Esō's words occurring on the Iyo stone mentioned at the beginning of this chapter: "Would it really be different here from the land of the long life?" In this expression, being in Japanese *jukoku*, 壽國, even the word *ten* has been omitted, and the hereafter has been seen even more in the perspective of an ideal piece of the earth. This also appears from the romantic description of the idyllic picture of this land: the place of the Iyo well. Here there is no question of a well or geyser as a dwelling-place of souls. Such a belief hardly exists in Japan. At the most people would deify the curative properties of the spring.[5]

When, after this examination, one classifies the above texts according to their age it is possible, even with this defective material, to establish a certain development. However, one will have to

[1] Op. cit., p. 323.
[2] Cf. Chapter III, pp. 153 ff.
[3] Cf. Chapter III, p. 156.
[4] Cf. footnote 1 on p. 169.
[5] Cf. Shimonaka Yasaburō, op. cit., part 1, p. 291, col. II.

keep realising that, in connection with variations amongst the peoples which conditioned Japan's structure of those times, many of these views will have existed side by side. With this proviso the following stages may be distinguished. At the beginning there was the belief in the *higan*: a vague awareness of the 'other side', such as is mentioned in the inscription of the Shaka-*sanzon*. At a later stage this 'other side' became the abode of the souls of the Tenjukoku-*mandara*. Later still this developed into an earthly idyll: the Iyo paradise. Finally, at the time of the final recension of the *Nihonshoki*, this paradise must have been idealised to such an extent that in its purity it could contrast with the uncleanness of the earthy. Thus, in the course of 150 years, the buddhistic ideal of the Pure Land had grown from a vague awareness of the life after death owing to very special Chinese and Buddhist contributions. Viewed from this steady growth it is unlikely that Shōtoku Taishi was acquainted with something like the Pure Land in the sense of the *Nihonshoki* text about the *jōdo*, which has been the starting point of this whole argument. It can be said only that the belief in the 'other side' of his time developed in that direction. The *jōdo* point of the *Nihon-shoki*, however, had not yet been reached. Otherwise the three inscriptions mentioned here would have used the term *jōdo* already. It is difficult to decide whether the inscriptions of the three monuments mentioned above also form three consecutive historical cross-sections in the development of one and the same transcendental faith, since it is unknown from which background these inscriptions derive. In any case all three may be accounted as typifying the 'other side' belief of Shōtoku's times.

Thus it is established that Shōtoku's 'other side' faith had not yet dissociated itself from the world before death. Nothing more is known from these sparse data about further details of this belief.

In the preceding chapters it has repeatedly been said that the few Buddhist notions which came to Japan were incorporated in the *ujigami* belief. It is, therefore, likely that this latter equally assisted in the formulation of Japan's first 'Buddhist' notions. That was specially the case when Buddhism and *ujigami* belief were least explicitly distinguished from each other and merged into each other without there being any clear dividing line. As has been seen it was exactly this latter which was the most striking characteristic of Japan's earliest Buddhism. That is why it is apparent that in the 'Buddhist' belief in heaven of Shōtoku's times there was a considerable element of *ujigami* belief. If, therefore, one wishes to acquaint oneself in detail with this belief in heaven it will be necessary to examine in the data of the *Kojiki* and *Nihonshoki* the conceptions of the *ujigami* belief, concerning which also the Tenjukoku-*mandara* and the other inscriptions are the concrete results. Naturally one should not cherish too high expectations of this examination, the more so since such an examination, even at the present day, is difficult enough. Of this Eder says:[1] "Über den Zustand der Totenseelen im Jenseits gibt uns der Volksglaube, soweit er nicht buddhistisch geformt ist, recht spärliche Auskunft." If this applies to present-day Japanese popular belief, it does *a fortiori* to Japanese antiquity. For there later, and Chinese, additions have rendered the original picture of this 'other side' belief nearly unrecognisable.

Now, it is mainly owing to Tsuda Sōkichi's critical and profound studies that even so a reconstruction of the genesis of this belief in the heaven of Japanese antiquity is possible. These provide the key which, through all Shōtoku myths, opens the door to the factual origin and the proper nature of Japanese Buddhism. On closer inspection of the *Kojiki* and the *Nihonshoki* it appears to the present author that, in the main, three concepts enable us to make this reconstruction. They are: 1. Takama *no hara*, 2. *yomi* and 3. *the land of tokoyo*. These three concepts will guide us further to the real core of the belief in heaven in the form in which Japan's earliest Buddhism has known it. They will therefore be more closely discussed in the following pages.

1 Takama *no hara*, 高天原.[2]

In several places in the present work it has been pointed out how the *Tenson-kōrin*, the descent of the 'celestial grandson', Ninigi *no mikoto*, forms the real beginning of Japan's history. This descent, then, took place from the Takama *no hara*. By the time it was codified in writing in the *Kojiki* and the *Nihonshoki* this word Takama *no hara* had undergone quite a development. The origin of the concept is closely connected with the birth of the Sun-god, the Hi *no*

[1] Cf. M. Eder, "Totenseelen und Ahnengeister in Japan", *Anthr.*, vol. 51, 1951, p. 108.

[2] Or Takama-ga-hara. According to Florenz by this the Japanese meant the blue vault of heaven. This is not entirely correct, as it formed only part of it. Cf. K. Florenz, op. cit., p. 10, footnote 1.

kami.[1] From this as a starting point, therefore, the concept can best be explained. According to Tsuda [2] the Japanese word *ame* or *ama* means 'sun', even though it is written with the Chinese character for heaven, 天, *ten*. Thus Takama *no hara* does not primarily mean: the high plain of heaven, but the plain of the high sun. Tsuda thinks that originally it was nothing else but the Sun-god himself.[3] Other gods, which later appeared as inhabitants of the Takama *no hara*, were always descendents, relatives or different forms of one and the same Sun-god. This close relationship appears especially between Takama *no hara* and Amaterasu. For she never left the Takama *no hara*. She caused her grandson Ninigi *no mikoto* to descend to earth there to initiate the Japanese nation. Furthermore, it has been seen in footnote 3 on p. 107, how her part-soul clothed the new emperors without her having to come to earth herself. It is also interesting that the component *taka* in Takama *no hara* is equally to be found in the names of 'heavenly' *musubi*, such as Takagi *no mikoto* and Takamimusubi. As the really deified powers of the Sun-goddess they were on the same level.[4] In a later stage the Takama *no hara* is to dissociate itself from the Sun-god himself and to become his habitation. Under Chinese influence it began gradually to become a true heaven.[5] But even then it did

[1] Cf. Tsuda Sōkichi, *Nihon Koten no Kenkyū*, vol. 1, pp. 385-390; p. 644.

[2] According to him *ame* or *ama* was an adjective of *hi* = sun: sunny; op. cit., p. 655. *Ame* was indeed always connected somehow with the sun. Thus the gods who had their being there all had a sun character. Afterwards, under Chinese influence and especially owing to the word being indicated by the character: 天 = *t'ien*, heaven, it acquired the meaning of place where the gods lived. Cf. Tsuda Sōkichi, op. cit., vol. 2, pp. 305-306. When the divine couple Izanami and Izanagi, not entirely strangers to Chinese influence, lived there too, *ame* had already the meaning of heaven.

[3] Cf. Tsuda Sōkichi, op. cit., vol. 1, pp. 655-656.

[4] Cf. Sasaya Ryōzō, "Musubi-gami no Shinkō", *K.G.Z.*, vol. 64, 1963, nos. 8, 9 (Aug., Sept.), p. 85.

[5] Cf. Tsuda Sōkichi, op. cit., vol. 2, p. 306. It may be doubted whether this belief in heaven had already taken root under Empress Suiko, since it was only during her government that, after a long interruption, the relations with China were revived. In that respect the influence of the Korean immigrants remained too limited to their own group to have brought about many changes in popular belief. This influence must, therefore, have increased especially after the Taika reform, when legislation inspired by China's example radically changed Japan's social pattern. Under its influence the Takama *no hara* of the Sun-god concept was extended to the plain of heaven, and in an even later stage to an even wider area, which became populated

not yet contain the wide heaven which embraces the whole earth, but only that small piece of sky which covers the area of Yamato. It was characterised by the same scenery as Yamato and owned, just as Yamato, the mountain Kagu, 香, which probably served as a bridge between Yamato and the Takama *no hara*.[1]

This miniature heaven presented an appearance similar to the earth below it. When the Emperor Jimmu proceeded with his army from Kyūshū to Yamato, Amaterasu accompanied him in her Takama *no hara*.[2] The military successes below were also booked in the Takama *no hara* because here, too, there was fighting against the gods of all the nations with which on earth the emperor was in conflict. These latter enemies also lived in their own—though not the same—Takama *no hara*. Afterwards all this strange 'upper land' of these alien gods merged into a proper heaven or land called Ashihara *no nakatsukuni*, 葦原中國. Ōnamuchi, 大穴牟遲, of Izumo, situated to the west of Yamato, became the divine ruler of this land, even though he remained under the jurisdiction of the Sun-god.[3] Thus the celestial situation reflected that of the earth beneath, where the ruler of Izumo was equally subject to the emperor. And thus the struggle of the small states on the Japanese islands was carried on equally fiercely in the small heavens above. As those on earth succeeded in establishing a great empire, Takama *no hara* became populated with ever more gods. Thus the deeds of the gods in the Takama *no hara*, as described in the first pages of the *Kojiki*

---

with all kinds of 'gods of heaven'. Ōnamuchi's Ashihara *no nakatsukuni* was made to accord with the Chinese pair of concepts: gods of heaven—gods of the earth (天神地祇) and destined to be the habitation of the earth gods. These two 'heavens' thus did not become heaven and hell, but two habitations of gods, the more important of which were the gods of heaven. In this way this pair of concepts must have obtained a place in Japanese mythology. Cf. Tsuda Sōkichi, op. cit., p. 345. This slavish borrowing is also evident from the fact that no one was able concretely to indicate who really were these heaven and earth gods (*ama-tsu-kami*, *kuni-tsu-kami*). Thus under Chinese influence the original sun-god heaven became the habitation of many gods who, from the eighth century, were required to explain the divine ancestry of many persons belonging to the nobility.

[1] Cf. Tsuda Sōkichi, op. cit., p. 246. Apart from the mountain Ame *no* Kagu there was also a river Ame *no* Yasu *no kawa*, 天安河; cf. *Kojiki*, 1st *maki*; Kuroita Katsumi, Maruyama Jirō, *Kokushitaikei Kojiki*, p. 20; K. Florenz, op. cit., pp. 4, 38.

[2] Cf. Tsuda Sōkichi, op. cit., vol. 2, p. 305.

[3] Cf. Tsuda Sōkichi, op. cit., vol. 2, p. 646.

and the *Nihonshoki*,[1] became the mythical reflection of the military successes of the emperors on the Japanese islands.[2]

It is possible then that the picture of the Tenjukoku-*mandara* refers to this idea of the Takama *no hara* and to one of the development stages described here? As we saw, the Takama *no hara* was, in its various phases of growth—just as the Ashihara *no nakatsukuni* —the exclusive domain of the Sun-god and other gods where there was no room for a mortal such as Shōtoku. That is why this idea of the Takama *no hara* can be of no further assistance to us in discerning something of the *tenjukoku* in Japan's most ancient 'shinto'.[3]

2 The *Yomi*, 夜見.[4]

This too is a concept which has undergone many developments. It is therefore possible with an accurate definition of this to grasp one of the phases of growth. Although *yomi* is connected with the dead this does not entitle us immediately to speak of a *land* of the dead, for in the whole historical growth of this concept the idea of a land of *yomi* is one of the last phases.

When placing the texts dealing with the *yomi* in the *Kojiki* and the *Nihonshoki* side by side one can establish the steady growth of this concept phase by phase.[5] The earliest phase is described in

[1] Cf. K. Florenz, op. cit., pp. 10-18 (*Kojiki*) and pp. 123-133 (*Nihonshoki*). In this genesis of heaven and earth it is interesting that the divine couple Izanagi and Izanami brought all this about again by the intervention of the *musubi*, viz. Takamimusubi. In court circles Izanagi also acquired before his name the epitheton *taka*. Cf. Sasaya Ryōzō, op. cit., p. 84.

[2] Tsuda is of the opinion that this idea of Takama *no hara* already existed in Suiko's time. He attempts to prove this on the basis of the Ise temple having been founded in the second half of the sixth century, as Ise was the place where Amaterasu appeared on earth from the Takama *no hara*. Cf. Suinin, 25th year, 3rd month, 10th day in the 6th *maki* of the *Nihonshoki*; Koroita Katsumi, Maruyama Jirō, *Kokushitaikei Nihonshoki*, vol. 1, p. 185. Here the building of a palace for Amaterasu is mentioned, of which it is said: "this is the place where Amaterasu descended from heaven for the first time". Although one would wish to accept his conclusion the convincing force of this argument is not clear. Cf. Tsuda Sōkichi, *Nihon Koten no Kenkyū*, vol. 1, p. 246.

[3] Or the place in the *ujigami* belief. Cf. our starting-point on p. 16 ff.

[4] *Yomi* phonetically written as: 黄泉, or 夜見. The two last characters, read as *yomi* or *yami*, express the characteristic darkness of *yomi* better. Tsuda Sōkichi, op. cit., vol. 2, p. 404.

[5] For these two texts see footnote 1 on p. 436, 2 on p. 438 and 1 on p. 439.

a *Nihonshoki* passage which, as appears from the *incipit 'issho iwaku'*, has been taken from another source and simply joined on to the story of the visit to the nether world by the 'father of the gods' Izanagi to the 'mother of the gods' Izanami. Although dealing here with an added text it appears to the present author that we have to do with a primeval datum, on the basis of which Izanagi's visit to the nether world has been more and more spun out in the *Nihonshoki* and the *Kojiki*. This *Nihonshoki* passage is the following: [1]

"A writing says: Izanagi *no mikoto* much wished to see his younger sister (Izanami). He therefore went to the place where she was provisionally lying in state.[2] There Izanami *no mikoto* went to meet him as if she were still alive and they spoke to each other. She said to Izanagi *no mikoto*: My husband and master, I beg of thee, do not look at me. Immediately after she had said this she became invisible and it became dark. Therefore Izanagi *no mikoto* struck a single light and looked at her. Izanami *no mikoto* was then already swollen and various kinds of thunders (*ikazuchi*, 雷) were above her. Izanagi *no mikoto* was frightened of them and rushed back. Then the thunders jumped up and went after him. Now by the road there stood a large peach tree. Izanagi *no mikoto* then hid himself under its branches. He picked the fruit and threw the peaches at the thunders. These then, all of them, fled. The origin of the custom of warding off evil spirits goes back to this. Then Izanagi *no mikoto* threw away his staff and said: 'Further than this the thunders may not go'. They called the staff Kunado *no kami*, 岐神. Its real name was the ancestral god Kunado. The names of the eight thunders (*ikazuchi*) were: the *ikazuchi* of the head is called the great *ikazuchi*, that of the chest the fire-thunder, that of the abdomen the earth-thunder, that of the back the young thunder, that of the posterior the black thunder, that of the fingers the *ikazuchi* of the mountains, that of the members above the foot the thunder of the plain and that of the genitals the cleaving thunder."

---

[1] Cf. *Nihonshoki*, 1st *maki*; Kuroita Katsumi, Maruyama Jirō, op. cit., vol. 1, pp. 20-21; W. G. Aston, op. cit., vol. I, p. 29; K. Florenz, op. cit., p. 142.

[2] In *furigana* it reads: *mogari no tokoro*, 殯斂之處, the place of the body lying in state. W. G. Aston, loc. cit., translates: "temporary burial place", and K. Florenz, loc. cit.: "Trauerhaus". The real tomb, therefore, is not meant here. The word *yomi* is not used.

This story, together with the visit to the nether world preceding it in the *Nihonshoki*, rounds off the 'life' of Izanami *no mikoto*, the mother of many gods, amongst whom was Amaterasu,[1] and through them the divine mother of the earth and everything that lives thereon.[2] Her husband's visit strongly reminds one of Orpheus' visit to Hades, yet there are differences. In the present text, namely, there is no question, in contrast to other tales, of a Hades or a nether world. For, as appears from our text, Izanami was in the *mogari no tokoro*, i.e. the place where the body lies in state before the final funeral.[3] There is no mention here of an abode or land of several souls. This is also, as a matter of fact, suggested by the eight *ikazuchi*, which are localised not somewhere in a nether world but in various parts of the deceased's body. Whether these bad ghosts were thunders or serpents—as Tsuda prefers it [4]— they

[1] Cf. *Nihonshoki*, 1st *maki*; Kuroita Katsumi, Maruyama Jirō, op. cit., vol. 1, p. 10: "Izanagi and Izanami consulted together and said: 'We ourselves have produced the eight great provinces, mountains, rivers, bushes and trees. Should we then not give life to him who is to be the ruler of all that is beneath heaven?' Then, together, they brought forth the sun-god, called *Ōhirume no muchi*, 大日靈貴, (the elevated lady of the great day (or sun)). According to another work she is also called Amaterasu *no ōkami*." Cf. W. G. Aston, op. cit., p. 18.

[2] This whole creation story is probably a hindsight construction which was to supply the real chief figure of *Kojiki* and *Nihonshoki* with a genealogy which she needed, it was thought, as much as the emperors themselves who, be it remembered, had, in many respects, turned *Kojiki* and *Nihonshoki* into genealogical works. Cf. K. Florenz, op. cit., pp. 11-12, footnote 8, especially Sir E. Satow's opinion. The present author agrees with Florenz that the first god mentioned in the *Kojiki*, viz. Ame *no* Minakanushi, 天之御中主, had nothing to do with monotheism, but was added only later to the original Japanese data under Chinese influence. Cf. Sasaya Ryōzō, op. cit., p. 83. The divine couple Izanagi and Izanami did not belong either to that original Japanese material, but were also added under Chinese influence, although their origin appears rather to have been in the warmer regions of South-east Asia. Cf. Nakashio Kiyoyuki, "Izanagi, Izanami nison to Fukugi Jōka no shinwa" (Izanagi and Izanami compared with the myths of Fukugi Jōka), *Kokugakuin Daigaku Kiyō*, vol. V, Tōkyō 1964, pp. 176 ff..

[3] Cf. footnote 2 on p. 436.

[4] Tsuda views these *ikazuchi* as bad spirits in the shape of snakes. According to him these snakes might have had something to do with sea serpents and refer to the strongly marine character of the *yomi no kuni*. Cf. Tsuda Sōkichi, *Nihon Koten no Kenkyū*, vol. 1, p. 397. On this belief in serpents as a typical sea religion see also Nakajima Etsuji, "Tokoyo-kuni-zakkō" (A study of '*Tokoyo no kuni*'), *K.G.Z.*, vol. 54, no. 1, April 1953, p. 77.

were not yet infernal devils. One might well interpret Izanagi's part here as the soul's journey of a Shaman.[1]

In the present author's view this story forms the real nucleus which possesses elements sufficient to develop into an actual nether world tale. The two phases of this development may then be observed in the *Nihonshoki* and the *Kojiki*. It would be too monotonous and require too much space if these two versions were to be reproduced here in their entirety. Let it suffice, therefore, to enumerate the main elements which were attached to the above framework. In the Izanami story of the *Nihonshoki* [2] no cemetery is mentioned any more but *yomotsu-kuni*, the land of *yomi*.[3] Furthermore, there was a special nether world food, the *yomotsu-hekuhiseri*, 飡泉之竈, correctly translated by Florenz as 'Yomi's Kochherd',[4] which prevented any return to earth. Darkness is emphasised here especially as an essential characteristic of this nether world. On no account should one remove it by lighting a light or throwing away

---

For further parallels which illustrate the close connection between the snake and water, cfr.: M. Éliade, *Traité d'Histoire des Religions*, p. 185, § 71: "Un serpent ou un génie-serpent se trouve toujours dans le voisinage des eaux ou il les controle; ils sont des génies protecteurs des sources de la vie, de l'immortalité, de la sainteté, ainsi que de tous les emblèmes en liaison avec la vie, la fécondité, l'héroisme, l'immortalité et les 'trésors'."

Perhaps a comparison with similar representations in India may throw some light on the background of these *ikazuchi*. In Indian literature (inter alia the *Atharvaveda*, the *Vājasaneyasamhitā* and the *Maitrayanī Samhitā* there is mention of 2, 3, and later even 5 and 7 breaths of life: *praṇa*, which like the *ikazuchi* are located in various parts of the body as the principles of life and movement therein. Just as the *ātman* leaves the body after death via the fontanelle, so the *ikazuchi* leave and unite themselves with the macrocosm from which they had separated themselves on behalf of that body. (Cf. the parallel of the Graeco-Roman concepts, footnote 1 on p. 169). It is difficult to determine in how far the root *ika* in *ikazuchi* has anything to do with the *ika* of *ikasu*—to revive, to keep alive. If indeed there is any connection then it is not difficult to see in the pursuit of Izanagi by Izanami's relinquished *ikazuchi* a new death of Izanami because she was deserted by her 'souffles vitaux'. Cf. J. Filliozat, *La Doctrine Classique de la Médecine Indienne*, Paris 1949, pp. 22 ff. and chiefly pp. 142-152.

[1] For the description of such a Shaman soul journey see: Alois Closs, "Das Religiöse im Schamanismus", *Kairos*, no. 1, 1960, p. 32.

[2] Cf. *Nihonshoki*, 1st *maki*; Kuroita Katsumi, Maruyama Jirō, op. cit., vol. 1, pp. 14-16; K. Florenz, op. cit., pp. 137-138.

[3] The *kanji*: 黄泉 = *yomi* is 'translated' by the *furigana* as *yomotsu-kuni*.

[4] Op. cit., p. 137.

a comb made of flint. The eight thunders are not mentioned here, but indeed the eight *yomotsu-shikome*, 泉津醜女, are mentioned, literally ghastly infernal women, whose duty it was to chase away Izanagi. Then the entry to the *yomotsu-kuni* is mentioned, viz. the *yomotsu-hirasaka*, 泉津平坂, the smooth slope of the *yomi*.

This *Nihonshoki* version of Izanagi's visit has been spun out even further in the *Kojiki*.[1] Here not only the *yomotsu-kuni* is indicated—of which especially the *Kojiki* in contradistinction to the *Nihonshoki* version encloses: 國=*kuni*, land—but mention is also made of a special entry, the *tono no kumido*, 殿縢戶, swing-door of the (*yomi*) palace. In contrast to the *Nihonshoki* the eight thunders are mentioned here. These chase Izanagi after the attempts of the eight witches and even of a whole *yomi* army of 1,500 soldiers have failed. Also Izanami consulted here with the god of the *yomi*, the *yomotsu-kami*, although it is not made clear who this *yomotsu-kami* really was. This picture of the land of *yomi* is even further expanded in other places. Thus Amaterasu's younger brother, Susa *no* O, was exiled to the nether world and became its ruler; [2] Izanami, too, is called the real chief divinity of the nether world.[3] Elsewhere special guardians of the roads of this country are mentioned, the *yomi-tsuchimori*, 泉守道者.[4] Then, according to the *Fudoki*, it is supposed to have a second subterranean entrance

---

[1] Cf. *Kojiki*, 1st *maki*; Kuroita Katsumi, Maruyama Jirō, *Kokushitaikei Kojiki*, pp. 11-13; K. Florenz, op. cit., pp. 21-25.

[2] As a punishment for all his crimes he was sent by the gods to the *ne no kuni*, 根國. Cf. *Nihonshoki*, 1st *maki*; Kuroita Katsumi, Maruyama Jirō, *Kokushitaikei Nihonshoki*, p. 38. According to Florenz, op. cit., p. 162, this would be the *yomotsu-kuni*. Furthermore Susa *no* O was ordered to rule there. Cf. *Nihonshoki*, 1st *maki*, Kuroita Katsumi, Maruyama Jirō, op. cit., vol. 1, p. 11; cf. K. Florenz, op. cit., p. 132. Here, too, not *yomi no kuni*, but *ne no kuni* is mentioned. Neither is *yomi no kuni* mentioned in the *Kojiki*, but *ne no katasu kuni*, 根堅洲國. Cf. *Kojiki*, 1st *maki*; Kuroita Katsumi, Maruyama Jirō, *Kokushitaikei Kojiki*, p. 27; K. Florenz, op. cit., p. 49. Therefore Izanami *no mikoto* is rather to be considered the real deity of the *yomi*. See the next footnote.

[3] It is expressly said of her in the *Kojiki* that she was called Yomotsu-ōkami, 黄泉津大神, the great god of the *yomi*. Cf. *Kojiki*, 1st *maki*; Kuroita Katsumi, Maruyama Jirō, op. cit., p. 13; K. Florenz, op. cit., p. 25.

[4] Cf. *Nihonshoki*, 1st *maki*; Kuroita Katsumi, Maruyama Jirō, *Kokushitaikei Nihonshoki*, vol. 1, p. 21. K. Florenz, op. cit., p. 143, translates this by "Weg-Wächter der Unterwelt".

in West Japan.[1] Thus it developed into a real Hades with many parallels all over the world.[2] In this way we obtain three phases of *yomi* belief. It appears that the most expanded one, viz. the *Kojiki* version, is also the latest, since in it are combined the two *Nihonshoki* versions mentioned first.

It seems to the present author that the first phase is not only the earliest of the three, but that it was also still generally accepted in the days of Shōtoku Taishi. One can also find this original, sober and unadorned concept a few pages further on in the *Nihonshoki* after the texts already quoted: [3] "There are those who say of the *yomotsu-hirasaka* that this *yomotsu-hirasaka* is not a special place. They call it only the time space within which a person dying gives up the ghost." If Florenz considers this a later rationalisation of the *yomi* concept,[4] the present author fails to see why it should not have stood at the beginning of the whole development. This point of view relies mainly on the following arguments.

First of all, Tsuda [5] points out that neither in ancient literature nor in any ritual are there any indications of such a nether world belief being alive among the people. According to him *yomotsu-kami*, the god of the nether world, was no more than an idealised human being whose role in the *Kojiki* story was to substantiate a political intention, i.e. no country, wheresoever it was, but it had to be under the rule of a sovereign. This idea of the nether world god was supposed to reinforce the factual position of emperorship. He thinks

---

[1] Probably this was one and the same entrance. For the *Kojiki* locates the *yomotsu-hirasaka* in Izumo and it is now supposed to be called Ifuyasaka, 伊賦夜坂. Cf. *Kojiki*, 1st *maki*; Kuroita Katsumi, Maruyama Jirō, *Kokushitaikei Kojiki*, p. 13; K. Florenz, op. cit., p. 13. In the *Fudoki*, too, a special entrance to the *yomi* is mentioned, situated in Izumo. This entrance was called *yomi no saka* (*yomi*- slope) or *yomi no ana* (*yomi*-hole). Cf. *Fudoki*; Takeda Iukichi, *Fudoki*, p. 132.

[2] For other parallels taken from the comparative study of religions see K. Florenz, op. cit., pp. 21-22, footnote 1.

Matsumae Takeshi compiled practically all parallel cases of a nether world belief which may exist anywhere in the world in his article: "Taiyo no fune to tokoyo no shinkō" (The sun-ship and the belief in the Tokoyo), *K.G.Z.*, vol. LXII, 1961, no. 2, 3 (Feb. /March), pp. 23-43, especially pp. 23-35.

[3] Cf. *Nihonshoki*, 1st *maki*; Kuroita Katsumi, Maruyama Jirō, *Kokushitaikei Nihonshoki*, vol. 1, p. 16; K. Florenz, op. cit., p. 139.

[4] Cf. K. Florenz, loc. cit., footnote 27.

[5] Cf. Tsuda Sōkichi, op. cit., vol. 1, p. 402.

that in this way it may be explained that hardly any religious practice is known from those days expressing the dependence on or the respect for such a *yomotsu-kami*.[1] *Yomi*, therefore, was originally only *yami*, i.e. a dark place where the body was buried. This argument of Tsuda's is not unassailable, since both in the *Nihonshoki* and in the *Kojiki* several—magical—usages are mentioned which do indeed imply such a belief: that of not kindling a light in the night and the emphasis on peaches as a remedy against all kinds of nether world forces. The following arguments are considered of greater importance.

In the tale of Izanagi and Izanami there is in the first place a strong reference to the ancient influence of matriarchy. For it cost Izanagi a good deal of trouble to avoid the magic influence of Izanami, incorporated, e.g., in the *ikazuchi*. One might also invert this, viz. by saying that, for a man of that period, it took a lot of trouble to get hold of a woman protected by so much magic. One is involuntarily reminded of the old *tsuchigumo*.[2]

Another argument for this great age as well as for the *yomi* may be seen in a parallelism with the Takama *no hara*, the land of the sun. The *yomi*, as total darkness, is the counterpart of *ama* or *ame*, the light itself. Both in the *Nihonshoki* and the *Kojiki* versions it appears that everything in the *yomi* is tabu which has to do with light. If the sun is the symbol of the day, the *yomi* is that of the night. Thence the *Nihonshoki* reduces the superstitious custom of people not kindling a light during the night to the close relationship which existed between night and *yomi*.[3] And just as *ame* as the sun developed into a land populated by gods, equally absolute darkness grew into such a land. From the same contrast between *ame* and *yomi* it is understandable why Amaterasu's great adversary, Susa *no* O, not only was exiled to the land of *yomi*, but came to occupy a ruler's position there.[4] That *yomi no kuni* originated from the absolute denial of all (sun-) light is no reason for equating this

---

[1] Ibid..

[2] For feminine influence see: Sugano Masao, "Tokoyo-yuku-shinwa no keisei" (The formation of the Visit to Hades myth), *K.G.Z.*, vol. LXII, 1961, no. 10, Oct., pp. 45 and 47.

[3] Cf. *Nihonshoki*, 1st *maki*; Kuroita Katsumi, Maruyama Jirō, op. cit., vol. 1, p. 15; cf. also K. Florenz, op. cit., p. 137; W. G. Aston, op. cit., vol. I, p. 24.

[4] This will do only if the identity of *yomi no kuni* and *ne no kuni* is accepted. Cf. p. 444.

without further ado with other 'nether worlds', such as for example *tokoyo no kuni*, which are not connected with darkness and the other unappetising peculiarities of the *yomi no kuni*, such as pus, maggots and decay, and in which worlds, on the other hand, there certainly is room for the sun. In the following pages this will be further pursued.

A last argument for the prevalence of *yomi* over *yomi no kuni* relies on the existence of the tumulus graves mentioned in the first chapter.[1] For these have been built with the purpose that the dead can continue their 'lives' with everything belonging to them, such as wives, war-horses and servants.[2] People did not shrink from burying alive, together with the beloved dead, hundreds of his or her servants in a circle round the grave in the form of a human hedge, *hitogaki*, 人垣.[3] That was already the case in the days of Queen Himiko.[4] This custom, which spread as far as China and Siberia, was still followed in the times of Shōtoku Taishi, for it was only abolished in 646 by the Taika reformation.[5] Nevertheless, even after this it continued its existence.[6] If one believed in a separate hereafter, such a custom would have been senseless. The close connection between the tumulus tombs and the *yomi* already follows from the fact that in the *Nihonshoki* passage quoted above on Izanagi's visit to Izanami a '*mogari no tokoro*' is mentioned as the place where Izanami was temporarily laid out. Now, such *mogari no tokoro* were customary with the tumulus tombs. Here the dead had to wait till the tumulus tomb was ready, which would often take years.[7] It is, therefore, not surprising that this custom of the *mogari no tokoro* was abolished in 646 by the same decree on

---

[1] Pp. 34 ff.

[2] Some remains of skeletons have been found in these tombs, which point to this custom. Cf. K. Florenz, op. cit., p. 262, footnote 48. Tsuda Sōkichi, op. cit., vol. 2, p. 403, attributes the origin of the *yomi no kuni* concept to the existence of these mass graves.

[3] Cf. *Kojiki*, 2nd *maki*; Kuroita Katsumi, Maruyama Jirō, *Kokushitaikei Kojiki*, p. 71; cf. K. Florenz, op. cit., p. 96: 'Menschenhecke'.

[4] Cf. Chapter II, p. 87.

[5] Here it is mentioned that live horses and men were buried at the same time. Cf. *Nihonshoki*, 25th *maki*, Taika, 2nd year, 3rd month, 22nd day; Kuroita Katsumi, Maruyama Jirō, op. cit., vol. 2, p. 235; cf. K. Florenz, op. cit., p. 348; W. G. Aston, op. cit., vol. II, p. 220.

[6] For this see: K. Florenz, op. cit., p. 262, footnote 48.

[7] The Emperor Ankō, for instance, was only interred three years after his death. Cf. J. E. Kidder, op. cit., p. 152.

funerals which regulated the building of tumulus tombs.[1] Perhaps that is why Izanami, too, was waiting in a *mogari no tokoro* for interment in a tumulus tomb. According to the *Kojiki* and the *Nihonshoki* she obtained, at any rate, a grave of her own.[2]

If, then, there was a close connection between *yomi* belief and tumulus tombs we know, owing to the existence of these monuments, that this *yomi* belief occupied an important place in the faith of Shōtoku's contemporaries. As witnesses to this *yomi* belief these tombs were certainly built, up to the time of the Taika reformation, when their size was made to accord with the rank of the deceased.[3] Furthermore, it is remarkable that the greatest concentration of these graves is to be found in the area where Shōtoku lived, viz. the Yamato region.[4] All these data together form the irrefutable proof of the fact that in Shōtoku's times people believed in a *yomi*, consisting of the grave of the deceased, rather than in a *yomi no kuni*. At the same time it follows from the close connection with the tumulus tombs that in the *yomi* belief we are dealing not only with a Chinese, but especially with an original Japanese detail.

If on the basis of these arguments the existence of the *yomi* has been proved, there are yet still further characteristics to be discovered in the *Kojiki* and the *Nihonshoki*, which give it an opening towards Buddhism. For in these works some other 'lands' are mentioned which, it appears, may also have something to do with *yomi no kuni*. These are, in the *Kojiki*, *ne no katasu kuni*, 根之堅洲國, and in the *Nihonshoki*, *ne no kuni*, 根國. Both these lands are mentioned in connection with the celestial savage Susa *no* O. In the *Kojiki* [5] Susa *no* O causes the whole company of gods to shudder with his lamentations in order to reach the 'land of my mother, *ne no katasu kuni*'. In the same *Kojiki* it is related how

---

[1] Cf. *Nihonshoki*, loc cit..

[2] According to the *Kojiki* and the *Nihonshoki* that tomb was located in various places. Cf. *Kojiki*, 1st *maki*; Kuroita Katsumi, Maruyama Jirō, *Kokushitaikei Kojiki*, p. 10; *Nihonshoki*, 1st *maki*; Kuroita Katsumi, Maruyama Jirō, *Kokushitaikei Nihonshoki*, p. 13; K. Florenz, op. cit., p. 133; W. G. Aston, op. cit., vol. 1, p. 21.

[3] Cf. *Nihonshoki*; Kuroita Katsumi, Maruyama Jirō, op. cit., pp. 233-234; cf. K. Florenz, op. cit., pp. 346-348; W. G. Aston, op. cit., vol. II, pp. 217-220.

[4] Cf. J. E. Kidder, op. cit., p. 147.

[5] Cf. *Kojiki*, 1st *maki*; Kuroita Katsumi, Maruyama Jirō, *Kokushitaikei Kojiki*, p. 16; cf. K. Florenz, op. cit., p. 30.

Ōnamuchi made the daughter of Susa *no* O, Suseri *hime*, 須勢理毗賣, his wife.[1] After a desperate struggle with the magic powers of this *ne no katasu kuni*—for here, as in the case of Izanagi's visit, we are concerned with the conquest of a woman—and pursued by Susa *no* O as far as *yomotsu-hirasaka*, situated on the borders of this land, Ōnamuchi succeeded in liberating his wife from the *ne no katasu kuni*.

Since we have come to know *yomi no kuni* as a nether world which began its existence in connection with Susa *no* O's mother Izanami and which is also bordered by the *yomotsu-hirasaka* and is no less known as land of horror, *yomi no kuni* and *ne no katasu kuni* are identical.

In connection with Susa *no* O the expression *ne no katasu kuni* does not occur in the *Nihonshoki*, but we do find *ne no kuni*. Here, too, Susa *no* O is emphatically called its ruler.[2] It is, therefore, not difficult to identify *ne no kuni* with *ne no katasu kuni* of the *Kojiki* and consequently with *yomi no kuni*. In the *Nihonshoki* this *ne no kuni* is called a subterranean, *sokotsu ne no kuni*,[3] and a distant,[4] very distant land, *kiwamete tooki ne no kuni*.[5]

Since *ne no kuni* is here referred to as a far off land it appears that the concept, *yomi* = place of the grave, has already been dropped. Analogous to the distant land of *tokoyo*, *yomi no kuni* has here become an intermediate form between *yomi* and *tokoyo no kuni*.[6] This facet is therefore certain to have been added later to the meaning of *ne no kuni*. Yet the real meaning of *ne no kuni* is not *nether*

[1] Cf. *Kojiki*, 1st *maki*; Kuroita Katsumi, Maruyama Jirō, op. cit., p. 27; cf. K. Florenz, op. cit., p. 49.

[2] Cf. *Nihonshoki*, 1st *maki*; Kuroita Katsumi, Maruyama Jirō, *Kokushi-taikei Nihonshoki*, vol. 1, p. 11: "He was sent down and made to rule the nether world." Cf. K. Florenz, op. cit., p. 132; W. G. Aston, op. cit., vol. I, p. 20.

[3] Cf. *Nihinshoki*, 1st *maki*; Kuroita Katsumi, Maruyama Jirō, op. cit., p. 38; cf. K. Florenz, op. cit., p. 162; W. G. Aston, op. cit., p. 50.

[4] Cf. *Nihonshoki*, 1st *maki*; Kuroita Katsumi, Maruyama Jirō, op. cit., p. 11; cf. K. Florenz, op. cit., p. 131; W. G. Aston, op. cit., p. 20.

[5] Cf. *Nihonshoki*, 1st *maki*; Kuroita Katsumi, Maruyama Jirō, op. cit., p. 12; cf. K. Florenz, op. cit., p. 132; W. G. Aston, op. cit., p. 20.

[6] This meaning of 'distant' applies to *tokoyo no kuni* rather than to *ne no kuni*. Cf. C. Ouwehand, *Namazu-e and their themes*, Leiden 1964, p. 94. On the basis, however, of South-east Asiatic equivalent expressions some authors ascribe the sense of 'distant' to *ne*. Cf. Matsumae Takeshi, op. cit., p. 41.

world, as one might perhaps expect because of the Chinese character: 根, root.[1] This character, however, is only of phonetic value. Basing himself on the equivalents now in use on Okinawa and in the Ryūkyū Archipelago, it is especially Yanagita Kunio who assigned the meaning of *honke*, 本家, to *ne*, i.e. the main family as root and basis of the whole family system.[2]

Although the present author would not wish to deny the relationship of these forms now in use on Okinawa and the Ryūkyū Archipelago it appears that in the *Kojiki* and the *Nihonshoki* a significance of *ne no kuni*, connected herewith and yet entirely its own, is implied, which to a high degree is conditioned by the religious situation of, i.a., Shōtoku's times. We may discern the real meaning of *ne no* (*katasu*) *kuni*, and consequently of *yomi no kuni*, in: *land of the mother*. This meaning is apparent in various places in the *Kojiki* and the *Nihonshoki*.

First of all Susa *no* O says, as we saw: "I want to go to the land of my mother, *ne no katasu kuni*." [3] It seems here that the 'land of my mother', *haha no kuni*, 妣國, and *ne no* (*katasu*) *kuni* are synonyms. The proof of this theory may be seen in the fact that the expression *ne no* (*katasu*) *kuni* is only used in connection with Susa no O, to whom *yomi no kuni* as the habitation of his mother Izanami was a true 'land of his mother'. If *ne no kuni* has that meaning then it is logical that this expression is not used for the land of Izanami herself. Interestingly enough this is indicated in the *Kojiki* and the *Nihonshoki* as: *mogari no tokoro* or *yomi no kuni*, because to her it was not a *ne no kuni*, i.e. land of the mother. Also the word *ine* = mother, which in some regions of Japan is still in use, may perhaps have something to do with this original meaning of *ne*.[4] Thus, really, the grave of *the* mother, Izanami, developed in the *Kojiki* and the *Nihonshoki* into the land of the mother: *ne no kuni*.

The fact that, in the *Nihonshoki*, *ne no kuni* is called subterranean is simply connected with the fact that Izanami's grave was also in the earth. Thus a very interesting parallelism is obtained. In this

---

[1] That is why Florenz's translation "das untere entlegene Land", e.g., op. cit., p. 49, is not entirely correct.

[2] Cf. C. Ouwehand, op. cit., pp. 94-95; Matsumae Takeshi, op. cit., p. 40.

[3] Cf. p. 443.

[4] This word occurs, for instance, in the Fukui and Ishikawa prefectures and on the island of Sado. Cf. Matsumae Takeshi, op. cit., p. 41. For other South-east Asiatic parallels see Matsumae Takeshi, op. cit., p. 42.

representation the *woman* Izanami was the force active and personified in the earth, in contrast to the *man* Izanagi active in the Takama *no hara*. The contrast Takama *no hara—yomi no kuni* was thus logically extended, apart from other parallels [1] of a comparative religious nature connected with this. The image of mother earth, well-known everywhere, was viewed in Japan as that of the mother in the earth.

This special idea of an Izanami loaded with tabus, living in the 'beyond' of this life, has assuredly been reinforced by the matriarchy and Shamanism of antiquity. The fact that in those days spiritual life and political dispensation began with the Shaman obtained its mythical significance in the figure of Izanami as the archetypal occurrence which was to support the day-to-day practice of the Shamans then living who, as may be remembered, themselves so often had to undertake their souls' journeys to the motherland which was so symbolical of matriarchy. As the land of the *deceased* mother, *ne no kuni* or *yomi no kuni* became a land of the dead. As the land, however, of the female giver of all life it became also a land of the origin of all that is living. In consequence it became a region where death, life and birth meet each other and where the circle of birth-life-death is finally closed.

It requires no argument that this identification of birth and death in the *ne no kuni* was of great importance to Buddhism. From this, in a subsequent phase, the idea of re-birth in this land itself could easily evolve. Notwithstanding the initial hideousness of *yomi no kuni* it was able to develop from these beginnings and find a connection with the Maitreyanistic Tuṣita heaven and the Amidistic Sukhāvatī. The circumstance that, in the imagination, this motherland had become far, very far distant, fitted in very well with this development. This concept and the last leap from *yomi no kuni* to Tuṣita heaven, as if from a hideous hell to an unimaginably beautiful earthly paradise, was considerably eased by the idea of the land of:

3 *Tokoyo*, 常世.

The word *tokoyo*, with its two different meanings, is capable of

[1] See especially M. Eliade, *Traité d'Histoire des Religions*, mainly the seventh chapter, "La Terre, la Femme et la Fécondité", pp. 211-229. A brief and clear description of these parallels is to be found in Dr. C. J. Bleeker, *Moedergodin der Oudheid*, The Hague 1960, pp. 21 ff..

giving us a false picture of the true nature of the land of *tokoyo*. Written as: 常世 its meaning is the eternal world, if, however, for phonetically the same word the characters: 常夜 are used *tokoyo* acquires nearly the same sense as *yomi*: eternal darkness. Which of these two meanings, then, is the most applicable to the land of *tokoyo*? In his work *Kojikiden*, 古事記伝, Motoori Norinaga, for instance, saw in the latter especially the original meaning of *tokoyo*. Herein he relies especially on the *Kojiki* in which Susa *no* O had provoked his sister Amaterasu so much that she withdrew into the celestial cavern. As a result both Takama *no hara* and Ashihara *no nakatsukuni* became pitch dark. Then the *Kojiki* continues: "*kore ni yorite tokoyo yuku*".[1] Since *tokoyo* is here written: 常夜 this sentence may be translated as: "as a result of this eternal night began".[2] The *furigana*, however, also gives the following reading of these characters: *tokoyami*: eternal darkness.[3] Now this expression here has only the meaning: "it became pitch dark", no more. From this one cannot derive the origin of a land,[4] the more so since *yomi no kuni*, too, is the result of a long development which had its starting point in the darkness of the grave itself. It seems, therefore, too far-fetched to attribute, on the basis of this text in which there is no question of land or nether world, the sense of land of eternal darkness to *tokoyo no kuni*.[5]

The real meaning of *tokoyo* in the term *tokoyo no kuni* is the first: land of the eternal world. It is described in that sense in both the *Kojiki* and the *Nihonshoki*. The *Kojiki* says of the dwarf god Sukunabikona, 少名毗古那, that he "crossed to the land of *tokoyo*".[6] Elsewhere two brothers of Iware *hiko* (= Jimmu) are mentioned in it, viz.: Mikenu *no mikoto*, 御毛沼命, and Inahi *no mikoto*, 稻氷命. The former, then, 'went and stood on the crest of the waves and crossed to the land of *tokoyo*"; the latter, however, "entered the

[1] Cf. *Kojiki*, 1st *maki*; Kuroita Katsumi, Maruyama Jirō, *Kokushitaikei Kojiki*, p. 20.

[2] Cf. K. Florenz, op. cit., pp. 37-38.

[3] Cf. *Kojiki*, loc. cit..

[4] Cf. Nakajima Etsuji, op. cit., p. 79.

[5] For this view see C. Ouwehand, op. cit., pp. 86-87.

[6] Cf. *Kojiki*, 1st. *maki*; Kuroita Katsumi, Maruyama Jirō, op. cit., p. 34; cf. also K. Florenz, op. cit., p. 57. The same is also found in the *Nihonshoki*, 1st *maki*; Kuroita Katsumi, Maruyama Jirō, *Kokushitaikei Nihonshoki*, vol. 1, p. 47; K. Florenz, op. cit., p. 172; W. G. Aston, op. cit., p. 60.

plain of the sea as the land of his mother".[1] It is difficult to decide whether the two countries mentioned here were identical. *Yomi no kuni* is sometimes indeed understood as 'mother-land', but that meaning is not known for *tokoyo no kuni*. In all these texts only the existence of the land of *tokoyo* is indicated. Its own character appears in the *Kojiki* as well as in the *Nihonshoki* from the journey to the land of *tokoyo* which, by the order of the very old Emperor Suinin,[2] was undertaken by a certain Tajimamori, 田道間守. Of this the *Nihonshoki* says: [3]

"The next year (i.e. the year after the death of the Emperor Suinin), spring, third month, twelfth day. Tajimamori returned from the land of *tokoyo* with eight sticks and eight bundles of eternally fragrant (lit.: *tokijiku no kagu*, 非時香, with the fragrance of timelessness) fruits.[4] Then Tajimamori lamented and cried. He said: 'I have carried out the emperor's order and went away to a far distant land. I went 10,000 *ri* across the waves. I went a long way over the weak water. This land of *tokoyo* is the mysterious (hidden) land of the *hijiri*,[5] inaccessible to ordinary people. My journey out and back has taken me ten years. Against expectation I braved high waves and returned to my own country. Thanks to the spirits of the imperial *hijiri* [6] I was able, though with difficulty, to accomplish my return. Now, however, the emperor has died without my being able to announce my return to him. If I, his servant, should stay alive, what would it avail?' He then turned to the emperor's tumulus tomb, cried aloud and died himself. When all the ministers heard this they shed tears. Tajimamori was the first ancestor of Miyake *no muraji*, 三宅."

[1] Cf. *Kojiki*, 1st *maki*; Kuroita Katsumi, Maruyama Jirō, *Kokushitaikei Kojiki*, p. 52; cf. K. Florenz, op. cit., p. 84.

[2] According to the *Kojiki* he died at the age of 153. Cf. *Kojiki*, 2nd. *maki*; Kuroita Katsumi, Maruyama Jirō, op. cit., p. 82.

[3] Cf. *Nihonshoki*, 4th *maki*, Suinin, 99th year; Kuroita Katsumi, Maruyama Jirō, *Kokushitaikei Nihonshoki*, vol. 1, pp. 192-193; cf. also W.G. Aston, op. cit., p. 187.

[4] According to the *Kojiki* text (cf. *Kojiki*, 2nd *maki*, Suinin Tennō; Kuroita Katsumi, Maruyama Jirō, *Kokushitaikei Kojiki*, p. 82) the tree from this fruit was called: *tokijiku no kagu no ko*: tree of eternal fragrance. The *Kojiki* adds that this tree was an orange tree. Cf. K. Florenz, op. cit., p. 102.

[5] This translation follows the *furigana* text. It reads, in Chinese characters: 神仙, *shinsen*. For the meaning of this expression see following page.

[6] Thus the *furigana* text. It reads, in Chinese characters: 聖帝, *seitei*, holy (wise) emperors.

In this story the land of *tokoyo* was not only an island which lay in and not under the sea, but it was also innocent of the horror of *yomi* and warranted, in accordance with its name, a long life as symbolised in the fruits of timelessness. This story is not very original, for earlier Chinese authors have used the same motif before. According to China's oldest historical work, the *Shih-chi*, by Szŭ-ma Ch'ien (145-ca. 86 B.C.), the Emperor Shih Huang, 始皇, (246-207 B.C.) sent a certain Hsü-fu, 徐福, to China's legendary East Sea,[1] in order to obtain from there an elixir of life similar to the above mentioned fruits. The Emperor Wu, 武, (140-87 B.C.) had also, though in vain, sent out Taoist hermits to such an island.[2] These Chinese parallels already indicate something of the origin of this Tajimamori tale. There are, however, still more signs in this text which indicate a Chinese origin. Thus the land of *tokoyo* is called a "mysterious land of the *hijiri*". The characters: 神仙, Sino-Jap.: *shinsen*, Chin.: *shên-hsien*; are rendered Japanese by the *furigana* text as *hijiri*. These *shên-hsien*, then, were the deified *hsien*, 仙, Chinese followers of Lao-tzŭ and, further, hermits who, especially until the foundation of the Ch'in dynasty (255-206 B.C.), enjoyed great popularity and lived in caverns, holes and special hermitages, called *ching-shê*, 精舍.[3]

This Chinese character also appears from the beautiful story of the fisherman Urashima *no ko*, 浦嶋子, which, in the *Nihonshoki*, is dated 478, the twenty-second year of Emperor Yūryaku.[4] This man caught a large turtle which changed into a wonderfully beautiful girl. Urashima *no ko* fell in love with her and made her his wife. Together they went—literally and figuratively—to sea. When they were sailing their ship past the land of *tokoyo* they saw the *hijiri*, here written as, 仙, *hsien*, walking about. This tale illustrates even better the Chinese character of the land of *tokoyo*. The *furigana* text here indicates *tokoyo no kuni* as the translation of the Chinese characters: 蓬萊山, Hōraisan, Chin. Fêng-lai-shan. This Fêng-lai-shan is known in Chinese literature and in a work preserved to the present day, the *Shih Chou chi*, 十洲記, the 'description of the ten

---

[1] Cf. J. J. M. de Groot, *Universismus*, p. 126.

[2] Cf. H. Coates, R. Ishizuka, *Honen the Buddhist Saint*, p. 590, footnote 10.

[3] Cf. J. J. M. de Groot, op. cit., pp. 98-99.

[4] Cf. *Nihonshoki*, 14th *maki*, Yūryaku, 22nd year, 7th month; Kuroita Katsumi, Maruyama Jirō, *Kokushitaikei Nihonshoki*, vol. 1, p. 388; cf W. G. Aston, op. cit., vol 1, p. 368.

islands', as one of the dream islands situated in the Eastern Sea, where only the *hsien* could enter.[1] It is therefore entirely by chance that in this text too *hsien* are mentioned. We are thus clearly dealing with one of the gardens of immortality of Chinese literature, one of which was also the eldorado of Hsi wang-mu mentioned on p. 175.

This idea of the land of *tokoyo*, imported from China, soon enjoyed great popularity in Japan too, probably under the influence of the horrific *yomi*. This is evident from the following story which the *Nihonshoki* relates under the third year of Empress Kōgyoku (644). It illustrates what excesses people were capable of, if only to avoid the *yomi*: [2]

"Third year, autumn, seventh month. A certain Ōfube *no* Ō, 大生部多, from the neighbourhood of the Fuji, 不盡, river in the east, exhorted the people in the hamlets and villages to worship an insect by saying: 'This is the god of *tokoyo* (or: of the eternal world). He who worships this god obtains from him riches and a long life'. Enchanters and enchantresses [3] then cheated them with the revelation of this god which runs: 'He who worships the god of *tokoyo* will—if he is poor—become rich, and—if he is old—become young'. They then exhorted the people more and more to lay down along the road everything valuable they had in their houses, such as *sake* (rice wine), vegetables and the six domestic animals.[4] They were made to shout: 'The new riches have come'. The people of the city and the countryside then took the insects of *tokoyo* and gave them a beautiful place. Singing and dancing they prayed to them for riches. They threw away their (own) riches. This, however, was no use. Very much of it was lost or destroyed. The Katono *no* Hata *no miyatsuko*, Kawakatsu, 葛野秦造河勝, was angry because of the people being swindled and beat Ōfube *no* Ō. Then the enchanters and enchantresses became frightened. They stopped their propaganda for this devotion (lit.: divine worship). A song was made at that time which runs: 'Utsumasa, 禹者麻佐, (= Kawakatsu) has

---

[1] Cf. J. J. M. de Groot, op. cit., pp. 125-126.

[2] Cf. *Nihonshoki*, 14th *maki*, Kōgyoku, 3rd year, 7th month; Kuroita Katsumi, Maruyama Jirō, op. cit., vol. 2, pp. 205-206; c.f. W. G. Aston, op. cit., vol. II, p. 188.

[3] Literally 巫覡, male and female *wu*.

[4] These were: horse, ox, sheep, pig, dog and chickens. Cf. W. G. Aston, op. cit., p. 188, footnote 3.

beaten off the god of gods who was said to be the god of *tokoyo*'. These insects usually live on orange trees or on the (bush) *hosoki* (creeping pepper).[1] They are more than 4 *sun* large(about an inch). They have a green colour with black spots and are very similar to silkworms."

On the one hand this story illustrates the enormous fear of the *yomi*, which at that time had seized everyone. On the other hand it gives a glimpse of the *tokoyo* belief of those days, i.e. about 20 years after Shōtoku Taishi's death. What the land of *tokoyo*, reserved only for a few, could not give the masses was guaranteed by the caterpillars who, be it remembered, lived on the same eternally fragrant trees as those in the land of *tokoyo* since, according to the *Kojiki*, these trees were none other than orange trees.[2]

The places in the *Kojiki* and the *Nihonshoki* mentioned here suffice as a picture of the nature of the *tokoyo* land. Other dates, for example from the *Fudoki*, can hardly add to or complete it.[3] Thus we have become acquainted with the *tokoyo no kuni* as a far distant Chinese island of eternal life, luxuriant plant growth and unrivalled prosperity, reserved for the *hijiri*, the Japanese counterparts of the

---

[1] Probably a bamboo-like grass is intended here, *mōsō*, 孟宗, Phyllostachys edulis, or a creeper. Cf. K. Florenz, op. cit., p. 339, footnote 21.

[2] This story is a further illustration of the excesses which often accompany the encounter of one ideology and culture with another totally unknown one. A parallel case is clearly that of the 'cargo cults' of the Admiralty Islands and New Guinea which also arose from the difficulty found in assimilating the encounter with a totally strange and superior civilization. The striking resemblance appears from what Margaret Mead sees in these 'cargo cults': "Mystical outbreaks in which a local prophet commanded the people to kill their pigs, destroy their property, and wait for the cargo." Cf. Margaret Mead, *New Lives for Old*, New York 1961, p. 186. The 'cargo' here consists of shiploads of western goods with which the ancestors would return to New Guinea. To this cargo belongs also the Salvation which Christianity has brought, the Redeemer figure of Christ himself. Cf. Margaret Mead, op. cit. On this see also F. Sierksma, *Een nieuwe hemel en een nieuwe aarde*, The Hague 1961, pp. 224 ff.

[3] In the *Fudoki*, too, *tokoyo no kuni* is called a land of riches and abundance. One may think, e.g., of the description of the Iyo well at the beginning of this Chapter, p. 384. That prosperity is also evident in the *Fudoki* of the land of Hitachi, which is compared, i.a., with what formerly "was called the land of *tokoyo*". Cf. *Fudoki*; Takeda Iukichi, op. cit., p. 47. In the *Fudoki* the marine character of this land appears from the land of Ise which "arose from the waves of *tokoyo*", Takeda Iukichi, op. cit., pp. 283-284.

shên-hsien. Although in the sources mentioned above it is known only as the land of the *hijiri*, whom we have come to know in the preceding chapter [1] as sun sages, yet afterwards this land acquired a special sun character. This is evident not only from the ships of souls which set out for the land of *tokoyo* with sacrifices to the dead, and which we have come to understand as sun ships.[2] Also the *marebito*, 客人, the divine visitors who, on the occasion of harvest festivals especially, came from this land to visit the southern regions of Japan, were often *avatāras* of the sun.[3] When comparing, then, this idea of *tokoyo no kuni*—undoubtedly imported by Korean immigrants—with the more Japanese complex of Takama *no hara*—*yomi no kuni*, then *tokoyo no kuni* appears not to fit into this complex at all. It is perhaps for exactly this reason that it was able eventually to break up and do away with the absolute contrast between Takama *no hara* and *yomi no kuni*. Thus *tokoyo no kuni* became a kind of catalyst owing to which the concept of *yomi no kuni* began to react and was able to develop towards various Buddhist conceptions of the hereafter. On the other hand, owing to this, complete identification could eventually come about between *yomi no kuni* and all the other lands of the dead and of heroes which existed in Japanese popular belief.[4] This identification is at the present day accepted by Japanese and Western authors with some reservation as regards a few conceptual gradations.[5] The beginning of this development is set out in the following diagram:

---

[1] P. 335.

[2] Cf. Chapter III, p. 210.

[3] For these and other sun characteristics see: Matsumae Takeshi, op. cit., p. 41.

[4] A clear picture of what is still alive of this in Japanese popular belief and in that of Japan's southern islands and the Ryūkyū Archipelago is provided by C. Ouwehand, op. cit., pp. 94-95. The enormous popularity of this *ne no kuni* is evident from the many names under which it occurred in Japan's southern islands. Cf. C. Ouwehand, op. cit., his map belonging to p. 87, footnote 7. The existence of these 'nether worlds' did not stop at the Ryūkyū islands. In many other South-east Asiatic areas parallels of this may be found. For this cf. Matsumae Takeshi, op. cit., pp. 39-42.

[5] Cf. Matsumoto Yoshio, "Kodaijin no takai-kannen" (The ideology of the ancients about the 'other' world), *Minzokugaku no tame ni*, no. 10, 1951, pp. 59-61; Yanagita Kunio, "Kaijingu kō" (Thoughts on the sea temple), *M.G.K.*, no. 2, pp. 104-105. On these and other views see also Matsumae Takeshi, op. cit., p. 40.

Takama no hara	*Yomi no kuni*		*Tokoyo no kuni*
1. = the sun itself became land of the sun	1. the grave itself became mass grave and land of the dead	a →	1. land of the sun (in later development)
2. eternal *light*	2. negation of light: absolute darkness	→	2. land of sunshine
3. only for sungod(s)	3. for gods of darkness and any dead	m → a ←	3. for the *hijiri*, immortals
4. above the earth (Yamato)	4. under the earth or the sea	→	4. far away in the sea
5. fatherland (Izanagi)	5. motherland (Izanami)	←	5. of ancestors
6. a divine life as on earth	6. dissolution of earthly life	→	6. a prosperous earthly life

In this diagram the points of connection with Buddhism are indicated by an arrow; a means: connection with Sukhāvatī of Amidism, m: connection with the Tuṣita heaven of Maitreyanism.[1] Since it was impossible for man to enter Takama *no hara* some correlation or other of this with one of the Buddhist 'lands' had little meaning.

It is evident from this diagram that *tokoyo no kuni* considerably softened several hard aspects of *yomi no kuni*; this is especially clear from the numbers 1, 2 and 6. In a later phase of development the sun concept, which positively and negatively forms the basis of Takama *no hara* and *yomi no kuni* (this is the reason why *yomi no kuni* has indeed something to do with sun belief!), was integrated with that of *tokoyo no kuni*, as also was the whole thought complex which is connected with number 5 of *yomi no kuni*. Thus really influenced by the belief in a *tokoyo no kuni*, brought to Japan by Korean or Chinese immigrants, the ancient *ujigami* belief came to approach Maitreyanism and Amidism, which had also found, be it remembered, so many points of contact in Korea and other North Asiatic areas. It is clear that the all-pervading sun faith was eventually to tip the scales of Japan's Buddhist development towards Amidism, which had itself also originated from the same sun faith.

[1] Cf. Chapter III, footnote 1 on p. 169.

After this digression on the vision of a hereafter alive in the *ujigami* belief, as it was reflected in the *Kojiki* and the *Nihonshoki*, we return to our starting point: Shōtoku Taishi's Buddhism and the Tenjukoku-*mandara*. With regard to this the following may be stated:

1) First of all it is now clear where Shōtoku Taishi went after his death. On p. 423 it was pointed out how emphatically the authors of the *Nihonshoki* made the monk Eji and his contemporaries say that Shōtoku Taishi was a *hijiri*. Since *tokoyo no kuni* was the exclusive domain of the *hijiri*, it is evident that they wanted to indicate by this that Shōtoku, too, had taken up his abode there. Admittedly the same text repeatedly mentions the 'Pure Land' as Shōtoku's habitation. But the whole of the above digression clearly shows that in Shōtoku's time this had ideologically not yet been reached. It has, therefore, been rejected as an anachronism.[1] If then Shōtoku came to a *tokoyo no kuni* this need not necessarily mean that here the belief in *yomi no kuni* could not also have played its part in the background. According to the inscription of the Tenjukoku-*mandara* Shōtoku's widow wanted to see him in this land "such as he lives there and has been reborn".[2] Now it is remarkable that in the same inscription, shortly before Shōtoku's death, his mother's is also mentioned. It was seen in the preceding pages not only how strong the *yomi* belief was in Shōtoku's time, but also that it was accepted as a motherland. In those days some people are sure to have believed of him that he had gone, just as did Susa *no* O, "to the land of his mother, *ne no kuni*", or, as Umako said of the deceased Buddhist Paekche king, Sŏng, "that he went to rest in a dark room",[3] which is nothing other than the *yomi*.

[1] Cf. p. 423.

[2] Cf. p. 381.

[3] In characters this reads: 玄室, dark room. The *furigana* text 'translates' this into Japanese as: *kuraki*, dark. For this text see further Chapter IV, p. 273. This whole expression reminds one of the Old Testament. That appears for instance from the preceding sentence: "like running water he does not return". The same expression may be found in II Kings, II, 14: "Omnes morimur et quasi aquae dilabimur in terram, quae non revertuntur." The Old Testament kingdom of the dead, moreover, was also envisaged in the earth or in a pit, i.e. equally a dark room. Cf. A. Van den Born and others, *Bijbels Woordenboek*, Roermond 1954-1957, sub voce *Dodenrijk*, p. 355, col. I.

Actually the close connection between water, death, and human revival

How then can one reconcile with one another these apparently contrary views of Shōtoku's hereafter? It has been seen how *tokoyo no kuni* managed to bridge the initial contrast between Takama *no hara* and *yomi no kuni* and how then later the hard aspects of *yomi no kuni* disappeared. The real synthesis between these two views, then, is to be found in:

2) The Tenjukoku-*mandara*. This was nothing but a truly syncretistic land, evolved from *tokoyo no kuni* on the one hand and a kind of Tuṣita heaven on the other. In it the *tokoyo no kuni* is recognisable in at least nineteen figures, some of which walk about as radiant *hijiri*, and then in an abundant fauna in which, here and there, a whirling camphor leaf reminds one of eternity. Round the broad branches of the *katsura* tree [1] are more birds, fishes and a hare as symbols of the *musubi*, active everywhere in nature. On all this radiates a sun, which makes one think of Rouault, while the moon hides somewhere in the branches of the *katsura* tree. Especially the scene in the top left-hand corner: *katsura* tree, hare, birds, and moon, remind one strongly of similar Chinese representations from the Han period relating to the kingdom of Hsi wang-mu.[2] It is also

in the shape of rebirth or resurrection which takes place in the water is to be found everywhere. M. Eliade calls this complex: "Symboles archétypales et universels; ils revèlent la situation de l'homme dans le cosmos, valorisant en même temps sa position en face de la divinité (de la réalité absolue) et de l'histoire." Cf. M. Eliade, *Traité d'histoire des Religions*, p. 175, § 65.

[1] This scenery may very well have a connection with the idea of the ten Islands of the Blessed, which chiefly flourished in popular Taoism. At the end of the sixth Chapter we shall see how this Chinese view also began to gain ground in the Japanese belief about the hereafter. Cfr.: J. J. M. de Groot, op. cit., pp. 125 ff., Suji Z., op. cit., p. 24.

The *katsura* tree (= Cercidiphyllum japonicum) is a deciduous tree, which grows 50 to 100 ft. in Japan and China. This tree is beautiful in its autumn tints.

[2] These animals had, as early as in the Chinese Han period, a symbolical meaning. Much of the pottery of this period shows how the hare often accompanies the ruler of the Chinese heroes' heaven, Hsi wang-mu. In his description of the western columns of the Inan sepulchral chamber Carl Hentze says: "Auf unserem Bilde wird diese Gottheit rechts und links von Hasen flankiert. In den Gefässen, die die Hasen vor sich stehen haben, bereiten sie das Kraut der Unsterblichkeit. Aus Texten und aus den Arbeiten von Edouard Chavannes wissen wir, dass es die Mondhasen sind, die das Kraut der Unsterblichkeit in Mörsern herstellen. Auf diese Weise wird rechts und links von der Si Wang Mu gezeigt, wie aus dem Dunkelmond neues Leben entsteht." Cf. Carl Hentze, "Die Wanderung der

remarkable that in the fourth division of this *mandara*, bottom right, a large hexagonal fruit is depicted—perhaps an orange cut through—, in which four Chinese characters recall the *tokijiku no kagu* fruits which Tajimamori brought with him. These characters 于多盍(?)時 may be translated: here is much fragrant time. So far we are dealing with a land which is very similar to *tokoyo no kuni*. Yet this is not the full description of the landscape, because there are, furthermore, four Buddhas or Bodhisattvas seated high on lotus pistils. Apparently a genuine lotus flower—in contrast to the usual representations—disappears against the yards high pistils towering above it. The place of these figures is so asymetrical and unsystematic that it is impossible to discover the lines which might indicate a known *maṇḍala* or heaven. The symbolical reference to the realm of Hsi wang-mu on the one hand, and the Buddhas seated on the lotus pistils on the other indicate a process in the Japanese belief in heaven which was still in full swing. Evidently it was attempted to turn a *tokoyo no kuni* into a Buddha land, although no correct image or model of the latter was available. Nevertheless, the *yomi* as an abode of horror can hardly be discovered here. As a land of death and origin and, through Buddhism, as a land of rebirth it—in the present author's opinion—rather pushed this growth towards Buddhism into the background, though strongly, as an incentive. Thus the thought of *yomi* compelled Buddhism to the solution of mankind's greatest problem: 'das Sein zum Tode'. Thus it is not surprising that in this way popular Buddhism became a funerary religion and remains such to the present day. From the standpoint of our 'superior' Western religion we may perhaps look down with a certain contempt on such a religion. In Shōtoku's time a religion was forming which stretched

---

Tiere um die heiligen Berge", *Symbolon, Jahrbuch für Symbolforschung*, Band 4, 1964, p. 20. On these hares see also in the same article p. 23. As concerning our Tenjukoku-*mandara* one might ask oneself whether the bird depicted thereon (a pheasant?) had not something in common with Hsi wang-mu herself, who was often presented as a bird in this same Chinese Han period. Cf. Carl Hentze, op. cit., p. 31. The close connection of Hsi wang-mu with the moon also stands out clearly on the Tenjukoku- *mandara*, because here hare and bird are depicted one on each side of the moon and this with the head facing towards it. That here both sun and moon are shown was not done just for ornament, as here in these two we have to do with symbols of death and new life at the same time. Of this there are parallels enough to be found all over the world. Cf. M. Eliade, op. cit., pp. 155 ff.

out a hand across death as the highest redemption from man's deepest need, a need similar to that from which St. Paul knew himself redeemed after Christ's Resurrection.

Thus the Tenjukoku-*mandara* has become a highly important phase, recorded by the embroidery needle, a cross-section of the meeting between Buddhism and the *ujigami* belief, although it is difficult to decide here how far the process: *yomi no kuni*—*tokoyo no kuni*—and, possibly, Tuṣita heaven had already advanced. This phase was most important because Buddhism, starting purely as a means loaded with magic, as in Iname's and Umako's case, began to stretch across terrestrial human existence as a true religion.

Although in this *maṇḍala* the strong accent on the Chinese ideal of the *tokoyo no kuni* is undoubtedly to be attributed to its Korean designers, we are able to observe here an important shift of accent in the nature of Shōtoku's Buddhism.

It is, moreover, interesting that this materialised thought of Shōtoku's is perhaps at the same time the only original idea which may be fully ascribed to him, an idea which perhaps reveals the syncretistic nature of any Japanese but at the same time is a very great one, since it instigated Buddhism to respond to the anthropological need and fear of those times. Although Shōtoku, down to the demythologising of his death, has retired rather into the oblivion of anonymity he may yet, even now, be called 'the father of the fatherland' in this sense, that he managed to surpass the Buddhism of Soga Iname and Umako.

Now that we have reached the end of this chapter the Buddhism of Shōtoku Taishi's time has become more clearly apparent through his demythologisation. In it the Empress Suiko—as the national *uji no kami* and Shaman—formed the central figure who, as a Shaman stretching past the fear of death, almost like her mythical archetype Izanami, managed to give new life to a Buddhism which had not yet quite freed itself from the *ujigami* belief. Thus, in accordance with the social structure of the period, she moulded Japan's religious climate. In this she was strongly supported by advisers such as the *uji no kami*, Soga *no* Umako, her nephew Shōtoku and no less by many Korean immigrants who had come to Japan for that purpose at the cost of great concessions to Paekche and later to other states. Owing, i.a., to the efforts of this latter group Japan came to grips with a Buddhism which contained everything of culture and religion which existed in East Asia. Fertilized by Japan's *ujigami* belief this, in its turn, was driven in two directions which were both to characterise its later history: Amidism and syncretism.

1. *Amidism.* The enormous fear of death and the *yomi*, which exists even now, grasped any means which might remove it. These means were found not only in the "caterpillars of eternal life", but also in the *tokoyo no kuni*, the Tuṣita heaven and Sukhāvātī. Initially it was Maitreyanism especially which, in its heaven, gave everyone [1] an answer which was willingly accepted. At a later stage Amidism was able to substitute for the Tuṣita heaven a solution even better suited to Japanese mentality, Sukhāvatī. This better adaptation was of a twofold kind: on the part of Amitābha himself it was better realized owing to this sun and light character which, as we saw, forms the true nature of Takama *no hara,* and also his redeeming grace the *bhakti*, which removed the harshness of the *yomi*. On the part of the believers the practice of *nenbutsu* [2] was added to it, which, without too much effort, ensured continued existence after death in Sukhāvatī. The Japanese philosophy of life which thus also came to form the basis of Amidism is even now one of the incentives which assisted many 'new' religions in arising in post-war Japan and in finding followers.[3]

2. *Syncretism.* In the preceding chapters, as well as in this one, it was shown that the factual growth of Buddhism in Japan only consisted of a syncretistic process.[4] At the beginning of this process there were

---

[1] This transition was easier since this heaven was also elsewhere in East Asia envisaged as a *tokoyo no kuni*. Cf. footnote 1 on p. 169.

[2] Cf. p. 176, footnote 4.

[3] On this cf. Werner Kohler, *Die Lotus-Lehre*, pp. 265 ff.. His remark in the caption under one of the photographs preceding p. 265 is of special interest. We are concerned here with the Risshō-kōsei-kai: "Die Alten werden besonders geehrt; denn sie leben angesichts des Todes. Wo sich die Alten einer Bewegung anvertrauen, wirken Kräfte, die den Tod überdauern."

[4] It is interesting to note that also with the conversion of the Germanic tribes in West Europe to Christianity similar syncretistic processes are to be seen. These live on in various so-called Christian festivals such as Christmas and the feast of All Saints as adaptations of the old Germanic Yule-tide and Halloween or Allhallows Day. Cfr. Sir J. Frazer, *The Golden Bough*, (abridged Edition), London 1950, p. 633 ff.
Of All Souls' he says: "Under a thin Christian cloak this conceals an ancient pagan festival of the dead." Cf. op. cit., p. 633.

a. a shortage of metaphysical interest and insight [1] into the great structure of the religions which initially came to Japan, and

b. the lack of a severe self-criticism which, if present, would make a sharp distinction between separate religions and which also would clearly delimit a popular belief's own contribution.[2]

c. Owing to which, but not only as a result of it, comes a quite different approach to reality. This chiefly consisted of a more intuitive acceptance of totality, an acceptance which was not the result of a previous analysis or synthesis. This acceptance of totality proceeded in considerable measure from the quite unique society of those times: the complete absorption by and subjection of the individual to the whole and to the absolute demands of his *uji*.[3]

---

[1] Later Zen attempted to make up this deficiency in a positive sense. Of this Arthur Koestler says: "Zen's arch-enemy, the thousand armed hydra which it fights to destroy, is rational thinking— verbal concepts, definitions, the operations of logic, classification by categories. The more extravagant koans are designed to undermine the pupil's confidence in his powers of conscious reasoning, and thus to clear away the obstacles to satori—the sudden flash of intuitive understanding which illuminates the path of Enlightenment. Hence the distrust of words, considered to be the germ-carriers of abstract thought." Arthur Koestler, *The Lotus and the Robot,* London 1960, p. 238.

[2] In connection with the spread of the doctrine of the Pure Land, G.B. Sansom says of this: "To account for this phenomenon in the religious life of the Japanese people is an extremely difficult task; but one thing is clear enough, and that is their lack of interest in metaphysical argument of theological subtleties, and preference for an emotional rather than a systematic approach to religious matters." G.B. Sansom, *A History of Japan to 1334,* Stanford, California, 1958, pp. 47-49.

[3] To this Japanese intuitive acceptance of totality applies what has been pointed out by Heinrich Köster with regard to Chinese Universism: "Im chinesischen Denken geht es . . . gerade nicht um eine vom Allgemeinen zum Besonderen fortschreitende Verknüpfung, sondern um ein Eingehen auf, um ein Entsprechen, um das In-eins-zusammenführen, kurz um eine universistische Denkweise. Nun ist aber das Wort Denkweise oder Denkform belastet mit Schlagworten wie: Asien denkt anders! Asiatisches Denken! u. dgl. mehr. Zweifelsohne sind die logischen Denkformen für die Chinesen wie für uns die gleichen. Kein begabter Chinese hat Schwierigkeiten, unsere arithmetischen, geometrischen oder trigonometrischen Sätze einzusehen und zu verstehen. Aber neben den rein logischen Denkformen gibt es die sogenannten weltanschaulichen Denkformen, d.h. bestimmte Weisen unseres Sehens und Vorstellens, Denkens, Fühlens und Erlebens, des Erarbeitens und des Gestaltens der Welt, sogenannte eigentümliche Strukturen

From these three a kind of syncretistic and new religion was born which kept changing while remaining, in its aversion from defined dogma, beyond the people's grasp. In this religion Buddhism and the *ujigami* belief had grown together and become entwined as versions of each other. A western dogmatic would perhaps only see in this slippery, constantly changing religion a corruption of pure values. To a Japanese, however, it has no other meaning than that of a mirror of his own mentality, which adapts itself each time to the new situation. Herein too there was indeed some dialectic, even though this can only be deduced from the mentality of a Zen monk. This religion was therefore not solely confined to the initial period of Buddhism, but manifested itself in every phase of Japanese religious history and played a part in nearly every religious renewal.[1]

---

unseres theoretischen, praktischen, technischen, ethischen und religiösen Verhaltens in der Wirklichkeit der Welt und der Menschen, kurz gesagt, besondere Weisen und Formen der Welterfahrung, und die sind meines Erachtens in China in einmaliger Weise *universistisch*." Heinrich Köster, "Was ist eigentlich Universismus?", *Sinologica*, vol. IX, nr. 2 (1967), p. 94.

[1] It would be worthwhile to establish and analyse this, period by period. Yet something has already been done in this field. Thus Umeda Yoshihiko set out the main lines and method for this study. Cf. Umeda Yoshihiko, "Shinbutsu-shugo-shi kenkyū-jōsetsu" (An introduction to the study of the syncretism of Shintō and Buddhism), *K. G. Z.*, vol. IV, 1963, no. 5, 6 (June), pp. 58-64, especially pp. 62 ff.. Others exhaustively studied specifically syncretistic doctrines. Suji Zennosuke has dealt with both in en exhaustive historical expose in his: *Nihon Bukkyō-shi no Kenkyū*, Tōkyō 1942, pp. 49-195. The same is found in: Kiyohara Sadao, *Shintō-shi*, pp. 60-100.

Although outside the framework of the present study two statements from Umeda's article may be mentioned here, from which it is evident that similar syncretistic tendencies still form the root of present-day Japanese popular religious experience. Cf. Umeda Yoshihiko, op. cit., pp. 60-61.

The first statement is as follows. When in the first years of the Meiji period (1868-1912) it was attempted, for the sake of imperial ideology, to cleanse Shintō of all Buddhist admixtures, this led not only to great material destruction of everything which smelt of syncretism, but also to rebellions in the north of the country, caused by the discontent on account of these measures. For many Buddhism and Shintō had died. These measures thus led to indifference and disbelief everywhere. On this cf. also Saki Akio, "Haisen to shūkyō no hakyoku" (Our defeat and the collapse of religion). This is the first paragraph of his article: "Sengo no shūkyō-hendō to mondai no shinten" (Post-war religious changes and the progress of problems),

All this confirms for our times what was done in this work for Shōtoku's, viz. the correctness of the thesis that the conversion of the Japanese people to whatever religion—including Christianity—begins on the basis of syncretism. Actually it is a grave question as to whether a Japanese with his capacity for acceptance of totality could live without this syncretism.

With regard to Christianity—Roman Catholicism as well as Protestantism—it must on this basis be said that, from the standpoint of religions in Japan, it can only become a generally accepted religion if it capitulates to syncretism, i.e. if it desists from being—what so far it has passed itself off as at all costs—a religion with an absolute and exclusive value of its own.[1] Should it give in to this, however, and replace Christ by Maitreya or Amitābha, Mary by Kannon, Heaven by the Pure Land and the Resurrection by rebirth, only then it could become a mass movement. One may ask oneself, however, what in that case would remain of Christianity. It has thus been illustrated here that Japanese syncretism creates for every religion which enters Japan and wishes to remain true to itself a dilemma between either isolation or total absorption by other religions.[2] In Japan this is perhaps a dilemma without a solution. Unless it might be that Christianity could muster the

---

N.S.K., vol. IV, p. 38. He indicates this syncretism with the words: *shinbutsu no shinjin*, 神仏の信心, the devotion to Buddhas and *kami*.

The second statement is closely connected with the preceding one. It is concerned with the post-war situation. When, namely, after the war, together with many other pre-war restrictions, the anti-syncretistic regulations, too, were withdrawn piecemeal and explosive growth of religions came about—some of them having a pre-war origin, others coming to life after it—which in propaganda and mass conversions beat all records in the history of religion. Umeda Yoshihiko, op. cit., p. 61, ascribes these successes to the circumstance that at long last there was once more an opportunity in Japan for proffering a syncretistic religion. It is therefore not surprising that in syncretism all these religions do not yield to each other.

[1] On the complex of problems connected with this cf. M. Heinrichs, *Katholische Theologie und asiatisches Denken*, Mainz, 1963, and the present author's review in *H.M.*, vol. XXXIV (1965), issue 2, pp. 115-122.

[2] It appears to the present author that here is the soft spot in the Japanese mentality from which this mentality is laid bare to us in its entirety. The success of the post-war religions is to be attributed to the fact that they chose this spot as their starting-point, from which they evolved, however imperfectly in our view, their own system.

courage to start anew in Japan to search for an answer to the *tokoyo no kuni*. There might be an answer in the Japanese theology of death and fear which precedes all other theologies, in the same way as in the history of Paul's conversion—factual and psychological—the Resurrection preceded all his later theology.

CONCLUSIONS

THE ORIGIN OF JAPAN'S EARLIEST BUDDHISM

What picture then is obtained of Japan's earliest religious mentality? An attempt will be made to round off this picture by means of an historical sketch and a general description of its type.

1. Historically viewed Japan's earliest Buddhism entered Japanese society in a natural manner through Korean immigrants. Thus it cannot be said that it came to Japan by virtue of a letter from King Sŏng of Paekche to the Japanese Emperor Senka in 538. It owes its origin to the immigration of inhabitants from Paekche, of whom Shiba Tattō and probably also Ikebe *no atae* Hida were the leaders. This Buddhism of the immigrants goes immediately back to the king of Paekche, Sŏng, who through the various immigrant communities in Japan was still able to influence religious life there.

The presentation of a statue and *sūtras* by Sŏng's emissaries to the Japanese ruler was therefore a second phase in the development of Japanese Buddhism. It took place not in the court of Kimmei, but in that of Senka. In this matter one cannot rely on the dating, which for that part of the sixth century was still to doubtful, since it was only introduced much later. This follows from other dates concerning the persons of Kimmei and Senka themselves.

It has been attempted to purge this actual course of events given in the *Nihonshoki* of various nationalist and anti-immigrant sentiments. These sentiments came about because the Japanese had had enough of the cultural and political assistance of this group of the population, which literally and figuratively had 'made' Japan. As a result of these interpolations the real origin of Japanese Buddhism disappeared from the oldest chronicles. Furthermore, the role of Shōtoku Taishi in them was reinforced and overdrawn at the expense of that of the immigrants, of Suiko and of Soga Umako.

Thus Buddhism may actually have arrived in Japan as early as under Emperor Keitai with Shiba Tattō and his saddlers. With them it went to the Takaichi region whence it radiated over the whole of Japan.

The monasteries were first populated from these non-Japanese communities. Consequently they were Korean islands within the Japanese landscape. This is evident both from their population and from their architecture of the first hundred years. As a result they were, in their strongly isolated position, less suitable to a confrontation with Japan's own religious mentality. From these monasteries no direct propaganda was carried out. They were, rather, centres of Buddhist experience. In a later stage they were to become the centres of the Nara schools. These looked as much as possible for affiliation with Indian Buddhism. Several founders of these Japanese establishments were immigrants. These schools were mostly replicas of various Mahāyānistic groupings, such as Mādhyamikas (the Sanron school), and the Vijñānavādin (Hossō and Kegon schools). They, too, isolated themselves within their own doctrinal oppositions without achieving any real contact with Japanese popular mentality. Thus they died a slow death and were outdone by other schools, such as the Tendai and the Shingon, who did indeed make sure of their popularity with the people. The Tendai [1] especially became the cradle of all the Buddhist currents which Japan witnessed, especially during its Middle Age. It is, however, interesting that this latter group too was organised in Japan by the descendent of an immigrant, Saichō, who afterwards obtained the honorific title of Dengyō Daishi, great teacher and propagator of the doctrine.

More than these monasteries several laymen from the above-mentioned immigrant groups took care to maintain a close contact with Japanese society. It is owing especially to their relations with Shiba Tattō, the leader of the saddlers, that the *shizoku* of the Soga became sympathetic to Buddhism. One of the main causes was also that it was exactly this *shizoku* which had from the earliest days faced everything new with an open mind. It was, too, the main protector of the immigrant groups. This sympathy led to the conversion of both the Soga *uji no kami*, Iname and Umako, who dominated the political stage of the whole of the second half of the sixth and the beginning of the seventh century.

These conversions were not identical with what we, from the Christian point of view, mean by it. Iname's conversion still left much to be desired, since it did not lead him to the essential core

[1] On this cf. footnote 5 on pp. 108 ff.

of Buddhism. Owing to defective means of communication, amongst which was his ignorance of Chinese and Korean, he was too insufficiently acquainted with this faith. His conversion did not advance much further than the magic power of a statue which was seen as a kind of new *ujigami* or *musubi*. But even for a considerable time after him people were still to see in the statue the meeting-point of all sorts of Buddhism and *ujigami* belief. Yet his conversion was of importance in so much as it also involved that of the whole of Soga society. For in matters religious this society was obliged to follow its *uji no kami*, Iname, without further ado, because he was the concrete personal form of the religious mentality of the Soga. The conversion of the Soga was a kind of conception of a small Buddhist core in Japanese *shizoku* society, which was then to develop into real Buddhism. That is why the small temples of Owarida, Mukuhara and Ishikawa, for example, were planned not only for Iname and Umako, but also for all the other members of the Soga *shizoku* as a meeting-place with the new Buddhist '*ujigami*'. This conversion was more or less undone by the first persecution which led to a disenchantment owing to the destruction of the statue, which showed that it had not been able to confirm the power attributed to it.

Umako's conversion went even further, since as the acceptance of something new it admittedly did not penetrate to the real depth of Buddhism, yet contained the germ of an entirely new religion in which *ujigami* belief and Buddhism began to integrate mutually. Also, with this conversion the *ujigami* belief itself was not at stake. Soga Umako distinguished himself from his Mononobe adversaries not in that he rejected the *ujigami* belief for the sake of Buddhism, but in that he—in contradistinction to them—integrated his Buddhism with his *ujigami* belief or enriched it with it. In this matter the burning question for the *ujigami* belief was whether or not to accept the first Buddhist data discovered by him. A conversion, in our Christian sense of the word as a radical break, would have meant for Umako the end of his existence as an *uji no kami*. Viewed from his historical significance that is unthinkable.

The above mentioned integration was rendered possible by the preceding history of both the *ujigami* belief and Buddhism which both, on meeting each other, had come to grow towards each other considerably. The *ujigami* belief, namely, was the continuation of Korean and North Chinese popular belief. This is evident if only from their mutual Shamanistic relationship. Buddhism, in its turn, had learned, especially in North and Central Asia, to adapt itself continually to changing situations. That adaptation came about not so much by re-interpreting anew the earliest basis of its origin on every occasion according to the demands of each period. North Chinese personalities, such as Tao-an and Hui-Yüan, formulated and managed Maitreyanism and Amidism as two currents which formed the Buddhist keystone of the popular religions which were alive there and strongly impregnated with Shamanism and ancestor worship. They met each other without there growing from this a genuine existential encounter. The distinctive Indian character of Buddhism was not achieved. This encounter between Buddhism and popular belief, begun on the North Asiatic continent, was continued in Japan.

This development, vaguely introduced by Fo-t'u-teng and more concretely by Tao-an and Hui-Yüan, was continued in the conversion of the two Soga and their *shizoku*. The powerful position of the Soga, their close relationship with the court, and separate courts of the empresses guaranteed the 'conversion' of the emperors. It is thus to be explained that the Buddhism of Emperor Yōmei, related to the Soga as he was, consisted in not much more than that he tended towards Buddhism, which signified a better approach to *ujigami* and a welcome complement to the *ujigami* belief. He integrated Buddhism not only in his own person, but also in the administration of the state and in the emperorship. That is why Tasuna became the first 'state' monk. To him Buddhism was a means charged with power to achieve other aims, such as the cure of diseases and the like. In him and in many of his successors it became a magic means which only he as the distributor of the spiritual reserves of the nation could set in motion. The Japanese character assumed by the Buddhism of the period therefore consisted mainly of this: that it became a manageable means towards the well-being of the nation, which was made coexistent with the *ujigami* belief. A syncretistic process of growing together was naturally the next phase in this development.

All this acquired even sharper outlines under Empress Suiko. She was still a Shaman, such as many which Japan had known. Her authority therefore rested not only on the circumstance that she was *uji no kami* of the nation, but above all on her Shamanism. Her authority was great enough to turn Buddhism into the state religion. As *uji no kami* she was, however, also strongly rooted in the *uji* structure. Thus she allowed the *ujigami* belief to continue its existence as the state religion at the same time. This was possible because this *ujigami* belief was not so very far removed from what was then called Buddhism. It was rendered more concrete in the cult of Amaterasu, which probably also had its beginnings in Suiko's days.

The figure of Shōtoku Taishi was launched in order to obscure her position and eclipse it. Criticism of these Shōtoku Taishi data has given us an insight into the Buddhism of the period. First of all, owing to it Suiko's function as a Shaman came more strongly to the fore. The inscriptions and monuments of that time reveal a Buddhism on its way towards Maitreyanism and Amidism. From being an arsenal of new powers, which were to guarantee happiness and prosperity in this life, it began to develop into a religion which searched for an answer to problems reaching beyond death. These problems were, in Shōtoku's time, already most oppressive owing to the *yomi* prospect which, with all its horrors, offered no kind of comfort to the common man. Yet there were already present in the same *yomi* several aspects which could prepare for a later Buddhist solution. One of them was certainly the idea connected with the matriarchy and Shamanism of the period: place of the mother as the place of origin and death. Since—as we saw in the third Chapter—in East Asiatic Buddhism the idea of *anatta* as the total annihilation of individuality was no longer being adhered to, Buddhism was able to continue to build on this with the concept of a re-birth in a land of the elect, which was cleansed of the horrors of the *yomi* and nevertheless—under conditions which were not difficult to fulfil—gave everyone access to it. This Shintō-Buddhist core created the possibility of a specifically East Asiatic as well as a Japanese answer to the great problems in connection with birth, life and death, which often—though in a more mythical wording—do not yield to those of a modern existentialist.

Thus Buddhism stepped out of the mists of antiquity as a doctrine of redemption, which was for the first time concretely expressed in Maitreyanism and which, together with other characteristics—such as its sun character—, so strongly reinforced the propagandist power of Amidism that this latter was able to establish itself without more ado as the Buddhism with the most Japanese character. It was pointed out in the introduction and in Chapter

VI that this 'belief in heaven' has been the constant which has been present through the whole of Japanese history up to the present day and even in the new, post-war religions is clearly evident as the real main artery of Japanese Buddhism.

2. What then are the special characteristics of this Buddhism? They can best be established on the basis of the topics in the introduction to the present work.

a. It is syncretistic. No existential meeting took place with the full personality of Buddhism, even though the meeting between the *ujigami* belief and Buddhism evolved not in books and writings but only on the personal plane, i.e. people had not penetrated to the otherness of Buddhism, but had got stuck on the way to its real core. On its part the *ujigami* belief had only recovered in Buddhism a better reflection of itself. All this, for a Buddhism which had not yet found itself, facilitated a growth towards the *ujigami* belief. Yet this was not all. As a result of this defective encounter a kind of new religion came about, rounded off on the one hand by the *ujigami* belief, on the other by Buddhism. The rounding off towards Buddhism developed into Maitreyanism and Amidism. That towards *ujigami* belief developed into what is now called Shintō. The old institutionalised *ujigami* belief admittedly continued its existence, but was made to move and was opened up by Buddhism. Owing to this Taoism and Confucianism could also be included.[1] In the marginal area in between these two main currents typically syncretistic practices and later also theories occurred. Thus the doctrine of the *honji-suijaku* came about, partly on the basis of Buddhist apologetical motifs, partly in imitation of earlier Chinese [2] doctrines. According to this doctrine the *kami* were only provisional and temporary epiphanies adopted by Buddhas and Bodhisattvas for the sake of the people's conversion. Thus the *kami* are the

[1] Suematsu Yasukazu, *Mimana Kōbōshi*, p. 270, considers the arrival of Taoism and Confucianism as a necessary condition owing to which alone Buddhism became possible in Japan. He writes: "It has to be admitted that, as a condition for the transfer of Buddhism, *kanji*, *kanbun* and education in Confucianism were required, in other words, Japanese Buddhism was planted in the soft earth of Confucianism." The Buddhism of which Suematsu speaks here is, however, not that of King Sŏng and Shiba Tattō, but is that of a much later period, perhaps that of the Nara schools. The magic Buddhism of Iname and Umako did not require such nourishing soil. Shōtoku's, however, had a greater need, since it built on typically Chinese ideology.

[2] Cf. footnote 4 on p. 242.

suijaku, the temporary and passing shape, the Buddhas and Bodhisattvas, however, are the *honji,* literally its archetype. Thus, for example, the *kami* of Kashima became the *suijaku* of Kannon.[1] Thus, also, Buddhas and Bodhisattvas became the *honji* of famous Shintō temples: Vairocāna Buddha of the Amaterasu temple of Ise, Amitābha and Śākyamuni, i.a., of the Ishikiyomizu temple in Kyōto, where many *kami* were worshipped etc.[2] This syncretism later acquired shape especially in the many Shintō versions which afterwards originated from the two Buddhist tantric sects, the Shingon-*shū* and the Tendai-*shū,* both of which had 'charted' for the first time the many Buddhas and Bodhisattvas of their tantrism on two *maṇḍalas.*[3] This was called *ryōbu-shintō,* the Shintō of the two *maṇḍalas.*[4] In this form it has continued up to the present day.

b. It is also Shamanistic. In *Le Chamanisme,* M. Eliade says that Buddhism has greatly stimulated Shamanism.[5] In Japan this was certainly not the case, since there Shamanism had existed for a long time before the arrival of Buddhism.[6] Here exactly the opposite took place. Here a Shaman, Suiko, guaranteed the existence of Buddhism by turning it into a state religion. Thus it came to belong also to the '*matsurigoto*' which, since the days of the first known Shamans, Himiko and Jingū, both religiously and constitutionally, was the real practical execution of what they had seen in their Shamanistic trances. It may thus be said that the Suiko Buddhism as a state religion emanated from her Shamanistic trance.

[1] For the concept of *honji-suijaku* cf. Inoue Tetsujirō, op. cit., p. 997, col. III, p. 998, col. I.

[2] For its size see: Kiyohara Sadao, *Shintō-shi,* pp. 77-96.

[3] Cf. Ryūjun Tajima, *Les deux Grands* Maṇḍalas *et la Doctrine de l'Esotérisme Shingon,* p. 55-214.

[4] Cf. Inoue Tetsujirō, op. cit., p. 1088, col. II.

[5] Cf. M. Eliade, *Le Chamanisme,* p. 433.

[6] In today's Shamanism in Japan many elements may be observed indicating a pre-Buddhist stage. Cf. M. Eder, "Schamanismus in Japan", *Paid.,* VI, Heft 7, May 1958, p. 373. So he says about the *gehōbako*: "In den meisten Gegenden tragen die Schamaninnen eine in ein Tuch eingeschlagene Kiste auf dem Rücken herum, wenn sie in die Häuser gerufen werden. Diese Kiste stellen sie dann vor sich hin, wenn sie sich zum Herbeirufen eines Gottes auf den Boden setzen. Sie stützen während der eigentlichen Funktion beide Hände oder Ellbogen darauf. Der Name dieser Kiste ist *gehōbako,* was wörtlich "Kiste ausserhalb des Gesetzes", nämlich der buddhistischen Lehre bedeutet. So ist die Kiste in ihrem Namen schon ihres Inhaltes wegen als zur vorbuddhistischen jedenfalls ausserbuddhistischen Volksreligion gehörig gekennzeichnet."

c. It grew towards Maitreyanism and Amidism. Thus these two form the terminal points of a development which, on the one hand, began with Tao-an (or, if preferred, Fo-t'u-teng); on the other hand, in Japanese *shizoku* society. This was set going in Japan by the Korean immigrations to Takaichi. In accordance with the same syncretistic process even now similar encounters with Christianity and other world religions still take place in Japan. The reflection of such processes may be found in the declarations of principle of several modern Japanese religions, such as the Seichō *no* Ie, 生長の家.[1] Many followers of these religions think that they are exceedingly suitable to act as mediators in various religious disputes, wheresoever in the world. This suitability is based on the open-mindedness with which Japan, since the days of Shiba Tattō, encountered and absorbed every religion. In all this, however, it remains a difficulty that, its congenital open-mindedness notwithstanding, this country yet remained too much its own self to be able completely to understand those religions in their otherness. For metaphysical depth and insight are lacking.

d. It is not divorced from the *ujigami* belief. Initially it even became part of it. Afterwards it looked for a connection with the most pressing problems which were alive in the *ujigami* belief of the period.

e. It managed to discover and gain for itself that point in the *ujigami* society of those days from which it could dominate and reform the whole of that society: viz. the *uji no kami*. In connection with the *shizoku* of the Soga these were Iname and Umako, and in the national connection the Emperor Yōmei and even more the Empress-shaman Suiko.

Thus the final end to a long road, which stretched geographically from India to Japan and historically covered more than twelve centuries, was the result of many dialogues on the Asiatic continent with the philosophies of life of every sort of peoples, dialogues which in Japan continued to exist in a 'frozen' state in the syncretism congenital to every Japanese and nearly unrenounceable.

---

[1] Cf. W. Kohler, *Die Lotus-Lehre*, p. 96. Under the fifth rule of life of Seicho *no* Ie it says: "Jedes Glied der Seicho-no-Ie-Bewegung soll sich zur aktiven Teilnahme entscheiden. Dabei geht es nicht nur um Japan; denn Japan ist nur Mittler zwischen Ost und West und soll als Nation die Wahrheit des Mahâyâna-Buddhismus verwirklichen. Auf diese Weise wird das Leben sinnvoll. Japan hat eine Mission, wir alle haben eine Mission."

SELECT BIBLIOGRAPHY

Only those works are mentioned which bear upon the main subject of this study. Less important works, written in Japanese, Chinese and Sanskrit figure, however, in the Index at the end of this work.

I ABBREVIATIONS

Anthr.	*Anthropos.*
B.E.F.E.O.	*Bulletin de l'École Française d'Extrême-Orient.*
C.G.	*Chōsen Gakuhō.*
C.u.R.	*Christus und die Religionen der Erde.*
Folk. St.	*Folklore Studies.*
H.J.A.S.	*Harvard Journal of Asiatic Studies.*
H.M.	*Het Missiewerk.*
H.o.R.	*History of Religions.*
J.A.	*Journal Asiatique.*
J.R.A.S.	*The Journal of the Royal Asiatic Society of Great Britain and Ireland.*
J.o.W.H.	*Journal of World History.*
K.E.	*Katholieke Encyclopedie.*
K.G.Z.	*Kokugakuin Zasshi.*
M.G.K.	*Minzoku-gaku Kenkyū.*
M.N.	*Monomenta Nipponica.*
M.S.	*Monumenta Serica.*
M.S.G.	*Mitteilungen der Schweizerischen Gesellschaft der Freunde Ostasiatischer Kultur.*
N.S.K.	*Nihon Shūkyō-shi Kōza.*
O.E.	*Oriens Extremus.*
Paid.	*Paideuma.*
Pr. du B.	*Présence du Bouddhisme.*
R.H.R.	*Revue de l'Histoire des Religions.*
T.A.S.J.	*The Transactions of the Asiatic Society of Japan.*
T.B.	*Memoirs of the Research Department of the Tōyō Bunko.*
T.P.	*T'oung Pao.*
T.P.J.S.	*Transactions and Proceedings of the Japan Society.*
Z.M.R.	*Zeitschrift für Missionswissenschaft und Religionswissenschaft.*

II JAPANESE WORKS AND ARTICLES

Abe Makoto, 阿部真琴, Imai Rintarō, 今井林太郎, Inoue Kaoru, 井上薫, e.a., *Daigaku Nihon-shi*, 大学日本史, Tōkyō 1957.

Anzu Sunahiko, 安津素彦, "Kami to Mikoto", 神と命, *K.G.Z.*, vol. 59, nos. 10, 11, p. 8-18.

Arai Tsuneyasu, 新井恒易, *Nihon no Matsuri to Geino*, 日本の祭と芸能, Tōkyō 1956.

Asaka Yukio, 淺香幸雄, e.a., Tennō no Rekishi, 天皇の歴史, Tōkyō 1959.
Asano Motohiro, 淺野素弘, "Waga Taishi shinkō", 我太子信仰, *Shūkyō Kōron*, vol. 25, no. 4, p. 40-42.
Chōsen Gakuhō, 朝鮮学報, Tōkyō 1951—.
Doi Tadao, 土井忠生, e.a., *Nihongo no Rekishi*, 日本語の歴史, Tōkyō 1959.
Egami Namio, 江上波夫, Oka Masao, 岡正雄, Yawata Ichirō, 入幡一朗, "Nihon-minzoku-bunka no genryū to Nihon-kokka no keisei", 日本民族分化の源流と日本國家の形成, *M.G.K.*, vol. 13, no. 3, p. 207-277.
Fukuda Tadashi, 福田正, *Tendaigaku-gairon*, 天台学概論, Tōkyō 1955.
Fukuō Takeichirō, 福尾猛市郎, Nihon-kazoku-seidoshi, 日本家族制度史, Tōkyō 1959.
Fusō ryakki, 扶桑略記, *Kokushitaikei*, 國史大系, part VI, Tōkyō 1906.
Gendai Shūkyō Kōza, 現代宗教講座, vol. 5, Tōkyō 1958.
Genkō Shakusho, 元享釈書, *Kokushitaikei*, 國史大系, part XIV, Tōkyō 1897.
Higuchi Kiyoyuki, 樋口清臣, "Jōdai gūshi-densetsu-chi no kenkyū", 上代宮址伝說地の研究, *K.G.Z.*, vol. 62, no. 9, p. 33-43.
Igarashi Sukehiro, 五十嵐祐宏, "Taishi-sokkin no hitobito", 太子側近の人々, *Shūkyō Kōron*, vol. 25, no. 4, p. 45-47.
Igata Sadachi, 鋳方貞亮, "Chōsen ni okeru tozaibo no kigen" 起鮮における稲栽培の起原, *C.G.*, vol. 18, p. 1-31.
Inoue Tetsujirō, 井上哲次郎, e.a., *Bukkyō Jiten*, 仏教事典, Tōkyō 1938.
Ishida Mōsaku, 石田茂作, "Kudara-jiin to Hōryūji", 百済寺院と法隆寺, C. G., no. 5, p. 77-86.
——, "Ibutsu yori mita Taishiden no hensen", 遺物より見た太子伝の變遷, *Shūkyō Kōron*, vol. 25, no. 4, p. 31 ff..
Itamoto Tarō, 坂本太郎, "Keitaiki-shijitsu", 繼休紀史実, *K.G.Z.*, vol. 62, no. 9, p. 43-54.
Iwahashi Koyata, 岩橋小弥太, "Temmu tennō to *Kojiki*", 天武天皇と古事記, *K.G.Z.*, vol. 63, no. 9, p. 50 ff.
Kadowaki Teiji, 問脇禎二, *Jimmu Tennō*, 神武天皇, Tōkyō 1957.
Kanaji Isamu, 金治勇, "Shōtoku Taishi no jōdokan", 聖徳太子の浄土観, *Shūkyō Kōron*, vol. 29, no. 9, p. 3 ff..
Kanazawa Shōzaburō, 金沢庄三郎, "Chōsen-kenkyū to *Nihonshoki*", 朝魚研究と日本書紀, *C.G.*, no. 1, p. 69-91.
——, "Nissengo-hikaku-zakkō" 日鮮語比較雑考, *C.G.*, no. 8, pp. 21-31.
——, "Sammai to Bosatsu", 三米と菩薩, *C.G.*, no. 11, p. 33-41.
Kanda Ichikyōsuke, 金田一京取, *Jikai*, 辞海, Tōkyō 1957.
Kaneko Taiei, 金子大栄, *Nihon Bukkyō-shikan*, 日本仏教史観, Tōkyō 1940.
Kasai Wajin, 笠井倭人, "*Sankoku-iji* Kudara-ōreki to *Nihonshoki*", 三國遺事百済王暦と日本書紀, *C.G.*, no. 24, p. 84-111.
Kiyohara Sadao, 清原貞雄, *Shintō-shi* 神道史, Tōkyō 1939.
Kokugakuin Daigaku Kiyō, 國学院大学紀要, Tōkyō 1939.
Kokugakuin Zasshi, 國学院雑誌, Tōkyō, 1894-
Kojiki see Kuroita Katsumi.

Kuroita Katsumi, 黒坂勝美, Maruyama Jirō, 丸山二郎, *Kokushitaikei*, no. 10, *Kojiki*, 國史大系古事記, Tōkyō 1962.
Kuroita Katsumi, Maruyama Jirō, *Kokushitaikei* nos. 1 and 2, *Nihonshoki*, 國史大系日本書紀, Tōkyō 1963.
——, *Kokushitaikei* nos. 3 and 4, *Shoku-Nihongi*, 國史大系續日本紀, Tōkyō 1962.
Matsukawa Jirō, 松川二郎, "Tennō-shijō no bōten", 天皇史上の盲点, *Tennō no Rekishi*, p. 20-122.
——, "Tennō-taii no rekishi", 天皇退位の歴史, *Tennō no Rekishi*, p. 271-298.
Matsumae Takeshi, 松前建, "Amateru-mitama no kami kō", 天照御魂神考, *K.G.Z.* vol. 62, no. 10, p. 49-55.
——, "Taiyō no fune to tokoyo no shinkō" 太陽の舟と常世の信仰, *K.G.Z.*, vol. 62, nos. 2, 3, p. 23-43.
Matsumoto Yoshio, 松本芳夫, "Kodaijin no takai-kannen", 古代人の他界観念, *Minzoku-gaku no tame ni*, no. 10, 1951, p. 59-61.
Minzoku-gaku kenkyū, 民族学研究, Tōkyō 1935-
Minzoku-gaku no tame ni, 民族学のために, Tōkyō.
Mishina Shōei, 三品彰英, "Kokuryō no gozoku ni tsuite", 高句麗の五族について, *C.G.*, no. 6, p. 13-57.
——, "*Kudara-ki, Kudara-shinsen, Kudara-hongi* ni tsuite" 百済記, 百済新撰, 百済本記について, *C.G.*, no. 24, p. 1-18.
——, "*Nihonshoki* Nissen-kankei kiji kōshō" 日本書紀日韓関係記事考証, *C.G.*, no. 14, p. 503-533.
——, "*Sankoku-iji*-kōshō" 三國遺事考証, *C.G.*, no. 29, p. 148-170.
Miyazaki Ichijō, 宮崎市定, "Sankanjidai no ikaisei ni tsuite", 三韓時代の位階制について, C.G., no. 14, p. 253-280.
Nagano Tadashi, 長野正, "Kōi-sōjō-monogatari no honjitsu", 皇位互讓物語の本質, *Tennō no Rekishi*, p. 257-270.
Naitō Masatsune, 内藤政恒, "Asuka-jidai no jiin", 飛鳥時代の寺院, *Shūkyō Kōron*, vol. 25, no. 4, p. 36-38.
Nakajima Etsuji, 中島悦次, "Tokoyo-kuni-zakkō", 常世國雑考, *K.G.Z.*, vol. 54, no. 1, p. 71-79.
Nakamura Kichiji, 中村吉治, *Nihon Shakai-shi*, 日本社会史, Tōkyō 1956.
Nara national Institute of Cultural Properties, *Asukadera Temple Site, Archeological survey carried out in 1956, 1957*, Nara 1958.
Nihonjin no Shūkyō-seikatsu, 日本人の宗教生活, part V, Tōkyō 1956.
Nihon Shūkyō-shi kōza, 日本宗教史講座, part II, III, IV, Tōkyō 1959.
Nishida Chōnan, 西田長男, *Nihonshoki* no rekishi-shisō", 日本書紀の歴史思想, *K.G.Z.*, vol. 57, no. 7, p. 165-177.
Oka Masao see: Egami Namio.
Okabe Nagaaki, 岡部長章, "Kigensetsu no mondai", 紀元節の問題, *Shūkyō Kōron*, vol. 27, no. 3, p. 2-8.
——, "Nichi-shi-kō to shijō no Taishi", 日支交と史上の太子, *Shūkyō Kōron*, vol. 25, no. 4, p. 65 ff.
——, "Shōwa no Hōryūji-mondai to Taishi-shinkō", 昭和の法隆寺問題と太子信仰, *Shūkyō Kōron*, vol. 25, no. 4, p. 25-30.

Ōno Tatsunosuke, 大野達之取, *Nihon Bukkyō-shisō-shi*, 日本仏教思想史, Tōkyō 1958.

Sakai Kaizō, 酒井改藏, "Kotaiō-himen no chimei ni tsuite", 好太王碑面の地名について, *C.G.*, no. 8, p. 51-63.

Sakaino Kōyō, 境野黄洋, *Shōtoku Taishi-den*, 聖徳太子伝, Tōkyō 1931.

Saki Akio, 佐木秋夫, "Sengo no shūkyō-hendō to mondai no shinten", 戦後の宗教変動と問題の進展, *N.S.K.*, vol. IV, p. 3-61.

Sasaki Nobutsuna, 佐左木信綱, *Shinkun Manyōshū*, 新訓萬葉集, Tōkyō 1958.

Sasaya Ryōzō, 笹谷良造, "Musubi-gami no shinkō", 產霊神の信仰, *K.G.Z.*, vol. 64, nos. 8, 9, p. 83-111.

Shibata Minoru, 柴田実, "Sōsen-sūhai no genryū", 祖先崇拝の源梳, *N.S.K.*, vol. III, p. 3-40.

Shigaku zasshi, 史学雑誌, Tōkyō 1889-

Shimonaka Yasaburō, 下中彌三郎, *Shintō Daijiten*, 神道大事典, 3 vols., Tōkyō 1940.

Shoku-Nihongi see Kuroita Katsumi.

Shūkyō Kōron, 宗教公論, Tōkyō 1934-

Suematsu Yasukazu, 末松保和, *Mimana Kōbōshi*, 任那興亡史, Tōkyō 1949.

Sugano Masao, 菅野雅雄, "Tokoyo-yuku shinwa no keisei", 黄泉行神話の刑成, *K.G.Z.*, vol. 62, n. 10, p. 42-48.

Suji Zennosuke, 辻善之取, "*Nihon Bukkyō-shi no Kenkyū*", 日本仏教史の研究, part II, Tōkyō 1942.

——, *Nihon Bunka-shi*, 日本分化史, part I, II, Tōkyō 1942.

Suzuki Shūchū, 鈴木宗忠, "Kenkoku-hi no mondai", 建国日の問題, *Shūkyō Kōron*, vol. 28, no. 2, p. 26-28.

Tagita Koya, 田北耕也, *Shōwa-jidai no senpuku-kirishitan*, 昭和時代の潜伏キリシタン, Tōkyō 1958.

Takahashi Tōru, 高橋享, "*Sankoku-iji* no ayamari oyobi Tangun-densetsu no hatten", 三國遺事の註及檀君伝説の発展, *C.G.*, no. 7, p. 63-90.

Takatori Masao, 高取正男, "Kodai minshū no shūkyō", 古代民衆の宗教, *N.S.K.*, vol. 2., p. 3-71.

Takeda Iukichi, 武田祐吉, *Fudoki*, 風土記, Tōkyō 1938.

Takeda Shizuko, 武田清子, "Tennōsei to shūkyō", 天皇制と宗教, *Gendai Shūkyō Kōza*, part 5, p. 166 ff.

Takazaki Masahide, 高崎正秀, "Kojiki-denshōron", 古事記伝承論, *K.G.Z.*, vol. 63, no. 9, p. 4-22.

Tanaka Jigohei, 田中治吾平, *Amaterasu Ōmikami no Kenkyū*, 天照大神の研究, Tōkyō 1959.

Tanaka Yoshito, 田中義能, *Shintō-gairon*, 神道概論, Tōkyō 1942.

Taya Raishun, 多屋頼俊, e.a., *Bukkyō-gaku Jiten*, 仏教学事典, Tōkyō 1957.

Tsuda Noritake, 津田敬武, *Shintō-kigenron* 神道起原論, Tōkyō 1920.

Tsuda Sōkichi, 津田左右吉, *Nihon Jōdaishi no Kenkyū*, 日本上代史の研究, Tōkyō 1963.

——, *Nihon Koten no Kenkyū*, 日本古典の研究, 2 vols., Tōkyō 1963.

——, *Shina-bukkyō no Kenkyū*, シナ仏教の研究, Tōkyō 1957.

Ui Hakuju, 宇井伯寿, *Nihon Bukkyō-gaishi*, 日本仏教概史, Tōkyō 1958.
Udō Masamoto, 鵜殿正元, "Kodai-Nihon no taiyō-shinkō to sono bungaku-hyōgen", 古代日本の大陽信仰とその文学表現, *K.G.Z.*, vol. 59, nos. 10, 11, p. 123-131.
Umeda Yoshihiko, 梅田義彦, "Shinbutsu-shugo-shi kenkyū-jōsetsu", 神仏習合史研究序說, *K.G.Z.*, vol. 4., nos. 5, 6, p. 58-64.
Umehara Sueji, 梅原末治, "Kodai-Nissenkan no bunbutsu no kōryū", 古代日鮮間の文物の交流, *C.G.*, no. 11, p. 1-19.
Yanagita Kunio, 柳田國男, "Kaijingū kō", 海神宮考, *M.G.K.*, vol. 15, no. 2, p. 104 ff.
——, *Nihon no Matsuri*, 日本の祭, Tōkyō 1956.
Yawata Ichirō see: Egami Namio.
Yoshioka Yoshitoyo, 吉岡義豊, *Dōkyō to Bukkyō*, 道教と仏教, Tōkyō 1959.

III WORKS AND ARTICLES IN OTHER LANGUAGES

Abegg E., "Der Buddha Maitreya", *M.S.G.*, VII, p. 7-37.
Anesaki M., "The Buddhist Ideals as conceived and carried out by the Prince Regent Shôtoku", M.N., no. VI, 1943, p. 1-12.
Anthropos, Internationale Zeitschrift für Völker und Sprachkunde, Wien, Fribourg 1906.
Aston W.G., "Nihongi, Chronicles of Japan from the earliest times to A.D. 697", *T.P.J.S.*, Suppl. I, vol. 1 and 2, London 1896.
Bairy M.A., *Japans neue Religionen in der Nachkriegszeit*, Bonn 1959.
Baruch W., "Maitreya d'après les sources de Sérinde", *R.H.R.*, vol. 132, 1946, p. 67-92.
Bleeker C.J., *Moedergodin in de Oudheid*, Den Haag 1960.
Born A. v. d., e.a., *Bijbels Woordenboek*, Roermond 1954-1957.
Bouteiller M., *Chamanisme et Guérison Magique*, Paris 1950.
Bulletin de l'École Française d'Extrême Orient, Paris-Hanoi 1901-
Cahier d'Histoire Mondial see: Journal of World History.
Casal U.A., *Die Sieben Glücksgötter*, Tokyo-Wiesbaden 1958.
——, *Hachiman, der Kriegsgott*, Tokyo 1962.
Closs A., "Das Religiöse im Schamanismus", *Kairos*, no. 1, 1960, p. 29-38.
Coates H. H., Ishizuka R., *Honen the Buddhist Saint*, Tokyo 1930.
Conze E., *Buddhism*, London 1952.
Cornelis É., *Valeurs Chrétiennes des Réligions non Chrétiennes*, Paris 1965.
Creel H. G., *La Naissance de la Chine*, Paris, 1937.
Cumont F., *Lux Perpetua*, Paris 1949.
Daniélou Alain, *Le Polythéisme Hindou*, Paris 1960.
Déchanet J.M., *La Voix du Silence, Paris*, 1961.
Démiéville P., "La Yogacara-bhūmi de Saṃgharakṣa", *B.E.F.E.O.*, XLIV, 1947-1950, p. 378-383.
Dutt N., "The Fundamental Principles of Mahāyāna", *Pr. du B.*, p. 324-327.
Eberhard W., *A History of China*, London 1950.
——, "Geschichte Chinas bis zum Ende der Hanzeit", *Historia Mundi*, part II, p. 565-606.
——, "Kultur und Siedlung der Randvölker Chinas", suppl. of *T.P.*, vol. XXXVI, 1942.

Eberhard W., *Das Toba-Reich Nord Chinas*, Leiden 1949.
Eckardt A., *Koreanica, Festschrift für Prof. Dr. André Eckardt*, Baden Baden 1960.
Eder M., "Die Reisseele in Japan und Korea", *Folkl. St.*, vol. XIV, 1955, p. 215-244.
——, "Schamanismus in Japan", *Paid.*, Heft VI, Mai 1958, p. 367-381.
Eliade M., *Le Chamanisme*, Paris 1951.
——, *Images et Symboles*, Paris 1952.
——, "Recent Works on Shamanism", *H.o.R.*, vol. 1, 1961, p. 153-187.
——, *Traité d'Histoire des Religions*, Paris 1959.
——, *Le Yoga*, Paris 1960.
Eliot C., *Hinduism and Buddhism*, London 1921.
Feifel E., Nagasawa K., *Geschichte der Chinesischen Literatur*, Darmstadt 1959.
Fenollosa E., *Epochs of Chinese and Japanese Art*, vol. I, New York 1912.
Filliozat J. see Renou L.
——, *La Doctrine Classique de la Médecine Indienne*, Paris 1949.
Findeisen H., *Schamanentum*, Stuttgart 1957.
Fischer J., Yokota T., *Das Sūtra Vimalakīrti*, Tokyo 1944.
Florenz K., *Die Historischen Quellen der Shinto Religion*, Göttingen 1919.
Folklore Studies, Journal of far Eastern Folklore, Tokyo 1942-
Franke O., *Geschichte des Chinesischen Reiches*, part II, Berlin 1936.
Fraser Sir J., *The Golden Bough*, abridged edition, London 1950.
Freiherr von Eickstedt E., "Rassentypen und Typendynamik von Asien", *Historia Mundi*, vol. I, p. 115-134.
Frauwallner E., *Philosophie des Buddhismus*, Berlin 1956.
Gaspardone E., "La chronologie ancienne du Japon", *J.A.*, Tome CCXXX, Avril Juin, 1938, p. 235-277.
Glasenapp H. von, *Buddhismus und Gottesidee*, Wiesbaden 1954.
——, *Der Buddhismus in Indien und im fernen Osten*, Berlin-Zürich 1936.
Goldammer Kurt, *Formenwelt des Religiösen*, Stuttgart 1960.
Graf O., "Ein Abriss der Religionsgeschichte Koreas", *C.u.R.*, vol. III, p. 375-391.
Granet M., *La Religion des Chinois*, Paris 1951.
——, *Danses et Légendes de la Chine Ancienne*, tome I et II, Paris 1959.
Groot J.J.M. de, *The Religious System of China*, vol. VI, book II, Leiden 1910.
——, *Universismus*, Berlin 1918.
Grousset R., *Les Civilisations de l'Orient*, Tome III et IV, Paris 1930.
——, *La Face de l'Asie*, Paris 1955.
Gundert W., *Japanische Religionsgeschichte*, Stuttgart 1935.
Gusinde M., "Stone Circles in Northern Japan", *Anthr.*, vol. 55. 1960, p. 441-455.
Harvard Journal of Asiatic Studies, Cambridge, Mass., 1936-
Heinrichs M., *Katholische Theologie und Asiatisches Denken*, Mainz 1963.
Hentze C., "Die Wanderung der Tiere um die heiligen Berge", *Symbolon*, Band IV, 1964, p. 20 ff.
History of Religions, Chicago 1961-

Historia Mundi, Ein Handbuch der Weltgeschichte in zehn Bänden, by Fritz Kern and many others, vols. I & II, München 1952.
Hoffmann H., *Die Religionen Tibets*, Freiburg/München 1956.
Holtom D.C., "The meaning of Kami", *M.N.*, vol. III, no. 1, no. 2 and vol. IV, no. 2, p. 351-394.
Humphrey C., *Buddhism*, London 1954.
Ikeuchi H., "A Study on the Fu-yü", *T.B.*, no. VI, 1932, p. 23-60.
Ishizuka R., see Coates H.H.
Iwasaki Tamihei, *Kenkyusha's New English-Japanese Dictionary*, Tokyo 1951.
Jensen A. E., *Mythos und Kult bei Naturvölkern*, Wiesbaden 1960.
Journal Asiatique, Paris 1822-
The Journal of the Royal Asiatic Society of Great Britain and Ireland, London 1834-
Journal of World History, Cahier d'histoire Mondial, Neuchâtel 1955-
Kairos, Zeitschrift für Religionswissenschaft und Theologie, Salzburg 1960-
Kamstra J. H., "Katholieke Theologie en Oosters Denken", *H.M.*, 44 (1965), no. 2, p. 115-121.
——, "Japans grösste Gefahr—die Sōkagakkai", *Z.M.R.*, 44 (1960), Heft 1 & 2, p. 41-51, 98-106.
——, "Ontstaan en groei van een mythe". *H.M.*, 46 (1967), no. 2, p. 98-113.
——, *The Hīna- and Mahāyānism of the Japanese Nara-sects* (manuscript), Nijmegen 1962.
Katsumata Senkichiro, *Kenkyusha's New Japanese-English Dictionary*, Tokyo 1954.
Kidder J. E., *Japan before Buddhism*, London 1959.
Kirfel W., *Symbolik des Buddhismus*, Stuttgart 1959.
Kitagawa J. M., "Prehistoric background of Japanese Religion", *H.o.R.*, vol. II, 1963, no. 2, p. 292-328.
Koestler A., *The Lotus and the Robot*, London 1960.
Kohler W., *Die Lotus-Lehre*, Zürich 1962.
König F., e.a., *Christus und die Religionen der Erde*, Band III, Wien 1956.
Lamotte E., *Histoire du Bouddhisme Indien*, Louvain 1958.
Lewin B., *Aya und Hata*, Wiesbaden 1962.
Lubac H. de, *Amida*, Paris 1955.
Lin Tsiu Sen, *China und Japan*, Band I, Zürich (after 1944).
Link E., "Biography of shih Tao-an", *T.P.*, XLVI, 1958.
Martin J. M., *Le Shintoïsme*, vols. 1 and 2, Hongkong 1924 and 1927.
Mead M., *New Lives for Old*, New York 1961.
Mathews R. H., *Chinese-English Dictionary*, Cambridge, Mass., 1963.
Memoirs of the Research Department of the Tōyō Bunko, the Oriental Library, Tōkyō 1927-
Mensching G., *Die Religion*, Stuttgart 1959.
Missiewerk Het, Nederlands tijdschrift voor Missiewetenschap, Nijmegen 1919-
Mitteilungen der Schweizerischen Gesellschaft der Freunde Ostasiatischer Kultur, Bern 1939-
Monumenta Nipponica, Tokyo 1938-

Monumenta Serica, Peking-Tokyo 1935-
Müller M., *Lotus-sūtra,* New York 1963.
Naberfeld E., *Grundriss der Japanischen Geschichte,* Tokyo 1940.
Nagasawa K., see: Feifel E.
Nebesky-Wojkowitz R. de, *Oracles and Demons of Tibet,* The Hague 1956.
Neumann K. E., *Die Reden Gotamo Buddhas,* München 1922.
Nikan N. A. and Mac Keon R., *The Edicts of Aśoka,* Chicago 1959.
Offner C. B., see: Straelen H. van.
Oriens Extremus, Zeitschrift für Sprache, Kunst und Kultur der Länder des Fernen Ostens, Hamburg 1954-
Ouwehand C., *Namazu-e and their themes,* Leiden 1964.
Paideuma, Mitteilungen zur Kulturkunde Frankfurt/M., 1938-
Pelliot P., "Le Ts'ien Tseu Wen ou Livre des mille mots", *T.P.*, XXIV (1926), p. 209.
Pratt J. B., *The Pilgrimage of Buddhism,* New York 1928.
Présence du Bouddhisme, Saigon 1958.
Radakrishnan S., *Indian Philosophy,* London 1929.
Reischauer A. K., *Studies in Japanese Buddhism,* New York 1928.
Renou L., Filliozat J., *L'Inde Classique,* tome II, Hanoi 1953.
Revue de l'Histoire des Religions, Paris 1880-
Romieux J., "Mythes du Japon ancien vus à la lumière de la linguistique comparative", *M.S.G.*, VIII, 1946, p. 63-93.
Sansom G. B., *Japan,* London 1946.
——, *A History of Japan to 1334,* Stanford, Cal., 1958.
Sasaki G., "Hînayâna Schools in China and Japan", *Pr.du B.*, p. 508 ff.
Saunders E. D., *Buddhism in Japan,* Philadelphia, 1960.
——, *Mudrā,* London 1960.
Schreiber G., "The History of the former Yen-dynasty", *M.S.*, XIV (1949-1955), p. 374-480; XV (1956), pp. 1-141.
Schröder D., "Zur Struktur des Schamanismus", *Anthr.*, vol. 50, 1955, p.830-880.
Schwientek J., "Der Synkretismus von Shinto und Buddhismus in Japan", *Anthr.*, vol. 22, 1927, p. 430-439.
Sierksma F., *Een nieuwe hemel en een nieuwe aarde,* 's-Gravenhage 1961.
Snellen J. B., "Shoku-Nihongi, Chronicles of Japan, continued from 697-791", *T.A.S.J.*, Sec. Ser. XI 1934, XIV 1937.
Straelen H. van, Offner C. B., *Modern Japanese Religions,* Tokyo 1963.
Suematsu Yasukazu, "Japan's Relations with the Asian Continent and the Korea Peninsula", *J.o.W.H.*, no. 3, 1958, p. 671-683.
Symbolon, Jahrbuch für Symbolforschung, Basel/Stuttgart 1961-
Szcześniak B., "Japanese-Korean Wars in A.D. 391-407 and their chronology", *J.R.A.S.*, 1946, parts 1 & 2, p. 54-66
Tajima R., *Les deux grands Maṇḍalas et la doctrine de l'ésotérisme Shingon,* Tōkyō/Paris 1959.
Tappe F., *Soziologie der Japanischen Familie,* Münster 1955.
T'oung Pao, Leiden 1890-
The Transactions of the Asiatic Society of Japan, Tōkyō 1872-

Transactions and Proceedings of the Japan Society, London 1896-
Tsui Chi, *Histoire de la Chine et de la civilisation chinoise*, Paris 1949.
Tsunoda R., *Japan in the Chinese Dynastic Histories*, South Pasadena 1951.
——, de Bary Wm., Keene D., *Sources of Japanese Tradition*, vol. I, New York 1964.
Visser M. W. de, *Ancient Buddhism in Japan*, 2 vols., Leiden 1935.
Vos F., *Volken van één stam*, (inaugural speech), 's-Gravenhage 1959.
——, "Kim Yusin, Persönlichkeit und Mythos", *O.E.*, Jahrg. I, 1954.
Vroklage B.A.G., *Godsdiensten der Primitieven*, Roermond 1949.
Waley A., *The Nine Songs*, London 1956.
Wedemeyer A., *Japanische Frühgeschichte*, Tokyo 1930.
Widengren G., *Mani und Manichäismus*, Stuttgart, 1961.
Wieger L., *Amidisme Chinois et Japonais*, 1928.
——, *Histoire des Croyances religieuses et des Opinions philosophiques en Chine*, Hien-hien 1927.
——, *Vinaya, Monachisme et Discipline*, Leiden 1951.
Wright A. F., "Fo-t'u-teng", *H.J.A.S.*, vol. 11, 1948, p. 312-371.
——, *Buddhism in Chinese History*, Stanford, Cal., 1959.
Yokota T., see: Fischer J.
Young J., *The Location of Yamatai*, Baltimore 1957.
Zeitschrift für Missionswissenschaft und Religionswissenschaft, Münster 1950-
Zimmer H., *Philosophies of India*, New York 1960.
Zürcher E., *The Buddhist Conquest of China*, Leiden 1959.
——, *Het Boeddhisme*, Amsterdam 1961.

CORRIGENDA

p. 162, line 17 *Mahāparanibbana-suttam*: *Mahāparinibbana-suttam*

p. 192, footnote 4, line 12 *Santalaceae, Santalum album*: Santalaceae, Santalum album

line 16 *euonymus*: euonymus

line 19 *Betula Schmidtii*: Betula Schmidtii

p. 243, footnote 3, 2nd line districts: provinces

p. 349, footnote 3, Bhaiṣajyaguru Vaidūrya: Bhaiṣajyaguru-vaidūrya

p. 380, first line 330: 380

INDICES

Italicized figures indicate the footnotes of the pages. No reference is made to quotations of *Kojiki* and *Nihonshoki*.

I. Index of Japanese Names and Terms

II. Index of Names and Terms other than Japanese